S0-BZX-784

Managing Human Resources

9th Edition

Arthur W. Sherman, Jr.
Professor of Psychology
California State University, Sacramento

George W. Bohlander
Professor of Management
Arizona State University

COLLEGE DIVISION South-Western Publishing Co.
Cincinnati Ohio

Publisher: Roger L. Ross
Developmental Editor: Brigid M. Harmon
Production Editor: Susan C. Williams
Production House: Carnes-Lachina Publication Services, Inc.
Cover and Interior Designer: Joseph M. Devine
Marketing Manager: Tania L. Hindersman
Photo Researcher: Kimberly A. Larson
Cover Painting: Stuart Davis (1894–1964). *Swing Landscape*, 1938.
Indiana University Art Museum, Bloomington, Indiana.
Photograph by Michael Cavanagh and Kevin Montague.

GJ83IA

Library of Congress Cataloging-in-Publication Data

Sherman, Arthur W.
Managing human resources / Arthur W. Sherman, Jr., George W. Bohlander.—9th ed.
p. cm.
Includes index.
ISBN 0-538-81075-0
1. Personnel management. I. Bohlander, George W. II. Title.
HF5549.C465 1992
658.3—dc20 91-18459
CIP

2 3 4 5 6 7 8 9 RN 9 8 7 6 5 4 3 2

Printed in the United States of America

To my wife, Leneve Sherman, and to our children, Beverly, Sandy, and Judy

To my wife, Ronnie Bohlander, and to our children, Ryan and Kathryn

About the Authors

Arthur W. Sherman, Jr.

Arthur W. Sherman, Jr., is Professor of Psychology, California State University, Sacramento. During most of his academic career he has taught undergraduate and graduate courses in organizational psychology, personnel psychology, personnel management, psychological testing, and professional development in psychology. Dr. Sherman has served as a personnel consultant to several organizations including the Department of Consumer Affairs of the State of California and the Social Security Administration. He has been a participant in seminars and workshops. For twelve consecutive years he was a lecturer in the management development program conducted by the CSUS School of Business Administration for the federal government.

During World War II and the Korean War, Dr. Sherman served in the U.S. Air Force as a Personnel Classification Officer, as an Aviation Psychologist, and as head of a test development unit for the Airman Career Program. Later he was active in the planning of the psychology curriculum at the U.S. Air Force Academy.

Dr. Sherman received an A.B. in psychology from Ohio University, an A.M. from Indiana University, and a Ph.D. in industrial and counseling psychology from the Ohio State University. His professional affiliations include the American Psychological Association, the Society for Industrial and Organizational Psychology, and the Academy of Management.

He has been an author of this book since its beginning as well as *Personnel Practices of American Companies in Europe,* published by the American Management Association.

George W. Bohlander

George W. Bohlander is Professor of Management at Arizona State University. He teaches undergraduate, graduate, and executive development programs in the field of human resources and labor relations. His areas of expertise include employment law, training and development, performance appraisal, public policy, and labor relations. He is the recipient of four outstanding teaching awards at ASU.

Dr. Bohlander is an active researcher and author. He has published over 30 articles and monographs covering various topics in the human resources area ranging from labor–management cooperation to employee productivity. His articles appear in such academic and practitioner journals as *Labor Studies Journal, Personnel Administrator, Labor Law Journal, Journal of Collective Negotiations in the Public Sector, Public Personnel Management, Personnel,* and *Employee Relations Law Journal.*

Before beginning his teaching career, Dr. Bohlander served as Personnel Administrator for General Telephone Company of California. His duties included recruitment and selection, training and development, equal employee opportunity, and labor relations. He was very active in resolving employee grievances and in arbitration preparation. Dr. Bohlander continues to be a consultant to both public- and private-sector organizations, and he has worked with such organizations as the U.S. Postal Service, Kaiser Cement, McDonnell-Douglas, Arizona Public Service, American Productivity Center, Rural Metro Corporation, and Del Webb. Dr. Bohlander is also an active labor arbitrator. He received his Ph.D. from the University of California at Los Angeles and his M.B.A. from the University of Southern California.

Preface

As we rapidly approach the close of the 20th century, it is gratifying to those of us who have studied work organizations to observe that increased attention and recognition are being given to human resources (HR) and their management. The HR manager has achieved a status that is equal to that of managers in charge of such major functions as marketing, production, and finance. There is an awareness among top management that HR managers can play a vital role in determining the success of an organization.

HR managers are no longer viewed primarily as being in charge of performing a service function such as recruiting and selecting personnel. Today they are not only invited to, but also expected to, assume an active role in the strategic planning and decision making at the upper echelons of their organizations. Their contributions to the achievement of organizational objectives have finally earned them the recognition that they deserve. Their contributions in the past also signal even greater potential for the future.

Students who are now preparing for careers in organizations will find that the study of human resources management (HRM) will provide a background of understanding that will be valuable in line, as well as staff, positions. There are many opportunities in HR staff positions. However, the HR functions are also performed by line managers and supervisors. In many ways the line managers and supervisors have an even greater opportunity to contribute to the organization through the manner in which they implement the policies and procedures regarding the management of HR. Throughout this book the important roles of managers and supervisors, as well as HR managers, are examined thoroughly.

As in previous editions, we have attempted to define more precisely the impact of the internal and external environments upon the activities of the HR manager. We emphasize that the management of human resources occurs in a culture that is highly dynamic. You are, therefore, advised at many points to be alert for changing conditions that will present new problems that require new solutions.

We have attempted to demonstrate wherever possible the contributions that HRM can make to productivity. Ethics, career development, equal employment opportunity, motivation, performance appraisal, leadership and communication, rights and responsibilities of employers and employees, complaint handling, and professionalization of HRM practitioners are among the topics that have received special emphasis.

We are continuing the orientation that we have had since the *first* edition of having a balanced approach to HRM that melds the principles of behavioral science with traditional personnel and labor relations philosophies and practices. In the process of preparing this current edition we have given increased emphasis to the growing body of laws, regulations, and court decisions that influence the daily activities of HR managers and their staffs.

We continue to use the language of the HRM practitioner and to emphasize current issues and problems of the "real world." Examples are provided wherever possible to help make the concepts a part of the reader's working knowledge. References are made to the practices of 398 organizations listed in a special index of this edition. New to this edition is a special feature called Highlights in HRM which illustrates actual HR policies and practices of public and private (large and small) organizations. Several Highlights in HRM features are provided in each chapter.

As with most authors, we have reported not only our own experiences, but also the experiences and published works of many academicians and practitioners. We have tried to cite those articles and books that we believe are both timely and authoritative, at the same time recognizing the publications that are considered to be classics. Reference citations are consolidated at the end of each chapter along with any special notes that may interest the reader.

ORGANIZATION OF THE TEXT

This book is divided into seven parts. In Part One we show why and how the various HRM functions have evolved, and examine the different environments that must be considered. Because of their importance in performing all of the HRM functions, equal employment opportunity and affirmative action are introduced early in the book in Chapter 3.

The chapters in Part Two focus on the way that the HR requirements are met through analyzing job requirements, planning, recruiting personnel, and selecting those individuals who are most likely to be successful. Once individuals are hired it is necessary to provide training, to assist in their career development, and to appraise their performance on the job. These topics are discussed in Part Three.

In Part Four we study the importance of implementing compensation and providing economic, physical, and emotional security for employees. The creation of a productive work environment is of fundamental concern to all managers. It is a topic that is emphasized in Part Five and throughout this text. In Part Five we focus on motivation, the role of communication in HRM, and employee rights and discipline.

Part Six, Strengthening Employee–Management Relations, discusses the dynamics of labor relations, collective bargaining, and contract administration. While these activities are typically handled by specialists in labor relations, all managers must be alert to the constraints of employee–management agreements.

In the last part of the book—Part Seven—there is a chapter on international HRM. The rapid growth of global enterprises in recent years demands that managers have an understanding of the types of differences that one encounters in operations outside one's homeland. Placement of this chapter in the last part of the book should not be construed as a reflection of its importance. Rather, we believe that its contents are likely to have more meaning for the reader who first understands the policies and practices that are typically found in organizations in the United States. The topic of the final chapter is the auditing of the HRM program. As with other organizational programs, there should be formal procedures for determining the extent to which HR objectives are being met.

Following Part Seven there is a major section containing 12 extended cases portraying current issues/problems in HRM. "Ill-Fated Love," "Toxic Substances at Lukens Chemical Industries," and "The EEO Charge" are a few of them.

The section of comprehensive cases is followed by:

- a name index
- an organization index
- a subject index

CHAPTER ORGANIZATION

Each chapter contains the following features that are designed to facilitate understanding and retention of the material presented:

- Learning Objectives.
- Terms to Identify—a list at the beginning of the chapter signals the key terms that will appear in boldface on the pages indicated.
- Figures—flow charts, summaries of research data, and other graphic materials are presented.
- Highlights in HRM—a new feature with practical examples of how organizations are performing HR functions.
- Illustrations—captioned photographs and cartoons are designed to reinforce points made in the text and to add interest to the presentation.
- Summary—provides a brief review at the end of each chapter.
- Discussion Questions—offer an opportunity to focus on critical points in the chapter.
- Mini-Cases—current HRM issues are presented in a real-life setting for student appraisal.
- Notes and References—each chapter contains an average of 50 or more references from academic and practitioner journals and books.

SUGGESTIONS FOR STUDYING THE BOOK

To gain maximum value from studying this textbook, we recommend that you first review the table of contents in order to acquire a perspective of the material that will be covered. Before reading each chapter, study the objectives, then scan through its pages to familiarize yourself with how the information is presented. Look at the headings as you go. Return to the beginning of the chapter and begin your reading. Look for the main ideas.

Also, give special attention to words that are printed in **boldface** type. These are important terms which are defined where they first appear in the chapter. Study carefully the figures and the Highlights in HRM which provide information that is essential to your full understanding of the concepts presented in the chapter. Make brief notes or mark the printed page as you prefer. When you have finished reading the chapter, look back at the list of Terms to Identify. Check your understanding of them. In addition, refer back to the chapter objectives to determine your comprehension of what you have read. Then answer the discussion questions at the end of the chapter. Finally, study the mini-cases at the end of the chapter to determine if you can apply what you have learned to a practical problem in HRM. Review each chapter frequently in order to reinforce your understanding of what you have learned.

From time to time your instructor may assign cases at the end of this textbook. These cases cover situations that a particular organization has encountered in managing its human resources. Generally they are broader in scope than the mini-cases at the end of the chapter.

SUPPLEMENTARY MATERIALS

Practical Study Experiences in Managing Human Resources. Additional opportunities to apply the theories and principles presented in this textbook may be found in *Practical Study Experiences in Managing Human Resources*, 9th Edition. This is a workbook with 80 projects designed to give students a variety of experiences similar to those they are likely to find on the job. It also contains review test questions that can be used to check the student's understanding of each chapter in this textbook.

Human Resources Simulation. The management of human resources in a nondiscriminatory and efficient manner is growing increasingly dependent upon the use of computer technology. In order to provide readers with hands-on computer experiences related to personnel activities, a software/printware package titled *Human Resources Simulation*, prepared by Dr. Larry E. Penley and Yolanda Penley, is available. Through simulation exercises, the user of this package can gain valuable knowledge in utilizing a computer in the areas of equal employment opportunity, training, HR planning, and others.

Multicolor Transparencies. Also available with this edition is a set of 130 multicolor transparencies. Only a few of these transparencies duplicate the illustrations in the textbook.

Achievement Tests. For this edition there are six tests that cover various parts of the textbook and a Final Examination that covers all 20 chapters in the textbook. Each of the six tests contains 24 true/false questions and 16 multiple-choice questions. The Final Examination has 48 true/false questions and 32 multiple-choice questions. None of the questions in the Achievement Tests duplicates a Review Question in *Practical Study Experiences in Managing Human Resources* or a question in the separate test bank.

Instructor's Resource Manual. This manual is more extensive than those of previous editions. For each chapter in the textbook, Section I of the manual for the 9th edition contains the following:

- Chapter synopsis and purpose.
- Chapter objectives (restated from this textbook).
- A very detailed lecture guide, based on the textbook chapter outline.
- Instructional aids that consist of an annotated list of audiovisual materials that are pertinent to the chapter's subject matter and are available from various sources.
- Answers to discussion questions in the textbook.
- Analysis of mini-cases in the textbook.
- Answers to projects in *Practical Study Experiences in Managing Human Resources*.
- Notes on the transparency masters, which are located at the back of the manual.

Section II of the manual contains the solutions to the extended cases in the textbook; Section III, the answers to the Achievement Tests; Section IV, the appendixes to the textbook; and Section V, the transparency masters (black-and-white versions of the multicolor transparencies mentioned earlier).

Test Bank. A separate manual, new with this edition, contains 1,460 test questions. There are 28 true/false, 42 multiple-choice, and 3 essay items per chapter, arranged by chapter topic using the major headings and page references from the text. Each objective question is coded to indicate whether it covers knowledge of key terms, understanding of concepts and principles, or application of principles. The Test Bank has been designed to facilitate use by instructors with differing requirements regarding content and format.

Testing Software. All items from the printed Test Bank and Achievement Tests are available on disk through South-Western's automated testing program, MicroSWAT III. This program allows you to create exams by selecting questions as provided by the program, modifying existing questions, or adding questions. MicroSWAT III will run on IBM PCs and compatibles with two double-sided disk drives and a minimum of 320K memory for DOS versions higher than 2.0 and lower than 3.0. For DOS versions 3.0 or higher, a minimum of 384K memory is required. The software will also run on a Tandy 1000 with a minimum of 320K memory, DOS 2.11 or higher, and two double-sided disk drives. MicroSWAT III is provided free of charge to instructors at educational institutions that adopt *Managing Human Resources*.

ACKNOWLEDGMENTS

We were fortunate in having the expertise of several reviewers each of whom read a few chapters. We appreciate their contributions in making this text as close as possible to the way things really are. Our thanks to:

William C. Bessey
Golden Gate University
Elmer H. Burack
University of Illinois at Chicago
Joseph H. Culver
University of Texas at Austin
Walter A. Fogel
University of California at Los Angeles
Rodger W. Griffeth
Louisiana State University
Edwin C. Leonard, Jr.
Indiana University/Purdue University at Fort Wayne
Desmond D. Martin
University of Cincinnati
Marcia P. Miceli
The Ohio State University
Larry E. Penley
Arizona State University
Dorothy Perrin Moore
The Citadel
Janet Thompson Reagan
California State University at Northridge
Sandy J. Wayne
University of Illinois at Chicago

In preparing the manuscript for this edition, we have drawn not only upon the current literature, but also upon the current practices of organizations that have furnished information and illustrations relating to their HR programs. We are indebted to the leaders in the field who have developed the available heritage of information and practices of HRM and who have influenced us through their writings and personal associations. We have also been aided by students in our classes, by former students of ours, by the participants in the management development programs with whom we have been associated, by HR managers, and by our colleagues. In particular, we would like to express our appreciation to the following individuals: Andrew J. Blaner, Luis R. Gomez-Mejia, Ph.D., Todd S. Hochman, Esq., Alexander J. Kavic, M.D., Sharon Watkins, and James F. White. We especially want to recognize the valuable contribution of Dr. Larry E. Penley, who authored the chapters on Motivating Employees (Chapter 14) and The Role of Communication in HRM (Chapter 15).

We are grateful to the team of individuals who helped to develop and produce this text. They include, at South-Western: Roger Ross, Publisher; Brigid Harmon, Developmental Editor; Susan Williams, Production Editor; Tania Hindersman, Marketing Manager; Joe Devine, Designer; and Kim Larson, Photo Researcher; and, at Carnes-Lachina: Ed Huddleston, Project Manager, and Laura Evans, Art Manager.

Our greatest indebtedness is to our wives—Leneve Sherman and Ronnie Bohlander—who have contributed in so many ways to this book over the years. Through their active participation in the preparation of the manuscript for this edition, they have been a source of invaluable guidance and assistance. Furthermore, by their continued enthusiasm and support, they have made the process a more pleasant and rewarding experience. We are most grateful to them for their many contributions to this publication, to our lives, and to our families.

Arthur W. Sherman, Jr.
California State University, Sacramento

George W. Bohlander
Arizona State University

Contents in Brief

Contents

PART ONE

HUMAN RESOURCES MANAGEMENT IN PERSPECTIVE

PART TWO

MEETING HUMAN RESOURCES REQUIREMENTS

PART FIVE

CREATING A PRODUCTIVE WORK ENVIRONMENT

PART SIX

STRENGTHENING EMPLOYEE–MANAGEMENT RELATIONS

PART SEVEN

INTERNATIONAL HUMAN RESOURCES MANAGEMENT AND HR AUDITS

CASES

Managing Human Resources

PART ONE

Human Resources Management in Perspective

The three chapters in Part One provide an overview of the field of human resources management. Chapter 1 describes the historical development of HR management, including the programs and policies required for HR departments to succeed. Chapter 2 discusses both the internal and the external factors that affect the supervision of an organization's human resources. It reviews important demographic changes in the U.S. work force and discusses how organizations are evolving to meet the needs of today's employees. Chapter 3 is concerned with the many federal laws, executive orders, and court rulings that influence how managers must treat present and prospective employees. It takes a look at equal employment opportunity and affirmative action, pervasive topics that have an impact on all HR activities. When managers and supervisors understand the environment of managing employees, they are in a better position to utilize these valuable organizational resources effectively.

CHAPTER 1

Development of Human Resources Management

After reading this chapter you will be able to:

1. *Describe the concept and approach underlying human resources management.*
2. *Trace the early development of the field of human resources management.*
3. *Cite the leaders and movements that contributed significantly to the field, as well as the nature of their contributions.*
4. *Describe the principal functions performed in human resources management and how these functions evolved.*
5. *Explain the importance of the strategic management approach in human resources management.*
6. *Identify the organizations and publications that contribute to the professional status of human resources management.*
7. *Describe the principal elements of a human resources program and their importance in managing human resources.*
8. *Describe the various responsibilities of the human resources department and the nature of its relationship with other departments.*
9. *Define the key terms in the chapter.*

TERMS TO IDENTIFY

personnel management (4)*
human resources management (HRM) (4)
scientific management (9)
Hawthorne studies (10)
human relations movement (11)
behavioral sciences (11)
organizational behavior (OB) (12)
organizational development (OD) (12)
certification (18)
HR objectives (24)
HR policies (24)
HR procedures (25)
HR information system (HRIS) (27)
HR budget (28)

If an organization is to achieve its goals, it must not only have the required resources, but it must also use them effectively. Traditionally, organizational resources have been divided into three categories—human, financial, and physical (buildings, machines, inventories, etc.). A fourth category of resources—technological resources, which include patents and processes that relate to both products and production methods—has been added more recently.[1] While human resources (HR) have always been critical to the success of any organization, they have assumed an increasingly greater importance that is being recognized inside and outside work organizations.

The human resources of an organization established to produce a product or provide a service typically include individuals with a wide variety and range of knowledge, skills, and abilities who are expected to perform job activities in a manner that contributes to the attainment of organizational goals. How effectively employees contribute to the organization depends in large part upon the quality of the organization's HR program and the ability and eagerness of management—from the CEO to first-line supervisors—to create an environment that fosters the effective use of the organization's human resources.

In the process of managing human resources, increasing attention is being given to the personal needs of the participants. Thus, throughout this book it is appropriate not only to emphasize the importance of the contributions that human resources management makes to the organization but also to give serious consideration to its effects on the individual and on society.

Increasingly, employees and the public at large are demanding that employers demonstrate greater social responsibility in managing their human resources. Com-

*The number in parentheses refers to the text page on which the term is introduced.

plaints that many jobs are devitalizing the lives and injuring the health of employees are not uncommon. Charges of discrimination against women, minorities, the physically handicapped, and the aged with respect to hiring, training, advancement, and compensation are being leveled against some employers. Issues such as comparable pay for comparable work, the rising costs of employee benefits, day care for children of employees, and alternative work schedules are concerns that many employers must address. Where employees are organized into unions, employers can encounter costly collective bargaining proposals, strike threats, and charges of unfair labor practices. Court litigation, demands for corrective action by governmental agencies, sizable damage awards in response to employee lawsuits, and attempts to erode the employment-at-will doctrine valued by employers are still other hazards that contemporary employers must try to avoid.

THE ROLE OF HUMAN RESOURCES MANAGEMENT

For many decades such responsibilities as selection, training, and compensation were considered basic functions constituting the area historically referred to as **personnel management.** These functions were performed without much regard for how they related to each other. From this narrow view we have seen the emergence of what is now known as human resources management. **Human resources management (HRM),** as it is currently perceived, represents the extension rather than the rejection of the traditional requirements for managing personnel effectively. An understanding of human behavior and skill in applying that understanding are still required. Also required are knowledge and understanding of the various personnel functions performed in managing human resources, as well as the ability to perform them in accordance with organizational objectives. An awareness of existing economic, social, and legal constraints upon the performance of these functions is also essential. Attention will be given to these constraints in the next chapter.

HRM, as it is practiced today, recognizes the dynamic interaction of personnel functions with each other and with the objectives of the organization. Most important, it recognizes that HR planning must be coordinated closely with the organization's strategic and related planning functions. As a result, efforts in HRM are being directed toward providing more support for the achievement of the organization's operating goals. These efforts are reflected in the statements from HR executives that are presented in Highlights in HRM 1.

The present status of the field of HRM has been achieved only after years of progress involving an evolutionary development. We hope this chapter will help readers not only to understand the forces that have contributed to this progress, but also to become more aware of the forces that may have an effect upon it today and in the future.

HIGHLIGHTS IN HRM

1 VOICES OF HR EXPERIENCE

"Human resources is part of the strategic planning process. Little is done that doesn't involve us in the planning, policy, or final stages of any deal."

Kathryn Connors, Corporate VP of Human Resources
Liz Claiborne, Inc.

"At no time in my career, which now spans 40 years, has more importance been placed by our top management on the human resources function."

H. Gordon Smith, Senior VP of Employee Relations
DuPont Company

"As a personnel executive you really have to understand the business and its priorities. You must know what is important to the business and how personnel can make things happen."

William Stopper, Director of Personnel Development
IBM Corporation

"If you are not looking at these people who are at the bottom of the line and looking to train and develop them, you're going to continue to have employment problems."

Von Johnston, Director of the People Division
Wal-Mart Stores

"We must be globally competitive in terms of human resources. If not, we won't be where we want to be five years from now."

E. Jeffrey Stoll, Director of Corporate Personnel Relations
Merck & Company

"To really get programs and attitudes and communication programs in place is an enormous challenge for human resources people. You don't see the results of your work for some time."

Rennie Roberts, Senior VP of Human Resources
American Express Company

"Our corporate values set J. P. Morgan apart from other firms. Two explicit values are flexibility and a team approach to doing business."

Helen Finnigan, Manager of Human Resources Policy and Consulting Unit
J. P. Morgan and Company, Inc.

"Although 3M desires a one-firm concept, we're challenged with managing a large firm with the value system of a small business."

Dennis L. Nowlin, Manager of Executive Development
3M

"How are we going to instill in our managers that it isn't the work force that has to change, but our corporate culture?"

Charlene Watler, Manager, Training and Development,
Employee Relations Department
Dow Jones & Company, Inc.

SOURCE: Stephanie Lawrence, "Voices of HR Experience, Part I," *Personnel Journal* 68, no. 4 (April 1989): 64–75; and Allan Halcrow, "Voices of HR Experience, Part II," *Personnel Journal* 68, no. 5 (May 1989): 38–49. Reproduced with permission.

EARLY STAGES OF DEVELOPMENT

HRM, at least in a primitive form, has existed since the dawn of group effort. Certain HR functions, even though informal in nature, were performed whenever people came together for a common purpose. During the course of this century, however, the processes of managing people have become more formalized and specialized, and a growing body of knowledge has been accumulated by practitioners and scholars. An understanding of the events contributing to the growth of HRM (see Figure 1–1) can provide a perspective for contemporary policies and practices.

The Factory System

During the 19th century, the development of mechanical power made possible a factory system of production. Power-driven equipment and improved production techniques enabled products to be manufactured more cheaply than had previously been possible in small shops and in homes. However, this process also created many jobs that were monotonous, unchallenging, and often unhealthy and hazardous. Moreover, factory workers lacked salable skills with which to bargain for improved working conditions or for economic security. This meant that they could be replaced by others who could be trained quickly to perform their jobs. (Even today the quality of work life and employment security are issues of concern for many factory workers.)

The concentration of workers in factories served to focus public attention on their conditions of employment. It also enabled workers to act collectively to achieve better conditions. Consequently, during the late 1880s, laws were passed in some states to regulate hours of work for women and children, to establish minimum wages for male labor, and to regulate working conditions that affect employee health and

FIGURE 1–1 IMPORTANT EVENTS IN THE DEVELOPMENT OF HRM

1786	Earliest authenticated strike in America by Philadelphia printers to gain minimum weekly wage of $6.
1842	*Commonwealth* v. *Hunt* decision, in which the conspiracy doctrine restricting collective bargaining was overturned by the Massachusetts Supreme Court.
1848	Passage of a law in Philadelphia setting a minimum wage for workers in commercial occupations.
1875	Initiation by the American Express Company of the first employer-sponsored pension plan.
1881	Beginning of Frederick W. Taylor's work in scientific management at the Midvale Steel Plant.
1883	Establishment of the United States Civil Service Commission.
1886	Founding of the American Federation of Labor (AFL).
1912	Passage in Massachusetts of the first minimum wage law.
1913	Establishment of the United States Department of Labor.
1913	Publication of Hugo Münsterberg's book *Psychology and Industrial Efficiency.*
1915	First course in personnel management offered at Dartmouth College for employment managers.
1917	First large-scale use of group intelligence tests—the Army *Alpha* and *Beta* tests.
1920	First text in personnel administration, by Ordway Tead and Henry C. Metcalf.
1924	Point method of job evaluation developed by the National Electric Manufacturers' Association and the National Metal Trades Association.
1927	Hawthorne studies begun by Mayo, Roethlisberger, and Dickson.
1935	Establishment of Congress of Industrial Organizations (CIO) by several unions previously affiliated with the AFL.
1939	Publication of the first edition of the *Dictionary of Occupational Titles.*
1941	Beginning of U.S. involvement in World War II, demanding the mobilization of individuals trained in personnel management and the rapid development of personnel programs in the defense forces and in industry.
1947	Establishment of the Industrial Relations Research Association (IRRA), a private organization to encourage and disseminate research on industrial relations.
1955	Merger of the AFL and CIO union organizations.
1967	Federal Women's Program established by U.S. Civil Service Commission to enhance the employment and advancement of women.
1975	Beginning of professional accreditation (now certification) program by the Personnel Accreditation Institute.
1978	Passage of the Civil Service Reform Act, which established the Office of Personnel Management (OPM), the Merit Systems Protection Board (MSPB), and the Federal Labor Relations Authority (FLRA).
1982	Beginning of the erosion of employment-at-will doctrine, with increasing attention to "just cause" terminations.
1985	Increased emphasis on employee participation and involvement in organizational decision making to improve productivity and competitive position.
1990	Heightened awareness of privacy rights of employees as employers use techniques to monitor employee performance.

Rubber workers at the B. F. Goodrich factory in Akron, Ohio, in 1913 strike to demand an eight-hour day and minimum wage.

safety. It was also at this time that laws were enacted to provide indemnity payments for injuries suffered in industrial accidents. Eventually, as the result of state legislation and collective bargaining, employment conditions began to improve. Even today, however, labor organizations, employees, and legislators believe there is still room for improvement.

The Mass Production System

Mass production was made possible by the availability of standardized and interchangeable parts designed to be used in assembly-line production. With this system came improvements in production techniques and the use of labor-saving machinery and equipment. The accompanying increases in overhead costs and wage rates, however, forced companies to seek ways of using production facilities and labor more efficiently.

CONTRIBUTIONS OF SCIENTIFIC MANAGEMENT Scientific management involves an objective and systematic approach to improving worker efficiency based on the collection and analysis of data. Frederick W. Taylor (1856–1915), whose contributions stimulated the scientific management movement, is often referred to as the father of scientific management. Among his contemporaries in this movement were Frank Gilbreth (1868–1924) and his wife, Lillian Gilbreth (1878–1972), Henry L. Gantt (1861–1919), and Harrington Emerson (1853–1931).[2] Dr. Lillian Gilbreth was one of the first women to gain an international reputation as a management consultant.[3] Professionally active until her death at age 94, she is the first psychologist to be honored on a U.S. postage stamp (Great Americans series, 1984).[4]

Taylor believed that work could be systematically analyzed and studied with the same scientific approach used by researchers in the laboratory. In his words, **scientific management** constituted "the substitution of exact scientific investigation and knowledge for the old individual judgment or opinion, either of the workman or the boss, in all matters relating to the work done in the establishment."[5] Taylor regarded accurate performance standards, based on objective data gathered from time studies and other sources, as important personnel management tools. These standards provided a basis for rewarding the superior workers financially and for eliminating the unproductive ones. According to Taylor, scientific management offered the best means for increasing workers' productivity and earnings and for providing higher profits to owners and lower prices to customers. His approach was in sharp contrast to the then prevailing practice of attempting to gain more work from employees by threatening them with the loss of their jobs. While the modern literature depicts Taylor as an authoritarian who equated worker motivation solely with money, one reviewer of Taylor's work shows that he anticipated several motivational strategies generally associated with the human relations movement, a topic which will be discussed later.[6]

CONTRIBUTIONS OF INDUSTRIAL/ORGANIZATIONAL PSYCHOLOGY By the early 1900s some of the knowledge and research from the field of psychology was beginning to be applied to the management of personnel. One of the best-known pioneers in industrial psychology was Hugo Münsterberg (1863–1916). His book *Psychology and Industrial Efficiency* (1913) called attention to the contributions that psychology could make in the areas of employment testing, training, and efficiency improvement.[7]

Just a few years after the publication of Münsterberg's book, many psychologists were called into military service for World War I. Most of them were engaged in various aspects of personnel selection and training; some were assigned to special projects in other personnel areas where their expertise could be utilized.

Many psychologists whose work before World War I had been largely theoretical and experimental followed Münsterberg's lead by making practical contributions to the personnel field in business and industry. Walter Dill Scott (1869–1955) received acclaim for his early work in the rating of sales personnel and for his classic book in personnel management, which he coauthored with Robert C. Clothier in 1923.[8]

James McKeen Cattell (1860–1944), another pioneer, is noted for his test development activities and his leadership in establishing The Psychological Corporation (1921), an organization that still offers personnel services.[9] These services include publishing and distributing employment tests and conducting validation studies for employers; the latter activity has become a very important aspect of HRM that will be examined in detail in Chapters 3 and 6. A contemporary of Cattell, Walter Van Dyke Bingham (1880–1952), gained prominence as an author of books on interviewing and aptitude testing that were widely used by personnel practitioners. Bingham later served as chief psychologist for the War Department, which included the Army and Air Force until the defense establishment was reorganized in 1947.[10]

LATER DEVELOPMENTS

The contemporary era of HRM began in the late 1920s. It was characterized by an increased concern for the human element in management. With this era came research in the area of human behavior and the development of new tools and techniques for managing people. It was also during this period that employer–employee relations began to become the subject of governmental regulations.

The Hawthorne Studies

Begun in the 1920s, the **Hawthorne studies** were an effort to determine what effect hours of work, periods of rest, and lighting might have on worker fatigue and productivity. These experiments constituted one of the first cooperative indus-

Women assemble telephone relays at the Hawthorne Works while production is monitored to gauge how environmental factors affect their work.

try/university research efforts. As the studies progressed, however, it was discovered that the social environment could have an equivalent if not greater effect on productivity than the physical environment.

Conducted by Elton Mayo (1880–1949), Fritz J. Roethlisberger (1898–1974), and W. J. Dickson (1904–) at the Western Electric Company's Hawthorne Works near Chicago, Illinois, these studies were a pioneering endeavor to examine factors affecting productivity.[11] While there has been considerable controversy over interpretation of the findings, HR specialists generally agree that the Hawthorne studies had a very important role in the development of HRM. The studies spurred efforts to humanize the workplace and to find more-sensitive ways to motivate workers, rather than to continue to regard them as assembly-line robots who could be kept producing through fear and discipline. Out of the interviewing techniques used by the Hawthorne researchers grew the nondirective approach to counseling, which recognizes the importance of feelings—something that until that time was generally considered somewhat inappropriate in employment situations.[12]

It is interesting to note that what the Hawthorne studies revealed about human relations had been anticipated some years earlier by a sociologist, Mary Parker Follett (1868–1933). In her writings she continually emphasized the important role of informal groups in work situations.[13]

The Human Relations Movement

Along with the work of Kurt Lewin (1890–1947) at the National Training Laboratories, the Hawthorne studies helped to give rise to the **human relations movement** by providing new insights into human behavior.[14] This movement focused attention on individual differences among employees and on the influence that informal groups may have upon employee performance and behavior. It also focused attention on the necessity for managers to improve their communications and to be more sensitive to the needs and feelings of their subordinates. Furthermore, the movement emphasized the need for a more participative and employee-centered form of supervision. The reader will observe later that various principles and practices currently applied in quality circles and other employee involvement programs grew out of the work of researchers and practitioners of the human relations movement.

Emergence of the Behavioral Sciences

As the human relations movement evolved, it became broader in scope. The understanding of human behavior was enhanced by contributions not only from the traditional disciplines of psychology, sociology, and anthropology, but also from social economics, political science, linguistics, and education. More important, the interrelationships of these various disciplines became more widely recognized, so that they are now referred to collectively as the **behavioral sciences.**

The behavioral science approach is oriented toward economic objectives, concerned with the total climate or milieu, and consistent with the development of interpersonal competence. It stresses a humanistic approach and the use of groups and participation in the achievement of organizational objectives, including the management of change.[15]

One of the major contributions of the behavioral science approach has been its application to **organizational behavior (OB),** which is concerned with employee behavior in work organizations. OB focuses on the relationships between individuals, groups, and the environment within an organization and their impact on employee behavior.

Efforts to create an organizational environment that will enlist cooperation and teamwork among employees have encouraged the growth of what has become known as **organizational development (OD).** The goal of OD is to bring about a change in the attitudes, values, and behavioral patterns of individuals and of the organizational environment in which they work. The reduction of mistrust and conflict, the encouragement of greater participation and productivity, and operating flexibility within the organization are among the specific outcomes sought from OD programs.

Growth of Governmental Regulations

Prior to the 1930s, employer relations with employees and with their labor organizations were subject to very few federal or state laws and regulations. However, political pressures for social reform created by the Depression of the 1930s gave rise to both federal and state legislation affecting these relations. Starting with the National Labor Relations Act in 1935, federal regulations have expanded to the point where they govern the performance of virtually every HR function. Some of the major federal laws and the functional areas of HRM they affect are listed in Figure 1–2.

Important federal legislation, executive orders, and major court decisions affecting HRM activities will be cited throughout this book. Special attention will be given in Chapter 3 to those laws, executive orders, and court decisions pertaining to equal employment opportunity. While emphasis must necessarily be given to federal laws and regulations, the reader should be aware that HR managers are also responsible for compliance with all state and local laws and regulations that govern work organizations. These are often more stringent than federal laws. Although employers are often critical of the demands these laws and regulations impose upon their operations, most of this legislation has been a response to employers' lack of social responsibility as manifested in their poor treatment of employees.

Increased Specialization of Functions

Initially, the management of human resources was limited largely to hiring, firing, and recordkeeping, functions carried out by managerial and supervisory personnel. Eventually, clerical personnel were employed to assist in keeping records relating to hours worked and to payroll.

FIGURE 1–2 IMPORTANT FEDERAL LEGISLATION GOVERNING HRM

1868	Passage by Congress of the first federal 8-hour day, covering laborers and mechanics employed by or working on behalf of the government.
1883	Civil Service Act, establishing a merit system of employment in the federal government.
1926	Railway Labor Act, supporting collective bargaining in the railroad industry.
1935	National Labor Relations Act (Wagner Act), giving workers the right to organize and bargain collectively.
1935	Social Security Act, which initially provided only for retirement benefits.
1938	Fair Labor Standards Act (FLSA), establishing a federal minimum wage with time and a half for overtime.
1947	Labor Management Relations Act (Taft-Hartley Act), placing curbs on union activities.
1959	Labor–Management Reporting and Disclosure Act (Landrum-Griffin Act), designed to eliminate improper actions toward union members by unions and management.
1963	Equal Pay Act, amendment to the FLSA, prohibiting wage differentials based on sex.
1964	Civil Rights Act of 1964, barring discrimination on the basis of race, color, religion, sex, or national origin.
1965	Executive Order 11246, requiring federal contractors to develop affirmative action programs for the employment of women and minorities.
1967	Age Discrimination in Employment Act, barring discrimination against employment of persons 40 to 70 years of age. (Later amended to 40 years of age or older.)
1970	Occupational Safety and Health Act (OSHA), establishing and enforcing safety and health standards.
1972	Equal Employment Opportunity Act, strengthening the Civil Rights Act of 1964 and providing for affirmative action programs.
1972	Vietnam Era Veterans' Readjustment Assistance Act, requiring federal contractors to undertake affirmative action programs for veterans.
1973	Vocational Rehabilitation Act, aiding handicapped workers.
1974	Employee Retirement Income Security Act (ERISA), reforming and regulating private pension systems.
1978	Pregnancy Discrimination Act, prohibiting discrimination against employment of pregnant women.
1982	Job Training Partnership Act, providing for employer participation in planning projects for the disadvantaged.
1986	Immigration Reform and Control Act, prohibiting unlawful employment of aliens and unfair immigration-related employment practices.
1986	Consolidated Omnibus Budget Reconciliation Act (COBRA), requiring employers to continue health coverage of employees, spouses, and dependents upon employee death, termination of employment, or divorce.
1988	Polygraph Protection Act, limiting an employer's ability to use lie detectors.
1988	Worker Adjustment and Retraining Notification Act, requiring employers to provide 60 days' notice before a facility closing or mass layoff.
1988	Drug-Free Workplace Act, requiring federal contractors or recipients of federal grants to take steps to ensure a drug-free workplace.
1990	Americans with Disabilities Act, prohibiting employers from discriminating against individuals with physical or mental handicaps or the chronically ill.

One of the first specialized jobs involving actual personnel work was that of welfare secretary. The welfare secretary's responsibility in an organization was to help workers and their families cope with personal problems of a financial, medical, housing, or similar nature.[16] In the decades following the establishment of this position, other functions were added to the personnel department's responsibilities.

By the 1940s the typical personnel department in a medium-sized or large organization included individuals with specific training and/or experience to carry out these specialized functions. As top management gradually recognized the importance of functions performed by HR departments in the achievement of organizational objectives, HR managers were elevated to higher levels. Today it is common for the corporate HR manager to occupy a position at the vice-president level.

The major HR functions performed in today's organizations have had a long history. We will briefly examine their development to provide a perspective for our study of contemporary HRM. While most of the books and articles cited in the Notes and References section (at the end of each chapter in this text) are current, the reader should always be aware that the philosophy and practices reflected in contemporary HRM have evolved from a history encompassing several decades.

RECRUITMENT AND SELECTION Early recruiting practices often varied with the supply of qualified applicants to fill openings. When there was a line of applicants seeking work, recruiting was often done at the entrance to company premises. For jobs requiring some degree of skill or training, advertisements or private employment agencies were used to attract applicants.

Employee selection was initially based on subjective decisions reached through face-to-face contact. The federal government was one of the first employers to attempt to select and promote employees on an objective basis by using competitive examinations. However, tests—the most objective of selection tools—did not become popular until the entry of the United States into World War I, when psychologists who had developed various tests of mental ability were given the assignment of constructing tests that could be used for the selection and classification of recruits. After World War I employers who were sold on the value of tests often used them without the technical competence required to evaluate the results.[17] As we pursue this topic further in later chapters, we will learn what corrective action has since been taken to overcome this problem.

TRAINING AND DEVELOPMENT Personnel training was emphasized by both industry and government during World Wars I and II. The most important innovation during World War II was the creation of the Training Within Industry (TWI) program for helping supervisors to become more effective in their positions. Experience and knowledge gained during both wars helped to make organizations aware of the potential contributions of formal training programs. In recent years, training programs have been broadened to include developmental activities and career planning for personnel at all levels.

PERFORMANCE APPRAISAL One of the first systems of performance appraisal was that developed by Walter Dill Scott to rate salespersons. Referred to as the *man-to-man rating scale,* this system compared the performance of salespersons against the performance levels of selected individuals that provided the benchmarks for the scale. In the decades since Scott developed his rating scale, a variety of appraisal methods have emerged, but because of their failure to meet technical standards and/or user acceptance, many of these methods have disappeared. Other methods with lesser deficiencies have emerged and are currently being used. The methods discussed in Chapter 9 are those that have lived through an evolutionary process.

COMPENSATION MANAGEMENT Not until the middle 1920s were objective job evaluation systems developed for determining hourly wage rates based on the worth of jobs. At about that time more employers also began to provide certain benefits and services for their employees, including health and recreation services, paid holidays, vacations, sick leave, and life insurance. Although these benefits were reduced drastically during the Depression of the 1930s, they were restored on an even greater scale beginning with World War II. In Chapter 12 on employee benefits, we will see that the types of benefits available today could not even have been thought possible in the early 1940s.

LABOR RELATIONS The sweeping layoffs caused by the Depression of the 1930s led society to realize that individual workers possessed little bargaining power and few employment rights in the face of big business. This realization led to the passage in 1935 of the National Labor Relations Act (Wagner Act), which offered encouragement for employees in the private sector to unionize and bargain collectively. With the large-scale unionization that followed passage of the Wagner Act, the bargaining power of employees increased dramatically.

Since the early 1960s, employees in the public sector have been receiving similar encouragement. Once unionized, employees in both sectors have bargained and even gone on strike for improved employment conditions. Labor relations continues to be a vital function of HRM. However, as we will observe in Part 6 of this text, the percentage of employees who belong to a union has been decreasing, and the power that unions once wielded has declined as a result of many forces.

Emphasis on Strategic Management

While top management has generally recognized the contributions of the HR program to the organization, there has been a growing need for HR managers to assume a broader role in overall organizational strategy. In short, "the HR function should be planned, organized, and evaluated on the basis of its contribution to the business."[18] Or, as expressed more pointedly, "Today's HR managers—whether located at corporate headquarters, at a manufacturing plant, or at a research and development facility—must remember the bottom line if they are to earn their board and keep."[19]

HRM in the 1990s should play a vital role in creating and sustaining the competitive advantage of an organization. In order to carry out their expanded role, many HR professionals will therefore need to acquire new competencies. This set of competencies is illustrated in Figure 1–3 and summarized as follows:

1. *Business Capabilities.* HR professionals will need to know the business of their organization thoroughly. This requires an understanding of its economic and financial capabilities.
2. *State-of-the-Art HRM Practices.* HR professionals will be the organization's behavioral science experts. In areas such as staffing, development, appraisal, rewards, organizational design, and communication, HR professionals should develop competencies that keep them abreast of developments.
3. *Management of Change Process.* HR professionals will have to be able to manage change processes so that HR activities are effectively merged with the business needs of the organization.

The ability to integrate business, HRM, and management of change is essential.[20] By helping their organization build a sustained competitive advantage through HRM and by learning to manage many activities well, HR professionals will become strategic business partners. Many of the most forward-looking CEOs are seeking top HR managers who can report directly to them and help them address key issues.[21]

Use of Consultants

HR managers frequently go outside the organization for professional assistance from qualified consultants. These consultants are hired to solve a variety of HR problems. In the past, most of the consulting firms specialized in one or two areas

FIGURE 1–3 COMPETENCIES OF HR PROFESSIONALS

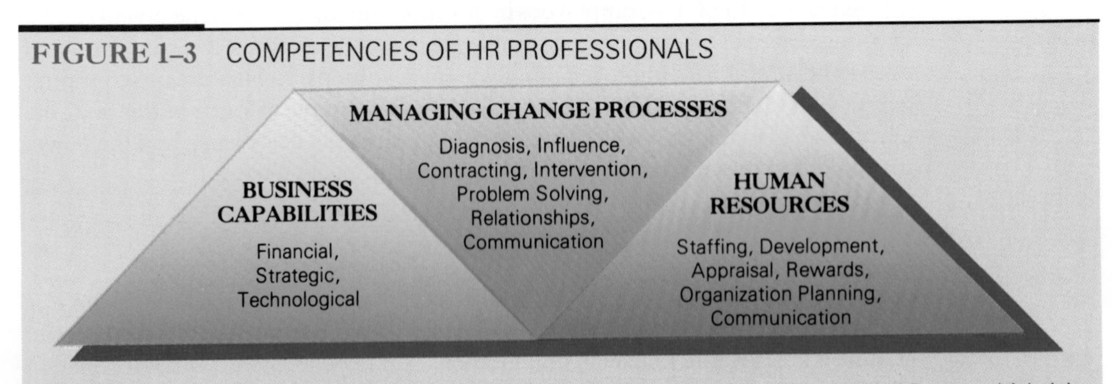

SOURCE: David Ulrich, Wayne Brockbank, and Arthur Yeung, "HR Competencies in the 1990s," *Personnel Administrator* 34, no. 11 (November 1989): 91–93. Reprinted with the permission from *HRMagazine* (formerly *Personnel Administrator*), published by the Society for Human Resource Management, Alexandria, VA.

of expertise, though many have broadened their expertise in order to meet the expanding needs of their clients more effectively. The areas for which consultants are used most frequently are pension plans, executive recruitment, health and welfare plans, psychological assessment, wage and salary administration, job evaluation, and executive compensation.

While consultants used by HR departments represent many different academic disciplines (economics, law, finance, and others), often they have advanced education in industrial/organizational psychology and organizational behavior and are frequently enlisted to help organizations in the areas of selection, training, employee motivation and satisfaction, performance appraisal, and design of organizational structures and working conditions. In utilizing the services of a consultant, it is important to select an experienced, reputable individual, to educate him or her about the corporate environment, and to have a clear understanding of what the consultant is to do.[22]

Professionalization of Human Resources Management

Because of the changes occurring in the work force and its environment, HR managers can no longer function simply as technical specialists who perform the various HRM functions. Instead, they must concern themselves with the total scope of HRM and its role within the organization and society as a whole. Therefore, HR managers today should be professionals with respect to both their qualifications and their performance.

One of the characteristics of a profession is the development through research and experimentation of an organized body of knowledge. This knowledge is exchanged through conferences, seminars, and workshops sponsored by professional associations. The latest information in the field is communicated through the literature published by the professional associations, as well as by various nonprofit organizations and educational institutions. Other characteristics of a profession include the establishment of a code of ethics and of certification requirements for its members. HRM exhibits all these characteristics.

PROFESSIONAL ASSOCIATIONS AND CERTIFICATION Today a number of professional organizations represent general, as well as specialized, areas of HRM. The professional association with the largest membership—more than 45,000—is the Society for Human Resource Management (SHRM), until September 1989 known as the American Society for Personnel Administration (ASPA). Its members come from organizations with a total work force of more than 53 million employees.[23] Affiliated with SHRM are local chapters in major cities throughout the United States, many of which sponsor student conferences, seminars, and workshops. The national annual meeting of the society is held in a different city each year. The society publishes *HR Magazine* (formerly *Personnel Administrator*) and *HR News* (formerly *Resource*), as well as various books and bulletins. While *HR Magazine* is available to the general public and is found in most libraries, *HR News* is available

Former Labor Secretary Elizabeth Dole addresses the national SHRM conference in June 1990.

only to members of SHRM. SHRM frequently collaborates with the Bureau of National Affairs, Inc. (BNA), in conducting surveys in various areas of HRM.

Other leading professional associations in the field include the International Personnel Management Association, the International Personnel Management Association for Personnel Women, the American Management Association (AMA), and The Conference Board (CB). AMA and CB are prominent nonprofit organizations that provide publications and educational services relating to HRM and other functional areas. Organizations that represent specialized areas of interest include the Human Resource Planning Society, the American Compensation Association, the American Society for Training and Development, the Association for Industrial Research, and the Society for Industrial and Organizational Psychology of the American Psychological Association. For professors in the field, there is the Personnel and Human Resources Division of the Academy of Management.[24] All of these organizations sponsor meetings and workshops that promote the professional growth of their members. They also provide opportunities for contact with other organizations, including government agencies.

The professionalization of a field generally leads to some form of **certification** for practitioners to enhance their status and to recognize their competency. The Human Resource Certification Institute of SHRM, established in 1975, has developed such a program for professionals in HRM. The program offers two types of certification, each of which reflects the number of specialties and the amount of experience and/or academic training possessed by the recipient. The certifications and the requirements for achieving them are as follows:

1. Professional in Human Resources (PHR)—four years' professional HRM experience or two years' HRM experience and a related bachelor's degree (or one year's HRM experience and a related graduate degree).
2. Senior Professional in Human Resources (SPHR)—eight years' professional HRM experience or six years' HRM experience and a related bachelor's degree (or five years' HRM experience and a related graduate degree). The most recent three years must include policy-developing responsibility.

To qualify for either of these certifications, an applicant must provide verification of experience and pass an intensive four-hour written examination to demonstrate mastery of knowledge. The certifications, which must be renewed every three years, serve largely to indicate the qualifications of recipients and encourage others to qualify for certification. As the reputation of the certification program grows and becomes even more widely recognized among the ranks of top management, it can become an important qualification for individuals seeking positions in HRM.[25]

CODE OF ETHICS It is typical for professional associations to develop a code of ethics that members are expected to observe. The code shown in Figure 1–4 was developed for HR managers by the SHRM. Many large corporations have their own code of ethics to govern corporate relations with employees and the public at large.

Adherence to a code often creates a dilemma for professionals, including those in HRM. Referring to principles in the SHRM code in Figure 1–4, Wallace observes:

> With an orientation toward profitable business, whom do HR professionals service? Who is the client—management or the individual employees? In the course of serving the employees and management and maintaining respect and regard for human values, whose needs are paramount? What happens when—which is frequently the case in HR work—the confidential issues of management and/or the employees are in conflict?[26]

These and similar questions are not easy to answer. However, the fact that there is a code does focus attention on ethical values and provides a basis for HR professionals to evaluate their plans and their actions.

The HR staff is of course concerned with monitoring ethics in its own operations. More recently, however, HR departments have been given a greater role in communicating the organization's values and standards, monitoring compliance with its code of ethics, and enforcing the standards throughout the organization. Many organizations have ethics committees and ethics ombudsmen to provide training in ethics to employees. The general objectives of ethics training are stated in Highlights in HRM 2.[27]

PROFESSIONAL LITERATURE Personal development in any profession requires keeping abreast of the current literature in the field. A number of periodicals contain articles on general or specialized areas of interest in HRM. Here are some of the more important journals students and practitioners should be familiar with:

Compensation and Benefits Review
Employee Relations Law Journal
Employee Responsibilities and Rights Journal
HR Magazine
Human Relations
Human Resource Management
Human Resource Management Review
Human Resource Planning
Industrial and Labor Relations Review
Industrial Relations
International Journal of Human Resources
Management
Journal of Applied Psychology
Journal of Collective Negotiation in the Public Sector
Journal of Labor Research
Journal of Management
Journal of Vocational Behavior
Labor Law Journal
Labor Studies Journal
Monthly Labor Review
Personnel
Personnel Administrator (now *HR Magazine*)
Personnel Journal
Personnel Psychology
Public Personnel Management
Supervisory Management
Training
Training and Development Journal

Other periodicals that cover the general field of business and management often contain articles pertaining to HRM. Among these are *Academy of Management Executive*, *Academy of Management Journal*, *Academy of Management Review*, *Business Horizons*, *California Management Review*, *Harvard Business Review*, *Journal of Business Ethics*, *Management Review*, *Business Week*, and *The Wall Street Journal*.

FIGURE 1–4 CODE OF ETHICS OF THE SHRM

SOCIETY FOR
HUMAN
RESOURCE
MANAGEMENT

Code of Ethics

As a member of the Society for Human Resource Management, I pledge myself to:

- **Maintain the highest standards of professional and personal conduct.**
- **Strive for personal growth in the field of human resource management.**
- **Support the Society's goals and objectives for developing the human resource management profession.**
- **Encourage my employer to make the fair and equitable treatment of all employees a primary concern.**
- **Strive to make my employer profitable both in monetary terms and through the support and encouragement of effective employment practices.**
- **Instill in the employees and the public a sense of confidence about the conduct and intentions of my employer.**
- **Maintain loyalty to my employer and pursue its objectives in ways that are consistent with the public interest.**
- **Uphold all laws and regulations relating to my employer's activities.**
- **Refrain from using my official positions, either regular or volunteer, to secure special privilege, gain or benefit for myself.**
- **Maintain the confidentiality of privileged information.**
- **Improve public understanding of the role of human resource management**

This Code of Ethics for members of the Society for Human Resource Management has been adopted to promote and maintain the highest standards of personal conduct and professional standards among its members. Adherence to this code is required for membership in the Society and serves to assure public confidence in the integrity and service of human resource management professionals.

SOURCE: Society for Human Resource Management. Reproduced with permission.

HIGHLIGHTS IN HRM

2 OBJECTIVES OF ETHICS TRAINING FOR EMPLOYEES

1. To increase awareness of the ethical principles and values behind everyday work decisions.
2. To increase awareness of the organization's standards of conduct and their application.
3. To identify key ethical issues facing employees in different divisions and functional areas.
4. To increase awareness of pressures that may lead to unethical conduct.
5. To alert employees to the importance of avoiding ethical misconduct and the need to report unethical practices.
6. To publicize the consequences to individuals if they are caught or suspected of misconduct.

SOURCE: Gary Edwards and Kirk Bennett, "Ethics and HR: Standards in Practice," *Personnel Administrator* 32, no. 12 (December 1987): 62–66. Reprinted with the permission from *HRMagazine* (formerly *Personnel Administrator*), published by the Society for Human Resource Management, Alexandria, VA.

The vast number of books and articles being published on HRM makes it virtually impossible even to locate, let alone read, all of the literature in the field. Consequently, students and practitioners will find three references invaluable in locating those books and articles they may have time to read and those with the most pertinent information. One is *Personnel Management Abstracts*, which contains abstracts from journals and books and an index of periodical literature.[28] The second is *Work Related Abstracts*, organized into broad categories with a cumulative guide to specific subjects, organizations, and individuals.[29] The third is *Human Resources Abstracts* (An International Information Service), which provides abstracts of current literature from more than 250 sources.[30] Also, the reader should not overlook various computerized compilations of periodical literature that are available in most libraries. One source is the ABI/INFORM, a computerized index to business information whose strength is its 150-word summaries of significant articles.

RESEARCH ORGANIZATIONS Throughout this book many of the findings from the efforts of a number of different research organizations and individuals will be reported. The primary function of these organizations is to conduct research and to make their findings available to all who are interested in them. Many such organizations may be found at universities. Probably the largest university research center in the behavioral sciences is the Institute for Social Research at the University

Important HRM information can be found in the BNA manual.

of Michigan. Its three divisions—the Survey Research Center, the Research Center for Group Dynamics, and the Center for Political Studies—have together published over 5,000 books, articles, and reports.

A number of state universities have centers for the study of labor and industrial relations, including those in California, Minnesota, Illinois, and New York. The School of Industrial and Labor Relations at Cornell University is also well known for its publications. Organizations sponsored by industry, such as the American Management Association (AMA) and The Conference Board (CB), publish research studies that benefit managers in HRM. Rand Corporation of Santa Monica, California, and the Brookings Institution of Washington, D.C., are also recognized for their contributions to this as well as other fields.

The Bureau of National Affairs, Inc. (BNA), Commerce Clearing House (CCH), and Prentice-Hall (PH) also conduct surveys relating to HRM policies and practices. Survey results from these organizations may be found in loose-leaf volumes that contain a wealth of information about policies and practices and the legal aspects of HRM. The student of HRM should become familiar with the various BNA, CCH, and PH publications that are updated regularly. These volumes are available in many college and university libraries, city libraries, and the libraries of the larger work organizations.

ACADEMIC TRAINING With so much attention focused on the behavioral sciences during the 1960s and 1970s, the subject of HRM suffered from neglect at some colleges and universities. Since then, however, equal employment opportunity, comparable worth, employee rights, concern for productivity, cost of employee benefits, and other current issues have rekindled interest in HRM courses and in HRM as a major field of study.

A random survey of HR professionals conducted in 1967 and 1968 and a repeated and expanded survey in 1987 reveal a shift in specific courses taken in college. Figure 1–5 shows a sizable increase in courses in introduction to personnel/HR, human relations, and wage and salary administration. Courses in organizational behavior, which were almost nonexistent at the time of the original study, rank second in frequency.

In the past, many HR professionals entered the field with degrees in liberal arts and sciences and perhaps a few business courses taken as electives. However, as certification requirements and other factors became essential for professional status, a bachelor's degree and even a master's degree in business have become more important. The degrees earned by the 1987 survey respondents, compared to those of respondents 20 years earlier, tended to be more in business areas such as personnel/HRM, general management, and general business.

In addition to business courses, it is desirable for students planning careers in HRM to take courses in such areas as personnel and organizational psychology, industrial sociology, economics, industrial engineering, and electronic data processing.

A knowledge of computer operations is essential for processing and reporting personnel data to gauge the performance of HR programs. While learning about the

FIGURE 1-5 COURSES TAKEN BY HR PROFESSIONALS

Specific courses taken at the university level by frequency, percentage, and rank

	1967–68			1987–88			Percentage Increase or Decrease
	Frequency	Percentage	Rank	Frequency	Percentage	Rank	
Introduction to Personnel/HR	54	40.9	2	103	59.5	1	+18.6
Organizational Behavior*	0	—	—	95	54.9	2	+54.9
Human Relations	44	25.8	4	87	50.3	3	+24.5
Wage and Salary Administration	30	22.7	5	68	39.3	4	+16.6
Industrial Psychology	61	46.2	1	65	37.6	5	−8.6
Labor Problems	49	37.1	3	58	33.5	6	−3.6
Job Evaluation	30	22.7	5	57	32.9	7	+10.2
Collective Bargaining	29	21.9	8	56	32.4	8	+10.5
Problems in Personnel/HR	30	22.7	5	41	23.7	9	+1.0
Industrial Sociology	16	12.1	10	30	17.3	10	+5.2
Time and Motion Study	25	18.9	9	15	8.7	11	−10.2
Other	0	—	—	30	17.3	—	—

*Organizational behavior was added to most college offerings a few years after the 1967–68 survey.

SOURCE: O. Jeff Harris and Art L. Bethke, "HR Professionals Two Decades Later," *Personnel Administrator* 34, no. 2 (February 1989): 66–71. Reprinted with the permission from *HRMagazine* (formerly *Personnel Administrator*), published by the Society for Human Resource Management, Alexandria, VA.

uses of computers, it is desirable for future HR professionals to become knowledgeable in research design and the use of statistics in research.

In the past three decades, graduate programs in business schools have expanded considerably. Undergraduates often ask if they should pursue a graduate course of study. To answer this question, a survey was conducted among HR practitioners who are certified members of SHRM. The survey asked them to indicate their level of agreement with the statement "A master's degree in personnel and/or labor will be increasingly important in the '80s and '90s." Of 304 respondents, 85 percent strongly agreed or agreed with the statement.[31]

THE PROGRAM FOR MANAGING HUMAN RESOURCES

The HR program constitutes the overall plan for managing HR and for guiding managers and supervisors in decisions relating to their subordinates. It establishes the objectives, policies, procedures, and budget pertaining to the HR functions to be performed. Although HR managers are responsible for coordinating and enforcing policies relating to HR functions, responsibility for performing these functions rests with all managers and supervisors within an organization.

Objectives

HR objectives are determined by the organization's objectives as a whole. More and more, HR objectives are reflecting the increasing social responsibilities of organizations, which include not only traditional responsibilities to customers, employees, and shareholders but also responsibilities to the community and the total society. Creating employment opportunities for the disadvantaged and providing a favorable work environment and greater financial security represent but a few ways in which organizations can exercise greater social responsibility.

Policies

Closely related to HR objectives are **HR policies** that serve to guide the actions required to achieve these objectives. Policies provide the means for carrying out the management processes, and as such are an aid to decision making. Like objectives, they may be idealistic or realistic, general or specific, flexible or inflexible, qualitative or quantitative, broad or narrow in scope. However, while objectives determine what is to be done, policies explain how it is to be done.

NEED FOR POLICIES Carefully developed policies are vital to HRM because employees are sensitive to any differences, no matter how slight, in the treatment they may receive compared with others. The quickest way to impair employee efficiency and morale is for a manager to show favoritism in decisions such as those relating to vacations, work schedules, raises and promotions, overtime, or disciplinary action. Decisions can be made more rapidly and more consistently if policies relating to these and other subjects have been formulated and communicated throughout the organization.

FORMULATION OF POLICIES The formulation of HR policies for approval by top management should be a cooperative endeavor among managers, supervisors, and members of the HR staff. Policy committees facilitate the pooling of experience and knowledge. Participation by operating managers is particularly essential because they are often more familiar with the specific areas in which problems arise, and also because their cooperation is required for policy enforcement. On the other hand, the manager and staff of the HR department have the responsibility for exercising leadership in formulating policies that are consistent with overall organizational objectives. They also must make certain that these policies are compatible with current economic conditions, collective bargaining trends, and laws and regulations at the federal, state, and local levels.

WRITTEN POLICY STATEMENTS Organizations can make their HR policies more authoritative by putting them in writing. To strengthen their effectiveness, these statements, which may be compiled into a policy manual, should include the reasons the policy is needed.[32] Written policy statements can serve as invaluable aids in orienting and training new personnel, administering disciplinary action, and resolving grievance issues with employees and their unions. When distributed to employees, these policy statements can provide answers to many questions that might otherwise have to be referred to supervisors. A sample policy statement relating to overtime is shown in Highlights in HRM 3.

In recent years, HR policy statements as well as employee handbooks have assumed the force of a legal contract between employer and employee. Just as employers refer to policy statements as a basis for their personnel actions, employees now cite company failure to adhere to established policies as a violation of their rights. It is therefore advisable for organizations to insert a disclaimer or waiver in employee manuals to the effect that the contents of the manual do not constitute a contract. The disclaimer should be prominently placed, not buried in a footnote. Wording the manual carefully (avoiding "always" and "never," for example), using a conversational tone rather than legalistic jargon, and having an outside labor counsel check the manual can help in avoiding problems.[33]

Procedures

HR procedures serve to implement policies by prescribing the chronological sequence of steps to follow in carrying out the policies. Procedures relating to employee selection, for example, might provide that individuals first be required to complete an application form, followed by an interview with an HR office representative. Grievances, promotions, transfers, and wage adjustments likewise must be administered according to established procedure in order to avoid the problems resulting from oversights. For example, as a step in the disciplinary procedure, the failure to give an employee written warning of a violation might prevent the organization from discharging the employee for a second violation.

HR procedures, like HR policies, must be treated as means to an end, not as ends in themselves. As we mentioned earlier, when organizations become more bureaucratic, complaints may be raised about excessive "red tape," inflexibility, and impersonality in making HR decisions. Unfortunately, when procedures become too detailed or numerous, they can impair rather than further the interests of the organization and its employees. To avoid this hazard, procedures must be reviewed periodically and modified to meet changes in conditions that may affect them.

HIGHLIGHTS IN HRM

3 SAMPLE POLICY STATEMENT

Subject: Overtime Hours and Pay

Purpose: To ensure equitable payment of overtime compensation to eligible employees in accordance with all applicable provisions of federal and state law.

Guidelines:

1. The company's workweek runs from Monday through Sunday, with normal operating hours scheduled from 8 A.M. Monday through 5 P.M. Friday. The normal daily work schedule for employees consists of an eight-hour day within a 24-hour period. The normal weekly schedule consists of a 40-hour week. Employees are entitled to a daily one-hour unpaid lunch period, and to two 15-minute paid break periods each day.
2. Business demands or production deadlines occasionally may require some employees to work overtime, which means more than eight hours in a 24-hour day or more than 40 hours in a week. Supervisors will try to inform employees well in advance of any overtime requirement. Employees may not work more than their scheduled daily or weekly hours without written authorization from their supervisor. In assigning overtime, supervisors will seek to distribute extra hours equitably among employees who have the required skills and abilities to perform the necessary work.
3. All employees considered "nonexempt" under the Fair Labor Standards Act will be paid at the rate of time and one-half ($1\frac{1}{2}$ times their regular rate of pay) for all hours worked in excess of 40 in one week. Scheduled holidays, vacation days, and time off for jury duty will be considered hours worked for purposes of calculating overtime. Unscheduled absences or time off for sickness, emergencies, or other personal reasons will not be considered hours worked for overtime purposes.
4. Nonexempt employees who work on company-recognized holidays will be paid their regular rate for the extra hours worked, in addition to their regular holiday pay. However, no "pyramiding" of paid holiday worktime—i.e., treating it as hours worked for weekly overtime computation purposes—is allowed.
5. Employees considered "exempt" under the Fair Labor Standards Act will be compensated for abnormal amounts of extra time worked. Exempt employees will be paid their straight-time rate for all extra authorized hours worked in excess of 46 in a week.
6. Compensatory time off is not available to any employee—exempt or nonexempt—for work in excess of regularly scheduled hours.
7. Nonexempt employees must record their daily work hours either on time clocks in their department or on time cards supplied by their supervisor. Occasional minor differences—i.e., five minutes or less—between a nonexempt worker's scheduled time and recorded worktime will be ignored. Exempt employees must complete and turn in to their supervisor a weekly report indicating how many hours they spent on exempt work and how many, if any, on nonexempt work.
8. Employees who falsify their own or another worker's time record will be subject to severe penalties, up to and including dismissal.

SOURCE: Reprinted with permission from *Employment Guide,* p. 29:103. Copyright 1986 by The Bureau of National Affairs, Inc.

Throughout this book the discussion of policies and procedures for the various HRM functions will reflect what is typical of the large or medium-sized organization. In smaller organizations HRM is often carried out on an informal basis, and attention to policies and formal procedures may vary considerably. Since most federal laws governing work organizations apply to large organizations, small organizations have greater latitude in the way they manage their employees and perform HR activities. The reader should also be aware that our descriptions of the implementation of various HR policies are probably closer to the "ideal" than to what is typically found in many organizations.

Human Resources Information Systems

Effective HRM requires an **HR information system (HRIS)** to provide current and accurate data for purposes of control and decision making. The system is composed of procedures, equipment, information, methods to compile and evaluate information, the people who use the information, and information management.[34]

HRIS has been enhanced by advancements in computer technology. According to one survey of a randomly selected group of subscribers to *Personnel Journal,* 99.8 percent of the respondents have automated one or more HR functions. The functions for which computers are used by these organizations, and the percentages of organizations using them, are as follows:

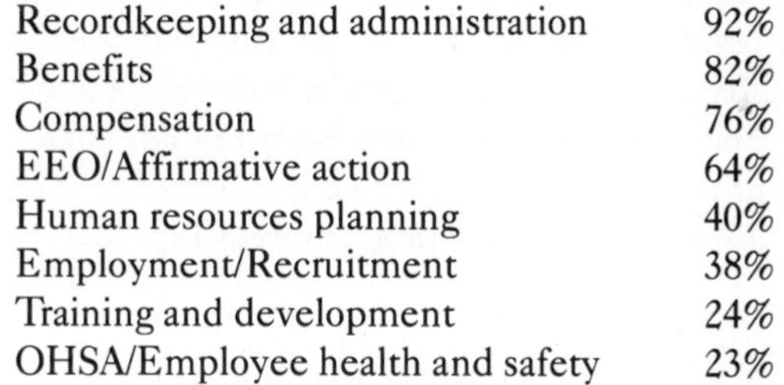

Recordkeeping and administration	92%
Benefits	82%
Compensation	76%
EEO/Affirmative action	64%
Human resources planning	40%
Employment/Recruitment	38%
Training and development	24%
OHSA/Employee health and safety	23%

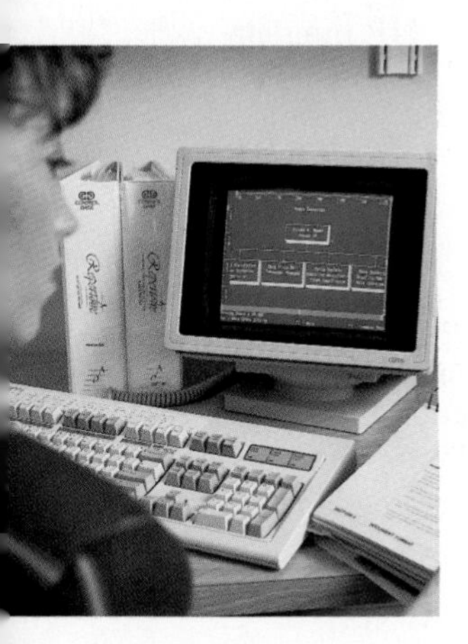

Many software packages are available for use by the human resources manager.

To date, computers in HRIS have been used primarily for storage and retrieval, but the trend is toward broader applications, including the production of basic reports, HR calculations, long-range forecasting and strategic planning, career/promotion planning, and evaluation of HR policies and practices.[35]

A well-designed HRIS can serve as the main management tool in the alignment of HR department goals with the goals of long-term strategic planning. As HR issues have been increasingly recognized as critical factors in strategic planning decisions, the ability of the HRIS to quantify, analyze, and model change has enhanced the status of the HRIS in many organizations.[36]

The entire range of computer hardware—mainframes, minicomputers, and microcomputers—is used for HRIS. Mainframe computers tend to be used in larger organizations and microcomputers (i.e., personal computers, or PCs) in smaller organizations. It is possible to combine both systems, linking microcomputers at individual workstations with a single mainframe. The price of the PC has made computing affordable for literally millions of individuals and small organizations.[37] Also, HRM software for PCs is available from many sources, making these kinds of systems even more useful for HR departments.

With a PC, the HR professional can take advantage of a variety of information services. An on-line service designed especially for HR departments is the Human Resource Information Network, a subsidiary of BNA. It provides up-to-the-minute information in several categories, including news, research, software, and services, covering all disciplines of HRM. SHRM also has an on-line database that permits users to access the SHRM library and quickly search the more than 24,000 citations of books and articles.[38]

In developing an effective HRIS, an organization must address privacy issues in advance. A data privacy policy can make the HRIS a positive factor in employee relations rather than a mistrusted disseminator of sensitive personnel information.[39] A comprehensive discussion of privacy issues will be presented in the next chapter.

Budget

Statements relating to objectives, policies, and procedures, or to a program as a whole can be meaningful only if they are supported financially through the budget. An **HR budget** is both a financial plan and a control for the expenditure of funds necessary to support the HR program. As such, it is one of the best indicators of management's real attitude toward the program. Thus, while an organization's selection policy may be to hire only fully qualified applicants to fill vacancies, its ability to observe this policy will depend on whether it budgets enough money to screen applicants carefully. Securing adequate funds for the HR budget further requires the HR staff to be able to convince top management that the HR program is cost-effective and is producing results.

HUMAN RESOURCES DEPARTMENT

We observed earlier that the HR manager is assuming a greater role in top-management planning and decision making. This trend reflects a growing awareness of the contributions that HRM can make to the success of the organization. Although managerial personnel at all levels are engaged in HRM activities, the top manager of the HR department has the primary responsibility for developing a program that will help the organization to meet its HRM objectives.

Responsibilities of the Human Resources Manager

Since the early 1960s, federal and state legislation and court decisions have had a major influence on HR policies and practices. More recently, concern over declining productivity, employee demands for a better work environment, and desire of workers for a better quality of life have added to the responsibilities of the HR manager. These influences have thus required HR managers not only to be more knowledgeable about many issues, but also to be more versatile in handling several activities. The major activities for which an HR manager is typically responsible are as follows:

1. *Policy Initiation and Formulation.* Proposal and drafting of new policies or policy revisions to cover recurring problems or prevent anticipated problems. Ordinarily, these are proposed to the senior executives of the organization, who actually issue the policy.
2. *Advice.* Counseling and advising line managers. The HR staff is expected to be fully familiar with HR policy, labor agreements, past practice, and the needs and welfare of both the organization and the employees in order to develop sound solutions to problems.
3. *Service.* Activities of HR administration such as recruiting, selection, testing, planning of training programs, grievance hearings, and so forth.
4. *Control.* Monitoring performance of line departments and other staff departments to ensure conformity with established HR policy, procedures, and practice.[40]

The HR manager's authority in carrying out these activities is restricted to staff authority (policy initiation and formulation and advice giving) and functional authority (service and control). Within the scope of functional authority, the HR manager generally has the right and is expected to issue policies and procedures for HR functions—i.e., selection, training, performance evaluation, etc.—throughout an organization. The only line authority the HR manager has is over subordinates in his or her department.

In-House Consultant

A major contribution that the HR department staff can make to the organization is to serve as in-house consultants to the managers and supervisors of other departments. Alerting top management to contemporary issues and changes within society that affect the organization is also an important responsibility. Closely related is the responsibility of monitoring new developments taking place in the HR field and, when feasible, getting top management to adopt them. Bohlander, White, and Wolfe found that while the HR department's primary role is still viewed by many executives and managers as service and advising, both executives and HR managers desire more involvement for the HR department in policy and control activities. They suggest that this finding may reflect the involvement of HRM in legal issues that affect the organization as a whole and the professionalization increasingly accorded HR departments.[41]

Any consultation provided by the HR staff must be based on managerial and technical expertise. Furthermore, it should be concerned with the operating goals of the managers and supervisors who are their consulting clients and should help them to make firm decisions. These managers and supervisors must be convinced that the HR staff is there to assist them in increasing their productivity rather than to impose obstacles to their goals. This requires not only the ability to consider problems from the viewpoint of the line managers and supervisors, but also skill in communicating with them.

Department Structure

In a small organization the HR department may consist only of a manager and a few assistants. In a larger organization many additional staff members may be required. Increased size eventually leads to the establishment of divisions. Figure 1–6 is a chart containing the divisions into which a large HR department may be organized.

The relative contribution of each function will help determine the need for new divisions, as well as the sequence in which they are established. In recent years, for example, changes in the legal environment have forced many organizations to establish a division to oversee and coordinate equal employment opportunity and affirmative action (EEO/AA) efforts. The passage of the Employee Retirement Income Security Act (ERISA), together with employee pressure for expanded benefits, similarly has led organizations to establish divisions to supervise these functions. Safety divisions have been formed to ensure compliance with the Occupational Safety and Health Act (OSHA). When an organization becomes unionized, a separate division is likely to be established to oversee the labor relations function.

Staff Jobs in HRM

The HR department organization chart (Figure 1–6) provides a comprehensive listing of the functions as organized by divisions. As you study the various functions, it may be helpful to think in terms of the variety of staff positions available to qualified and interested individuals. This listing of jobs includes those typically found in a large organization.

In smaller organizations there will naturally be fewer positions in HRM. As a result, a staff employee may be responsible for performing a wider variety of functions. Among the staff jobs mentioned or implied in various chapters of this book are the following:

Human Resources Information Manager/Specialist	Chap. 1
EEO/AA Coordinator/Specialist	Chap. 3
Job Analyst	Chap. 4
Organizational Planning Manager	Chap. 5
Recruiter	Chap. 5
Employment Manager/Specialist/Interviewer	Chap. 6
Training Director/Specialist	Chap. 7
Orientation Manager/Specialist	Chap. 7

FIGURE 1–6 ORGANIZATION OF A HUMAN RESOURCES DEPARTMENT

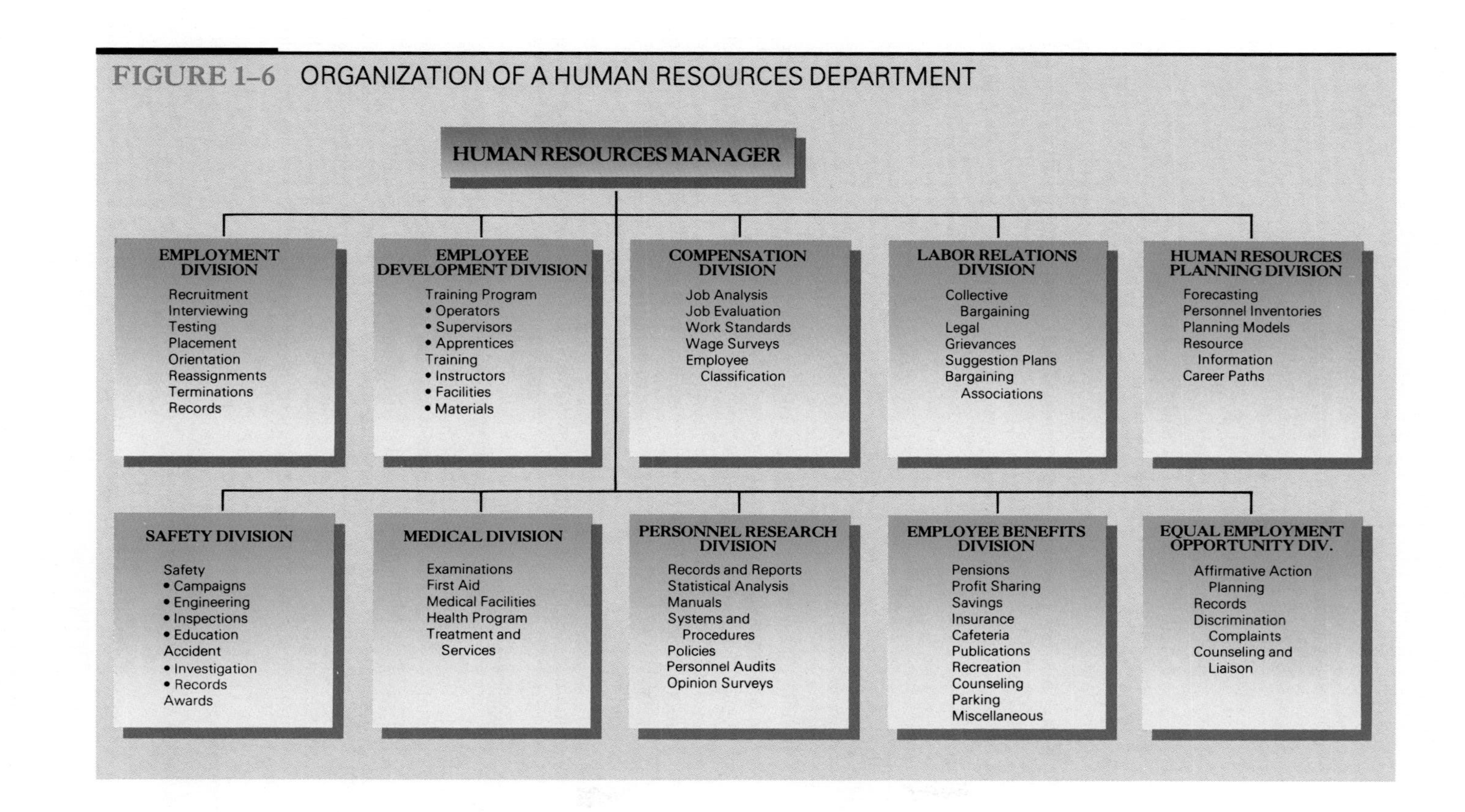

Director of Management Development	Chap. 8
Career Development Specialist	Chap. 8
Compensation Manager/Specialist	Chap. 10
Benefits Administrator/Specialist	Chap. 12
Recreation Director	Chap. 12
Safety Director/Specialist	Chap. 13
Employee Counselor	Chap. 13
Labor Relations Director/Specialist	Chap. 18
Employee Opinion Analyst	Chap. 20

As in all fields, employment opportunities in HRM vary from time to time. The various HR journals listed earlier often contain articles that discuss current opportunities. The *Occupational Outlook Handbook*, published by the Bureau of Labor Statistics and available in virtually all libraries, is a valuable source of current information.

SUMMARY

HRM represents a new concept of and approach to performing personnel functions. It still requires the performance of those personnel functions that have evolved over the years in response to emerging needs. But instead of treating these functions as separate and distinct, HRM considers them interrelated parts of a management system. HRM recognizes that HR planning must be integrated closely with strategic organizational planning. Accordingly, HR managers are becoming more involved in the decision making of top management.

The contemporary field of HRM is the product of evolutionary development reflecting the concepts of scientific management and the human relations movement. The most recent conceptual development has been the emergence of behavioral science, which continues to contribute to a better understanding of organizational behavior and to programs for organizational development.

The evolution of the field of HRM is also characterized by a growth in its professional status. This status is reflected in the code of ethics developed by the Society for Human Resource Management. It is further seen in the programs initiated by the Human Resources Certification Institute for certifying practitioners in the field of HRM and in the growth of literature and research efforts within the field. Since the early 1960s, the responsibilities of the HR manager have increased. This has led to the expansion of the activities of the HR department, requiring specialization in many different areas.

DISCUSSION QUESTIONS

1. In what respects does HRM differ from the traditional approach to personnel management?

2. Why is HRM playing an increasingly important role in organizations?
3. What specific HRM responsibilities do line managers and supervisors have?
4. Cite some of the more recent federal laws governing human resources management and their areas of impact.
5. Give some specific examples from your own experience and observations of how microcomputers can be used in the performance of the various HR functions described in this chapter.
6. What contributions has the Society for Human Resource Management made to HRM?
7. What should be the role of the HR staff in its relations with personnel outside the HR department?
8. Of those functions performed in HRM, which do you consider to be most important? State your reasons.

NOTES AND REFERENCES

1. Andrew J. DuBrin, R. Duane Ireland, and J. Clifton Williams, *Management & Organization* (Cincinnati: South-Western, 1989), 4–5. See also Lee Dyer, ed., *Human Resource Management—Evolving Roles and Responsibilities* (Washington, DC: Bureau of National Affairs, 1988).

2. Harrington Emerson, *The Twelve Principles of Efficiency* (New York: The Engineering Magazine Co., 1913). See also Alex W. Rathe, ed., *Gantt on Management* (New York: American Management Association, 1961).

3. For the collected works of the Gilbreths see William R. Spriegel and Clark E. Myers, eds., *The Writings of the Gilbreths* (Homewood, IL: Richard D. Irwin, 1953). For many years Dr. Lillian Gilbreth combined a career as a management consultant with that of a homemaker and the mother of twelve children, who her husband alleged were "cheaper by the dozen." For an entertaining account of the lives of Lillian and Frank Gilbreth as parents, see Frank B. Gilbreth, Jr., and Ernestine Gilbreth Carey, *Cheaper by the Dozen* (New York: Grosset & Dunlap, 1948).

4. John Bales, "Lillian Gilbreth Honored on U.S. Postage Stamp," *APA Monitor* (February 1984): 2. Dr. Gilbreth's portrait appears on a 40¢ stamp.

5. Frederick W. Taylor, "What Is Scientific Management?" in *Classics in Management*, ed. Harwood F. Merrill (New York: American Management Association, 1960), 80. See also Edwin A. Locke, "The Ideas of Frederick W. Taylor: An Evaluation," *Academy of Management Review* 7, no. 1 (January 1982): 14–24.

6. Hindy Lauer Schacter, "Frederick Winslow Taylor and the Idea of Worker Participation—A Brief Against Easy Administrative Dichotomies," *Administration and Society* 21, no. 1 (May 1989): 20–30.

7. Hugo Münsterberg, *Psychology and Industrial Efficiency* (Boston: Houghton Mifflin, 1913).

8. Walter Dill Scott and Robert C. Clothier, *Personnel Management: Practices and Point of View* (New York: A. W. Shaw, 1923). See also Edmund C. Lynch, *Walter Dill Scott, Pioneer in Personnel Management* (Austin: Bureau of Business Research, University of Texas, 1968), 22–23.

9. For extensive references to Cattell, see Ernest R. Hilgard, ed., *American Psychology in Historical Perspective* (Washington, DC: American Psychological Association, 1978). The address of the Psychological Corporation is 555 Academic Court, San Antonio, TX 78204-0952.

10. Walter Van Dyke Bingham and Bruce Victor Moore, *How to Interview* (New York: Harper & Brothers, 1931). See also Bingham, *Aptitudes and Aptitude Testing* (New York: Harper & Brothers, 1937).

11. F. J. Roethlisberger and W. J. Dickson, *Management and the Worker* (Cambridge, MA: Harvard University Press, 1939).

12. John G. Adair, "The Hawthorne Effect: A Reconsideration of the Methodological Artifact," *Journal of Applied Psychology* 69, no. 2 (May 1984): 334–345. This article includes a comprehensive bibliography of articles that contain critiques and reinterpretations of the Hawthorne experiments. See also Berkeley Rice, "The Hawthorne Defect: Persistence of a Flawed Theory," *Psychology Today* 16, no. 2 (February 1982): 70–74.

13. For an appreciation of Mary Parker Follett's contributions see Elliot M. Fox, "Mary Parker Follett: The Enduring Contribution," *Public Administration Review* 28, no. 6 (November–December 1968): 520–529.

14. Kurt Lewin, *The Research Center for Group Dynamics* (New York: Beacon House, 1947). See also Alfred J. Marrow, *The Practical Theorist: The Life and Work of Kurt Lewin* (New York: Basic Books, 1969).

15. Harold M. F. Rush, *Behavioral Science: Concepts and Management Application,* Personnel Policy Study No. 216 (New York: National Industrial Conference Board, 1969), 2.

16. Henry Eilbert, "The Development of Personnel Management in the United States," *Business History Review* 33, no. 3 (Autumn 1959): 345–364.

17. Harold E. Burtt, *Principles of Employment Psychology,* rev. ed. (New York: Harper & Brothers, 1942), 62–66. A special edition of the 1942 edition was published in 1978 by Greenwood Press, Westport, CT, as a classic work. Author's note: A former doctoral student of Burtt, Dr. Frank Stanton, president emeritus of CBS, Inc., and Mrs. Ruth Stanton honored Professor Harold Burtt on his 100th birthday on April 26, 1990, by donating $1.25 million to Ohio State University to establish the Harold E. Burtt Chair in Industrial Psychology. As an author of ten books and a university professor for over 40 years, Dr. Burtt has had widespread influence in the area of personnel and industrial psychology.

18. Lloyd Baird and Ilan Meshoulam, "A Second Chance for HR to Make the Grade," *Personnel* 63, no. 4 (April 1986): 45–48. See also Raymond E. Miles and Charles C. Snow, "Designing Strategic Human Resources Systems," *Organizational Dynamics* 13, no. 1 (Summer 1984): 36–52.

19. Jack F. Gow, "Human Resources Managers Must Remember the Bottom Line," *Personnel Journal* 64, no. 4 (April 1985): 30–32; and David J. McLaughlin, "Take the Personnel Challenge," *Personnel Journal* 63, no. 6 (June 1984): 78–81. See also Harish Jain and Victor Murray, "Why the Human Resources Management Function Fails," *California Management Review* 26, no. 4 (Summer 1984): 95–110; and James F. Rand, "HR Management: An Integrative Perspective," *Personnel* 63, no. 6 (June 1986): 50–53. For an interesting discussion of different ways to define "strategy" see Henry Mintzberg, "The Strategy Concept I: Five Ps for Strategy," *California Management Review* 30, no. 1 (Fall 1987): 11–24.

20. David Ulrich and Arthur Yeung, "A Shared Mindset," *Personnel Administrator* 34, no. 3 (March 1989): 38–45.

21. John Hoerr, "Human Resources Managers Aren't Corporate Nobodies Anymore," *Business Week* (December 2, 1985): 58–59.

22. Joanne Wisniewski, "Are Consultants Set Up to Fail?" *Personnel Journal* 68, no. 10 (October 1989): 56–63.

23. Source is Membership Department, Society for Human Resource Management.

24. Addresses of these associations may be found in the latest edition of the *Encyclopedia of Associations* (Detroit, MI: Gale Research), available in most libraries.

25. Cheryl Haigley, "Professionalism in Personnel," *Personnel Administrator* 29, no. 6 (June 1984): 103–106. See also James W. Walker and Gregory Moorhead, "CEOs: What They Want from HRM," *Personnel Administrator* 32, no. 12 (December 1987): 50–59. The Human Resource Certification Institute was originally known as the Personnel Accreditation Institute.

26. Fran A. Wallace, "Walking a Tightrope: Ethical Issues Facing HR Professionals," *Personnel* 62, no. 6 (June 1985): 32–36. See also Ernest A. Archer, "Human Resource Professionalism: An Unexpected Source of Conflict," *Personnel Administrator* 31, no. 7 (July 1986): 97–104.

27. Gary Edwards and Kirk Bennett, "Ethics and HR: Standards in Practice," *Personnel Administrator* 32, no. 12 (December 1987): 62–66. See also *Bulletin to Management,* 38, no. 45 (Washington, DC: Bureau of National Affairs, November 5, 1987): 360.

28. Issued quarterly, *Personnel Management Abstracts* includes abstracts of articles and recent books, a subject and author index of articles, and a list of journals abstracted with addresses of publishers.

29. Issued monthly, *Work Related Abstracts* extracts significant information from over 250 management, labor, government, professional, and university publications.

30. *Human Resources Abstracts* is published quarterly in March, June, September, and December by Sage Periodicals Press.

31. Earl Harper and David B. Stephens, "Personnel and Labor Relations Master's Degrees for the '80s and '90s," *Personnel Administrator* 27, no. 11 (November 1982): 53–56.

32. See *How to Develop a Company Personnel Manual* (Chicago: Dartnell, n.d.).

33. Nancy Croft Baker, "The Need for Caution in Handbook Changes," *ASPA/Resource* 7, no. 12 (December 1988): 6. See also Thomas M. Hestwood, "Making Policy Manuals Useful and Relevant," *Personnel Journal* 67, no. 4 (April 1988): 43–46.

34. Joel E. Ross, *Management by Information System* (Englewood Cliffs, NJ: Prentice-Hall, 1970), 106.

35. Morton E. Grossman and Margaret Magnus, "The Growing Dependence on HRIS," *Personnel Journal* 67, no. 9 (September 1988): 53–59.

36. John E. Spirig, "Selling HRIS to Top Management," *Personnel* 65, no. 10 (October 1988): 26–34; and Cynthia Diers, "The Evolving HRIS Manager," *Personnel* 66, no. 9 (September 1989): 28–32.

37. Stephen G. Perry, "The PC-Based HRIS," *Personnel Administrator* 33, no. 2 (February 1988): 60–63. See also Perry, "An HRIS for the '90s," *Personnel Journal* 69, no. 8 (August 1990): 75–78; and Stephen E. Forrer and Zandy B. Leibowitz, *Using Computers in Human Resources* (San Francisco: Jossey-Bass, 1991), Chapters 1 and 7.

38. The source of the Human Resource Information Network is Executive Telecom System, Inc., 9585 Valparaiso Court, Indianapolis, IN 46268. The source of SHRM Database is *ASPA Resource* (December 1988).

39. Barbara A. Bland-Acosta, "Developing an HRIS Privacy Policy," *Personnel Administrator* 33, no. 7 (July 1988): 52–59.

40. George W. Bohlander, Harold C. White, and Michael N. Wolfe, "The Three Faces of Personnel—or, PAIR Department Activities as Seen by Executives, Line Managers, and Personnel Director," *Personnel* 60, no. 4 (July–August 1983): 12–22. See also John A. Byrne, Edward A. Emerman, David J. McLaughlin, Leonard A. Schlesinger, and Carole K. Barnett, "Selecting the Head of HR: A Roundtable Discussion," *Human Resource Management* 27, no. 4 (Winter 1988): 413–431.

41. Bohlander, White, and Wolfe, "The Three Faces of Personnel." See also James H. Morrison, "Profiling the New HR Management Style," *Personnel Administrator* 33, no. 6 (June 1988): 88–92; and Barbara Whitaker Shimko, "All Managers Are HR Managers," *HR Magazine* 35, no. 1 (January 1990): 67–70.

CHAPTER 2

The Environment for Human Resources Management

After reading this chapter you will be able to:

1. *List the various elements that constitute an organization's external and internal environments and discuss their possible impact on the management of human resources.*
2. *Identify demographic and cultural changes occurring within society and their implications for HRM.*
3. *Describe the federal regulatory system as it pertains to HRM.*
4. *Explain the relationship between job trends and HRM.*
5. *Describe the various approaches to improving the quality of work life.*
6. *Identify the characteristics of a supportive organizational culture.*
7. *Define the key terms in the chapter.*

TERMS TO IDENTIFY

environment *(37)**
external environment *(38)*
environmental scanning *(39)*
issues management *(39)*
internal environment, or organizational climate *(43)*
sociotechnical system *(44)*
organizational politics *(44)*
telecommuting *(53)*
psychology of entitlement *(54)*
work ethic *(55)*
quality of work life (QWL) *(58)*
participative management *(59)*
organizational culture *(60)*
intrapreneurs *(64)*

An HRM program functions in a complex environment both inside and outside the organization. In order to have an effective HR program, HR managers must give careful attention to all aspects of the environment. Rapid changes are occurring within society and the environment in which organizations operate. These changes present challenges that require early solutions if an HR program is to be successful and make its full contribution to the organization and to all its members. In this chapter we will consider the kinds of changes that are anticipated and their implications for HRM. How to improve an organization's internal environment is one of the major challenges confronting employers today, so we will give special emphasis to ways the internal environment may be changed to improve the quality of work life.

ELEMENTS OF AN ORGANIZATION'S ENVIRONMENT

The **environment** of an organization consists of the conditions, circumstances, and influences that affect the organization's ability to achieve its objectives. Figure 2–1 shows that every organization exists in an environment that has both external and internal components. It also illustrates that both the external and the internal environment are composed of five elements: physical, technological, social, political, and economic. As shown by the arrows, the five elements of the external environment influence how the HR functions will be performed. The internal environment influences both the HR policies and procedures and the individuals who make up the work force of the organization. One could further argue that

*The number in parentheses refers to the text page on which the term is introduced.

performance of the HR functions also has some influence on the external environment. In fact, more than a decade ago, the president of the Conference Board of Canada made the following observation:

> For an increasing number of HR executives, their role goes beyond the sensing and interpreting of the impact of the environment on the organization. For them it is equally important to participate in and influence the environment.[1]

The External Environment

The environment that exists outside the organization, the **external environment,** has a significant impact on HRM policies and practices. It helps to determine

FIGURE 2–1 THE ENVIRONMENTS FOR MANAGING HUMAN RESOURCES

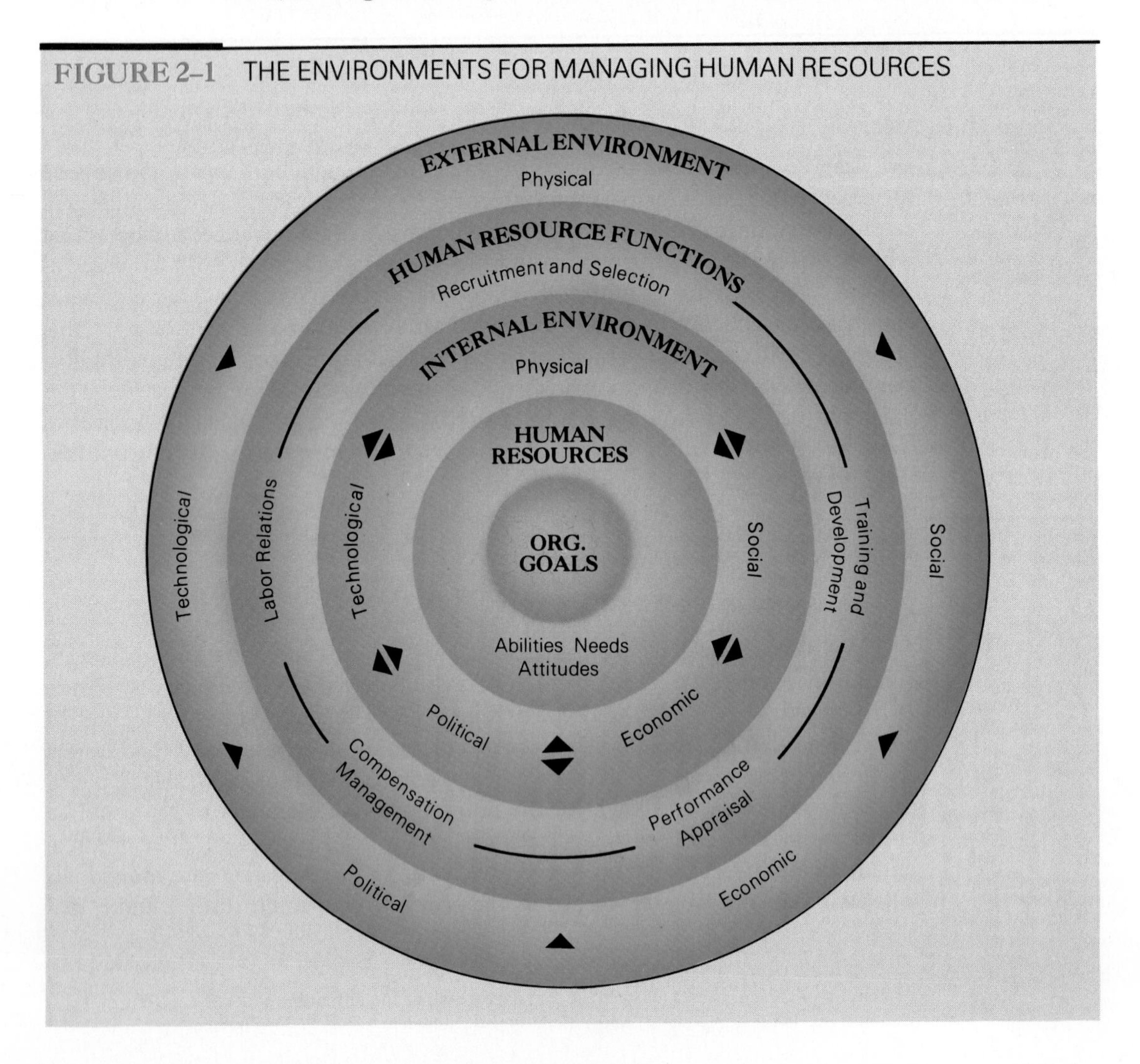

the values, attitudes, and behavior that employees bring to their jobs. This is why many organizations engage in **environmental scanning,** which involves analyzing the environment and changes occurring within it. Their purpose is to determine its possible impact on organizational policies and practices. Another closely related practice is **issues management,** by which managers attempt to keep abreast of current issues. This may include bringing the organization's policies in line with prevailing public opinion.

PHYSICAL ELEMENT The physical element of the external environment includes the climate, terrain, and other physical characteristics of the area in which the organization is located. The physical element can help or hinder an organization's ability to attract and retain employees. Housing, commuting, and living costs can vary from one location to another and can have a significant impact on the compensation employees will expect. Recent population shifts to the Sunbelt and to small towns and rural areas can be attributed, at least in part, to the desire of the migrants to work and live in what they perceive to be a more desirable physical environment. Ironically, this movement has created congestion, pollution, and other problems of population growth in the areas to which people are moving.

TECHNOLOGICAL ELEMENT We live in an extremely competitive age. Only through technological innovation can organizations develop new products and services and improve existing ones in order to stay competitive. Technology also provides a basis for an organization to attain the productivity and quality it needs to gain a competitive advantage.

Perhaps the most important technology of the day is the computer. The invention of semiconductors made possible the miniaturization of computers with greatly increased capabilities. Advancements in computer technology have enabled organizations to cope with the information explosion. With computers, unlimited amounts of data can be stored, retrieved, and used in a wide variety of ways, from simple recordkeeping to controlling complex equipment. In our everyday living we see bank tellers, airline reservation clerks, and supermarket cashiers using computers to perform their jobs. At the bank's automated teller machine and at the library's computerized card catalog we become computer operators ourselves.

Less visible are the computers that monitor employees' speed, efficiency, and accuracy. Companies such as AT&T, United Airlines, Equitable Life Insurance, and American Express use sophisticated devices to measure employee work output.[2] But while large businesses and computer firms tout computerized monitoring as an effective means of improving productivity, the computerized control systems used for this purpose have been linked to increased stress, loss of job privacy rights, health risks, and job dissatisfaction among employees. Supporters argue that such systems improve the consistency, clarity, and objectivity of performance measurement, and so are an improvement over stressful, subjective evaluations by human supervisors.

The introduction of computer-controlled robots represents one of the most significant technological innovations of this century. The Robot Institute of America

"As director of personnel, I feel *I* should purchase the robots!"

From *The Wall Street Journal*—Permission, Cartoon Features Syndicate

defines a robot as "a reprogrammable, multifunctional manipulator designed to move materials, parts, tools, and specialized devices through variable programmed motions for the performance of a variety of tasks."[3] In simpler language, "A robot is like a computer with muscles. . . . The computer provides the information, or brain power, and the robot's metal limbs do the physical work it orders."[4] Robots are commercially available for a number of industrial tasks, including arc and spot welding, spray painting, plastic molding, brick making, deburring of metal parts, die casting, and palletizing.[5] Robots have been particularly beneficial for tasks that present safety and health risks to employees.

Industry has adopted robots for a number of uses.

The introduction of robots into a work force will obviously affect the number of employees, and those employees who are displaced will require retraining. Management at Westinghouse has found it essential to develop what it calls a "sense of ownership" in all employees who will be involved with robots.[6] Because of the implications of robotization for HRM, the HR manager should play a major role in planning for it. Communication with employees clearly plays a crucial role in minimizing negative feelings about automation. Employees must feel that management has a real commitment to supporting them as they adjust to changes. Relevant training programs, commitment by supervisors to training, and willingness to adjust production deadlines during training periods are important indicators of that commitment.[7]

Technological advancements have tended to reduce the number of jobs that require little skill and to increase the number of jobs that require considerable skill. We thus experience the paradox of having pages and pages of newspaper advertisements for applicants with technical or scientific training while several million job seekers without such training register for work with employment agencies.

SOCIAL ELEMENT Increasingly, employers are being expected to demonstrate a greater sense of responsibility toward employees and toward society as a whole. Employees, furthermore, are expecting the same freedoms, rights, and benefits on the job that they enjoy as members of society. Employers who fail to accept this fact are encountering difficulties with their employees. In addition, employers are being constrained by legislation and court decisions that support their employees' rights in the workplace.

Many employees today are concerned less with the acquisition of wealth than with the pursuit of happiness. They are seeking ways of living that are less complicated but more meaningful. These new life-styles cannot help but have an impact on the way employees must be motivated and supervised. Consequently, HRM has become more complex than it was when employees were concerned primarily with economic survival.

POLITICAL ELEMENT Governments have a significant impact on HRM. Each of the functions performed in the management of human resources—from employee recruitment to termination—is in some way affected by laws and regulations established at the state and federal levels.

As mentioned earlier, HR managers must follow all laws and government regulations, federal, state, and local, relating to HRM. In this book we will emphasize *federal* laws and regulations, however, because they apply to all organizations within the United States, except those specifically exempted from their provisions. Occasionally, state laws will be mentioned to illustrate differences among the states and to emphasize that HR managers must abide by state as well as federal laws and regulations in performing their various HRM functions.

While federal legislation and the agencies to enforce it have existed for many decades—e.g., the Interstate Commerce Commission (1887) and the Federal Communications Commission (1934)—those agencies regulating the activities relating to HRM are relatively new. Unlike agencies overseeing particular industries, the newer agencies regulate a specific management function across several industries, such as equal employment opportunity, labor relations, and worker safety and health.

Today's HR manager must understand the federal regulatory system in order to function effectively in the face of what has been described as a "seemingly incoherent body of agency directives, inspections, reviews, regulations, and determinations."[8] Figure 2–2 shows that regulation begins with social and political problems that prompt lawmakers to pass laws empowering agencies to take regulatory actions which in turn trigger management responses. Finally, the courts oversee the process by settling disputes between the litigating parties. Careful study of Figure 2–2 will give the reader a better understanding of how acts of Congress (laws) and presidential executive orders influence the activities of the HR manager.

FIGURE 2–2 THE REGULATORY MODEL

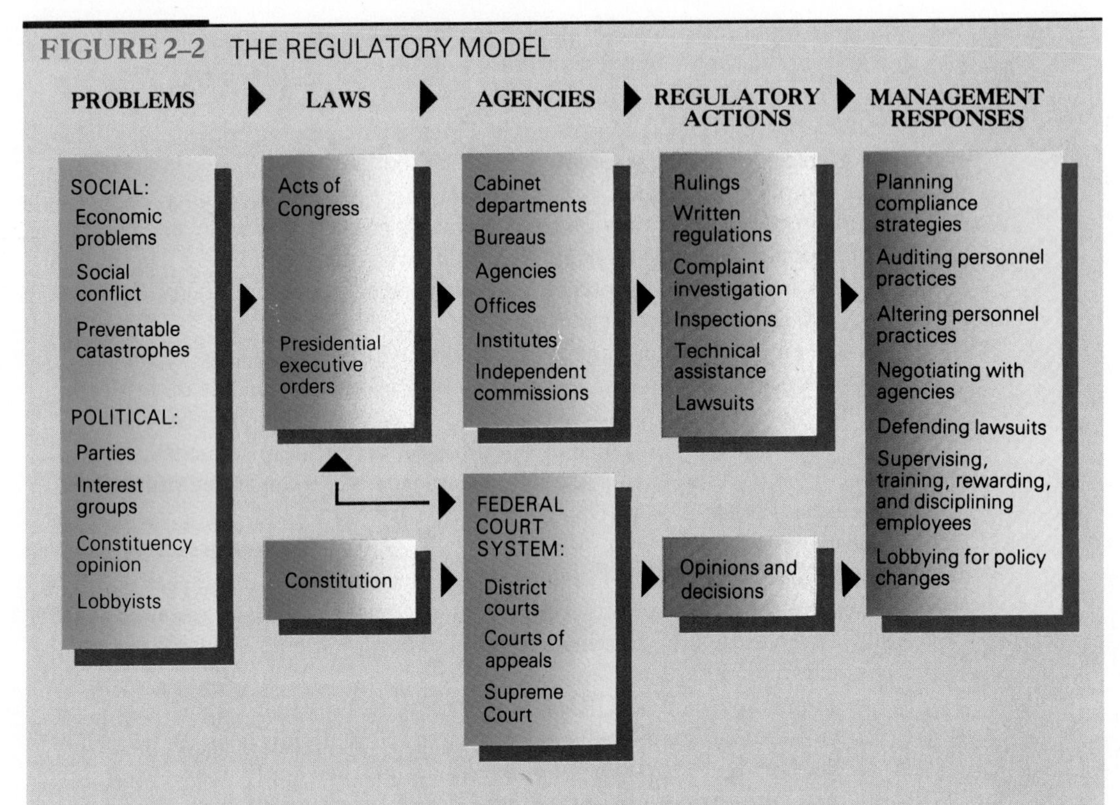

SOURCE: From James Ledvinka and Vida Scarpello, *Federal Regulation of Personnel and Human Resource Management*, 2d ed. (Boston: PWS-KENT Publishing, 1990), 18. Reprinted with permission.

Federal regulations in particular are made more complex by the different interpretations placed upon them. The federal agency charged with administering a certain law typically develops guidelines for its interpretation which are published in the *Federal Register.*[9] This interpretation may differ from what Congress intended in passing the law. Furthermore, subsequent court decisions may provide still a different interpretation. To keep abreast of the latest interpretations, most HR managers find it advisable to use one of the principal labor information services listed at the end of this chapter (see note 10).[10] We will refer in this book to federal laws and court decisions that are currently viewed as having a major influence on HRM. Be aware, however, that each week brings news of pending legislation and court decisions that change the course of HRM policies and practices.

ECONOMIC ELEMENT Closely interrelated with the political element is the economic element. Many of the nation's economic ills today are of political origin. It has been typical of our lawmakers to appropriate funds to support generous programs and benefits for their constituents without levying the necessary taxes to cover the costs. During the 1970s, this deficit spending, coupled with the monetary policies of the federal government, created a sharp increase in inflation. Inflation eased somewhat after 1981, but average inflation in the 1980s remained above the average levels experienced during the 1950s and 1960s. By eroding purchasing power, inflation constitutes a form of taxation in disguise. Unfortunately, the burden has fallen most heavily upon those in the lower- and fixed-income groups.

Inflation has had a significant impact on HR programs, necessitating periodic upward adjustments in employee compensation and benefit payments. Unions, which are an important part of the economic environment, seek through collective bargaining to keep abreast of inflation. Their efforts sometimes lead to severe strikes for which they and the public pay a high price. Some employees with strong bargaining power have been able to keep up with inflation at the expense of others, widening economic disparities within our society in the process. Government efforts to control inflation can create recessions, which increase unemployment and business failures. These conditions then precipitate political pressure for corrective action that can lead to more inflation.

Economic conditions often dictate whether an organization will need to hire or lay off employees. They also affect an employer's ability to increase employees' pay and/or benefits. While economic recessions can force the curtailment of operations in the private sector, they may have the opposite effect in the public sector. Unemployment generated by a recession usually necessitates the expansion of agencies that provide welfare and workfare services. Expanding federal programs to combat a recession may mean that these agencies need more employees to supervise the programs.

Competition with foreign rivals has been a serious problem for the United States since the early 1980s. Year-to-year gains have enabled Japan, Germany, France, Taiwan, Brazil, South Korea, and other foreign competitors to beat American producers on price, quality, or both. In every country of the world, political leaders are under pressure to provide jobs for their unemployed—not just jobs, but "decent jobs" that will provide the standard of living to which their citizens aspire. These jobs can be created only if employers are able to compete successfully in the domestic and foreign markets.

The Internal Environment

The environment that exists within an organization is known as the **internal environment,** or **organizational climate.** Like the external environment, the internal environment consists of physical, technological, social, political, and economic elements. These elements affect and are affected by the policies, procedures, and employment conditions that HR managers oversee. Therefore, the program developed for managing human resources must take into account the internal as well as the external environment.

PHYSICAL ELEMENT The physical element of the internal environment includes such factors as air quality, temperature, noise, dust, radiation, and other conditions affecting employee health and safety. One study of government employees revealed a high percentage of dissatisfaction with aspects of the physical environment of the workplace. Seventy-one percent of employees were dissatisfied with air quality and temperature; 54 percent with elevator operation; 46 percent with workplace appearance; 46 percent with maintenance and repairs; and 28 percent with washroom cleanliness.[11] These responses would seem to indicate that there is much room for improvement in such areas, and organizations would be well advised to be attentive to this aspect of the internal environment.

TECHNOLOGICAL ELEMENT The technological element of the internal environment interrelates closely with the physical one. It consists of the layout of the workplace; the process by which the work is performed; and the tools, equipment, and machinery used to perform the work. These factors in turn determine both the way work is to be processed and the requirements of the jobs to be performed.

The way in which work is organized affects interpersonal relations and interaction among employees within a work area. It influences the formation of informal work groups and the degree of cooperation or conflict among employees. Technological systems increasingly are being integrated with the social systems in an organization, creating what is referred to as a **sociotechnical system.** Under this system, job design is based on human as well as technological considerations.

SOCIAL ELEMENT The social element reflects the attitudes and behaviors of managers and employees, individually and in groups. Because of their influential place in the organizational hierarchy, top managers play an extremely important role in determining the quality of the social element. The rules and regulations they devise, the concern they have for employees, the rewards and support they provide, and the tolerance they have for varying opinions are major factors in determining the organizational climate. In recent years there has been considerable interest in what has been labeled "the corporate culture." We will examine later in this chapter how the culture prescribes the type of climate, as well as the course that HRM will take.

POLITICAL ELEMENT Politics is an important social influence process that is found in all organizations. **Organizational politics** is the management of influence to obtain ends not sanctioned by the organization or to obtain sanctioned ends through nonsanctioned means. It thus has the potential for being helpful or harmful to organizations and individuals.

A study by Allen and others shows that there are several tactics used in organizational politics. These include attacking or blaming others, using (or withholding or distorting) information to overwhelm another person, building images, building support for ideas, praising others, creating power coalitions, associating with the influential, and performing services or favors to create obligations. Which of these tactics individuals will use depends upon their nature or disposition and the particular situation confronting them. The characteristics of a good politician, according to managers interviewed in the study, could also be considered the attributes of an effective leader. Managers are advised to learn more about the processes of organizational politics to enable them to play a larger role in its management.[12] In every organization there are many politicians, from the shop floor up to Mahogany Row. Politics and power tactics are thus considered a part of organizational life.

Power is the capacity to influence the behavior of others. The degree of power that managers possess is determined in part by where they fit in the formal organization structure, the number of subordinates they supervise, and the authority delegated to them. Power may also be derived from personal expertise and from informal leadership skills that enable managers to enlist the loyalty and support of others.

Power is an important aid in HRM. It can provide a means of gaining the type of performance and behavior desired of employees. The more power HR managers have in their organizations, the more successful they will be in getting other managers to carry out their own HR responsibilities and to comply with established policies and procedures.

ECONOMIC ELEMENT The economic element of an organization's internal environment reflects the organization's financial condition. The more favorable this condition, the more financial resources the organization will have to support its human resources, including employee compensation and benefits. Furthermore, when the financial health of an organization is strong, there is a tendency to expand HRM activities such as training and development, employee assistance programs, and recreational activities. If the organization is growing, there is the possibility of expansion leading to employee recruitment, selection, and orientation. Conversely, when financial resources are low, organizations tend to reduce HR budgets and cut back the HR services it offers to its employees.

CHANGES THAT CHALLENGE MANAGERS OF HUMAN RESOURCES

In the preceding section we briefly mentioned some of the environmental changes that may precipitate changes in an HR program. Increasingly, HR managers are involved in issues management directed toward early identification of trends that may require adjustments in HR policies and procedures. Beginning in the fall of 1986, SHRM began an organizational effort known as the Issues Management Program. After reviewing the trends and patterns of development of more than 200 specific "issues," SHRM identified five basic areas where change is occurring. These five areas are shown in Highlights in HRM 1. The goals of the departments

HIGHLIGHTS IN HRM

1 CURRENT ISSUES IN HUMAN RESOURCES MANAGEMENT

EMPLOYER/EMPLOYEE RIGHTS

This is clearly an important and growing area of debate and concern. To some degree, it reflects the shift in employer/employee negotiating from the bargaining table to the courtroom as organizations and individuals attempt to define rights, obligations, and responsibilities. Among the many specific issues that are covered in the broad area are:

- Job as an entitlement
- Employment at will
- Privacy (testing)
- Whistle-blowing
- Mandated benefits
- Smoking
- Plant closing notification
- Right to know
- Comparable worth
- Right to manage
- AIDS

EDUCATION/TRAINING/RETRAINING

As organizations trim personnel and gear up for the tough competition within the global economy, the skills and competence of the available pool of employees are becoming a pivotal issue. This issue spans the range of skill development from the earliest stages of the education experience to the challenges of retraining an aging work force. If "human resources are our most important asset," it is here that the investments must be made if that asset is to be productive. Among the key issues in this area are:

- Literacy
- Employee education/training
- Management development
- Plant closings
- Dropout prevention
- Retraining
- Industry obsolescence

CHANGING DEMOGRAPHICS

The next 20 years will bring a constant aging of the work force. This has major implications for all aspects of human resource management as it alters traditional experience and expectations regarding the labor pool. Among the issues in this area are:

- Shrinking pool of entry-level workers
- Retirement health-benefits funding
- Increasing number of "nonpermanent/contract" employees
- Social security
- "Plateauing" and motivation
- Elder care
- Pension-fund liabilities

WORK AND FAMILY RELATIONSHIPS

There is a new and important perception that the individual at work is not "detached" from family concerns and responsibilities. Due, in part, to the rapid increase of women in the workplace, as well as a growing interest in and concern with the family, there is increasing demand for recognition and support of family-related employee concerns. Among the issues in this area are:

- Day care
- Child care leave
- Alternative work plans
- Elder care
- Parental leave
- Cafeteria plans
- Mandated benefits

PRODUCTIVITY/COMPETITIVENESS

The calls for increased productivity, quality, and competitiveness will only grow in intensity over the coming years. A persistent trade deficit and continued successes in the global market of our international competitors will serve to intensify the quest for a more productive work force. Among the issues in this area are:

- Productivity improvement
- Worker participation
- Foreign competition
- Mergers
- Quality programs and measurement
- Incentive/performance pay
- Globalization
- Down-sizing

SOURCE: Catherine Downes Bower and Jeffrey J. Hallett, "Issues Management at ASPA," *Personnel Administrator* 34, no. 1 (January 1989): 40–43. Reprinted with the permission from *HRMagazine* (formerly *Personnel Administrator*), published by the Society for Human Resource Management, Alexandria, VA.

of SHRM are now directly related to these areas so that the society can provide the services most relevant to the needs of its members.

While our discussion of changes that challenge HR managers will incorporate key issues from the SHRM Issues Management Program, we will use the following categories: demographic changes, job trends, cultural changes, and change in organizational effectiveness.

Demographic Changes

Among the most significant challenges to HR managers are the demographic changes occurring in the United States. Because they affect the work force of an employer, these changes—in population growth, the age and gender distribution of the population, and education trends—are important topics for discussion.

POPULATION GROWTH AND ETHNIC BACKGROUND Population growth is the single most important factor governing the size and composition of the labor force. The U.S. civilian labor force totaled about 125 million in 1990 and is expected to reach 141 million in the year 2000. Though this projected increase of

13 percent for the 10-year period sounds quite high, it is substantially lower than the 35 percent increase for the period 1972–1986.[13] This difference represents a slowing in both the number of people joining the labor force and the rate of labor force growth.

It is predicted that American workers will continue to be a diverse group. In the year 2000, minorities will make up an even larger share of the U.S. labor force than they did in 1986. Blacks will increase their share from 11 to 12 percent, Hispanics from 7 to 10 percent, and Asians and others from 3 to 4 percent. These groups are expected to account for about 58 percent of the labor force growth between 1986 and 2000. The arrival of immigrants also has significant implications for the labor force, since they tend to be of working age but have different educational and occupational backgrounds from those of the U.S. population as a whole.[14]

AGE DISTRIBUTION OF THE POPULATION Past fluctuations in the birthrate will produce abrupt changes in the makeup of major U.S. labor force groups during the 1990s. The number of younger workers (16 to 24 years of age) will decline until the mid-1990s, then turn upward as the children of the baby-boom generation enter the work force. The number of older workers (55 and above) will decline through the mid-1990s, then start to rise sharply as the baby boomers themselves approach retirement age.

Contrary to popular belief, the number of older workers is expected to be only slightly higher in 2000 than it was in 1986. Declining labor force participation of older persons will largely offset the increase in the number of persons in this population group. The youth share of the labor force is projected to drop to only 16 percent by 2000, down from 20 percent in 1986 and 23 percent in 1972. Many organizations with a primary interest in this age group—fast-food restaurants and other retail establishments, for example—can expect to see the population from which they draw part-time workers, as well as customers, shrink throughout most of the 1986–2000 period.[15]

Despite the fact that the pool of younger workers is shrinking and labor shortages loom ahead, public policy discourages the employment of older workers beyond traditional retirement age, regardless of substantial evidence of the value of their training and experience. Many employers, however, are making positive efforts to attract more older workers, especially those who have taken early retirement, by expanding the number of part-time hours available and offering sabbaticals and job sharing. They are also providing retraining programs for older employees. Among employers benefiting from such efforts are Varian Associates, a $1-billion-a-year high-tech equipment maker; Grumman, a $3.4-billion defense contractor; Corning Glass Works, and Wells Fargo Bank.[16]

But there are a number of barriers to overcome before organizations can succeed in making continued employment attractive to older workers. The economic disincentives of the social security tax for wage earners between ages 65 and 70 need to be reduced, and discriminatory pension arrangements must be eliminated. Also, many employers fall victim to the myth that older people don't want to work or are incapable of it. There is a continuing need to counteract this and other inaccurate perceptions of the older worker.[17]

Imbalance in the age distribution of our labor force has significant implications for employers. It means that those who constitute the population bulge are experiencing greater competition for advancement from others of approximately the same age. This situation challenges the ingenuity of managers to develop career patterns for members of this group and to motivate their performance. In addition, providing pension and social security benefits for this group when they reach retirement age early in the next century will present a very serious problem for employers and society. Because of the drop in the birthrate following the baby boom, the labor force available to support the retirees will be smaller. The solutions to this and other problems created by the imbalance in the age distribution of our labor force will require long-range planning on the part of both organization and government leaders.

GENDER DISTRIBUTION OF THE WORK FORCE According to projections by the Bureau of Labor Statistics, women will continue to join the U.S. labor force in growing numbers. Women made up only 39 percent of the labor force in 1972; by 2000 they are expected to account for over 47 percent. The increase of women in the labor force is a trend that employers must continue to recognize. Employers will be under constant pressure to ensure equality for women with respect

Genentech, Inc., runs a day care facility for the children of its employees.

to employment, advancement opportunities, and compensation. They also will need to accommodate working mothers and fathers through parental leaves, part-time employment, flexible work schedules, job sharing, telecommuting, and child care assistance. Increasingly, benefit programs are being designed to meet the needs of the two-wage-earner family.[18]

Because more women are working, employers are more sensitive to the growing need for policies and procedures to eliminate sexual harassment in the workplace. Some organizations have special orientation programs to acquaint all personnel with the problem and to warn potential offenders of the consequences. Many employers are demanding that managers and supervisors enforce their sexual harassment policy vigorously. (The basic components of such policies will be presented in Chapter 3.)

Typically, sexual harassment involves one individual taking advantage of another. One psychological counselor, however, has observed that "instead of a single individual [being charged with harassment], I'm seeing more cases in which the whole environment is a source of sexual harassment." Characteristic of the "whole environment" syndrome are risqué jokes, pornographic magazines and slides in video presentations, and pinup posters. While some employers argue that it isn't always easy to define what constitutes an environment of sexual harassment, a spokesman for DuPont says that to be safe, "we tell people: it's harassment when something starts bothering somebody."[19]

RISING LEVELS OF EDUCATION In recent years the educational attainment of the U.S. labor force has risen dramatically. Between 1972 and 1986 the proportion of the labor force age 18 to 64 with at least one year of college increased from 28 to 41 percent, while the proportion with four years of college or more increased from 14 to 21 percent. The emphasis on education is expected to continue, and opportunities for high school dropouts will be increasingly limited.[20] At the same time, college graduates may find that to be employed will require taking a job that does not fully utilize the knowledge and skills they acquired in college. To compensate their employees for this lack of parity, employers must try harder to improve the quality of work life. We will discuss some suggested improvements later in the chapter.

It is important to observe that while the educational level of the work force has continued to rise over the past several decades, employers are having to cope with individuals who are functionally illiterate—i.e., unable to read, write, calculate, or solve problems at a level that enables them to perform even the simplest technical tasks. The U.S. Department of Education estimates that the functionally illiterate now account for 30 percent of unskilled, 29 percent of semiskilled, and 11 percent of all managerial, professional, and technical employees. In a speech to the Commonwealth Club of California, David Kearns, chairman and CEO of Xerox Corporation, said: "The American work force is in grave jeopardy. We are running out of qualified people. If current demographic and economic trends continue, American business will have to hire a million new workers a year who can't read, write, or count."[21]

Another, related problem is technological illiteracy. Nearly 40 states now have some kind of technology education program. In New York State all junior high school students are required to take a one-year introductory technology course. The program stresses hands-on laboratory work, problem-solving activities, and a curriculum that treats technology as a set of systems.[22]

Many of the larger employers have instituted programs in basic skills. Ford Motor Company offers reading courses at 25 plants. AT&T spends $6 million a year on remedial courses for employees. Aetna Life and Casualty spent $750,000 to teach 500 employees basic reading, writing, and math skills. Domino's Pizza Distribution Corporation developed a videodisk program designed to improve employees' reading and math skills while also teaching them how to make pizza dough.[23]

Job Trends

HR managers are interested in job trends because of their effects on all of the HRM functions. Government studies show that as incomes and living standards have risen, the desire for services has grown more rapidly than the desire for goods. As a result, employment in service-producing industries has been increasing faster than employment in goods-producing industries. Furthermore, imports of foreign-made goods have been limiting the growth of goods-producing industries in the United States.

INCREASING SERVICE JOBS Employment is expected to continue to increase much faster in service-producing industries than in goods-producing industries, as shown in Figure 2–3. The largest projected change in employment

FIGURE 2–3 PROJECTED CHANGES IN EMPLOYMENT IN MAJOR INDUSTRIES, 1988–2000

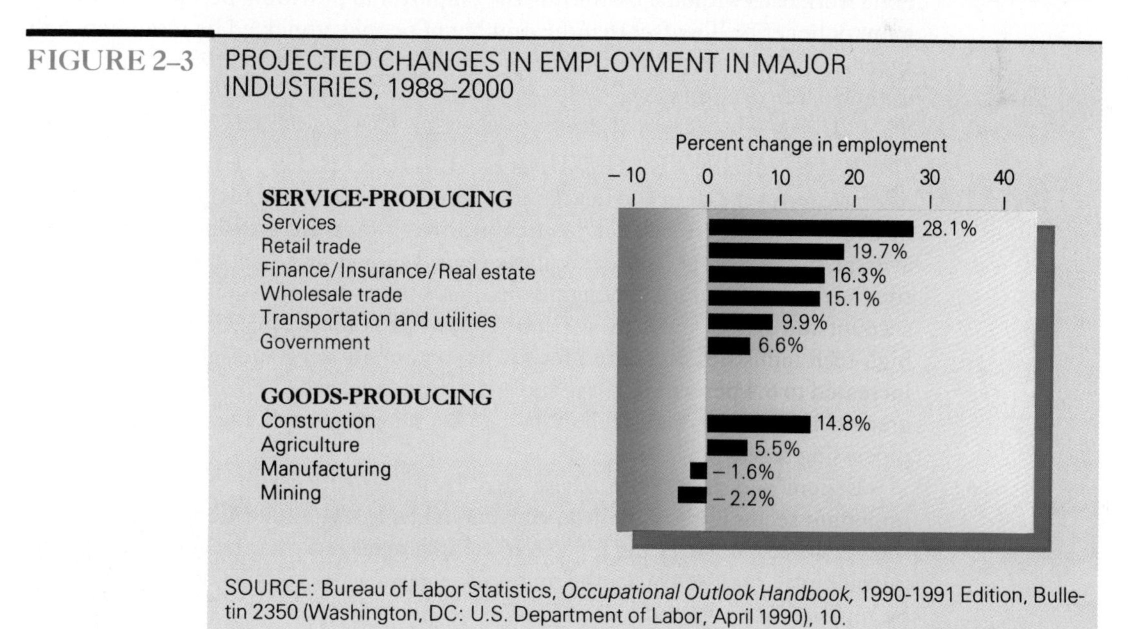

SOURCE: Bureau of Labor Statistics, *Occupational Outlook Handbook,* 1990-1991 Edition, Bulletin 2350 (Washington, DC: U.S. Department of Labor, April 1990), 10.

is in services, retail and wholesale trade, and finance/insurance/real estate. The service industries employ a wide range of workers in food and beverage preparation, security, personal and health services, and various nonprofit organizations.

Employment in the goods-producing industries peaked in the late 1970s and has not recovered from the recessionary period of the early 1980s. Construction is the only goods-producing area expected to show an increase in employment between 1986 and 2000 in response to projected economic conditions and demographic trends. Employment in manufacturing is expected to decline by 4 percent in that period. Most of the jobs that will disappear will be production jobs. The number of professional, technical, and managerial positions in manufacturing firms will actually increase.[24]

Since there are proportionately larger numbers of clerical and service jobs at the lower pay levels, special effort may be required to attract and retain employees in these jobs. Career ladders will be needed to enable the more capable employees to advance, and to provide greater psychological rewards for those unable to do so. On the other hand, for professional, technical, and managerial jobs, employers will have to develop recruiting and selection programs appropriate to the type of applicants being sought. Effective HR planning that involves career ladders and development programs will be essential to help employees reach these positions through internal promotion.

By using temporary workers—usually from an agency such as Manpower, Thomas, Olsten, or Kelly—organizations can have the benefit of finding individuals who have been screened and trained. Temporaries can be used effectively to handle extra workloads without committing the employer to providing permanent employment or benefits. The fact that the number of people employed by temporary help agencies in the United States has been increasing annually since 1983 is an indicator of their value to employers.[25]

JOBS IN HIGH-TECHNOLOGY INDUSTRIES High technology is often touted as the source of new employment opportunities to help replace jobs lost in declining "smokestack" industries. Although they are growing faster than the average for all sectors, and particularly the manufacturing sector, high-tech industries such as computers, bioengineering, and telecommunications are expected to account for only a small proportion of new jobs through 1995. Employment in high-tech industries accounted for 6.1 percent of all wage and salary jobs in 1972, increased to 6.4 percent in 1984, and is projected to reach 7.0 percent by 1995. The greatest increases in high-tech industries are projected to be in computer and data processing services.[26]

Etzioni and Jargowsky advise that basic industries will continue to be an important sector in the American economy. The HRM implications for a two-track society (basic industries and high tech) are that managers must be adept at supervising blue-collar, white-collar, and professional employees and that not all workers can be retrained for high-tech jobs. They conclude that "there is no reason to expect, favor, or promote . . . a high-tech society and the closing of basic industries."[27]

SALLY FORTH. Reprinted with special permission of North America Syndicate

TELECOMMUTING One of the more recent changes and potentially the most far-reaching is telecommuting. **Telecommuting** is the use of microcomputers to do work in the home that is traditionally done in the workplace. Using computer and telephone hookups with the office some miles away, employees perform their job tasks.

Not all jobs lend themselves to at-home work, but many do: travel agent, architect, writer, salesperson, data entry clerk, insurance agent, real estate agent, bookkeeper, accountant, computer programmer, word-processing secretary, engineer, and others. Numerous organizations have some sort of telecommuting program. Among them are Control Data, J. C. Penney, American Express, International Banking Corporation, Blue Cross/Blue Shield of South Carolina, Chevron Chemical Company, and Pacific Bell.[28]

Managers of telecommuters must be innovative thinkers and risk takers. According to Jack Nilles, who coined the term *telecommuter,* "The major obstacle to telecommuting in the last 15 years has been conservative management with industrial revolution mindsets."[29] Many employers have been reluctant to consider telecommuting because they fear they will lose control if employees are not physically present. However, it appears that with careful selection of personnel, this is not a problem. In fact, many employers report that there is a tendency for telecommuters to become workaholics.[30] In choosing telecommuters, organizations should try to limit them to people whose jobs do not require interaction with others, have been with the organization for some time, have the appropriate psychological characteristics to work at home, and above all are self-starters. Preparing managers to supervise employees who are not physically present is a special requirement for success.[31] Managers have to work harder at planning and communicating with their subordinates, and they have to be clearer about their objectives.

What potential benefits do HR managers see in telecommuting? The most common responses of over 100 HR managers surveyed in the Raleigh-Durham, North Carolina, area were decreased production costs, increased employee satisfaction, and increased productivity.[32] In a *Wall Street Journal* survey conducted by

Roper, more than 2,000 adults were asked to rank the pros and cons of working at home. Their responses are shown in Figure 2–4. Over one-fourth of the respondents said the benefits of working at home outweighed the drawbacks, indicating that reluctant employers are a big reason the home-office boom hasn't materialized.[33]

Cultural Changes

The attitudes, beliefs, values, and customs of people in a society are an integral part of their culture. Naturally, their culture affects their behavior on the job and the environment within the organization, influencing their reactions to work assignments, leadership styles, and reward systems. Like the external and internal environments of which it is a part, culture is undergoing continual change. HR policies and procedures, therefore, must be adjusted to cope with this change.

EMPLOYEE RIGHTS Since World War II, the United States has enjoyed periods of unprecedented prosperity. Americans have come to expect a continuing rise in their standard of living. Such expectations, in turn, are increasingly being perceived as entitlements, creating what some writers refer to as a **psy-**

FIGURE 2–4 PRO'S AND CONS OF WORKING AT HOME

Percentage of people who consider these to be the major advantages and disadvantages:

BENEFITS		DRAWBACKS	
More control over one's work schedule	53%	Not having necessary supplies or equipment	51%
Wear more comfortable clothes	36%	Having too many family interruptions	38%
Avoiding a commute	35%	Mixing work with family life too much	37%
Not having a boss close by	28%	Being distracted by household chores	32%
Being able to care for children	20%	Not having interaction with co-workers	27%
No interruptions from co-workers	20%	Not having a regular routine	23%
Job seems less like work	20%	Having trouble quitting after a full day	16%
Not minding overtime as much	15%	Feeling work is less important if done at home	14%

SOURCE: Thomas R. King, "Working at Home Has Yet to Work Out," *Wall Street Journal* (December 22, 1989): B1. Reprinted by permission of *The Wall Street Journal,* © Dow Jones & Company, Inc., 1989. All Rights Reserved Worldwide.

Federal law mandates that women performing the same job as men receive equal pay.

chology of entitlement. According to Louis Davis, there is a growing belief that individuals are not at fault if their expectations are not met—rather, it is the institution or society that is to blame.[34] This belief represents a substantial shift from what traditionally was referred to as the **work ethic,** in which personal success was attributed to individual effort in meeting certain obligations. The work ethic held that "If I am not successful, something must be wrong with me!" With the decline of the work ethic, many individuals now believe that "Something is wrong but not necessarily wrong with me. It might have nothing to do with me but with the situation in which I find myself."[35] The result is that what were once considered privileges to be earned are now being regarded as entitlements, or rights.

In the past two decades federal legislation has radically changed the rules for management of employees by granting them many specific rights. Among these are laws granting the right to equal employment opportunity (Chapter 3), union representation if desired (Chapter 18), a safe and healthful work environment (Chapter 13), a pension plan that is fiscally sound (Chapter 12), equal pay for men and women performing essentially the same job (Chapter 10), and privacy in the workplace. An expanded discussion of the specific areas in which rights and responsibilities are of concern to employers and employees, including the often-cited employment-at-will doctrine, will be presented in Chapter 16.

CONCERN FOR PRIVACY HR managers and their staffs, as well as others in positions of responsibility in organizations, generally recognize the importance of discretion in handling all types of information about employees. Since the passage of the federal Privacy Act of 1974, increased attention to privacy has been evident. While the Act applies almost exclusively to records maintained by federal government agencies, it has drawn attention to the importance of privacy and has led to the passage of privacy legislation in several states.

Employer responses to the issue of information privacy vary widely. IBM was one of the first companies to show concern for how personal information about employees was handled. It began restricting the release of information as early as 1965 and in 1971 developed a comprehensive privacy policy. Cummins Engine Company, Dow Corning Corporation, Avid, Inc., and Corning Glass Works are among other employers that have developed privacy programs.[36] We will discuss the content of such programs and present some recommended privacy guidelines in Chapter 16.

CHANGING ATTITUDES TOWARD WORK Changing attitudes toward authority have become prevalent in today's labor force. Employees increasingly expect to exercise certain freedom from management control without jeopardizing their job security or chances for advancement. They are more demanding, more questioning, and less willing to accept the "I am the boss" approach.

Another well-established trend is for employees to define success in terms of personal self-expression and the fulfilling of their potential on the job while still receiving adequate compensation for their efforts. A greater proportion of the work force strives to have challenging jobs. More people are also seeking rewarding careers and multiple careers rather than just being satisfied gaining employment.

Workers also seem to value free time more than in earlier decades. Many polls report that Americans feel they have less free time than they once did. Contrary to their reported feelings, however, a Use of Time Project at the Survey Research Center of the University of Maryland found that Americans today actually have more free time than ever before. Men have 40 hours of free time a week and women have 39 hours. Free time is defined as what is left over after subtracting the time people spend working and commuting to work, taking care of their families, doing housework, shopping, sleeping, eating, and doing other personal activities. According to the report, free time has increased because women are doing much less housework than they did several decades ago, and because the number of actual work hours that workers record in their daily diaries—not the number of "official" hours of work—has fallen significantly for both men and women. The average findings, however, do hide much individual variation. Working parents, especially, are under severe time pressures. On balance, though, more people are gaining free time than are losing it.[37]

PERSONAL AND FAMILY LIFE ORIENTATION We noted earlier that HRM has become more complex than it was when employees were concerned primarily with economic survival. Today's employees have greater expectations from society and from their employment. Etzioni reports that having time to develop a satisfying personal life and pursue cultural and other nonwork-related interests is valued by workers today as much as having a full-time job.[38] Employers are thus being forced to recognize the fact that as individuals strive for a greater balance in their lives, employers will have to alter their attitudes and their HRM policies to satisfy employee desires.

Work and the family are connected in many subtle and not so subtle social, economic, and psychological ways. Because of the new forms that the family has taken—e.g., the two-wage-earner and the single-parent family—work organizations find it necessary to provide employees with more flexibility and options. Day care, part-time work, pregnancy leave, parental leave, executive transfers, spousal involvement in career planning, and assistance with family problems have become important considerations for HR managers.

Change in Organizational Effectiveness

Of major concern to most Americans is the fact that the United States now ranks twelfth among the top 13 industrialized nations in "growth in output per worker."

U.S. annual growth in output per worker averaged 1 percent for the period 1981–1985. In recent years productivity in basic manufacturing operations has improved slightly. Following a cycle of down-sizing, the forging of new union agreements, and the closing or modernization of obsolete plants, the U.S. manufacturing sector has recovered from the 1970s slowdown and was back on a 3 percent growth track in the late 1980s.[39] More recently there have been periods of decline.

Intense international competition has forced U.S. organizations to enhance quality, as well as productivity, to regain their competitive edge. Through quality improvements, companies such as Hewlett-Packard, Boeing, A. O. Smith, Cummins Engine, and Maytag have substantially improved productivity and bolstered their competitive advantage. Quality improvement requires an organization to make major changes in its philosophy, its operating mechanisms, and its HR program. A survey asked 307 executives from Fortune 1000 companies and 308 executives from smaller firms (20+ employees) to rate the importance of eight quality-improvement techniques. Those techniques that stressed human factors—employee motivation, change in corporate culture, and employee education—received higher ratings than those emphasizing processes or equipment. Companies known for product and service quality strongly believe that employees are the key to product quality. They believe that proper attention to employees will naturally improve quality and productivity.[40] In other words, they believe that HRM is the most promising strategy for reversing the productivity slide.

To test the validity of this belief, an empirical study was designed by two researchers. The study was conducted at two autonomous divisions of a large service/recreational corporation, each with a separate profit center. Using a list of activities the company believed to be important and a set of critical employee attitude statements, an employee opinion survey was developed and administered. The results showed that when an organization is committed to good HR department programs and activities, employees will see this commitment in a positive manner. Attitudes will be affected in a meaningful way, thus contributing to organizational effectiveness in many ways. These findings add empirical support to the literature and surveys of HR and other managers that have been reported.[41]

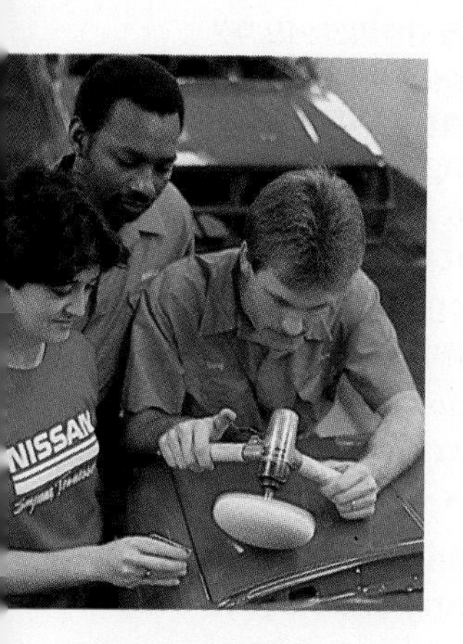

Teamwork on the production line at the Nissan plant in Smyrna, Tennessee.

The fact that many companies in the United States have found it difficult to compete successfully with those in Japan has stimulated interest in uncovering differences between the two countries. Cultural and sociological differences between Japanese and American workers may explain to some extent why workers in Japan are credited with being more productive and dedicated to their work. For example, the Japanese tradition in the larger companies of providing lifetime employment and avoiding layoffs, even at a financial sacrifice, has generated a sense of loyalty and commitment to employers among Japanese workers. Cole, in his research of Japanese management, concludes that Japanese workers tend to identify more than American workers with their employers and their employers' goals. However, he found them to be little different from American workers with respect to their dedication to the work ethic or to doing a decent job.

One of the keys to the increased productivity of Japanese workers lies in the coordinated efforts of individuals—through interdependence, collaboration, and teamwork.[42] Another is the Japanese philosophy of employee management, which rests on respect for the worker's intelligence and need for self-esteem. Some Japanese subsidiaries, such as Nissan in Smyrna, Tennessee, and GM-Toyota in Fremont, California, have been able to apply this philosophy to the management of their American employees. These companies have translated the philosophy into action by encouraging their American workers to participate in decision making and to identify with company goals.

Many American companies have adopted certain aspects of Japanese management practices to their advantage. It should be observed, however, that the Japanese business and management system has been undergoing significant changes. Lifetime employment, seniority-based promotion systems, and company-wide unions—all characteristic of Japanese-style management—have been called into serious question by some writers.[43]

IMPROVING THE QUALITY OF WORK LIFE

Improving an organization's external environment is, to a large extent, beyond an employer's control. However, improving the organization's internal environment is definitely within the realm of an employer's influence. A major challenge confronting employers today is that of improving the **quality of work life (QWL).** This challenge stems not only from the need to meet foreign competition, but also from the demographic and cultural changes that have just been discussed.

Many of our largest private and public organizations are making changes to try to improve the QWL of their employees. These efforts consist of looking for ways to make work more rewarding and reduce anxieties and stresses of the work environment. Several different approaches are being used, including restructuring work organization and job design, increasing employee involvement in shaping the organization and its functions, and developing a corporate culture that will encourage members to behave in ways that will maximize productivity, strengthen human relationships, meet employee expectations, and sustain desired attitudes and beliefs.[44]

Work Organization and Job Design

If QWL is to be improved, there is no better place to start than with the way work is organized and the way jobs are designed. Since each industry and its jobs present special problems to be solved, it is only possible to present some general prescriptions. Mansell and Rankin of the Ontario (Canada) Quality of Working Life Centre have developed criteria for designing organizational structures and processes, including jobs, for high QWL. These criteria are presented in Highlights in HRM 2. We will discuss specific ways of making jobs more meaningful and more

HIGHLIGHTS IN HRM

2 CRITERIA FOR ORGANIZATIONAL STRUCTURES AND PROCESSES

1. Decisions are made at the lowest level possible. Self-regulation for individuals and groups is a primary goal.
2. Individuals or integrated groups of workers are responsible for a "whole job." People do not work on fragmented, meaningless tasks.
3. The potential (technical and social) of individuals, of groups, and of the overall organization is developed to the fullest.
4. Hierarchies are minimized and artificial barriers do not exist between people or between functions.
5. Quality and quality control are built directly into the primary production system.
6. Safety and health are built directly into the total system.
7. Support systems and structures promote and support self-regulation, integration, and flexibility. For example, information systems provide immediate feedback directly to those who need the information in order to perform their job; information is not used to retain power or to police others.
8. Problems are resolved on the basis of joint control and shared responsibility between all groups. Structures and processes for the sharing of decision-making powers are guaranteed at all levels in the organization.

SOURCE: Jacquie Mansell and Tom Rankin, *Changing Organizations: The Quality of Working Life Process* (Toronto, Ontario, Canada: Ontario Quality of Working Life Centre, September 1983), 10–11. Reproduced with permission of the authors.

satisfying in Chapter 4. Other aspects of job design and such work arrangements as job rotation, flexible working hours, and job sharing that contribute to QWL will also be discussed in that chapter.

Participative Management

Essential to QWL is the development of **participative management.** Basically, participative management involves enabling employees to participate in decisions relating to their work and employment conditions. It thereby creates a psychological partnership between management and employees.

The concept of participative management is not a new one. The human relations movement helped to initiate efforts toward greater employee participation. Unfortunately, many early attempts to have employees participate were largely cosmetic in nature. These attempts were long on method and technique and short on sincerity, largely because many managers feared the erosion of their authority. Even today the efforts of some organizations to provide a more participative environment are viewed with suspicion by their employees.

Despite the reluctance of management and the suspicions of employees, participative management is the wave of the future. If only for reasons of survival, both sides must recognize that they have a mutual interest in working together to reduce costs and avoid becoming victims of foreign and domestic competition. Thus, there is a strong incentive to form joint union–management committees to probe ways of reducing costs and improving quality. Caterpillar, Champion International, and General Motors, through their QWL programs, are making substantial progress in providing avenues for employee input. Other organizations with employee participation programs will be examined in detail in Chapters 14 and 15.

Enlightened business leaders recognize that basic changes in relations between employers and employees are essential. Many are also convinced that bringing workers into the decision-making process offers the most significant explanation for the success of Japanese companies they seek to emulate. Employee participation in the context of our culture and environment is equally essential in the United States. Today's workers are better educated and more demanding. Having become accustomed to privileges and freedoms in our democratic society, they are not about to relinquish what they believe to be their rights in the workplace.

Supportive Organizational Culture

Over the years much has been written about the organizations that are noted for the quality of their products and services and their relationships with people both outside and inside the organization. The names of early leaders of American businesses, such as Thomas Watson of IBM, Harley Procter of Procter & Gamble, General Johnson of Johnson & Johnson, and John Patterson of NCR, as well as many others, are legend in management literature. These individuals are well known for the attention they gave to HR and the work environment they created and nurtured. While it is not possible to detail here the legacy of these early leaders, the credo of social objectives of Johnson & Johnson, reproduced in Highlights in HRM 3, conveys the attitudes characteristic of these individuals. In recent years the success of Japanese companies in maintaining the loyalty of employees has increased attention to the need to reexamine what is happening to American firms.

In the past decade, organizational culture has been viewed as an intangible but real and important factor in determining the organizational climate.[45] Kilmann and associates emphasize that "culture is the glue that not only holds our organizations together, but our theories about them as well." **Organizational culture** is defined as the shared philosophies, values, assumptions, beliefs, expectations, attitudes, and norms that knit an organization together. It may also be defined as "the way things are done around here."[46] For example, everyone at Hewlett-Packard knows that employees are expected to be innovative. Everyone at International Business

HIGHLIGHTS IN HRM

3 SOCIAL OBJECTIVES OF JOHNSON & JOHNSON

Our Credo

We believe our first responsibility is to the doctors, nurses and patients,
to mothers and fathers and all others who use our products and services.
In meeting their needs everything we do must be of high quality.
We must constantly strive to reduce our costs
in order to maintain reasonable prices.
Customers' orders must be serviced promptly and accurately.
Our suppliers and distributors must have an opportunity
to make a fair profit.

We are responsible to our employees,
the men and women who work with us throughout the world.
Everyone must be considered as an individual.
We must respect their dignity and recognize their merit.
They must have a sense of security in their jobs.
Compensation must be fair and adequate,
and working conditions clean, orderly and safe.
We must be mindful of ways to help our employees fulfill
their family responsibilities.
Employees must feel free to make suggestions and complaints.
There must be equal opportunity for employment, development
and advancement for those qualified.
We must provide competent management,
and their actions must be just and ethical.

We are responsible to the communities in which we live and work
and to the world community as well.
We must be good citizens — support good works and charities
and bear our fair share of taxes.
We must encourage civic improvements and better health and education.
We must maintain in good order
the property we are privileged to use,
protecting the environment and natural resources.

Our final responsibility is to our stockholders.
Business must make a sound profit.
We must experiment with new ideas.
Research must be carried on, innovative programs developed
and mistakes paid for.
New equipment must be purchased, new facilities provided
and new products launched.
Reserves must be created to provide for adverse times.
When we operate according to these principles,
the stockholders should realize a fair return.

Johnson & Johnson

SOURCE: Johnson & Johnson. Reproduced by permission.

Machines knows that "IBM means service." Everyone at Mary Kay Cosmetics knows the philosophy of the chairman emeritus of the board, Mary Kay Ash:

> People come first at Mary Kay Cosmetics—our beauty consultants, sales directors and employees, our customers, and our suppliers. We pride ourselves as a "company known for the people it keeps." Our belief in caring for people, however, does not conflict with our need as a corporation to generate a profit. Yes, we keep our eye on the bottom line, but it's not an overriding obsession. To me, P and L doesn't only mean profit and loss—it also means *people* and *love.*[47]

In her book *Mary Kay on People Management*, she describes how managers can develop an organizational culture and can provide leadership that is based on the golden rule. Unlike most management books, which are written by and for men, her book is written for men *and* women who aspire to be effective managers.[48]

We do find an increasing number of larger American firms receiving widespread acclaim for their supportive cultures, including Wal-Mart, Herman Miller, and

This stylish hallway in Herman Miller's Design Yard stimulates discussion and creativity.

others that have been recognized in a series of *Fortune* articles. While each of these companies has its own unique culture, team spirit is a characteristic they all share. In addition to what observers have noted about these and other companies, the findings from two research studies of employees show a positive correlation between employees' perception of being valued and cared about by the organization and (a) conscientiousness in carrying out conventional job responsibilities, (b) expressed emotional involvement in the organization, and (c) innovation on behalf of the organization in the absence of anticipated reward or personal recognition.[49]

THE IMPORTANCE OF CULTURE After studying 80 large American companies, Deal and Kennedy report in the book *Corporate Culture: The Rites and Rituals of Corporate Life* that those with consistently high performance were companies with strong cultures.[50] Similarly, in their *In Search of Excellence: Lessons from America's Best-Run Companies*, Peters and Waterman report that of the 62 companies they studied, "without exception, the dominance and coherence of culture proved to be an essential quality of the excellent companies."[51] In their more recent books, *Thriving on Chaos: Handbook for Management Revolution* (by Peters) and *The Renewal Factor: How to Best Get and Keep the Competitive Edge* (by Waterman), they emphasize the tapping of the enormous latent energy of people committed to excellence.[52] There is a strong emphasis in both books on people as a source of renewal, and both stress that renewal requires continuing change.

ELEMENTS OF CULTURE Deal and Kennedy made an exhaustive study of the organizational literature from the 1950s to the early 1980s to understand better the elements that make up a strong culture. They found that there are five elements, which they describe as follows:

1. *Business Environment.* Each organization carries on certain kinds of activities—e.g., selling, inventing, conducting research. Its business environment is the single greatest influence in shaping its culture.
2. *Values.* These are basic concepts and beliefs that define "success" in concrete terms for employees—e.g., "If you do this, you too will be a success."
3. *Heroes.* People who personify the culture's values provide tangible role models for employees to follow. Companies with strong cultures have many heroes.
4. *Rites and Rituals.* The systematic and programmed routines of day-to-day life in the company (rituals) show employees the kind of behavior that is expected of them and what the company stands for.
5. *Cultural Network.* Through informal communication the corporate values are spread throughout the organization.[53]

A strong culture not only spells out how people are to behave most of the time, it also enables people to feel better about what they do, so they are more likely to work harder.

KEEPING CULTURE CONTEMPORARY We observed earlier in this chapter that there are many changes taking place in our society that affect HRM. Organizations with strong cultures must be able to adapt to these changes and at the same time retain their basic philosophy. An organizational culture established by the U.S. Department of Labor or the management team of the City of St. Louis in the 1960s might not be healthy in the 1990s. The increased heterogeneity of the work force and changes in life-styles are affecting the performance and attitudes of employees.[54]

One recent change that organizations have fostered is to encourage employees to become entrepreneurs or innovators on the job. Since they remain in the employ of the organization but are given freedom to create new products, services, production methods, etc., they are referred to as **intrapreneurs.** Pinchot defines this people-based approach to innovative management as allowing "entrepreneurs . . . freedom and incentive to do their best in small groups within large corporations." Often the results of such activities lead to the organization of a new division or subsidiary.[55] Among the better-known divisions or subsidiaries devoted to intrapreneurship are the Colgate Venture Company, General Foods' Culinova Unit, and Scott Paper's Do-It-Yourself Group.[56]

Employers are beginning to recognize that if the spirit of intrapreneurism is to exist beyond the lifespan of a fad, it must be nurtured. Not only should intrapreneurs be given special recognition, but incentives and rewards should be established individually. To quote one writer, "A major roadblock to the nurturing of intrapreneurs is often the compensation manager whose traditional interests are control and consistency."[57]

The challenge for management in the coming decades will be to maintain a balance between rapid change and the need for stability. Since the focus of HR professionals is on human performance and everything that affects it, HR managers should not lose sight of their responsibility to keep the culture open and flexible.

SUMMARY

The internal and external environments of an organization can have a significant impact on the productivity of its human resources and on their management. For this reason HR managers must be aware of the impact these environments—and the changes occurring within them—may have on their programs. The failure of management in many organizations to anticipate and cope effectively with these changes has been one of the principal causes for the declining rate of productivity in the United States.

While changes are taking place in many areas that affect HRM, those of major concern are the demographic nature of the work force, job trends, and such cultural changes as increased demands for employee rights, changing attitudes toward work, and personal and family life orientation.

To improve the internal environment and thereby increase productivity, many organizations are making greater efforts to enhance the quality of work life. These efforts include giving greater attention to work organization, job design, participative management, and the building of a supportive organizational culture. All of these efforts reflect the increasing responsiveness of employers to the changes that affect the management of their human resources.

DISCUSSION QUESTIONS

1. What impact will the growing proportion of women and the rising level of education in the work force have on HRM?
2. What are some of the problems employers may encounter with respect to the federal regulation of HRM?
3. What are some of the jobs that can be performed by telecommuting? How is telecommuting likely to affect superior–subordinate relationships?
4. How do employee demands for more rights affect HRM?
5. It is generally recognized that today's employees are seeking a more balanced life-style. What effect does this have on HR policies and procedures?
6. Describe the culture of an organization with which you have been associated. What are its values, who are its heroes, and what rites and rituals does it use to reinforce the culture?
7. What can the management of an organization do to encourage intrapreneuring? Can you name some of the outstanding intrapreneurs in American industry?
8. What is your opinion concerning the governmental regulation of HRM? Do you consider the amount of regulation to be excessive, insufficient, about right? What would your viewpoint be if you were an employer? A union leader?

MINI-CASE 2–1 Work Satisfaction in an Assembly Plant

During a case-gathering interview, Dr. Steele, an industrial psychologist, was asked to indicate what he considered to be the basic causes of worker dissatisfaction in his company's assembly plants. Following are some of his observations on the subject:

> In my opinion, the question of how to provide work satisfaction defies any simplistic answer. We have had more work stoppages and poor-quality workmanship in some of our most modern plants than in some of our more antiquated ones. In some plants where we have the most problems, the work force is relatively young, but in other plants where we have had fewer problems the workers are equally young. I believe that individual differences have a great deal to do with the satisfaction a particular worker derives from a job.

For example, in one of our small plants where truck cab and chassis units are assembled, we experimented with four different assembly methods to determine which would be preferable from the standpoint of worker satisfaction and production efficiency. First, we used the traditional assembly-line method. Next, we tried making subassemblies and putting these assemblies together. Then we tried having the workers follow the vehicle down the line, performing the various assembly operations in sequence. Finally, we organized work teams to build the entire vehicle in a work area. What we discovered from this experience was that each of the methods was preferred by some of the workers.

Individual differences appeared to be a major factor in determining a particular worker's preferences. Unfortunately, because of our tremendous volume of production, we are forced to use the assembly-line method. We couldn't begin to meet the demand for our cars and trucks, for example, with the production methods used by Volvo. Consequently, I believe that by improving relations between people in our organization and by reducing adversarial relationships between employees and management we can perhaps make the greatest contribution to improving worker satisfaction. In our organization, therefore, we are seeking to learn more about how people work together and how we can help them to work together better.

QUESTIONS

1. Should management be concerned about job satisfaction for its employees? Why or why not?
2. What is there in each of the four assembly methods that might have made these methods preferable to some of the workers?
3. How closely, if at all, do the views of Dr. Steele correspond with the results of the Hawthorne studies discussed in Chapter 1?

MINI-CASE 2–2 Organizational Excellence

In recent years, many books and articles have been written about the importance of excellence in all phases of operation of an organization. Most of these publications, several of which are cited in this chapter, have shown by many examples what various organizations have done to achieve the high degree of excellence for which they are known.

One of the more recent books, *The 100 Best Companies to Work For in America,*[58] is unique in that its authors use the reported attitudes and feelings of employees as a basis for their overall determination of a company's excellence. As they state: "It's one thing to listen to presidents or chairmen talk about the great companies they head . . . it's something else to talk with the head of the mailroom at Time, Inc., or to an usher at the Los Angeles Dodgers stadium and to see the pride they felt about working for their companies."

The report of "The 100 Best" is based on visits to 114 companies in 27 different states in which at least a half-dozen employees and sometimes several dozen employees were interviewed. On the basis of the interviews, each company was rated on a five-point scale on the following factors: pay, benefits, job security, chance to move up, and ambience (unique qualities that set it apart from all others). Most interesting are the descriptive quotes from the employees, including capsule comments for each company, such as:

	PLUS	MINUS
Delta	A family feeling despite its huge size.	Nobody leaves so it's hard to move up.
Exxon	The prestige of working for Number One.	A highly bureaucratic environment.
Intel	A chance to be one of the best and brightest.	They yell at each other a lot.
3M	It's a good place for people who like to tinker with ideas.	You won't like it if you don't like small towns.
Los Angeles Dodgers	They're winners off the field and on.	You can't tell your friends from Brooklyn where you work.
J. C. Penney	They still believe in the golden rule.	It may seem as if it's from another era.

On the basis of their findings from "The 100 Best," the authors draw a composite picture of the ideal company. Good pay and strong benefits are basic. Beyond them are many other qualities, such as "Making people feel that they are part of a team, or in some cases a family."

QUESTIONS

1. What other qualities would you expect employees to include in a description of the ideal company?
2. How accurate do you believe employee responses are in describing the internal environment and the culture of a company?
3. The authors report that the best companies have achieved a sense of "we are all in it together." What factors are most likely to contribute to this feeling?

NOTES AND REFERENCES

1. James R. Nininger, "Human Resource Priorities in the 1980s," *Canadian Business Review* 7, no. 4 (Winter 1980): 11.

2. Gary T. Marx and Sanford Sherizen, "Corporations That Spy on Their Employees," *Business and Society Review* 60 (Winter 1987): 32–37; and Rebecca Grant and Christopher Higgins, "Monitoring Service Workers via Computer: The Effect on Employees, Productivity, and Service," *National Productivity Review* 8, no. 2 (Spring 1989): 101–112.

3. Thomas P. Verney, Charles J. Hollon, and George Rogol, "HR Planning for Robots in the Work Place," *Personnel* 63, no. 2 (February 1986): 8–9.

4. Edward Cornish, "Those Undemanding Robots Make Unerring Workers," *Sacramento Bee* (January 13, 1985): G6.

5. Robert U. Ayres and Steven M. Miller, "Robotic Realities: Near-Term Prospects and Problems," *Annals of the American Academy of Political and Social Science* 470 (November 1983): 33.

6. Fred K. Foulkes and Jeffrey L. Hirsch, "People Make Robots Work," *Harvard Business Review* 84, no. 1 (January–February 1984): 94–102. See also Charles J. Hollon and George N. Rogol, "How Robotization Affects People," *Business Horizons* 28, no. 3 (May–June 1985): 74–80; Linda Argote, Paul S. Goodman, and David Schkade, "The Human Side of Robotics: How Workers React to a Robot," *Sloan Management Review* 24, no. 3 (Spring 1983): 31–40; Alcott Arthur, "Robots, RIFS, and Rights," *Journal of Business Ethics* 4, no. 3 (June 1985): 197–203; and Verney, Hollon, and Rogol, "HR Planning for Robots in the Work Place."

7. David Herold, "Don't Shoot Your Robot in the Foot," *Robotics World* 7, no. 1 (January/February 1989): 2. See also Jeffrey R. Edwards, "Computer Aided Manufacturing and Worker Well-Being: A Review of Research," *Behaviour and Information Technology* 8, no. 3 (1989): 157–174.

8. James Ledvinka and Vida Scarpello, *Federal Regulation of Personnel and Human Resource Management*, 2d ed. (Boston: PWS-Kent Publishing, 1990), 18.

9. The *Federal Register* provides a uniform system for making available to the public those regulations and legal notices issued by federal agencies. These include presidential proclamations and executive orders and federal agency documents having general applicability and legal effect, documents required to be published by act of Congress, and other federal agency documents of public interest. It is published daily, Monday through Friday, except holidays.

10. Prentice-Hall, Commerce Clearing House, and The Bureau of National Affairs, Inc., are the leading publishers of such services.

11. *Government Executive*, October 1989 as cited in *USA Today* (January 25, 1990): 1A.

12. Bronston T. Mayes and Robert W. Allen, "Toward a Definition of Organizational Politics," *Academy of Management Review* 2, no. 4 (October 1977): 672–678; and Robert W. Allen, Dan L. Madison, Lyman W. Porter, Patricia A. Renwick, and Bronston T. Mayes, "Organizational Politics: Tactics and Characteristics of Its Actors," *California Management Review* 22, no. 1 (Fall 1979): 77.

13. "Tomorrow's Jobs," *Occupational Outlook Handbook*, 1990–1991 edition (Washington, DC: Bureau of Labor Statistics, Bulletin no. 2350, April 1990), 8.

14. Ibid.

15. Ibid.

16. Anthony Ramirez, "Making Better Use of Older Workers," *Fortune* 119, no. 3 (January 30, 1989): 179–187.

17. Ibid. See also "Age as an Asset," *USA Today* (December 13, 1989): B1; and Bureau of National Affairs, "Employers Prepare—Gray Wave Is Coming," *BNA Fair Employment Practices* (March 16, 1989): 33.

18. Aaron Bernstein, "Business and Pregnancy: Good Will Is No Longer Enough," *Business Week* (February 2, 1987): 37; "20 Corporations That Listen to Women," *Ms Magazine* (November 1987): 45–52; and Walecia Konrad, "Welcome to the Woman-Friendly Company Where Talent Is Valued and Rewarded," *Business Week* (August 6, 1990): 48–55.

19. Joseph Pereira, "Women Allege Sexist Atmosphere in Offices Constitutes Harassment," *Wall Street Journal* (February 10, 1988): 23.

20. *Occupational Outlook Handbook*, 1990–1991, 9.

21. Ron Zemke, "Workplace Illiteracy—Shall We Overcome?" *Training* 26, no. 6 (June 1989): 33–39.

22. Mimi Bluestone and Douglas A. Harbrecht, "Reading, 'Riting, 'Rithmetic—and Now Tech Ed," *Business Week* (October 19, 1987): 114–116.

23. Ron Zemke, "Workplace Illiteracy," 33–39.

24. *Occupational Outlook Handbook*, 1990–1991, 10.

25. *Sacramento Bee* (January 31, 1988).

26. Valerie A. Personick, "A Second Look at Industry Output and Employment Trends Through 1995," *Monthly Labor Review* 108, no. 11 (November 1985): 37.

27. Amitai Etzioni and Paul Jargowsky, "High Tech, Basic Industry, and the Future of the American Economy," *Human Resource Management* 23, no. 3 (Fall 1984): 229–240.

28. Dorothy Kroll, "Telecommuting: A Revealing Peek Inside Some of the Industry's First Electronic Cottages," *Management Review* 73, no. 11 (November 1984): 18–23.

29. Lynne F. McGee, "Setting Up Work at Home," *Personnel Administrator* 33, no. 12 (December 1988): 58–62.

30. Bob Shallit, "A Few Firms Tiptoe Toward Freeing Workers from Office," *Sacramento Bee* (July 13, 1986): E1.

31. William Atkinson, "Home/Work," *Personnel Journal* 64, no. 11 (November 1985): 104–109. See also Atkinson, *Working at Home: Is It for You?* (Homewood, IL: Dow Jones–Irwin, 1985); and Robert O. Metzger and Mary Ann Von Glinow, "Off-Site Workers: At Home and Abroad," *California Management Review* 30, no. 3 (Spring 1988): 101–111.

32. Barbara J. Risman and Donald Tomaskovic-Devey, "The Social Construction of Technology: Microcomputers and the Organization of Work," *Business Horizons* 32, no. 3 (May–June 1989): 71–75.

33. Thomas R. King, "Working at Home Has Yet to Work Out," *Wall Street Journal* (December 22, 1989): B1.

34. Louis E. Davis, "Individuals and the Organization," *California Management Review* 22, no. 3 (Spring 1980): 8.

35. Ibid.

36. For practical recommendations on how to avoid lawsuits over invasion of privacy, see John Corbett O'Meara, "The Emerging Law of Employees' Right to Privacy," *Personnel Administrator* 30, no. 6 (June 1985): 159–165.

37. John P. Robinson, "Time's Up," *American Demographics* 11, no. 7 (July 1989): 33–35.

38. Amitai Etzioni, "Opting Out: The Waning of the Work Ethic," in *Working Changes and Choices*, ed. James O'Toole, Jane L. Scheiber, and Linda C. Wood (New York: Human Sciences Press, 1981), 156–157.

39. Thomas Rollins and Jerrold R. Bratkovich, "Productivity's People Factor," *Personnel Administrator* 33, no. 2 (February 1988): 50–57.

40. Y. K. Shetty, "The Human Side of Product Quality," *National Productivity Review* 8, no. 2 (Spring 1989): 175–182. See also Rosabeth Moss Kanter, Barry A. Stein, and Todd Jick, *The Challenge of Organizational Change—How People Experience It and Manage It* (New York: Free Press, 1991).

41. George W. Bohlander and Angelo J. Kinicki, "Where Personnel and Productivity Meet," *Personnel Administrator* 33, no. 9 (September 1988): 122–130.

42. Walter H. Gmelch and Val D. Miskin, "The Lost Art of High Productivity," *Personnel* 63, no. 4 (April 1986).

43. John Naisbitt and Patricia Aburdene, *Re-inventing the Corporation* (New York: Warner Books, 1985), 240.

44. Robert T. Golembiewski and Ben-chu Sun, "QWL Improves Worksite Quality: Success Rates in a Large Pool of Studies," *Human Resource Development Quarterly* 1, no. 1 (Spring 1990): 35–43.

45. Edgar H. Schein, "Are You Corporate Cultured?" *Personnel Journal* 65, no. 11 (November 1986): 82–96.

46. Ralph H. Kilmann, Mary J. Saxton, Roy Serpa, and Associates, *Gaining Control of the Corporate Culture* (San Francisco: Jossey-Bass, 1985), 15–16. An interesting technique for studying an organization's culture may be found in W. Jack Duncan, "Organizational Culture: 'Getting a Fix' on an Elusive Concept," *Academy of Management Executive* 3, no. 3 (August 1989): 229–236.

47. Mary Kay Ash, *Mary Kay on People Management* (New York: Warner Books, 1984), xix. See also Mary Kay Ash, *Mary Kay* (New York: Harper & Row, 1981); and Richard E. Hattwick, "Mary Kay Ash," *The Journal of Behavioral Economics* 16 (Winter 1987): 61–69.

48. Ash, *Mary Kay on People Management*, xviii–xix.

49. Kenneth Labich, "Hot Company, Warm Culture," *Fortune* 119, no. 5 (February 27, 1989): 74–78; and John Huey, "Wal-Mart—Will It Take Over the World?" *Fortune* 119, no. 3 (January 30, 1989): 52–61. See also Robert Eisenberger, Peter Fasolo, and Valerie Davis-LaMastro, "Perceived Organizational Support and Employee Diligence, Commitment, and Innovation," *Journal of Applied Psychology* 75, no. 1 (1990): 51–59.

50. Terrence E. Deal and Allan A. Kennedy, *Corporate Cultures: The Rites and Rituals of Corporate Life* (Reading, MA: Addison-Wesley, 1982), 7. See also Benjamin Schneider, ed., *Organizational Climate and Culture* (San Francisco: Jossey-Bass, 1990).

51. Thomas J. Peters and Robert H. Waterman, Jr., *In Search of Excellence: Lessons from America's Best-Run Companies* (New York: Harper & Row, 1982), 75.

52. Tom Peters, *Thriving on Chaos: Handbook for Management Revolution* (New York: Alfred A. Knopf, 1987); and Robert H. Waterman, Jr., *The Renewal Factor: How to Best Get and Keep the Competitive Edge* (New York: Bantam Books, 1987).

53. Deal and Kennedy, *Corporate Cultures*, 13–15.

54. Meryl P. Gardner, "Creating a Corporate Culture for the Eighties," *Business Horizons* 28, no. 1 (January–February 1985): 59–63. See also Larry B. Meares, "A Model for Changing Organizational Culture," *Personnel* 63, no. 7 (July 1986): 38–46.

55. G. Pinchot, "Intrapreneurialism for Corporations," *The Futurist* (February 1984): 82–83. See also Peter F. Drucker, *Innovation and Entrepreneurship—Practice and Principles* (New York: Harper & Row, 1985); and Philip R. Harris, *Management in Transition* (San Francisco: Jossey-Bass, 1985), Chapter 3. For an interesting biography of probably America's greatest intrapreneur, see Stuart W. Leslie, *Boss Kettering—Wizard of General Motors* (New York: Columbia University Press, 1983).

56. Ronald Alsop, "Consumer-Product Grants Relying on 'Intrapreneurs' in New Ventures," *Wall Street Journal* (April 22, 1988): 25.

57. Kirkland Ropp, "Bringing Up Baby: Nurturing Intrapreneurs," *Personnel Administrator* 32, no. 6 (June 1987): 92–96. See also W. Jack Duncan, Peter M. Guites, Andrew C. Ruchs, and T. Douglas Jacobs, "Intrapreneurship and the Reinvention of the Corporation," *Business Horizons* 31, no. 3 (May–June 1988): 16–21.

58. Robert Levering, Milton Moskowitz, and Michael Katz, *The 100 Best Companies to Work For in America* (Reading, MA: Addison-Wesley, 1985).

CHAPTER 3

Equal Employment Opportunity and Affirmative Action

After reading this chapter you will be able to:

1. *Explain why equal employment opportunity and affirmative action are important parts of employment law.*
2. *Discuss how equal employment opportunity affects HRM.*
3. *Identify the major laws and court decisions affecting equal employment opportunity and affirmative action.*
4. *Describe the various types of discrimination.*
5. *Calculate the four-fifths, disparate impact rule.*
6. *Explain the steps in the filing and investigation of an equal employment opportunity charge.*
7. *Describe the procedure for establishing an affirmative action plan.*
8. *Define the key terms in the chapter.*

TERMS TO IDENTIFY

- equal employment opportunity *(72)*
- protected classes *(76)*
- reasonable accommodation *(80)*
- handicapped individual *(81)*
- fair employment practices (FEPs) *(84)*
- *Uniform Guidelines on Employee Selection Procedures* *(85)*
- disparate impact, or adverse impact *(86)*
- four-fifths rule *(86)*
- bottom-line concept *(88)*
- disparate treatment *(89)*
- sexual harassment *(90)*
- bona fide occupational qualification (BFOQ) *(91)*
- business necessity *(92)*
- EEO-1 report *(94)*
- charge form *(96)*
- affirmative action *(99)*
- reverse discrimination *(100)*

Within the field of HRM perhaps no topics have received more attention during the past 30 years than equal employment opportunity (EEO) and affirmative action (AA). **Equal employment opportunity,** or the employment of individuals in a fair and nonbiased manner, has consumed the attention of the media, the courts, practitioners, and legislators. Not surprisingly, along with this attention have come a myriad of legal requirements affecting all aspects of the employment relationship. These mandates create legal responsibilities for an organization and each of its managers to comply with various laws and administrative guidelines. All functional areas of HRM should be performed according to legal standards.

When managers ignore the legal aspects of HRM, they risk incurring costly and time-consuming litigation, negative public attitudes, and damage to organizational morale. In one highly publicized case, the Big Eight accounting firm Price Waterhouse was sued by a female manager for alleged sexual stereotyping. The manager claimed she was denied a partnership in the firm because other managers believed her to be overly "macho" and "hardnosed." The U.S. Supreme Court ruled in her favor, noting that "gender must be irrelevant to employment decisions" and sex stereotyping is discriminatory.[1]

Equal employment opportunity is not only a legal topic; it is also an emotional issue. It concerns all individuals regardless of their sex, race, religion, age, national origin, color, or position in an organization. Supervisors should be aware of their personal biases and how these attitudes can influence their dealings with subordinates. It should be emphasized that both intentional and covert discrimination in employment is illegal.

In recent decades, employers have been compelled to develop employment policies that incorporate different laws, executive orders (EOs), administrative regulations, and court decisions (case law) designed to end job discrimination. The role of these legal requirements in shaping employment policies will be emphasized in this chapter. We will also discuss the process of affirmative action, which attempts to correct past practices of discrimination by actively recruiting minority group members.

HISTORICAL PERSPECTIVE OF EEO LEGISLATION

Equal employment opportunity as a national priority has emerged slowly in the United States. Not until the mid-1950s and early 1960s did nondiscriminatory employment become a strong social concern. Three factors seem to have influenced the growth of EEO legislation: (1) a growing body of laws and government regulations covering discrimination; (2) changing attitudes toward employment discrimination; and (3) published reports highlighting the economic problems of women, minorities, and older workers.

Early Legal Developments

Since as early as the 19th century, the public has been aware of discriminatory employment practices in the United States. In 1866, Congress passed the Civil Rights Act, which extended to all persons the right to enjoy full and equal benefits of all laws regardless of race. Unfortunately this Act had little effect on employment policies, since job discrimination was widely practiced and accepted during that period.

Beginning in the 1930s and 1940s, more-specific federal policies covering nondiscrimination began to emerge. In 1933, Congress enacted the Unemployment Relief Act, which prohibits employment discrimination on account of race, color, or creed. In 1941, President Franklin D. Roosevelt issued Executive Order 8802, which was to ensure that every American citizen, "regardless of race, creed, color, or national origin," would be guaranteed equal employment opportunities in World War II defense contracts. Over the next 20 years a variety of other legislative efforts were promoted to resolve inequities in employment practices. These occurred largely at the federal level, through executive orders issued by Presidents Eisenhower, Kennedy, and Johnson.

While various EEO policies were instituted, these early efforts did little to correct employment discrimination. First, at both the state and federal levels, nondiscrimination laws often failed to give any enforcement power to the agency charged with upholding the law. Rather, when discrimination was found, conciliation was used as a remedy, and this often proved to be ineffective. Second, the laws that were passed frequently neglected to list specific discriminatory practices or methods for their correction. Third, employers covered by the Acts were only required to comply voluntarily with the equal employment opportunity legislation. Without a compulsory requirement, employers often violated legislation with impunity. Despite these faults, however, early executive orders and laws laid the groundwork for passage of the Civil Rights Act of 1964.

Changing National Values

The United States was founded on the principles of individual merit, hard work, and equality. The Constitution grants to all citizens the right to life, liberty, and the pursuit of happiness. The Fifth, Thirteenth, and Fourteenth Amendments expand these guarantees by providing for due process of law (Fifth Amendment), outlawing slavery (Thirteenth Amendment), and guaranteeing equal protection under the law (Fourteenth Amendment). A central aim of political action has been to establish justice for all people of the nation.

In spite of these constitutional guarantees, employment discrimination has a long history in the United States. Organizations that claim to offer fair treatment to employees have openly or covertly engaged in discriminatory practices. Well-known organizations such as Rockwell International Corporation, the United Steel Workers Union, and the City of Los Angeles have violated equal employment laws.[2] While in theory the American dream of economic prosperity has existed for all citizens, in reality many have believed that women and minorities should be excluded from equal consideration.

Public attitudes changed dramatically with the beginning of the civil rights movement. During the late 1950s and early 1960s, minorities—especially blacks—publicized their low economic and occupational position through marches, sit-ins, rallies, and clashes with public authorities. The low employment status of women also gained recognition during this period. Supported by concerned individuals and church and civic leaders, the civil rights movement and the women's movement received wide attention through television and print media. These movements had a pronounced influence on changing the attitudes of society at large, of the business community, of civic leaders, and of government officials, resulting in improvements in the civil rights of all individuals. No longer was blatant discrimination to be accepted.

Economic Disparity

The change in government and societal attitudes toward discrimination was further prompted by increasing public awareness of the economic imbalance between nonwhites and whites. Even today, civil rights activists cite government statistics to emphasize this disparity. For example, the December 1989 unemployment rate for black males over 20 years old was 10.8 percent, compared to 3.9 percent for white males the same age. When employed, nonwhites tend to hold unskilled or semiskilled jobs characterized by unstable employment, low status, and low pay. In 1988, the median weekly earnings of white males were $465; for black males, $326;

NAACP youth council marches for jobs in Baltimore, Maryland, 1960.

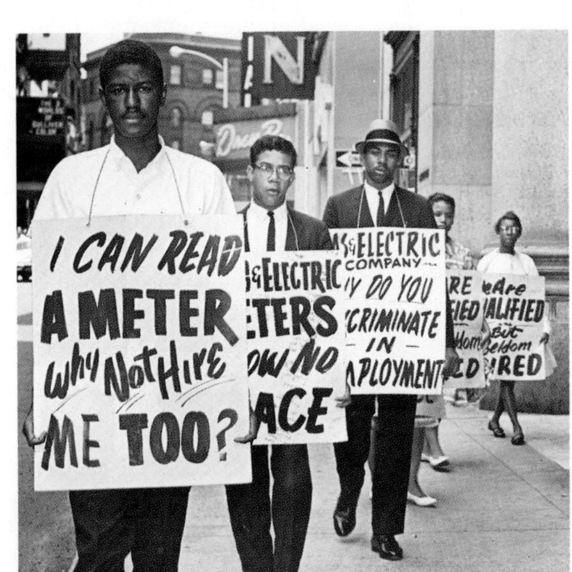

and for Hispanic males, \$307.[3] The inequities in unemployment rates and income figures have been consistent in the preceding years as well, lending additional support for legislative change.

GOVERNMENT REGULATION OF EQUAL EMPLOYMENT OPPORTUNITY

Significant laws have been passed barring employment discrimination. These laws influence all of the HRM functions, including recruitment, selection, performance appraisal, promotion, and compensation. Because all managers are involved in employment activities, knowledge of these statutes is critical. Furthermore, continuous training in EEO legislation is a requirement for successful employee supervision. For example, the Bank of America has developed a comprehensive HR policy concerning employees stricken with acquired immune deficiency syndrome (AIDS). This policy serves as a basis for an elaborate, ongoing managerial communication and training program.[4] Organizations cannot afford to have managers make HRM decisions without considering the possible legal implications of their actions for the organization or themselves.

Major Federal Laws

Major federal equal employment opportunity laws have attempted to correct social problems of interest to particular groups of workers, called **protected classes.** Defined broadly, these include individuals of a minority race, women, older persons, and those with physical or mental disabilities. Separate federal laws cover each of these groups. Figure 3–1 lists the major federal laws and their provisions governing equal employment opportunity.

EQUAL PAY ACT OF 1963 The Equal Pay Act outlaws discrimination in pay, employee benefits, and pensions based on the worker's gender. Employers are prohibited from paying employees of one gender at a rate lower than that paid to

FIGURE 3–1 MAJOR FEDERAL LAWS AFFECTING EQUAL EMPLOYMENT OPPORTUNITY

Law	Provisions
Equal Pay Act of 1963	Requires all employers covered by the Fair Labor Standards Act and others to provide equal pay for equal work, regardless of sex.
Title VII of Civil Rights Act of 1964 (amended in 1972)	Prohibits discrimination in employment on the basis of race, color, religion, sex, or national origin. Created the Equal Employment Opportunity Commission (EEOC) to enforce the provisions of Title VII.
Age Discrimination in Employment Act of 1967 (amended in 1986)	Prohibits private and public employers from discriminating against persons 40 years of age or older in any area of employment because of age. Exceptions are permitted where age is a bona fide occupational qualification.
Equal Employment Opportunity Act of 1972	Amended Title VII of Civil Rights Act of 1964. Strengthens EEOC's enforcement powers and extends coverage of Title VII to government employees, faculty in higher education, and other employers and employees.
Pregnancy Discrimination Act of 1978	Broadens the definition of sex discrimination to include pregnancy, childbirth, or related medical conditions. Prohibits employers from discriminating against pregnant women in employment benefits if they are capable of performing their job duties.
Americans with Disabilities Act of 1990	Prohibits discrimination in employment against persons with physical or mental disabilities or the chronically ill. Employers must make reasonable accommodation to the employment needs of the disabled. Covers employers with 25 or more employees 2 years after passage and employers with 15 or more employees 4 years after passage.

members of the other gender for jobs of equal work. Jobs are considered equal when they require substantially the same skill, effort, and responsibility under similar working conditions and in the same establishment. For example, male and female flight attendants working for United Airlines must not be paid differently because of their gender. However, other airlines may pay their flight attendants wage rates that differ from those at United, based on different job content or economic conditions.

Employers do not violate the Equal Pay Act when differences in wages paid to men and women for equal work are based on seniority systems, merit considerations, or incentive pay plans. However, these exceptions must not be based on the employee's gender or serve to discriminate against one particular gender. Employers may not lower the wages of one gender to comply with the law, but must raise the wages of the gender being underpaid.

The Equal Pay Act was passed as an amendment to the Fair Labor Standards Act (FLSA) and is administered by the Equal Employment Opportunity Commission. It covers employers engaged in interstate commerce and most government employees.

CIVIL RIGHTS ACT OF 1964 Title VII of the Civil Rights Act of 1964 is the broadest and most significant of the antidiscrimination statutes. The Act bars discrimination in all HR activities, including hiring, training, promotion, pay, employee benefits, or other conditions of employment.[5] Discrimination is prohibited on the basis of race, color, religion, sex, or national origin. Also prohibited is discrimination based on pregnancy. The law protects hourly employees, supervisors, professional employees, managers, and executives from discriminatory practices. Section 703(a) of Title VII of the Civil Rights Act specifically provides that:

> It shall be unlawful employment practice for an employer:
>
> 1. To fail or refuse to hire or to discharge any individual, or otherwise to discriminate against any individual with respect to his [or her] compensation, terms, conditions, or privileges of employment because of such individual's race, color, religion, sex, or national origin; or
> 2. To limit, segregate, or classify his [or her] employees or applicants for employment in any way which would deprive or tend to deprive any individual of employment opportunities or otherwise adversely affect his [or her] status as an employee because of such individual's race, color, religion, sex, or national origin.

While the purpose and the coverage of Title VII are extensive, the law does permit various exemptions. For example, as with the Equal Pay Act, managers are permitted to apply employment conditions differently if those differences are based on such objective factors as merit, seniority, or incentive payments. Nowhere does the law require employers to hire, promote, or retain workers who are not qualified to perform their job duties. And managers may still reward employees differently, provided these differences are not predicated on the employees' race, color, sex, religion, or national origin.

The Civil Rights Act of 1964, as amended by the Equal Employment Opportunity Act of 1972, covers a broad range of organizations. The law includes under its jurisdiction the following:

1. All private employers in interstate commerce who employ 15 or more employees for 20 or more weeks per year.
2. State and local governments.
3. Private and public employment agencies, including the U.S. Employment Service.
4. Joint labor–management committees that govern apprenticeship or training programs.
5. Labor unions having 15 or more members or employees.
6. Public and private educational institutions.

Certain employers are excluded from coverage of the Civil Rights Act. Broadly defined, these are:

1. Persons elected to public office.
2. United States government-owned corporations.
3. Bona fide, tax-exempt private clubs.
4. Religious organizations employing persons of a specific religion.
5. Organizations hiring native Americans on or near a reservation.

The Civil Rights Act of 1964 established the Equal Employment Opportunity Commission to administer the law and promote equal employment opportunity. The commission's structure and operations will be reviewed later in this chapter.

AGE DISCRIMINATION IN EMPLOYMENT ACT OF 1967 A special study by the U.S. Department of Labor notes that by the year 2000, the average age of the work force will be 39 years.[6] Since older workers are less likely to agree to relocate or adapt to new job demands, they are prone to employer discrimination. To make employment decisions based on age illegal, the Age Discrimination in Employment Act (ADEA), as amended, was passed in 1967. The Act prohibits specific employers from discriminating against persons 40 years of age or older in any area of employment, including selection, because of age. Employers affected are those with 20 or more employees, unions with 25 or more members, employment agencies, and federal, state, and local governments.

Exceptions to the law are permitted where age is a bona fide occupational qualification (BFOQ). (BFOQs are discussed more fully later in the chapter.) A BFOQ may exist where an employer can show that advanced age may affect public safety or organizational efficiency. A BFOQ will not exist where an employer argues that younger employees foster a youthful or more energetic organizational image. Employers must also be careful to avoid making offhanded remarks like "the old man," "old codger," or "we need new blood," since these can be used as proof of discrimination in age-bias suits.[7]

EQUAL EMPLOYMENT OPPORTUNITY ACT OF 1972 In 1972, the Civil Rights Act of 1964 was amended by the Equal Employment Opportunity Act. Two important changes were made. First, the coverage of the Act was broadened to include all of the organizations noted previously. Second, the law strengthened the enforcement powers of the EEOC by allowing the agency itself to sue employers in court to enforce the provisions of the Act. Regional litigation centers were established to provide faster and more effective court action.

PREGNANCY DISCRIMINATION ACT OF 1978 Prior to the passage of the Pregnancy Discrimination Act, pregnant women could be forced to resign or take a leave of absence because of their condition. In addition, employers did not have to provide disability or medical coverage for pregnancy. The Pregnancy Discrimination Act amended the Civil Rights Act of 1964 by stating that pregnancy is a disability and that pregnant employees in covered organizations must be treated on an equal basis with employees having other medical conditions. Under the law, it would be illegal for employers to deny sick leave for morning sickness or related pregnancy illness if sick leave were permitted for other medical conditions such as flu or surgical operations.

Furthermore, the law prohibits discrimination in the hiring, promotion, or termination of women because of pregnancy. Women must be evaluated on their ability to perform the job, and employers may not set arbitrary dates for mandatory pregnancy leaves. Leave dates are to be based on the individual pregnant employee's ability to work.

Houston Police Chief Elizabeth Watson worked until two days before the birth of her child in December 1990.

AMERICANS WITH DISABILITIES ACT OF 1990 Discrimination against the disabled is prohibited in federally funded activities by the Vocational Rehabilitation Act. However, the disabled were not among the protected classes covered by the Civil Rights Act of 1964. To remedy this shortcoming, Congress in 1990 passed the Americans with Disabilities Act, prohibiting employers from discriminating against individuals with physical and mental handicaps or the chronically ill. The law defines a disability as "(a) a physical or mental impairment that substantially limits one or more of the major life activities; (b) a record of such impairment; or (c) being regarded as having such an impairment." Note that the law also protects persons "regarded" as having a disability—for example, individuals with disfiguring burns. The Act does not include:

1. Homosexuality or bisexuality.
2. Gender-identity disorders not resulting from physical impairment, or other sexual-behavior disorders.
3. Compulsive gambling, kleptomania, or pyromania.

4. Psychoactive substance use disorders resulting from current illegal use of drugs.
5. Current illegal use of drugs.
6. Infectious or communicable diseases of public health significance (applied to food-handling jobs only, and excluding AIDS).

The Act requires employers to make a reasonable accommodation to disabled persons who are otherwise qualified to work, unless doing so would cause undue hardship to the employer. **Reasonable accommodation** "includes making facilities accessible and usable to disabled persons, restructuring jobs, permitting part-time or modified work schedules, reassigning to a vacant position, changing equipment, and/or expense," considering the (1) nature and cost of the accommodation and (2) financial resources, size, and profitability of the facility and parent organization. Furthermore, employers cannot use selection procedures that screen out or tend to screen out disabled persons unless the selection procedure "is shown to be job-related for the position in question and is consistent with business necessity," and acceptable job performance cannot be achieved through reasonable accommodation.

The Act incorporates the procedures and remedies found in Title VII of the Civil Rights Act allowing employees the right to seek reinstatement, back pay, and other injunctive relief against an employer who violates the law. The Act covers employers with 25 or more employees beginning two years after enactment and extends coverage to employers with 15 or more employees two years after that. The EEOC will enforce the law in the same manner that Title VII of the Civil Rights Act is now enforced.

Other Federal Laws and Executive Orders

Because the major laws affecting equal employment opportunity do not cover agencies of the federal government and because state laws do not apply to federal employees, it has been necessary for the President to issue executive orders to protect federal employees. Executive orders are also used to provide equal employment opportunity to individuals employed by government contractors. Since many large employers, like General Dynamics, AT&T, Allied-Signal, and Motorola, and numerous small companies have contracts with the federal government, managers are expected to know and comply with the provisions of executive orders and other laws. The federal laws and executive orders that apply to government agencies and government contractors are summarized in Figure 3–2.

VOCATIONAL REHABILITATION ACT OF 1973 Often considered a forgotten group, handicapped persons experience discrimination because of negative attitudes regarding their ability to perform work, as well as the physical limitations imposed by organizational facilities.[8] The Vocational Rehabilitation Act was passed in 1973 to correct these problems by requiring private employers with federal contracts over $2,500 to take affirmative action to hire and promote individuals with

FIGURE 3–2 EQUAL EMPLOYMENT OPPORTUNITY LAWS AND EXECUTIVE ORDERS APPLICABLE TO AGENCIES OF AND CONTRACTORS WITH THE FEDERAL GOVERNMENT

LAW	PROVISIONS
Vocational Rehabilitation Act of 1973 (amended in 1974)	Prohibits federal contractors from discriminating against handicapped individuals in any program or activity receiving federal financial assistance. Requires federal contractors to develop affirmative action plans to hire and promote handicapped persons.
Vietnam Era Veterans' Readjustment Assistance Act of 1974	Prohibits discrimination against Vietnam era veterans by employers with government contracts of $10,000 or more. Mandates affirmative action to employ and advance disabled and qualified veterans.
Executive Order 11246 (1965), as amended by Order 11375 (1966)	Prohibits employment discrimination based on race, color, religion, sex, or national origin by government contractors with contracts exceeding $10,000. Requires contractors employing 50 or more workers to develop affirmative action plans when government contracts exceed $50,000 a year.
Executive Order 11478 (1969)	Obligates the federal government to ensure that all personnel actions affecting employees or applicants for employment be free from discrimination based on race, color, religion, sex, and national origin.

a mental or physical disability. Recipients of federal financial assistance, such as public and private colleges and universities, are also covered. Employers must make a reasonable accommodation to hire handicapped individuals but are not required to employ unqualified persons. In applying the safeguards of this law, the term **handicapped individual** means ". . . any person who (1) has a physical or mental impairment which substantially limits one or more of such person's major life activities, (2) has a record of such an impairment, or (3) is regarded as having such an impairment." This definition closely parallels the definition of handicapped individual provided in the Americans with Disabilities Act just discussed.

Individuals may be regarded as substantially limited when they experience difficulty in securing, retaining, or advancing in employment because of their handicap.[9] Since the Act was passed, a growing number of mental and physical impairments have been classified as handicaps within the meaning of the law. For example, handicaps such as blindness or paralysis are clearly covered. But other, less obvious impairments such as diabetes, high blood pressure, or heart disease also fall within the definition of handicap established under the Act.

In 1987, the Supreme Court ruled in *Nassau County, Florida* v. *Arline* that employees afflicted with contagious diseases, such as tuberculosis, are handicapped individuals and subject to the Act's coverage.[10] In cases where persons with contagious diseases are "otherwise qualified" to do their jobs, the law requires employers to make a reasonable accommodation to enable the handicapped to perform their jobs.[11] In *Chalk* v. *U.S. District Court,* the Ninth Circuit Court of Appeals ruled that individuals with AIDS are also handicapped within the meaning of the Rehabilitation Act.[12] Therefore, discrimination on the basis of AIDS violates the law, and employers must accommodate the employment needs of AIDS victims.[13] Public interest in AIDS has presented management with a challenge to address work-related concerns about AIDS.[14] Many organizations, including BankAmerica Corporation, have developed specific policies to deal with the issue of AIDS in the workplace (see Highlights in HRM 1).

The Rehabilitation Act does not require employers to hire or retain a handicapped person if he or she has a contagious disease that poses a direct threat to the health or safety of others and the individual cannot be accommodated. Also, employment is not required when some aspect of the employee's handicap prevents that person from carrying out essential parts of the job or if the person is not otherwise qualified.[15]

Nevertheless, because of the success experienced in the employment of handicapped persons, the slogan "Hire the handicapped—it's good business" has become standard policy for many organizations. This slogan does not suggest that handicapped persons can be placed in any job without careful consideration being given to their disabilities, but rather that it is good business to hire qualified handicapped persons who can work safely and productively. Members of the HR staff should be trained to assess individual types and degrees of limitations and should be aware of how these restrictions relate to different jobs in the organization. In many cases the restructuring of jobs or the use of special equipment permits handicapped persons to qualify for employment.

VIETNAM ERA VETERANS' READJUSTMENT ASSISTANCE ACT OF 1974 To ensure equal employment opportunity to qualified disabled veterans and veterans of the Vietnam War, Congress passed the Vietnam Era Veterans' Readjustment Assistance Act of 1974. The law applies to employers with government contracts of $10,000 or more, and it requires employers to take affirmative action in the hiring and promotion of veterans. Veterans are defined as *disabled* if their disability is rated at 30 percent or more. In addition, contractors and subcontractors must list all suitable job openings with appropriate state-run employment security offices. These offices are to give priority status to veterans when making employment referrals. Small government-contract employers who make extensive use of state employment offices for recruiting employees should be aware of this requirement.

HIGHLIGHTS IN HRM

1 BANKAMERICA CORPORATION'S POLICY ON ASSISTING EMPLOYEES WITH LIFE-THREATENING ILLNESSES*

BankAmerica recognizes that employees with life-threatening illnesses—including but not limited to cancer, heart disease, and AIDS—may wish to continue to engage in as many of their normal pursuits as their condition allows, including work. As long as these employees are able to meet acceptable performance standards and medical evidence indicates that their conditions are not a threat to themselves or others, managers should be sensitive to their conditions and ensure that they are treated consistently with other employees. At the same time, BankAmerica has an obligation to provide a safe work environment for all employees and customers. Every precaution should be taken to ensure that an employee's condition does not present a health and/or safety threat to other employees or customers.

Consistent with this concern for employees with life-threatening illnesses, BankAmerica offers the following range of resources available through Personnel Relations:

- Management and employee education and information on terminal illnesses and specific life-threatening illnesses.
- Referral to agencies and organizations which offer supportive services for life-threatening illnesses.
- Benefit consultation to assist employees in effectively managing health, leave, and other benefits.

Guidelines

When dealing with situations involving employees with life-threatening illnesses, managers should:

1. Remember that an employee's health condition is personal and confidential. Reasonable precautions should be taken to protect information regarding an employee's health condition.
2. Contact Personnel Relations if you believe that you or other employees need information about terminal illness or a specific life-threatening illness or if you need further guidance in managing a situation that involves an employee with a life-threatening illness.
3. Contact Personnel Relations if you have any concern about the possible contagious nature of an employee's illness.
4. Contact Personnel Relations to determine if a statement should be obtained from the employee's attending physician that continued presence at work will pose no threat to the employee, co-workers, or customers. BankAmerica reserves the right to require an examination by a medical doctor appointed by the company.
5. If warranted, make reasonable accommodation for employees with life-threatening illnesses consistent with the business needs of the division/unit.
6. Make a reasonable attempt to transfer employees with life-threatening illnesses who request a transfer and are experiencing undue emotional stress.

7. Be sensitive and responsive to co-workers' concerns and emphasize employee education available through Personnel Relations.
8. No special consideration should be given beyond normal transfer requests for employees who feel threatened by a co-worker's life-threatening illness.
9. Be sensitive to the fact that continued employment for an employee with a life-threatening illness may sometimes be therapeutically important in the remission or recovery process or may help to prolong that employee's life.
10. Employees should be encouraged to seek assistance from established community support groups for medical treatment and counseling services. Information on these can be requested through Personnel Relations or Corporate Health Programs.

*This policy applies to all BankAmerica Corporation subsidiaries, one of which is Bank of America.

SOURCE: William H. Wagel, "AIDS: Setting Policy, Educating Employees at Bank of America," *Personnel* (August 1988). Used with permission.

EXECUTIVE ORDER 11246 Federal agencies and government contractors with contracts of $10,000 or more must comply with the antidiscrimination provisions of Executive Order 11246. The order prohibits discrimination based on race, color, religion, sex, or national origin in all employment activities. Furthermore, it requires that government contractors or subcontractors having 50 or more employees with contracts in excess of $50,000 develop affirmative action plans; these will be discussed later in the chapter.

Executive Order 11246 created the Office of Federal Contract Compliance Programs (OFCCP) to ensure equal employment opportunity in the federal procurement area. The agency issues nondiscriminatory guidelines and regulations similar to those issued by the EEOC. Noncompliance with OFCCP policies can result in the cancellation or suspension of contracts. The OFCCP is further charged with requiring that contractors provide job opportunities to the handicapped, disabled veterans, and veterans of the Vietnam War.

Fair Employment Practice Laws

Federal laws and executive orders provide the major stipulations governing equal employment opportunity. In addition, almost all states and many local governments have passed laws barring employment discrimination. Referred to as **fair employment practices (FEPs),** these statutes are often more comprehensive than the federal laws. While state and local laws are too numerous to review here, managers should be aware of them and how they affect HRM in their organizations.

State and local FEPs also promote the employment of individuals in a fair and unbiased way. They are patterned after federal legislation, although they frequently extend jurisdiction to employers exempt from federal coverage and, therefore, pertain mainly to smaller employers. While Title VII of the Civil Rights Act exempts employers with fewer than 15 employees, many states extend antidiscrimination laws to employers with one or more workers. Therefore, managers and entrepreneurs operating a small business must pay close attention to these laws. Local or state legislation may bar discrimination based on physical appearance, marital status, sexual preferences, arrest records, color blindness, or political affiliation.

States with FEPs establish independent governmental agencies to administer and enforce the statutes. The Ohio Civil Rights Commission, Massachusetts Commission Against Discrimination, Colorado Civil Rights Division, and Pittsburgh Commission on Human Relations are examples. State agencies play an important role in the investigation and resolution of employment discrimination charges. FEP agencies and the Equal Employment Opportunity Commission often work together to resolve discrimination complaints.

Uniform Guidelines on Employee Selection Procedures

In the past, employers have been uncertain about the appropriateness of specific selection procedures, especially those related to testing. To remedy this concern, in 1978 the Equal Employment Opportunity Commission, along with three other government agencies, adopted the current ***Uniform Guidelines on Employee Selection Procedures.***[16] Since it was first published in 1970, the *Uniform Guidelines* has become a very important procedural manual for HR managers because it applies to employee selection procedures in the areas of hiring, retention, promotion, transfer, demotion, dismissal, and referral. It is designed to assist employers, labor organizations, employment agencies, and licensing and certification boards in complying with the requirements of federal laws prohibiting discriminatory employment.

Essentially the *Uniform Guidelines* recommends that an employer be able to demonstrate that selection procedures are valid in predicting or measuring performance in a particular job. It also defines discrimination as follows:

> The use of any selection procedure which has a disparate impact on the hiring, promotion, or other employment or membership opportunities of members of any race, sex, or ethnic group will be considered to be discriminatory and inconsistent with these guidelines, unless the procedure has been validated in accordance with these guidelines (or, certain other provisions are satisfied).[17]

VALIDITY When using a test or other selection instrument to choose individuals for employment, employers must be able to prove that the selection instrument bears a direct relationship to job success. This proof is established through validation studies that show the job-relatedness or lack thereof for the selection instrument under study.[18] The *Uniform Guidelines*, along with several of the court cases we discuss later, provides strict standards for employers to follow as they validate selection procedures. The different methods of testing validity are reviewed in detail in Chapter 6.

DISPARATE IMPACT For an applicant or employee to pursue a discrimination case successfully, the individual must establish that the employer's selection procedures resulted in a disparate impact on a protected class. **Disparate impact** (also commonly referred to as **adverse impact**) refers to the rejection for employment, placement, or promotion of a significantly higher percentage of a protected class when compared to a nonprotected class.[19]

There are four ways to show that disparate impact exists:

1. *Restricted Policy*. Any evidence that an employer has a selection procedure that excludes members of a protected class, whether intentional or not, constitutes disparate impact.
2. *Population Comparisons*. This involves comparing the percentage of protected-class employees in an organization with the percentage of that class in the general population of the surrounding community.
3. *Disparate Rejection Rate*, or *Four-Fifths Rule*. According to the *Uniform Guidelines*, a selection program has a disparate impact when the selection rate for any racial, ethnic, or sex class is less than four-fifths (or 80 percent) of the rate of the class with the highest selection rate. The Equal Employment Opportunity Commission has adopted the **four-fifths rule** as a rule of thumb to determine disparate impact in enforcement proceedings. The four-fifths rule is not a legal definition of discrimination; rather, it is a method by which the EEOC or other enforcement agencies monitor serious discrepancies in hiring, promotion, or other employment decisions. Highlights in HRM 2 explains how disparate impact is determined and gives a realistic example of how the four-fifths rule is computed.
4. *Statistical Evidence*. Employees may use statistical evidence to show underrepresentation of women and minorities in job discrimination claims. In *Watson* v. *Fort Worth Bank and Trust* (1988), the Supreme Court ruled that Clara Watson, a black bank teller seeking promotion to supervisor, could use, as proof of job discrimination, statistical evidence showing that white supervisors hired only 3.5 percent of black applicants but 14.8 percent of white applicants.[20] This ruling expands antidiscrimination laws, making it easier for women and minority workers to prove disparate impact discrimination in hirings and promotions.[21]

Using statistical data to show evidence of discrimination does, however, have its limitations. In 1989, the Supreme Court held in *Wards Cove Packing* v. *Atonio* that a disparate impact case cannot be established merely by showing that the percentage of minorities in skilled jobs is not as great as in nonskilled jobs.[22] This case arose when nonwhites, namely Filipinos and native Alaskans, holding unskilled cannery jobs complained that noncannery jobs—those paying higher wages—were held predominantly by whites. The plaintiffs' statistical case was based primarily on a comparison between the large percentage of minorities holding cannery jobs and the mostly white composition of the noncannery work force. The Supreme Court rejected the plaintiffs' arguments, making clear that the appropriate statistical comparison was between the racial composition of the jobs at issue and the composition of qualified persons in the local labor market. Thus, in *Wards Cove Packing*, the

HIGHLIGHTS IN HRM

2 DETERMINING DISPARATE IMPACT: THE FOUR-FIFTHS RULE

Employers can determine disparate impact by using the method outlined in the interpretive manual on the *Uniform Guidelines on Employee Selection Procedures.*

A. Calculate the rate of selection for each group (divide the number of persons selected from a group by the number of total applicants from that group).
B. Observe which group has the highest selection.
C. Calculate the impact ratios by comparing the selection rate for each group with that of the highest group (divide the selection rate for a group by the selection rate for the highest group).
D. Observe whether the selection rate for any group is substantially less (i.e., usually less than four-fifths, or 80 percent) than the selection rate for the highest group. If it is, disparate impact is indicated in most circumstances.

Example:

	Job Applicants		No. Hired	Selection Rate Percent Hired
Step A	Whites	100	52	52/100 = 52%
	Blacks	50	14	14/50 = 28%

Step B The group with the highest selection rate is whites, 52 percent.

Step C Divide the black selection rate (28%) by the white selection rate (52%). The black rate is 53.8 percent of the white rate.

Step D Since 53.8 percent is less than four-fifths, or 80 percent, disparate impact is indicated.

SOURCE: Adoption of Questions and Answers to Clarify and Provide a Common Interpretation of the *Uniform Guidelines on Employee Selection Procedures, Federal Register* 44, no. 43 (March 2, 1979): 11998.

Court made it more difficult for minorities and women to win discrimination cases based on statistics.

While the *Uniform Guidelines* has not required an employer to conduct validity studies of selection procedures where no disparate impact exists, it does encourage employers to use selection procedures that are valid. Organizations that validate their selection procedures on a regular basis and use interviews, tests, and other procedures in such a manner as to avoid disparate impact will generally be in compliance

Canneries employ large numbers of unskilled workers.

with the principles of equal employment legislation. Affirmative action programs also reflect employer intent. The motivation for using valid selection procedures, however, should be the desire to achieve effective management of human resources rather than the fear of legal pressure.

BOTTOM-LINE CONCEPT The 1978 revision of the *Uniform Guidelines* introduced the **bottom-line concept,** which specifies that an employer is not required to evaluate individually each component of the selection process unless there is disparate impact. However, the end result of the selection process must be predictive of future job performance if disparate impact is present. The *Uniform Guidelines* also requires that if disparate impact is present, employers consider alternative selection devices and maintain detailed records from which disparate impact can be detected.

SIGNIFICANT COURT CASES The *Uniform Guidelines* has been given added importance through three leading Supreme Court cases. Each case is noteworthy because it elaborates on the concepts of disparate impact, validity testing, and job-relatedness. Managers of both large and small organizations must constantly be alert to new court decisions and be prepared to implement those rulings. The Bureau of National Affairs, Commerce Clearing House, and Prentice-Hall provide legal information on a subscription basis to interested managers.

The benchmark case in employment selection procedures is *Griggs* v. *Duke Power Company* (1971). Willie Griggs had applied for the position of coal handler with the

Duke Power Company. His request for the position was denied because he was not a high school graduate—a requirement for the position. Griggs claimed the job standard was discriminatory because it did not relate to job success and because the standard had a disparate impact on a protected class.

In the *Griggs* decision, the Supreme Court established two important principles affecting equal employment opportunity.[23] First, the Court ruled that employer discrimination need not be overt or intentional to be present. Rather, employment practices can be illegal even when applied equally to all employees. For example, under this ruling, cities requiring all firefighters to be six feet tall would impose a disparate impact on Asians and women, limiting their employment opportunities. Disparate impact differs from **disparate treatment,** which occurs when protected-class members receive unequal treatment or are evaluated by different standards. For example, allowing men to apply for craft jobs and denying this opportunity to women would be disparate treatment.

Second, under *Griggs*, employment practices must be job-related. When discrimination charges arise, employers have the burden of proving that employment requirements are job-related or constitute a business necessity. Where employers use education, physical, or intelligence standards as a basis for hiring or promotion, these requirements must be absolutely necessary for job success. Under Title VII, good intent, or absence of intent to discriminate, is not a sufficient defense.

In 1975, the Supreme Court decided *Albemarle Paper Company* v. *Moody*.[24] The Albemarle Paper Company required job applicants to pass a variety of employment tests, some of which were believed to be poor predictors of job success. The *Albemarle* case is important because in it the Supreme Court strengthened the principles established in *Griggs*. Specifically, more-stringent requirements are placed on employers to demonstrate the job-relatedness of tests. Where tests are used for hiring or promotion decisions (tests are defined to include performance appraisals), they must be valid predictors of job success. To ensure the validity of selection, the Court defined the proper method for employers to use when validating selection tools. The Supreme Court's ruling in *Albemarle* placed great importance on the EEOC *Uniform Guidelines* for employee selection procedures. Today HR managers follow these procedures to ensure the legality of their HRM practices.

In *Washington* v. *Davis,* decided in 1976, the Supreme Court continued to address employers' use of tests in employment decisions.[25] However, in contrast to the cases noted before, in *Washington* v. *Davis* the Court upheld the use of tests for hiring police officers in Washington, D.C. The case was initially filed because a large percentage of blacks and women, compared with whites, failed the screening test. Because of their low success rate, the unsuccessful job candidates (plaintiffs) believed the tests had a disparate impact on their chances of being employed. The Court ruled that the test was job-related and predicted successful job performance. Because a test screened out a disproportionate number of a protected class does not automatically mean the test is illegal, provided it is job-related.

OTHER EQUAL EMPLOYMENT OPPORTUNITY ISSUES

Federal laws, executive orders, court cases, and state and local statutes provide the broad legal framework for equal employment opportunity. Within these major laws, specific issues are of particular interest to supervisors and HR managers. The situations discussed here occur in the day-to-day supervision of employees.

Sexual Harassment

Sexual situations in the work environment are not new to organizational life. Sexual feelings are a part of group dynamics, and people who work together may come to develop these kinds of feelings for one another. Unfortunately, however, often these encounters are unpleasant and unwelcome, as witnessed by the many reported instances of sexual harassment. In a 1988 survey conducted by the U.S. Merit System Protection Board, 42 percent of women and 14 percent of men who responded said they had experienced some form of sexual harassment on the job.[26]

The EEOC guidelines on sexual harassment are specific, stating that "unwelcome advances, requests for sexual favors, and other verbal or physical conduct of a sexual nature" constitute **sexual harassment** when submission to the conduct is tied to continuing employment or advancement. The conduct is also illegal when it interferes with an employee's work performance or creates an "intimidating, hostile, or offensive working environment." If a supervisor promotes a female employee only after she agrees to an after-work date, the conduct is clearly illegal. Also, dirty jokes, vulgar slang, swearing, and personal ridicule and insult constitute sexual harassment when an employee finds them offensive.[27]

In 1986 the Supreme Court issued its first sexual harassment decision, in *Meritor Savings Bank* v. *Vinson*.[28] This ruling provided employers with the Court's interpretation of how sexual harassment is viewed under the EEOC guidelines. It is noteworthy that both the Supreme Court and the EEOC hold employers strictly accountable to prevent the sexual harassment of both female and male employees. The EEOC considers an employer guilty of sexual harassment when the employer knew about or should have known about the unlawful conduct and failed to remedy it or take corrective action. Employers are also guilty of sexual harassment when they allow nonemployees (customers or salespersons) to sexually harass employees. Where charges of sexual harassment have been proved, the EEOC has imposed remedies including back pay, reinstatement, and payment of lost benefits, interest charges, and attorney's fees. Sexual harassment involving physical conduct can invite criminal charges, and damages may be assessed against both the employer and the individual offender.

Despite legislation against it, however, sexual harassment is still common in the work place. HR managers and supervisors must take special precautions to try to prevent it. Highlights in HRM 3 presents the Court's suggestions and the EEOC guidelines for an effective policy to minimize sexual harassment in the work environment.[29]

HIGHLIGHTS IN HRM

3 BASIC COMPONENTS OF AN EFFECTIVE SEXUAL HARASSMENT POLICY

1. Develop a comprehensive organization-wide policy on sexual harassment, and present it to all current and new employees. Stress that sexual harassment will not be tolerated under any circumstances. Emphasis is best achieved when the policy is publicized and supported by top management.
2. Hold training sessions with supervisors to explain Title VII requirements, their role in providing an environment free of sexual harassment, and proper investigative procedures when charges occur.
3. Establish a formal complaint procedure in which employees can discuss problems without fear of retaliation. The complaint procedure should spell out how charges will be investigated and resolved.
4. Act immediately when employees complain of sexual harassment. Communicate widely that investigations will be conducted objectively and with appreciation for the sensitivity of the issue.
5. When an investigation supports employee charges, discipline the offender at once. For extremely serious offenses, discipline should include penalties up to and including discharge. Discipline should be applied consistently across similar cases and among managers and hourly employees alike.
6. Follow up on all cases to ensure a satisfactory resolution of the problem.

Bona Fide Occupational Qualification

Under Title VII of the Civil Rights Act of 1964, employers are permitted limited exemptions from antidiscrimination regulations if employment preferences are based on a bona fide occupational qualification. A **bona fide occupational qualification (BFOQ)** permits discrimination where employer hiring preferences are a reasonable necessity for the normal operation of the business. However, a BFOQ is a suitable defense against a discrimination charge only where age, religion, sex, or national origin is an actual qualification for performing the job. For example, an older person could legitimately be excluded from consideration for employment as a model for teenage designer jeans. It is reasonable to expect the San Francisco 49ers of the National Football League to hire male locker-room attendants or for Macy's department store to employ females as models for women's fashions. Likewise, religion is a BFOQ in organizations that require employees to share a particular religious doctrine.

The EEOC does not favor BFOQs, and both the EEOC and the courts have construed the concept narrowly. The exception does not apply to discrimination based on race or color. Where an organization claims a BFOQ, it must be able to prove that hiring on the basis of sex, religion, age, or national origin is a business necessity. **Business necessity** has been interpreted by the courts as a practice that is necessary to the safe and efficient operation of the organization.

Religious Preference

Freedom to exercise religious choice is guaranteed under the Constitution. Title VII of the Civil Rights Act also prohibits discrimination based on religion in employment decisions, though it permits employer exemptions. The Act defines religion to "include all aspects of religious observance and practice, as well as belief."

Title VII does not require employers to grant complete religious freedom in employment situations. Employers need only make a reasonable accommodation to a current employee's or job applicant's religious observance or practice without incurring undue hardship on the conduct of the business. What constitutes reasonable accommodation has been difficult to define. In 1977, in the leading case of *TWA* v. *Hardison*, the Supreme Court attempted to settle this dispute by ruling that employers had only to bear a minimum cost to show accommodation.[30] The Court said that to require otherwise would be discrimination against other employees for whom the expense of permitting time off for religious observance was not incurred. The *Hardison* case is important because it supported union–management seniority systems where the employer had made a reasonable attempt to adjust employee work schedules without undue hardship. While *Hardison* permits reasonable accommodation and undue hardship as a defense against religious discrimination charges, the EEOC will investigate complaints on a case-by-case basis; and employers are still responsible for supporting their decisions to deny an employee's religious requests.[31]

Immigration Reform and Control

Good employment is the magnet that attracts many people to the United States. Unfortunately, illegal immigration has adversely affected welfare services and educational and social security benefits. To preserve our tradition of legal immigration while closing the door to illegal entry, in 1986 Congress passed the Immigration Reform and Control Act. The Act was passed to control unauthorized immigration by making it unlawful for a person or organization to hire, recruit, or refer for a fee persons not legally eligible for employment in the United States.

Employers must comply with the law by verifying and maintaining records on the legal rights of applicants to work in the United States. The *Handbook for Employers*, published by the U.S. Department of Justice, lists five things that employers must do to comply with the law:

1. Have employees fill out their part of Form I-9.
2. Check documents establishing employees' identity and eligibility to work.
3. Complete the employer's section of Form I-9.
4. Retain Form I-9 for at least three years.

5. Present Form I-9 for inspection to an Immigration and Naturalization or Department of Labor officer upon request.[32]

Section 102 of the law also prohibits discrimination. Employers with four or more employees may not discriminate against any individual (other than an unauthorized alien) in hiring, discharge, recruiting, or referring for a fee because of that individual's national origin, or in the case of a citizen or intending citizen, because of citizenship status.[33] Employers found to have violated the Act will be ordered to prohibit the discriminatory practice. They may also be directed to hire, with or without back pay, individuals harmed by the discrimination and pay a fine of up to $1,000 for each person discriminated against. Charges of discrimination based on national origin or citizenship are filed with the Office of Special Counsel in the Department of Justice.

ENFORCING EQUAL EMPLOYMENT OPPORTUNITY LEGISLATION

Along with prohibiting employment discrimination, Title VII of the Civil Rights Act created the Equal Employment Opportunity Commission. As the federal government's leading civil rights agency, the EEOC is responsible for ensuring that covered employers comply with the intent of this Act. It accomplishes this goal primarily by (1) issuing various employment guidelines and monitoring the employment practices of organizations and (2) protecting employee rights through the investigation and prosecution of discrimination charges.

It is important to remember that the EEOC's guidelines are not federal law but only administrative rules and regulations. However, the different guidelines have been given weight by the courts as they interpret the law and, therefore, should not be taken lightly. In addition to enforcing Title VII, the EEOC has the authority to enforce the Age Discrimination in Employment Act and the Equal Pay Act. Executive Order 12067, which requires the coordination of all federal equal employment opportunity regulations, practices, and policies, is also administered by the EEOC.

The Equal Employment Opportunity Commission

The EEOC consists of five commissioners and a general counsel, all appointed by the President of the United States and confirmed by the Senate. The President appoints commissioners for staggered five-year terms, and no more than three members of the commission can be of the same political party. One commissioner is appointed to be the EEOC chairperson, who is responsible for the overall administration of the agency. The commission's work consists of formulating EEO policy and approving all litigation involved in maintaining equal employment opportunity.

Appointed for a four-year term, the general counsel is responsible for investigating discrimination charges, conducting agency litigation, and providing legal opinions, in addition to reviewing EEOC regulations, guidelines, and contracts.

The day-to-day operation of the commission is performed through administrative headquarters, districts, and area offices. *District offices* handle discrimination charges and all compliance and litigation enforcement functions. *Area offices* are less than full-service organizations and generally serve as charge-processing and initial investigation units. Much of the EEOC's work is delegated to the district offices and other designated representatives. District directors have authority to receive or consent to the withdrawal of Title VII charges, issue subpoenas, send notices of the filing of charges, dismiss charges, enter into and sign conciliation agreements (voluntary employer settlements), and send out notices of the employee's right to sue. Employees who wish to file discrimination charges and employers responding to complaints will work with district or area office personnel.

Recordkeeping and Posting Requirements

Organizations subject to Title VII are required by law to maintain specific employment records and reports. In addition, employers are required to post selected equal employment opportunity notices and to summarize the composition of their work force in order to determine the distribution of protected individuals. These records are for establishing minority-group statistical reports. Equal employment opportunity legislation covering federal contractors and subcontractors has special reporting requirements for these employers. Those failing to comply with recordkeeping and posting requirements or willfully falsifying records can incur penalties including fines and imprisonment.

It is important to note that recordkeeping requirements are both detailed and comprehensive. For example, managers must generate and retain for specific time periods different employment data under each of the following laws: Title VII, the Age Discrimination in Employment Act, and the Equal Pay Act. Where federal contractors are required to have written affirmative action programs, these must be retained along with supporting documents (e.g., names of job applicants, rejection ratios, seniority lists).

Employers of 100 or more employees (except state and local government employers) and government contractors and subcontractors subject to Executive Order 11286 must file annually an **EEO-1 report** (Employer Information Report). Figure 3–3 shows Section D of the EEO-1 report, which requires the reporting of minority employees. This comprehensive report is the EEOC's basic document for determining an employer's work-force composition. In preparing the EEO-1 report, the organization may collect records concerning racial or ethnic identity either by visual survey or through postemployment questionnaires, if not prohibited by state fair employment practice law.[34]

To show evidence of its equal employment opportunity and affirmative action efforts, an organization should retain copies of recruitment letters sent to minority

FIGURE 3–3 SECTION D, EEO-1 REPORT

Section D — EMPLOYMENT DATA

Employment at this establishment--Report all permanent, temporary, or part-time employees including apprentices and on-the-job trainees unless specifically excluded as set forth in the instructions. Enter the appropriate figures on all lines and in all columns. Blank spaces will be considered as zeros.

JOB CATEGORIES	NUMBER OF EMPLOYEES										
		MALE					FEMALE				
	OVERALL TOTALS (SUM OF COL. B THRU K) A	WHITE (NOT OF HISPANIC ORIGIN) B	BLACK (NOT OF HISPANIC ORIGIN) C	HISPANIC D	ASIAN OR PACIFIC ISLANDER E	AMERICAN INDIAN OR ALASKAN NATIVE F	WHITE (NOT OF HISPANIC ORIGIN) G	BLACK (NOT OF HISPANIC ORIGIN) H	HISPANIC I	ASIAN OR PACIFIC ISLANDER J	AMERICAN INDIAN OR ALASKAN NATIVE K
Officials and Managers											
Professionals											
Technicians											
Sales Workers											
Office and Clerical											
Craft Workers (Skilled)											
Operatives (Semi-Skilled)											
Laborers (Unskilled)											
Service Workers											
TOTAL											
Total employment reported in previous EEO-1 report											

(The trainees below should also be included in the figures for the appropriate occupational categories above)

Formal On-the-job trainees		A	B	C	D	E	F	G	H	I	J	K
	White collar											
	Production											

1. NOTE: On consolidated report, skip questions 2-5 and Section E.
2. How was information as to race or ethnic group in Section D obtained?
   1 ☐ Visual Survey 3 ☐ Other—Specify ....
   2 ☐ Employment Record ....
3. Dates of payroll period used –
4. Pay period of last report submitted for this establishment
5. Does this establishment employ apprentices?
   This year? 1 ☐ Yes 2 ☐ No
   Last year? 1 ☐ Yes 2 ☐ No

agencies, announcements of job openings, and other significant information concerning employee recruitment. Other employment records to keep include data on promotions, demotions, transfers, layoffs or terminations, rates of pay or other terms of compensation, and selections for training or apprenticeship programs. Title VII requires retention of all personnel or employment records, including application forms, for at least six months or until resolution of any HR action, whichever occurs later.

During the employment process, employers are permitted to collect racial data on job applicants for compiling statistical reports. These data must be collected on a separate information sheet, not on the formal job application form. Where a charge of discrimination has been filed, the respondent organization must retain all HR records relevant to the case until final disposition of the charge.

The law requires EEOC posters to be prominently displayed.

Posters explaining to individuals what their employment rights are and how to file complaints of discrimination have been developed by the EEOC and other administrative agencies (see Highlights in HRM 4). The law requires that employers display these posters in prominent places easily accessible to employees. HR employment offices, cafeterias, centrally located bulletin boards, or time clocks are popular locations. Posting requirements should not be taken lightly. For example, EEO posters show the time limits for filing a charge of discrimination. Failure to post these notices may be used as a basis for excusing the late filing of a discrimination charge.

Processing Discrimination Charges

Employees or job applicants who believe they have been discriminated against may file a discrimination complaint, or **charge form,** with the EEOC. Filing a charge form initiates an administrative procedure that can be lengthy, time-consuming, and costly for the employer. Both parties—the plaintiff (employee) and the defendant (organization)—must be prepared to support their beliefs or actions. If litigation is needed, employers will normally take an aggressive approach to defend their position.

Figure 3–4 summarizes the process of filing a discrimination charge with the EEOC. Under the law, charges must be filed within 180 days of the alleged unlawful practice. The processing of a charge includes notifying the employer that a charge of employment discrimination has been filed. Employers will receive a copy of the charge within ten days of filing. Organizations may not retaliate against individuals for their legal right to file charges or to support other employees during EEOC proceedings. The commission has the power to prosecute employers in court if retaliation takes place.

In states that have FEP laws with appropriate enforcement machinery, the discrimination charge will be deferred to the state agency for resolution before action is taken by the EEOC. The EEOC will accept the recommendation of the state agency because deferral states must comply with federal standards. If the state agency fails to resolve the complaint or if the 60-day deferral period lapses, the case is given back to the EEOC for final investigation.

EEOC investigations are conducted by a fully trained equal opportunity specialist (EOS) who has extensive experience in investigative procedures, theories of discrimination, and relief and remedy techniques. The EOS will gather facts from both sides through telephone calls, letters and questionnaires, field visits, or jointly arranged meetings. While it is generally advisable for them to cooperate in EEOC investigations, employers may legally resist the commission's efforts by refusing to submit documents or give relevant testimony. However, the EEOC may obtain this information through a court subpoena. Employers who then refuse to supply the information will face contempt-of-court charges.

HIGHLIGHTS IN HRM

4 EEO AND THE LAW

Equal Employment Opportunity is the

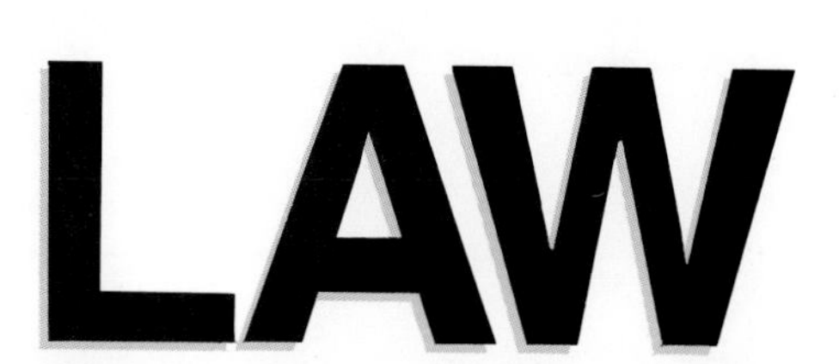

Private Employment, State and Local Governments, Educational Institutions

Race, Color, Religion, Sex, National Origin:
Title VII of the Civil Rights Act of 1964, as amended, prohibits discrimination in hiring, promotion, discharge, pay, fringe benefits, and other aspects of employment, on the basis of race, color, religion, sex or national origin.

Applicants to and employees of most private employers, state and local governments and public or private educational institutions are protected. Employment agencies, labor unions and apprenticeship programs also are covered.

Age:
The Age Discrimination in Employment Act of 1967, as amended, prohibits age discrimination and protects applicants and employees 40 years of age or older from discrimination on account of age in hiring, promotion, discharge, compensation, terms, conditions, or privileges of employment. The law covers most private employers, state and local governments, educational institutions, employment agencies and labor organizations.

Sex (wages):
In addition to sex discrimination prohibited by Title VII of the Civil Rights Act (see above), the Equal Pay Act of 1963, as amended, prohibits sex discrimination in payment of wages to women and men performing substantially equal work in the same establishment. The law covers most private employers, state and local governments and educational institutions. Labor organizations cannot cause employers to violate the law. Many employers not covered by Title VII, because of size, are covered by the Equal Pay Act.

If you believe that you have been discriminated against under any of the above laws, you immediately should contact:

The U.S. Equal Employment Opportunity Commission
Washington, D.C. 20507
or an EEOC field office by calling toll free 800-USA-EEOC.
(For the hearing impaired, EEOC's TDD number is 202-663-4399.)

Employers holding Federal contracts or subcontracts

Race, Color, Religion, Sex, National Origin:
Executive Order 11246, as amended, prohibits job discrimination on the basis of race, color, religion, sex or national origin, and requires affirmative action to ensure equality of opportunity in all aspects of employment.

Handicap:
Section 503 of the Rehabilitation Act of 1973, as amended, prohibits job discrimination because of handicap and requires affirmative action to employ and advance in employment qualified handicapped individuals who, with reasonable accommodation, can perform the functions of a job.

Vietnam Era and Special Disabled Veterans:
38 U.S.C. 2012 of the Vietnam Era Veterans Readjustment Assistance Act of 1974 prohibits job discrimination and requires affirmative action to employ and advance in employment qualified Vietnam era veterans and qualified special disabled veterans.

Applicants to and employees of companies with a Federal government contract or subcontract are protected under the authorities above. Any person who believes a contractor has violated its nondiscrimination or affirmative action obligations under Executive Order 11246, as amended, Section 503 of the Rehabilitation Act or 38 U.S.C. 2012 of the Vietnam Era Veterans Readjustment Assistance Act should contact immediately:

The Office of Federal Contract Compliance Programs (OFCCP)
Employment Standards Administration, U.S. Department of Labor, 200 Constitution Avenue, N.W., Washington, D.C. 20210
(202) 523-9368, or an OFCCP regional or district office, listed in most telephone directories under U.S. Government, Department of Labor.

Programs or activities receiving Federal financial assistance

Handicap:
Section 504 of the Rehabilitation Act of 1973, as amended, prohibits employment discrimination on the basis of handicap in any program or activity which receives Federal financial assistance. Discrimination is prohibited in all aspects of employment against handicapped persons who, with reasonable accommodation, can perform the essential functions of a job.

Race, Color, National Origin, Sex:
In addition to the protection of Title VII of the Civil Rights Act of 1964, Title VI of the Civil Rights Act prohibits discrimination on the basis of race, color or national origin in programs or activities receiving Federal financial assistance. Employment discrimination is covered by Title VI if the primary objective of the financial assistance is provision of employment, or where employment discrimination causes or may cause discrimination in providing services under such programs. Title IX of the Education Amendments of 1972 prohibits employment discrimination on the basis of sex in educational programs or activities which receive Federal assistance.

If you believe you have been discriminated against in a program of any institution which receives Federal assistance, you should contact immediately the Federal agency providing such assistance.

1/90

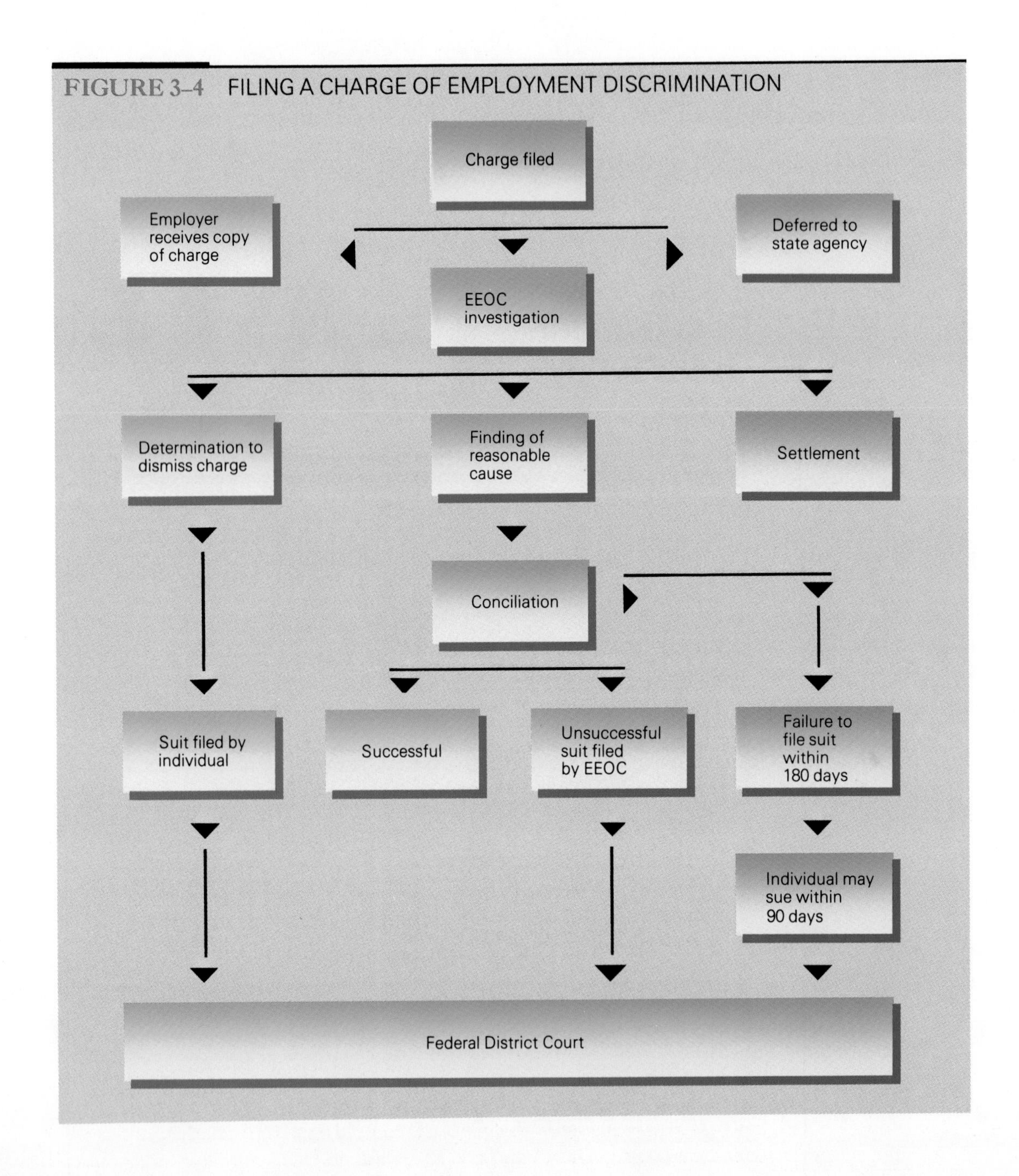

FIGURE 3–4 FILING A CHARGE OF EMPLOYMENT DISCRIMINATION

Once the investigation is under way or completed, several decision points occur. First, the employer may offer a settlement to resolve the case without further investigation. If the offer is accepted, the case is closed. Second, the EEOC may find no violation of law and dismiss the charge. The charging party will be sent a *right-to-sue* notice, which permits the individual to start private litigation in federal court within 90 days. Third, if the EEOC finds "reasonable cause" of discrimination, the commission will attempt to conciliate (settle) the matter between the charging party and the employer. The conciliation process is a voluntary procedure and will not always lead to a settlement.

Employers should keep in mind that when the EEOC negotiates a settlement, it will attempt to obtain full remedial, corrective, and preventive relief.[35] Back pay, reinstatement, transfers, promotions, seniority rights, bonuses, and other "make whole" perquisites of employment are considered to be appropriate remedies. These settlements can frequently be costly.

If the employer and the EEOC cannot reach a negotiated settlement, the commission has the power to prosecute the organization in court. However, this decision is made on a case-by-case basis and may depend on the importance of the issue. Failure of the EEOC to take court action or to resolve the charge in 180 days from filing permits private employees to pursue litigation within 90 days after receiving a right-to-sue letter issued by the commission.

AFFIRMATIVE ACTION

Equal employment opportunity legislation requires managers to provide the same opportunities to all job applicants and employees regardless of race, color, religion, sex, national origin, or age. While EEO law is largely a policy of nondiscrimination, **affirmative action** requires employers to analyze their work force and develop a plan of action to correct areas of past discrimination. Affirmative action is achieved by having organizations follow specific guidelines and goals to ensure that they have a balanced and representative work force.[36] To achieve these goals, employers must make an affirmative effort to recruit, select, train, and promote members of protected classes. Employers must locate not only minority candidates who are qualified, but also those who, with a reasonable amount of training or physical accommodation, can be made to qualify for job openings.

Establishing Affirmative Action Programs

Employers establish affirmative action programs for several reasons. As noted in Figure 3–2, affirmative action programs are required by the OFCCP for employers with federal contracts greater than $50,000. These programs may also be required by federal court order where an employer has been found guilty of past discrimination. Finally, many employers wisely develop their own affirmative action programs to ensure that protected-class members receive fair treatment in all aspects of employment. General Electric, the City of Portland, and Hilton Hotels use these programs as a useful way of monitoring the progress of employees while demonstrating good-faith employment effort. The EEOC recommends that organizations developing affirmative action programs follow specific steps, as shown in Highlights in HRM 5.

In pursuing affirmative action efforts, employers may be accused of **reverse discrimination,** or giving preference to members of protected classes to the extent that unprotected individuals believe they are suffering discrimination. When these charges occur, organizations are caught between attempting to correct past discriminatory practices and handling present complaints from unprotected members alleging that HR policies are unfair. It is exactly this "Catch-22" which has made affirmative action one of the most controversial issues of the past 50 years. Two highly publicized cases illustrate the controversy.

In *University of California Regents* v. *Bakke* (1978), the Supreme Court settled one of the most famous reverse discrimination cases.[37] Allen Bakke, a white male, was denied admission to the medical school of the University of California at Davis. He charged that the university was guilty of reverse discrimination by admitting minority group members he believed were less qualified than he. Bakke alleged that the university discriminated against him by giving preferred consideration to minority applicants.

The central issue before the Court was equal treatment under the law as guaranteed in the equal protection clause of the Fourteenth Amendment. The Court ruled that applicants must be evaluated on an individual basis, and race can be one factor used in the evaluation process as long as other competitive factors are considered. The Court stated that affirmative action programs were not illegal per se as long as rigid quota systems were not specified for different protected classes.

Demonstrators protest the Bakke decision outside the Supreme Court.

One year later the Supreme Court decided *United Steelworkers of America* v. *Weber.*[38] In 1974, Kaiser Aluminum and its union, the United Steelworkers, joined in a voluntary affirmative action program designed to increase the number of black workers in craft jobs at Kaiser's Louisiana plant. The program specified that 50 percent of all new craft trainees would be black regardless of employment seniority. The plan was to remain in place until the percentage of black craft employees matched the percentage of blacks in the local labor market. Brian Weber, a white production employee, was passed over for craft training in favor of a less-senior black worker. Weber filed suit charging a violation of Title VII.

The Supreme Court ruled against Weber, holding that under Title VII, voluntary affirmative action programs are permissible where they attempt to eliminate racial imbalances in "traditionally segregated job categories." The Court nevertheless encouraged employers to adopt voluntary affirmative action programs as positive employment policy. In *Weber,* the Supreme Court did not

HIGHLIGHTS IN HRM

5 BASIC STEPS IN DEVELOPING AN EFFECTIVE AFFIRMATIVE ACTION PROGRAM

1. Issue written equal employment policy and affirmative action commitment.
2. Appoint a top official with responsibility and authority to direct and implement the program.
3. Publicize the policy and affirmative action commitment.
4. Survey present minority and female employment by department and job classification.
5. Develop goals and timetables to improve utilization of minorities and women in each area where utilization has been identified.
6. Develop and implement specific programs to achieve goals.
7. Establish an internal audit and reporting system to monitor and evaluate progress in each aspect of the program.
8. Develop supportive in-house and community programs.

SOURCE: *Affirmative Action and Equal Employment: A Guidebook for Employers,* vol. 1 (Washington, DC: Equal Employment Opportunity Commission, 1974), 16–17.

endorse all voluntary affirmative action programs, but it did give an important push to those programs voluntarily implemented and designed to correct past racial imbalances.

The Future of Affirmative Action

Support for affirmative action plans from the public, the judiciary, and business has been checkered at best. For example, in *Firefighters Local 93* v. *City of Cleveland,* the Supreme Court stated that voluntary programs to eradicate racial discrimination may include minority individuals who are not actually victims of discrimination.[39] In 1989, however, the Court dealt affirmative action a blow when it ruled in *City of Richmond* v. *Croson* that state and local governments cannot reserve a percentage of their business for minority contractors based only upon a "general assumption" of discrimination in the construction industry.[40] Writing for the majority, Justice Sandra O'Connor stated, "None of the evidence presented by the city points to any identified discrimination in the Richmond construction industry. Adoption of such quotas nationwide would obliterate the goal of a colorblind America."[41]

While affirmative action programs have achieved success in many important instances, these programs still face specific challenges. The following issues contribute to this condition:

"Yes, we do have an affirmative-action program, but it doesn't cover right-brained people."

From *The Wall Street Journal*—Permission, Cartoon Features Syndicate

1. Lack of a unified national consensus that affirmative action is a worthy employment goal.
2. Realization that some employers give only enough attention to the affirmative action concept to forestall legal or punitive government action.
3. The belief that somehow affirmative action is un-American and that goals and timetables are offensive employment measures.
4. The belief that affirmative action reduces productivity by promoting those who are least productive while discriminating against qualified individuals.

As the decade of the 1990s finds more minority, women, handicapped, and older employees in the work force, these negative attitudes toward affirmative action will decline. Organizations are beginning to adopt an approach of "fair employment" toward protected classes that may improve opportunities for all those seeking employment both at present and in the future.

SUMMARY

Congress passed the Civil Rights Act of 1964 to redress inequities in employment. This far-reaching law prohibits employment discrimination on the basis of race, color, religion, sex, or national origin. Every manager must keep the law in mind when making employment decisions regarding hiring, training, promotions, compensation issues, and other employment conditions.

Effective management requires knowing the legal aspects of the employment relationship. Besides the Civil Rights Act, pertinent legislation includes the Equal Pay Act, Age Discrimination in Employment Act, Pregnancy Discrimination Act, Vocational Rehabilitation Act, Americans with Disabilities Act, and various executive orders. These measures grant special protection to different categories of employees and place specific obligations on employers. The United States court system continually interprets employment law, and HR managers must formulate organizational policy in response to court decisions. Violations of the law will invite discrimination charges from protected individuals or a self-initiated investigation from government agencies.

To ensure that organizations comply with antidiscrimination legislation, the EEOC and OFCCP were established to monitor employer actions. These agencies serve two basic purposes. First, they require employers to keep accurate and comprehensive employment records and to report these data at designated intervals or when faced with charges of discrimination. Failure to maintain records is punishable under law. Second, the agencies investigate discrimination charges and seek relief for wronged individuals.

Government regulations covering equal employment opportunity and affirmative action have helped to increase the importance of the HR department's role in most organizations. Nowhere is this more critical than in HR planning activities. Affirmative action programs are an important part of the planning process and the effective utilization of employees.

DISCUSSION QUESTIONS

1. EEO legislation was prompted by significant social events. List those events and describe how they influenced the passage of various EEO laws.
2. Cite and describe the major federal laws and court decisions that affect the employment process of both large and small organizations.
3. What is the *Uniform Guidelines on Employee Selection Procedures*? To whom do the guidelines apply, and what do they cover?
4. What is meant by disparate impact? How is it determined? Give an example in calculating the four-fifths rule.
5. After receiving several complaints of sexual harassment, the HR department of a city library decided to establish a sexual harassment policy. What should be included in the policy, and how should it be implemented?
6. Describe the structure of the EEOC.
   a. What purpose does the EEOC serve?
   b. What are some of its reporting and posting requirements?
7. Explain how affirmative action differs from equal employment opportunity.
8. What are the arguments for and against affirmative action programs? If you were asked to implement such a program, what steps would you follow?

MINI-CASE 3–1 The Unhappy Resignation

Over the past several months John Oliver, a seventh-year customer service representative for Mesa Gas and Electric Company, had made many requests for time off to see his personal physician. Customer service supervisor Cathy Avery had observed during this period that John often looked ill, and she asked him on several occasions if he felt all right. John always replied that he was "just tired" and that "nothing major" was wrong.

Two weeks later Tom Glithero, customer service manager, questioned Cathy about John's requests for time off. Tom mentioned that through a mutual friend of his and John's he learned John was seeing a doctor about a possible AIDS infection. When John next requested to see his doctor, Cathy confronted him with her new-found information. John immediately became defensive and said that he didn't have to tell her about his "personal business." Only after a long conversation and a promise of confidentiality did John admit that he had been diagnosed as having the AIDS virus.

The promise was not kept, however, when Cathy immediately told another supervisor and asked for advice on how to handle, as she said, "this problem." Unfortunately, in a short time everyone in John's immediate work group knew of his medical condition. It wasn't long before employees began expressing fear of working with John. He slowly became isolated from other employees, now having to contend not only with his medical condition but with the negative reactions of his unhappy co-workers. Under this pressure John finally resigned his position.

QUESTIONS

1. What recourse, if any, does John Oliver have to get his job back?
2. What do you think about the way Cathy Avery handled the situation?
3. If you were the director of human resources for Mesa Gas and Electric, what elements would you feel should be in a policy governing employees with illnesses like AIDS?

MINI-CASE 3–2 Discrimination at Interplace

Interplace Transworld Recruit and Recruit U.S.A., two Japanese-owned firms, have been charged by the Equal Employment Opportunity Commission with discrimination. Both firms recruit applicants for employers in the United States and Japan. Interplace is a Los Angeles–based nationwide employment agency with offices in several major U.S. cities. The EEOC has charged these firms with systematic discrimination on the basis of race, age, national origin, and sex. To support its charge, the EEOC has uncovered a series of company memos that specify race, age, and sex preferences for job applicants. The EEOC has also obtained internal documents from both firms that advise employees how to code the sex, race, and job requests from clients—for example, "see Adam" when a client wished a male employee, or "talk to Harvo" when a Japanese worker was desired.

The EEOC became aware of this situation after an article appearing in the *San Francisco Chronicle* detailed the existence of the job coding memos. As a first step in its investigation, the commission obtained a court order preventing the firms from altering or destroying records or taking them out of the country. In response, the firms have filed court papers denying they ever failed to hire anyone on the basis of sex or national origin.

These Japanese companies are not the only firms to come under EEOC investigation. Female secretaries at Sumitomo Corporation have charged that they lost promotions to Japanese co-workers. Honda of America Mfg., Inc., last year settled an EEOC charge of racial and sexual discrimination. The total settlement: $6 million.

SOURCE: Reported in "EEOC Documents Widespread Bias in Memos of Japanese-owned Companies," *BNA's Employment Relations Weekly* (June 12, 1989): 753; and "White People, Black People Not Wanted Here," *Business Week* (July 10, 1989): 31.

QUESTIONS

1. In your opinion, should Japanese-owned companies recruiting applicants to work in Japan be subject to U.S. employment law?
2. Explain the procedure the EEOC uses in processing discrimination charges.

NOTES AND REFERENCES

1. Bureau of National Affairs, "Price Waterhouse Ruling Viewed as Major Weakening of Employer Position," *BNA's Employee Relations Weekly* 7, no. 19 (May 8, 1989): 579–580.

2. Bureau of National Affairs, "EEOC Sues Rockwell over Policy of Firing Aliens Who Report Newly Legal Status," *BNA's Employee Relations Weekly* 7, no. 26 (June 26, 1989): 812.

3. "Current Labor Statistics–Table 7," *Monthly Labor Review* 112, no. 4 (April 1989): 64; and U.S. Department of Commerce, Bureau of the Census, *Statistical Abstracts of the United States 1990,* 110th ed. (Washington, DC: U.S. Government Printing Office, 1990), 409.

4. William H. Wagel, "AIDS: Setting Policy, Educating Employees at Bank of America," *Personnel* 65, no. 8 (August 1988): 5–8.

5. David P. Twomey, *Equal Employment Opportunity Law,* 2d ed. (Cincinnati, OH: South-Western, 1990), 1–2.

6. *Workforce 2000: Work and Workers for the 21st Century,* Executive Summary (Washington, DC: U.S. Department of Labor, n.d.), 19.

7. Sydney P. Freedberg, "Forced Exits? Companies Confront Wave of Age-Discrimination Suits," *Wall Street Journal* (October 13, 1987): 37.

8. Jennifer S. MacLeod, "The Real Nature of the Handicap Problem and What Can Be Done About It," *Employment Relations Today* 11, no. 2 (Summer 1984): 164.

9. Michael D. Levin-Epstein, *Primer of Equal Employment Opportunity* (Bureau of National Affairs, 1987), 74–77.

10. *Nassau County, Florida* v. *Arline,* U.S. 43 FEP 81 (1987).

11. Jose G. Fagot-Diaz, "Employment Discrimination Against AIDS Victims: Rights and Remedies Available Under the Federal Rehabilitation Act of 1973," *Labor Law Journal* 39, no. 3 (March 1988): 157–159. As currently defined, an "otherwise qualified" employee is one who can perform "the essential functions" of the job under consideration.

12. George W. Johnson, "Coping with AIDS: Today's Major Workplace Issue," *Labor Law Journal* 40, no. 5 (May 1989): 302–306.

13. Over two-thirds of the states have defined AIDS as a handicap under their fair employment practice statutes.

14. Michael D. Whitty, "AIDS, Labor Law, and Good Management," *Labor Law Journal* 40, no. 3 (March 1989): 183–187.

15. Michael W. Sculnick, "Handicap Discrimination—Guidelines for Alleviating Employer Concerns," *Employment Relations Today* 11, no. 4 (Winter 1984–85): 337–339.

16. Equal Employment Opportunity Commission, Civil Service Commission, Department of Labor, and Department of Justice, Adoption by Four Agencies of *Uniform Guidelines on Employee Selection Procedures* (1978), as reproduced in the *Federal Register* 43, no. 166 (August 25, 1978): 38290–38315. Discussion relating to the adoption of the *Uniform Guidelines* by four agencies comprises several pages. The guidelines are published on pages 38295–38309. Further clarification and expansion on the guidelines may be found in the *Federal Register* 44, no. 43 (March 2, 1979): 11996–12009.

17. *Uniform Guidelines,* sec. 3A.

18. For a good review of the legal aspects of employment testing, see Clint Bolick, "Legal and Policy Aspects of Testing," *Journal of Vocational Behavior* 33, no. 3 (December 1988): 320–330.

19. *Uniform Guidelines,* sec. 40. Disparate impact need not be considered for groups that constitute less than 2 percent of the relevant labor force.

20. *Watson* v. *Fort Worth Bank and Trust,* 108 U.S. 2777 (1988).

21. James Fraze, "Supreme Court Ruling Expands U.S. Anti-Bias Laws," *Resource* 9 (American Society for Personnel Administration, August 1988): 1.

22. *Wards Cove Packing Co.* v. *Atonio,* 109 U.S. 2115 (1989). See also Bill Shaw, Gary A. Moore, and Michael K. Braswell, "Wards Cove Packing Company, Inc. *v.* Atonio," *Labor Law Journal* 41, no. 3 (March 1990): 183–188.

23. *Griggs* v. *Duke Power Company,* 401 U.S. 424 (1971).

24. *Albemarle Paper Company* v. *Moody,* 422 U.S. 405 (1975).

25. *Washington* v. *Davis,* 426 U.S. 229 (1976).

26. Eileen Putman, "Sex Harassment on U.S. Payroll," *Sacramento Bee* (June 30, 1988): 1.

27. Robert K. Robinson, Delany J. Kirk, and Elvis C. Stephens, "Hostile Environment: A Review of the Implications of *Meritor Savings Bank* v. *Vinson,*" *Labor Law Journal* 38, no. 3 (March 1987): 179–183.

28. *Meritor Savings Bank, VSB* v. *Vinson,* 106 U.S. 2399 (1986).

29. For a good review of employer sexual harassment policy, see Dawn Bennett-Alexander, "Sexual Harassment in the Office," *Personnel Administrator* 33, no. 6 (June 1988): 174–188.

30. *TWA* v. *Hardison,* 432 U.S. 63 (1977).

31. Robert M. Preer, Jr., "Reasonable Accommodation of Religious Practice: The Conflict Between the Courts and the EEOC," *Employee Relations Law Journal* 15, no. 1 (Summer 1989): 67–99.

32. U.S. Department of Justice, Immigration and Naturalization Service, *Handbook for Employers: Instructions for Completing Form I-9* (Washington, DC: U.S. Government Printing Office, 1987).

33. Charles E. Mitchell, "Illegal Aliens, Employment Discrimination, and the 1986 Immigration Reform and Control Act," *Labor Law Journal* 40, no. 3 (March 1989): 177–182.

34. Steven C. Kahn, "Developing a Record-Keeping System," *Employment Relations Today* 2, no. 3 (Fall 1984): 269–275.

35. James C. Sharf, "Litigating Personnel Measurement Policy," *Journal of Vocational Behavior* 33, no. 3 (December 1988): 235–271. See also *Policy Statement on Remedies and Relief for Individual Cases of Unlawful Discrimination,* approved by the Equal Employment Opportunity Commission (February 5, 1985).

36. Martin K. Denix, "Employers' Procedural Rights in the Disclosure of Affirmative Action Plans," *Employee Relations Law Journal* 13, no. 4 (Spring 1988): 625–636. See also Eric Matusewitch, "Pitfalls of Informal Affirmative Action," *Personnel Journal* 69, no. 1 (January 1990): 84–90.

37. *University of California Regents* v. *Bakke,* 438 U.S. 265 (1978).

38. *United Steelworkers of America* v. *Weber,* 443 U.S. 193 (1979).

39. *Firefighters Local 93* v. *City of Cleveland,* 106 U.S. 3063 (1986).

40. *City of Richmond* v. *Croson,* 109 S.Ct. 706 (1989).

41. "Court Curbs Business Aid to Minorities," *Arizona Republic* (January 24, 1989): 1.

PART TWO

Meeting Human Resources Requirements

The three chapters in Part Two focus on HR staffing concerns. Chapter 4 deals with establishing job requirements and designing jobs that are both technologically efficient and psychologically satisfying to employees. Chapter 5 discusses HR planning and the recruitment of employees to fill those jobs. Chapter 6 is concerned with the many issues involved in selecting employees whose personal characteristics fit with the requirements of the job. When these three interrelated HR functions are performed effectively, the organization will have developed jobs that are meaningful to employees and will have acquired a work force capable of contributing to organizational success.

CHAPTER 4

Job Requirements

After reading this chapter you will be able to:

1. *Discuss the relationship of job requirements to the performance of HRM functions.*
2. *Describe the methods by which job analysis typically is accomplished.*
3. *Distinguish between job descriptions and job specifications.*
4. *Explain why job specifications must be based on job-related requirements.*
5. *List the various factors that must be taken into account in designing a job.*
6. *Describe the different quality-of-work-life programs.*
7. *Discuss the various job characteristics that motivate employees.*
8. *Define the key terms in the chapter.*

TERMS TO IDENTIFY

job *(109)*
position *(110)*
property right *(110)*
job requirements *(111)*
job specification *(111)*
job description *(112)*
job analysis *(114)*
functional job analysis (FJA) *(117)*
position analysis questionnaire (PAQ) *(117)*
critical incident method *(118)*
job design *(124)*
industrial engineering *(124)*
human engineering *(126)*
job enlargement *(127)*
job enrichment *(128)*
job characteristics model *(129)*
employee participation teams *(130)*
flextime *(132)*

In previous chapters, we discussed the effects of the external and internal settings on HR managers and the importance of equal employment opportunity in employment decisions. The interaction between an organization and its environment has important implications for internal organization and structure. For example, as the organization interacts with its environment, it will organize human resources to achieve specific objectives and perform different functions. The organization will formally group the activities to be done by its human resources into basic units. These basic units of the organization structure are referred to as *jobs*.

In this chapter, we will discuss how jobs may be designed so as to best contribute to the objectives of the organization and at the same time satisfy the needs of the employees who are to perform them. The value of job analysis, which defines clearly and precisely the requirements of each job, will be stressed. We will emphasize that these job requirements provide the foundation for making objective and legally defensible decisions in managing human resources. The chapter concludes by reviewing several innovative job design techniques that increase employee job satisfaction while improving organizational performance.

THE ROLE AND IMPORTANCE OF JOBS

Work must be divided into manageable units and ultimately into jobs that can be performed by employees. A **job** consists of a group of related activities and duties. Ideally, the duties of a job should consist of natural units of work that are similar and related. They should be clear and distinct from those of other jobs to minimize misunderstanding and conflict among employees and to enable employees to recognize what is expected of them. For some jobs, several employees may be required, each of whom will occupy a separate position. A **position** consists of different duties and responsibilities performed by only one employee. In a city library, for example, four employees (four positions) may be involved in reference work, but all of them have only one job (reference librarian).

Role of Jobs in the Organization

Within an organization, each job is designed to facilitate the achievement of the organization's objectives. This is accomplished by coordinating the contents of jobs in order to perform particular functions or activities. Since all organizations experience change, individual jobs and the relationships between jobs should be continually studied to ensure an efficient work arrangement. Furthermore, delineation of jobs within the organization facilitates the division of work. If the duties of each job are made clear and distinct from those of other jobs, it is less likely that any activity required to be performed within the organization will be neglected or duplicated.

During recent years, the contribution that jobs make to organizational success has become an important new concern of managers. The cause of this concern is the effect that unproductive job duties and responsibilities have on organizational productivity. As the renowned management scholar Peter Drucker notes, "All available evidence indicates that work rules and job restrictions are the main cause of the 'productivity gap' of American (and European) manufacturing industry."[1] Therefore, it is not surprising that approaches like job redesign, use of employee work teams, and flexible work schedules are touted as significant new means to improve worker productivity and organizational performance.

Role of Jobs for Employees

Jobs provide employees with a primary source of income. Their jobs also determine their standard of living and establish the basis for possible upward social mobility, depending on the demands and titles of their jobs as well as their rates of pay. Because a job consumes a significant portion of an employee's life, the duties of the job and the conditions under which they are performed should satisfy the personal needs of the employee. Organizations as diverse as the City of New York and Hallmark Cards have made employee job satisfaction one goal of their job design efforts.

As employees have gained greater protection from loss of employment through various laws, they have come to regard a job more and more as a form of property right. A **property right** is a right that cannot be taken away without just cause or due process. As noted in Chapter 2, erosion of the employment-at-will doctrine has magnified the importance placed on the fair and just dismissal of employees while exposing organizations to increased liability when wrongful discharge suits are successfully litigated. An employee's rights both to receive a fair hearing before being subjected to disciplinary action and to appeal an employer's action to an

An engineer manufactures hard disks for use in computer disk drives.

arbitrator, an adjudication body, or a court of law become more significant under the "job as property" concept. If the employer's action is not to be reversed through the appeals process, it must be supported by objective evidence. Effective disciplinary procedures and the due process rights of employees will be discussed in Chapter 16.

Changing Role of Jobs in Society

The creation of jobs contributes to the economic prosperity of a community or a nation as a whole. Yet according to a special study reported by the U.S. Department of Labor, the last years of this century will bring new developments in technology, international competition, demography, and other factors that will alter the nation's job structure.[2] Manufacturing jobs will continue to decline and new jobs in service industries will demand much higher skill levels. The future workplace will need employees with strong skills in communications and mathematical and technical knowledge.[3] Unfortunately, a large number of new job entrants will lack the qualifications needed to perform successfully in the growth occupations. This situation, unless corrected, portends a shift of jobs from the United States to those countries able to provide a well-trained work force and, consequently, a likely decline in the American standard of living.

RELATIONSHIP OF JOB REQUIREMENTS TO HRM FUNCTIONS

Job requirements are the different duties, tasks, and responsibilities that make up a job. Not surprisingly, job requirements influence many of the HR functions that are performed as a part of managing employees. When job requirements are modified in any way, it may be necessary to make corresponding changes in HRM activities.

Recruitment

Before they can find capable employees for an organization, recruiters need to know the job specifications for the positions they are to fill. A **job specification** is a statement of the knowledge, skills, and abilities required of the person performing the job. The job specification for a senior personnel analyst, for example, might include the following:

1. Graduation from a four-year college with major course work (minimum 15 hours) in human resources management.
2. Three to five years' experience in employee classification and compensation or selection or recruitment.
3. Two years' experience in developing/improving job-related compensation and testing instruments and procedures.[4]

Because job specifications establish the qualifications required of applicants for a job opening, they serve an essential role in the recruiting function. These qualifications typically are contained in the notices of job openings. Whether posted on organization bulletin boards or included in help-wanted advertisements or employment agency listings, job specifications provide a basis for attracting qualified applicants and discouraging unqualified ones.

Selection

In addition to job specifications, HR recruiters and supervisors will use job descriptions to select and orient employees to jobs. A **job description** is a statement of the tasks, duties, and responsibilities of a job.

In the past, job specifications used as a basis for selection sometimes bore little relation to the duties to be performed under the job description. Examples of such nonjob-related specifications abounded. Applicants for the job of laborer were required to have a high school diploma. Firefighters were required to be at least six feet tall. And applicants for the job of truck driver were required to be male. These kinds of job specifications served to discriminate against members of certain protected classes, many of whom were excluded from these jobs.

Since the landmark *Griggs* v. *Duke Power* case (see Chapter 3), employers must be able to show that the job specifications used in selecting employees for a particular job relate specifically to the duties of that job. An organization must be careful to ensure that managers with job openings do not hire employees based on "individualized" job requirements that satisfy personal whims but bear little relation to successful job performance.

" 'Overqualified'? You don't mean you *believe* all that stuff!"

From *The Wall Street Journal*—Permission, Cartoon Features Syndicate

Training and Development

Any discrepancies between the knowledge, skills, and abilities (often referred to as KSA) demonstrated by a jobholder and the requirements contained in the description and specification for that job provide clues to training needs. Also, career development as a part of the training function is concerned with preparing employees for advancement to jobs where their capacities can be utilized to the fullest extent possible. The formal qualification requirements set forth in high-level jobs serve to indicate how much more training and development are needed for employees to advance to those jobs.

Performance Appraisal

The requirements contained in the description of a job provide the criteria for evaluating the performance of the holder of that job. The results of performance appraisal may reveal, however, that certain requirements established for a job are not completely valid. As we have already stressed, these criteria must be specific and job-related. If the criteria they use to evaluate employee performance are vague and not job-related, employers may find themselves being charged with unfair discrimination.

Compensation Management

In determining the rate to be paid for performing a job, the relative worth of the job is one of the most important factors. This worth is based on what the job demands of an employee in terms of skill, effort, and responsibility, as well as the conditions and hazards under which the work is performed. The systems of job evaluation by which this worth may be measured are discussed in Chapter 10.

Labor Relations

Long before it was required by law, consistent and equitable treatment of employees was required by union agreements. To avoid grievances and conflicts with unions, employers often found it advantageous to prepare written job descriptions. These job descriptions served as a basis for determining which jobs in the organization were subject to union jurisdiction. This jurisdiction can be especially important if more than one union is contesting the right to perform certain work. For example, the Carpenters' Union may argue that its members have the exclusive right to install metal windowsills in new homes. The Sheet Metalworkers' Union, however, may claim that the installation of metal sills falls solely within their jurisdiction to handle metal goods. If activities such as this are included in the description of a particular job, the union representing employees in that job can usually claim jurisdiction over those activities.

JOB ANALYSIS

Job analysis is sometimes called the cornerstone of HRM because the information it collects serves so many HRM functions. **Job analysis** is the process of obtaining information about jobs by determining what the duties, tasks, or activities of those jobs are. The procedure involves undertaking a systematic investigation of jobs by following a number of predetermined steps specified in advance of the study.[5] When completed, job analysis results in a written report summarizing the information obtained from the analysis of 20 or 30 individual job tasks or activities.[6] HR managers will use these data to develop job descriptions and job specifications. The job specification may be prepared as a separate document or included as a part of the job description. Figure 4–1 illustrates the elements of the job analysis system and the functions for which it is used.

As contrasted with job design, which reflects subjective opinions about the *ideal* requirements of a job, job analysis is concerned with objective and verifiable information about the *actual* requirements of a job. The job descriptions and job specifications developed through job analysis should be as accurate as

FIGURE 4–1 THE JOB ANALYSIS SYSTEM

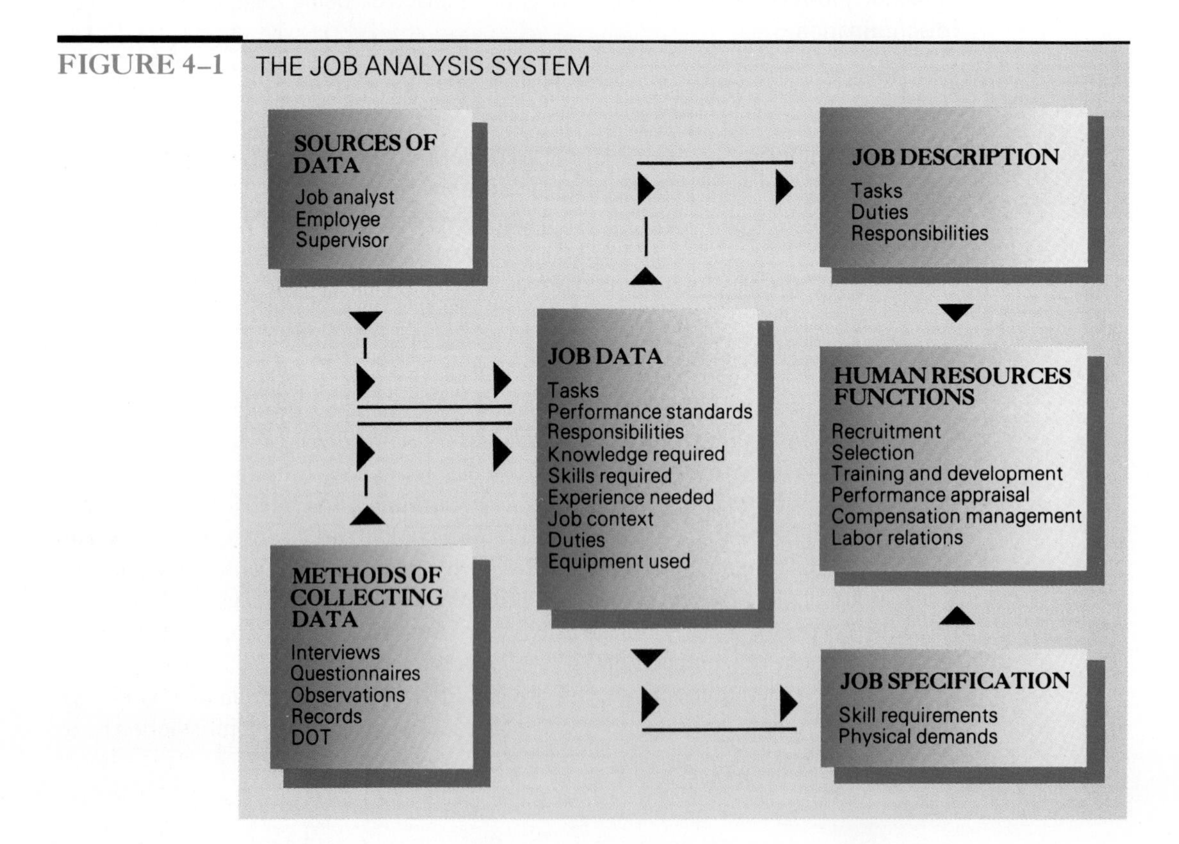

possible if they are to be of value to those who make HRM decisions. These decisions may involve any of the HR functions—from recruitment to termination of employees.

The Job Analyst's Responsibilities

Conducting job analysis is usually the primary responsibility of the HR department. If this department is large enough to have a division for compensation management, job analysis may be performed by members of that division. For example, in the HR department of General Telephone Company of California, job analysis is performed by the section titled Compensation and Organization.

Staff members of the HR department who specialize in job analysis have the title of job analyst or personnel analyst. Since the job carrying this title requires a high degree of analytical ability and writing skill, it sometimes serves as an entry-level job for college graduates who choose a career in HRM. The job description for a job analyst, shown in Figure 4–2, is taken from the *Dictionary of Occupational Titles*.

Although job analysts are the personnel primarily responsible for the job analysis program, they usually enlist the cooperation of the employees and supervisors in the departments where jobs are being analyzed. It is these supervisors and employees who are the sources of much of the information about the jobs. If at all possible, these supervisors and employees may be asked to prepare rough drafts of the job descriptions and specifications the job analysts need.

FIGURE 4–2 JOB DESCRIPTION FOR A JOB ANALYST

166.267–018 JOB ANALYST (profess. & kin.) personnel analyst.
Collects, analyzes, and prepares occupational information to facilitate personnel, administration, and management functions of organization. Consults with management to determine type, scope, and purpose of study. Studies current organizational occupational data and compiles distribution reports, organization and flow charts, and other background information required for study. Observes jobs and interviews workers and supervisory personnel to determine job and worker requirements. Analyzes occupational data, such as physical, mental, and training requirements of jobs and workers, and develops written summaries, such as job descriptions, job specifications, and lines of career movement. Utilizes developed occupational data to evaluate or improve methods and techniques for recruiting, selecting, promotion, evaluating, and training workers, and administration of related personnel programs. May specialize in classifying positions according to regulated guidelines to meet job classification requirements of civil service system and be known as POSITION CLASSIFIER (gov. ser.).

SOURCE: U.S. Department of Labor, Employment and Training Administration, *Dictionary of Occupational Titles,* 4th ed. (Washington, DC: U.S. Government Printing Office, 1977), 99–100.

Gathering Job Information

Job data may be obtained in several ways. The more common methods of studying jobs are interviews, questionnaires, observation, and diaries.

INTERVIEWS The job analyst may question individual employees and supervisors about the job under review.

QUESTIONNAIRES The job analyst may circulate carefully prepared questionnaires to be filled out individually by jobholders and supervisors. These forms will be used to obtain data in the areas of job duties and tasks performed, purpose of the job, physical setting, requirements for performing the job (skill, education, experience, physical and mental demands), equipment and materials used, and special health and safety concerns.

OBSERVATION The job analyst may learn about the jobs by observing and recording on a standardized form the activities of jobholders. Videotaping jobs for later study is an approach used by some organizations.

DIARIES Jobholders themselves may be asked to keep a diary of their work activities during an entire work cycle. Diaries are normally filled out at specific times of the work shift (e.g., every half-hour or hour) and maintained for a two- to four-week period.

Controlling the Accuracy of Job Information

If job analysis is to accomplish its intended purpose, the job data collected must be accurate. Care must be taken to ensure that all important facts are included. A job analyst should be alert for employees who tend to exaggerate the difficulty of their jobs in order to inflate their egos and their paychecks. When interviewing employees or reviewing their questionnaires, the job analyst must look for any responses that do not agree with other facts or impressions the analyst has received.

Whenever a job analyst doubts the accuracy of information provided by employees, he or she should obtain additional information from them, from their supervisors, or from other individuals who are familiar with or perform the same job. It is common practice to have the descriptions for each job reviewed by the jobholders and their supervisors. The job description summaries contained in the *Dictionary of Occupational Titles* can also serve as a basis for the job analyst's review.

The DOT and Job Analysis

Commonly referred to as the DOT, the *Dictionary of Occupational Titles* was first compiled by the then U.S. Employment Service in 1939. Now in its fourth edition (1977), the DOT contains standardized and comprehensive descriptions of about 20,000 jobs. The purpose of the DOT is to "group occupations into a systematic occupational classification structure based on interrelationships of job tasks and requirements." This grouping of occupational classifications is done under a coding system.[7]

The DOT has helped to bring about a greater degree of uniformity in the job titles and descriptions used by employers in different sections of the country. This uniformity has facilitated the movement of workers from sections of the country that may be experiencing widespread unemployment to areas where employment opportunities are greater. The DOT code numbers also facilitate the exchange of statistical information about jobs. In addition, these code numbers are useful in reporting research in the HR area, in vocational counseling, and in charting career paths through job transfers and/or advancements.

Approaches to Job Analysis

The systematic and quantitative definition of job content that job analysis provides is the foundation of many HRM practices, serving to justify job descriptions and other HRM selection procedures.[8] It should be emphasized that a major goal of modern job analysis is to help the organization establish the *job-relatedness* of its selection requirements. Therefore, these procedures help both large and small employers to meet their legal duty under EEO law. Section 14.C.2 of the *Uniform Guidelines* states: "There shall be a job analysis which includes an analysis of the important work behaviors required for successful performance. . . . Any job analysis should focus on work behavior(s) and the tasks associated with them." Several different job analysis approaches are used, each with specific advantages and disadvantages. Three of the more popular methods are functional job analysis, the position analysis questionnaire system, and the critical incident method.

FUNCTIONAL JOB ANALYSIS Developed by the U.S. Training and Employment Service, the **functional job analysis (FJA)** approach utilizes an inventory of the various types of functions or work activities that can constitute any job. FJA thus assumes that each job involves performing certain functions. Specifically, there are three broad worker functions that form the bases of this system: (1) data, (2) people, and (3) things. These three categories are subdivided to form a hierarchy of worker-function scales as shown in Figure 4–3. The job analyst, when studying the job under review, will indicate the functional level for each of the three categories (for example, "copying" under "DATA") and then reflect the relative involvement of the worker in the function by assigning a percentage figure to each function (i.e., 50 percent to "copying"). This is done for each of the three areas, and the three functional levels must equal 100 percent. The end result is a quantitatively evaluated job. FJA can easily be used to describe the content of jobs and assist in writing job descriptions and specifications, and it is used as a basis for the DOT code.

THE POSITION ANALYSIS QUESTIONNAIRE SYSTEM The **position analysis questionnaire (PAQ)** was developed by three industrial psychol-

FIGURE 4–3 DIFFICULTY LEVELS OF WORKER FUNCTIONS

DATA (4th Digit)	PEOPLE (5th Digit)	THINGS (6th Digit)
0 Synthesizing	0 Mentoring	0 Setting-up
1 Coordinating	1 Negotiating	1 Precision working
2 Analyzing	2 Instructing	2 Operating-controlling
3 Compiling	3 Supervising	3 Driving-operating
4 Computing	4 Diverting	4 Manipulating
5 Copying	5 Persuading	5 Tending
6 Comparing	6 Speaking-signaling*	6 Feeding-offbearing
	7 Serving	7 Handling
	8 Taking Instructions —Helping	

*Hyphenated factors are single factors.

SOURCE: U.S. Department of Labor, Employment and Training Administration, *Handbook for Analyzing Jobs* (Washington, DC: U.S. Government Printing Office, 1972), 5.

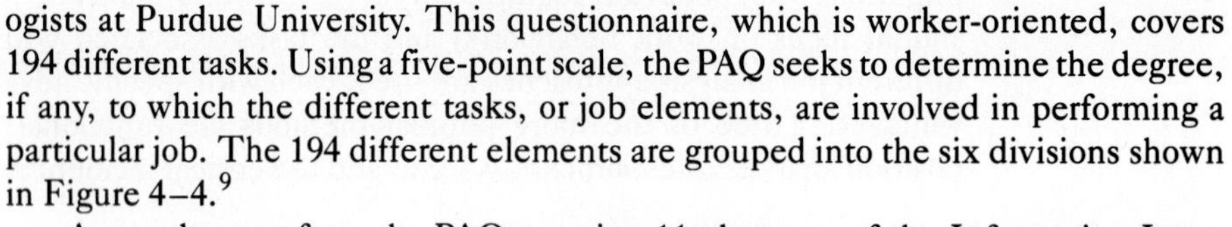

ogists at Purdue University. This questionnaire, which is worker-oriented, covers 194 different tasks. Using a five-point scale, the PAQ seeks to determine the degree, if any, to which the different tasks, or job elements, are involved in performing a particular job. The 194 different elements are grouped into the six divisions shown in Figure 4–4.[9]

A sample page from the PAQ covering 11 elements of the Information Input Division is shown in Figure 4–5. The person making an analysis with this questionnaire would rate each of the elements using the five-point scale shown in the upper right-hand corner of the sample page. The results obtained with the PAQ are quantitative and can be subjected to statistical analysis. The PAQ also permits dimensions of behavior to be compared across a number of jobs and permits jobs to be grouped on the basis of common characteristics.

Interviewing is one way of obtaining information for a job analysis.

CRITICAL INCIDENT METHOD The objective of the **critical incident method** is to identify critical job tasks. Critical job tasks are those important duties and job responsibilities performed by the jobholder that lead to job success. Information about critical job tasks can be collected through interviews with employees or supervisors or through self-report statements written by employees.

Suppose, for example, that the job analyst is studying the job of reference librarian. The interviewer will ask the employee to describe the job on the basis of what is done, how the job is performed, and what tools and equipment are used. The reference librarian may describe the job as follows:

FIGURE 4–4 DIVISIONS AND NUMBER OF JOB ELEMENTS IN THE PAQ

DIVISION	NUMBER OF JOB ELEMENTS
Information Input (where and how does the worker get the information used in the job)	35
Mental Processes (what reasoning, decision making, planning, etc., are involved in the job)	14
Work Output (what physical activities do the workers perform, and what tools or devices do they use)	49
Relationships with Other Persons (what relationships with other people are required in the job)	36
Job Context (in what physical and social contexts is the work performed)	19
Other Job Characteristics	41

> I assist patrons by answering their questions related to finding books, periodicals, or other library materials. I also give them directions to help them find materials within the building. To perform my job I may have to look up materials myself or refer patrons to someone who can directly assist them. Some individuals may need training in how to use reference materials or special library facilities. I also give library tours to new patrons. I use computers and a variety of reference books to carry out my job.

After the job data are collected, the analyst will then write separate task statements that represent important job activities. For the reference librarian one task statement might be

> Listens to patrons and answers their questions related to locating library materials.

Typically the job analyst will write five to ten important task statements for each job under study. The final product will be written task statements that are clear, complete, and easily understood by those unfamiliar with the job. The critical incident method is an important job analysis method since it teaches the analyst to focus on employee behaviors critical to job success.

Job Descriptions

As previously noted, a job description is a written description of a job and the types of duties it includes. Since there is no standard format for job descriptions, they tend to vary in appearance and content from one organization to another. However, most job descriptions will contain at least three parts: the job title, a job identification section, and a job duties section. If the job specifications are not prepared as a separate document, they are usually stated in the concluding section of the job description. Highlights in HRM 1 shows a job description for an HR employment assistant. This sample job description includes both job duties and job

FIGURE 4–5 A SAMPLE PAGE FROM THE POSITION ANALYSIS QUESTIONNAIRE

INFORMATION INPUT

	Extent of Use (U)
NA	Does not apply
1	Nominal/very infrequent
2	Occasional
3	Moderate
4	Considerable
5	Very substantial

1 INFORMATION INPUT

1.1 Sources of Job Information

Rate each of the following items in terms of the extent to which it is used by the worker as a source of information in performing his job.

1.1.1 Visual Sources of Job Information

1 U Written materials (books, reports, office notes, articles, job instructions, signs, etc.)

2 U Quantitative materials (materials which deal with quantities or amounts, such as graphs, accounts, specifications, tables of numbers, etc.)

3 U Pictorial materials (pictures or picturelike materials used as *sources* of information, for example, drawings, blueprints, diagrams, maps, tracings, photographic films, x-ray films, TV pictures, etc.)

4 U Patterns/related devices (templates, stencils, patterns, etc., used as *sources* of information when *observed* during use; do *not* include here materials described in item 3 above)

5 U Visual displays (dials, gauges, signal lights, radarscopes, speedometers, clocks, etc.)

6 U Measuring devices (rulers, calipers, tire pressure gauges, scales, thickness gauges, pipettes, thermometers, protractors, etc., used to obtain visual information about physical measurements; do *not* include here devices described in item 5 above)

7 U Mechanical devices (tools, equipment, machinery, and other mechanical devices which are *sources* of information when *observed* during use or operation)

8 U Materials in process (parts, materials, objects, etc., which are *sources* of information when being modified, worked on, or otherwise processed, such as bread dough being mixed, workpiece being turned in a lathe, fabric being cut, shoe being resoled, etc.)

9 U Materials *not* in process (parts, materials, objects, etc., not in the process of being changed or modified, which are *sources* of information when being inspected, handled, packaged, distributed, or selected, etc., such as items or materials in inventory, storage, or distribution channels, items being inspected, etc.)

10 U Features of nature (landscapes, fields, geological samples, vegetation, cloud formations, and other features of nature which are observed or inspected to provide information)

11 U Man-made features of environment (structures, buildings, dams, highways, bridges, docks, railroads, and other "man-made" or altered aspects of the indoor or outdoor environment which are *observed or inspected* to provide job information; do not consider equipment, machines, etc., that an individual uses in his work, as covered by item 7)

SOURCE: E. J. McCormick, P. R. Jeanneret, and R. C. Mecham, *Position Analysis Questionnaire,* © copyright 1979 by Purdue Research Foundation, West Lafayette, IN 47907. Reprinted with permission.

HIGHLIGHTS IN HRM

1 JOB DESCRIPTION FOR AN EMPLOYMENT ASSISTANT

Job Identification

JOB TITLE: Employment Assistant

Division:	Southern Area
Department:	Human Resources Management
Job Analyst:	Virginia Sasaki
Date Analyzed:	12/3/90
Wage Category:	Exempt
Report to:	HR Manager
Job Code:	11-17
Date Verified:	12/17/90

Brief Listing of Major Job Duties

JOB STATEMENT

Performs professional human resources work in the areas of employee *recruitment* and *selection, testing, orientation, transfers,* and maintenance of employee human resources files. May handle special assignments and projects in *EEO/Affirmative Action, employee grievances, training,* or *classification and compensation.* Works under general supervision. Incumbent exercises initiative and independent judgment in the performance of assigned tasks.

Job Duties and Responsibilities

JOB DUTIES

1. Prepares recruitment literature and job advertisements for applicant placement.
2. Schedules and conducts personal interviews to determine applicant suitability for employment. Includes reviewing mailed applications and résumés for qualified personnel.
3. Supervises administration of testing program. Responsible for developing or improving testing instruments and procedures.
4. Presents orientation program to all new employees. Reviews and develops all materials and procedures for orientation program.
5. Coordinates division job posting and transfer program. Establishes job posting procedures. Responsible for reviewing transfer applications, arranging transfer interviews, and determining effective transfer dates.
6. Maintains a daily working relationship with division managers on human resource matters, including recruitment concerns, retention or release of probationary employees, and discipline or discharge of permanent employees.
7. Distributes new or revised human resources policies and procedures to all employees and managers through bulletins, meetings, memorandums, and/or personal contact.
8. Performs related duties as assigned by the human resources manager.

JOB SPECIFICATION

Job Specifications and Requirements

1. Four-year college or university degree with major course work in human resources management, business administration, or industrial psychology; OR a combination of experience, education, and training equivalent to a four-year college degree in human resources management.
2. Considerable knowledge of principles of employee selection and assignment of personnel.
3. Ability to express ideas clearly in both written and oral communications.
4. Ability to independently plan and organize one's own activities.
5. Knowledge of human resource computer applications desirable.

specifications and should satisfy most of the job information needs of managers who must recruit, interview, or orient a new employee. Job descriptions may list specific physical or mental restrictions that are job-related and for which physical or mental accommodation is not possible. For example, the job may require the jobholder to read extremely fine print or to tour customer facilities including climbing stairs.

THE JOB TITLE Selection of a job title is important for several reasons. First, the job title provides psychological importance and status to the employee. *Sanitation Engineer* is a more psychologically appealing title than *Garbage Collector.* Second, if possible, the title should provide some indication of what the duties of the job entail. Titles like *Meat Inspector, Electronics Assembler, Salesperson,* or *Engineer* obviously hint at the nature of the duties of these jobs. The job title also should indicate the relative level occupied by its holder in the organizational hierarchy. For example, the title *Junior Engineer* implies that this job occupies a lower level than that of *Senior Engineer.* Other titles that indicate the relative level in the organizational hierarchy are *Welder's Helper* and *Laboratory Assistant.*

Certain kinds of job titles should be avoided altogether. For example, a series of identical titles with qualifiers, such as *Inventory Clerk I* and *Inventory Clerk II,* makes it difficult to distinguish one job from another.[10] Job titles qualified by the terms "man" or "woman" are also being discarded to avoid the implication that the jobs can be performed only by members of one gender. Thus, a Repairman is now a *Repairer;* a Foreman or a Forelady, a *Supervisor;* and a Steward or a Stewardess, a *Flight Attendant.*

THE JOB IDENTIFICATION SECTION The job identification section of a job description usually follows the job title. It includes such items as the departmental location of the job, the person to whom the jobholder reports, and the date the job description was last revised. Sometimes it also contains a payroll or code number, the number of employees performing the job, the number of employees in the department where the job is located, and the DOT code number. The "Statement of the Job" usually appears at the bottom of this section and serves to distinguish the job from other jobs—something the job title may fail to do.

THE JOB DUTIES SECTION The statements covering job duties are typically arranged in order of importance. These statements should indicate the weight, or value, of each duty. Usually, but not always, the weight of a duty can be gauged by the percentage of time devoted to it.[11] The statements should stress the responsibilities all the duties entail and the results they are to accomplish. It is general practice also to indicate the tools and equipment used by the employee in performing the job.

JOB SPECIFICATIONS As stated earlier, the personal qualifications an individual must possess in order to perform the duties and responsibilities contained in a job description are compiled in the job specification. Typically the job specification covers two areas: (1) the skill required to perform the job and (2) the physical demands the job places upon the employee performing it.

Skills relevant to a job include education or experience, specialized training, personal traits or abilities, and manual dexterities. The physical demands of a job refer to how much walking, standing, reaching, lifting, or talking must be done on the job. The condition of the physical work environment and the hazards employees may encounter are also among the physical demands of a job.

Problems with Job Descriptions

HR managers consider job descriptions a valuable tool for performing HRM functions. Nevertheless, several problems are frequently associated with these documents, including the following:

1. They are often poorly written, providing little guidance to the jobholder.
2. They are not updated as job duties or specifications change.
3. They may violate the law by containing specifications not related to job success.
4. The job duties they include are written in vague rather than specific terms.
5. They can limit the scope of activities of the jobholder.[12]

Writing Clear and Specific Job Descriptions

When writing a job description, it is essential to use statements that are terse, direct, and simply worded. Unnecessary words or phrases should be eliminated. Typically, the sentences that describe job duties begin with a verb in its present tense, with the implied subject of the sentence being the employee performing the job. The term *occasionally* is used to describe those duties that are performed once in a while. The term *may* is used in connection with those duties performed only by some workers on the job.

Even when set forth in writing, job descriptions and specifications can still be vague. To the consternation of many employers, however, today's legal environment has created what might be called an "Age of Specifics." Federal guidelines and court decisions now require that the specific performance requirements of a job be based on *valid* job-related criteria.[13] Personnel decisions that involve either job applicants or employees and are based on criteria that are vague or not job-related are increasingly being challenged successfully. Managers of small businesses, where employees may perform many different job tasks, must be particularly concerned about writing specific job descriptions.

Values of Written Job Requirements

Spelling out job requirements in job descriptions and job specifications is essential in order for members of the HR staff to perform their duties. Job descriptions, in particular, are of value to both the employees and the employer. From the employees' standpoint, job descriptions can be used to help them learn their job duties and to remind them of the results they are expected to achieve. From the employer's standpoint, written job descriptions can serve as a basis for minimizing the misunderstandings that occur between supervisors and their subordinates concerning job requirements. They also establish management's right to take corrective action when the duties covered by the job description are not performed as required.

JOB DESIGN

An outgrowth of job analysis, **job design** is concerned with structuring jobs in order to improve organization efficiency and employee job satisfaction. The design of a job should reflect both technological and human considerations. It should facilitate the achievement of organizational objectives and the performance of the work the job was established to accomplish. At the same time, the design should recognize the capacities and needs of those who are to perform it.

As Figure 4–6 illustrates, job design is a combination of four basic considerations: (1) the organizational objectives the job was created to fulfill; (2) industrial engineering considerations, including ways to make the job technologically efficient; (3) human engineering concerns, including workers' physical and mental capabilities; and (4) quality-of-work-life changes. Quality-of-work-life considerations in job design or redesign are reflected in contemporary programs. Three of the more popular programs are job enrichment, job enlargement, and employee participation teams, all of which are discussed later in the chapter.

Industrial Engineering Considerations

The study of work is an important contribution of the scientific management movement. **Industrial engineering,** which evolved with this movement, is concerned with analyzing work methods and establishing time standards. Specifically, it involves both analyzing the elements of the work cycle that compose a particular job activity and determining the time required to complete each element. For

FIGURE 4–6 BASIS FOR JOB DESIGN

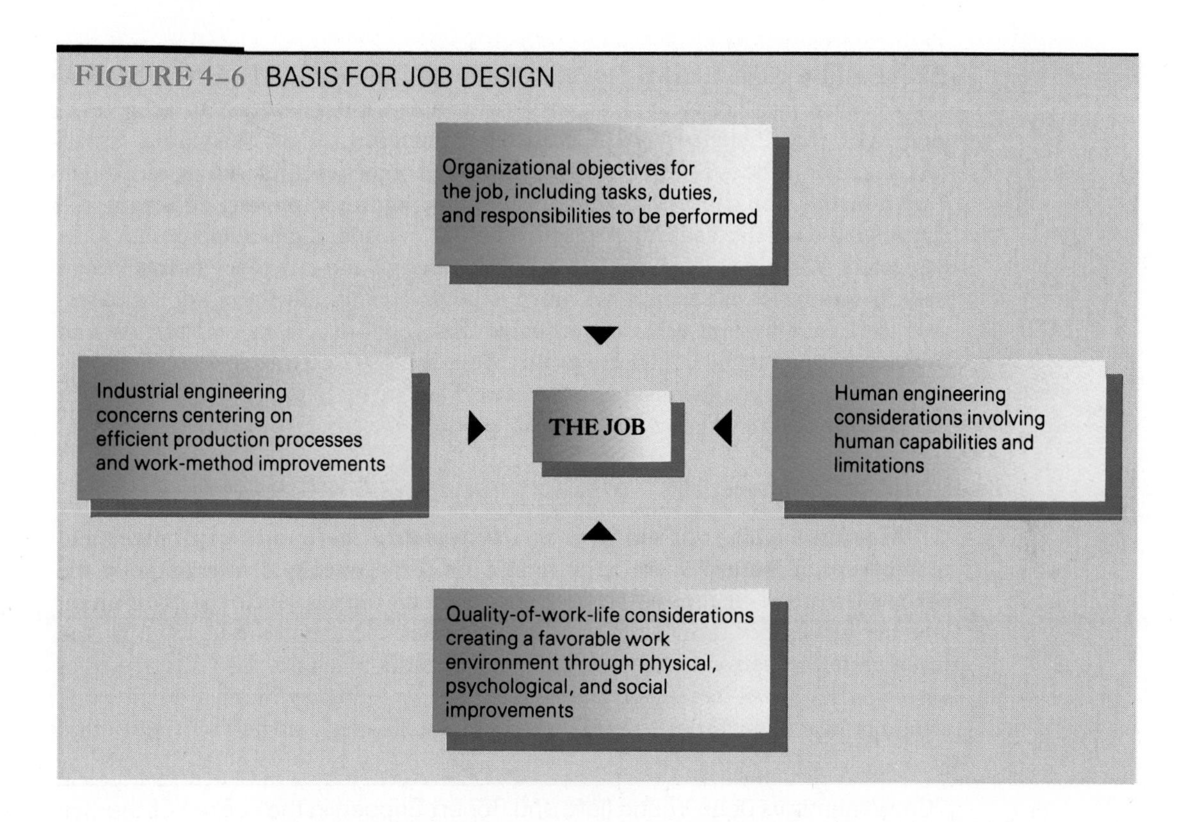

example, the Methods Improvement Group of First Interstate Bank employs the principles of industrial engineering to improve the work flow of its tellers. This may include eliminating any seemingly duplicate processes in the work cycle, or it may involve combining the tasks of two employees.

DEVELOPMENT OF TIME STANDARDS Identifying and timing the elements in a work cycle are generally the responsibilities of the industrial engineering staff. They study the work cycle to determine which, if any, of its elements can be modified, combined, rearranged, or eliminated to reduce the time needed to complete the cycle.

To establish time standards, the industrial engineering staff measures and records the time required to complete each element in the work cycle, using a stopwatch or work sampling techniques. By combining the times for each element, they determine the total time required. This time is subsequently adjusted to allow for the skill and effort demonstrated by the observed worker and for interruptions that may occur in performing the work. The adjusted time becomes the time standard for that particular work cycle. This standard then provides an objective basis for evaluating and improving employee performance and for determining incentive pay.

BENEFITS AND LIMITATIONS OF INDUSTRIAL ENGINEERING Since jobs are created primarily to enable an organization to achieve its objectives, the efficiency goals of industrial engineering cannot be ignored. Industrial engineering does constitute a disciplined and objective approach to job design. Unfortunately, the concern of industrial engineering for improving efficiency and simplifying work methods may cause the human considerations in job design to be neglected. What may be improvements in job design and efficiency from an engineering standpoint can sometimes prove to be psychologically unsound. For example, the assembly line with its simplified and repetitive tasks embodies sound principles of industrial engineering, but these tasks are often not psychologically rewarding for those who must perform them. Thus, to be effective, job design must also provide for the satisfaction of human needs.

Human Engineering Considerations

Human engineering attempts to accommodate the human capabilities and deficiencies of those who are to perform a job. It is concerned with adapting the entire job system—the work, the work environment, the machines, the equipment, and the processes—to match human characteristics. In short, it seeks to fit the machine to the person rather than the person to the machine. Also referred to as *human factors engineering*, *ergonomics*, and *engineering psychology*, human engineering attempts to minimize the harmful effects of carelessness, negligence, and other

Crew members John Young (left) and Robert Crippen in the cockpit of the space shuttle *Columbia*.

human fallibilities—effects that otherwise may cause product defects, damage to equipment, or even the injury or death of employees.

Machine design must take into consideration the physical ability of operators to use the machines and to react through vision, hearing, and touch to the information that the machines convey. The National Aeronautics and Space Administration (NASA) widely employed the principles of human engineering to improve the visual and auditory display of information through dials, instruments, and indicators on the space shuttle *Columbia*. Designing equipment controls to be compatible with both the physical characteristics and reaction capabilities of the people who must operate them and the environment in which they work is increasingly important in the design of work systems.[14] While human engineering ordinarily focuses on what is the best arrangement for a large percentage of workers, it can also aid in the design of jobs for specific groups, such as the handicapped or the elderly.

Job Design and the Problem of Overspecialization

Organizations typically combine similar duties and tasks into a job to facilitate the selection, training, and supervision of personnel who are to perform it. In doing so, organizations may unintentionally create jobs that are monotonous to perform. The employees performing such jobs face a problem referred to as overspecialization.

Recognizing the problems created by overspecialization, some employers have initiated programs to consolidate the duties of several jobs under a single title. For example, the jobs of typist, receptionist, and file clerk might be consolidated under the single title of *Clerk Typist.* This process is essentially one of enlarging the job duties of employees to relieve the boredom and feeling of low achievement that overspecialization creates.

Behavioral Considerations

Management thought pertaining to job design has evolved from preoccupation with work simplification, standardization, and division of labor to concerns with human needs in job performance.[15] This change has been caused in part by the limitations of overspecialization and industrial engineering noted earlier. Another major challenge confronting employers today is that of improving the quality of work life (QWL). In large and small organizations, efforts are under way to use job design to improve the well-being of employees while also improving organizational effectiveness. These efforts consist of making work more rewarding psychologically and reducing anxieties and stresses of the work environment. They include job enrichment programs, changes in job characteristics, creation of employee participation teams, and adjustments in traditional work schedules.

JOB ENLARGEMENT **Job enlargement,** sometimes referred to as the *horizontal loading* of jobs, consists of increasing the number and variety of tasks a job includes. The tasks that are added are similar to current job duties; however, the new duties relieve boredom by offering additional variety to the jobholder. For example, a salesclerk's job may be enlarged by having that individual perform inventory control, merchandise returns, or shipping and receiving duties.

JOB ROTATION Employees participate in job rotation when they do entirely different jobs on a rotating schedule. For example, new employees hired as customer service representatives (CSRs) at America West Airlines are trained in reservations/sales, in-flight services (flight attendant), and airport services (ramp work and ticketing). CSRs alternate between these jobs on a weekly schedule determined by a seniority bidding system. Other organizations may allow employees to rotate between jobs on a daily, weekly, or monthly basis depending on organizational and employee needs.

JOB ENRICHMENT Any effort that makes work more rewarding or satisfying by adding more meaningful tasks to an employee's job is called **job enrichment.** Originally popularized by Frederick Herzberg, job enrichment is touted as fulfilling the high motivational needs of employees, such as self-fulfillment and self-esteem, while achieving long-term job satisfaction and performance goals.[16] Job enrichment, or the *vertical expansion* of jobs, may be accomplished by increasing the autonomy and responsibility of employees. Herzberg discusses five factors for enriching jobs and thereby motivating employees: achievement, recognition, growth, responsibility, and performance of the whole job versus only parts of the job. These factors allow employees to assume a greater role in the decision-making process and become more involved in planning, organizing, directing, and controlling their own work. The job of secretary, for example, might be enriched by having the jobholder conduct quality checks on his or her own work, handle the manager's appointment calendar, draft letters or memos, or attend meetings for the manager. Vertical job enrichment can also be accomplished by organizing workers into teams and giving these teams greater authority for self-management.

In spite of the benefits to be achieved through job enrichment, it must not be considered a panacea for overcoming production problems and employee discontent. Job enrichment programs are more likely to succeed in some jobs and work situations than in others. They are *not* the solution to such problems as dissatisfaction with pay, with employee benefits, or with employment insecurity. Moreover, not all employees object to the mechanical pacing of an assembly line, nor do all employees seek additional responsibility or challenge.[17] Some prefer routine jobs because they can let their minds wander while performing their work.

Furthermore, managerial attitudes can be a factor that limits the success of a job enrichment program. Granting employees more job responsibility and allowing them to make job decisions once made by supervisors can be demotivating and unsettling to managers. First-level managers who feel threatened with the possible loss of their jobs can be formidable sources of resistance to change.[18] This point is well illustrated by the following statement, made to one of the authors of this text at the completion of a job enrichment program: "Now that you've enriched the jobs of my employees, what's left for me to do?" Moreover, where supervisors hold low beliefs about participative decision making, this may discourage employees from participating in the redesign of work.[19]

JOB CHARACTERISTICS Job design studies explored a new field when behavioral scientists focused on identifying various job dimensions that would improve simultaneously the efficiency of organizations and the job satisfaction of employees. Perhaps the theory that best exemplifies this research is the one advanced by Hackman and Oldham.[20] Their **job characteristics model** proposes that three psychological states of a jobholder result in improved work performance, internal motivation, and lower absenteeism and turnover. The motivated, satisfied, and productive employee is one who (1) experiences *meaningfulness* of the work performed, (2) experiences *responsibility* for work outcomes, and (3) has *knowledge of the results* of the work performed. Achieving these three psychological states serves as reinforcement to the employee and is a source of internal motivation to continue doing the job well. As Hackman and Oldham state:

> The net result is a self-perpetuating cycle of positive work motivation powered by self-generated rewards, that is predicted to continue until one or more of the three psychological states is no longer present, or until the individual no longer values the internal rewards that derive from good performance.[21]

Hackman and Oldham believe that five core job dimensions produce the three psychological states. As Figure 4–7 illustrates, three of these job characteristics foster meaningful work, while one contributes to responsibility and one to knowledge of results. The five job characteristics are as follows:

1. *Skill Variety*. The degree to which a job entails a variety of different activities, which demand the use of a number of different skills and talents by the jobholder.
2. *Task Identity*. The degree to which the job requires completion of a whole and identifiable piece of work, that is, doing a job from beginning to end with a visible outcome.
3. *Task Significance*. The degree to which the job has a substantial impact on the lives or work of other people, whether in the immediate organization or in the external environment.
4. *Autonomy*. The degree to which the job provides substantial freedom, independence, and discretion to the individual in scheduling the work and in determining the procedures to be used in carrying it out.
5. *Feedback*. The degree to which carrying out the work activities required by the job results in the individual being given direct and clear information about the effectiveness of his or her performance.[22]

It is important to realize that each of the five job characteristics affects employee performance differently. Therefore, employees will experience the greatest motiva-

FIGURE 4–7 THE JOB CHARACTERISTICS MODEL OF WORK MOTIVATION

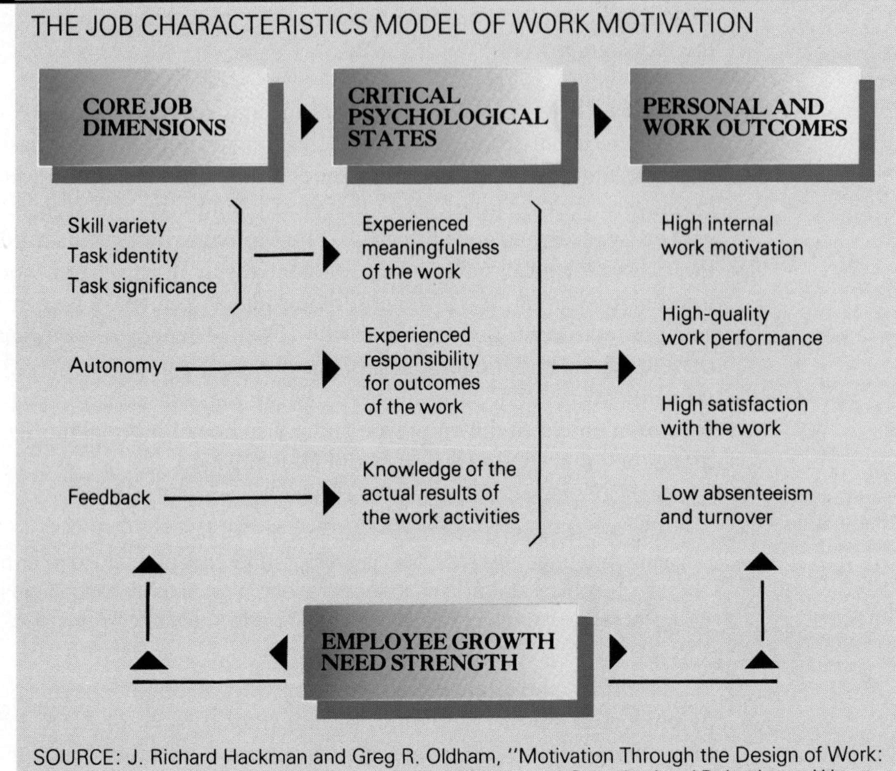

SOURCE: J. Richard Hackman and Greg R. Oldham, "Motivation Through the Design of Work: Test of a Theory." Reprinted from the August, 1976 issue of *Organizational Behavior and Human Performance,* copyright 1976.

tion when all five characteristics are present, since the job characteristics combine to produce the three psychological states.

The job characteristics model appears to work best when certain conditions are met. One of these conditions is that employees must have the psychological desire for the autonomy, variety, responsibility, and challenge of enriched jobs. When this personal characteristic is absent, employees may resist the job redesign effort. In addition, job redesign efforts almost always fail when employees lack the physical or mental skills, abilities, or education needed to perform the job. Forcing enriched jobs on individuals lacking these traits can result in frustrated employees.

EMPLOYEE PARTICIPATION TEAMS A logical outgrowth of job enrichment and the job characteristics model has been the growth of **employee participation teams.** Participation teams are groups of employees who rotate jobs as they complete the production or service process. Team members acquire multiple skills, enabling them to perform a variety of job tasks. Participation can also include joint

Factory employees at this Saturn auto manufacturing plant participate in group discussions and decision making.

decision making in which employees are encouraged to help solve organizational problems.[23]

Employee participation teams incorporate the motivational factors of job enrichment and the core job dimensions from the job characteristics model to produce a work environment that is intrinsically fulfilling to employees. One key ingredient of teams is their ability to foster among all team members a sense of ownership, involvement, and responsibility for completing the assigned tasks. Because of the growing attention being paid to work teams, they will receive an extended treatment in Chapter 14.

Adjustments in Work Schedules

Another form of job design is to alter the normal workweek of five 8-hour days in which all employees begin and end their workday at the same preset time. Employers may depart from the traditional workday or workweek in their attempt to improve organizational productivity and morale by giving employees increased control over the hours they work. The more common alternative work schedules include the four-day workweek, flextime, and job sharing.

THE FOUR-DAY WORKWEEK Under the four-day workweek (or *compressed workweek*), the number of days in the workweek is shortened by lengthening the number of hours worked per day. This schedule is best illustrated by the four-day, 40-hour week, generally referred to as 4/10 or 4/40. Employees working a four-day workweek might work ten hours a day, Monday through Thursday. Although the 4/10 schedule is probably the best known, other compressed arrangements include reducing weekly hours to 38 or 36 hours.

Organizations that operate batch processing systems (e.g., oil companies like Exxon or Shell Oil) use shorter workweeks to coordinate work schedules with production schedules. Compressed workweeks may assist with scheduling arrangements by improving plant and equipment utilization. The keying of work schedules to processing time for a specific operation rather than to a standard workweek reduces startup and closedown time and often results in higher weekly output.

According to a 1987 survey by the Society for Human Resource Management, two of the strongest advantages for the compressed work schedule were that it "accommodates the leisure-time activities of the employees" and "facilitates the employee's scheduling of medical, dental, and other types of appointments."[24] Other advantages included the improvement of employee job satisfaction and morale and the facilitation of recruitment.

The major disadvantage of the compressed workweek, according to the survey, was the increased amount of stress on supervisors. Few other disadvantages were identified by survey respondents. There was no apparent problem of employee fatigue from working ten-hour days, and the coordination of work activities between departments was not hampered.

FLEXTIME **Flextime,** or flexible working hours, permits employees the option of choosing daily starting and quitting times provided that they work a certain number of hours per day or week. With flextime, employees are given considerable latitude in scheduling their work. However, there is a "core period" during the morning and afternoon when *all* employees are required to be on the job.

Some variations of flextime allow employees to work as many or as few hours per day as they desire, so long as the total hours worked per week meet the minimum specified by management, usually 40 hours. Flexible working hours are most common in service-type organizations—financial institutions, government agencies, or other organizations with large clerical operations. The regional office of Sentry Insurance Company in Scottsdale, Arizona, has found that flextime provides many advantages for employees working in claims, underwriting, and HR areas. Highlights in HRM 2 illustrates the flextime schedule used by Sentry Insurance.

Flextime provides both employees and employers with several advantages. By allowing employees greater flexibility in work scheduling, employers can reduce some of the traditional causes of tardiness and absenteeism. Employees can adjust their work to accommodate their particular life-styles and, in doing so, gain greater job satisfaction.[25] Employees can also schedule their working hours for the time of day when they are most productive. In addition, variations in arrival and departure times can help reduce traffic congestion at the peak commuting hours. In some cases, employees require less time to commute, and the pressures of meeting a rigid schedule are reduced.

From the employer's standpoint, flextime can be most helpful in recruiting and retaining personnel. It has proved invaluable to organizations wishing to improve

HIGHLIGHTS IN HRM

2 SENTRY INSURANCE COMPANY'S FLEXTIME SCHEDULE

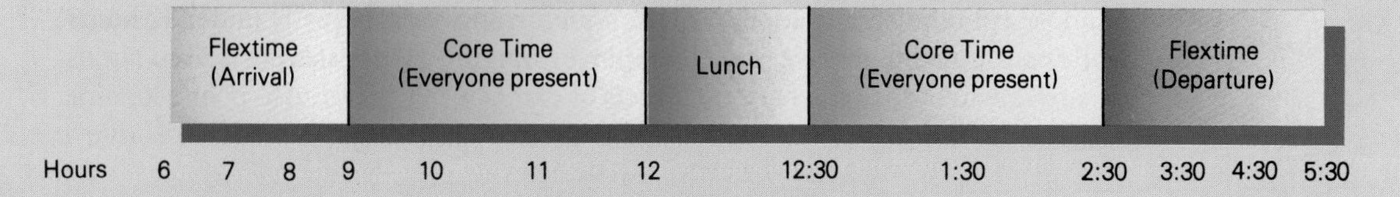

- Employees arriving at 6:00 A.M. would leave at 2:30 P.M.
- Employees arriving at 9:00 A.M. would leave at 5:30 P.M.

service to customers or clients by extending their hours. Research demonstrates that flextime can have a positive impact on the performance measures of reliability, quality, and quantity of work.[26]

There are, of course, several disadvantages to flextime. First, it is not suited to some jobs. It is not feasible, for example, where specific workstations must be staffed at all times. Second, it can create problems for supervisors in communicating with and instructing employees. Flextime schedules may also force these supervisors to extend their workweek if they are to exercise control over their subordinates. Finally, keeping premises open for a longer period will increase energy consumption, resulting in higher costs for the employer.

JOB SHARING The arrangement whereby two part-time employees perform a job that otherwise would be held by one full-time employee is called job sharing. Government agencies at all levels are showing interest in job sharing, as are private employers. Both Steelcase Inc. and Carter Hawley Hale Stores have formulated procedures for employees to share jobs. Employers note that without job sharing, two good employees might otherwise be lost.

Job sharing is suited to the needs of families where one or both spouses desire to work only part-time. It is suited also to the needs of older workers who want to phase into retirement by shortening their workday. For the employer, the work of part-time employees can be scheduled to conform to peaks in the daily workload. Job sharing can also limit layoffs in hard economic times. A final benefit is that employees engaged in job sharing have time off during the week to accommodate personal needs, so they are less likely to be absent.

Job sharing does have several problems, however. Employers may not want to employ two people to do the work of one because the time required to orient and train a second employee constitutes an added burden. They may also want to avoid

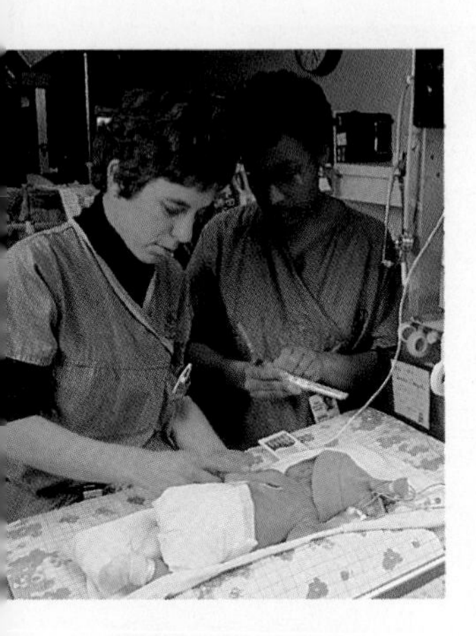

Employees in the health care industry must work shifts to provide their patients with constant care.

prorating the employee benefits between two part-time employees. This problem may be reduced, however, by permitting the employees to contribute the difference between the health insurance (or life insurance) premiums for a full-time employee and the pro rata amount the employer would otherwise contribute for a part-time employee.

A variation of job sharing is work sharing. A work sharing program permits all employees in the organization to shorten their workweeks (usually under 32 hours) while continuing to receive normal employee benefits. Work sharing is used almost exclusively to reduce the harmful effects of extensive layoffs due to poor economic conditions.

SHIFT WORK In order to meet various service requirements, some industries, such as transportation, communications, and health care, must provide continuous operations. For economic reasons, some businesses—for example, refinery operations—must maintain 24-hour production schedules. Employees working in these organizations are subject to round-the-clock work schedules, or shift work. The most common shift schedules are days (7 A.M. to 3 P.M.), evenings (3 P.M. to 11 P.M.), and nights (11 P.M. to 7 A.M.). Employees doing shift work may have their shifts rotated on a daily, weekly, or monthly basis. Rotating employees through the different shifts permits everyone to share in the favored daytime hours. Employees can be assigned to shifts by management; in unionized organizations, the seniority rights of employees will dictate their ability to choose their work hours.

SUMMARY

The job is the basic unit of an organization structure. Information on the duties of the job and the qualifications employees must possess to perform it is contained in job descriptions and job specifications, respectively. Gathered through the process of job analysis, these data provide the criteria upon which employment and HRM decisions must be based. It is the prevailing opinion of the courts that HRM decisions on employment, performance appraisal, and promotions must be based on specific criteria that are job-related. These criteria can be determined objectively only by analyzing the requirements of each job.

To improve the internal environment of organizations and thereby increase American productivity, greater efforts are being made by many organizations to enhance the quality of work life. These efforts include the establishment of job enrichment programs, the use of job characteristics that motivate, the use of employee participation teams, and adjustments in the traditional work schedule. Job enrichment programs provide opportunities for employees to exercise more autonomy in performing their jobs, thus giving them greater job satisfaction. Job characteristics—skill variety, task identity, task significance, autonomy, and feedback—create positive psychological states in employees, enabling them to be more productive. Employee participation teams allow employees to make suggestions to improve operations and services, thereby giving them a greater commitment to the organization. Changes in work schedules—which include the four-day work-week, flextime, and job sharing—permit employees to adjust their work periods to accommodate their particular life-styles. Employers can select from among these HR techniques to accommodate diverse employee needs while fostering organizational effectiveness.

DISCUSSION QUESTIONS

1. What does job analysis entail, and who within an organization participates in the job analysis process?
2. How do the functional approaches to job analysis differ from the traditional approach?
3. The courts have been fairly consistent in ruling that selection, performance appraisal, and similar decisions must be based on job-related criteria. What are the implications of these rulings for job analysis?
4. To what extent, if any, can the absence of formal job descriptions contribute to employees' desire to unionize?
5. As a project, prepare a description of a job at which you are currently working or have worked. Develop specifications listing the minimum qualifications required for the job. How do the qualifications required for the job compare with your own qualifications? Are/were you underemployed or overemployed?
6. Considering your present job, or a recent job, how would you incorporate into the position the five job characteristics that motivate employees? Could all five characteristics be included?
7. As a small business employer, explain how nontraditional work schedules might make it easier for you to recruit employees.
8. Assume the role of a supervisor. What are the advantages and disadvantages you see with flextime?

MINI-CASE 4–1 Redesigning City Jobs

When Mary Garcia received her promotion to HR director for the City of Gilbert, she was faced with an immediate problem. For the previous 18 months, employee turnover had risen substantially, and supervisors reported general job dissatisfaction among different employee groups. Unfortunately, this occurred during a period of economic prosperity when other employment opportunities were available and regional unemployment was low. Replacing lost employees was becoming more costly and time-consuming for the City of Gilbert, since qualified applicants were more difficult to find. Numerous job requisition orders were several weeks past due.

Exit interviews with terminating employees showed that, in the main, workers believed that the city offered competitive wages and benefits but that many jobs were routine and offered little challenge. Employees complained of being underutilized, with almost no chance to demonstrate their skills and talents. As one employee stated during her exit interview, "It's just plain boring to work around here."

Upon further examination, Mary found out that two years earlier, specific jobs in the city had been redesigned as the result of an industrial engineering study. Newly hired industrial engineers were able to demonstrate that by simplifying various jobs, the city could save $97,000 annually. Because taxpayers were forcing city managers to be cost-conscious, saving financial resources was an important city goal and an important objective for elected officials. It was approximately six months after the jobs were redesigned that turnover and job dissatisfaction began to increase. Mary also learned that several city managers sponsored the job redesign efforts.

As a specialist in HR management, Mary Garcia is well aware of behavioral considerations in job redesign. As an undergraduate business student, she had taken a class in quality-of-work-life programs and the motivational dimensions of jobs. In fact, her study of the turnover issue has led her to believe that overspecialization is the cause of the problem. She is considering approaching her superior, the city manager, with a proposal to once again redesign the affected jobs. This time, however, changes would be made with employees' concerns in mind.

QUESTIONS

1. What arguments could be advanced in favor of the changes suggested by Mary?
2. What are some of the job design programs available for implementation? What are their advantages and disadvantages? Which program(s) would you recommend?

MINI-CASE 4–2 Reality in the Use of Job Descriptions

In the Tormaru Electronics Company's American subsidiary, the duties of each manager were not determined entirely by their job descriptions. The assignments they might perform from time to time also depended on their particular abilities and their past performance. Those who had performed well were likely to receive additional responsibilities, and those who had not were often relieved of certain responsibilities. The less effective managers consequently were likely to suffer the loss of responsibility and status rather than the loss of their jobs.

Because of this fact, the duties being performed by a particular executive might not coincide with those the executive's job title traditionally included. The HR manager, for example, admitted that she spent less than half her time with traditional personnel activities and a significant portion of her time working with the company's suppliers to help them overcome delivery-schedule problems. Thus, rigid adherence to formal job descriptions frequently did not determine the assignment a particular manager might be given.

Quite obviously, the management practices of this subsidiary of Tormaru Electronics differ from those of most American companies. Yet, in competing with American companies, it has been quite successful. Furthermore, its workers had been sufficiently satisfied with their employment conditions to vote down union efforts to organize them.

QUESTIONS

1. What are the potential advantages and disadvantages of the company's practice not to limit a manager's assignment to the duties set forth in the description of that individual's job?
2. If job specifications were part of the job description, what legal problems might the company face?
3. If you were the HR manager of this company, would you recommend changes to this practice? Explain.

NOTES AND REFERENCES

1. Peter F. Drucker, "Worker's Hands Bound by Tradition," *Wall Street Journal* (August 2, 1988): 20.
2. *Workforce 2000: Work and Workers for the 21st Century,* Executive Summary (Washington, DC: U.S. Department of Labor, n.d.), 1.
3. "Where the Jobs Are Is Where the Skills Aren't," *Business Week* (September 19, 1988): 104–108.
4. Adapted from job description, *Senior Personnel Analyst,* City of Mesa, Arizona (May 1989). Provided by John Smoyer, Personnel Director, City of Mesa.
5. Ronald A. Ash, "Job Analysis in the World of Work," in *The Job Analysis Handbook for Business, Industry, and Government,* ed. Sidney Gael (New York: John Wiley & Sons, 1988), 3.
6. Richard Henderson, *Compensation Management,* 5th ed. (Englewood Cliffs, NJ: Prentice-Hall, 1989), 114–118.
7. U.S. Department of Labor, *Dictionary of Occupational Titles,* 4th ed. (Washington, DC: U.S. Government Printing Office, 1977), xiv.
8. Robert D. Gatewood and Hubert S. Field, *Human Resource Selection* (Chicago: Dryden Press, 1987), 174–177.
9. Ernest J. McCormick and Daniel R. Ilgen, *Industrial Psychology,* 7th ed. (Englewood Cliffs, NJ: Prentice-Hall, 1980), 42.
10. Jai V. Ghorpade, *Job Analysis: A Handbook for the Human Resource Director* (Englewood Cliffs, NJ: Prentice-Hall, 1988), 97–98.
11. Philip C. Grant, "What Use Is a Job Description?" *Personnel Journal* 67, no. 2 (February 1988): 46.
12. Philip C. Grant, "Why Job Descriptions Don't Work," *Personnel Journal* 67, no. 1 (January 1988): 53–59.
13. Chapter 3 discussed the *Uniform Guidelines on Employee Selection Procedures* and the necessity for performance standards to be based on valid job-related criteria.
14. Michael A. Campion and Paul W. Thayer, "How Do You Design a Job?" *Personnel Journal* 68, no. 1 (January 1989): 43–46.
15. Bernard J. Reilly and Joseph A. DiAngelo, Jr., "A Look at Job Redesign," *Personnel* 65, no. 2 (February 1988): 61.
16. For Herzberg's original article on job enrichment, see Frederick Herzberg, "One More Time: How Do You Motivate Employees?" *Harvard Business Review* 46, no. 2 (January–February 1968): 53–62.
17. Martin Kilduff and Dennis T. Regan, "What People Say and What They Do: The Differential Effects of Informational Cues and Task Design," *Organizational Behavior and Human Decision Processes* 41, no. 1 (February 1988): 83–84.
18. Jay Gilberg, "Managerial Attitudes Toward Participative Management Programs: Myths and Reality," *Public Personnel Management* 17, no. 2 (Summer 1988): 111.
19. Newton Margulies and Stewart Black, "Perspectives on the Implementation of Participative Approaches," *Human Resource Management* 26, no. 3 (Fall 1987): 385–412. For the original article on the job characteristics model, see J. Richard Hackman and Greg R. Oldham, "Motivation Through the Design of Work: Test of a Theory," *Organizational Behavior and Human Performance* 16, no. 2 (August 1976): 250–279.

20. Hackman and Oldham, "Motivation Through the Design of Work," 250–279.
21. Ibid., 256.
22. Ibid., 257–258.
23. Dean Tjosvold, "Participation: A Close Look at Its Dynamics," *Journal of Management* 13, no. 4 (Winter 1987): 739–740. See also Carlla S. Smith and Michael T. Brannick, "A Role and Expectancy Model of Participative Decision-making: A Replication and Theoretical Extension," *Journal of Organizational Behavior* 11, no. 2 (March 1990): 91–104.
24. *1987 American Society for Personnel Administration and Commerce Clearing House Survey* (June 26, 1987): 4.
25. Ibid., 8.
26. Ibid., 9.

CHAPTER 5

Human Resources Planning and Recruitment

After reading this chapter you will be able to:

1. *Discuss the relationship between strategic organizational planning and human resources planning (HRP).*
2. *List the three key elements of the HRP model.*
3. *Explain the advantages and disadvantages of staffing job vacancies with personnel from within the organization.*
4. *Identify the principal external recruitment sources and explain when these sources are likely to be utilized.*
5. *Describe the barriers to job opportunities encountered by members of protected classes and the means by which these barriers are being overcome.*
6. *Define the key terms in the chapter.*

TERMS TO IDENTIFY

human resources planning (HRP) *(140)*

employment forecasting *(144)*

quantitative, or top-down, approach to forecasting *(144)*

trend analysis *(144)*

indexation *(145)*

qualitative, or bottom-up, approach to forecasting *(145)*

expert forecasts *(145)*

staffing tables *(145)*

skills inventories *(145)*

management inventories *(146)*

job posting and bidding *(149)*

labor market *(151)*

tight labor market *(152)*

realistic job preview (RJP) *(160)*

In earlier chapters we stressed that the structure of an organization and the design of the jobs within it affect the organization's ability to reach its objectives. These objectives, however, can be achieved only through the efforts of people. It is essential, therefore, that jobs within the organization be staffed with personnel who are qualified to perform them. Meeting these staffing needs requires effective planning for human resources.

Once the HR planning function is fulfilled, then the staffing of the organization must be completed through the recruitment process. Employment recruiting has acquired a new importance for managers since both manufacturing and service organizations are finding it increasingly difficult to find qualified applicants to fill job openings. According to a 1989 Society for Human Resource Management (SHRM) special report on the U.S. labor shortage, employers are entering a period in which jobs ranging from the unskilled to the professional and technical will be harder to staff;[1] and this condition is not likely to abate in the near future. No longer can managers rely solely upon unsolicited applications to fill openings. Changing employment conditions mandate that HR managers consider a variety of recruitment alternatives to attract the right employees to the organization. The process of planning for HR needs, sources of applicants, and methods of attracting applicants will be discussed in this chapter.

HUMAN RESOURCES PLANNING

Human resources planning (HRP) is the process of anticipating and making provision for the movement of people into, within, and out of an organization. Its purpose is to use these resources as effectively as possible and to have available the required number of people with the qualifications to fill positions *where* and *when* openings occur.

Importance of Human Resources Planning

Consider these facts:

- The U.S. labor force will grow by 21 million, or 18 percent, by the year 2000.
- Between 80 and 90 percent of the new labor force entrants will be minorities and women.
- Immigrants will account for more than 23 percent of the change in the labor force composition over the 1986–2000 period.
- The average age of the work force will be 39 by the year 2000.
- The five occupations expected to experience faster-than-average growth are technicians, service workers, professional workers, sales workers, and executive and managerial employees. These occupations require the highest education and skill levels.
- 2.5 million functionally illiterate Americans enter the work force yearly.[2]

These dramatic shifts in the composition of the labor force will require HR managers to become more involved in HRP. Each of these changes will affect employee recruitment while requiring additional HRP in the areas of employee selection, training, compensation, and motivation. Although planning has always been an essential process of management, increased emphasis on HRP provides the foundation for establishing an effective HRM program and for coordinating the HRM functions being performed within it. As one HR vice-president noted, "The scope and mission of the HR function will be under pressure to change and be responsive to market conditions, international competitive pressures, and business readjustments."[3] HRP becomes especially critical when organizations consider mergers, the relocation of plants, or the closing of operating facilities.

An organization may incur several intangible costs as a result of inadequate HRP or the lack of HRP. For example, inadequate HRP can cause vacancies to remain unstaffed. The resulting loss in efficiency can be costly, particularly when lead time is required to train replacements. Situations also may occur in which employees are laid off in one department while applicants are hired for similar jobs in another department. This may cause overhiring and result in the need to lay off those employees who were recently hired. Finally, lack of HRP makes it difficult for employees to make effective plans for career or personal development. As a result, some of the more competent and ambitious ones may seek other employment where they feel they will have better career opportunities.

HRP AND STRATEGIC PLANNING As organizations plan for their future, HR managers must be concerned with meshing HRP with strategic business planning.[4] Strategic planning is the process of setting major organization objectives and developing comprehensive plans to achieve these objectives.[5] It involves deciding on the primary direction of the organization including its structure, its process, and the interrelationship of its human resources. Part of the strategic planning process involves determining if people are available, internally or externally, to implement the strategic organization plan.

HRP and strategic planning become effective when there is a reciprocal and interdependent relationship between the two functions. In this relationship, top management and strategic planners recognize that strategic planning decisions affect—and are affected by—HR functions.[6] The HR department and its activities are viewed as credible and important along with other management functions such as production, marketing, service, and finance. Likewise, HR managers recognize the contribution they can make to organizational growth and development and are proactive in developing HR programs and policies that foster the organization's strategic mission.[7] This positive linkage occurs when the HR manager becomes a member of the organization's management steering committee or strategic planning group. Once this interactive and dynamic structure exists, HR managers are recognized as contributing strategic planners alongside other top managers.[8]

IBM has been a forerunner in the integration of HRP and strategic planning. At IBM, this process takes place at three levels—plant, division, and corporate. Each year the corporation's HR department develops a five-year HR strategic plan and a two-year tactical plan based on tentative business goals. These goals are formulated only after IBM conducts an internal and external analysis of the company's strengths and weaknesses. Major business decisions are not approved until the vice-president of HR concurs with the business plan.[9] Highlights in HRM 1 illustrates how proactive HRP and strategic planning influence HR activities, thereby contributing to organizational effectiveness.

HRP AND ENVIRONMENTAL SCANNING Environmental scanning is the systematic, regular monitoring of the major external forces influencing the organization.[10] In theory, HRP requires an integration of the environment with all of the HRM functions. As the IBM example illustrates, the HRP process will be integrated with the strategic planning process through environmental scanning. This procedure is necessary because any strategies developed must be consistent with those environmental trends and contemporary issues that may have an impact on the organization. HRP, in turn, must anticipate the possible impact of these strategies upon HRM.

Organizations can select any number of environmental factors to scan; however, the following five are monitored most frequently:

1. Economic factors (including general and regional conditions and competition trends)
2. Technological changes (including robotics and office automation)
3. Political/legislative issues (including laws and administrative rulings)
4. Social concerns (including child care and educational priorities)

HIGHLIGHTS IN HRM

1 BENEFITS OF INTEGRATING HRP AND STRATEGIC PLANNING

1. Facilitates the movement of employees into, through, and out of the organization, thereby ensuring proper staffing levels.
2. Anticipates the training needs of future and present employees.
3. Enables organization to know the skills, abilities, and knowledge levels of current employees, by maintaining employee and manager skills inventories.
4. Directs employee efforts to meaningful activities contributing to increased productivity, by demanding that employee appraisal systems coincide with strategic goals.
5. Establishes appropriate compensation levels (wages and benefits) to attract qualified employees. This helps control costs by preventing the overpaying—or underpaying—of employees.
6. Allows the HR department to be proactive in meeting organizational needs, by requiring the continual monitoring of environmental factors affecting the organization and its HR needs.
7. Puts emphasis on management development and the training of managers and executives needed in future years.

Senior citizens are becoming a new recruiting source to fill minimum wage positions.

5. Demographic trends (including age, composition, and literacy of the work force)

The labor force trends listed earlier, for example, illustrate the importance of monitoring demographic changes in the population as a part of HRP. Such changes can affect the composition and performance of an organization's work force. These changes are important because EEO/AA plans must take into account the demographic composition of the population in the area where the organization is located. Furthermore, with a "maturing" American work force, HRP must consider the many implications of this demographic fact on recruitment and replacement policies. McDonald's and other fast-food chains, for example, have made a stronger effort to hire more older workers to offset shortages of younger workers.

Elements for Effective HRP

HR managers follow a systematic process, or model, when undertaking HRP, as shown in Figure 5–1. The three key elements of the process are making forecasts, performing supply analysis, and balancing supply and demand considerations. Careful attention to each factor will help either top managers or supervisors to meet their staffing requirements.

FIGURE 5–1 HUMAN RESOURCES PLANNING MODEL

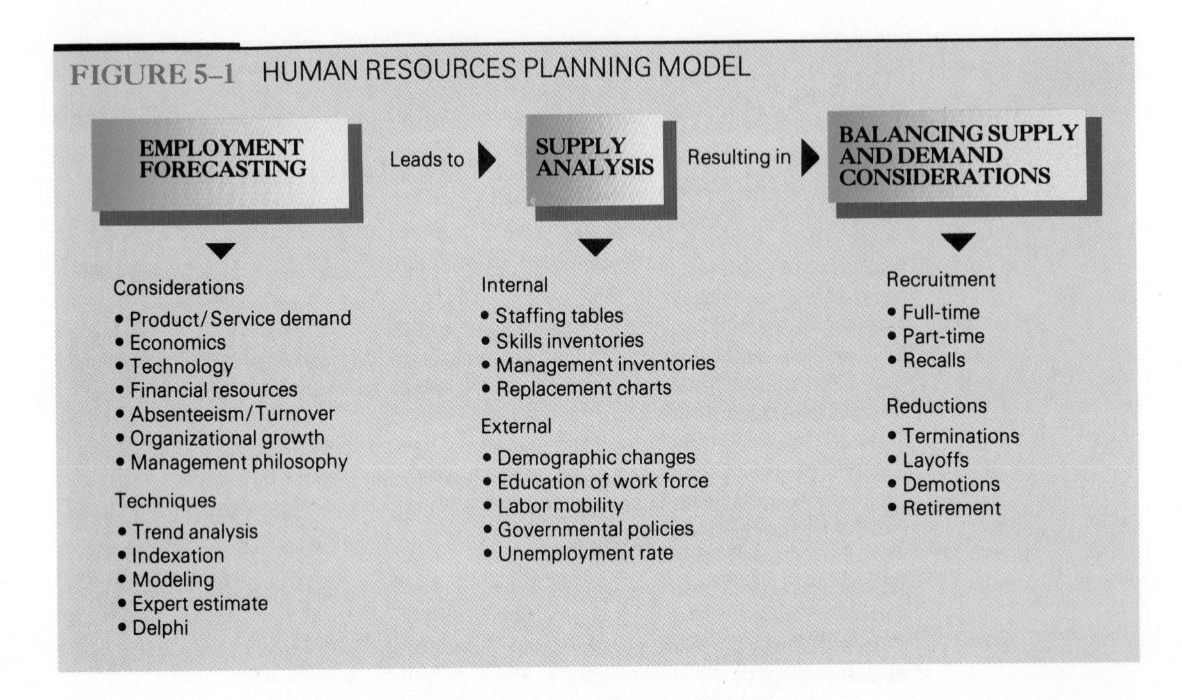

FORECASTING **Employment forecasting,** a key component of HRP, is the HR activity of estimating in advance the *number* and *type* of people needed to meet organizational objectives. When concentrating on resource needs, forecasting is primarily quantitative in nature and in large organizations is accomplished by highly trained specialists. Quantitative approaches to forecasting can employ sophisticated analytical models, although forecasting may be as informal as having one person who knows the organization anticipate future HR requirements. Organizational demands will ultimately determine which technique to use. Regardless of the method, however, forecasting should not be neglected even in relatively small organizations.

Forecasting is frequently more an art than a science, providing inexact approximations rather than absolute results. The ever-changing environment in which an organization operates contributes to this problem. For example, estimating changes in product or service demand is a basic forecasting concern, as is anticipating changes in national or regional economics. A hospital anticipating internal changes in technology, organization, or administration must consider these environmental factors in its forecasts of staffing needs. Also, the forecasted staffing needs must be in line with the organization's financial resources.

There are two approaches to HR forecasting: quantitative and qualitative. The **quantitative,** or **top-down, approach to forecasting** involves the use of statistical or mathematical techniques; it is the approach used by theoreticians and professional planners. One example is **trend analysis,** which forecasts employment requirements based on past HR growth. If, for example, an average of ten new employees were hired every month for each of the past ten years, then 120 employees would be required for the forthcoming year. **Indexation,** or ratio analysis, is a method of forecasting that determines employment growth based on some organizational index.[11] The ratio of employees to sales is a common indexing technique, since there is a strong correlation between sales and the number of employees the firm needs. An organization with sales of $50 million may operate efficiently with 2,500 employees; but if its sales increase to $60 million, 3,000 employees may be needed.

Other, more sophisticated statistical planning methods include modeling or multiple-predictive techniques. Whereas trend analysis relies on a single factor (e.g., sales) to predict employment needs, the more advanced methods combine several factors, such as interest rates, gross national product, disposable income, and sales, to predict employment levels. Because of the high costs of developing these forecasting methods, they are used only by large organizations like Ford Motor Company or the U.S. government.

The **qualitative,** or **bottom-up, approach to forecasting** is less statistical, attempting to reconcile the interests, abilities, and aspirations of individual employees with the current and future staffing needs of an organization. HR practitioners experienced in training, counseling, and management development techniques use this approach. Qualitative forecasting can be used to evaluate employee performance and promotability, as well as management and career development.

In both large and small organizations, HR planners may rely on expert forecasts to anticipate staffing requirements. **Expert forecasts** are the opinions (judgments) of supervisors, department managers, or others knowledgeable about the organization's future employment needs.

One variation of the expert forecasting method, the Delphi technique, attempts to decrease the subjectivity of forecasts by soliciting and summarizing the judgments of a preselected group of individuals.[12] The final forecast thus represents a composite group judgment. The Delphi technique requires a great deal of coordination and cooperation in order to ensure satisfactory forecasts. This method works best in organizations where dynamic technological changes affect staffing levels.

Ideally, HRP should include the use of both quantitative and qualitative approaches. In combination, the two approaches serve to complement each other, providing a more complete forecast by bringing together the contributions of both the theoreticians and the practitioners.

SUPPLY ANALYSIS Once an organization has forecast its future requirements for employees, it must then determine if there are sufficient numbers and types of employees available to staff anticipated openings. Supply analysis will encompass two sources—internal and external. An internal supply analysis may begin with the preparation of staffing tables. **Staffing tables** are a pictorial representation of all organizational jobs along with the numbers of employees currently occupying those jobs and future (monthly or yearly) employment requirements. In conjunction with staffing tables, **skills inventories** are prepared on hourly employees that list each individual's education, past work experience, vocational interests, specific abilities and skills, compensation history, and job tenure. Well-prepared and up-to-date skills inventories allow an organization to quickly match forthcoming job openings with employee backgrounds. Organizations like Zenith Data Systems and the State of Illinois use computers and special programs to perform this task. When data are gathered on management employees, these inventories are called **management inventories.**

Both skills and management inventories can be used to develop employee replacement charts, which list current jobholders and identify possible replacements should openings occur. Figure 5–2 shows an example of how an organization might develop a replacement chart for the executives in one of its divisions. Note that this chart provides information on the current job performance and promotability of possible replacements. Replacement charts are very useful planning tools for locating hard-to-find employees or key management personnel.

When it lacks an internal supply of employees for promotions, or when it is staffing entry-level positions, an organization must consider the external supply of labor. Many factors influence labor supply, including demographic changes in the population, national and regional economics, education level of the work force, demand for specific employee skills, population mobility, and governmental policies. National and regional unemployment rates are often considered a general barometer of labor supply.

Fortunately, labor market analysis is aided by various published documents. Unemployment rates, labor force projection figures, and population characteristics are reported by the U.S. Department of Labor.[13] Chambers of commerce and individual state development and planning agencies also may assist with labor market analysis.[14] The *Monthly Labor Review,* published by the U.S. Department of Labor, frequently contains articles on jobholder characteristics and predicted changes in the work force.[15]

BALANCING SUPPLY AND DEMAND CONSIDERATIONS HRP should strive for a proper balance not only between forecasting techniques and their application, but also between the emphasis placed on *demand considerations* and that placed on *supply considerations*. Demand considerations are based on the forecast of trends in business activity. Supply considerations involve the determination of where and how candidates with the required qualifications are to be found to fill vacancies. Because of the difficulty in locating applicants for the increasing number of jobs that require advanced training, this phase of planning is receiving more attention. Greater planning effort is also needed in recruiting members of protected classes for managerial jobs and technical jobs that require advanced levels of education.

When organizations experience a demand for workers, several staffing possibilities exist. Hiring full-time employees, having employees work overtime, recalling those laid off, and using temporary employees are options. The Internal Revenue Service relies heavily on temporary employees between January and April when tax returns are received for processing. However, when HRP shows a surplus of jobholders, organizations may use terminations, work sharing, layoffs, or demotions or rely on attrition (a gradual reduction of employees through resignations, retirements, or

FIGURE 5–2 AN EXECUTIVE REPLACEMENT CHART

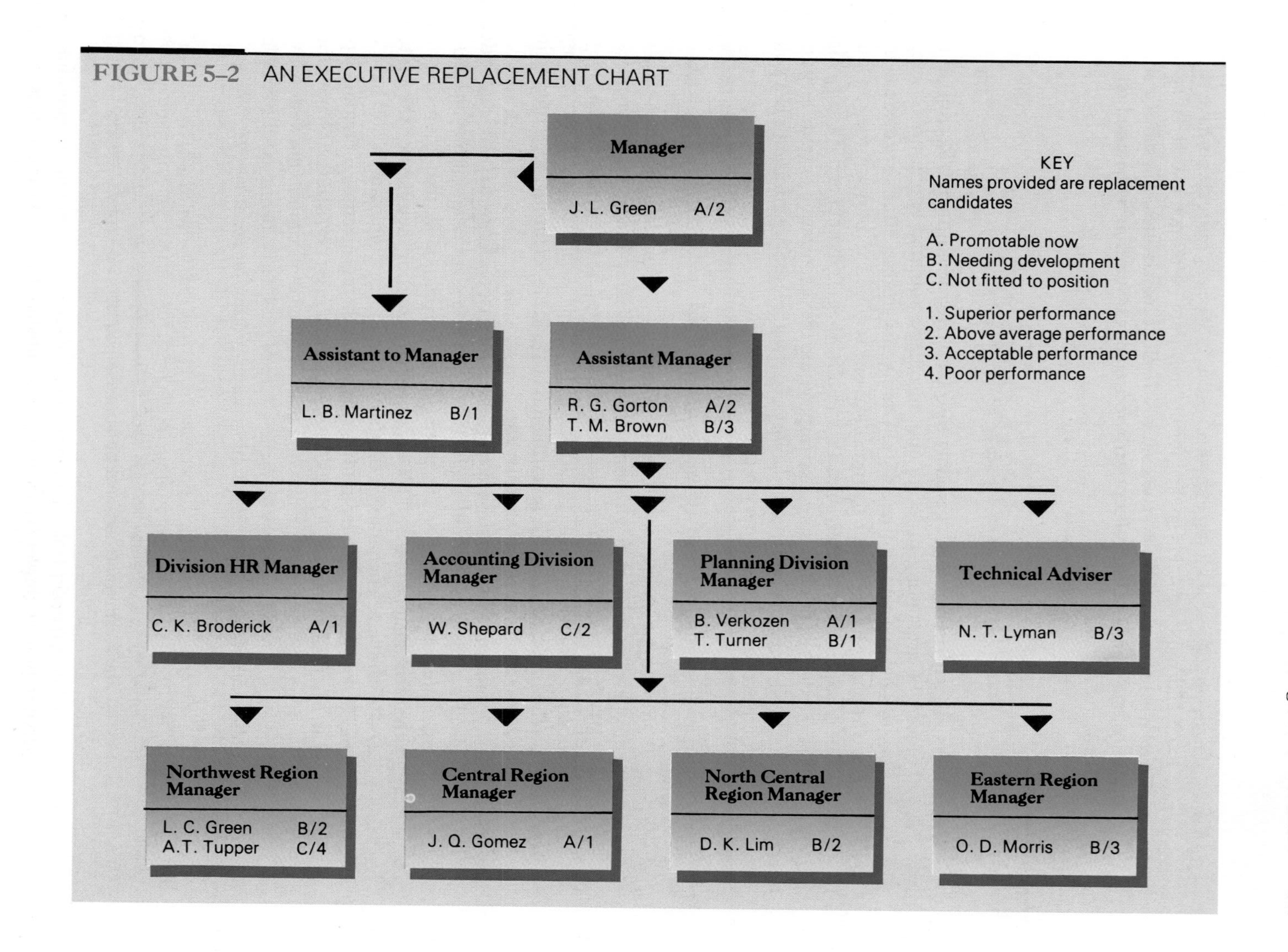

deaths) to achieve work force balance. Since 1980, early retirements have become a more and more common means for organizations to reduce excess labor supply. Organizations as diverse as state colleges, health care facilities, and travel companies encourage employees to accept early retirement by offering sweetened retirement benefits.

RECRUITING WITHIN THE ORGANIZATION

Effective HRP leads naturally into employee recruitment. Recruiting is the process of attempting to locate and encourage potential applicants to apply for existing or anticipated job openings. During this process, efforts are made to inform the applicants fully about the qualifications required to perform the job and the career opportunities the organization can offer them. Whether or not a particular job vacancy will be filled by someone from within the organization or from outside will, of course, depend upon the availability of personnel, the organization's HR policies, and the requirements of the job to be staffed.

Advantages of Recruiting from Within

Most organizations try to follow a policy of filling job vacancies above the entry-level position through promotions and transfers. In one study, organizations filled 85 percent of their management openings and 58 percent of their white-collar openings through internal recruitment.[16] By filling vacancies in this way, an organization can capitalize on the investment it has made in recruiting, selecting, training, and developing its current employees.

Promotion serves to reward employees for past performance and is intended to encourage them to continue their efforts.[17] It also gives other employees reason to anticipate that similar efforts by them will lead to promotion, thus improving morale within the organization.[18] This is particularly true for members of the protected classes who have encountered difficulties in finding employment and have often faced even greater difficulty in advancing within an organization. A promotion policy is an essential part of the EEO/AA programs that most organizations have adopted.

If an organization's promotion policy is to have maximum motivational value, however, employees must be made aware of it. The following is an example of a policy statement that an organization might prepare on the subject:

> "Promotion from within" is generally recognized as a foundation of good employment practice, and it is the policy of our museum to promote from within whenever possible when filling a vacancy. The job vacancy will be posted for five calendar days to give all qualified full- and part-time personnel an equal opportunity to apply.

While a transfer lacks the motivational value of a promotion, it sometimes can serve to protect employees from layoff or broaden their job experiences. Furthermore, the transferred employee's familiarity with the organization and its operations can eliminate the orientation and training costs that recruitment from the outside would entail. Most important, management has knowledge of the transferee's performance record. This knowledge is likely to be a more accurate predictor of the candidate's success than the data gained about outside applicants through the selection process.

Methods of Locating Qualified Job Candidates

The effective use of internal sources requires a system for locating qualified job candidates and for enabling those who consider themselves qualified to apply for the opening. Qualified job candidates within the organization can be located by computerized record systems, by job posting and bidding, and by recall of those who have been laid off.

COMPUTERIZED RECORD SYSTEMS Computers have made possible the creation of data banks that contain the complete records and qualifications of each employee within an organization. Similar to the skills inventories mentioned earlier, these computerized records allow an organization to screen its entire work force in a matter of minutes to locate suitable candidates to fill an internal opening. These data can also be used to predict the career paths of employees and to anticipate when and where promotion opportunities may arise. Since the value of the data depends on how current the data are, the record system must include provisions for recording changes in employee qualifications and job placements as they occur.

JOB POSTING AND BIDDING Organizations may communicate information about job openings through a process referred to as **job posting and bidding.** This process consists largely of posting vacancy notices on bulletin boards, but may include use of designated posting centers, employee publications, special "announcement handouts," direct mail, and public-address messages. Intel Corporation has computerized its job posting and bidding program by maintaining voluntary lists of employees looking for upgraded positions. As a position becomes available, the list of employees seeking that position is retrieved from the computer and their records are reviewed to select the best-qualified candidate.

The system of job posting and bidding can provide many benefits to an organization. However, these benefits may not be realized unless employees believe the system is being administered fairly.[19] Therefore, to reap the full advantages of job posting, organizations should follow the administrative guidelines for job posting and bidding programs presented in Highlights in HRM 2.

Furthermore, job bidding is more effective when it is part of a career development program in which employees are made aware of opportunities available to them within the organization. For example, HR departments may provide new employees with literature on job progression that describes the lines of job advancement,

HIGHLIGHTS IN HRM

2 ELEMENTS OF AN EFFECTIVE JOB POSTING AND BIDDING PROCEDURE

1. Establish and widely distribute applicant eligibility requirements for employees wishing to use the bidding procedure.
2. Develop job notices that are complete, including the job's major duties and responsibilities and any special (unusual) tasks that must be performed.
3. List the minimum abilities, skills, experience, education, or special knowledge needed by applicants.
4. Communicate the availability of jobs to all affected employees. Use several notice methods if possible.
5. Establish posting periods and state any filing constraints if appropriate.
6. Develop an applicant-review procedure and feedback system that employees will accept.
7. Establish an appeals procedure for those employees wishing to challenge selection decisions.

training requirements for each job, and skills and abilities needed as they move up the job-progression ladder.

RECALL FROM LAYOFF When economic conditions necessitate the "down-sizing" of an organization, some employees are laid off. Usually, when the economic outlook brightens again and job openings occur, employees who were laid off while in good standing are recalled to their jobs.

In the case of unionized organizations, the criteria for determining an employee's eligibility for layoff are typically set forth in the union agreement. As a rule, seniority on the job receives significant weight in determining which employees are laid off first. Similar provisions in the union agreement provide for the right of employees to be recalled for jobs they are still qualified to perform. Organizational policy, as well as provisions in the labor agreement, should therefore establish and define clearly the employment rights of each individual and the basis upon which layoff selections will be made and reemployment effected. The rights of employees during layoffs, the conditions concerning their eligibility for recall, and their obligations in accepting recall should also be clarified. It is common for labor agreements to preserve the reemployment rights of employees laid off for periods of up to two years, providing that they do not refuse to return to work if recalled sooner.

The order of employee layoffs is usually based on seniority and/or ability. In some organizations, especially those with labor agreements, seniority may be the primary consideration. In other organizations, such factors as ability and fitness may take precedence over seniority in determining layoffs.

It has become customary, however, for employers to give some degree of recognition to seniority even among employees who are not unionized. Unions generally advocate recognition of seniority because they feel that their members should be entitled to certain rights proportionate to the years they have invested in their jobs. Nevertheless, whenever seniority provides a basis for determining or even influencing HR decisions, the discretion of management is reduced accordingly. One of the major disadvantages of overemphasizing seniority is that the less competent employees receive the same rewards and security as the more competent ones. Also, the practice of using seniority as the basis for deciding which workers to lay off may well have a disparate impact on women and minority workers, who often have less seniority than other groups.

Limitations of Recruiting from Within

Sometimes certain jobs at the middle and upper levels that require specialized training and experience cannot be filled from within the organization and must be filled from the outside. This is especially common in small organizations. Also, for certain openings it may be necessary to hire individuals from the outside who have gained from another employer the knowledge and expertise required for these jobs.

Even though HR policy encourages job openings to be filled from within the organization, potential candidates from the outside should occasionally be considered in order to prevent the inbreeding of ideas and attitudes. Applicants hired from the outside, particularly for certain management positions, can be a source of new ideas and may bring with them the latest knowledge acquired from their previous employers. Indeed, excessive reliance upon internal sources can create the risk of "employee cloning." Furthermore, it is not uncommon for firms in competitive fields such as high technology to attempt to gain secrets from competitors by hiring away their employees.

RECRUITING OUTSIDE THE ORGANIZATION

Unless there is to be a reduction in the work force, a replacement from outside must eventually be found to fill a job left vacant when the jobholder moved to a new slot in the organization. Thus, when the president of the organization retires, a chain reaction of promotions may subsequently occur. This creates other managerial openings throughout the organization. The question to be resolved, therefore, is not whether to bring people into the organization, but rather at which level they are to be brought in.

The Labor Market

The **labor market,** or the area from which applicants are to be recruited, will vary with the type of job to be filled and the amount of compensation to be paid for the job. Recruitment for executive or technical jobs requiring a high degree of knowledge and skill may be national or even international in scope. Colleges and universities like Cornell, Scottsdale Community College, and the University of Oregon conduct national employment searches to fill top administrative positions. Recruitment for jobs that require relatively little skill, however, may encompass a relatively small geographic area. The unwillingness of people to relocate may cause them to turn down offers of employment, thereby eliminating them from employment consideration beyond the local labor market. However, by offering an attractive level of compensation and by helping to defray moving costs, employers may induce some applicants to move.

The ease with which employees can commute to work will also influence the boundaries of the labor market. Insufficient public transportation or extreme traffic congestion on the streets and freeways can limit the distance employees are willing to travel to work, particularly to jobs of low pay. Also, population migration from the cities to the suburbs has had its effect on labor markets. If suitable employment can be obtained near where they live or they can work at home (see Chapter 2), many suburbanites are less likely to accept or remain in jobs in the central city.

One organization, Kentucky Fried Chicken (KFC), has adopted several nontraditional recruiting strategies to attract needed managerial and hourly employees. Faced with high turnover and labor shortages in the central Florida labor market, KFC recruited from outside established geographical boundaries. Areas with high unemployment were chosen as recruitment locations and jobs were offered in other areas. KFC also recruited from inner-city areas for hourly positions in its suburban stores. Anticipating the potential transportation problems of inner-city employees, it established a van service and provided public-transportation coupons to recruits.[20]

Outside Sources of Recruitment

The outside sources from which employers recruit will vary with the type of job to be filled. A computer programmer, for example, is not likely to be recruited from the same source as a machine operator. Trade schools can provide applicants for entry-level positions, though these recruitment sources are not as useful when skilled employees are needed.[21]

The condition of the labor market may also help to determine which recruiting sources an organization will use. During periods of high unemployment, organizations may be able to maintain an adequate supply of qualified applicants from unsolicited résumés alone. A **tight labor market,** one with low unemployment, may force the employer to advertise heavily and/or seek assistance from local employment agencies. How successful an organization has been in reaching its affirmative action goals may be still another factor in determining the sources from which to recruit. Typically, an employer at any given time will find it necessary to utilize several recruitment sources.

Several studies have suggested that an employee's recruitment source can affect that employee's subsequent tenure and job performance with an organization.[22] In general, applicants who find employment as "walk-ins" or through referral by a current employee tend to remain with the organization longer and have higher-quality performance than those employees recruited through the formal recruitment sources of advertisements and employment agencies. Informal recruiting sources may also yield higher selection rates than formal sources. In one study, an examination of recruitment sources showed that women and blacks use formal recruiting sources more frequently than men, nonminorities, and Hispanics.[23] Employers are cautioned, however, that relying only on one or two recruitment sources to secure job applicants could have an adverse effect on protected classes.

ADVERTISEMENTS One of the most common methods of attracting applicants is through advertisements. While newspapers and trade journals are the media used most often, radio, television, billboards, posters, and even sound trucks have also been utilized. Advertising has the advantage of reaching a large audience of possible applicants. Some degree of selectivity can be achieved by using newspapers and journals directed toward a particular group of readers. Professional journals, trade journals, and publications of unions and various fraternal or nonprofit organizations fall into this category.

As Highlights in HRM 3 illustrates, the preparation of recruiting advertisements not only is time-consuming, but also requires creativity in developing design and message content. Well-written advertisements highlight the major assets of the

"Your references reveal you to be a nice sort of person. The hitch is that in this company, it's dog eat dog."

From *The Wall Street Journal*—Permission, Cartoon Features Syndicate

The IRS uses television commercials to recruit seasonal employees.

position while showing the responsiveness of the organization to the job and career needs of the applicants.

Also, there appears to be a correlation between the accuracy and completeness of information provided in advertisements and the recruitment success of the organization. Among the information often included in advertisements is that the recruiting organization is an *equal opportunity employer.*

Advertising can sometimes place a severe burden on an organization's employment office. Even though the specifications for the openings are described thoroughly in the advertisement, many applicants who know they do not meet the job requirements may still be attracted. They may apply in hopes that the employer will not be able to find applicants who meet the specifications.

PUBLIC EMPLOYMENT AGENCIES Each of the 50 states maintains an employment agency that is responsible for administering its unemployment insurance program. Many of the state agencies bear such titles as Department of Employment or Department of Human Resources. They are subject to certain regulations and controls administered by the U.S. Employment Services (USES).

State agencies maintain local public employment offices in most communities of any size. Individuals who become unemployed must register at one of these offices and be available for "suitable employment" in order to receive their weekly unemployment checks. Consequently, public employment agencies are able to refer to employers with job openings those applicants with the required skills who are available for employment.

USES has developed a nationwide computerized job bank that lists job openings and to which state employment offices are connected. The computerized job bank helps facilitate the movement of job applicants to different geographic areas. Most of these offices now have a local *job bank book* that is published as a daily computer

HIGHLIGHTS IN HRM

3 EIGHT POINTS FOR DEVELOPING EFFECTIVE NEWSPAPER ADVERTISEMENTS

1. Determine the readership and geographic area served by the newspaper. Consider placing ads in sections of the paper such as the sports, entertainment, or television section to reach people who are currently employed and who may not be reading the classified section.
2. Use small community newspapers or weekly classified publications that only reach a specific market segment or geographical area.
3. Develop ads that are creative and distinctive. Employ eye-catching images and borders. Use language that is clear and creates interest in the position.
4. Consult your organization's marketing or advertising department for suggestions for copy and graphics that will attract readers' attention.
5. Use different copy formats to reach different types of applicants.
6. To reach impulse applicants, consider using weekend telephone numbers to attract applicants currently employed or those without prepared résumés.
7. Attach "clip-out" coupons to the ad that applicants can send in to the organization to obtain additional information about the advertised position. The convenience of this feature might attract potential applicants who have given only slight consideration to a job change.
8. Make sure that job specifications clearly define applicant skill, ability, and educational requirements.

SOURCE: Adapted from Catherine D. Fyock, "New Ways to Say 'Help Wanted,' " *Personnel Administrator* 33, no. 9 (September 1988): 100.

printout. Employer openings are listed along with other pertinent information, such as number of openings, pay rates, and job specifications. The local job bank makes it possible for employment interviewers in an agency to have a list of all job openings in the geographic area for which applicants assigned to them might qualify. Furthermore, applicants looking for a specific job can review the computer printout and apply directly to the organization having the opening.

In addition to matching unemployed applicants with job openings, public employment agencies may assist employers with employment testing, job analysis, evaluation programs, and community wage surveys.

PRIVATE EMPLOYMENT AGENCIES Charging a fee enables private employment agencies to tailor their services to the specific needs of their clients. It is common for agencies to specialize in serving a specific occupational area or professional field. For example, Remedy Perm Personnel Services places clerical, data processing, and accounting personnel with requesting organizations. Depending upon who is receiving the most service, the fee may be paid by either the employer or the job seeker or both. It is not uncommon for private employment agencies to charge an employer a 25–30 percent fee, based on the position's annual salary, if they hire an applicant found by the agency.

Private employment agencies differ in the services they offer, their professionalism, and the caliber of their counselors. If counselors are paid on a commission basis, their desire to do a professional job may be offset by their desire to earn a commission. Thus, they may encourage job seekers to accept jobs for which they are not suited. As one management consultant has noted, "Take the time to find a recruiter who is knowledgeable, experienced, and professional. Discuss openly your philosophies and practices with regard to recruiting strategies, including advertising, in-house recruiting, screening procedures, and costs for these efforts. Find a recruiter who is flexible and who will consider your needs and wants."[24]

EXECUTIVE SEARCH FIRMS In contrast to public and private employment agencies, which help job seekers find the right job, executive search firms (often called *headhunters*) help employers find the right person for a job. They seek out candidates with qualifications that match the requirements of the positions their client firm is seeking to fill. Executive search firms do not advertise in the media for job candidates, nor do they accept a fee from the individual being placed.

The fees charged by search firms may range from 30 to 40 percent of the annual salary for the position to be filled. For the recruitment of senior executives, this fee is paid by the client firm whether or not the recruiting effort results in a hire. It is for this practice that search firms receive the greatest criticism.

Nevertheless, according to one survey, one out of four new chief executive officers (CEOs) is still selected from outside candidates, and a large number of new CEOs were placed in those positions through the services of an executive search firm.[25] Since high-caliber executives are in short supply, a significant number of the nation's largest corporations, including Texaco, Pillsbury, MONY Financial Services, and the Rockefeller Foundation, use search firms to fill their top positions.

EDUCATIONAL INSTITUTIONS Educational institutions typically are a source of young applicants with formal training but with relatively little full-time work experience. High schools are usually a source of employees for clerical and blue-collar jobs. Community colleges, with their various types of specialized training, can provide candidates for technical jobs. These institutions can also be a source of applicants for a variety of white-collar jobs, including those in the sales and retail fields. Some management-trainee jobs are also staffed from this source.

For technical and managerial positions, colleges and universities are generally the primary source. However, the suitability of college graduates for open positions often depends on their major field of study. Organizations seeking applicants in the technical and professional areas, for example, are currently faced with a shortage of qualified candidates. To attract graduates in areas of low supply, HR managers are

Job fairs held at colleges attract many applicants looking for entry-level positions.

employing innovative recruitment techniques such as low-interest loans, internships, work-study programs, and scholarships. Writing on the subject of educational assistance programs, one professional journal noted that "the object is to ensure the company meets its personnel needs by targeting potential employees at a younger age, and nurturing their educational—and professional—development through college and even high school."[26]

Some employers fail to take full advantage of college and university resources because of a poor recruitment program. Consequently, their recruitment efforts fail to attract many potentially good applicants. Another common weakness is the failure to maintain a planned and continuing effort on a long-term basis. Furthermore, some recruiters sent to college campuses are not sufficiently trained or prepared to talk to interested candidates about career opportunities or the requirements of specific openings. Attempts to visit too many campuses instead of concentrating on selected institutions and the inability to use the campus placement office effectively are other recruiting weaknesses. Mismanagement of applicant visits to the plant or company headquarters and the failure to follow up on individual prospects or to obtain hiring commitments from higher management are among other mistakes that have caused employers to lose well-qualified prospects.

EMPLOYEE REFERRALS The recruitment efforts of an organization can be aided by employee referrals, or recommendations made by current employees. HR managers have found that the quality of employee-referred applicants is normally quite high, since employees are generally hesitant to recommend individuals who might not perform well. The effectiveness of this recruitment effort can be increased by paying commissions to employees when they make a successful "recruitment sale." Other recruitment incentives used by organizations include complimentary dinners, discounts on merchandise, all-expense-paid trips, and free insurance.[27]

Negative factors associated with employee referrals include the possibility of "inbreeding" and the violation of EEO regulations. Since employees and their referrals tend to have similar backgrounds, employers who rely heavily on employee referrals to fill job openings may intentionally or unintentionally screen out, and thereby discriminate against, protected classes. Furthermore, organizations may choose not to employ relatives of current employees. The practice of hiring relatives, referred to as nepotism, can invite charges of favoritism, especially in appointments to desirable positions.

UNSOLICITED APPLICATIONS AND RÉSUMÉS Many employers receive unsolicited applications and résumés from individuals who may or may not be good prospects for employment.[28] Even though the percentage of acceptable applicants from this source may not be high, it is a source that cannot be ignored. In fact, it is often believed that individuals who on their own initiative contact the employer will be better employees than those recruited through college placement services or newspaper advertisements.

Good public relations dictates that any person contacting an organization for a job be treated with courtesy and respect. If there is no possibility of employment in the organization at present or in the future, the applicant should be tactfully and frankly informed of this fact. Telling applicants, "Fill out an application, and we will keep it on file," when there is no hope for their employment is not fair to the applicant.

PROFESSIONAL ORGANIZATIONS Many professional organizations and societies offer a placement service to members as one of their benefits. Listings of members seeking employment may be advertised in their journals or publicized at their national meetings. A placement center is usually established at national meetings for the mutual benefit of employers and job seekers.

LABOR UNIONS Labor unions can be a principal source of applicants for blue-collar and some professional jobs. Some unions, such as those in the maritime, printing, and construction industries, maintain hiring halls that can provide a supply of applicants, particularly for short-term needs. Employers wishing to use this recruitment source should contact the local union under consideration for employer eligibility requirements and applicant availability.

TEMPORARY HELP AGENCIES The temporary services industry is one of the fastest-growing recruitment sources. An estimated nine out of ten U.S. companies use temporary employees, and the U.S. Department of Commerce predicts that of all American industries, temporary services will be one of the strongest employers through the 1990s.[29] Organizations such as Citibank, General Mills, and Avis use "temps" for occasional short-term assignments. Small business managers use temporary help when they cannot justify hiring a full-time employee. One study showed that organizations use temporary employees mostly for (1) vacation fill-ins, (2) peak work periods, and (3) pregnancy-leave or sick-leave replacements.[30] Temporary employees, however, are being used more and more to fill positions once staffed by permanent employees. This practice is growing because temporaries can be laid off quickly, and with less cost, when work lessens. The use of temporaries thus becomes a viable way to maintain proper staffing levels. Also, the employment costs of temporaries are often lower than those of permanent employees because temps are not provided with benefits and can be dismissed without the need to file unemployment insurance claims. Used predominantly in office clerical positions, temporaries are becoming more and more common in legal work, engineering, computer programming, and other jobs requiring advanced professional training.

EMPLOYEE LEASING Contract Staffing of America, Staff Services, Inc., and Action Staffing are three of a growing number of employee leasing firms. Employee leasing, also called contract staffing or staff leasing, became popular after 1982 with passage of the Tax Equity and Fiscal Responsibility Act.[31] Unlike temporary help agencies, which supply workers only for limited periods, employee leasing companies place their employees with subscribers on a permanent basis.

In its most common form, employee leasing is a process whereby an employer terminates a number of employees who are then hired by a third party—the employee leasing company—which then leases the employees back to the original organization. However, leasing companies hire workers on a continual basis and then lease them to requesting organizations. The leasing company performs all the HR duties of an employer—hiring, payroll, performance appraisal, benefits administration, and other day-to-day HR activities[32]—and in return is paid a placement fee of normally 5 to 10 percent of payroll cost. Some leasing companies charge payroll cost plus a fixed fee per employee that might be $5–$25 per week.[33]

Organizational Recruiters

Who performs the recruitment function depends mainly on the size of the organization. For large employers like Raytheon or the City of Denver, professional HR recruiters are hired and trained to find new employees. In smaller organizations, recruitment may be done by an HR generalist; or if the organization has no HR position, recruitment may be carried out by managers and/or supervisors.

Regardless of who does the recruiting, it is important to remember that recruiters have an influence on applicants' job decisions. Recruiters are often a main reason why applicants select one organization over another. One study showed that recruiters may have significant impacts on perceived job attractiveness, regard for job and company, and intention to accept a job.[34] Therefore, choosing personable, enthusiastic, competent recruiters would seemingly have an impact on the success of an organization's recruitment program.

Realistic Job Previews

Another way for organizations to increase the effectiveness of their recruitment efforts is to provide job applicants with a realistic job preview. A **realistic job preview (RJP)** informs applicants about all aspects of the job, including both the desirable and undesirable facets of the position. In contrast, a typical job preview only presents the job in positive terms. The RJP may also include a tour of the working area combined with a discussion of any negative health or safety considerations. Proponents of the RJP believe that applicants who are given realistic information regarding a position are more likely to remain on the job and be successful, because there will be fewer unpleasant surprises. In fact, since 1980 a number of research studies on RJP report these positive results:

- Improved employee job satisfaction
- Reduced voluntary turnover
- Enhanced communication through honesty and openness
- Realistic job expectations[35]

Like other HR techniques, however, RJPs must be tailored to the needs of the organization and should include a balanced presentation of positive and negative job information.[36] (RJPs are discussed further in Chapter 15.)

RECRUITMENT OF PROTECTED CLASSES

In meeting their legal obligation to provide equal employment opportunity, employers often develop a formal EEO/AA program. An essential part of any EEO/AA policy must be an affirmative effort to recruit members of protected classes. The steps that the EEOC recommends for organizations to follow in developing such a program were discussed in Chapter 3.

Recruitment of Women

Women constitute the largest numbers among the protected classes. In 1987, they accounted for almost 45 percent of all workers.[37] Women will be the major source of new entrants into the U.S. labor force over the next 13 years. They will make up 63 percent of the net labor force growth, or 13.2 million workers, by the year 2000.[38] Within this group, Hispanic women will increase their labor force participation by 85 percent between 1986 and 2000.[39] However, even with the large numbers of women in the labor force, employers today often have difficulty in recruiting women for clerical, secretarial, and other jobs in which they have traditionally been employed. Furthermore, women still encounter barriers to landing the better-paying jobs that have been traditionally performed by men or in rising to positions of top managerial responsibility.

It is essential for employers to recognize that a majority of women, just like men, work because of economic necessity. Contrary to a once-common belief, most women do not go to work merely to "get out of the house" or to fulfill psychological needs. Sixty percent of all women in the work force in 1987 were responsible for supporting themselves, and three out of five were heads of households. These women had the employment disadvantage of having completed, on average, fewer years of school than married women not in the work force, and they were concentrated in lower-skilled, lower-paying jobs.[40]

A major employment obstacle for women is the stereotyped thinking that persists within our society. For example, a recent study comparing male and female personality types concluded that females are still viewed as possessing fewer characteristics of the "ideal" manager profile.[41] Still another barrier has been that women in the past were not as likely as men to have professional training and preparation for entrance or advancement into management positions. This situation is changing, however, with a significant increase in the enrollment of women in programs leading to degrees in management. In addition, more women are enrolling in management seminars and certification programs that will further prepare them for higher managerial positions.

Entrance of Men into Traditional Jobs for Women

EEO/AA requirements have also led to the recruitment of men for jobs traditionally held by women. More and more men are working as secretaries, phone operators, flight attendants, and nurses. While the entrance of males into jobs once exclusively held by women will deprive women of employment opportunities, in the long run both groups may benefit. The willingness of men and women to assert themselves in jobs traditionally held by one sex will help make employment conditions better and more equal for both sexes. Higher wages, better working conditions, and greater job status for both men and women could be the result.

More men, such as this directory assistance operator, are working in traditionally female jobs.

Recruitment of Minorities

Since the passage of the Civil Rights Act of 1964, many members of minority groups have been able to realize a substantial improvement in their social and economic well-being. Increasing numbers of blacks and Hispanics are now in the upper income-tax brackets by virtue of their entrance into professional, engineering, and managerial positions. However, the proportion of minorities in these areas is still substantially below their proportions in the total population. Unemployment among minorities, particularly the youth, continues to be at a critically high level. Undoubtedly, these rates are considerably higher during periods of economic downturn when employment opportunities become harder to find.

For many minorities who live predominantly in the inner cities, employment opportunities still remain exceedingly limited because of educational and societal disadvantages. Also, because their social environment can sometimes lie apart from the mainstream, traditional recruitment methods may prove ineffective in reaching them. Community action agencies, civil rights organizations, or church groups within the communities can provide a means for recruiters to reach inner-city residents. Special media advertising targeted to this group also may prove effective.

Unless minorities can be retained within an organization, EEO/AA programs are likely to prove ineffective. If minority employees are to be retained, they, like any employees, must be made to feel welcome in their jobs, as well as to feel that their efforts contribute to the success of the organization.

Recruitment of the Handicapped

According to the 1985 Current Population Survey, only 10.2 percent of severely disabled adults of working age are in the U.S. labor force. However, two-thirds of disabled adults without jobs say they want to work.[42] The handicapped have often been rejected for employment because of the mistaken belief that there were no jobs within an organization that they might be able to perform effectively. Fears that the handicapped might have more accidents or that they might aggravate existing disabilities have also deterred their employment. The lack of special facilities for physically handicapped persons, particularly those in wheelchairs, has been a further employment restriction. However, physical obstructions are being eliminated as employers are making federally legislated improvements to accommodate handicapped workers.

Physical handicaps may constitute limitations only with respect to specific job requirements. An employee in a wheelchair who might not be able to perform duties that involve certain physical activities may be quite capable of working at a bench or a desk. Some employers have even found ways to use handicapped workers' "disabilities" to an advantage. The Air Force, for example, estimates that the work of five blind inspectors of jet engine blades saves it several millions of dollars a year. Their keen sense of touch enables them to spot minor defects on blades which, if installed in a jet engine, might lead to mechanical failure and even the loss of life.

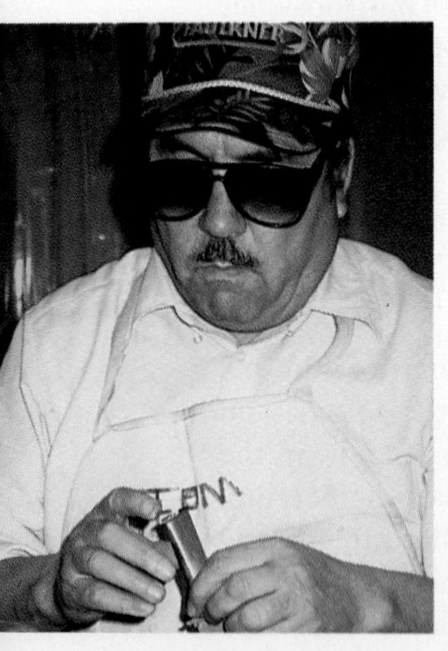

A blind Air Force employee checks for possible nicks in a TF-39 jet engine blade.

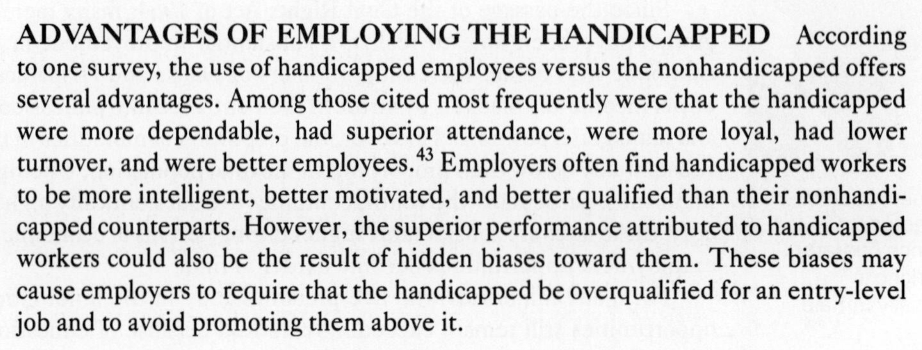

ADVANTAGES OF EMPLOYING THE HANDICAPPED According to one survey, the use of handicapped employees versus the nonhandicapped offers several advantages. Among those cited most frequently were that the handicapped were more dependable, had superior attendance, were more loyal, had lower turnover, and were better employees.[43] Employers often find handicapped workers to be more intelligent, better motivated, and better qualified than their nonhandicapped counterparts. However, the superior performance attributed to handicapped workers could also be the result of hidden biases toward them. These biases may cause employers to require that the handicapped be overqualified for an entry-level job and to avoid promoting them above it.

THE LESS-PUBLICIZED HANDICAPS In addition to the widely recognized forms of handicaps, there are others that can limit hiring and advancement opportunities. One such handicap is unattractiveness, against which employers can be biased even if unconsciously. Unattractive individuals are said to be those whose facial features are considered unpleasant but who do not possess physical disfiguration that would put them in the physically handicapped category. Another less-publicized handicap in gaining and retaining employment is obesity. In extreme cases, however, courts have held obesity to be a legitimate physical handicap.

Finally, there is the handicap of illiteracy. It is estimated that approximately 27 million Americans—one out of every five adults—are functionally illiterate. These individuals lack the reading and writing abilities needed to handle the minimal demands of daily living or job performance. Further, there may be as many as 45 million more adults who are only marginally literate.[44] Even if these figures are somewhat exaggerated, employers are encountering increasing numbers of employees, including college graduates, whose deficient reading and writing skills limit their performance on the job. About one-fifth of Motorola's production workers require basic literacy training, and half need further instruction to be able to operate automated equipment.[45] In order to maintain an effective work force, Motorola currently teaches reading, math, and communication skills to employees who are deficient in them.

Recruitment of Older Persons

There is a definite trend by organizations toward hiring older persons. The move has come as a result of changing work force demographics and a change in the attitudes of employers and employees. Organizations realize that older workers have proven employment experience, have job "savvy," and are reliable employees. Older individuals are an excellent recruitment source to staff part-time and full-time positions that are hard to fill.

As the demand for skilled employees increases, organizations are offering flexible work schedules and additional training to attract older workers.[46] At Sterile Design, Inc., older employees work four-hour "mini-shifts" packing hospital and medical supplies. Aerospace Corporation hires "casual employees" who work less than 20 hours a week or less than 1,000 hours a year. This allows these employees the opportunity to continue receiving pension benefits in addition to their earnings. No longer can organizations pursuing an effective employment strategy ignore older persons as a potential recruitment source.

SUMMARY

HRP is the foundation upon which many HRM functions are based. The HRP activity consists of forecasting employment needs, matching these needs against the supply of employees available to fill openings, and balancing supply and demand considerations. Organizations use a variety of quantitative (top-down) or qualitative (bottom-up) approaches to forecast employment requirements.

Recruitment requires effective planning to determine the specific HR needs of the organization. Also to be determined are the requirements of the jobs to be staffed, which establish the qualifications of the applicants to be recruited and selected. Employers usually find it advantageous to fill by means of internal promotion as many openings as possible above the entry level. However, filling some jobs above the entry level requires them to rely upon outside sources. These outside sources are also utilized to fill jobs with special qualifications, to avoid excessive inbreeding, and to acquire new ideas and technology. Which outside sources and methods will be used in recruiting will depend on the recruitment goals of the organization, the conditions of the labor market, and the specifications of the jobs to be filled.

The legal requirements governing EEO make it mandatory that employers exert a positive effort to recruit and promote members of protected classes so that their representation at all levels within the organization will approximate their proportionate numbers in the labor market. These efforts include recruiting not only those members who are qualified, but also those who can be made qualified with reasonable training and assistance.

DISCUSSION QUESTIONS

1. Identify the three key elements of the human resources planning model, and discuss the relationship among them.
2. Distinguish between the quantitative and the qualitative approaches to forecasting the need for human resources.
3. What are the comparative advantages and disadvantages of filling openings from internal sources?
4. Describe the relationships between the recruitment function and the functions of selection, performance appraisal, and compensation management.
5. In what ways do executive search firms differ from the traditional employment agencies?
6. Explain how realistic job previews (RJPs) operate. Why do they appear to be an effective recruitment technique?
7. Discuss some of the employment problems faced by members of protected classes.
8. An employment agency seeking to recruit salespeople for an insurance company advertised for applicants in the local newspaper. The position was described as a "management trainee" job with an insurance company. The advertisement did not list the name of either the employment agency or the insurance company but gave only the telephone number of the agency. What are the possible reasons for this practice? What would be your reaction upon reading the ad? Upon learning all the facts about the job?

MINI-CASE 5–1 Filling Job Openings

Reports issued by the U.S. Department of Labor as well as independent research groups conclude that many employers will face a labor shortage during the 1990s. This condition may extend beyond the year 2000. The implications of this labor force trend will be significant for individual managers and supervisors of small businesses, as well as HR departments in large organizations. For managers, this will mean longer delays in the filling of available job openings. Employers may be forced to hire individuals with inadequate or marginal skills. The end result could be lower organizational productivity and quality concerns.

To compensate for the labor shortages, HR departments will strive to attract qualified job applicants through innovative compensation and selection programs. Training demands are likely to increase in correlation with the need to upgrade the skill levels of new hires. Perhaps one of the greatest challenges faced by HR departments will be to attract and recruit qualified or qualifiable job applicants through a variety of recruitment sources.

QUESTIONS

1. Assume you are the HR director for a medium-sized organization. What recruitment sources would you use to fill available job openings in the following areas: (1) clerical, (2) managerial, and (3) technical/professional?
2. Besides the major sources mentioned in the chapter, what other sources are available for recruiting job applicants?

MINI-CASE 5–2 Writing Newspaper Advertisements

This assignment requires you to use your creative abilities to the fullest. As almost all HR managers will admit, writing newspaper advertisements is a difficult and challenging task. To create an ad that is both thorough and eye-catching requires ingenuity, thoughtfulness, and possibly even a stroke of genius.

Your job is to create a newspaper advertisement for the position of stenographer at the Greenriver Public Service Company, an electric utility operating in a major metropolitan area. The company offers a full range of employee benefits and competitive wages. Career advancement is available and the position reports to the Director of Operations. Job duties and responsibilities would be similar to those of any high-level stenographic position. The advertisement should be done on 8-1/2" x 11" paper and should be suitable for presentation in a classroom discussion. Be creative and have fun.

NOTES AND REFERENCES

1. Martha I. Finney, "The ASPA Labor Shortage Survey," *Personnel Administrator* 34, no. 2 (February 1989): 35–42.

2. Martha I. Finney, "Planning Today for the Future's Changing Shape," *Personnel Administrator* 34, no. 1 (January 1989): 44–45. See also Gilbert Fuchsberg, "Many Businesses Responding Too Slowly to Rapid Work Force Shifts, Study Says," *Wall Street Journal* (July 19, 1990): B1; and Kenneth A. Kovach and John A. Pearce, "HR Strategic Mandates for the 1990s," *Personnel* 67, no. 4 (April 1989): 50–55.

3. James W. Walker and Gregory Moorhead, "CEOs: What They Want from HRM," *Personnel Administrator* 32, no. 12 (December 1987): 51.

4. Wayne F. Cascio and Donald H. Sweet, *Human Resource Planning Employment and Placement* (Washington, DC: Bureau of National Affairs, 1989).

5. Leslie W. Rue and Phyllis G. Holland, *Strategic Management,* 2d ed. (New York: McGraw-Hill, 1989), 6–13.

6. Paul F. Butler, "Successful Partnerships: HR and Strategic Planning at Eight Top Firms," *Organizational Dynamics* 17, no. 2 (Autumn 1988): 27–42.

7. Lloyd Baird and Ilan Meshoulam, "Managing Two Fits of Strategic Human Resources Management," *Academy of Management Review* 13, no. 1 (March 1988): 125.

8. For a review of strategic HR management literature, see Cynthia A. Lengnick-Hall and Mark L. Lengnick-Hall, "Strategic Human Resources Management: A Review of the Literature and a Proposed Typology," *Academy of Management Review* 13, no. 3 (July 1988): 454–470.

9. "Human Resources Managers Aren't Corporate Nobodies Anymore," *Business Week* (December 2, 1985): 59.

10. Elmer H. Burack, *Creative Human Resource Planning and Applications: A Strategic Approach* (Englewood Cliffs, NJ: Prentice-Hall, 1988), 11–12.

11. Donald L. Caruth, Robert M. Noe III, and R. Wayne Mondy, *Staffing the Contemporary Organization* (New York: Quorum Books, 1988), 114.

12. John F. Preble, "The Selection of Delphi Panels for Strategic Planning Purposes," *Strategic Management Journal* 5, no. 2 (April–June 1985): 157–170.

13. For example, see U.S. Department of Labor, Bureau of Labor Statistics, *Geographic Profiles of Employment and Unemployment, 1986,* Bulletin 2279 (May 1987).

14. For example, each month the Arizona Department of Economic Security publishes the *Arizona Labor Market Information Newsletter,* providing information on labor market conditions in Arizona.

15. The *Monthly Labor Review* is published each month by the U.S. Department of Labor, Bureau of Labor Statistics.

16. Stephen L. Mangum, "Recruitment and Job Search: The Recruitment Tactics of Employers," *Personnel Administrator* 27, no. 6 (June 1982): 90–102.

17. Jay Wickliff, "Beyond Staffing," *Personnel* 65, no. 5 (May 1988): 54.

18. Caruth, Noe, and Mondy, *Staffing the Contemporary Organization,* 131.

19. David Gold and Beth Madigan, "Job Posting Boosts Worker Morale," *Resource* 8, no. 6 (June 1989): 7.

20. "Innovative Recruiting Practices at Kentucky Fried Chicken Attract Middle Managers and Reduce Turnover" (Presented at the annual meeting of the American Society for Personnel Administration, Kansas City, 1987).

21. R. Wayne Mondy, Robert M. Noe, and Robert E. Edwards, "Successful Recruitment: Matching Sources and Methods," *Personnel* 64, no. 9 (September 1987): 42–46.

22. Jean Powell Kirnan, John A. Farley, and Kurt F. Geisinger, "The Relationship Between Recruiting Source, Applicant Quality, and Hire Performance: An Analysis by Sex, Ethnicity, and Age," *Personnel Psychology* 42, no. 2 (Summer 1989): 293–308. See also David F. Caldwell and A. Austin Spivey, "The Relationship Between Recruiting Source and Employee Success: An Analysis by Race," *Personnel Psychology* 36, no. 1 (Spring 1983): 67–72.

23. Kirnan, Farley, and Geisinger, "Relationship Between Recruiting Source, Applicant Quality, and Hire Performance," 293.

24. Donald A. Levenson, "Needed: Revamped Recruiting Services," *Personnel* 65, no. 7 (July 1988): 52.

25. "The New Headhunters," *Business Week* (February 6, 1989): 65.

26. Holly Rawlinson, "Scholarships Recruit Future Employees Now," *Recruitment,* a supplement of *Personnel Journal* (August 1988): 14.

27. Allan Halcrow, "Employees Are Your Best Recruiters," *Personnel Journal* 67, no. 11 (November 1988): 42–49.

28. For an excellent article on the contents of job résumés, see William H. Holly, Jr., Early Higgins, and Sally Speights, "Résumés and Cover Letters," *Personnel* 65, no. 12 (December 1988): 49–51.

29. "The Temporary Services: A Lasting Impact on the Economy," *Personnel Administrator* 33, no. 1 (January 1988): 60–62.

30. Jack L. Simonetti, Nick Nykodym, and Louella M. Sell, "Temporary Employees," *Personnel* 65, no. 8 (August 1988): 52.

31. George Munchus III, "Employee Leasing: Benefits and Threats," *Personnel* 65, no. 7 (July 1988): 59–61.

32. Howard E. Potter, "Getting a New Lease on Employees," *Management Review* 78, no. 4 (April 1989): 28–31.

33. "Give Your Employees a Break—by Leasing Them," *Business Week* (August 14, 1989): 135.

34. Michael M. Harris and Laurence S. Fink, "A Field Study of Applicant Reactions to Employment Opportunities: Does the Recruiter Make a Difference?" *Personnel Psychology* 40, no. 1 (Winter 1987): 781.

35. For a review of the literature on realistic job previews, see Mary K. Suszko and James A. Breaugh, "The Effects of Realistic Job Previews on Applicant Self-Selection and Employee Turnover, Satisfaction, and Coping Ability," *Journal of Management* 12, no. 4 (Winter 1986): 513–523.

36. John P. Wanous, "Installing a Realistic Job Preview: Ten Tough Choices," *Personnel Psychology* 42, no. 1 (Spring 1989): 117–133.

37. U.S. Department of Labor, Women's Bureau, *Facts on Women Workers,* Fact Sheet No. 88-2 (1988), 1.

38. U.S. Department of Labor, Women's Bureau, *Facts on U.S. Working Women,* Fact Sheet No. 88-1 (January 1988), 1.

39. Ibid.

40. *Facts on Women Workers,* 2–3.

41. Kenneth P. Carson, "Effects of Applicant Gender and Trait Characteristics on Selection Decision Behavior and Outcome" (unpublished manuscript, September 1989), 1–14. See also Madeline E. Heilman, Caryn J. Block, Richard F. Martell, and Michael C. Simon, "Has Anything Changed? Current Characterizations of Men, Women, and Managers," *Journal of Applied Psychology* 74, no. 6 (December 1989): 935–942.

42. *Out of the Job Market: A National Crisis* (President's Committee on Employment of the Handicapped, n.d.), 13.

43. Donald J. Peterson, "Paving the Way for Hiring the Handicapped," *Personnel* 58, no. 2 (March–April 1981): 51.

44. "Functional Illiteracy: It's Your Problem, Too," *Supervisory Management* 34, no. 6 (June 1989): 22.

45. "Managing Now for the 1990s," *Fortune* (September 26, 1988): 46.

46. Benson Rosen and Thomas H. Jerdee, "Investing in the Older Worker," *Personnel Administrator* 34, no. 4 (April 1989): 70–74. See also David V. Lewis, "Make Way for the Older Worker," *HR Magazine* 36, no. 5 (May 1990): 75–77.

CHAPTER 6

Selection

After reading this chapter you will be able to:

1. *Define the concepts of reliability and validity.*
2. *Describe the three types of validity used in the selection process.*
3. *Distinguish between the different types of interviews according to the degree of structure.*
4. *List the guidelines for the interviewing process that interviewers should know.*
5. *Identify the types of preemployment questions that should be avoided during the interview.*
6. *Describe the categories of tests according to the characteristics that are measured.*
7. *Describe the factors to be considered and strategies used in reaching hiring decisions.*
8. *Define the key terms in the chapter.*

TERMS TO IDENTIFY

reliability *(171)*
validity *(171)*
criterion-related validity *(172)*
concurrent validity *(173)*
predictive validity *(173)*
cross-validation *(173)*
validity generalization *(174)*
content validity *(174)*
construct validity *(175)*
structured interview *(183)*
nondirective interview *(183)*
depth interview *(184)*
patterned interview *(184)*
stress interview *(185)*
stereotyping *(188)*
halo error *(189)*
face validity *(192)*
job-knowledge tests *(195)*
job-sample, or work-sample, tests *(195)*
selection ratio *(197)*

The recruiting process typically yields a number of applicants whose qualifications must be measured against the requirements of the job. Making a selection from applicants from inside or outside the organization to fill existing or projected job openings is a major HR function with far-reaching effects.

Today greater attention is being given to the selection process than ever before. Individuals hired after thorough screening against carefully developed job specifications learn their job tasks readily, are productive, and generally adjust to their jobs with a minimum of difficulty. As a result, the individual, the organization, and society as a whole benefit from a careful selection process.

Where the job tenure of employees is protected by a union agreement or by civil service regulations, there is an additional incentive for management to have sound selection policies and procedures since it is usually more difficult to discharge unsatisfactory employees who have such protection.

The greatest impetus to improve the selection process has come from equal employment legislation, court decisions, and the *Uniform Guidelines,* discussed in Chapter 3. What was once the exclusive concern of the employment office may now be carried into the courtroom. Among other factors affecting selection are scarcity of labor supply in high-technology labor markets, increasing geographic immobility of career couples, and changing staffing needs due to promotion and turnover.[1]

While the selection program typically is the responsibility of the HR department, managerial and supervisory personnel in all the departments of an organization also have an important role in the selection process. The final decision in hiring is usually theirs. It is important, therefore, that they understand the objectives and policies relating to selection. They should also be thoroughly trained in the most effective and acceptable approaches for evaluating applicants and should be motivated to use them.

MATCHING PEOPLE AND JOBS

Those responsible for making selection decisions should have adequate information upon which to base them. Information about the jobs to be filled, knowledge of the ratio of job openings to the number of applicants, and as much relevant information as possible about the applicants themselves are essential for making sound decisions.

Use of Job Specifications

In Chapter 4, we discussed the process of analyzing and developing specifications for jobs. Such factors as skill, effort, responsibility, and physical demands provide the basis for determining what types of information should be obtained from the applicant, from previous employers, or from other sources. The job specifications also form the basis for the administration of any applicable employment tests. Research has demonstrated that complete and unambiguous job information reduces the influence of racial and sex stereotypes and helps the interviewer to differentiate between qualified and unqualified applicants.

Ordinarily, the managers and supervisors in an organization are well acquainted with the requirements pertaining to skill, physical demands, and other factors for jobs in their respective departments. Interviewers and other members of the HR department who participate in selection should maintain a close liaison with the various departments so that they can become thoroughly familiar with the jobs.

The Selection Process

In most organizations, selection is a continuous process. Turnover inevitably occurs, leaving vacancies to be filled by applicants from inside or outside the organization or by individuals whose qualifications have been assessed previously. It is common to have a waiting list of applicants who can be called when permanent or temporary positions become open.

The number of steps in the selection process and their sequence will vary, not only with the organization but also with the type and level of jobs to be filled. Each step should be evaluated in terms of its contribution. The steps that typically make up the selection process are shown in Figure 6–1. Not all applicants will go through all of these steps. Some may be rejected after the preliminary interview, others after taking tests, and so on.

As shown in Figure 6–1, organizations use several different means to obtain information about applicants. These include application blanks, interviews, tests, medical examinations, and background investigations. Regardless of the method

FIGURE 6–1 STEPS IN THE SELECTION PROCESS

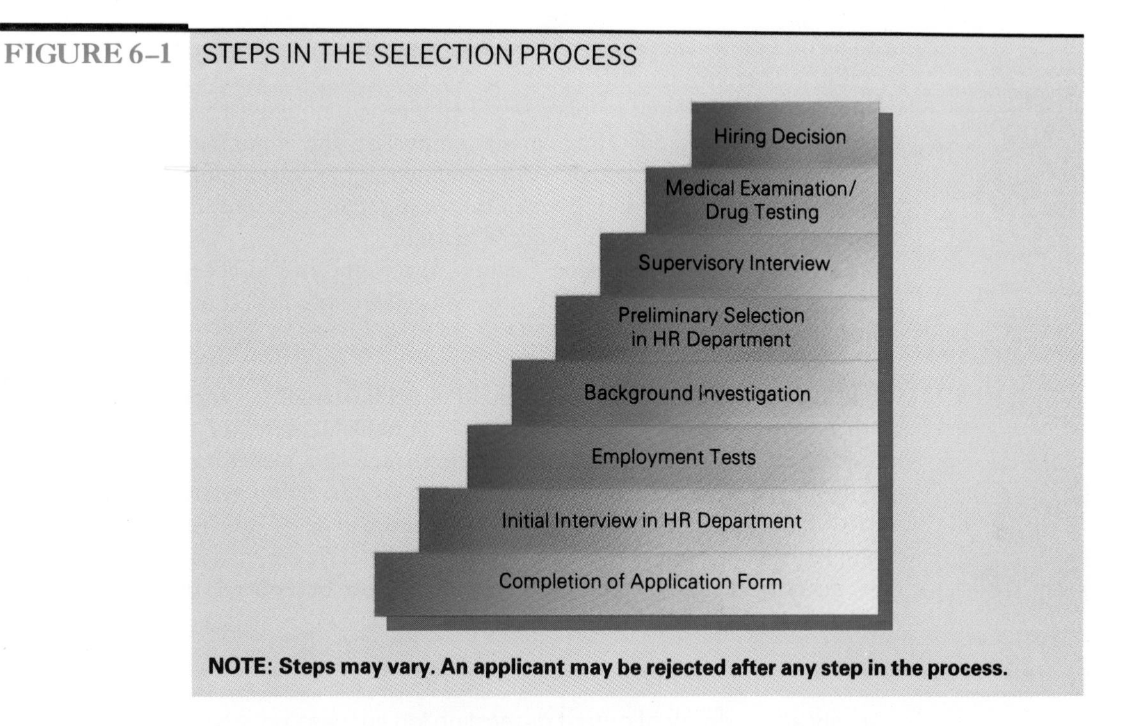

used, it is essential that it conform to accepted ethical standards, including privacy and confidentiality, as well as legal requirements. Above all, it is essential that the information obtained is sufficiently reliable and valid.

Obtaining Reliable and Valid Information

The degree to which interviews, tests, and other selection procedures yield comparable data over a period of time is known as **reliability.** For example, unless interviewers judge the capabilities of a group of applicants to be the same as they did yesterday, their judgments are unreliable (i.e., unstable). Likewise, a test that gives widely different scores when it is administered to the same individual a few days apart is unreliable.

Reliability also refers to the extent to which two or more methods (interviews, tests, etc.) yield similar results or are consistent. Interrater reliability—agreement between two or more raters—is one measure of consistency. Unless the data upon which selection decisions are based are reliable, in terms of both stability and consistency, they cannot be used as predictors.

In addition to having reliable information pertaining to a person's suitability for a job, the information must be as valid as possible. **Validity** refers to *what* a test or other selection procedure measures and *how well* it measures it. In the context of personnel selection, validity is essentially an indicator of the extent to which data from a procedure (interview, test, etc.) are related to or predictive of job performance or some other relevant criterion. Like a new medicine, a selection procedure must be validated before it is used. There are two reasons for validating a procedure. First, validity is directly related to increases in employee productivity, as we will demonstrate later. Second, EEO regulations emphasize the importance of validity in selection procedures. Although we commonly refer to "validating" a test or interview procedure, validity in the technical sense refers to the inferences made from the use of a procedure, not the procedure itself.

The *Uniform Guidelines* (see Chapter 3) recognizes and accepts different approaches to validation. These are criterion-related validity, content validity, and construct validity.

CRITERION-RELATED VALIDITY The extent to which a selection tool predicts or significantly correlates with important elements of work behavior is known as **criterion-related validity.** Performance on a test, for example, is compared to actual production records, supervisory ratings, training outcomes, and other measures of success that are appropriate to each type of job. In a sales job, for example, it is common to use sales figures as a basis for comparison. In production jobs, quantity and quality of output may provide the best criteria of job success.

Quality and quantity of output determine job success on the production line.

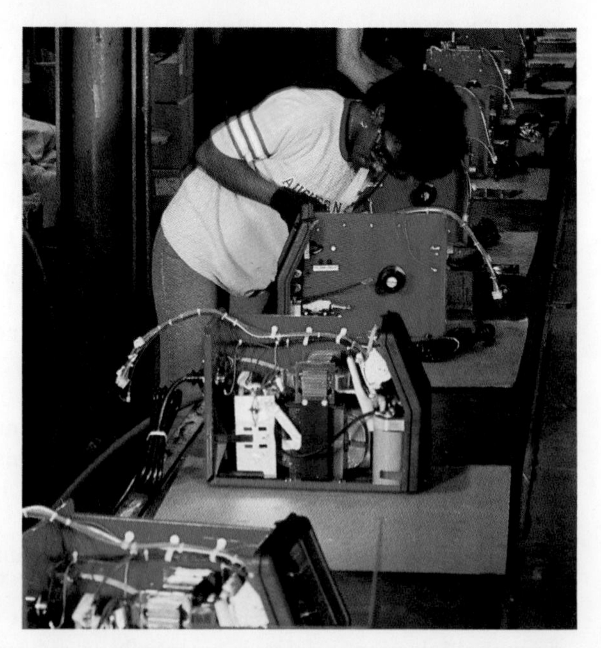

There are two types of criterion-related validity, concurrent and predictive. **Concurrent validity** involves obtaining criterion data at about the same time that test scores (or other predictor information) are obtained from *current employees*. For example, a supervisor is asked to rate a group of clerical employees on the quantity and quality of their performance. Within a few days these employees are given a clerical aptitude test that is then validated. **Predictive validity,** on the other hand, involves testing *applicants* and obtaining criterion data *after* they have been on the job for some indefinite period. For example, applicants are given a clerical aptitude test, which is then filed away for later study. After the individuals have been on the job for several months, supervisors, who should not know the employees' test scores, are asked to rate them on the quality and quantity of their performance. Test scores are then compared with the supervisors' ratings.

Regardless of the method used, cross-validation is essential. **Cross-validation** is a process in which a test or test battery is administered to a different sample (drawn from the same population) for the purpose of verifying the results obtained from the original validation study.

Correlational methods are generally used to determine the relationship between predictor information such as test scores and criterion data. The correlation scatterplots in Figure 6–2 illustrate the difference between a selection test of zero validity (A) and one of high validity (B). Each dot represents a person. Note that in scatterplot A there is no relationship between test scores and success on the job; in other words, the validity is zero. In scatterplot B, those who score low on the test

FIGURE 6–2 CORRELATION SCATTERPLOTS

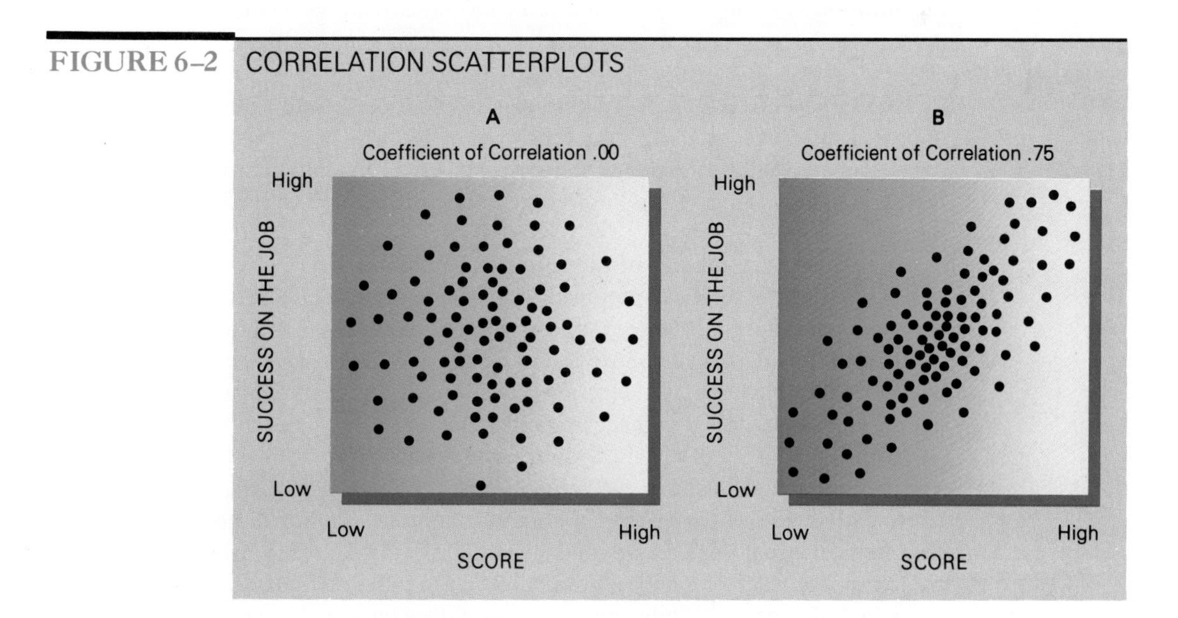

tend to have low success on the job, whereas those who score high on the test tend to have high success on the job, indicating high validity. In actual practice we would apply a statistical formula to the data to obtain a coefficient of correlation referred to as a validity coefficient. Correlation coefficients range from 0.00, denoting a complete absence of relationship, to +1.00 and to –1.00, indicating a perfect positive or perfect negative relationship, respectively.

A thorough survey of the literature shows that the averages of the maximum validity coefficients are 0.45 where tests are validated against *training* criteria and 0.35 where tests are validated against job *proficiency* criteria. These figures represent the predictive power of single tests.[2] A higher validity may be obtained by combining two or more tests or other predictors (interview, biographical data, etc.), using the appropriate statistical formulas. The higher the overall validity, the greater the chances of hiring individuals who will be the better performers. The criterion-related method is generally preferred to other validation approaches because it is based on empirical data.

For several decades, personnel psychologists believed that validity coefficients had meaning only for the specific situation (job and organization). More recently, as a result of several research studies—many involving clerical jobs—it appears that validity coefficients can often be generalized across situations, hence the term **validity generalization.** Where there are adequate data to support the existence of validity generalization, the development of selection procedures can become less costly and time-consuming. The process involves analyzing jobs and situations and, on the basis of these analyses, consulting tables of generalized validities from previous studies using various predictors in similar circumstances. It is advisable for organizations to employ the services of an industrial/organizational psychologist experienced in test validation to develop the selection procedures.[3]

CONTENT VALIDITY Where it is not feasible to use the criterion-related approach, often because of limited samples of individuals, the content method is used. **Content validity** is assumed to exist when a selection instrument, such as a test, adequately samples the knowledge and skills needed to perform a particular job.

The closer the content of the selection instrument to actual work samples or behaviors, the greater the content validity. For example, a civil service examination for accountants has high content validity when it requires the solution of accounting problems representative of those found on the job. Asking an accountant to lift a 60-pound box, however, is a selection procedure that has content validity only if the job description indicates that accountants must be able to meet this requirement.

Content validity is the most direct and least complicated type of validity to assess. It is generally used to evaluate job knowledge and skill tests, to be described later. Unlike the criterion-related method, content validity is not expressed in correlational terms. Instead, an index which indicates the relationship between the content of the test items and performance on the job is computed from evaluations of a panel of experts.[4] While content validity does have its limitations, it has made a positive contribution to job analysis procedures and to the role of expert judgment in sampling and scoring procedures.

CONSTRUCT VALIDITY The extent to which a selection tool measures a theoretical construct, or trait, is known as **construct validity.** Typical constructs are intelligence, mechanical comprehension, anxiety, etc. They are in effect broad, general categories of human functions that are based on the measurement of many discrete behaviors. For example, the *Bennett Mechanical Comprehension Test* consists of a wide variety of tasks that measure the construct of mechanical comprehension.

Measuring construct validity requires showing that the psychological trait is related to satisfactory job performance and that the test accurately measures the psychological trait. There is a lack of literature covering this concept as it relates to employment practices, probably because it is difficult and expensive to validate a construct and also show how it is job-related.

SOURCES OF INFORMATION ABOUT JOB CANDIDATES

Many sources of information are used to provide as reliable and valid a picture as possible of an applicant's potential for success on the job. In this section, we will study the potential contributions of application forms, biographical information blanks, background investigations, lie detector tests, honesty tests, and medical examinations. Because interviewing plays such a major role in selection and because testing presents unique challenges, there will be expanded discussions of these sources of information later in the chapter. Assessment centers, which are often used in managerial selection, will be discussed in Chapter 8.

Application Forms

Most organizations require application forms to be completed because they provide a fairly quick and systematic means of obtaining a variety of information about the applicant. As with interviews, the EEOC and the courts have found that many questions asked on application forms disproportionately discriminate against females and minorities and often are not job-related. Application forms, therefore, should be developed with great care and revised as often as necessary. Because of differences in state laws on fair employment practices (FEPs) (see Chapter 3), organizations operating in more than one state will find it difficult to develop one form that can be used nationally.

Application forms serve several purposes. They provide information for deciding whether an applicant meets the minimum requirements for experience, education, etc. They provide a basis for questions the interviewer will ask about the applicant's background. They also offer sources for reference checks. For certain jobs a short application form such as that shown in Figure 6–3 is appropriate. For scientific, professional, and managerial jobs a more extended form is likely to be used. A study of Figure 6–3 will reveal that while the form is brief, it asks for information from the applicant that is highly relevant to job performance. It also provides information regarding the employer's conformity with various laws and regulations.

Even when applicants come armed with elaborate résumés, it is important that they complete an application form early in the process. Robert Half, founder of the worldwide Robert Half recruiting firm, estimates that 30 percent of job candidates lie on their résumés. He warns that one should "beware of the 'cookie-cutter, too slick look' of a résumé. An employer has to be wary of someone who's allowed others to put words in his or her mouth."[5]

FIGURE 6–3 A SHORT APPLICATION FORM

EMPLOYMENT APPLICATION

SOCIAL SECURITY NO. ________

NAME ________ FIRST NAME ________ MIDDLE INITIAL ________ LAST NAME ________ STREET ADDRESS ________

APT. NO. OR BOX ________ CITY ________ STATE ________ ZIP ________ AREA CODE ________ TEL. NO. ________

ARE YOU 18 OR OLDER? ☐ YES ☐ NO, IF NOT, AGE ________ EVER WORKED IN A McDONALD'S RESTAURANT BEFORE? IF YES, DATES AND LOCATION ________

AVAILABILITY:

TOTAL HOURS AVAILABLE PER WEEK ________

HOURS AVAILABLE:	M	T	W	T	F	S	S
FROM							
TO							

ARE YOU LEGALLY ABLE TO BE EMPLOYED IN THE U.S. ☐ YES ☐ NO HOW DID YOU HEAR OF JOB? ________ HOW FAR DO YOU LIVE FROM STORE? ________ DO YOU HAVE TRANSPORTATION TO WORK? ________

SCHOOL MOST RECENTLY ATTENDED:

NAME ________ LOCATION ________ PHONE ________

TEACHER OR COUNSELOR ________ DEPT. ________ LAST GRADE COMPLETED ________ GRADE POINT AVERAGE ________

GRADUATED ☐ YES ☐ NO NOW ENROLLED? ☐ YES ☐ NO SPORTS OR ACTIVITIES ________

TWO MOST RECENT JOBS: (IF NOT APPLICABLE, LIST U.S. MILITARY, WORK PERFORMED ON A VOLUNTARY BASIS OR PERSONAL REFERENCES)

COMPANY ________ LOCATION ________

PHONE ________ JOB ________

SUPERVISOR ________ DATES WORKED: FROM ________ TO ________

SALARY ________ REASON FOR LEAVING ________ MGMT. REFERENCE CHECK DONE BY ________

COMPANY ________ LOCATION ________

PHONE ________ JOB ________

SUPERVISOR ________ DATES WORKED: FROM ________ TO ________

SALARY ________ REASON FOR LEAVING ________ MGMT. REFERENCE CHECK DONE BY ________

PHYSICAL: ANY HEALTH PROBLEMS OR PHYSICAL DISABILITIES WHICH COULD AFFECT YOUR EMPLOYMENT? ☐ YES ☐ NO

DO YOU NOW HAVE OR HAVE YOU HAD, WITHIN THE LAST SIX MONTHS, ANY CONTAGIOUS OR COMMUNICABLE DISEASES, OR GASTRO—INTESTINAL INFECTIONS, OR HAVE YOU EVER HAD HEPATITIS OR SALMONELLA? ☐ YES ☐ NO EXPLAIN ANY YES ANSWERS IN DETAIL: ________

* DURING THE PAST 7 YEARS, HAVE YOU EVER BEEN CONVICTED OF A CRIME, EXCLUDING MISDEMEANORS AND TRAFFIC VIOLATIONS? ☐ YES ☐ NO IF YES, DESCRIBE IN FULL ________

* A conviction will not necessarily bar you from employment.

1. I certify that the information contained on this application is correct to the best of my knowledge and understand that deliberate falsification of this information is grounds for dismissal in accordance with the policy of this independent McDonald's franchise. 2. I authorize the references listed above to give you any and all information concerning my previous employment and pertinent information they may have, personal or otherwise, and release all parties from all liability for any damage that may result from furnishing same to you. 3. I acknowledge that, if I become employed, I will be free to terminate my employment at any time for any reason and this McDonald's franchise retains the same rights. No McDonald's representative of this McDonald's franchise has the authority to make any contrary agreement.

DATE ________ **SIGNATURE** ________

This McDonald's franchise is an equal opportunity employer. The Civil Rights Act of 1964 and State and Local laws prohibit discrimination on the basis of race, color, religion, sex, national origin or veterans status. In addition, State and Local laws prohibit discrimination on the basis of disability and the Age Discrimination in Employment Act of 1978 and some State and Local laws prohibit discrimination on the basis of age with respect to individuals who are at least 40 years of age. It is our policy to comply fully with these Acts and information requested on this application will not be used for any purpose prohibited by law.

YOUR APPLICATION WILL BE CONSIDERED ACTIVE FOR 30 DAYS-FOR CONSIDERATION AFTER THAT YOU MUST REAPPLY. THIS RESTAURANT IS OWNED AND OPERATED BY AN INDEPENDENT McDONALD'S LICENSEE.

LICENSEE

OB PRODUCT NO. 4850113 (REV. 2/90)

APPLICANTS — PLEASE DETACH THIS TEAR OFF SECTION AND TAKE WITH YOU.

If hired, Federal Law requires that you furnish documentation showing your identity and that you are legally authorized to work in the United States.

SEE BACK OF THIS TAB FOR SPECIFIC DOCUMENTS NEEDED.

McDonald's

- FLEXIBLE HOURS
- ADVANCEMENT OPPORTUNITIES
- COMPETITIVE WAGES
- WAGE REVIEWS
- PERFORMANCE REVIEW
- PAID TRAINING
- FRIENDLY WORK ENVIRONMENT
- UNIFORMS
- LIBERAL MEAL BENEFITS
- EMPLOYEE ACTIVITIES
- SERVICE AWARDS

APPLICANTS — PLEASE DETACH THIS TEAR OFF SECTION AND TAKE WITH YOU.

SOURCE: McDonald's Corporation. Reprinted with permission.

One technique for anticipating problems of misrepresentation is to ask applicants to transcribe specific résumé material onto an application form. The applicant is then asked to sign a statement that the information contained on the form is true and that he or she accepts the employer's right to terminate the candidate's employment if any of the information is subsequently found to be false.[6]

Biographical Information Blanks

One of the oldest methods for predicting job success uses biographical information about job applicants. As early as 1917, the Life Insurance Agency Management Association constructed and validated a biographical information blank (BIB) for life insurance salespersons. It covers such items as hobbies, club memberships, sales experience, and investments. Certain responses to these items were found to be predictive of success on the job.

Both the BIB and the application form can be scored like tests. The development of a scoring system requires that the items that are valid predictors of job success be identified and that weights be established for different responses to these items. By totaling the scores for each item, it is possible to obtain a composite score on the blank as a whole for each applicant. Studies have shown that an objective scoring of BIB and application forms is one of the most potentially valid methods that can be used to predict job success. This method has been useful in predicting all types of behavior including employee theft.[7]

Background Investigations

When the interviewer is satisfied that the applicant is potentially qualified, information about previous employment as well as other information provided by

CATHY COPYRIGHT 1978 CATHY GUISEWITE. Reprinted with permission of Universal Press Syndicate. All rights reserved.

the applicant is investigated. Former employers, school and college officials, credit bureaus, and individuals named as references may be contacted for verification of pertinent information such as length of time on job, type of job, performance evaluation, highest wages, academic degrees earned, and credit rating. An Employment Management Association survey found that 93 percent of companies participating in the survey investigate information supplied by job applicants.[8] The most common ruse, according to employers, is to exaggerate one's college background. "The pressure for higher education has pushed some people over the line," says Richard Bond, director of placement at the Adolph Coors Company. According to the National Credential Verification Service of Minneapolis, "It's very easy to get a college degree without ever going to college. The practice of falsification is rampant."[9]

CHECKING REFERENCES Most organizations use both the mail and the telephone to check references. Generally, telephone checks are preferable because they save time and provide for greater candor. The most reliable information usually comes from supervisors, who are in the best position to report on an applicant's work habits and performance. It is often advisable, however, to obtain written verification of information relating to job titles, duties, and pay levels from the former employer's HR office.

Since enactment of the Family Educational Rights Privacy Act of 1974 (FERPA), which gave students and their parents the right to inspect student personnel files, university administrators and faculty have been reluctant to provide anything other than general and often meaningless positive statements about student performance. The principles involved in FERPA came to apply to employees and their personnel records as well. As a result, three-fourths of SHRM employers surveyed prefer using the telephone to check references.[10]

Inadequate reference checking is one of the major causes of high turnover, employee theft, and white-collar crime. By using sources in addition to former employers, organizations can obtain valuable information about an applicant's character and habits. For example, it is legal to use court records, litigation, bankruptcy, and workers' compensation records of applicants as long as the prospective employer is consistent in the use of information from these records.[11]

In recent years there have been a growing number of cases in which organizations have been charged with "negligently" hiring or retaining employees who later commit crimes. Typically, the suits charge that the organization has failed to adequately check references, criminal records, or general background that would have shown the employee's likelihood for aberrant behavior. Rulings in the cases, which range from theft to homicide, are making employers even more aware of the importance of checking applicant references.[12]

REQUIRING SIGNED REQUESTS FOR REFERENCES As a legal protection to all concerned, it is important to ask the applicant to fill out forms permitting information to be solicited from former employers and other reference sources. Even with these safeguards, many organizations are reluctant to put into writing an evaluation of a former employee. One reason is that several firms have been sued by former employees who discovered that they had been given poor recommendations. As a result of such experiences, some employers even hesitate to answer questions and/or verify information about former employees over the phone.

Individuals have a legal right to examine letters of reference about them (unless they waive the right to do so) where protected by the Privacy Act of 1974 or state laws. While the Privacy Act applies only to the records maintained by federal government agencies, it has influenced many employers to "clean up" personnel files and open them up to review and challenge by the employees concerned. Furthermore, over half of the states have privacy legislation.[13]

USING CREDIT REPORTS The use of consumer credit reports by employers as a basis for establishing an applicant's eligibility for employment has become more restricted. Under the federal Fair Credit Reporting Act, an employer must advise applicants if such reports will be requested. If the applicant is rejected on the basis of the report, the applicant must be advised of this fact and be provided with the name and address of the reporting agency.

If an employer plans to use a more comprehensive type of consumer report, such as an investigative consumer report, the applicant must be advised in writing. An investigative consumer report includes information based upon personal interviews with the applicant's friends, neighbors, or associates. The applicant must be told that, upon written request, additional disclosure concerning the complete nature and scope of the investigation will be provided.[14]

The Polygraph

The polygraph, or lie detector, is a device that measures the changes in breathing, blood pressure, pulse, etc., of a person who is being questioned. It consists of a rubber tube around the chest, a cuff around the arm, and sensors attached to the fingers that record the physiological changes in the examinee as the examiner asks questions that call for an answer of "yes" or "no." Questions typically cover such items as whether a person uses drugs, has stolen from an employer, or has committed a serious undetected crime. Foremost-McKesson, a pharmaceutical manufacturer, reported some years ago that about one-quarter of its applicants who undergo polygraph tests are screened out.[15]

Administering a polygraph test.

The use of lie detectors both to screen out undesirable job applicants and to curtail internal theft met with strong resistance for many years. The reliability of the polygraph device and the skill of the examiners appeared to be the central issues. While 30 states and the District of Columbia passed laws requiring the licensing of polygraphers,[16] there was continuing pressure to place more restrictions on the use of lie detectors.

The growing swell of objections to the use of polygraphs in employment situations culminated in the passage of the federal Employee Polygraph Protection

Act of 1988. The Act prohibits most private employers from using a lie detector for prehire screening and random testing. It defines the term lie detector to include the polygraph, deceptograph, voice stress analyzer, psychological stress evaluator, and any similar mechanical or electrical device used to render a diagnostic opinion about the honesty or dishonesty of an individual. There are some exemptions, as stated in the poster reproduced in Highlights in HRM 1.

Other provisions of the Act set qualification standards for polygraph examiners, conditions for examinations, and disclosure of information where the use of the polygraph is authorized. Because of the new law, employers will have to resort to such alternatives as written tests of honesty and background checks of applicants. Among the organizations most affected are Wall Street firms and banks, which have relied heavily on polygraphs in the past.[17]

Honesty Testing

Prior to the enactment of the federal polygraph law, employers in states where preemployment polygraph examinations are illegal were using paper-and-pencil honesty tests. The new federal law has stimulated new interest in honesty tests, which have been on the market for several years. They have commonly been used in settings such as retail stores where employees have access to cash or merchandise. Common areas of inquiry include beliefs about frequency and extent of theft in our society, punishment for theft, and perceived ease of theft.[18]

Development of honesty tests has taken place largely outside the mainstream of industrial/organizational psychology. A comprehensive review of ten honesty tests reveals a need for further research in this area to determine the validity of judgments made from scores on these tests.[19] Meanwhile, HRM specialists should use the results from such tests very cautiously and most certainly in conjunction with other sources of information.

Graphology

Graphology, a term that refers to a variety of systems of handwriting analysis, is being used by some employers to make employment decisions. Graphologists obtain a sample of handwriting and then examine such characteristics as the size and slant of letters, amount of pressure applied, and placement of the writing on the page. From their observations they draw inferences about the writer's personality traits, temperament, cognitive abilities, social traits, etc. Graphology has been used since the 1930s in France, Germany, Switzerland, and more recently in Israel in making employment decisions.[20] Now handwriting analysis is quietly spreading through corporate America. Richard Klimoski, a professor of industrial psychology at Ohio State University, notes that "handwriting analysis is popular because it sounds like a heaven-sent solution to employment problems."

Organizations using handwriting analysis say they prefer it to typical personality tests because it only requires job candidates to take a few minutes to jot down a short essay. By contrast, a battery of personality tests and interviews with psychologists can take several hours and can cost as much as $1,000.[21] In the academic community,

HIGHLIGHTS IN HRM

1 EMPLOYEE POLYGRAPH PROTECTION ACT

U.S. DEPARTMENT OF LABOR

EMPLOYMENT STANDARDS ADMINISTRATION

Wage and Hour Division
Washington, DC 20210

NOTICE

EMPLOYEE POLYGRAPH PROTECTION ACT

The Employee Polygraph Protection Act prohibits most private employers from using lie detector tests either for pre-employment screening or during the course of employment.

PROHIBITIONS

Employers are generally prohibited from requiring or requesting any employee or job applicant to take a lie detector test, and from discharging, disciplining, or discriminating against an employee or prospective employee for refusing to take a test or for exercising other rights under the Act.

EXEMPTIONS*

Federal, State and local governments are not affected by the law. Also, the law does not apply to tests given by the Federal Government to certain private individuals engaged in national security-related activities.

The Act permits polygraph (a kind of lie detector) tests to be administered in the private sector, subject to restrictions, to certain prospective employees of security service firms (armored car, alarm, and guard), and of pharmaceutical manufacturers, distributors, and dispensers.

The Act also permits polygraph testing, subject to restrictions, of certain employees of private firms who are reasonably suspected of involvement in a workplace incident (theft, embezzlement, etc.) that resulted in economic loss to the employer.

EXAMINEE RIGHTS

Where polygraph tests are permitted, they are subject to numerous strict standards concerning the conduct and length of the test. Examinees have a number of specific rights, including the right to a written notice before testing, the right to refuse or discontinue a test, and the right not to have test results disclosed to unauthorized persons.

ENFORCEMENT

The Secretary of Labor may bring court actions to restrain violations and assess civil penalties up to $10,000 against violators. Employees or job applicants may also bring their own court actions.

ADDITIONAL INFORMATION

Additional information may be obtained, and complaints of violations may be filed, at local offices of the Wage and Hour Division, which are listed in the telephone directory under U.S. Government, Department of Labor, Employment Standards Administration.

THE LAW REQUIRES EMPLOYERS TO DISPLAY THIS POSTER WHERE EMPLOYEES AND JOB APPLICANTS CAN READILY SEE IT.

**The law does not preempt any provision of any State or local law or any collective bargaining agreement which is more restrictive with respect to lie detector tests.*

where formal and rigorous validity tests are conducted, use of graphology for employment decisions has been and continues to be viewed with considerable skepticism.

Medical Examination

The medical examination is one of the later steps in the selection process because it can be costly. The use of the preemployment medical examination varies according to industry, but about one-half of the companies surveyed by the Bureau of National Affairs give preemployment examinations to prospective employees.[22]

A medical examination is generally given to ensure that the health of applicants is adequate to meet the job requirements. It also provides a baseline against which subsequent medical examinations may be compared and interpreted. The last objective is particularly important in determinations of work-caused disabilities under workers' compensation law.

In the past, requirements for such physical characteristics as strength, agility, height, and weight were often determined by an employer's unvalidated notion of what should be required. Many such requirements that tend to discriminate against women have been questioned and modified so as to represent typical job demands.

While there is much publicity about AIDS, corporate testing for the presence of the HIV virus is conducted in only 6 percent of the companies surveyed by the American Management Association. Nearly two-thirds of those firms reporting that they were conducting HIV tests were health care providers; an additional 14 percent were government and military units.[23]

Drug Testing

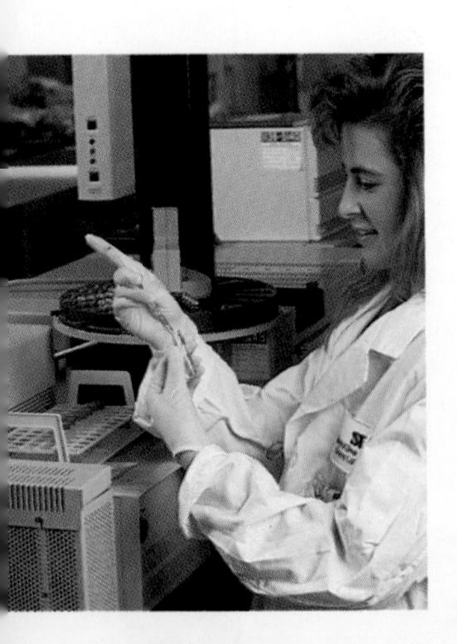
Testing urine samples for controlled substances in a lab.

A growing number of employers use drug tests to screen applicants and current employees for drug use. Urine sampling is the preferred form of drug testing; it is used by 96 percent of AMA-surveyed employers who do drug testing. More sophisticated tests are used to validate positive findings. Some of the sharpest criticism of drug testing attacks the technology and standards by which tests are conducted—a topic we will discuss in detail in Chapter 16, in the context of employee rights.

The wide range of firms that report using drug tests include Federal Express, General Electric, Georgia Power, Southern Pacific Railroad, Trans World Airlines, and the New York Times Company. With most employers, applicants who test positive have virtually no chance of being hired. However, employees who test positive are typically referred for treatment or counseling or receive some sort of disciplinary action.[24]

Since passage of the Drug-Free Workplace Act of 1988, applicants and employees of federal contractors, Department of Defense contractors, and those under Department of Transportation regulations are subject to testing for illegal drug use. (See Chapter 13 for an extended discussion of this topic, including a sample policy statement for a drug-free workplace.)

THE EMPLOYMENT INTERVIEW

Traditionally, the employment interview has had a very important role in the selection process. Various surveys over the past several decades have shown that it is considered to be the most important step in selection.[25] Depending upon the type of job, applicants may be interviewed by one person or by several members of the organization. While researchers have raised serious doubts about the validity of the interview as a selection method, two researchers state that the interview is popular because (1) it is especially practical when there are only a small number of applicants; (2) it does other things well, such as serving as a public relations tool; and (3) interviewers maintain great faith and confidence in their judgments. They suggest that research should focus on differences among interviewers rather than the validity of the interview as a method. In other words, some interviewers' judgments are more valid than others' in the evaluation of applicants.[26]

Interviewing Methods

Employment or selection interviews differ according to the methods used to obtain information and to find out an applicant's attitudes and feelings. The most significant difference lies in the amount of structure, or control, that is exercised by the interviewer. In the highly **structured interview,** the interviewer determines the course that the interview will follow as each question is asked. In the less-structured interview, the applicant plays a larger role in determining the course the discussion will take. An examination of the different types of interviews from the least structured to the most structured will reveal the differences.

NONDIRECTIVE INTERVIEW In the **nondirective interview,** the interviewer carefully refrains from influencing the applicant's remarks. The applicant is allowed the maximum amount of freedom in determining the course of the discussion. The interviewer asks broad, general questions, such as "Tell me more about your experiences on your last job," and permits the applicant to talk freely with a minimum of interruption. Generally, the nondirective interviewer listens carefully and does not argue, interrupt, or change the subject abruptly. The interviewer also uses questions sparingly, phrases responses briefly, and allows pauses in the conversation; the pausing technique is the most difficult for the beginning interviewer to master. The greater freedom afforded to the applicant in the nondirective interview is particularly valuable in bringing to the interviewer's attention any information, attitudes, or feelings that may often be concealed by more structured questioning. However, because the applicant determines the course of the interview and no set procedure is followed, little information that comes from these interviews enables interviewers to cross-check agreement with other interviewers. Thus the reliability and validity of the nondirective interview may be expected to be minimal. This method is most likely to be used in interviewing candidates for high-level positions and in counseling, which we will discuss in Chapter 15.

DEPTH INTERVIEW The **depth interview** goes beyond the nondirective interview by providing additional structure in the form of questions covering different areas of the applicant's life that are related to employment. A form available from Martin M. Bruce, Ph.D., Publishers, provides 34 questions covering work, school achievement, and other areas, to be answered in depth by the applicant. Some of the questions are as follows:

1. What do you consider your most important skills?
2. What sort of supervision brings out the best in you?
3. What would you like to have learned at school that you were not taught?
4. Tell me about the people in your last job.
5. What do you hope to be doing ten years from now?
6. What responsibility did you have in your most recent job?[27]

PATTERNED INTERVIEW The most highly structured type of interview is the **patterned interview**, in which the interviewer adheres closely to a highly detailed set of questions on specially prepared forms. A portion of one of the commercially available patterned interview forms is shown in Figure 6–4. The questions in black ink are asked of the applicant during the course of the interview. The questions in color beneath the lines are not asked of the applicant, but are directed at the interviewers to help them obtain complete information, interpret its significance, and be aware of any inconsistencies. The interpretations are recorded later on a summary sheet that is completed on the basis of information obtained from the interview and from other sources. The training required to conduct the patterned

FIGURE 6–4 A SECTION OF THE McMURRY PATTERNED INTERVIEW FORM

How many times did you draw unemployment compensation? ________ **When?** ________ **Why?** ________
Does applicant depend on self?

How many weeks have you been unemployed in the past five years? ________ **How did you spend this time?** ________
Did conditions in applicant's occupation justify this time?
Did applicant use time profitably?

What accidents have you had in recent years? ________
Is applicant accident-prone? Any disabilities which will interfere with work?

SCHOOLING

How far did you go in school? Grade: 1 2 3 4 5 6 7 8 High School: 1 2 3 4 College: 1 2 3 4 Date of leaving school ________
Is applicant's schooling adequate for the job?

If you did not graduate from high school or college, why not? ________
Are applicant's reasons for not finishing sound?

What special training have you taken? ________
Will this be helpful? Indications of perseverance? Industry?

Extracurricular activities (exclude military, racial, religious, nationality groups) ________
Did applicant get along well with others?

What offices did you hold in these groups? ________
Indications of leadership?

interview, as well as the fact that the procedure is standardized, probably has contributed to its moderate to highly valid results.[28]

INCREASING USE OF HIGHLY STRUCTURED INTERVIEWS More attention is being given to the highly structured type of interview as a result of EEO requirements. For example, staff members of Weyerhaeuser Company's HR department have developed a structured interviewing process with the following characteristics:

1. Is based exclusively on job duties and requirements critical to job performance.
2. Has four types of questions that may be used: situational questions, job-knowledge questions, job sample/simulation questions, and worker-requirements questions.
3. Has sample answers to each question determined in advance. Interviewee responses are rated on a five-point scale defined explicitly in advance.
4. Has an interview committee so that interviewee responses are evaluated by several raters.
5. Is consistently applied to each applicant. All procedures are consistently followed to ensure that each applicant has exactly the same chance as every other applicant.
6. Is documented for future reference and in case of legal challenge.[29]

A highly structured interview is more likely to provide the type of information needed for making sound decisions. It also helps to reduce the possibility of legal charges of unfair discrimination. Employers must be aware that the interview is highly vulnerable to legal attack and that more litigation in this area can be expected in the future.

Special Interviewing Methods

Most employment interviewers will use the methods that have just been discussed. However, there are other methods that are utilized for special purposes. One type of interview, commonly used by government agencies and the military services, involves a panel of interviewers who question and observe a single candidate. This is called a panel, or board, interview.

In a typical panel interview the candidate meets with three to five interviewers who take turns asking questions. After the interview they pool their observations to reach a consensus about the suitability of the candidate. HRM specialists using this method at Philip Morris USA and Virginia Power report that panel interviews provide several significant advantages over traditional one-to-one interviews, including higher validity due to multiple inputs, greater acceptance of the decision, and faster decision time.[30]

Another type of interview, developed during World War II as a technique for selecting military espionage personnel, places the candidate under considerable pressure and hence is known as the **stress interview.** It usually involves rapid-fire questions by several interviewers who verbally attack the interviewee. While it may be useful in selecting personnel for intelligence or similar jobs, its usefulness for other jobs is questionable. One writer remarks that "the onslaught of bad manners called stress interviewing must ensure a splendid crop of witless masochists in the companies that go for it."[31]

In a third type of interview—the group interview—several applicants interact with each other in the presence of selected personnel from the organization. This type of interview, which may reveal competence in interpersonal relationships, is often included as part of an assessment center evaluation, which will be discussed in Chapter 8.

Guidelines for Employment Interviewers

Organizations should exercise considerable caution in the selection of employment interviewers. Qualities that are desirable include humility; the ability to think objectively; freedom from overtalkativeness, extreme opinions, and biases; maturity; and poise. Experience in associating with people from a variety of backgrounds is also desirable.

A training program should be provided on a continuing basis for employment interviewers and at least periodically for managers and supervisors in other departments. Many books on employment interviewing are available as guides. For the HR specialist who desires to explore the topic in depth, a wealth of information is available in journals.

Since 1964, five separate reviews of research studies on the employment interview have been published.[32] Each of these reviews discusses and evaluates numerous studies concerned with such questions as "What traits can be assessed in the interview?" and "How do interviewers reach their decisions?" Highlights in HRM 2 presents some of the major findings of these studies.[33] It shows that information is available that can be used to increase the validity of interviews.

Figure 6–5 illustrates the variables and processes involved in the employment interview that have been studied. The figure shows that a number of applicant characteristics may influence the perception of the interviewer and influence the hiring decision. In addition, many interviewer and situational factors may also influence the perceptual and judgmental processes. For example, knowing the race and sex of an applicant may shape the expectations, biases, and behaviors of an interviewer, which in turn may affect the interview outcome. Even a limited understanding of the variables shown in Figure 6–5 can help increase the effectiveness of the typical employment interviewer.

Interviewer training programs should include practice interviews conducted under guidance. Practice interviews may be recorded on videotape and evaluated later in a group training session. Some variation in technique is only natural. However, the following list presents 13 ground rules for employment interviews that are commonly accepted and supported by research findings. Their apparent simplicity should not lead one to underestimate their importance.

HIGHLIGHTS IN HRM

2 SOME MAJOR FINDINGS FROM RESEARCH STUDIES ON THE INTERVIEW

1. Structured interviews are more reliable than unstructured interviews.
2. Interviewers are influenced more by unfavorable than by favorable information.
3. Interrater reliability is increased when there is a greater amount of information about the job to be filled.
4. A bias is established early in the interview, and this tends to be followed by either a favorable or an unfavorable decision.
5. Intelligence is the trait most validly estimated by an interview, but the interview information adds nothing to test data.
6. Interviewers can explain why they feel an applicant is likely to be an unsatisfactory employee but not why the applicant may be satisfactory.
7. Factual written data seem to be more important than physical appearance in determining judgments. This increases with interviewing experience.
8. An interviewee is given a more extreme evaluation when preceded by an interviewee of opposing value.
9. Interpersonal skills and motivation are probably best evaluated by the interview.
10. Allowing the applicant time to talk makes rapid first impressions less likely and provides a larger behavior sample.
11. Nonverbal as well as verbal interactions influence decisions.
12. Experienced interviewers rank applicants in the same order, although they differ in the proportion that they will accept. There is a tendency for experienced interviewers to be more selective than less experienced ones.

1. *Establish the objectives and scope of each interview.* Examine the purposes of the interview, and determine the areas and specific questions to be covered. Review job requirements, application-form data, test scores, and other available information before seeing the applicant.
2. *Establish and maintain rapport.* This is accomplished by greeting the applicant pleasantly, by displaying sincere interest in the applicant, and by listening carefully.
3. *Be an active listener.* Strive to understand, comprehend, and gain insight into what is only suggested or implied. A good listener's mind is alert, and face and posture usually reflect this fact.
4. *Pay attention to body language.* An applicant's facial expressions, gestures, body position, and movements often provide clues to that person's attitudes and feelings. Interviewers should be aware of what they themselves are communicating nonverbally.

FIGURE 6–5 VARIABLES IN THE EMPLOYMENT INTERVIEW

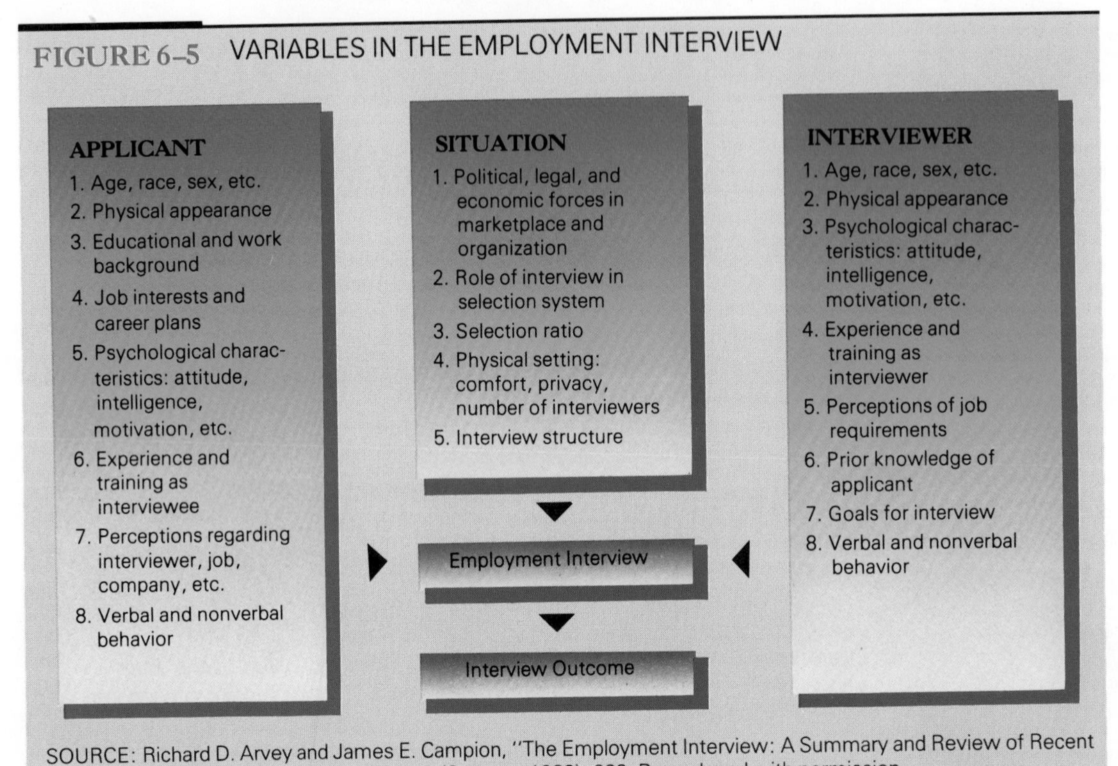

SOURCE: Richard D. Arvey and James E. Campion, "The Employment Interview: A Summary and Review of Recent Literature," *Personnel Psychology* 35, no. 2 (Summer 1982): 283. Reproduced with permission.

5. *Provide information as freely and honestly as possible.* Answer fully and frankly the applicant's questions.
6. *Use questions effectively.* To elicit a truthful answer, questions should be phrased as objectively as possible and with no indication of what response is desired.
7. *Separate facts from inferences.* During the interview, record factual information. Later, record your inferences or interpretations of the facts. Compare your inferences with those of other interviewers.
8. *Recognize biases and stereotypes.* One typical bias is for interviewers to consider strangers who have interests, experiences, and backgrounds similar to their own to be more acceptable. **Stereotyping** involves forming generalized opinions of how people of a given gender, race, etc., appear, think, feel, and act. The influence of sex-role stereotyping is central to sex discrimination in employment.
9. *Avoid the influence of "beautyism."* Discrimination against unattractive persons is a persistent and pervasive form of employment discrimination.

10. *Avoid the halo error.* Judging an individual favorably or unfavorably on the basis of one strong point (or weak point) on which you place high value is the **halo error.**
11. *Control the course of the interview.* Provide the applicant with ample opportunity to talk, but maintain control of the situation in order to reach the interview objectives.
12. *Standardize the types of questions asked.* Avoid discrimination by asking the same questions of all applicants for a particular job.
13. *Keep careful notes.* Record facts, impressions, and any relevant information, including what was told to the applicant.

Types of Preemployment Questions to Ask

The entire subject of preemployment questioning is complex. There are differing and sometimes contradictory interpretations by the courts, the EEOC, and the OFCCP about what is lawful and unlawful. Under federal laws there are no questions that are expressly prohibited. However, the EEOC looks with disfavor on direct or indirect questions related to race, color, age, religion, sex, or national origin. Some

"We need more people like you in our organization!"

SWP

of the questions that interviewers once felt free to ask can be potentially hazardous. Federal courts have severely limited the area of questioning. An interviewer, for example, can ask about physical handicaps if the job involves manual labor, but not otherwise. Several states have fair employment practice laws that are more restrictive than federal legislation. In general, if a question is job-related, is asked of everyone, and does not discriminate against a certain class of applicants, it is likely to be acceptable to government authorities.

Particular care has to be given to questions asked of female applicants about their family responsibilities. It is inappropriate, for example, to ask, "Who will take care of your children while you are at work?" or "Do you plan to have children?" or "What is your husband's occupation?" or "Are you engaged?" It is, in fact, inappropriate to ask applicants of either gender questions about matters that have no relevance to job performance.

Employers have found it advisable to provide interviewers with instructions on how to avoid potentially discriminatory questions in their interviews. The examples of appropriate and inappropriate questions shown in Highlights in HRM 3 may serve as guidelines for application forms, as well as preemployment interviews. Complete guidelines may be developed from current information available from district and regional EEOC offices and from state FEP offices. Once the individual is hired, the information needed but not asked in the interview may be obtained if there is a valid need for it and if it does not lead to discrimination.

EMPLOYMENT TESTS

Since the development of the Army Alpha Test of mental ability during World War I, tests have played an important part in the HR programs of both public and private organizations. Before the passage of the Civil Rights Act of 1964, over 90 percent of companies surveyed by the Bureau of National Affairs reported using tests. By 1976, however, only 42 percent were using tests. But an SHRM survey in 1988 shows that 84 percent of the organizations responding to a survey include testing in their employment decision-making procedures.[34] This resurgence of employment testing from the mid-1970s figure indicates both that employers today are less fearful of lawsuits and that there is a return to a focus on individual competence. Objective standards are coming back in both education and employment. Concurrently, methodological changes have made it easier to demonstrate test validity.[35]

The most popular selection tests are those used to determine secretarial and clerical skills (83 percent of companies). Other tests include general aptitude (39 percent), psychological/personality (32 percent), mechanical aptitude (29 percent), management skills (28 percent), and industrial skills (25 percent).[36]

A renewed interest in testing may indicate that employers who at one time abandoned tests because of EEO requirements now realize their value as a selection procedure. Too often the interview is misused to measure or predict skills and abilities that can be measured or predicted more accurately by tests.[37]

HIGHLIGHTS IN HRM

3 PREEMPLOYMENT QUESTIONS: TO ASK OR NOT TO ASK

	INAPPROPRIATE QUESTIONS	MORE APPROPRIATE QUESTIONS
1.	Do you have any physical defects?	Do you have any physical disabilities or impediments which might in any way hinder your ability to perform the job for which you have applied?
2.	Have you had any recent or past illness or operations?	Have you had any recent or past illness or operations which might, in any way, hinder your ability to perform the job for which you have applied?
3.	What was the date of your last physical exam?	Are you willing to take a physical exam at our expense if the nature of the job requires one?
4.	Are you a U.S. citizen?	Do you have the legal right to live and work in the U.S.?
5.	Date of birth?	Are you over 18?
6.	Age?	Are you over 18?
7.	Emergency information: (Relationship)?	Emergency information: Name, address, telephone no.
8.	Do you possess a legal driver's license?	Only for applicants who desire a job driving a company vehicle: Do you possess a legal and current driver's license?
9.	What are your hobbies? Interests?	Do you have any hobbies or interests which have a direct bearing on the job you are seeking?
10.	Have you ever been arrested for a misdemeanor or felony?	Have you, since the age of 18, ever been convicted of a misdemeanor or felony? (Note: A conviction will not necessarily bar you from employment. Each conviction will be judged on its own merits with respect to time, circumstances, and seriousness.)
11.	Dates attended high school? Grammar school?	Did you complete grammar school? High school?
12.	Date graduated or last attended high school? Grammar school?	Same as item 11.
13.	In what extracurricular activities did you participate? Clubs?	While in school, did you participate in any activities, or belong to any clubs, which have a direct bearing upon the job for which you are applying?

INAPPROPRIATE QUESTIONS	MORE APPROPRIATE QUESTIONS
14. College subjects of interest?	While in college, did you take any courses that directly relate to the job for which you are applying?
15. What salary earnings do you expect?	If you are employed, are you willing to accept the prevailing wage for the job you are seeking?
16. Memberships (with or without EEO disclaimer)?	Have you ever belonged to a club, organization, society, or professional group which has a direct bearing upon your qualification for the job which you are seeking?

SOURCE: E. C. Miller, "An EEO Examination of Employment Applications." Reprinted from the March, 1980 issue of *Personnel Administrator,* copyright 1980, The American Society for Personnel Administration, 606 North Washington Street, Alexandria, VA 22314.

Tests have played a more important part in government personnel programs where hiring on the basis of merit is required by law. Government agencies experienced the same types of problems with their testing programs as did organizations in the private sector. However, their staffs were forced to improve their testing programs rather than to abandon them.

Many organizations utilize professional test consultants to improve their testing programs and to meet EEO requirements. While it is often advisable to use consultants, especially if an organization is considering the use of personality tests, the HR staff should have a basic understanding of the technical aspects of testing and the contributions that tests can make to the HR program.

The Nature of Employment Tests

An employment test is an objective and standardized measure of a sample of behavior that is used to gauge a person's abilities, aptitudes, interests, or personality in relation to other individuals.[38] The proper sampling of behavior—whether verbal, manipulative, or some other type—is the responsibility of the test author. It is also the responsibility of the test author to develop tests that meet accepted standards of reliability.[39]

Data concerning reliability are ordinarily presented in the manual for the test. While high reliability is essential, it offers no assurance that the test provides the basis for making valid judgments. It is the responsibility of the HR staff to conduct validation studies before a test is adopted for regular use. Other considerations are cost, time, ease of administration and scoring, and the apparent relevance of the test to the individuals being tested—commonly referred to as **face validity.** While face validity is desirable, it is no substitute for technical validity, described earlier in this

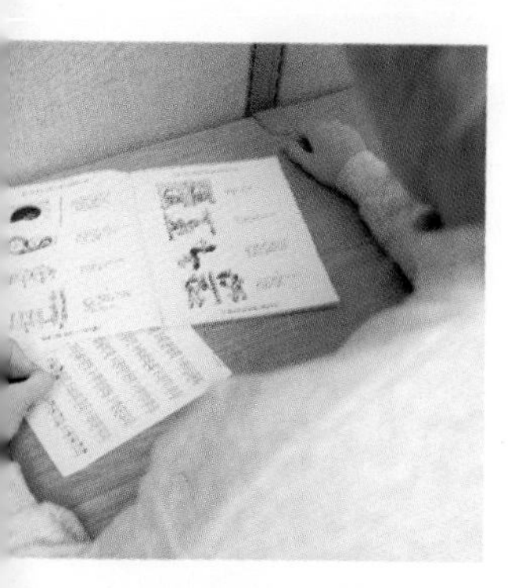

This paper-and-pencil test measures the mechanical aptitude of an applicant.

chapter. Adopting a test just because it appears relevant is bad practice; many a "good-looking" test has poor validity.

Classification of Employment Tests

Employment tests may be classified in different ways. Most of them are *group tests*, in contrast to *individual tests* which usually require one examiner for each person being tested. Another classification relates to the manner in which the individual responds to the test items. For example, *paper-and-pencil tests* require the examinee to respond by writing or marking answers on a booklet or answer sheets. On the other hand, *performance tests* or *instrumental tests* require the examinee to manipulate objects or equipment. Paper-and-pencil tests are the most common, since they can be administered easily to groups, as well as to individuals, with minimum cost. In recent years some paper-and-pencil tests have been adapted for administration by computer, thus providing automatic scoring and accumulation of data for analysis. More sophisticated uses of the computer in testing cognitive, perceptual, and psychomotor abilities are receiving increased attention from research psychologists.

COMMERCIALLY AVAILABLE TESTS In addition to the classifications just mentioned, there is a more fundamental breakdown of tests according to the characteristics they measure. Highlights in HRM 4 lists the types of tests available from commercial sources, along with what they are designed to measure and some of the jobs for which they are used. The publishers of tests in these various categories provide descriptions in their catalogs to help employers select the appropriate tests.

HR managers who need to examine paper-and-pencil tests can obtain specimen sets that include a test manual, a copy of the test, an answer sheet, and a scoring key. The test manual provides the essential information about the construction of the test, its recommended use, and instructions for administering, scoring, and interpreting the test.

Test users should not rely entirely on the material furnished by the test author and publisher. Since 1934, a major source of consumer information about commercially available tests—the *Mental Measurements Yearbook* (MMY)—has been available in most libraries. Published periodically, the MMY contains descriptive information plus critical reviews by experts in the various types of tests. The reviews are useful in evaluating a particular test for tryout in employment situations.

Other sources of information about tests include *Test Critiques*, a set of volumes containing professional reviews of tests, and *Tests: A Comprehensive Reference for Assessments in Psychology, Education, and Business*. The latter describes more than 3,100 tests published in the English language. Another source, *Principles for the Validation and Use of Personnel Selection Procedures*, published by the Society for Industrial and Organizational Psychology, Inc., is a valuable guide for employers who use tests. Other publications are available that present detailed information on how to avoid discrimination and achieve fairness in testing. A review of Chapter 3 will remind the reader of the major issues in the achievement of fairness.[40]

HIGHLIGHTS IN HRM

4 TYPES OF STANDARDIZED TESTS COMMERCIALLY AVAILABLE FOR USE IN PERSONNEL TESTING

TYPE OF TEST	WHAT IS MEASURED	EXAMPLES OF JOBS FOR WHICH USED
General mental ability	Academic intelligence or scholastic aptitude.	Managerial or executive jobs; technical and clerical jobs.
Multiaptitude	Several different aptitude areas such as verbal, numerical, spatial, and mechanical comprehension.	Wide variety of jobs from executive to unskilled.
Dexterity	Finger dexterity, tweezer dexterity, assembly.	Watch repairers, precision electronic assemblers, telephone installers.
Clerical aptitude	Verbal aptitude, numerical aptitude, perceptual speed.	Clerical jobs, inspectors, checkers, packers.
Mechanical aptitude	Mechanical comprehension, spatial relationships.	Variety of engineering and mechanical jobs.
Personality	Range of personality characteristics including emotional adjustment, self-confidence, and perseverance.	Salespersons, managers, and supervisors.
Supervisory and managerial abilities	Attitudes and perceptions, administrative skills, decision-making abilities.	Managerial and supervisory jobs.
Interest inventories	Major interest areas such as scientific, literary, investigative, and computational.	Career planning.

CUSTOM-MADE TESTS Some large organizations do not rely on commercial sources for tests. For various reasons they develop their own tests. Test security is probably a major reason. Another good reason is that a tailor-made test is usually better suited to the jobs and to the organization. Most organizations, however, do not construct their own mental-ability, aptitude, and personality tests. If they do build tests, the tests are more likely to be job-knowledge and job-sample tests.

Government agencies and licensing boards usually develop **job-knowledge tests,** a type of achievement test designed to measure a person's level of understanding about a particular job. Most civil service examinations, for example, are used to determine whether an applicant possesses the information and understanding that will permit placement on the job without further training.[41] Job-knowledge tests also have had a major role in the enlisted personnel programs of the U.S. Army, Navy, and Air Force. They should be considered as useful tools for private and public organizations.

Job-sample tests, or **work-sample tests,** require the examinee to perform tasks that are actually a part of the work required on the job. Like job-knowledge tests, job-sample tests are constructed from a carefully developed outline that experts agree includes the major job functions; the tests are thus considered content-valid. They are often used to measure skills for office/clerical jobs. Job-sample tests have also been devised for many diverse jobs: a map-reading test for traffic control officers, a lathe test for machine operators, a complex coordination test for pilots, an in-basket test for managers, a group discussion test for supervisors, a judgment and decision-making test for administrators, to name a few. The City of Miami Beach has used job-sample tests for jobs as diverse as plumber, planner, and assistant chief accountant. The city reports that this type of test is cost-effective, reliable, valid, fair, and acceptable to applicants.[42]

REACHING A SELECTION DECISION

While all of the steps in the selection process are important, the most critical step is the decision to accept or reject applicants. Because of the cost of placing new employees on the payroll, the short probationary period in many organizations, and EEO/AA considerations, the final decision must be as sound as possible. Thus it requires systematic consideration of all the relevant information about applicants. It is common to use summary forms and checklists to ensure that all of the pertinent information has been included in the evaluation of applicants.

Many employers have introduced a step to the selection process by which to determine more carefully how well the applicant understands what the job entails. A realistic job preview, discussed in Chapter 5, may be used to cover the nature of the job in detail, to describe working conditions, and to point out desirable and undesirable aspects of the job. Several researchers have reported that RJPs are effective in reducing turnover and in having a positive influence on employee attitudes.[43]

Summary of Information About Applicants

Fundamentally, an employer is interested in what an applicant *can do* and *will do*. An evaluation of candidates on the basis of assembled information should focus on these two factors, as shown in Figure 6–6.[44] The "can-do" factors include knowledge and skills, as well as the aptitude (the potential) for acquiring new knowledge and skills. The "will-do" factors include motivation, interests, and other personality characteristics. Both factors are essential to successful performance on the job. The employee who has the ability *(can do)* but is not motivated to use it *(will not do)* is little better than the employee who lacks the necessary ability.

It is much easier to measure what individuals *can do* than what they *will do*. The *can-do* factors are readily evident from test scores and verified information. What the individual *will do* can only be inferred. Responses to interview and application-form questions may be used as a basis for obtaining information for making inferences about what an individual *will do*.

Decision Strategy

The strategy used for making personnel decisions for one category of jobs may differ from that used for another category. The strategy for selecting managerial and executive personnel, to be discussed in Chapter 8, will differ from that used in selecting clerical and technical personnel. While many factors are to be considered in hiring decisions, the following are some of the questions that HR staffs must consider:

1. Should the individuals be hired according to their highest potential or according to the needs of the organization?
2. At what grade or wage level should the individual be started?
3. Should initial selection be concerned primarily with an ideal match of the employee to the job, or should potential for advancement in the organization be considered?
4. To what extent should those who are not qualified but are qualifiable be considered?
5. Should overqualified individuals be considered?
6. What effect will a decision have on meeting affirmative action goals?

FIGURE 6–6 EMPLOYERS SHOULD CONSIDER "CAN-DO" AND "WILL-DO" FACTORS IN SELECTING PERSONNEL

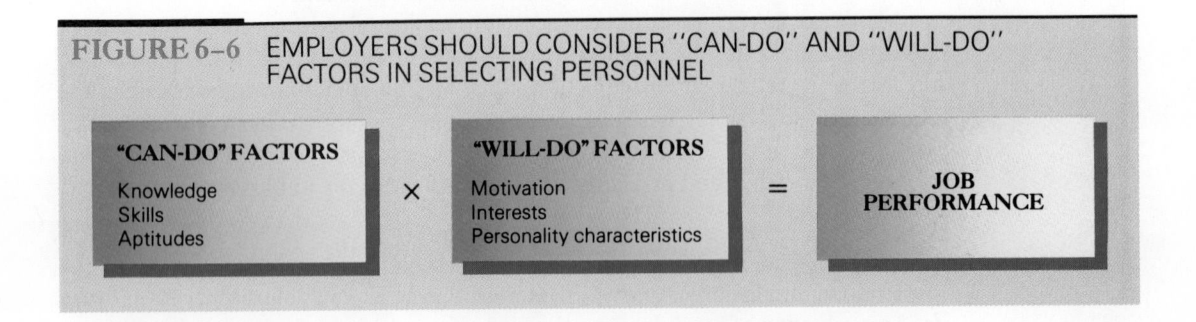

In addition to these types of factors, HR staffs must also consider which approach they will use in making hiring decisions. There are two basic approaches to selection, clinical and statistical.

CLINICAL APPROACH In the clinical approach to decision making, those making the selection decision review all the data on applicants. Then, based on their understanding of the job and the individuals who have been successful in that job, they make a decision. Different individuals often arrive at different decisions about an applicant when they use this approach because each evaluator assigns different weights to the applicant's strengths and weaknesses. Furthermore, personal biases and stereotypes are frequently covered up by what appear to be rational bases for acceptance or rejection.

STATISTICAL APPROACH In contrast to the clinical approach, the statistical approach to decision making is entirely objective. It involves identifying the most valid predictors and weighting them through sophisticated statistical methods. Quantified data such as scores or ratings from interviews, tests, and other procedures are then combined according to their weighted value. Individuals with the highest combined scores are selected. A comparison of the clinical approach with the statistical approach in a wide variety of situations has shown that the statistical approach is superior.[45] Although this superiority has been recognized for many decades, the clinical approach continues to be the one most commonly used. This is a surprising circumstance in light of the widespread utilization of technology in production, finance, and marketing.[46]

While the most valid predictors should be used, there is a related factor that contributes to selecting the best-qualified persons. It is selectivity, or having an adequate number of applicants or candidates from which to make a selection. Selectivity is typically expressed in terms of a **selection ratio,** which is the ratio of the number of applicants to be selected to the total number of applicants. A ratio of 0.10, for example, means that 10 percent of the applicants will be selected. A ratio of 0.90 means that 90 percent will be selected. If the selection ratio is low, only the most promising applicants will normally be hired. When the ratio is high, very little selectivity will be possible since even applicants having mediocre ability will have to be hired if the vacancies are to be filled.

It should be noted that how much of a contribution any predictor will make to the improvement of a given selection process is a function not only of the validity of the predictor and the selection ratio, but also of the proportion of persons who are judged successful using current selection procedures.[47]

The statistical approach requires that a decision be made about where the cutoff lies—that point in the distribution of scores above which a person should be considered and below which the person should be rejected. The score that the applicant must achieve is the cutoff score. Depending upon the labor supply, it may be necessary to lower or raise the cutoff score.

The effects of raising and lowering the cutoff score are illustrated in Figure 6–7. Each dot in the center of the figure represents the relationship between the test score (or a weighted combination of test scores) and the criterion of success for one individual. In this instance, the test has a fairly high validity, as represented by the elliptical pattern of dots. Note that the high-scoring individuals are concentrated in the satisfactory category on job success, whereas the low-scoring individuals are concentrated in the unsatisfactory category.

If the cutoff score is set at A, only the individuals represented by areas 1 and 2 will be accepted. Nearly all of them will be successful. If more employees are needed (i.e., an increase in the selection ratio), the cutoff score may be lowered to point B. In this case, a larger number of potential failures will be accepted, as shown in quadrants 2 and 4. Even if the cutoff is lowered to C, the total number of satisfactory individuals selected (represented by the dots in areas 1, 3, and 5) exceeds the total number selected who are unsatisfactory (areas 2, 4, and 6). Thus, the test serves to maximize the selection of probable successes and to minimize the selection of probable failures. This is all we can hope for in predicting job success: the probability of selecting a greater proportion of individuals who will be successful rather than unsuccessful.

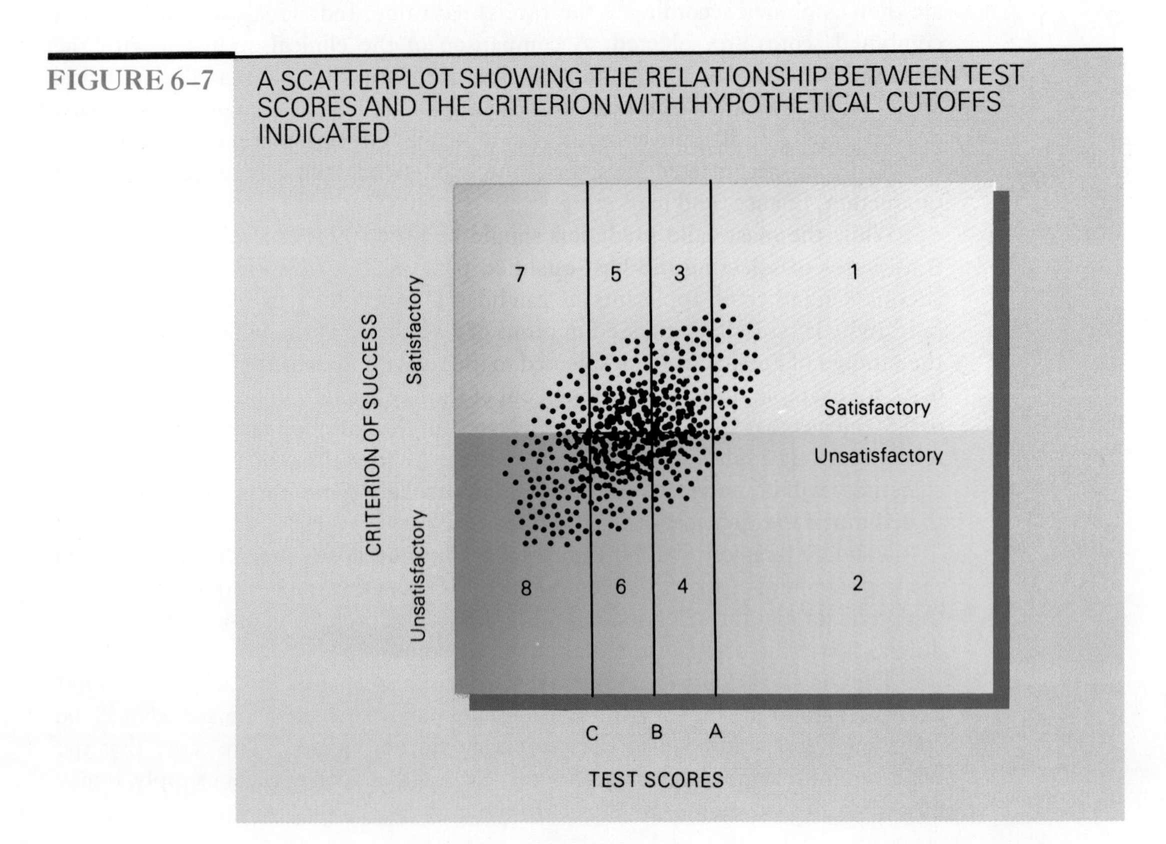

FIGURE 6–7 A SCATTERPLOT SHOWING THE RELATIONSHIP BETWEEN TEST SCORES AND THE CRITERION WITH HYPOTHETICAL CUTOFFS INDICATED

The Final Decision

After a preliminary selection has been made in the employment department, those applicants who appear to be most promising are then referred to departments having vacancies. There they are interviewed by the managers or supervisors, who usually make the final decision and communicate it to the employment department. Because of the weight that is usually given to their choices, managers and supervisors should be trained so that their role in the selection process does not negate the more scientific efforts of personnel in the HR department.

Notifying applicants of the decision and making job offers is generally the responsibility of the HR department. This department should confirm the details of the job, working arrangements, wages, etc., and specify a deadline by which the applicant must reach a decision. If, at this point, findings from the medical examination are not yet available, an offer is often made contingent upon the applicant's passing the examination.

In government agencies, the selection of individuals to fill vacancies is made from lists or registers of eligible candidates. Ordinarily, three or more names of individuals at the top of the register are submitted to the requisitioning official. This arrangement provides some latitude for those making a selection and, at the same time, preserves the merit system.

SUMMARY

The selection process should provide as much reliable and valid information as possible about applicants so that their qualifications can be carefully matched with job specifications. The information that is obtained should be clearly job-related or predictive of success on the job and free from potential discrimination.

Interviews and tests are customarily used in conjunction with application forms, background investigations, medical examinations, and other sources of information. The interview is an important source of information about job applicants. Those who conduct interviews should receive special training to acquaint them with interviewing methods and EEO considerations. The training should also make them more aware of the major findings from research studies on the interview and how they can apply these findings. While the popularity of tests has declined somewhat since the passage of EEO laws, their value should not be overlooked. Tests are more objective than the interview and can provide a broader sampling of behavior.

In the process of making decisions, all "can-do" and "will-do" factors should be assembled and weighted systematically so that the final decision can be based on a composite of the most reliable and valid information. While the clinical approach to decision making is used more than the statistical approach, it lacks the accuracy of the latter approach. Whichever approach is used, the goal is to select a greater proportion of individuals who will be successful on the job.

DISCUSSION QUESTIONS

1. What is meant by the term *criterion* as it is used in personnel selection? Give some examples of criteria used for jobs with which you are familiar.
2. What are some of the problems that arise in checking references furnished by job applicants? Are there any solutions to these problems?
3. Compare briefly the major types of employment interviews described in this chapter. Which type would you prefer to conduct? Why?
4. What characteristics do job-knowledge and job-sample tests have that often make them more acceptable to the examinees than other types of tests?
5. In what ways does the clinical approach to selection differ from the statistical approach? How do you account for the fact that one approach is superior to the other?
6. Personality tests, like other tests used in employee selection, have been under attack for several decades. What are some of the reasons why applicants find personality tests objectionable? On what basis could their use for selection purposes be justified?
7. The term *intelligence* is not commonly used in personnel work, and the concept of IQ (intelligence quotient) is never used. Can you suggest any reasons for this practice?
8. The Supreme Court has consistently interpreted Title VII of the Civil Rights Act of 1964 as prohibiting not only intentional discrimination but also neutral practices which have a discriminatory effect. Thus, practices that are discriminatory in intent *and* effect are prohibited by Title VII. What are some employment practices that are discriminatory in effect, even if not in intent? What should be done with respect to these practices?

MINI-CASE 6–1 Avoiding Discrimination in the Selection Interview

In this chapter we have observed that the interview is used widely as a method for learning as much as possible about job applicants. While conducting an interview, one must be very careful not to ask questions that are or could be interpreted to be discriminatory under equal and/or fair employment laws.

Study the following questions that employment interviewers might ask in the course of a preemployment interview. Evaluate each question in relation to equal opportunity employment laws. Is it acceptable or not? Rephrase those questions that you believe can be made generally acceptable under federal and/or state laws relating to discrimination in employment.

1. Do you have any hobbies?
2. From the ring on your finger I assume that you are married. Am I correct?
3. What type of work does your husband do?
4. I notice on your application form that you are a college graduate. Did you take any courses that are related to the job you are seeking?
5. Do you have any physical handicaps?
6. Do you own your own home, or do you rent?

7. Would you be willing to take a physical examination at our expense?
8. You stated that you are a veteran. Did you have any experience in the military service that relates to the job we are discussing?
9. Have you ever been arrested?

QUESTIONS

1. What are the general rules concerning what may be asked of applicants in a preemployment interview?
2. How can an interviewer avoid asking questions that are or may be construed to be discriminatory?

MINI-CASE 6–2 Working in Harmony

The job of manager in a business organization has frequently been compared with that of a symphony orchestra conductor. Both are concerned with getting each member in the organization to play his or her part and to blend each contribution into a team that works together productively and harmoniously. In order to produce the highest quality of music for its listeners, the San Francisco Symphony Orchestra, with over 100 musicians, gives considerable attention to the recruitment and selection of personnel to fill vacancies. Since 1911, highly accomplished musicians have been striving to become a part of this world-famous organization, and many of them have not achieved their goal.

Whenever a position in the orchestra becomes vacant, an announcement is placed in the magazine *International Musician,* which has subscribers in orchestras and on campuses across the country. After reviewing the résumés it receives, an orchestra screening committee selects qualified applicants and invites them to San Francisco for an audition. Those not selected are invited to submit a tape to be considered along with their résumés; the committee listens to the tapes and invites the most-promising candidates to audition as well.

On the day of the auditions, the candidates arrive at Davies Symphony Hall. Numbers are drawn to establish the order of appearance. Candidates are then provided with practice rooms so they can warm up for the first selection stage—the preliminary audition. Under the terms of the Master Agreement between the San Francisco Symphony Association and the Musicians Union Local #6, the preliminary audition involves ten members of the orchestra who listen to the candidates; five of them are drawn from the principal chairs, and five are members-at-large from the orchestra.

When it is a candidate's turn to audition, he or she is ushered onto the stage behind a screen so as not to be seen by the members of the orchestra sitting in the auditorium. Each candidate for a certain chair plays the same selection, designated in the repertoire for auditionees that was mailed to them. The repertoire typically includes a solo work that demonstrates the candidate's virtuosity. Immediately after a candidate's performance, which usually lasts about 10 to 15 minutes, the selection committee votes on a "yes" or "no" basis. Ballots are collected and counted at once by the union steward and the symphony personnel manager. Candidates who receive six "yes" votes are advised to be available for the final audition on the following day.

In the audition of the finalists, the music director joins the committee. The candidates again appear on stage, one at a time, and play the prescribed selection; however, no screen is used. After hearing a candidate play, the music director may work with the candidate and have the candidate play with members of the appropriate section of the orchestra.

A discussion to evaluate the performance of each finalist follows the last audition. Committee members each express their opinions, and after they are finished, the music director states his opinions. Further discussion and then voting take place. Each committee member votes "yes" or "no." Any candidate receiving six or more "yes" votes qualifies. The music director does not vote but can select or decline to select any qualifying candidate. (Additional provisions exist if a current member of the orchestra is a finalist receiving eight or more qualifying votes.) If the music director selects a finalist for the vacancy, a contract is offered. Should the finalist decline, the music director may select any other qualifying candidate, or may choose not to.

QUESTIONS

1. Why does the orchestra have candidates perform behind a screen for the preliminary audition? Would it be advisable to use this same procedure in the typical employment interview? What would be the advantages and disadvantages of such a procedure in the interview?
2. Why are candidates not permitted to choose their own music? How does this procedure compare with that used in evaluating job candidates in other types of organizations?
3. The music director can select or decline to select any qualifying candidate. Is this a desirable practice? Why or why not?
4. Should a typical business organization be this selective when considering individuals for an executive position? Why or why not?

NOTES AND REFERENCES

1. Charles G. Tharp, "A Manager's Guide to Selection Interviewing," *Personnel Journal* 62, no. 8 (August 1983): 636–639. See also Robert M. Guion and Wade M. Gibson, "Personnel Selection and Placement," in *Annual Review of Psychology* (Palo Alto, CA: Annual Reviews Inc., 1988): 349–374; Edwin A. Fleishman, "Some New Frontiers in Personnel Selection Research," *Personnel Psychology* 41, no. 4 (Winter 1988): 679–701; and Neal Schmitt and Ivan Robertson, "Personnel Selection," in *Annual Review of Psychology* (Palo Alto, CA: Annual Reviews Inc., 1990).

2. Edwin E. Ghiselli, "The Validity of Aptitude Tests in Personnel Selection," *Personnel Psychology* 26, no. 4 (Winter 1973): 461–477.

3. Sheldon Zedeck and Wayne F. Cascio, "Psychological Issues in Personnel Decisions," *Annual Review of Psychology* 35 (1984): 461–518. See also F. L. Schmidt and J. E. Hunter, "Employment Testing: Old Theories and New Research Findings," *American Psychologist* 36, no. 10 (October 1981): 1128–1137; Schmidt, Hunter, and K. Pearlman, "Progress in Validity Generalization: Comments on Callender and Osburn and Further Developments," *Journal of Applied Psychology* 67, no. 6 (December 1982): 835–845; and Margaret E. Giffin, "Personnel Research on Testing, Selection, and Performance Appraisal," *Public Personnel Management* 18, no. 2 (Summer 1989): 127–137.

4. Wayne F. Cascio, *Applied Psychology in Personnel Management,* 3d ed. (Reston, VA: Reston Publishing, 1987), 149–152.

5. *Wall Street Journal* (May 27, 1988): 5C.

6. Robert P. Vecchio, "The Problem of Phony Résumés: How to Spot a Ringer Among the Applicants," *Personnel* 61, no. 2 (March–April 1984): 22–27.

7. Richard R. Reilly and Georgia T. Chao, "Validity and Fairness of Some Alternative Employee Selection Procedures," *Personnel Psychology* 35, no. 1 (Spring 1982): 1–62. See also Hannah R. Rothstein, Frank L. Schmidt, Frank W. Erwin, William A. Owens, and C. Paul Sparks, "Biographical Data in Employment Selection: Can Validities Be Made Generalizable?" *Journal of Applied Psychology* 75, no. 2 (1990): 175–184; and Fleishman, "Some New Frontiers."

8. *BNA Policy and Practice Series—Personnel Management* (Washington, DC: Bureau of National Affairs, 1989), 201:283.

9. "How Many Imposters Have You Hired?" *U.S. News & World Report* (July 13, 1981): 71–72.

10. Thomas J. Von der Embse and Rodney E. Wyse, "Those Reference Letters: How Useful Are They?" *Personnel* 62, no. 1 (January 1985): 42–46; and Erwin S. Stanton, "Telephone Reference Checks," *Personnel Journal* 67, no. 11 (November 1988): 123–129.

11. Carole Sewell, "Pre-employment Investigations: The Key to Security in Hiring," *Personnel Journal* 60, no. 5 (May 1981): 376–377.

12. "Firms Face Lawsuits for Hiring People Who Then Commit Crimes," *Wall Street Journal* (April 30, 1987): 29.

13. *Fair Employment Practices Bulletin,* no. 414 (Washington, DC: Bureau of National Affairs, February 12, 1981), 4. See also Suzanne Cook, "Privacy Rights: Whose Life Is It Anyway?" *Personnel Administrator* 67, no. 9 (April 1987): 58–69.

14. *BNA Policy and Practice Series—Personnel Management,* 1988, 201:279. See also Gilbert Fuchsberg, "More Employers Check Credit Histories of Job Seekers to Judge Their Character," *Wall Street Journal* (May 30, 1990): B1.

15. "Personal Business," *Business Week* (July 27, 1981): 85–86.

16. With some exceptions for jobs in law enforcement, government agencies, or drug-dispensing firms, the following states have banned compulsory or involuntary polygraphing in employment situations: Alaska, California, Connecticut, Delaware, Georgia, Hawaii, Idaho, Iowa, Kansas, Maine, Maryland, Massachusetts, Michigan, Minnesota, Montana, Nebraska, Nevada, New Jersey, New York, Oregon, Pennsylvania, Rhode Island, Tennessee, Texas, Utah, Vermont, Virginia, Washington, West Virginia, and Wisconsin; and the District of Columbia. Several states have some restrictions. See *BNA Policy and Practice Series—Personnel Management,* 1988, 201:251.

17. Albert R. Karr, "Law Limiting Use of Lie Detectors Is Seen Having Widespread Effect," *Wall Street Journal* (July 1, 1988): 13.

18. Paul R. Sackett, "Honesty Testing for Personnel Selection," *Personnel Administrator* 30, no. 9 (September 1985): 67–76.

19. Paul R. Sackett and Michael M. Harris, "Honesty Testing for Personnel Selection: A Review and Critique," *Personnel Psychology* 37, no. 2 (Summer 1984): 221–245.

20. M. Susan Taylor and Kathryn K. Sackheim, "Graphology," *Personnel Administrator* 33, no. 5 (May 1988): 71–76.

21. Michael J. McCarthy, "Handwriting Analysis as Personnel Tool," *Wall Street Journal* (August 25, 1988): 17.

22. *BNA Policy and Practice Series—Personnel Management,* 1988, 201:254.

23. Stephen J. Vodanovich and Milano Reyna, "Alternatives to Workplace Testing," *Personnel Administrator* 33, no. 5 (May 1988): 78–84; and Eric Rolfe Greenberg, "Workplace Testing: Who's Testing Whom?" *Personnel* 66, no. 5 (May 1989): 39–45.

24. Greenberg, "Workplace Testing," 39–45.

25. Ernest J. McCormick and Daniel R. Ilgen, *Industrial Psychology,* 7th ed. (Englewood Cliffs, NJ: Prentice-Hall, 1980), Chapter 10.

26. Richard D. Arvey and James E. Campion, "The Employment Interview: A Summary and Review of Recent Research," *Personnel Psychology* 35, no. 2 (Summer 1982): 281–322.

27. *Selection Interview Form (Revised),* © 1977 by Benjamin Balinsky, Ph.D. Published by Martin M. Bruce, Ph.D., Publishers, 50 Larchwood Road, Larchmont, NY 10538. Reproduced with permission.

28. Robert N. McMurry, *Tested Techniques of Personnel Selection,* rev. ed. (Chicago: Dartnell, n.d.). See also *The Employment Interview—Theory, Research, and Practice,* ed. Robert W. Eder and Gerald R. Ferris (Newbury Park, CA: Sage Publications, 1989).

29. Elliott D. Pursell, Michael A. Campion, and Sarah R. Gaylord, "Structured Interviewing: Avoiding Selection Problems," *Personnel Journal* 59, no. 11 (November 1980): 907–912.

30. David J. Weston and Dennis L. Warmke, "Dispelling the Myths About Panel Interviews," *Personnel Administrator* 33, no. 5 (May 1988): 109–111.

31. R. B. Buzzard, "How Science Will Be Helping Men at Work," *Occupational Psychology* 45, no. 3 (1971): 183–191.

32. E. C. Mayfield, "The Selection Interview—A Reevaluation of Published Research," *Personnel Psychology* 17, no. 3 (Autumn 1964): 239–260; Lynn Ulrich and Don Trumbo, "The Selection Interview Since 1949," *Psychological Bulletin* 63, no. 2 (February 1965): 100–116; Orman R. Wright, Jr., "Summary of Research on the Selection Interview Since 1964," *Personnel Psychology* 22, no. 4 (Winter 1969): 391–414; Neal Schmitt, "Social and Situational Determinants of Interview Decisions: Implication for the Employment Interview," *Personnel Psychology* 29, no. 1 (Spring 1976): 79–101; and Richard D. Arvey and James E. Campion, "The Employment Interview: A Summary and Review of Recent Literature," *Personnel Psychology* 35, no. 2 (Summer 1982): 281–322.

33. These are only a few of the findings from the many studies cited in the review articles listed in note 32. The student who desires to study a comprehensive evaluation of research as it relates to the employment interview may wish to consult Edward C. Webster, *The Employment Interview—A Social Judgment Process* (Ontario, Canada: S.I.P. Publications, 1982); and Eder and Ferris, *The Employment Interview*. A book designed for executives that contains many helpful suggestions is Auren Uris, *88 Mistakes Interviewers Make and How to Avoid Them* (New York: AMACOM, 1988).

34. *Resource* (Alexandria, VA: American Society for Personnel Administration, June 1988), 2.

35. Chris Lee, "Testing Makes a Comeback," *Training* 25, no. 12 (December 1988): 49–59.

36. *Resource*, 2.

37. Robert M. Guion and Andrew S. Mada, "Eyeball Measurement of Dexterity: Tests as Alternatives to Interviews," *Personnel Psychology* 34, no. 1 (Spring 1981): 31–36.

38. For books with comprehensive coverage of testing, including employment testing, see Anne Anastasi, *Psychological Testing*, 5th ed. (New York: Macmillan, 1982); and Lee J. Cronbach, *Essentials of Psychological Testing*, 4th ed. (New York: Harper & Row, 1984).

39. Standards that psychological tests and testing programs should meet are described in *Standards for Educational and Psychological Tests* (Washington, DC: American Psychological Association, 1985).

40. The latest edition of the *Mental Measurements Yearbook* is the tenth edition, published in August 1989. It may be ordered from the University of Nebraska Press, 901 North 17th Street, Lincoln, NE 68588-0529. *Test Critiques and Tests: A Comprehensive Reference* is published by ProEd, 8700 Shoal Creek Blvd., Austin, TX 78758. The address of the administrative office of the Society for Industrial and Organizational Psychology is 617 E. Golf Road, Suite 103, Arlington Heights, IL 60005.

For publications that focus on the topic of fairness, see Richard D. Arvey and Robert H. Faley, *Fairness in Selecting Employees*, 2d ed. (Reading, MA: Addison-Wesley, 1988); and *Journal of Vocational Behavior* 33, no. 3 (December 1988). The entire issue, which is edited by Linda S. Gottfredson and James C. Sharf, is devoted to the topic of fairness in employment testing.

41. It is interesting to note that the origins of the civil service system go back to 2200 B.C., when the Chinese emperor examined officials every three years to determine their fitness for continuing in office. In 1115 B.C. candidates for government posts were examined for their proficiency in music, archery, horsemanship, writing, arithmetic, and the rites and ceremonies of public and private life. See Philip H. DuBois, *A History of Psychological Testing* (Boston: Allyn & Bacon, 1970), Chapter 1.

42. Wayne F. Cascio and Niel F. Phillips, "Performance Testing: A Rose Among Thorns?" *Personnel Psychology* 32, no. 4 (Winter 1979): 751–766.

43. Paula Popovich and John P. Wanous, "The Realistic Job Preview as a Persuasive Communication," *Academy of Management Review* 7, no. 4 (October 1982): 570–578. See also James A. Breaugh, "Realistic Job Previews: A Critical Appraisal and Future Research Directions," *Academy of Management Review* 8, no. 4 (October 1983): 612–619.

44. These two factors are emphasized in a system developed by Robert N. McMurry, *Tested Techniques of Personnel Selection*, rev. ed. (Chicago: Dartnell, n.d.). The system includes a summary sheet for rating the applicant on "can-do" and "will-do" factors and for summarizing the ratings.

45. P. E. Meehl, *Clinical v. Statistical Prediction* (Minneapolis: University of Minnesota Press, 1954); and J. Sawyer, "Measurement and Prediction, Clinical and Statistical," *Psychological Bulletin* 66, no. 3 (September 1966): 178–200.

46. Charles F. Schanie and William L. Holley, "An Interpretative Review of the Federal Uniform Guidelines on Employee Selection Procedures," *Personnel Administrator* 25, no. 6 (June 1980): 44–48.

47. Cascio, *Applied Psychology in Personnel Management*, 284–287. In addition to Cascio's book, the statistically oriented reader may wish to consult George F. Dreher and Paul R. Sackett, *Perspectives on Employee Staffing and Selection* (Homewood, IL: Richard D. Irwin, 1983).

PART THREE

Developing Effectiveness in Human Resources

Part Three contains three chapters that deal with the training and development of employees. Chapter 7 discusses the process by which an organization plans for its training activities, and it describes the many available nonmanagerial and managerial training programs to improve employees' skills and abilities. Chapter 8 looks at career development and explains how individuals can implement their own career development program. Chapter 9 provides a comprehensive review of the employee performance appraisal process, offering several suggestions for carrying out a successful employee appraisal interview. Employees perform more effectively when they receive the proper training for their jobs and their work performance is evaluated in an objective and honest manner.

CHAPTER 7

Training

After reading this chapter you will be able to:

1. *List some of the characteristics of an effective orientation program.*
2. *Describe the scope of organizational training programs.*
3. *Identify and describe the three phases of the systems approach to training.*
4. *Identify the types of training methods used primarily with nonmanagerial personnel, as well as the most effective use of each method.*
5. *List the different types of training methods for developing managers.*
6. *Identify the preconditions for and the basic principles of learning.*
7. *Describe the characteristics of successful trainers.*
8. *Define the key terms in the chapter.*

TERMS TO IDENTIFY

orientation (207)
socialization (208)
organizational analysis (216)
task analysis (216)
person analysis (216)
instructional objectives (217)
on-the-job training (OJT) (218)
computer-assisted instruction (CAI) (220)
computer-managed instruction (CMI) (220)
apprenticeship training (222)
cooperative training (223)
internship programs (223)
in-basket technique (225)
leaderless group discussions (225)
behavior modeling, or interaction management (226)
reinforcement (228)
behavior modification (228)
transfer of training (229)

HR training has become increasingly vital to the success of modern organizations. Rapidly changing technology requires that employees possess the knowledge, skills, and abilities (KSA) needed to cope with new processes and production techniques. The growth of organizations into large, complex operations whose structures are continually changing makes it necessary for managers, as well as employees, to develop the KSA that will enable them to handle new and more demanding assignments.

Training is an ongoing process that begins with orientation and continues throughout an employee's tenure with an organization. Its importance is reflected in the amount organizations spend for training programs. In one year, 614 organizations that subscribe to *Personnel Journal* spent a total of more than $5.3 billion on training and development. Training and development dollars are invested in a variety of programs ranging from employee orientation to management development and in an array of training methods.[1]

There has been a definite trend for organizations to create career development programs. We will give special attention to these programs in the next chapter. In this chapter our emphasis will be on the orientation of employees, the design and evaluation of training programs, training methods, and the application of learning theory.

ORIENTATION

The first step in the training process is to get new employees off to a good start. This is generally accomplished through a formal orientation program. **Orientation**

An orientation meeting is often the first step in the training process.

is the *formal* process of familiarizing new employees with the organization, their job, and their work unit. Its purpose is to enable new employees to get "in sync" so that they become productive members of the organization.

Through a properly conducted orientation program, new employees become socialized to an organization. **Socialization** is the process in which new employees acquire the knowledge, skills, and attitudes that make them successful members of the organization. When socialization is effective, there is a uniting of individual and organizational goals.[2]

Benefits of Orientation

In some organizations a formal new-hire orientation program is almost nonexistent or, when it does exist, is performed in a casual manner. This is unfortunate, since there are a number of very practical and cost-effective benefits from conducting a well-run program. Some of the benefits frequently reported by employers include the following:

1. Lower turnover
2. Increased productivity
3. Improved employee morale
4. Lower recruiting and training costs
5. Facilitation of learning
6. Reduction of the new employee's anxiety

The more time and effort spent in helping new employees feel welcome, the more likely they are to identify with the organization and become valuable members of it. Unlike training, which emphasizes the *what* and *how*, orientation stresses the *why*. It is designed to develop in employees a particular attitude about the work they will be doing and their role in the organization. It defines the philosophy behind the rules and provides a framework for job-related tasks.[3]

Continuous Process

Since an organization is faced with ever-changing conditions, its plans, policies, and procedures must change with these conditions. Unless current employees are kept up-to-date with these changes, they may find themselves embarrassingly unaware of activities to which new employees are being oriented. While the discussion that follows focuses primarily on the needs of new employees, it is important that *all* employees be continually reoriented to changing conditions.

Cooperative Endeavor

For a well-integrated orientation program, cooperation between line and staff is essential. The HR department ordinarily is responsible for coordinating orientation activities and for providing new employees with information about conditions of employment, pay, benefits, and other areas not directly under a supervisor's direction. However, the supervisor has the most important role in the orientation program. New employees are interested primarily in what the supervisor says and does and what their new co-workers are like. Before the arrival of a new employee, the supervisor should inform the work group that a new worker is joining the unit. It is also common practice for supervisors or other managerial personnel to recruit co-workers to serve as volunteer "sponsors" for incoming employees. In addition to providing practical help to newcomers, this approach conveys a strong message of caring.[4]

Careful Planning

An orientation program can make an immediate and lasting impression on an employee that can mean the difference between the employee's success and failure on the job. Thus, careful planning with emphasis on program goals, topics to be covered, and methods of organizing and presenting them is essential. Successful programs emphasize the individual's needs for information, understanding, and a feeling of belonging.

USE A CHECKLIST To avoid overlooking items that are important to employees, many organizations devise checklists for use by those responsible for conducting some phase of orientation. The use of a checklist in the initial orientation of new employees compels a supervisor to be more attentive to each new employee at a time when personal attention is critical to building a long-term relationship. Highlights in HRM 1 suggests items to include in an orientation checklist for supervisors.

FOCUS ON WHAT'S IMPORTANT Those who plan orientation programs should not expect the new employee to assimilate immediately all kinds of details about the organization. There are many things that the new employee will need to know, but most of them can be learned over a period of time. Orientation should focus on matters of immediate concern, as illustrated in Highlights in HRM 1. New employees should be given a clear understanding of the job, safety rules, and any

HIGHLIGHTS IN HRM

1 SUPERVISORY ORIENTATION CHECKLIST

1. A formal greeting, including introduction to fellow employees
2. Explanation of job procedures, duties, and responsibilities
3. Training to be received
4. Supervisor and organization expectations regarding attendance, personal conduct, and appearance
5. Job standards and production/service levels
6. Performance appraisal criteria
7. Conditions of employment, including hours of work, pay periods, overtime requirements, etc.
8. Organization and work unit rules, regulations, and policies
9. Safety regulations
10. Those to notify or turn to if problems or questions arise
11. Chain of command for reporting purposes
12. An overall explanation of the organization's operation and purpose
13. Offers of help and encouragement

other important matters. The initial emphasis should be on making the new employee feel welcome and needed.[5]

DEVELOP AN ORIENTATION PACKET In orientation sessions new employees are often given a packet of materials to read at their leisure. Some of the materials such a packet might include are listed in Highlights in HRM 2. Because statements regarding such matters as tenure, basis for dismissal, and benefits may be viewed by employees and the courts as legally binding on the employer, it is advisable to have the legal department review the packet of materials and write disclaimers to the effect that they do not constitute an employment contract.

REDUCE EMPLOYEE ANXIETY Those planning an orientation program should take into account the anxiety employees feel during their first few days on the job. It is natural to experience some anxiety, but if employees are too anxious, training costs, turnover, absenteeism, and even production costs may increase. Early in the orientation program the following steps should be taken to reduce the anxiety level of new employees:

1. Assure new hires that they have a very good chance for success.
2. Encourage them to ask questions and seek help.
3. Tell them to disregard the comments of negative employees and "jokesters."
4. Encourage them to become acquainted with their supervisors.

HIGHLIGHTS IN HRM

2 ITEMS FOR AN ORIENTATION PACKET

1. Current organization chart
2. Projected organization chart
3. Map of the facility
4. List of key terms unique to the industry, company, and/or job
5. Copy of policy handbook
6. Copy of union contract
7. Copy of specific job goals and descriptions
8. List of holidays
9. List of employee benefits
10. Copies of performance appraisal forms, dates of appraisals, and appraisal procedures
11. Copies of other required forms (e.g., supply requisition and expense reimbursement)
12. List of on-the-job training opportunities
13. Sources of information
14. Detailed outline of emergency and accident-prevention procedures
15. Copy of each important organization publication
16. Telephone numbers and locations of key personnel and operations
17. Copies of insurance plans

SOURCE: Walter D. St. John, "The Complete Employee Orientation Program," *Personnel Journal* (May 1990). Reprinted with permission.

Some employers think it does no harm to allow new employees to be oriented by their peers. One danger of failing to ensure that new workers are oriented by their supervisors and not their peers is that unsafe work practices and unacceptable behaviors that conflict with the organization's policies can be perpetuated. The behaviors these employees develop can undermine the organization's policies and procedures.[6]

Follow-up and Evaluation

Supervisors should always consult with their new employees after the first day and frequently throughout the first week on the job. When all of the items on the orientation checklist for the employee have been addressed, both the supervisor and the employee should sign it, and the record should then be placed in the employee's personnel file. After the employee has been on the job for a month, and again after a year, an HR staff member should follow up to determine how effective the orientation has been. Evaluations can then be conducted through in-depth interviews, questionnaires and surveys, and discussion groups.

TRAINING PROGRAMS

Many new employees come equipped with most of the KSA needed to start work. Others may require extensive training before they are ready to make much of a contribution to the organization. A majority, however, will require some type of training at one time or another to maintain an effective level of job performance.

Training can be defined as any procedure initiated by an organization to foster learning among its members. The primary purpose of a training program is to help the organization achieve its overall objectives. At the same time, an effective training program should help trainees to satisfy their own personal goals.

Scope of Training Programs

The primary reason that organizations train new employees is to bring their KSA up to the level required for satisfactory performance. As they continue on the job, additional training provides opportunities for them to acquire new knowledge and skills. As a result of the training, employees may be even more effective on the job and may qualify for jobs at a higher level.

Automation and computerization have had and will continue to have a major impact on training programs. Economic, social, and political forces likewise have implications for training programs. A Work in America Institute study identifies these implications as follows:

1. Increased global and domestic competition is leading to a greater need for competitive strategies, which often include training as an essential element.
2. Rapid advances in technology have created an acute need for people with specialized technical skills.
3. Widespread mergers, acquisitions, and divestitures, which realign corporate structures but do not necessarily give people the ability to carry out their new responsibilities, require long-term training plans.
4. A better-educated work force, which values self-development and personal growth, has brought an enormous desire for learning plus a growing need for new forms of participation at work.
5. The obsolescence of some occupations and the emergence of new occupations resulting from the changing nature of the economy, the shift from manufacturing to service industries, and the impact of research, development, and technology require flexible training policies to prevent increased turnover and lower productivity.[7]

TRAINING BEYOND JOB REQUIREMENTS Within any large organization there are likely to be hundreds of jobs, each of which involves a variety of knowledge and skills. Thus, training programs may cover a wide range of content reflecting the particular demands of the jobs. In addition to providing training for specific jobs, many employers offer training opportunities that go beyond the immediate job requirements.

A survey of a large number of organizations reveals that the content of training programs varies widely. Figure 7–1 illustrates the diversity of subjects covered as well as the percentage of organizations providing different types of training. New employee orientation, discussed earlier, heads the list. The other types of training are designed for personnel occupying positions at different levels in the organization.

Educational assistance is valued highly by employees. Many organizations, including Intel, New York's Marine Midland Bank, the State of California, and American Express, have an educational assistance program that covers the tuition for courses of specific and direct benefit to an individual's present job performance. Educational assistance may pay off in other ways as well. A Detroit Burger King that in one year spent $10,000 for tuition and other costs for employees attending a local community college saved much more than that in reduced turnover. The annual turnover rate for college-enrolled workers was 58 percent, compared with a 240

FIGURE 7–1 ORGANIZATIONAL TRAINING SUBJECTS

TYPES OF TRAINING	% PROVIDING
New employee orientation	75.8
Performance appraisal	63.5
Time management	61.4
Leadership	58.8
Word processing	56.6
Stress management	53.1
Team building	51.5
Hiring/Selection	51.0
New equipment operation	50.6
Goal setting	49.2
Problem solving	46.0
Safety	46.0
Product knowledge	45.9
Interpersonal skills	44.2
Motivation	44.2
Managing change	42.8
Train-the-trainer	42.7
Listening skills	41.4
Planning	41.0
Personal computer applications	39.4

SOURCE: Chris Lee, "Where Do Training Dollars Go?" Reprinted with permission from the Oct. 1987 issue of *Training,* the Magazine of Human Resources Development. Copyright 1987, Lakewood Publications, Inc., Minneapolis, MN, (612) 333-0471. All Rights Reserved.

percent rate for other workers. Also, productivity rose 3 percent and tardiness and absenteeism declined.[8]

LITERACY EDUCATION The U.S. Department of Education estimates that some 27 million American adults are functionally illiterate. Experts define an illiterate individual as one having a sixth-grade education or less. The department reports that illiteracy will grow in the work force because each year one million teenagers leave school without elementary skills and another 1.3 million non-English-speaking persons arrive in the United States.[9] These figures have important implications for society at large and for organizations that must assimilate these individuals into the work force.

To combat the problem of illiteracy, Polaroid and United Technologies Corporation have developed remedial training programs in math, English, and spelling. Standard Oil of Indiana hired a schoolteacher to give classes in grammar and spelling to newly hired secretaries, while RJR Nabisco offers employees at its Planters Peanuts factory in Suffolk, Virginia, four hours of elementary school courses a week on company time. A further development is that community colleges have been actively working with industry to develop cooperative programs to fight illiteracy. All of these efforts are attempts by organizations to reduce losses in productivity resulting from the poor performance of illiterate employees—losses that in the United States alone annually run into the hundreds of millions of dollars.[10]

A Systems Approach to Training

Since the primary goal of training is to contribute to the organization's overall goals, training programs should be developed with an eye to corporate strategy. Part of the organization's strategy must include recognition of the growing pressure from government and society to attend to the needs of workers who have been displaced by structural shifts in the economy, geographical relocation of jobs, international competition, technological changes, and industry deregulation. Ford Motor Company and General Motors even train their displaced workers who must seek jobs at other organizations.[11]

The problem with some training programs is that one method or gimmick can sometimes become the main focus of the program. The objectives may also be hazy, or evaluation may be inadequate. In a critical review of training programs a decade ago, the HR scene was described as being caught up with fads that satisfy the organization's need to "do something." The reviewers noted that

> The popularity of a program, as indicated by trainee satisfaction, has frequently overshadowed the importance of examining whether the training is bringing about a relatively permanent change in the employee's self-awareness, decision making/problem solving skills, or motivation.[12]

Although one of the same reviewers almost a decade later noted improvements in making training more strategically oriented,[13] managers should still be aware that enthusiasm for a new approach may distract HR personnel from their primary training goals. A recommended solution to this problem is to use a systems approach to training that involves a step-by-step progression through (1) the formulation of instructional objectives, (2) the development of learning experiences to achieve these objectives, (3) the establishment of performance criteria, and (4) the gathering of information to use in evaluating training programs. A model that is useful to designers of training programs is presented in Figure 7–2. Note that the model

FIGURE 7–2 AN INSTRUCTION SYSTEM MODEL

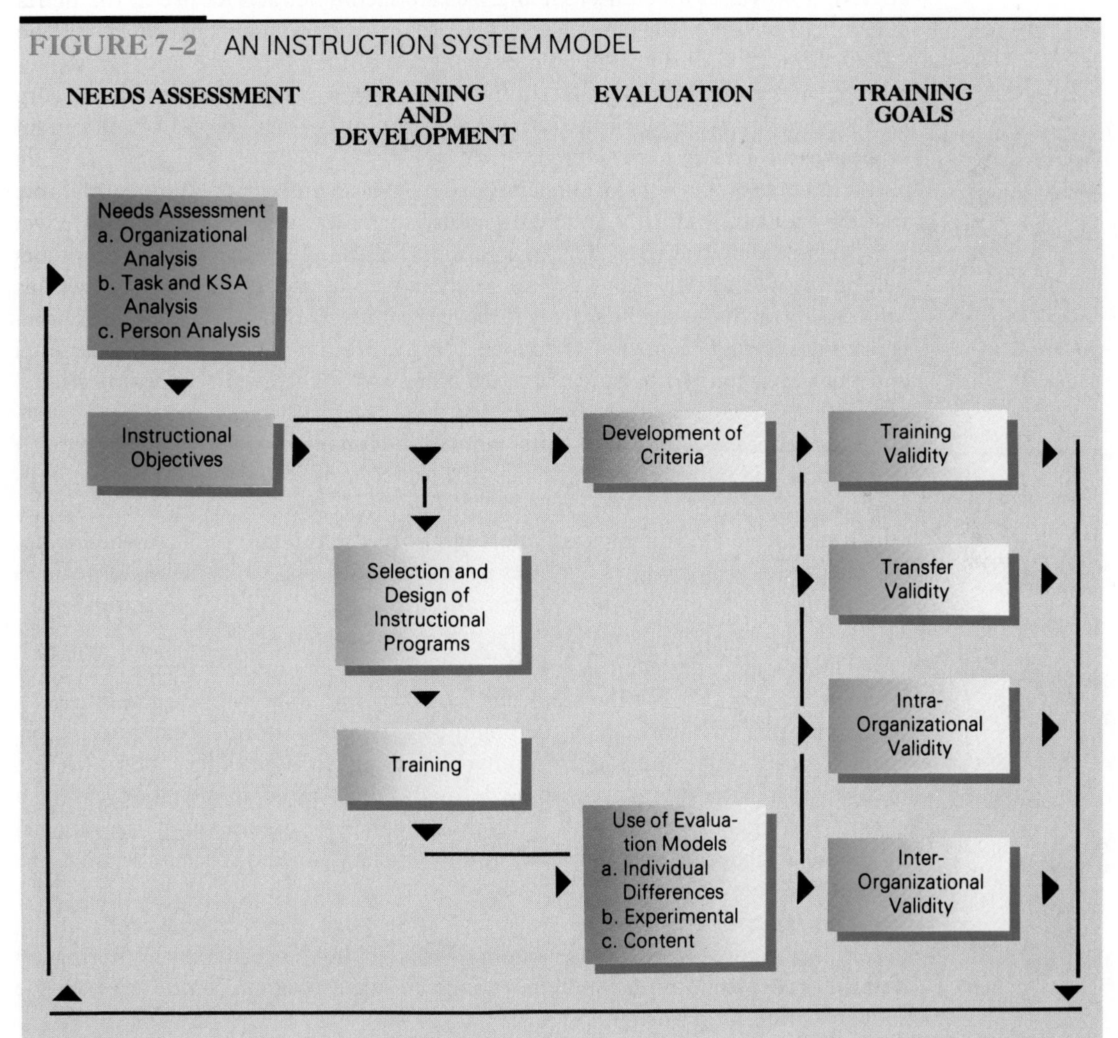

SOURCE: From *Training in Organizations: Needs Assessment, Development, and Evaluation,* 2d ed., by I. L. Goldstein. Copyright © 1986, 1974 by Wadsworth, Inc. Reprinted by permission of Brooks/Cole Publishing Company, Pacific Grove, CA 93950.

consists of four phases: needs assessment, training and development, evaluation, and training goals.[14]

NEEDS ASSESSMENT PHASE Managers and HR staffs should be alert to indications of what kind of training is needed and where it is needed. The failure of workers to meet production quotas, for example, might signal a need for training. Likewise, an excessive number of rejects or a waste of material might suggest inadequate training. Managers should be careful to approach training needs systematically, however. Three different analyses are recommended for use in the needs assessment phase: organizational analysis, task analysis, and person analysis.

Organizational analysis is an examination of the goals, resources, and environment of the organization to determine where training emphasis should be placed. The resources—technological, financial, human, etc.—that are available to meet objectives also must be considered.

HR policies and organizational climate have an impact on the goals of the training program. Similarly, external factors, such as public policy as reflected in laws, regulations, and court decisions, also influence where the training emphasis will be placed. Organizations typically collect data to use in the analysis, such as information on direct and indirect labor costs, quality of goods or services, absenteeism, turnover, and number of accidents. The availability of potential replacements and the time required to train them are other important factors in organizational analysis.

Designing a specific training program requires an organization to review the job description that indicates the activities performed in a particular job and the conditions under which they are performed. This review is followed by a **task analysis,** which involves determining what the content of the training program should be, based on a study of the tasks or duties involved in the job. Task analysis appears to be shifting from an emphasis on what is currently required to what will in the future be required for an employee to be effective in a particular job.[15]

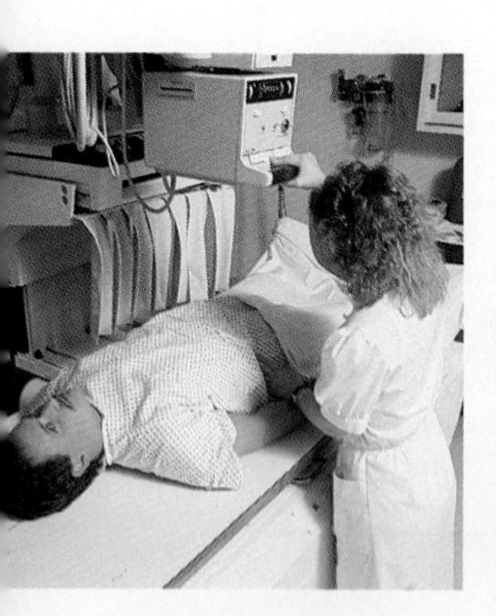

Taking an X-ray involves several steps.

The first step in task analysis is to list all the tasks or duties included in the job. The second step is to list the steps performed by the employee to complete each task. Once the job is understood thoroughly, the type of performance required (i.e., speech, recall, discrimination, manipulation), along with the skills and knowledge necessary for job performance, can be defined. For example, in the task of taking a chest X-ray, a radiologist correctly positions the patient (manipulation), gives special instructions (speech), and checks the proper distance of the X-ray tube from the patient (discrimination).

The types of performance skills and knowledge that trainees need can be determined by observing and questioning skilled jobholders and/or by reviewing job descriptions. This information helps trainers to select program content and choose the most effective training method.

Once the organizational and task analyses have been made, it is necessary to perform a **person analysis.** Person analysis involves determining whether or not task performance is acceptable and studying the characteristics of individuals and groups who will be placed in the training environment. It is important to determine what prospective trainees can and cannot do so that the training program can be designed to emphasize the areas in which they are deficient.

After all the analyses have been made, a picture of the training needs emerges. The desired outcomes of training programs should then be stated formally in **instructional objectives.** Generally, these objectives involve the acquisition of skills or knowledge or the changing of attitudes.[16] Robert Mager, an internationally known training expert, emphasizes the importance of instructional objectives by noting that

> Before you prepare for instruction, before you select instructional procedures or subject matter or material, it is important to be able to state clearly just what you intend the results of that instruction to be. A clear statement of instructional objectives will provide a sound basis for choosing methods and materials and for selecting the means for assessing whether the instruction will be successful.[17]

One type of instructional objective, the performance-centered objective, is widely used because it lends itself to an unbiased evaluation of results. For example, the stated objective for one training program might be that "the trainee will be able to operate a typewriter at the rate of 40 WPM with less than 1 percent error for a period of 10 minutes." Performance-centered objectives typically include precise terms, such as "to calculate," "to repair," "to adjust," "to construct," "to assemble," and "to classify."

TRAINING AND DEVELOPMENT PHASE Once the training needs have been determined and the instructional objectives specified, the next step is to develop the type of environment necessary to achieve these objectives. This includes formulating a specific training strategy and preparing instructional plans.[18] A major consideration in creating a training environment is choosing a method that will enable the trainee to learn most effectively.[19] The methods commonly used in training personnel at all levels—managerial, supervisory, and nonmanagerial—will be discussed later in the chapter.

EVALUATION PHASE Training, like any other HRM function, should be evaluated to determine its effectiveness. Unfortunately, however, few organizations have adequate systems to evaluate the effectiveness of their training programs.

While evaluation methods are improving, too many conclusions about training effectiveness are still based on the subjective reactions of trainers and trainees. It is easy to collect glowing comments from trainees, but this information, however gratifying to the HR staff, may not be very useful to the organization. Training is not provided for its entertainment value. The real issue is whether the training effort will translate to improved behavior or job performance.[20]

Not only should trainees be tested before and after training, but the same evaluations should also be made of individuals in a control group. The control group contains employees who have *not* received the training but who match the trainees in such areas as experience, past training, and job level. Some of the criteria used in evaluating the effectiveness of training are increased productivity, greater total sales, decreased costs and waste, and similar evidence of improved performance.

An evaluation should be undertaken to provide data for a specific decision, such as whether or not to adopt or continue a training course, or how to improve the course. This latter question was addressed by a large midwestern police force as it evaluated a training program for police officer recruits. The objectives of this evaluation were (1) to determine the extent to which the training content was job-related and (2) to identify what changes in training content were needed to improve job-relatedness.[21] Planning the evaluation around specific objectives increases the likelihood that findings will produce meaningful changes. Training directors often limit themselves by not being able to prove their effectiveness objectively in terms of the specific benefits of training to the organization and the costs of obtaining those benefits.

MEETING TRAINING GOALS To help determine the effectiveness of training, the evaluation phase must address the worth of the training program. As the last column of Figure 7–2 shows, a number of goals are possible. The choice of which goal to pursue depends on the information one seeks and the constraints under which one operates. Goldstein describes the four choices as follows:

1. *Training Validity*. Whether the trainees learn during training.
2. *Transfer Validity*. Whether what has been learned in training translates to enhanced performance in the organization.
3. *Intra-organizational Validity*. Whether the performance of a new group of trainees in the organization that developed the training program is consistent with the performance of the original training group in the same organization.
4. *Inter-organizational Validity*. Whether a training program found effective in one organization can be used successfully in another organization.[22]

TRAINING NONMANAGERIAL EMPLOYEES

A wide variety of methods are available for training personnel at all levels. Some of the methods have a long history of usage. Newer methods have emerged over the years out of a greater understanding of human behavior, particularly in the areas of learning, motivation, and interpersonal relationships. More recently, technological advances, especially in electronics, have resulted in training devices that in many instances are more effective and economical than traditional training methods.

On-the-Job Training

On-the-job training (OJT) is one of the most common methods of training nonmanagerial employees. OJT has the advantage of providing "hands-on" experience under normal working conditions and an opportunity for the trainer—a supervisor or senior employee—to build good relationships with new employees.

Although it is used by all types of organizations, OJT is often one of the most poorly implemented training methods. Three common drawbacks include (1) the lack of a well-structured training environment, (2) poor training skills of supervisors, and (3) the absence of well-defined job performance criteria.[23] To overcome these problems, training experts suggest the following:

1. Develop realistic goals and/or measures for each OJT area.
2. Plan a specific training schedule for each trainee, including setting periods for evaluation and feedback.
3. Help supervisors to establish a nonthreatening atmosphere that is conducive to learning.
4. Conduct periodic evaluations, after training is completed, to prevent regression.[24]

Off-the-Job Training

In addition to on-the-job training, it is usually necessary to provide workers with training in settings away from their ordinary workplace. Some methods involve training employees away from their usual workstations but still within the organization's facilities. Other methods involve training employees in locations outside the organization.

CONFERENCE OR DISCUSSION METHOD A method of individualized instruction frequently used where the training involves primarily the communication of ideas, procedures, and standards is the *conference* or *discussion method.* This method allows for considerable flexibility in the amount of employee participation.

CLASSROOM TRAINING METHOD *Classroom training* enables the maximum number of trainees to be handled by the minimum number of instructors. This method lends itself particularly to training in areas where information and instructions can be presented in lectures, demonstrations, videotapes, and films. Where it is not possible to obtain videotapes, audiotapes can be very valuable. For example, to instruct flight-crew trainees, airlines might play a cockpit tape taken from a doomed aircraft. After listening to the tape, the trainees discuss the behavior of the crew during the crisis. By listening to the recorded statements of others and observing their failure to operate as a team, pilot trainees develop an understanding of the need for balancing their sense of self-reliance with an ability to listen to subordinates.[25]

A special type of classroom facility is used in *vestibule training.* Trainees are given instruction in the operation of equipment like that found in operating departments. The emphasis is on instruction rather than production.

PROGRAMMED INSTRUCTION METHOD One method of instruction uses a book, manual, or teaching machine to present programmed subject matter. *Programmed instruction* breaks down subject matter content into highly organized, logical sequences that demand continuous responses on the part of the trainee. After being presented with a small segment of information, the trainee is required to answer a question, either by writing it in a response frame or by pushing a button. If the response is correct, the trainee is told so and is presented with the next step (frame) in the material. If the response is incorrect, further explanatory information is given and the trainee is told to try again.

A major advantage of programmed instruction is that it incorporates a number of established learning principles, which we discuss later in the chapter. With programmed instruction, training is individualized, trainees are actively involved in the instructional process, and feedback and reinforcement are immediate.

COMPUTER-BASED TRAINING According to a recent study of organizations with 50 or more employees, about 46 percent use computers in their training efforts. Users of computer-based training (CBT) include banks, utilities, educational institutions, government agencies, manufacturers, and health care providers. CBT encompasses two distinct techniques: computer-assisted instruction and computer-managed instruction.[26] A **computer-assisted instruction (CAI)** system delivers training material directly through a computer terminal in an interactive format. The memory and storage capabilities of computers make it possible to provide drill and practice, problem solving, simulation, gaming forms of instruction, and certain very sophisticated forms of individualized tutorial instruction.

A **computer-managed instruction (CMI)** system is normally used in conjunction with CAI, thereby providing an efficient means of managing the training function. CMI uses a computer to generate and score tests and to determine the level of trainee proficiency. CMI systems can also track the performance of trainees and direct them to appropriate study material to meet their specific needs. With CMI, the computer takes on some of the routine aspects of training, freeing the instructor to spend time on course development or individualized instruction.

CBT is being used more and more to train users of human resources information systems (HRIS). Trainees begin with relatively simple tasks, such as entering a new employee in the personnel file, then proceed to more complex procedures as they master each task. The training data are often simulated, but the procedures are real. Some of the advantages of CBT are listed in Highlights in HRM 3.[27]

SIMULATION METHOD Sometimes it is either impractical or unwise to train workers on the actual equipment that is used on the job. An obvious example is the training of personnel to operate aircraft, spacecraft, and other highly technical and expensive equipment. The simulation method emphasizes realism in equipment and its operation at minimum cost and maximum safety. For example, locomotive engineers can receive rigorous training through the use of a locomotive simulator. Employing advanced computer technology, the simulator can realistically

HIGHLIGHTS IN HRM

3 ADVANTAGES OF COMPUTER-BASED TRAINING

1. Learning is self-paced.
2. Training comes to the employee.
3. All trainees get exactly the same training.
4. New employees do not have to wait for a scheduled training session.
5. Training can focus on specific needs as revealed by built-in tests.
6. Trainees can be referred to on-line help or written material.
7. It is easier to revise a computer program than to change classroom training materials.
8. Recordkeeping is facilitated.
9. The computer program can be linked to video presentations.

SOURCE: Adapted from Ralph E. Ganger, "Computer-based Training Improves Job Performance," *Personnel Journal* 68, no. 6 (June 1989): 116–123. Reproduced with permission.

depict train-track dynamics, provide taped train sounds and visuals, and duplicate a variety of operations for trains of up to 240 cars and 15 engines.[28]

USE OF OTHER TRAINING DEVICES To teach skills and procedures for many production jobs, certain training devices may be used. For example, devices that look like a portable TV use slides or videotape to illustrate the steps in the manufacture and assembly of electronic and other components. Closed-circuit television and video recording equipment (such as camcorders) are also standard training devices. Closed-circuit television allows an instructional program to be transmitted to many locations simultaneously. The use of camcorders permits on-the-spot recording and immediate feedback to the trainees.

Two newer training techniques, the *videodisk* and *training by telephone* (or *teletraining*), incorporate positive learning principles while providing flexibility to organizational trainers. Interactive videodisks, an extension of CBT, have an advantage over other programmed learning techniques in that they allow immediate access to any segment of the instructional program. This is especially useful for individualized instruction of trainees with different levels of knowledge and ability. Videodisks are currently used to teach doctors to diagnose illness, to help dairy farmers to increase productivity, and to teach CPR trainees in firefighting and other emergency services jobs to revive victims of heart attacks.[29] More-recent applications tackle the difficult managerial skills of leadership, supervision, and interpersonal relations.

Teletraining is used by the Iowa Department of Social Services to provide orientation to new employees. The United Bank of Colorado presents monthly sales

The view from inside the locomotive simulator cab.

market training by telephone to 30 banks throughout the state. What are the benefits of teletraining? They include scheduling flexibility, reduced time and expense of staff travel, increased access to experts, and the ability to reach dispersed groups of trainees in remote locations. Hewlett-Packard "brings the academic world to the workplace" by using satellite technology to tap training from colleges and universities.[30]

Apprenticeship Training

A system of training in which the worker entering industry is given thorough instruction and experience, both on and off the job, in the practical and theoretical aspects of the work in a skilled trade is known as **apprenticeship training.** Apprenticeship programs are based on voluntary cooperation between management and labor, between industry and government, and between the organization and the school system. Although apprenticeship wages are less than those of fully qualified workers, this method does provide training with pay for individuals interested in qualifying for jobs such as machinist, appliance repairer, laboratory technician, and electrician. Since 1978, U.S. Department of Labor regulations have required apprenticeship-program operators to take affirmative action in recruiting and hiring women and to establish goals and timetables for doing so.

Cooperative Training, Internships, and Governmental Training

Cooperative training programs combine practical on-the-job experience with formal classes. The term *cooperative training* is also used in connection with high school programs that incorporate part-time work experiences.

Internship programs, jointly sponsored by colleges, universities, and a variety of organizations, offer students the chance to get real-world experience while finding out how they will perform in work organizations. Organizations benefit by getting student-employees with new ideas, energy, and eagerness to accomplish their assignments. Arizona State University and other universities allow students to earn college credits based on successful job performance and fulfillment of established program requirements.[31]

The federal government and various state governments sponsor a multitude of training programs for new and current employees. Frequently, these training efforts are aimed at the development of basic job skills for individuals lacking marketable skills.

A recurring criticism of government training programs is that they encourage waste and fraud, and that trainers and vocational counselors rely on out-of-date information in designing instructional programs. Recent government programs address these concerns by requiring that training programs be "run on a business-like basis, with annual operating plans, quarterly budgets, and criteria for making sure the training gets people jobs."[32]

Under the Job Training Partnership Act (JPTA), a federally sponsored training program stipulates that most local programs must place 55 percent of their participants in jobs. The federally funded Job Corps sets guidelines for its training centers, half of them managed by private, for-profit companies under Labor Department contracts. State programs experiencing success include Pennsylvania's Customized Job Training program and California's retraining program for unemployed workers.[33]

TRAINING MANAGERS AND SUPERVISORS

Some of the training methods discussed in the preceding section may also be used to train managers and supervisors. However, because of the broader KSA required of managerial and supervisory personnel, other methods are also used.

On-the-Job Experiences

Management skills and abilities cannot be acquired just by listening and observing or by reading about them. They must be acquired through actual practice and experience in which there are opportunities to perform under pressure and to learn from mistakes. On-the-job experiences are used most commonly by organizations to develop executives. Such experiences should be well planned and supervised and should be meaningful and challenging to the participant. Methods of providing on-the-job experiences include the following:

1. *Coaching*—involves a continuing flow of instructions, comments, and suggestions from the superior to the subordinate.
2. *Understudy Assignment*—grooms an individual to take over the supervisor's job by gaining experience in handling important functions of the job.
3. *Job Rotation*—provides, through a variety of work experiences, the broadened knowledge and understanding required to manage more effectively.
4. *Lateral Transfer*—involves horizontal movement through different departments along with upward movement in the organization.
5. *Project and Committee Assignments*—provide an opportunity for the individual to become involved in the study of current organizational problems and in planning and decision-making activities.
6. *Staff Meetings*—enable participants to become more familiar with problems and events occurring outside their immediate area by exposing them to the ideas and thinking of other managers.
7. *Planned Career Progressions* (discussed in Chapter 8)—utilize all these different methods to provide employees with the training and development necessary to progress through a series of jobs requiring higher and higher levels of knowledge and/or skills.

Although these methods are used most often to train managers for higher-level positions, they also provide valuable experiences for those who are being groomed for other types of positions in the organization.

Off-the-Job Experiences

While on-the-job experiences constitute the core of management training, certain methods of development away from the job can be used to supplement these experiences. Off-the-job experiences may be provided on either an individual or a group basis and may be taught by means of special programs or seminars. They may include time management, assertiveness training, business writing skills, strategic planning, employee appraisal, creative thinking, stress management, interpersonal skills, listening skills, and management of change.

CASE STUDY METHOD Particularly useful in classroom learning situations are *case studies*. These documented examples, which may have been developed from actual experiences within their organizations, can help managers to learn how to gather and interpret facts, to become conscious of the many variables on which a management decision may be based, and, in general, to improve their decision-making skills.

IN-BASKET TRAINING METHOD Another method used to simulate a problem situation is the **in-basket technique.** With this technique the participants are given several documents, each describing some problem or situation requiring an immediate response. They are thus forced to make decisions under the pressure of time and also to determine what priority to give each problem. In-basket exercises are a common instructional technique used in assessment centers, which are discussed in Chapter 8.

LEADERLESS GROUP DISCUSSIONS A popular assessment center activity is **leaderless group discussions.** With this technique, trainees are gathered in a conference setting to discuss an assigned topic either with or without designated group roles. The participants are given little or no instruction in how to approach the topic, nor are they told what decision to reach. Leaderless group trainees are evaluated on their initiative, leadership skills, and ability to work effectively in a group setting.

MANAGEMENT GAME METHOD Training experiences have been brought to life and made more interesting through the development of *management games*. Players are faced with the task of making a series of decisions affecting a hypothetical organization. The effects that every decision has on each area within the organization can be simulated with a computer that has been programmed for the game. A major advantage of this technique is the high degree of participation that it requires.

The game method does not always require a computer, however. Some years ago, Motorola developed a game called "EEO: It's Your Job" to teach the basic principles of equal employment opportunity. Originally devised to fill Motorola's own affirmative action needs, it is now commercially available for use in training

Managers learn EEO principles with Motorola's game "EEO: It's Your Job."

programs.[34] A game kit accommodates up to 24 players at a single session, divided into teams of four. The players get caught up in the competitive spirit of a game and at the same time absorb and remember government regulations. They also become aware of how their own daily decisions affect their employer's compliance with these regulations. The game is reinforced with a slide presentation.

ROLE-PLAYING METHOD *Role playing* consists of assuming the attitudes and behavior—that is, playing the role—of others, often a supervisor and a subordinate who are involved in a personnel problem. Role playing can help participants improve their ability to understand and cope with the problems of those they deal with in their daily work. It should also help them to learn how to counsel others by helping them see situations from a different point of view. Role playing is used widely in training health care personnel to be sensitive to the concerns of patients.

LABORATORY TRAINING METHOD Laboratory training, which typically involves interpersonal interactions in a group setting, has as its primary goal the development of greater sensitivity on the part of its participants, including self-insight and an awareness of group processes. It also provides the opportunity to improve human relations skills by having managers or supervisors better understand themselves and others. This is achieved by encouraging trainees to share their experiences, feelings, emotions, and perceptions with other trainees or fellow employees. The ability to participate constructively in group activities is another benefit of this technique.

One variant of laboratory training is *sensitivity training*. As the term would indicate, this training increases a person's awareness of his or her own behavior as it is seen by other training participants. Highly popular in the 1970s, sensitivity training came to be viewed as a form of brainwashing because of its often unwarranted intrusion into employees' personal lives. As the popularity of sensitivity training declined, a wide variety of "New Age" seminars and self-improvement courses emerged. However, a problem with these programs is that some individuals find that the content of the programs conflicts with their own personal moral, ethical, and religious beliefs. As a result, they resent being forced by their employer to participate. In February 1988 the EEOC issued a policy statement that referred specifically to such cases. The EEOC intends to treat religious objections to New Age programs according to the traditional guidelines of Title VII of the Civil Rights Act of 1964. In considering whether to offer such a program, an employer should examine the ethical and legal ramifications of the program.[35]

BEHAVIOR MODELING METHOD Training programs designed simply to change supervisors' attitudes are no longer as useful as they might have been in the past. Supervisors now must be shown how to put their attitudes to work. One such approach is **behavior modeling,** or **interaction management,** which emphasizes the need to involve supervisory trainees in handling real-life employee problems and to provide immediate feedback on their own performance.[36] The main purpose of behavior modeling is to achieve behavioral change. There are four basic steps in behavior modeling:

1. Supervisory trainees view films or videotapes in which a model supervisor is portrayed dealing with an employee in an effort to improve or maintain the employee's performance. The example shows specifically how to deal with the situation.
2. Trainees participate in extensive practice and rehearsal of the behaviors demonstrated by the models. The greatest percentage of training time is spent in these skill-practice sessions.
3. As the trainee's behavior increasingly resembles that of the model, the trainer and other trainees provide social reinforcers such as praise, approval, encouragement, and attention. Videotaping behavior rehearsals provides feedback and reinforcement.
4. Emphasis throughout the training period is placed on transferring the training to the job.[37]

Does behavior modeling work? Several controlled studies have demonstrated success in changing the behavior of supervisors, as well as measurable increases in worker productivity. One study provided objective evidence that behavior modeling of marketing representatives actually resulted in increased sales.[38]

PSYCHOLOGICAL PRINCIPLES OF LEARNING

The success of a job training program depends on more than the organization's ability to identify training needs and the care with which it prepares the program. If the trainees do not learn what they are supposed to learn, the training has not been successful. However, training experts believe that if trainees do not learn, it is probably because some important learning principle has been overlooked. Because the success or failure of a training program is frequently related to this simple fact, those who develop instructional programs should recognize that they need to attend to the basic psychological principles of learning. Trainers as well should understand that the different methods or techniques used in training personnel vary in the extent to which they utilize these principles.

Preconditions for Learning

Two preconditions for learning will affect the success of those who are to receive training: readiness and motivation. Trainee readiness refers to both maturity and experience factors in the trainee's background. Prospective trainees should be screened to determine that they have the background knowledge or the skills necessary to absorb what will be presented to them. Recognizing individual differences in readiness is as important in organizational training as it is in any other teaching situation. It is often desirable to group individuals according to their capacity to learn, as determined by test scores, or to provide an alternative type of instruction for those who need it.

The receptiveness and readiness of participants in workshops and similar training programs can be increased by having them complete questionnaires telling why they are attending the workshop and what they want to accomplish. Participants may also be asked to give copies of their completed questionnaires to their supervisors. Highlights in HRM 4 offers an example of a preprogram worksheet used by Analog Devices.

The other precondition for learning is that trainees be properly motivated. That is, for optimum learning trainees must recognize the need for acquiring new information or for having new skills, and they must maintain a desire to learn as training progresses. As one management consultant advises, "It's not enough just to 'tell.' You also have to 'sell' trainees on the material they are supposed to learn if training is to succeed."[39]

While most workers are motivated by certain common needs, they differ from one another in the relative importance of these needs at any given time. For example, new college graduates often have a high desire for advancement, and they have established specific goals for career progression. Training objectives that are clearly related to trainees' individual needs will increase the motivation of employees to succeed in training programs.

Basic Principles of Learning for Trainers

After trainees are placed in the learning situation, their readiness and motivation should be assessed further. In addition, trainers should understand the following basic principles of learning.

MEANINGFULNESS OF PRESENTATION One principle of learning is that the material to be learned should be presented in as meaningful a manner as possible. The material should be arranged so that each experience builds upon preceding ones and so that the trainee is able to integrate the experiences into a usable pattern of knowledge and skills.

REINFORCEMENT Anything that strengthens the trainee's response is called **reinforcement.** It may be in the form of approval from the trainer or the feeling of accomplishment that follows the performance; or it may simply be confirmation by a teaching machine that the trainee's response was correct. Reinforcement is generally most effective when it occurs immediately after a task has been performed.

In recent years some industrial organizations have used **behavior modification,** a technique that operates on the principle that behavior that is rewarded—positively reinforced—will be exhibited more frequently in the future, whereas behavior that is penalized or unrewarded will decrease in frequency.[40] Behavior modification will be discussed more thoroughly in Chapter 14.

HIGHLIGHTS IN HRM

4 TRAINING AND DEVELOPMENT PREPROGRAM WORKSHEET

Program Title	Program Date

Instructions: Please review and complete the questions below with your supervisor, referencing the program objectives in the Training & Development Guide.

1. The following are work situations in which I want to improve my skills.

2. As a result of this program, I want to achieve the following:

3. Any other related information:

Signature of Participant	Signature of Supervisor	Date

Requirements for Program Attendance. To help ensure your learning and use of new skills:

BRING one copy of this form to the program.
GIVE one copy to your supervisor.
SEND one copy to Training & Development, *at least five days before the program.*

SOURCE: Reprinted with permission of Analog Devices, Norwood, Massachusetts.

TRANSFER OF TRAINING Unless what is learned in the training situation is applicable to what is required on the job, the training will be of little value. The ultimate effectiveness of learning, therefore, is to be found in the answer to the question "To what extent does what is learned *transfer* to the job?" **Transfer of training** to the job can be facilitated by having conditions in the training program come as close as possible to those on the job. Another approach is to teach trainees how they can apply to the job the behaviors they have learned. Furthermore, once training is completed, the supervisor should ensure that the work environment supports, reinforces, and rewards the trainee for applying the new skills or knowledge.[41]

Other Principles of Learning

Other principles of learning have also been developed over the past several decades, primarily as a result of laboratory studies. The principles apply in varying degrees to different types of material to be learned. They have been found to have application in many job training programs.

KNOWLEDGE OF PROGRESS As an employee's training progresses, motivation may be maintained and even increased by providing ***knowledge of progress***, or feedback. Progress, as determined by tests and other records, may be plotted on a chart; the plot is commonly referred to as a learning curve. Figure 7–3 presents an example of a learning curve that is common in the acquisition of many job skills.

In many learning situations there are times when progress does not occur. Such periods show up on the curve as a fairly straight horizontal line, called a ***plateau***. A plateau may be the result of reduced motivation or ineffective methods of task performance. It is a natural phenomenon of learning, and there is usually a spontaneous recovery, as Figure 7–3 shows.

DISTRIBUTED LEARNING Another factor that determines the effectiveness of training is the amount of time devoted to practice in one session. Should

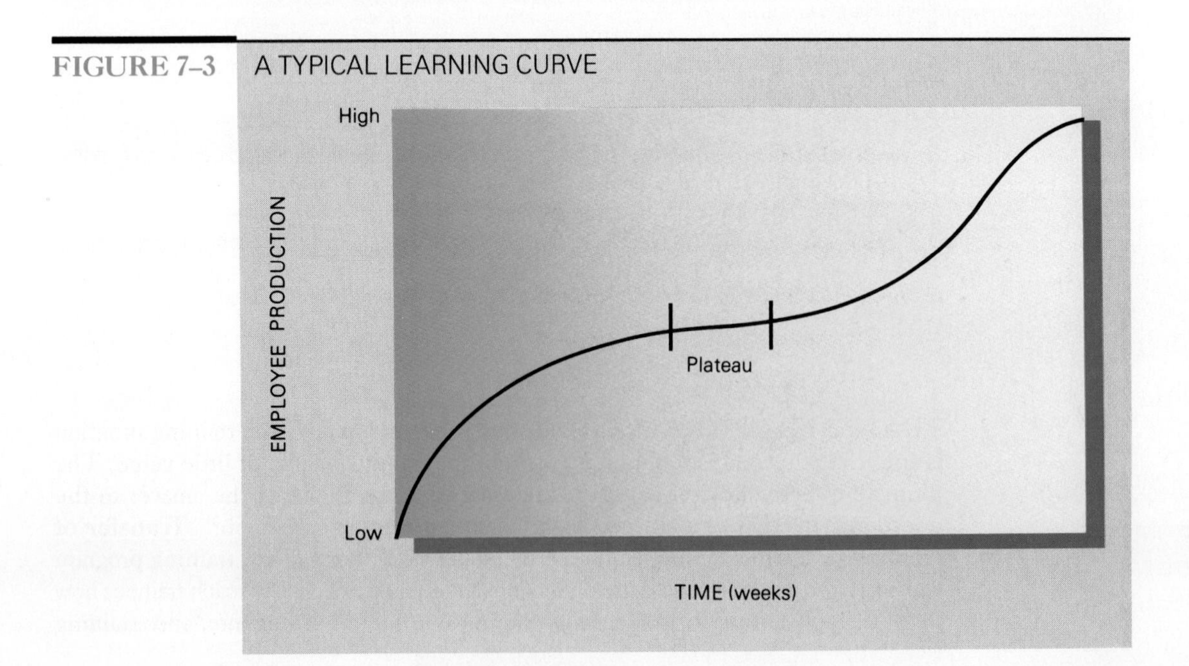

FIGURE 7–3 A TYPICAL LEARNING CURVE

Typists acquire their skills through part learning.

trainees be given training in five two-hour periods or in ten one-hour periods? It has been found in most cases that spacing out the training will result in faster learning and longer retention. This is the principle of distributed learning. Since the efficiency of the distribution will vary with the type and complexity of the task, trainers should refer to the rapidly growing body of research in this area when they require guidance in designing a specific training situation.[42]

WHOLE VERSUS PART LEARNING Most jobs and tasks can be broken down into parts that lend themselves to further analysis. Determining the most effective manner for completing each part then provides a basis for giving specific instruction. Typing, for example, is made up of several skills that are part of the total process. The typist starts by learning the proper use of each finger; eventually, with practice, the individual finger movements become integrated into a total pattern. Practice by moving individual fingers is an example of part learning. In evaluating *whole versus part learning*, it is necessary to consider the nature of the task to be learned. If the task *can* be broken down successfully, it probably *should* be broken down to facilitate learning; otherwise, it probably should be taught as a unit.

PRACTICE AND REPETITION Those things we do daily become a part of our repertoire of skills. Trainees should be given frequent opportunity to practice their job tasks in the way that they will ultimately be expected to perform them. The individual who is being taught to operate a machine should have an opportunity to practice on it. The supervisor who is being taught "how to train" should be given supervised practice in training.

Characteristics of Successful Trainers

The success of any training effort will depend in large part on the teaching skills and personal characteristics of those responsible for conducting the training. What separates the good trainers from the mediocre ones? Often a good trainer is one who shows a little more effort or demonstrates more instructional preparation. However, training is also influenced by the trainer's personal manner and characteristics. According to one survey, trainees list the following as traits of successful trainers:[43]

1. *Knowledge of Subject.* Employees expect trainers to know their job or subject thoroughly.
2. *Adaptability.* Some individuals learn faster or slower than others, and instruction should be matched to the trainee's learning ability.
3. *Sincerity.* Trainees appreciate sincerity in trainers.
4. *Sense of Humor.* Learning can be fun. Very often a point can be made with a story or anecdote.
5. *Interest.* Good trainers have a keen interest in the subject they are teaching. This interest is readily conveyed to trainees.
6. *Clear Instructions.* Naturally, training is accomplished more quickly and retained longer when trainers give clear instructions.

7. *Individual Assistance.* When training more than one employee, successful trainers always provide individual assistance.
8. *Enthusiasm.* A dynamic presentation and a vibrant personality show trainees that the trainer enjoys training. Employees tend to respond positively to an enthusiastic climate.[44]

For training programs to be most successful, organizations should reward valuable trainers. Too often the only place for trainers to advance is into managerial positions, thus diverting their expertise away from the training program and sending the message that training is not really as important as the organization would like its trainees to believe. High-performing technical experts should be given raises and perks comparable to what they would receive if they were moving up into management ranks. The importance of their work should be recognized by giving them varied job assignments and making sure they have the resources and authority they need to solve problems.[45]

SUMMARY

Because of rapid changes in technology and the growth of organizations into large, complex operations, training and development programs have become even more vital to an organization's success. In recent years such programs have broadened their scope to include the career development of personnel at all levels. A development program begins with the important process of orientation.

In designing training programs, organizations should follow a systems approach. This involves three phases: the needs assessment phase, the training and development phase, and the evaluation phase. From the wide variety of methods available for training both managerial and nonmanagerial personnel, the organization should select those methods that best fulfill the training objectives and that utilize as many of the principles of learning as possible. While new methods must always be explored, the focus should be on the objectives to be attained through training. In planning and conducting training programs, trainers should give special attention to the psychological principles of learning and the characteristics of successful trainers.

DISCUSSION QUESTIONS

1. Why is employee orientation an important process? What are some benefits of a properly conducted orientation program?
2. A new employee is likely to be anxious the first few days on the job.
   a. What are some possible causes of this anxiety?
   b. How may the anxiety be reduced?
3. What economic, social, and political forces have made employee training even more important than in the past?

4. What analyses should be made to determine the training needs of an organization? After the needs are determined, what is the next step?
5. Indicate what training methods you would use for each of the following jobs. Give reasons for your choices.
   a. file clerk
   b. computer operator
   c. automobile service station attendant
   d. pizza maker
   e. nurse's aide
6. Compare computer-assisted instruction with the lecture method in regard to the way they involve the different psychological principles of learning.
7. Suppose that you are the manager of an accounts receivable unit in a large company. You are switching to a new system of billing and recordkeeping and need to train your three supervisors and 28 employees in the new procedures. What training method(s) would you use? Why?
8. Participants in a training course are often asked to evaluate the course by means of a questionnaire. What are the pro's and cons of this approach? Are there better ways of evaluating a course?

MINI-CASE 7–1 Orientation of New Employees at Visitech

Visitech opened its first optical store in Dallas in October 1983. At the forefront of the revolution in the eyeware industry, Visitech has an on-site computerized and automated optical laboratory at each store that fabricates prescription glasses upon request. Customers can select their frames and watch as their lenses are being made in the laboratory.

Because of the company's rapid growth, Ms. Ronnie Gorton was recently promoted to store manager of a new facility to be opened in New Mexico. Visitech stores employ about 20 employees performing a variety of jobs. New store managers receive a week of managerial training in Dallas stressing human relations skills and customer services. One training session in particular discusses the importance of first impressions and how initial employee beliefs and experiences influence their job behavior. The training instructor emphasizes the importance of establishing a strong employee–supervisor relationship through a well-managed orientation program. The positive work attitudes that Visitech's strong employee relations program promotes are especially important in light of the optical industry's growing emphasis on service. Visitech has a formal employee orientation program. The HR department is responsible for introducing new employees to the company and its benefits, but store managers are required to orient all new employees to store operations and their individual jobs. Supervisors are granted considerable freedom to perform this task.

The New Mexico store is scheduled to open in two weeks. As a new store manager, Ronnie Gorton is concerned about meeting new employees and getting them started on the right foot.

SOURCE: Based on a consulting experience of one of the authors. All names are fictitious.

QUESTIONS

1. If you were Ms. Gorton, why would you be concerned about the orientation program?
2. What should be covered during the orientation, and how should the orientation be designed?
3. What principles of learning should be applied to the orientation process?

MINI-CASE 7–2 How Much Structure in Management Development Courses?

Diversified Products, Inc., with operating divisions in North America and abroad, recognized a need to provide its managers with a refresher course in HR management.

The company believed that its managers needed to be made more aware of government regulations affecting their relations with employees and to be better able to document decisions affected by these regulations. Also, improvements in their leadership and motivation skills were considered necessary for them to cope better with the changes in the attitudes and behavior of their younger subordinates.

The company decided to develop a course to be conducted by company personnel, making use of some guest instructors from the outside. Sessions lasting eight days each were held at a resort hotel for groups of 15 to 20 managers drawn from a variety of positions and locations in the corporation. Since these managers worked under highly structured conditions, it was believed that an unstructured course would be a beneficial change for them. Accordingly, at the first session of each course, participants were given a list of possible topics to discuss. They were told that it would be up to them to choose how the course was to be conducted. They were to decide on the nature of the topics, whether or not the class would be divided into discussion groups, and who would be invited as outside resource people.

Experience over a period of time with a number of groups revealed that it usually took three to four days for participants to begin to make progress. By this time their reactions to the unstructured nature of the course were about evenly divided. Roughly half of them were highly enthusiastic about the course, whereas the remainder hated it. Some disliked it so much that they abandoned the sessions and returned to work.

It proved almost impossible to determine, in advance of the course, which managers would react unfavorably to the unstructured format of the sessions. This determination could not be made until several sessions had been conducted. In spite of the negative reactions, top management and the HR staff considered the unstructured course format to be sufficiently worthwhile to justify its continuance.

QUESTIONS

1. How do you account for the sharp difference in the reactions of participants to the course?
2. What is to be gained by making the course unstructured?
3. Do you agree with the company's decision to continue the course with an unstructured format?

NOTES AND REFERENCES

1. Morton E. Grossman and Margaret Magnus, "The $5.3 Billion Tab for Training," *Personnel Journal* 68, no. 7 (July 1989): 54–56.

2. Stephen R. Hiatt, *The Effects of Social Orientation on Socialization Outcomes of New Nurses in Hospitals* (unpublished dissertation, Arizona State University, December 1983), 9. See also Richard Pascale, "Fitting New Employees into the Company Culture," *Fortune* 109, no. 11 (May 1984): 28.

3. Stephen B. Wehrenberg, "Skill and Motivation Divide Training vs. Orientation," *Personnel Journal* 68, no. 5 (May 1989): 111–113. See also Joy Van Eck Peluchette and Thomas N. Martin, "Employee Orientation," *Personnel Administrator* 34, no. 3 (March 1989): 60–65.

4. "Orientation: Positive First Impressions," *BNA Bulletin to Management* 38, no. 3 (January 15, 1987): 24.

5. David F. Jones, "Developing a New Employee Orientation Program," *Personnel Journal* 63, no. 3 (March 1984): 86–87.

6. George F. Truell, "Tracking Down the 'Aroundhereisms'—or, How to Foil Negative Orientation," *Personnel* 58, no. 4 (July–August 1981): 23–31. For an interesting discussion of the importance of orientation for younger employees, see James W. Sheehy, "New Work Ethic Is Frightening," *Personnel Journal* 69, no. 6 (June 1990): 28–36.

7. Adapted from Jill Cassner-Lotto and Associates, *Successful Training Strategies* (San Francisco: Jossey-Bass, 1988), 2.

8. Labor Letter, *Wall Street Journal* (January 31, 1989): 1.

9. "Functional Illiteracy: It's Your Problem, Too," *Supervisory Management* 34, no. 6 (June 1989): 22; and Kenneth N. Wexley, "Personnel Training," *Annual Review of Psychology* (Palo Alto, CA: Annual Reviews, Inc., 1984): 51–55.

10. "How Business Is Joining the Fight Against Functional Illiteracy," *Business Week* (April 16, 1984): 94. See also Richard G. Zalman, "The 'Basics' of In-house Skills Training," *HR Magazine* 36, no. 2 (February 1991): 74–78.

11. J. A. Sonnenfeld and C. A. Ingols, "Working Knowledge: Charting a New Course for Training," *Organizational Dynamics* 15, no. 1 (Summer, 1986): 63–79; and Gary P. Latham, "Human Resource Training and Development," *Annual Review of Psychology* (Palo Alto, CA: Annual Review, Inc., 1988): 554. See also "Automation Needs a Speedup and So Does Retraining," *Business Week* (September 29, 1986): 132.

12. Kenneth N. Wexley and Gary P. Latham, *Developing and Training Human Resources in Organizations* (Glenview, IL: Scott, Foresman, 1981), 6.

13. Latham, "Human Resource Training and Development," 546.

14. Irwin L. Goldstein, *Training in Organizations: Needs Assessment, Development, and Evaluation,* 2d ed. (Monterey, CA: Brooks/Cole, 1986), 15. See also Dana Gaines Robinson and James C. Robinson, *Training for Impact—How to Link Training to Business Needs and Measure the Results* (San Francisco: Jossey-Bass, 1989).

15. Latham, "Human Resource Training and Development," 554.

16. Frank O. Hoffman, "The Hierarchy of Training Objectives," *Personnel* 62, no. 8 (August 1985): 12.

17. Robert F. Mager, *Preparing Instructional Objectives* (Belmont, CA: David S. Lake Publishers, 1984), vi. See also Robert F. Mager, *Making Instruction Work or Skillbloomers* (Belmont, CA: David S. Lake, 1988).

18. Rosemary S. Caffarella, "A Checklist for Planning Successful Training Programs," *Training and Development Journal* 39, no. 3 (March 1985): 81–83.

19. Ron Zemke and John Gunkler, "28 Techniques for Transforming Training into Performance," *Training* 22, no. 4 (April 1985): 48–63.

20. Darlene F. Russ-Eft and John H. Zenger, "Common Mistakes in Evaluating Training Effectiveness," *Personnel Administrator* 30, no. 4 (April 1985): 57–62.

21. J. Kevin Ford and Steven P. Wroten, "Introducing New Methods for Conducting Training Evaluation and for Linking Training Evaluation to Program Redesign," *Personnel Psychology* 37, no. 4 (Winter 1984): 651–665.

22. Goldstein, 23

23. Robert F. Sullivan and Donald C. Miklas, "On-the-Job Training That Works," *Training and Development Journal* 39, no. 5 (May 1985): 118.

24. Ibid., 118–121. See also Marcia Ann Pulich, "The Basics of On-the-Job Training and Development," *Supervisory Management* 29, no. 2 (January 1984): 7–11. See also William J. Rothwell and H. C. Kazanas, "Planned OJT Is Production OJT," *Training and Development Journal* 44, no. 10 (October 1990): 53–56.

25. Judith Valente and Bridget O'Brian, "Airline Cockpits Are No Place to Solo," *Wall Street Journal* (August 2, 1989): B1.

26. Jack Gordon, "Computers in Training," *Training* 22, no. 10 (October 1985): 54; and Stephen Schwade, "Is It Time to Consider Computer-based Training?" *Personnel Administrator* 30, no. 2 (February 1985): 25–35.

27. Ralph E. Ganger, "Computer-based Training Improves Job Performance," *Personnel Journal* 68, no. 6 (June 1989): 116–123.

28. "Locomotive Simulator Brings Realism to Engineer Training," *Wall Street Journal* (November 25, 1983): 11.

29. Ralph Pribble, "Enter the Videodisk," *Training* 22, no. 3 (March 1985): 91–96.

30. Cynthia Levinson, "Training by Telephone," *Training* 22, no. 7 (July 1985): 63–66.

31. Jack Mendelson, "The Management Internship: An Application of Social Learning Theory" (Paper presented at Academy of Management Annual Meetings—1985, San Diego, CA, August 11–14 1985).

32. "The Forgotten Americans," *Business Week* (September 1, 1985): 50–55.

33. Labor Letter, *Wall Street Journal* (December 17, 1985): 1; and "There Really Are Jobs After Retraining," *Business Week* (January 28, 1985): 76–77.

34. Corporate Affirmative Action and Compliance Department, Motorola, Inc., 1303 E. Algonquin Road, Schaumburg, IL 60196.

35. Jack Gordon, "Where's the Line Between Training and Intrusion?" *Training* 26, no. 3 (March 1989): 27–39.

36. Phillip J. Decker, "The Effects of Rehearsal Group Size and Video Feedback in Behavior Modeling Training," *Personnel Psychology* 36, no. 4 (Winter 1983): 763–773.

37. Ibid., 763. While four basic steps in behavior modeling are normally discussed, some authors note a fifth step—the use of retention aids.

38. Stephen Wehrenberg and Robert Kuhnle, "How Training Through Behavior Modeling Works," *Personnel Journal* 59, no. 7 (July 1980): 576–580; and Herbert H. Meyer and Michael S. Raich, "An Objective Evaluation of a Behavior Modeling Training Program," *Personnel Psychology* 36, no. 4 (Winter 1983): 755–761.

39. Philip C. Grant, "Employee Motivation: The Key to Training," *Supervisory Management* 34, no. 6 (June 1989): 16–21. See also Debra J. Cohen, "What Motivates Trainees," *Training and Development Journal* 44, no. 1 (November 1990): 91–93.

40. Fred Luthans and Robert Kreitner, *Organizational Behavior Modification and Beyond: An Operant and Social Learning Approach* (Glenview, IL: Scott, Foresman, 1985), 127.

41. Dana Gaines Robinson and James C. Robinson, "Breaking Barriers to Skill Transfer," *Training and Development Journal* 39, no. 1 (January 1985): 82–83. See also Timothy T. Baldwin and J. Kevin Ford, "Transfer of Training: A Review and Directions for Future Research," *Personnel Psychology* 41, no. 1 (Spring 1988): 63–105.

42. *The Journal of Applied Psychology* is an excellent source of research studies of this type. Its articles are indexed in *Psychological Abstracts*.

43. Les Donaldson and Edward E. Scannell, *Human Resource Development: The New Trainers Guide* (Reading, MA: Addison-Wesley, 1983), 142–151.

44. For other suggestions on successful training, see Carol Haig, "A Line Manager's Guide to Training," *Personnel Journal* 63, no. 10 (October 1984): 42–45; and Leslie A. Bryan, "Making the Manager a Better Trainer," *Supervisory Management* 29, no. 4 (April 1984): 2–8.

45. Beverly Geber, "The Care and Feeding of Trainers," *Training* 25, no. 8 (August 1988): 41–46.

CHAPTER 8

Career Development

After reading this chapter you will be able to:

1. *Describe the type of climate that helps to make career development programs successful.*
2. *Discuss how job opportunities may be inventoried.*
3. *Describe the methods used for identifying and developing managerial talent.*
4. *Cite the ways in which employers can facilitate the career development of women and minorities.*
5. *Identify the stages of individual career development.*
6. *List the factors that should be considered in choosing a career.*
7. *Explain how to keep a career in perspective.*
8. *Define the key terms in the chapter.*

TERMS TO IDENTIFY

transfer *(241)*
relocation services *(242)*
outplacement services *(242)*
job progressions *(243)*
career paths *(243)*
career counseling *(244)*
assessment center *(245)*
fast-track program *(248)*
mentors *(249)*
mentoring functions *(249)*
dual-career couples *(254)*

The functions of human resources management that we have discussed so far have a fairly long history. Typically they have been carried out with organizational needs as the primary concern. Since the mid-1970s, however, increasing attention has been given to the need of employees to have satisfying careers. The term "career," as it is now used by professionals in HRM and related fields, refers to the sequence of jobs that individuals hold during their work histories, regardless of their occupation or organizational level. No longer does the term pertain only to high-status or rapid-advancement occupations.

Increased competition for promotion, constant innovation in technology, pressures for equal employment opportunities, corporate right-sizing and restructuring, and employees' desire to get the most out of their careers are all major forces pushing organizations to offer career development programs. The desire of employers to make better use of their employees' knowledge and skills and to retain those who are valuable to the organization is also an important consideration. There is a growing awareness among employers that a career development program can benefit not only managers, supervisors, and their subordinates, but the entire organization as well.[1]

PHASES OF A CAREER DEVELOPMENT PROGRAM

Organizations have traditionally engaged in human resources planning and development. As we noted in Chapter 5, this activity involves charting the moves of large numbers of employees through various positions in an organization and identifying future staffing needs. Career development programs, with their greater emphasis on the individual, introduce a personalized aspect to the process.

A common approach to establishing a career development program is to integrate it with the existing HR functions and structures in the organization. Integrating the HR program with the career development program reinforces both programs. Figure 8–1 illustrates how HR structures relate to some of the essential aspects of the career development process. For example, in planning careers, employees need organizational information—information that strategic planning, forecasting, succession planning, and skills inventories can provide. Similarly, as they obtain information about themselves and use it in career planning, employees need to know how management views their performance and the career paths within the organization.[2]

FIGURE 8–1 TWO-WAY SUPPORT: CAREER DEVELOPMENT/HUMAN RESOURCES

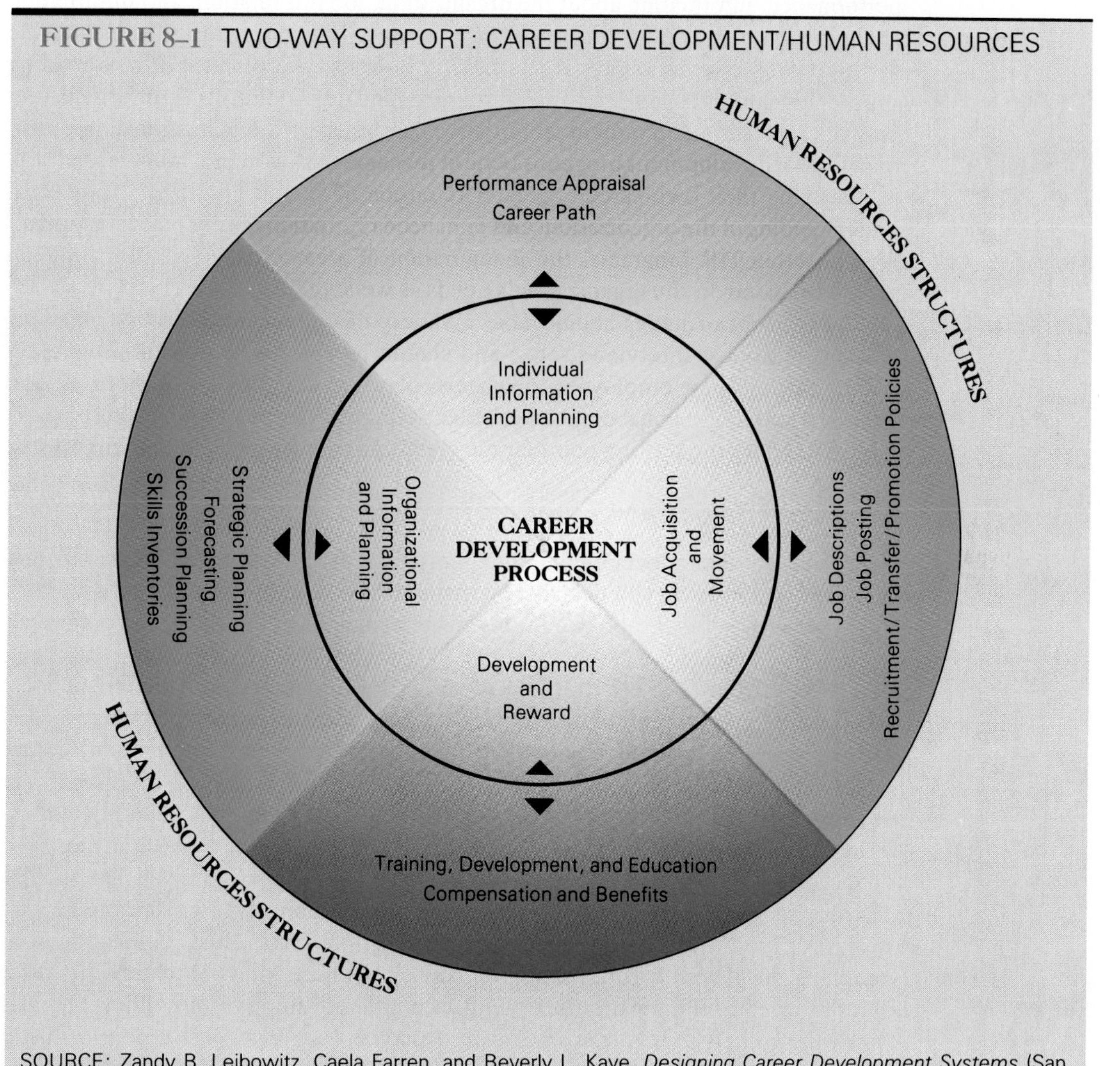

SOURCE: Zandy B. Leibowitz, Caela Farren, and Beverly L. Kaye, *Designing Career Development Systems* (San Francisco: Jossey-Bass, 1986), 41. Reproduced with permission.

Determining Individual and Organizational Needs

A career development program should be viewed as a dynamic process that attempts to meet the needs of managers, their subordinates, and the organization. Individual employees are responsible for initiating their own career planning. It is up to them to identify their knowledge, skills, abilities, interests, and values and seek out information about career options so that they can set goals and develop career plans. Managers should encourage subordinates to take responsibility for their own careers, offering continuing assistance in the form of feedback on individual performance, information about the organization, job information, and information about career opportunities that might be of interest. The organization is responsible for supplying information about its mission, policies, and plans and for providing support for employee self-assessment, training, and development. Significant career growth can occur when individual initiative combines with organizational opportunity. Career development programs benefit managers by giving them increased skill in managing their own careers, greater retention of valued employees, increased understanding of the organization, and enhanced reputations as people-developers.[3] As with other HR programs, the inauguration of a career development program should be based on the organization's needs as well.

Assessment of needs should take a variety of approaches (surveys, informal group discussions, interviews, etc.) and should involve personnel from different groups, such as new employees, managers, plateaued employees, minorities, and technical and professional employees. Identifying the needs and problems of these groups provides the starting point for the organization's career development efforts.

Creating Favorable Conditions

While a career development program requires many special processes and techniques, which we will describe later, some basic conditions must be present if it is to be successful. These conditions create a favorable climate for the program.

MANAGEMENT SUPPORT If career development is to succeed, it must receive the complete support of top management. Ideally, senior line managers and HR department managers should work together to design and implement a career development system.[4] The system should reflect the goals and culture of the organization, and the HR philosophy should be woven throughout. An HR philosophy can provide employees with a clear set of expectations and directions for their own career development. Many HR philosophies are expressed in slogans such as "People are the key to the company's success; development must therefore be well managed," or "The best managers are made, not born; therefore, development of people is the key to accomplishing objectives." These kinds of statements offer clues to whether the organization endorses a promote-from-within philosophy and thus will be likely to invest in retraining its people.[5]

For a program to be effective, managerial personnel at all levels must be trained in the fundamentals of job design, performance appraisal, career planning, and counseling. As HR development personnel at McCormack and Dodge advise, "Line managers must be the heart and soul of a career development program. The average manager, however, needs guidance and a defined structure."[6] Managers also need to be appraised on how well they are doing their job of career development.

GOAL SETTING Before individuals can engage in meaningful career planning, they must not only have an awareness of the organization's philosophy, but they must also have a clear understanding of the organization's more immediate goals. Otherwise, they may plan for personal change and growth without knowing if or how their own goals match those of the organization. For example, if the technology of a business is changing and new skills are needed, will the organization retrain to meet this need or hire new talent? Is there growth, stability, or decline in the number of employees needed? How will turnover affect this need? Clearly, an organizational plan that answers these kinds of questions is essential to support individual career planning.

CHANGES IN HRM POLICIES To ensure that its career development program will be effective, an organization may need to alter its current HRM policies. For example, a policy of lifelong job rotation can counteract obsolescence and maintain employee flexibility. Another policy that can aid development involves job transfers and promotions.

A **transfer** is the placement of an employee in another job for which the duties, responsibilities, status, and remuneration are approximately equal to those of the previous job. A transfer may require the employee to change work group, workplace, work shift, or organizational unit; and it may even necessitate moving to another geographic area. Transfers make it possible for an organization to place its employees in jobs where there is a greater need for their services and where they can acquire new knowledge and skills. A downward transfer, or demotion, moves an individual into a lower-level job that can provide developmental opportunities; but such a move is ordinarily considered unfavorable, especially to the individual who is demoted.

A promotion may involve a move to a larger office.

A promotion is a change of assignment to a job at a higher level in the organization. The new job normally provides an increase in pay and status and demands more skill or carries more responsibility. Promotions enable an organization to utilize the skills and abilities of its personnel more effectively, and the opportunity to gain a promotion serves as an incentive for good performance. The two principal criteria for determining promotions are *merit* and *seniority*. The problem the organization faces is to determine how much consideration to give to each factor. Even when not restricted by a labor agreement, management may find itself giving considerable weight to seniority because of the difficulties of effectively measuring merit and communicating to employees that the measurement is fair.

Transfers and promotions require the individual to adjust to new job demands and usually a different work environment. A transfer that involves moving to a new location within the United States or abroad places greater demands on employees, because it requires them to adapt not only to a new work environment but also to new living conditions. Those with families have the added responsibility of helping family members adjust to the new living arrangements. Even though some employers, such as Holiday Inns and Federal Express, provide all types of **relocation services,** including moving, help in selling a home, cultural orientation, and language training, there is always some loss of productive time. Pretransfer training, whether in job skills or related to life-style, has been suggested as one of the most effective ways to reduce lost productivity.[7]

Many organizations now provide **outplacement services** to help terminated employees find a job somewhere else. These services can be used to enhance a productive employee's career, as well as to terminate an employee who is unproductive. If an organization cannot meet its career development responsibilities to its productive workers, HR policy should provide assistance to them in finding more suitable career opportunities elsewhere. For unproductive employees, outplacement is a method of termination that preserves their dignity, recognizes their past contributions, and enables them to find a new job quickly and relatively painlessly. Professional outplacement counseling has been added to many employee benefit packages as another form of employee assistance.[8] The skills that are needed for outplacement counseling, as well as other types of counseling, will be examined in Chapter 15.

ANNOUNCEMENT OF THE PROGRAM The career development program should be announced widely throughout the organization. The objectives and opportunities can be communicated in several ways, including the following:

1. Publication in newsletters
2. Inclusion in employee manuals
3. Publication in a special career guide or as part of career planning workshops
4. Inclusion in videotaped or live presentations

At the very least, a manual that spells out the basic job families, career progression possibilities, and related requirements should be given to each manager and made available to every employee.

Inventorying Job Opportunities

While career development usually involves many different types of training experiences (discussed in the preceding chapter), the most important of them occur on the job. It is here that the individual is exposed to a wide variety of experiences, and it is here that contributions are made to the organization.

JOB COMPETENCIES It is important for an organization to study its jobs carefully to identify and assign weights to the knowledge and skills that each one requires. This can be achieved with job analysis and evaluation systems such as those used in compensation programs. The system used at Sears Roebuck measures three basic competencies for each job: *know-how, problem solving,* and *accountability.*

Know-how is broken down into three types of job knowledge: technical, managerial, and human relations. Problem solving and accountability also have several dimensions. Scores for each of these three major competencies are assigned to each job, and a total value is computed for each job. For any planned job transfer, the amount of increase (or decrease) the next job represents in each of the skill areas, as well as in the total point values, can be computed. This information is then used to make certain that a transfer to a different job is a move that requires growth on the part of the employee.

Sears designs career development paths to provide the following experiences: (1) an increase in at least one skill area on each new assignment, (2) an increase of at least 10 percent in total points on each new assignment, and (3) assignments in several different functional areas.[9]

JOB PROGRESSIONS Once the skill demands of jobs are identified and weighted according to their importance, it is then possible to plan **job progressions.** A new employee with no experience is typically assigned to a "starting job." After a period of time in that job, the employee can be promoted to one that requires more knowledge and/or skill. While most organizations concentrate on developing job progressions for managerial, professional, and technical jobs, progressions can be developed for all categories of jobs. These job progressions then can serve as a basis for developing **career paths**—the lines of advancement within an organization—for individuals.

Many organizations prepare interesting and attractive brochures to describe the career paths that are available to employees. General Motors has prepared a *Career Development Guide* that groups jobs by fields of work such as engineering, manufacturing, communications, data processing, financial, personnel, and scientific. These categories give employees an understanding of the career possibilities in the various fields.

TRAINING NEEDS There are likely to be points in one's career path where training beyond that received on the job is essential. Such points should be identified and appropriate training made available to prevent progress from being impaired by a lack of knowledge or skills. Because the training needs of individual employees differ, these needs must be monitored closely.

Gauging Employee Potential

Probably the most important objective of any career development program is to provide the tools and techniques that will enable employees to gauge their potential for success in a career path. This objective may be achieved in various ways, all of which naturally involve the active participation of the employees themselves. Informal counseling by HR staff and supervisors is used widely. Many organizations give their employees information on educational assistance, EEO/AA programs and policies, salary administration, and job requirements. Career planning workbooks and workshops are also popular means of helping employees identify their potential and the strength of their interests.

CAREER PLANNING WORKBOOKS Several organizations have put together workbooks to guide their employees individually through systematic self-assessment of values, interests, abilities, goals, and personal development plans. General Motors' *Career Development Guide* contains a section called "What do you want your future to be?" in which the employee makes a personal evaluation. General Electric has developed an extensive set of manuals for its career development program, including two workbooks to help employees explore life issues that affect career decisions. Syntex's workbook, *How to Work for a Living and Like It,* may be used by individuals on their own or in a group workshop.

Some organizations prefer to use workbooks written for the general public. Popular ones include *Where Do I Go from Here with My Life?* by John Crystal and Richard N. Bolles—a workbook follow-up to Bolles's *What Color Is Your Parachute?* Andrew H. Souerwine's *Career Strategies: Planning for Personal Growth* and John Holland's *Self-Directed Search* are also used frequently.[10] These are also recommended to students for help in planning their careers.

CAREER PLANNING WORKSHOPS Workshops offer experiences similar to those provided by workbooks. However, they have the advantage of providing a chance to compare and discuss attitudes, concerns, and plans with others in similar situations. Some workshops focus on current job performance and development plans. Others deal with broader life and career plans and values.

CAREER COUNSELING **Career counseling** involves talking with employees about their current job activities and performance, personal and career interests and goals, personal skills, and suitable career development objectives. Employees usually participate voluntarily, although some organizations make counseling a part of the annual performance appraisal (the subject of the next chapter). As employees approach retirement, they may be encouraged to participate in preretirement programs, which often include counseling along with other helping activities. Career counseling may be provided by the HR staff, superiors, specialized staff counselors, or outside professionals. Chapter 15 includes an expanded discussion of the types of skills required for career counseling. Preretirement programs will be discussed in Chapter 12.

CAREER DEVELOPMENT PROGRAMS FOR SPECIAL GROUPS

Organizations differ widely in the types of career development programs they offer. Some organizations have formal programs for all levels of employees covering a broad array of topics. Others have offerings limited to career counseling incorporated into annual performance reviews.[11] The more extensive career development programs also frequently include programs geared to special groups, such as management development programs, or programs for women, minorities, or dual-career couples. Let us examine some of these special programs more closely.

Management Development Programs

Contemporary organizations must have competent managers who can cope with the growing complexity of the problems affecting their operations. A formal management development program helps to ensure that developmental experiences both on and off the job are coordinated and in line with the individual's and the organization's needs.

INVENTORYING MANAGEMENT REQUIREMENTS AND TALENT An important part of a management development program is an inventory of managerial positions. The inventory directs attention to the developmental needs of employees both in their present jobs and in managerial jobs to which they may be promoted. An equally important part of the program is identifying employees who may be groomed as replacements for managers who are reassigned, retire, or otherwise vacate a position. Replacement charts, discussed in Chapter 5, provide the information needed to fill vacancies in key positions.

THE ROLE OF MANAGERS Identifying and developing talent in individuals is a role that all managers should take seriously. As they conduct formal appraisals, they should be concerned with their subordinates' potential for managerial jobs and encourage their growth in that direction. In addition to immediate superiors, there should be others in the organization who have the power to evaluate, nominate, and sponsor employees with promise. Companies that emphasize developing human assets as well as turning a profit typically have the talent they need and some to spare. Some companies—Citicorp, Xerox, Procter & Gamble, and General Motors, to name a few— have become "academy" companies that unintentionally provide a source of talented managers to organizations that lack good management development programs.

USE OF ASSESSMENT CENTERS Pioneered in the mid-1950s by Dr. Douglas Bray and his associates at AT&T, corporate-operated assessment centers have proliferated from just over 100 organizations to 2,000 organizations in an eight-year period.[12] An **assessment center** is a process (not a place) in which individuals are evaluated as they participate in a series of situations that resemble what they might be called upon to handle on the job. The popularity of the assessment center can be attributed to its capacity for increasing an organization's ability to select employees who will perform successfully in management positions or to assist and promote the development of skills for their current position. These centers may use in-basket exercises, role playing, and other approaches to employee development that we discussed in Chapter 7.

The schedule of the various activities at the California Highway Patrol Academy assessment center is shown in Figure 8–2. Participation in these activities provides samples of behavior that are representative of what is required for advancement. At the end of the assessment-center period, the assessors' observations are combined and integrated to develop an overall picture of the strengths and needs of the participants. A report is normally submitted to top management, and feedback is given to the participants.

Increasing attention is being given to the validity of assessment-center procedures. As with employment tests, the assessments provided must be valid. Before the assessment center is run, the characteristics or dimensions to be studied should be determined through job analyses. The exercises used in the center should reflect the job for which the person is being evaluated; i.e., the exercises should have content

The California Highway Patrol Academy.

FIGURE 8–2 CALIFORNIA HIGHWAY PATROL ASSESSMENT-CENTER PROGRAM

One week prior to conduct of every three centers	Five-day training for all assessors.
Monday—A.M.	Assessors review exercises. Participant orientation.
Monday—P.M.	Leaderless Group Discussion Exercise. Participants divided into two groups of six each, observed by three assessors; each assessor observes two participants. Assessors prepare final report on this exercise. In-basket exercise. Each participant works individually for three hours on a 31-item in-basket. Assessors review and score in-basket, and prepare for in-basket interview the following day.
Tuesday—P.M.	Participants take a 40-minute reading test (*Davis Reading Test*). Assessors review in-basket observations with participants and prepare final report on this exercise.
Wednesday—A.M.	Participants complete an individual analysis exercise and prepare for a seven-minute presentation to the panel of assessors on solution to the problem. Participants begin presentations to panel of assessors.
Wednesday—P.M.	Presentations continue through afternoon. Participants released to return to work site. Assessors prepare final reports on this exercise. Administrator prepares for discussion of each candidate the following day.
Thursday—All day	Assessors meet in teams of three to integrate observations of each participant's overall exercises to reach a consensual rating on each skill evaluated and to make specific developmental recommendations.
Within 45 days	Assessors meet with participants and their supervisors at the participant's work site to discuss observations of assessor panel.
Within 60 days	Participants and supervisors develop a career plan to assist participant in skill development.

Note: All exercises and training take place on-site at the CHP Academy.

SOURCE: California Highway Patrol Academy. Reproduced with permission.

validity. While the assessment-center methodology lends itself readily to content validation, predictive validity has also been observed in many instances. A strong positive relationship is found between assessments and future performance on the job.[13]

While assessment centers have proved quite valuable in identifying managerial talent and in helping with the development of individuals, it should be noted that the method tends to favor those who are strong in interpersonal skills and have the ability to influence others. Some individuals find it difficult to perform at their best in a situation that for them is as threatening as taking a test. The manner in which assessment-center personnel conduct the exercises and provide feedback to the participants will play a major role in determining how individuals react to the experience.

Management positions are the usual targets of assessment centers. However, adaptations of the assessment-center method can be used for nonmanagerial positions, such as those in sales. One adaptation involves playing videotaped scenarios for applicants, then using a multiple-choice test to find out how they would respond to the situations depicted. Other adaptations involve the use of role-playing situations and panel interviews in which three- or four-member panels record and evaluate the candidate's responses to questions and then meet to reach a consensus in their evaluations.[14]

DETERMINING INDIVIDUAL DEVELOPMENT NEEDS Because the requirements of each management position and the qualifications of the person performing it are different, no two managers will have identical developmental needs. For one individual, self-development may consist of developing the ability to write reports, give talks, or lead conferences. For another, it may require learning to communicate and relate more effectively with others in the organization. Periodic performance appraisals can provide a basis for determining each manager's progress. Conferences in which these appraisals are discussed are an essential part of self-improvement efforts.

In helping individuals plan their careers, it is important for organizations to recognize that younger managers today seek meaningful training assignments that are interesting and involve challenge, responsibility, and a "piece of the action."

In fact, the organizations with reputations for the best management make extensive use of job challenge to develop their executive talent. Those positions that force managers to deal with sudden, unexpected changes or call for skills the managers do not have are the jobs whose candidates require the most development.[15] Younger managers today also have a greater concern for the contribution that their work in the organization will make to society. Unfortunately, they are frequently given responsibilities they view as rudimentary, boring, and composed of too many "make-work" activities. Some organizations are attempting to retain young managers with high potential by offering a **fast-track program** that enables them to advance more rapidly than those with less potential. A fast-track program may provide for a relatively rapid progression—lateral transfers or promotions—through a number of managerial positions requiring exposure to different organizational functions, as well as providing opportunities to make decisions, preferably in profit centers.

MENTORING When one talks with men and women about their employment experiences, it is common to hear them mention individuals at work who influenced them. They frequently refer to immediate superiors who were especially helpful as career developers. But they also mention others at higher levels in the organization who provided guidance and support to them in the development of their careers. These executives and managers who coach, advise, and encourage employees of lesser rank are called **mentors.**

Informal mentoring goes on daily within every type of organization. Generally, the mentor initiates the relationship, but sometimes an employee will approach a potential mentor for advice. Most mentoring relationships develop over time on an informal basis.[16] However, in the 1980s there was a rapid growth of formal mentoring plans that call for the assignment of a mentor to those employees considered for upward movement in the organization. Under a good mentor, learning focuses on goals, opportunities, expectations, standards, and assistance in fulfilling one's potential.[17]

Analysis of a large number of research studies revealed that the **mentoring functions** can be divided into two broad categories: *career functions* and *psychosocial functions*. The functions are listed in Figure 8–3. Career functions are those aspects of the relationship that enhance career advancement; psychosocial functions are those aspects that enhance the protégé's sense of competence, identity, and effectiveness in a professional role. Both kinds of functions are viewed as critical to management development.[18]

Organizations with formal mentoring programs include Federal Express, The Jewel Companies, NCR Corporation, Johnson & Johnson, the Government Accounting Office, and Merrill Lynch.[19] Merrill Lynch's mentoring effort started out as part of a six-month management readiness program. A formal mentoring program

FIGURE 8–3 MENTORING FUNCTIONS

CAREER FUNCTIONS	PSYCHOSOCIAL FUNCTIONS
Sponsorship	Role modeling
Exposure and visibility	Acceptance and confirmation
Coaching	Counseling
Protection	Friendship
Challenging assignments	

SOURCE: From Kathy E. Kram, *Mentoring at Work* (Glenview, IL: Scott, Foresman, 1985). Reprinted by permission of the author.

was developed in order to (1) help generate high-level management support and visibility, (2) build bridges between high-level managers and employees, (3) help participants learn about the firm's culture, (4) increase networking, and (5) provide opportunities for talented people-developers to be seen. A mentor volunteers to serve as a counselor/adviser to four individuals during a six-month term. Mentors agree to meet with their protégés about once a month in either group or individual sessions. Both parties report that the mentoring relationship is one of the most beneficial parts of the management development program.[20]

Problems associated with recent events such as the merger explosion and the emergence of the cross-cultural corporation could be ameliorated by the use of assigned mentors to improve communication and ensure the continuity of the corporate culture. Not only have formal mentoring programs been valuable for management development, but more organizations are turning to them to help women, Hispanics, and blacks move more quickly up the corporate ladder.[21]

Career Development for Women

In Chapter 5 we discussed some of the current trends in the employment of women in jobs that until recently were held predominantly by men. Included among these jobs are management-level positions. Organizations are currently under considerable pressure, as a result of EEO/AA requirements, to increase the proportion of women they employ at this level.

ELIMINATING BARRIERS TO ADVANCEMENT Women in management have been handicapped by not being part of the so-called *old boys' network*, an informal network of interpersonal relationships that has traditionally provided a means for senior (male) members of the organization to pass along news of advancement opportunities and other career tips to junior (male) members. Women have also typically lacked role models to serve as mentors, because not many women as yet have reached the upper ranks of management.

To combat their difficulty in advancing to management positions, women in several organizations have developed their own *women's networks*. At Ralston Purina in St. Louis, a women's network that any female employee may join serves as a system for encouraging and fostering women's career development and for sharing information, experiences, and insights. Corporate officers are invited to regularly scheduled network meetings to discuss such matters as planning, development, and company performance. Network members view these sessions as an opportunity to let corporate officers know of women who are interested in and capable of furthering their careers. Other corporations where women's networks have been established include Hoffman-LaRoche, Metropolitan Life Insurance, Atlantic Richfield, Scholastic Magazines, and CBS.[22]

An organization that is devoted to helping employers break down barriers to upward mobility for women is Catalyst, a New York City–based not-for-profit organization. Catalyst not only courts corporate officers but also offers career advice, job placement, continuing education, and related professional development for women of all ages. At its New York headquarters, Catalyst houses an extensive library and audiovisual center regarded as the country's leading resource for information on women and work.

The advancement of women in management has been hindered by a series of sex-role stereotypes that have shaped the destiny of women and working women in particular. Some of the more prominent myths were discussed in Chapter 5. Fortunately, there is substantial evidence that stereotyped attitudes toward women are changing. As women pursue career goals assertively and attitudes continue to change, the climate for women in management will be even more favorable. The attitudes of younger male managers tend to be more progressive than those of older male managers. As the younger men move into positions of greater responsibility and power, their organizations should be more receptive to the advancement of women managers. Also, the recent U.S. Supreme Court ruling in *Price Waterhouse* v. *Hopkins* (1989), which states unequivocally that sex stereotyping is discriminatory, will be an additional force to push organizations in a progressive direction.

PREPARING WOMEN FOR MANAGEMENT Although progress has been slow, opportunities for women to move into management positions are definitely improving. In addition to breaking down the barriers to advancement, the development of women managers demands a better understanding of women's needs and the requirements of the management world.

Many employers now offer special training to women who are on a management career path. They may use their own staff or outside firms to conduct this training. Opportunities are also available for women to participate in seminars and workshops that provide instruction and experiences in a wide variety of management topics.

In the past several years the number of women enrolled in college and university degree programs in management has increased significantly. At the same time, more women trained in management have joined management-department faculties at business schools, thus creating an environment that fosters the development of women as professionals capable of assuming higher-level positions in work organizations.

In addition to formal training opportunities, women today are provided with a wealth of information and guidance in books and magazines. Business sections in bookstores are stocked with numerous books written especially for women who want a better idea of the career opportunities available to them. Many books are devoted to the pursuit of careers in specific fields.[23]

Popular magazines that contain many articles about women and jobs include *Working Woman, New Woman, Savvy, The Executive Female,* and *Enterprising Women.* These magazines are also recommended reading for men who want a better understanding of the problems that women face in the world of work.

ACCOMMODATING FAMILIES One of the major problems women have faced is that of having both a managerial career and a family. Women managers whose children are at an age requiring close parental attention often experience conflict between their responsibility to the children and their duty to the employer. If the conflict becomes too painful, they may decide to forgo their careers, at least temporarily, and leave their jobs.

In recent years many employers, including DuPont, Digital Equipment Corporation, Quaker Oats Company, Corning Glass Works, and Pacific Telesis, have inaugurated programs that are mutually advantageous to the career-oriented woman and the employer. These programs, which include alternative career paths, extended leave, flextime, job sharing, and telecommuting, provide new ways to balance career and family. The number of employers moving to protect their investment in top-flight women is still small, but more of them are defining a separate track for women managers.[24]

In a provocative article in the *Harvard Business Review,* Felice Schwartz, founder and president of Catalyst, offers justification for two separate groups, "career-primary" women and "career and family" women. She advises helping women in the latter group to be productive but not necessarily upwardly mobile.[25] Many women, as well as men, criticize Schwartz's approach as perpetuating the inequities of a double standard and as pitting women against women—those with children against those without. On the other side, there are those who believe that this approach at least gives women choices.

Career Development for Minorities

Many organizations have specific career planning programs for minority employees, often mandated as part of the organization's affirmative action commitments. These programs are intended to equip employees with career planning skills and development opportunities that will help them compete effectively for advancement.

Telecommuting allows a woman to keep her job and be at home with her children.

We observed in Chapter 5 that many employers make a special effort to recruit minorities. Once individuals from minority groups are on the job, it is important for employers to provide opportunities for them to move ahead in the organization as they improve their job skills and abilities.

ADVANCEMENT OF MINORITIES TO MANAGEMENT POSITIONS The area of employment that has been the slowest to respond to affirmative action appeals is the advancement of minorities to middle- and top-management positions. For example, while blacks constituted almost 10 percent of the employed U.S. civilian population in 1989, they held only 5.6 percent of executive, administrative, and managerial positions. With 7 percent of the employed civilian population, Hispanics held 4 percent of executive, administrative, and managerial positions.[26]

Excerpts from a *Newsweek* article present some of the major problems faced by the black manager who aspires to higher levels in an organization:

> The careers of young black executives take off like a rocket, only to stall as they reach middle-management ranks. . . . Making it to the top fast may be even worse. . . . They arouse unrealistic expectations and may quickly become overly anxious about their performance. . . . Even after nominal acceptance, many black executives experience a profound alienation from corporate life. . . . [However,] black executives are coping. Support groups like the Black Professionals Organization at United Airlines alert management to black employees' concerns. . . . Slowly, black managers seem to be changing the system.[27]

While minority managers do play a part in creating a better climate for groups that are discriminated against in advancement opportunities, top management and the HR department have the primary responsibility to create conditions in the organization that are favorable for recognizing and rewarding performance based on objective, nondiscriminatory criteria.

PROVIDING INTERNSHIPS One approach to helping minority students prepare for management careers is to give them employment experiences while they are still in college. An *internship program* offers students an opportunity to learn on the job and gain hands-on experience. One organization, Inroads, Inc., offers qualified minority college students a package of tutoring, counseling, and summer internships with large corporations. It has about 500 corporate sponsors that pay an annual fee for each intern they sponsor. The program only considers students who graduate in the top 10 percent of their high school class. In college, the students must maintain a 2.7 grade-point average out of a possible 4.0. Participants report that Inroads has raised their aspirations and has taught them how to adjust to the corporate world.[28]

ORGANIZING TRAINING COURSES Training opportunities for minority managers are offered by such organizations as the American Management Association. Specifically addressing the advancement difficulties of blacks, it conducts a course titled "Self-Development Strategies for Black Managers" in several cities throughout the country. Major topics include realities of corporate life, race-related stresses, effective interpersonal relationships, situational leadership, handling of racial discrimination, and personal self-assessment.

Dual-Career Couples

As noted in Chapter 2, the employment of both members of a couple has become a way of life in North America. Economic necessity and social forces have encouraged this trend to the point that there are now over 34 million dual-earner couples.[29] An increasing number of them are in the category of **dual-career couples,** in which both members follow their own careers and actively support each other's career development.

As with most life-styles, the dual-career arrangement has its positive and negative sides. A significant number of organizations are concerned with the problems facing dual-career couples and offer assistance to them. Flexible working schedules are the most frequent organizational accommodation to these couples. Other arrangements include leave policies where either parent may stay home with a newborn, policies that allow work to be performed at home, day care on organization premises, and job sharing.[30]

RELOCATION AND OTHER PROBLEMS The difficulties that dual-career couples face include the need for child care, the allocation of time, and emotional stress. However, the main problem these couples face is the threat of relocation. Many large organizations now offer some kind of job-finding assistance for spouses of employees who are relocated, including payment of fees charged by employment agencies, job counseling firms, and executive search firms. Organizations are also developing networking relationships with other employers to find jobs for the spouses of their relocating employees. These networks can provide a way to "share the wealth and talent" in a community while simultaneously assisting in the recruitment efforts of the participating organizations.[31]

UPDATING HR POLICIES When both spouses pursue careers, employers that hope to recruit and retain them need to examine their traditional HR policies. Long-standing policies that neglect consideration of the dual-career couple as a unique employee group can be very counterproductive. For example, a firm following a traditional policy against nepotism may be obliged to lose or transfer an employee in whom considerable investment has been made if that employee marries a fellow employee in the same unit. Another firm may be eager to hire a renowned research chemist but be unable to do so because she is unwilling to take the job unless her husband, a mathematician, can find a position commensurate with his skills at the same location. A plan that employers can use in developing new policies and practices for dual-career couples is shown in Highlights in HRM 1.

Traditional practices and possible new practices covering recruitment, nepotism, transfers, scheduling, and training/development are suggested for three types of couples.

HIGHLIGHTS IN HRM

1 HR POLICIES AND THE DUAL-CAREER COUPLE

POLICIES	TRADITIONAL PRACTICES	POSSIBLE NEW PRACTICES		
		TYPE I	TYPE II	TYPE III
		Same career, same organization	*Different careers, same organization*	*Different organizations*
Recruitment	Focus on individual's inducements and rewards.	Establish procedures for evaluating recruits as a couple.	Find a way to locate positions for spouses of prospects. Evaluate prospects' value to the firm as a couple.	Establish system for finding spouses positions in surrounding firms.
Nepotism	No one may supervise a family member.	Establish means for couples to work in the same office and be each other's supervisor.	Provide for one family member to supervise another's unit.	No change.
Transfers	Offer to the individual, usually expected to accept.	Use a transfer-the-couple procedure. Extend transition allowances.	Establish way to transfer both. Extend transition allowances.	Establish system for locating jobs for spouses. Extend transition allowances.
Scheduling	Design only to meet company needs. Often prohibits two people from same office to be on leave at same time.	Allow flexibility in scheduling to meet both couple's and company's demands. Allow joint leaves.	Allow flexibility in scheduling to meet both couple's and company's demands.	Allow flexibility in scheduling to meet both couple's and company's demands.

Training	Train only in specific skill areas. Management development based on corporate needs.	Establish joint training programs, shared career development paths.	Provide joint orientation with special attention to needs of the dual-career couple. Establish programs on shared career development.	Provide joint orientation with special attention to needs of the couple. Establish shared career development programs.

SOURCE: Reprinted from Carol B. Gilmore and William R. Fannin, "The Dual Career Couple: A Challenge to Personnel in the Eighties," *Business Horizons* 25, no. 3 (May–June 1982): 38. Copyright 1982 by the Foundation for the School of Business at Indiana University. Used with permission.

HR managers need to recognize that dual-career couples have unique needs. They should review all HR policies and procedures with a view to making changes where possible to meet the needs of both members of the couple. As dual-career couples become a more significant part of the work force, organizations ready to meet their needs should fare better in the competition for highly qualified professional personnel.[32]

PERSONAL CAREER DEVELOPMENT

We have observed that there are numerous ways for an employer to contribute to an individual employee's career development and at the same time meet the organization's HR needs. The organization can certainly be a positive force in the development process, but the primary responsibility for personal career growth still rests with the individual. One's career may begin before and often continue after a period of employment with an organization. To help employees achieve their career objectives, HRM professionals should have an understanding of the stages one goes through in developing a career and the actions one should take to be successful.

Stages of Career Development

Knowledge, skills, abilities, and attitudes as well as career aspirations change as one matures. While the work that individuals in different occupations perform can vary significantly, the challenges and frustrations that they face at the same stage in their careers are remarkably similar. A model describing these stages is shown in Figure 8–4. The stages are (1) preparation for work, (2) organizational entry, (3) early

FIGURE 8–4 STAGES OF CAREER DEVELOPMENT

Stage 1: Preparation for Work

Typical Age Range: 0–25
Major Tasks: Develop occupational self-image, assess alternative occupations, develop initial occupational choice, pursue necessary education.

Stage 2: Organizational Entry

Typical Age Range: 18–25
Major Tasks: Obtain job offer(s) from desired organization(s), select appropriate job based on accurate information.

Stage 3: Early Career

Typical Age Range: 25–40
Major Tasks: Learn job, learn organizational rules and norms, fit into chosen occupation and organization, increase competence, pursue goals.

Stage 4: Midcareer

Typical Age Range: 40–55
Major Tasks: Reappraise early career and early adulthood, reaffirm or modify goals, make choices appropriate to middle adult years, remain productive in work.

Stage 5: Late Career

Typical Age Range: 55–retirement
Major Tasks: Remain productive in work, maintain self-esteem, prepare for effective retirement.

SOURCE: From *Career Management* by J. H. Greenhaus, copyright © 1987 by The Dryden Press, a division of Holt, Rinehart and Winston, Inc., reprinted by permission of the publisher.

career, (4) midcareer, and (5) late career. The typical age range and the major tasks of each stage are also presented.

The first stage—preparation for work—encompasses the period prior to entering an organization, often extending until age 25. It is a period in which individuals must acquire the knowledge, abilities, and skills they will need to compete in the marketplace. It is a time when careful planning, based on sound information, should be the focus. The second stage, typically from ages 18 to 25, is devoted to soliciting job offers and selecting an appropriate job. During this period one may also be involved in preparing for work. The next three stages entail fitting into a chosen occupation and organization, modifying goals, making choices, remaining productive, and finally, preparing for retirement. In the remainder of the chapter we will examine some of the activities of primary concern to the student, who is likely to be in the early stages.

Graduation marks the transition from stage one to stage two.

Developing Personal Skills

In planning a career, one should not attend only to acquiring specific job knowledge and skills. Job know-how is clearly essential, but there are other skills one must develop to be successful as an employee. To succeed as a manager or supervisor, one must achieve a still higher level of proficiency in such major areas as communication, time management, organization of work, interpersonal relationships, and the broad area of leadership.

Hundreds of self-help books have been written on these topics, and a myriad of opportunities to participate in workshops are available, often under the sponsorship of one's employer.[33] One should not overlook sources of valuable information such as articles in general-interest magazines and professional journals. For example, the pointers on the basic skills of successful career management listed in Highlights in HRM 2 are taken from a *Personnel Journal* article in which the eight skills are discussed.

Choosing a Career

When asked about career choice, Peter Drucker said, "The probability that the first job choice you make is the right one for you is roughly one in a million. If you decide your first choice is the right one, chances are that you are just plain lazy."[34] The implications of this statement are that one must often do a lot of searching and changing to find a career path that is psychologically and financially satisfying.

USE OF AVAILABLE RESOURCES A variety of resources are available to aid in the process of choosing a satisfying career. Counselors at colleges and universities, as well as those in private practice, are equipped to assist individuals in evaluating their aptitudes, abilities, interests, and values as they relate to career selection. There is a broad interest among business schools in a formal instructional program in career planning and development, and other units in the institutions, such as placement offices and continuing education centers, offer some type of career planning assistance.

ACCURACY OF SELF-EVALUATION Successful career development depends in part on an individual's ability to conduct an accurate self-evaluation. In making a self-evaluation, one needs to consider those factors that are personally significant. An open model for career decision making, shown in Highlights in HRM 3, includes the most important factors to be considered in career decisions. It is "open" in that it provides spaces for additional factors. Note that it is divided into internal and external factors. On a scale of 0 to 5, the individual is to give a personal

HIGHLIGHTS IN HRM

2 BASIC SKILLS OF SUCCESSFUL CAREER MANAGEMENT

1. Develop a positive attitude.
2. Take responsibility for your own career.
3. Establish goals.
4. Be aware of success factors.
5. Present yourself in a positive manner.
6. Be in the right place at the right time.
7. Establish a relationship with a mentor or guide.
8. Adopt the mind-set of your superiors.

SOURCE: Lewis Newman, "Career Management: Start with Goals," *Personnel Journal* 68, no. 4 (April 1989): 91–92. Reproduced with permission.

weighting to indicate the relative importance of each factor to career decisions. Models such as this one help to ensure that an individual does not overlook factors that may be critical in the process of choosing a career.

SIGNIFICANCE OF INTEREST INVENTORIES Psychologists who specialize in career counseling typically administer a battery of tests such as those mentioned in Chapter 6. The *Strong Vocational Interest Blank (SVIB),* developed by E. K. Strong, Jr., during the 1920s, was among the first of the interest tests.[35] Somewhat later, G. Frederic Kuder developed inventories to measure degree of interest in mechanical, clerical, scientific, and persuasive activities, among others.

Strong found that there are substantial differences in interests that vary from occupation to occupation, and that a person's interest pattern, especially after age 21, tends to become quite stable. By taking his test, now known as the *Strong-Campbell Interest Inventory (SCII),* one can learn the degree to which his or her interests correspond with those of successful people in a wide range of occupations. Those results that are profiled on the basis of computer scoring also reveal one's personality type, using Holland's categories. According to Holland, most persons can be categorized into the following six types:

1. Realistic
2. Investigative
3. Artistic
4. Social
5. Enterprising
6. Conventional

HIGHLIGHTS IN HRM

3 CAREER DECISION-MAKING MODEL

INTERNAL FACTORS

Aptitudes and Attributes

____ Academic aptitudes and achievement
____ Occupational aptitudes and skills
____ Social skills
____ Communication skills
____ Leadership abilities
____ ____________________
____ ____________________

Interests

____ Amount of supervision
____ Amount of pressure
____ Amount of variety
____ Amount of work with data
____ Amount of work with people
____ ____________________
____ ____________________

Values

____ Salary
____ Status/prestige
____ Advancement opportunity
____ Growth on the job
____ ____________________
____ ____________________

EXTERNAL FACTORS

Family Influence

____ Family values and expectations
____ Socioeconomic level
____ ____________________
____ ____________________
____ ____________________
____ ____________________
____ ____________________
____ ____________________
____ ____________________

Economic Influence

____ Overall economic conditions
____ Employment trends
____ Job market information
____ ____________________
____ ____________________
____ ____________________
____ ____________________

Societal Influence

____ Perceived effect of race, sex, or ethnic background on success
____ Perceived effect of physical or psychological handicaps on success
____ ____________________

SOURCE: Lila B. Stair, *Careers in Business: Selecting and Planning Your Career Path* (Homewood, IL: Richard D. Irwin, 1980), 8. © 1980 by Richard D. Irwin, Inc. Reproduced with permission of National Textbook Company, 4255 W. Touhy, Lincolnwood (Chicago), IL 60646-1975.

These categories characterize not only a type of personality, but also the type of working environment that a person would find most congenial. In the actual application of Holland's theory, combinations of the six types are examined. For example, a person may be classified as Realistic-Investigative-Enterprising (RIE). Jobs in the

RIE category include mechanical engineer, watch repairer, and air-traffic controller.[36] To facilitate searching for occupations that match one's category, such as RIE, Holland has devised a series of tables that correlate the Holland categories with jobs in the *Dictionary of Occupational Titles* (DOT), described in Chapter 4.

EVALUATION OF LONG-TERM EMPLOYMENT OPPORTUNITIES In making a career choice, one should attempt to determine the probable long-term opportunities in the occupational fields one is considering. While even the experts can err in their predictions, one should give at least some attention to the opinions that are available. A source of information that has proved valuable over the years is the *Occupational Outlook Handbook,* published by the U.S. Department of Labor and available at most libraries. Many libraries also have publications that provide details about jobs and career fields. In recent years, a considerable amount of computer software has been developed to facilitate access to information about career fields and to enable individuals to match their abilities, aptitudes, interests, and experiences with the requirements of occupational areas.

Choosing an Employer

Once an individual has made a career choice, even if only tentatively, the next major step is deciding where to work. The choice of employer may be based primarily on location, immediate availability of a position, starting salary, and other basic considerations. However, the college graduate who has prepared for a professional or managerial career is likely to have more sophisticated concerns. Hall proposes that people frequently choose an organization on the basis of its climate and how it appears to fit their needs. According to Hall:

> People with high needs for achievement may choose aggressive, achievement-oriented organizations. Power-oriented people may choose influential, prestigious, power-oriented organizations. Affiliative people may choose warm, friendly, supportive organizations. We know that people whose needs fit with the climate of an organization are rewarded more and are more satisfied than those who fit in less well, so it is natural to reason that fit would also be a factor in one's choice of an organization.

Hall suggests further that because the relevant theory and measurement technology are available, the prediction of organizational choice is a promising area for researchers.[37]

Keeping a Career in Perspective

For most people, work is a primary factor in the overall quality of their lives. It provides a setting for satisfying practically the whole range of human needs and is

"First of all, you spelled 'résumé' wrong."

thus of considerable value to an individual. Nevertheless, it is advisable to keep one's career in perspective so that other important areas of life are not neglected.

Developing hobbies outside of work is important to a balanced life-style.

OFF-THE-JOB INTERESTS Satisfaction with one's life is a product of many forces. Some of the more important ingredients are physical health, emotional well-being, harmonious personal relationships, freedom from too much stress, and achievement of one's goals. While a career can provide some of the satisfaction that one needs, most people find it necessary to turn to interests and activities outside their career. Off-the-job activities not only provide a respite from daily work responsibilities, but also offer satisfaction in areas unrelated to work.

MARITAL AND/OR FAMILY LIFE The career development plans of an individual as well as an organization must take into account the needs of spouses and children. As we have said, the one event that often poses the greatest threat to family needs is relocation. Conflict between a desire to advance in one's career and a strong desire to stay in one place and put down family roots often borders on the disastrous. Many employers now provide complete assistance in this area, including relocation counseling, in an effort to reduce the severity of the pain that can accompany relocations.

While relocation may be the most serious threat to employees with families, there are also other sources of conflict between career and family. Some of the work-related sources of conflict are numbers of hours worked per week, frequency of overtime, and the presence and irregularity of shift work. In addition, ambiguity and/or conflict within the employee's work role, low level of leader support, and disappointments due to unfulfilled expectations affect one's life away from the job. Some of the family-related sources of conflict include having to spend an unusually large amount of time with the family and its concerns, spouse employment patterns, and dissimilarity in a couple's career orientations. Greenhaus and Beutell, who have examined research studies that identify the sources of work conflict, point out the need for refined measuring devices that can be used to study work–family interface more accurately. They emphasize that public policy decisions should rest on a solid foundation of accumulated knowledge.[38]

MAINTAINING A BALANCE Those who are "married" to their jobs to the extent that they fail to provide the attention and caring essential to marriage and family relationships can be said to lack an appreciation for the balance needed for a satisfying life. One should always be aware that "to be a success in the business world takes hard work, long hours, persistent effort, and constant attention. To be a success in marriage takes hard work, long hours, persistent effort, and constant attention. . . . The problem is giving each its due and not shortchanging the other."[39]

SUMMARY

Increased competition for promotion and advancement, pressures for equal employment opportunities, desire to get the most out of a career, better employee utilization, and other demands have resulted in the growth of career development programs. To succeed, such programs require management support, well-defined goals, effective communication, and compatible HR policies. It is essential that a career development program include a comprehensive inventory of job opportunities with carefully organized progressions from one job to the next. The process of choosing a career path should involve maximum participation of the individual concerned. This may be achieved through the use of workbooks, workshops, and career counseling.

Career development programs often contain segments designed to further the advancement of special groups within an organization. Management development programs, for example, help to provide a source of leadership talent that is custom-made for the organization.

Managers should be trained to identify talent for further evaluation in assessment centers. The use of mentors to facilitate the career development process is a valuable and popular approach. Special programs for women and minorities help overcome the barriers to advancement that individuals in these groups have traditionally encountered. The special needs of dual-career couples must also be addressed in a manner that is satisfactory to both the couple and the employer.

To help employees achieve their career objectives, HR professionals should understand the process by which individuals typically make career choices and be aware of some of the more scientific approaches to career selection that may be used. How to choose an organization and how to keep one's career in perspective are other questions that should be addressed.

DISCUSSION QUESTIONS

1. What are the reasons for the trend toward increased emphasis on career development programs?
2. Bank of America maintains a special suite of offices at its world headquarters in San Francisco for its retired executives. Two of the bank's former chief executives use their offices regularly.
   a. Of what value is this arrangement to the corporation? To the individuals?
   b. How might retired executives in any organization assist in the career development of current employees?
3. Why is it that some of the organizations with the best development programs experience the greatest loss of young management personnel?
4. One recruiter has said, "Next to talent, the second most important factor in career success is taking the time and effort to develop visibility." What are some ways of developing visibility?
5. Over 50 percent of all MBAs leave their first employer within five years. While the change may mean career growth for the individuals, it represents a loss to the employers. What are some of the probable reasons for their leaving?
6. What are some of the barriers that have limited advancement opportunities for women in many organizations?
7. What do you believe are the major advantages of the life-style of dual-career couples? The major disadvantages? Give reasons for your responses.
8. In your opinion, what personal characteristics are employers looking for in individuals whom they are considering for long-term employment and probable advancement in the organization? To what extent can one develop these characteristics?

MINI-CASE 8–1 Preparing a Career Development Plan

Sue Ann Scott was a telephone operator at the headquarters of a large corporation. A high school graduate, she had no particular skills other than a pleasing voice and personality. Nevertheless, Sue Ann wanted very much to improve her economic position. Recognizing her educational limitations, she began taking accounting courses on a random basis in an evening adult education program. Unfortunately, she did not have any particular plan for career development.

Sue Ann also took advantage of the corporation's job bidding system by applying for openings that were posted, even though in many instances she did not meet the specifications listed for them. After being rejected several times, she became discouraged. Her depressed spirits were observed by Mrs. Burroughs, one of the department managers in the corporation. Mrs. Burroughs invited Sue Ann to come to her office for a talk about the problems Sue Ann was having. Sue Ann took full advantage of the opportunity to express her frustrations and disappointments. As she unburdened herself, it became apparent that, besides lacking special skills and career objectives, during interviews she tended to apologize for having "only a high school education." This made it difficult for the interviewers to select her over other candidates who were putting their best foot forward. Mrs. Burroughs suggested that perhaps Sue Ann might try taking a more positive approach during her interviews. For example, she could stress her self-improvement efforts at night school and the fact that she was a dependable and cooperative person who was willing to work hard to succeed in the job for which she was applying.

Following Mrs. Burroughs' advice, Sue Ann selected a job for which she felt she could qualify. She made a very forceful and positive presentation during her interview, stressing the favorable qualities that she possessed. As a result of this approach, she was selected for the job of invoice clerk. While this job did not pay much more than that of telephone operator, it did offer an avenue for possible advancement into the accounting field where the accounting courses she was taking would be of value.

QUESTIONS

1. What are some of the possible reasons why Ms. Scott did not seek or receive advice from her immediate supervisor?
2. After reviewing the chapter, suggest all possible ways that Sue Ann Scott can prepare herself for career advancement.

MINI-CASE 8–2 Career-Path Roadblocks

A major problem confronting the Able Company was that of providing job experiences for new, young managers that would equip them to eventually take over positions in upper management. Unfortunately, a number of middle-management positions in which this experience could be gained were "plugged up" by older managers who would be occupying these positions until their retirement some five or six years away. The company was anxious to open up some of these positions without adversely affecting the self-esteem or future performance of the managers occupying them. Furthermore, the company wished to avoid, if possible, the appearance that it was "kicking these managers upstairs."

Able finally decided to solve this problem by creating new positions of staff assistants to its vice-presidents. The older managers were to be appointed to these new positions where their past experience could be utilized. To maintain the morale and productivity of the new staff assistants, the vice-presidents were encouraged to give them more than the usual amount of personal attention. The vice-presidents followed up at periodic intervals on the projects assigned to the older managers and complimented them on their progress and assistance. As a result, most of the older managers were able to make contributions that were well in line with the salaries they were receiving. Unfortunately, there was a limit to the number of staff assistants that were needed and to the amount of time that senior executives could spend with them. Consequently, it was not possible to open up all the positions that were needed to provide developmental experiences for all the younger managers going up the promotional ladder.

QUESTIONS

1. Are there any other ways for the company to provide meaningful job assignments or career development activities for the younger managers to move up the corporate ladder?
2. What should the company policy be with respect to those managers who have moved as far upward as possible but who are several years away from retirement?

NOTES AND REFERENCES

1. Douglas T. Hall, *Careers in Organizations* (Santa Monica, CA: Goodyear Publishing, 1976), 36; and Zandy B. Leibowitz, Caela Farren, and Beverly L. Kaye, *Designing Career Development Systems* (San Francisco: Jossey-Bass, 1986), 7.
2. Leibowitz et al., 40–42. See also Lorraine M. Carulli, Cheryl L. Noroian, and Cindy Levine, "Employee-Driven Career Development," *Personnel Administrator* 34, no. 3 (March 1989): 6–70.
3. Leibowitz et al., 5–7.
4. Milan Moravec, "A Cost Effective Career Planning Program Requires a Strategy," *Personnel Administrator* 27, no. 1 (January 1982): 28–32.
5. Manuel London and Edward M. Mone, eds., *Career Growth and Human Resource Strategies* (Westport, CT: Quorum Books, 1988), 99–104.
6. Carulli et al.
7. Mitchell W. Fields and James B. Shaw, "Transfers Without Trauma," *Personnel Journal* 64, no. 5 (May 1985): 58–63. See also "Cushioning the Shocks of Job Relocation," Personal Business, *Business Week* (February 4, 1985): 89–90.
8. Thomas M. Camden, "Use Outplacement as a Career Development Tool," *Personnel Administrator* 27, no. 1 (January 1982): 35–37.
9. K. J. Nilan, S. Walls, S. L. Davis, and M. E. Lund, "Creating Hierarchical Career Progression," *Personnel Administrator* 32, no. 6 (June 1987): 168–183; and R. J. Sahl, "Succession Planning: A Blueprint for Your Company's Future," *Personnel Administrator* 32, no. 9 (September 1987): 101–108.
10. For other sources of career information and how to select a professional career counselor, see Berkeley Rice, "Why Am I in This Job?" *Psychology Today* 19, no. 1 (January 1985): 54–59. For a book that provides guidance as well as an opportunity for self-analysis, see Julie Griffin Levitt, *Your Career—How to Make It Happen*, 2d ed. (Cincinnati, OH: South-Western, 1990); and Monica E. Breidenbach, *Career Development—Taking Charge of Your Career* (Englewood Cliffs, NJ: Prentice-Hall, 1989).
11. Daniel C. Feldman, *Managing Careers in Organizations* (Glenview, IL: Scott, Foresman, 1988), 184.
12. Leland C. Nichols and Joseph Hudson, "Dual-Role Assessment Center: Selection and Development," *Personnel Journal* 60, no. 5 (May 1981): 380–386.
13. Frederic D. Frank, David W. Bracken, and Michael R. Struth, "Beyond Assessment Centers," *Training and Development Journal* 42, no. 3 (March 1988): 65–67. See also Virginia R. Boehm, "Designing Developmental Assessment Centers: Step by Step," in London and Mone.
14. Frank et al.
15. Morgan W. McCall, Jr., Michael M. Lombardo, and Ann M. Morrison, "Great Leaps in Career Development," *Across the Board* 26, no. 3 (March 1989): 54–61.
16. Caela Farren, Janet Dreyfus Gray, and Beverly Kaye, "Mentoring: A Boon to Career Development," *Personnel* 61, no. 6 (November–December 1984): 20–24.

17. George S. Odiorne, "Mentoring—An American Management Innovation," *Personnel Administrator* 30, no. 5 (May 1985): 63–70.

18. Kathy E. Kram, *Mentoring at Work: Developmental Relationships in Organizational Life* (Glenview, IL: Scott, Foresman, 1985), 22–24. See also James A. Wilson and Nancy S. Elman, "Organizational Benefits of Mentoring," *The Executive* IV, no. 4 (November 1990): 88–94.

19. Odiorne, "Mentoring"; and Michael G. Zey, "A Mentor for All Reasons," *Personnel Journal* 67, no. 1 (January 1988): 46–51.

20. Farren et al.

21. Zey, "A Mentor for All Reasons"; and Raymond A. Noe, "Women and Mentoring: A Review and Research Agenda," *Academy of Management Review* 13, no. 1 (January 1988): 65–78. See also "Chipping Away at the Glass Ceiling," *Nation's Business* 79, no. 5 (May 1991): 20–21.

22. "How Networks Work for Women," *Management Review* 70, no. 8 (August 1981): 43–45.

23. The interested reader should find the following books very informative: Helen Gurley Brown, *Having It All* (New York: Simon and Schuster, 1982); Johanna Hunsaker and Phillip Hunsaker, *Strategies and Skills for Managerial Women* (Cincinnati, OH: South-Western, 1986); and Norma Carr-Ruffino, *The Promotable Woman—Becoming a Successful Manager,* rev. ed. (Belmont, CA: Wadsworth, 1985).

24. Elizabeth Ehrlich, "The Mommy Track," *Business Week* (March 20, 1989): 126–134; and "Is the Mommy Track a Blessing or Betrayal?" *Business Week* (May 15, 1989): 98–99.

25. Felice Schwartz, "Management Women and the New Facts of Life," *Harvard Business Review* 89, no. 1 (January–February 1989): 65–82.

26. U.S. Department of Commerce, Bureau of the Census, *Statistical Abstracts of the United States* (Washington, DC: U.S. Government Printing Office, 1990), 389.

27. Ibid. For an excellent book written especially for black managers, see Floyd Dickens, Jr., and Jacqueline B. Dickens, *The Black Manager—Making It in the Corporate World* (New York: AMACOM, 1982).

28. David Mills, "Program to Employ Minorities Is Criticized As It Drifts Toward Aiding the Middle Class," *Wall Street Journal* (July 28, 1983): 23.

29. John Naisbitt and Patricia Aburdene, *Reinventing the Corporation* (New York: Warner Books, 1985), 209.

30. Donna H. Green and Thomas J. Zenisek, "Dual Career Couples: Individual and Organizational Implications," *Journal of Business Ethics* 2, no. 3 (August 1983): 171–184.

31. Patricia A. Mathews, "The Changing Work Force: Dual-Career Couples and Relocation," *Personnel Administrator* 29, no. 4 (April 1984): 55–62. See also Maria Helene Sekas, "Dual-Career Couples—A Corporate Challenge," *Personnel Administrator* 29, no. 4 (April 1984): 37–45.

32. Carol B. Gilmore and William R. Fannin, "The Dual Career Couple: A Challenge to Personnel in the Eighties," *Business Horizons* 25, no. 3 (May–June 1982): 36–41.

33. A discussion of the major skill areas can be found in George S. Odiorne, *Personal Effectiveness* (Westfield, MA: MBO, 1979). See also Stephen P. Robbins, *Training in Interpersonal Skills—Tips for Managing People at Work* (Englewood Cliffs, NJ: Prentice-Hall, 1989).

34. Mary Harrington Hall, "A Conversation with Peter Drucker," *Psychology Today* 1, no. 10 (March 1968): 22.

35. E. K. Strong, Jr., of Stanford University, was active in the measurement of interests from the early 1920s to the time of his death in 1963. Since then his work has been carried on by the staff of the Measurement Research Center, University of Minnesota. The *Strong-Campbell Interest Inventory (SCII)* is distributed by Consulting Psychologists Press, Inc., P.O. Box 60070, Palo Alto, CA 94306, to qualified persons under an exclusive license from the publisher, Stanford University Press.

36. John I. Holland, *Making Vocational Choices: A Theory of Careers,* 2d ed. (Englewood Cliffs, NJ: Prentice-Hall, 1984).

37. Douglas T. Hall, *Careers in Organizations* (Santa Monica, CA: Goodyear Publishing, 1976), 36. See also Douglas T. Hall and Associates, *Career Development in Organizations* (San Francisco: Jossey-Bass, 1986).

38. Jeffrey H. Greenhaus and Nicholas J. Beutell, "Sources of Conflict Between Work and Family Roles," *Academy of Management Review* 10, no. 1 (January 1985): 76–88.

39. Richard W. Ogden, *How to Succeed in Business and Marriage* (New York: AMACOM, 1978), 2.

CHAPTER 9

Appraising and Improving Performance

After reading this chapter you will be able to:

1. *Discuss the relationship between performance appraisal and other HR functions.*
2. *Describe the various objectives of performance appraisal programs.*
3. *Identify the basic considerations in selecting standards for appraisal.*
4. *List the factors brought out in major court decisions involving performance appraisal procedures.*
5. *Discuss the primary performance appraisal methods.*
6. *Describe the types of errors that arise in the use of rating methods.*
7. *Identify the different approaches to performance appraisal interviewing.*
8. *Define the key terms in the chapter.*

TERMS TO IDENTIFY

peer appraisals *(272)*
appraisal by subordinates *(273)*
leniency or strictness error *(274)*
anchors *(274)*
error of central tendency *(274)*
recency error *(274)*
rating scale method *(281)*
global rating *(281)*
mixed standard scales *(282)*
behaviorally anchored rating scale (BARS) *(282)*
essay method *(284)*
management by objectives (MBO) *(284)*
tell-and-sell method *(293)*
tell-and-listen method *(293)*
problem-solving method *(293)*

In the preceding chapters, we discussed the programs that an organization uses to procure and develop a productive work force. In this chapter we turn to performance appraisal programs, which must be developed if an organization is to maintain its productivity. Of course, performance appraisal takes place in every organization whether there is a formal program or not. Supervisors are constantly observing the way their subordinates carry out their assignments and forming impressions about the relative worth of these employees to the organization. Most organizations, however, do seem to use a formal program. In a study of 324 organizations, 94 percent reported having such a program[1]—a clear indication that performance appraisal is seen as a valuable activity.

The success or failure of a performance appraisal program depends on the philosophy underlying it and the attitudes and skills of those responsible for its administration. Many different methods can be used to gather information about the performance of subordinates. However, gathering information is only the first step in the appraisal process. The information must then be evaluated in the context of organizational needs and communicated to employees so that it will result in high levels of performance.

PERFORMANCE APPRAISAL PROGRAMS

Formal programs for performance appraisal and merit ratings are by no means new to organizations. The federal government began evaluating employees in 1842, when Congress passed a law mandating yearly performance reviews for department clerks. From this early beginning, performance appraisal systems have spread to large and small organizations in both the public and private sectors. Advocates see these HR programs as the only logical means to appraise, develop, and thus effectively utilize the knowledge and abilities of employees.

A performance appraisal program benefits both the organization and the subordinates whose performance is being appraised. For the organization, employee appraisal is a management feedback system that provides input that can be used for the entire range of HRM activities. For example, performance appraisal is directly related to a number of other major HR functions, such as managerial planning and employee compensation. Appraisal systems have the capability to influence employee behavior, thereby leading directly to improved organizational performance.[2] For the individual, appraisal provides the feedback essential to good performance. Newer approaches to performance appraisal stress training as well as development and growth plans for employees. A development approach to appraisal recognizes that the purpose of a manager is to improve job behavior, not simply to evaluate past performance.

Having a sound basis for improving performance is one of the major benefits of an appraisal program. Performance appraisal data may also be used to assess the effectiveness of other aspects of the HR program. Performance appraisal reports have been found to be valuable measures of employee success that may be used in validating selection tests and in determining the relative worth of jobs under a job evaluation program. Such reports may be useful in defending HRM actions that have led to the filing of a grievance or a charge of discrimination. Finally, it is important to recognize that the success of the entire HR program depends on knowing how the performance of employees compares with the goals established for them. This knowledge is best derived from a carefully planned and administered HR appraisal program.

New demands for performance accountability have focused greater attention on performance appraisal. Bernardin and Beatty discuss four developments that have arisen in response to these demands.[3]

The first development concerns the regulation of HR functions. Because of government EEO/AA decisions, employers must maintain accurate, objective records of employee performance in order to defend themselves against possible charges of discrimination in connection with such HRM actions as termination, promotion, and salary determination.

The second development is a response to employee concerns about the fairness and accuracy of performance appraisal as a basis for determining raises and promotions. Involving employees in the planning stage of the appraisal process and in helping to develop performance measures is a way of addressing these concerns.

The third development addresses the problem of increased costs and diminished organizational performance arising from underutilization or mismanagement of human resources. To attack this problem, organizations must develop appraisal systems that measure employee performance against objective, job-related standards.

The fourth development concerns the low productivity growth of the United States over the past 15 years compared to that of other major industrial countries.

This trend was discussed in Chapter 2. Strengthening appraisal systems by linking individual performance and rewards to measurable organizational goals is seen as one way to beat the "productivity dilemma."

Developing an Appraisal Program

The HR department ordinarily has the primary responsibility for overseeing and coordinating the appraisal program. Managers from the operating departments should also be actively involved, particularly in helping to establish the objectives for the program. Furthermore, employees are more likely to accept and be satisfied with the performance appraisal system when they have the chance to participate in its development.

OBJECTIVES OF AN APPRAISAL PROGRAM The Travelers Insurance Company has the following objectives for its performance appraisal program. They are similar to the objectives of other organizations.

1. To give employees the opportunity to regularly discuss performance and performance standards with their supervisor.
2. To provide the supervisor with a means of identifying the strengths and weaknesses of an employee's performance.
3. To provide a format enabling the supervisor to recommend a specific program designed to help an employee improve performance.
4. To provide a basis for salary recommendations.[4]

Research has shown that performance appraisals are used most widely as a basis for compensation decisions.[5] The practice of "pay-for-performance" is found in all types of organizations. Besides using them to determine salaries, many enterprises use information from appraisals to recommend job improvements and to provide development feedback to employees. Employee placement decisions, such as those regarding promotions, transfers, or demotions, are often based on appraisal reports. An increasing number of organizations are using appraisal reports as documentation for personnel decisions. As we have said, organizations are recognizing the growing need to document employee performance as a defense against possible charges of wrongful termination or unfair employment practices. Figure 9–1 shows the more common uses of performance appraisals.

APPRAISERS OF PERFORMANCE Managers and supervisors traditionally have served as appraisers of their subordinates' performance. In most instances they are in the best position to perform this function, although it may not always be possible for them to do so. Supervisors often complain that they do not have the time to fully observe the performance of employees. The result is a less-than-objective appraisal. These managers must then rely on performance records or the observations of others to complete the appraisal. For example, American Express uses individuals as telephone monitors to gauge the quality of conversation between a

FIGURE 9–1 PRIMARY USES OF PERFORMANCE APPRAISALS

	SMALL ORGANIZATIONS, %	LARGE ORGANIZATIONS, %	ALL ORGANIZATIONS, %
Compensation	80.2	66.7	74.9
Performance improvement	46.3	53.3	48.4
Feedback	40.3	40.6	40.4
Documentation	29.0	32.2	30.2
Promotion	26.1	22.8	24.8
Training	5.1	9.4	7.3
Transfer	8.1	6.1	7.3
Discharge	4.9	6.7	5.6
Layoff	2.1	2.8	2.4
Personnel research	1.8	2.8	2.2
Manpower planning	0.7	2.8	1.5

SOURCE: Alan H. Locher and Kenneth S. Teel, "Appraisal Trends," *Personnel Journal* 67, no. 9 (September 1988): 140. Reproduced with permission.

service-center representative or credit analyst and a customer. This information is then given to the supervisor for use in completing the employee's performance appraisal.

Occasionally, appraisals are made by persons other than a supervisor. Individuals of equal rank who work together are sometimes asked to evaluate each other. These **peer appraisals** provide information which differs to some degree from ratings by a superior. Peers can readily identify leadership and interpersonal skills along with other strengths or weaknesses of their co-workers. A superior asked to rate a patrol officer on a dimension such as "dealing with the public" may not have much opportunity to observe it. Fellow officers, on the other hand, have the opportunity to observe this behavior regularly.

One advantage of peer appraisals is the belief that they furnish more accurate and valid information than appraisals by superiors. This advantage is exemplified by the appraisal program called Teams Evaluation and Management System (TEAMS). TEAMS attempts to answer the question "Who can most accurately judge job performance, the manager who often sees employees putting their best foot forward, or those who work with their fellow associates on a regular basis?"[6] Peers complete TEAMS evaluation forms on the employee. These forms incorporate safeguards to minimize the possibility of biasing caused by popularity, friendship, or other factors. The forms are then compiled into a single profile, which is given to the supervisor for use in the final appraisal.[7]

GRANTLAND ® reproduced by permission of Grantland Enterprises, Inc.

Despite the evidence that peer appraisals are possibly the most accurate method of judging employee behavior, this system is not widely used.[8] The reasons commonly cited include the following:

1. Peer ratings are simply a popularity contest.
2. Managers are reluctant to give up control over the appraisal process.
3. Those receiving low ratings might retaliate against their peers.
4. Peers rely on stereotypes in ratings.

Employers using peer appraisals must also be sure to safeguard confidentiality in handling the review forms. Any breach of confidentiality can create interpersonal rivalries or hurt feelings and bring about hostility toward fellow employees.

Sometimes employees are asked to evaluate themselves on a self-appraisal form.[9] Self-appraisals are beneficial when managers seek to increase employees' involvement in the review process. A self-appraisal system requires an employee to complete the appraisal form prior to the performance interview. During the performance interview, the supervisor and the employee discuss job performance and agree on a final appraisal. This approach also works well when the supervisor and the employee jointly establish future performance goals or employee development plans.

Critics of self-appraisal argue that self-raters are more lenient than managers in their assessments and tend to present themselves in a highly favorable light.[10] However, several research studies have shown that self-assessments are as valid as, if not better than, test scores, school grades, or external evaluations. The results of one study at a university showed a high agreement between faculty members' and chairpersons' ratings. The authors of this study point out that self-appraisal systems work best in organizations with a participative style of management.[11]

Appraisal by subordinates has been used in some instances to give superiors feedback on how their subordinates view them. Subordinates are in a good position to evaluate their managers since they are in frequent contact with their superiors and occupy a unique position from which to observe many performance-related behaviors. Those performance dimensions judged most appropriate for subordinate appraisals include leadership, oral communication, delegation of authority, coordination of team efforts, and interest in subordinates. However, dimensions related to managers' specific job tasks, such as planning and organizing, budgeting, creativity, and analytical ability, are not seen as appropriate for subordinate appraisal.

In a study including both profit and not-for-profit organizations, three-quarters of the managers responding said they would value the feedback from employees for personal development issues.[12] However, over 70 percent of the managers disapproved of subordinate appraisals where they would involve such issues as pay and performance and where the subordinate's input would count heavily in the appraisals of managers.

RATING ERROR With any rating method, certain types of errors can arise that should be considered. The halo error discussed in Chapter 6 is also common with respect to rating scales, especially those that do not include carefully developed descriptions of the employee behaviors being rated.[13] Provision for comments on the rating form, as shown in Figure 9–2, tends to reduce halo error.

It is common for some raters to give unusually high or low ratings. This gives rise to the **leniency** or **strictness error.**[14] One way to reduce this error is to clearly define the characteristics or dimensions and to provide meaningful descriptions of behavior, known as **anchors,** on the scale. Another approach is to require ratings to conform to some pattern. For example, it may be required that 10 percent of ratings be poor (or excellent). This is similar to the requirement in some schools that instructors grade on a curve.

Raters who are reluctant to assign either extremely high or extremely low ratings commit the **error of central tendency.** To such individuals it is a good idea to explain that, among large numbers of employees, one should expect to find significant differences in behavior, productivity, and other characteristics.

When the appraisal is based largely on the employee's recent behavior, good or bad, the rater has committed the **recency error.** The resulting performance review will be biased either favorably or unfavorably depending on the way performance information is selected, evaluated, and organized by the rater.[15] Without work-record documentation for the entire appraisal period, the rater is forced to recall recent employee behavior to establish the rating. The recency error can be minimized by having the rater routinely document employee accomplishments and failures throughout the whole appraisal period. Rater training also will help reduce this error.

Furthermore, raters should be aware of any stereotypes they may hold toward particular groups—male/female, black/white, etc.—because the observation and interpretation of performance can be clouded by these stereotypes. Results from a study examining how individual differences in stereotypes of women affect performance ratings suggested that women evaluated by raters who have traditional stereotypes of women will be at a disadvantage in obtaining merit pay increases and

FIGURE 9–2 RATING SCALE WITH PROVISION FOR RATER COMMENTS

Appraise employee's performance in PRESENT ASSIGNMENT. Check (✓) most appropriate square. Appraisers are *urged to freely use* the "REMARKS" sections for significant comments descriptive of the individual.

Factor	Rating	Remarks
1. KNOWLEDGE OF WORK: Understanding of all phases of his/her work and related matters.	Needs instruction or guidance. / Has required knowledge of own and related work. / Has exceptional knowledge of own and related work. ☐ ☐ ☐ ☑ ☐	Is particularly good on gas engines.
2. INITIATIVE: Ability to originate or develop ideas and to get things started.	Lacks imagination. / Meets necessary requirements. / Unusually resourceful. ☐ ☑ ☐ ☐ ☐	Has good ideas when asked for an opinion, but otherwise will not offer them. Somewhat lacking in self-confidence.
3. APPLICATION: Attention and application to his/her work.	Wastes time. Needs close supervision. / Steady and willing worker. / Exceptionally industrious. ☐ ☐ ☑ ☐ ☐	Accepts new jobs when assigned.
4. QUALITY OF WORK: Thoroughness, neatness, and accuracy of work.	Needs improvement. / Regularly meets recognized standards. / Consistently maintains highest quality. ☐ ☐ ☐ ☐ ☑	The work he turns out is always of the highest possible quality.
5. VOLUME OF WORK: Quantity of acceptable work.	Should be increased. / Regularly meets recognized standards. / Unusually high output. ☐ ☐ ☑ ☐ ☐	Would be higher if he did not spend so much time checking and rechecking his work.

promotions.[16] This problem will be aggravated when employees are appraised on the basis of poorly defined performance standards and subjective performance traits.

TRAINING OF APPRAISERS A weakness of many performance appraisal programs is that managers and supervisors are not adequately trained for the appraisal task and provide little meaningful feedback to subordinates. Because they lack precise standards for appraising subordinates' performance, their appraisals often tend to become overly lenient to the point of having little meaning. Latham and Wexley stress the importance of performance appraisal training by noting that

> Observer bias in performance appraisals can be largely attributed to well-known rating errors . . . that occur in a systematic manner when an individual observes and evaluates another. In order to minimize the occurrence of rating error and costly litigation battles, organizations, regardless of the appraisal instrument they use, are well advised to expose people who evaluate employees to a training program to minimize rating errors.[17]

Training programs are most effective when they follow a systematic process that begins with an explanation of the objectives of the performance appraisal system.[18] The mechanics of the rating system are also explained, including how frequently the appraisals are to be conducted, who will conduct them, and what the standards of performance are. It is important for the rater to know the purpose for which the appraisal form is to be used. For example, using the form for compensation decisions rather than development purposes may affect how the rater evaluates the employee, and it may change the rater's opinion of how the appraisal form should be completed. In addition, appraisal training should alert raters to the weaknesses and problems of appraisal systems so they can be avoided.

Appraisal training should focus on eliminating the *subjective errors* made by managers in the rating process. Organizations like Sears and Allied Chemical have developed formal training programs, complete with workbooks, to reduce the subjective errors commonly made during the rating process. This training can pay off. As one study concluded, "Rater training has generally been shown to be effective in reducing rating errors, especially if the training is extensive and allows for rater practice."[19]

Finally, a training program for raters should provide some general points to consider for planning and conducting the review. A checklist can be used to assist supervisors in preparing for the appraisal interview. A checklist suggested by AT&T is shown in Highlights in HRM 1. The AT&T checklist reflects the growing tendency of organizations to have employees assess their own performance prior to the appraisal interview.

Establishing Performance Standards

Before any appraisal is conducted, the standards by which performance is to be evaluated should be clearly defined and communicated to the employee. These

HIGHLIGHTS IN HRM

1 SUPERVISOR'S CHECKLIST FOR THE PERFORMANCE APPRAISAL

Scheduling

1. Schedule the review and notify the employee ten days or two weeks in advance.
2. Ask the employee to prepare for the session by reviewing his or her performance, job objectives, and development goals.
3. Clearly state that this will be the formal annual performance appraisal.

Preparing for the Review

1. Review the performance documentation collected throughout the year. Concentrate on work patterns that have developed.
2. Be prepared to give specific examples of above- or below-average performance.
3. When performance falls short of expectations, determine what changes need to be made. If performance meets or exceeds expectations, discuss this and plan how to reinforce it.
4. After the appraisal is written, set it aside for a few days and then review it again.
5. Follow whatever steps are required by your organization's performance appraisal system.

Conducting the Review

1. Select a location that is comfortable and free of distractions. The location should encourage a frank and candid conversation.
2. Discuss each item in the appraisal one at a time, considering both strengths and shortcomings.
3. Be specific and descriptive, not general or judgmental. Report occurrences rather than evaluating them.
4. Discuss your differences and resolve them. Solicit agreement with the evaluation.
5. Jointly discuss and design plans for taking corrective action for growth and development.
6. Maintain a professional and supportive approach to the appraisal discussion.

SOURCE: Adapted from "The Performance-Management Process, Part 1 and 2," *Straight Talk,* AT&T, Vol. 1, nos. 8 and 9 (December 1987).

standards must be based on job-related requirements. As discussed in Chapter 4, job standards should be based on job analysis and the resulting job descriptions and job specifications. When performance standards are properly established, they will translate job requirements into levels of acceptable/unacceptable employee performance.[20]

In establishing performance standards, there are three basic considerations:

The performance of postal workers is measured against predetermined standards.

1. *Relevance.* This refers to the extent to which standards relate to the objectives of the job.[21] For example, if a standard that 95 percent of all customer complaints are to be resolved in one day is appropriate to the job of customer service representative, then the standard is said to be relevant to performance.
2. *Freedom from Contamination.* A comparison of performance among production workers, for example, should not be contaminated by the fact that some have newer machines than others. A comparison of the performance of traveling salespersons should not be contaminated by the fact that territories differ in sales potential.
3. *Reliability.* This refers to the stability or consistency of a standard, or the extent to which individuals tend to maintain a certain level of performance over time. In ratings, reliability may be measured by correlating two sets of ratings made by a single rater or by two different raters.[22] For example, two employment interviewers may interview the same group of applicants and predict their job success. The interviewer ratings could be compared to determine interrater reliability.

Performance standards will permit managers to specify and communicate precise information to employees regarding quality and quantity of output. Therefore, when performance standards are written, they should be defined in quantifiable and measurable terms. For example, "ability and willingness to handle customer orders" is not as good a performance standard as "all customer orders will be filled in 4 hours with a 98 percent accuracy rate." When standards are expressed in specific, measurable terms, comparing the employee's performance against the standard results in a more justifiable appraisal. For example, the U.S. Postal Service is able to appraise its employees by evaluating their performance against the following standards:

- Window clerks are expected to generate $165.00 in sales revenue hourly (stamps, retail products, etc.).
- Distribution clerks (manual) are expected to sort approximately 600 letters hourly.
- Mail carriers are expected to case 18 letters or 8 flats per minute in office.

Performance Appraisal and the Law

Since performance appraisals are used as one basis for HRM actions, they must meet certain legal requirements. As the courts have made clear, a central issue is to have carefully defined and measurable performance standards. In one landmark case involving test validation, *Albemarle Paper Company* v. *Moody* (discussed in Chapter 3), the U.S. Supreme Court found that employees had been ranked against a vague standard, open to each supervisor's own interpretation. The court stated that "there is no way of knowing precisely what criteria of job performance the supervisors were considering, whether each supervisor was considering the same criteria, or whether indeed, any of the supervisors actually applied a focused and stable body of criteria of any kind."[23] This decision has prompted organizations to try to eliminate vagueness in descriptions of traits such as attitude, cooperation, dependability, initiative, and leadership. For example, the trait "dependability" can be made much less vague if it is spelled out in terms of employee tardiness and/or unexcused absences. In general, reducing room for subjective judgments will improve the entire appraisal process.

Furthermore, other court decisions show that employers might face legal challenges to their appraisal systems when appraisals indicate acceptable or above-average performance but employees are later disciplined for poor performance. In these cases the performance appraisal form undermines the legitimacy of the subsequent personnel decision. As one commentator noted, "A discharged employee may claim that a failure to inform him or her during a performance review of both the unsatisfactory performance and the possibility of discharge constitutes negligence on the part of the employer."[24]

Therefore, in light of recent court rulings, HR managers suggest that performance appraisals should meet the following legal guidelines:

- Performance ratings must be job-related, with performance standards developed through job analysis.
- Employees must be given a written copy of their job standards in advance of appraisals.
- Managers who conduct the appraisal must be able to observe the behavior they are rating. This implies having a measurable standard to which to compare employee behavior.
- Supervisors should be trained to use the appraisal form correctly. They should be instructed in how to apply appraisal standards when making judgments.
- Appraisals should be discussed openly with employees and counseling or corrective guidance offered to help poor performers improve their performance.
- An appeals procedure should be established to enable employees to express disagreement with the appraisal.[25]

To comply with the legal requirements of performance appraisals, employers must ensure that managers and supervisors document appraisals and reasons for subsequent HRM actions (see Chapter 16 on documentation). This information may prove decisive should an employee take legal action. An employer's credibility is strengthened when it can support performance appraisal ratings by documenting instances of poor performance.[26]

Why Performance Appraisal Programs Fail

In actual practice, formal performance appraisal programs sometimes yield disappointing results, for a number of reasons. The primary culprits are lack of top-management support, lack of job-relatedness standards, rater bias, too many appraisal forms to complete on each individual, and using the program for conflicting purposes. For example, if an appraisal program is used to provide a written appraisal for salary action and at the same time to motivate subordinates to improve their work, the two purposes may be in conflict. As a result, the appraisal interview essentially becomes a salary discussion in which the superior seeks to justify the action taken. Consequently, the discussion has little influence on the subordinate's future job performance.

As with all HR functions, if the support of top management is lacking, the appraisal program will not be successful. Even the best-conceived program will not work in an environment where appraisers are not encouraged by their superiors to take the program seriously. To underscore the importance of this responsibility, top management should announce that effectiveness in appraising subordinates is a standard by which the appraisers themselves will be evaluated.

Other reasons why performance appraisal programs can fail to yield the desired results include the following:

1. Managers feel that little or no benefit will be derived from the time and energy spent in the process.
2. Managers dislike the face-to-face confrontation of appraisal interviews.
3. Managers are not sufficiently skilled in conducting appraisal interviews.
4. The judgmental role of appraisal conflicts with the helping role of developing employees.

Performance appraisal at some organizations is a once-a-year activity in which the appraisal interview becomes a source of friction for both appraisers and employees. An important principle of performance appraisal is that continuous feedback and employee coaching must be a positive daily activity.[27] The annual or semiannual performance review should simply be a logical extension of the day-to-day supervision process.

One of the main concerns of employees is the fairness of the performance appraisal system, since the process is central to so many HRM decisions. Employees who believe the system is unfair may consider the appraisal interview a waste of time and leave the interview with feelings of anxiety or frustration. Also, they may view compliance with the appraisal system as perfunctory and thus play only a passive role during the interview process. By addressing these employee concerns during the planning stage of the appraisal process, the organization will help the appraisal program to succeed in reaching its goals.

Finally, organizational politics can introduce a bias even in fairly administered employee appraisals. For example, managers may distort ratings upward because they desire higher salaries for their employees or because higher subordinate ratings make them look good as managers. Managers may want to get rid of troublesome employees, dumping them on another department by altering the rating. These are not errors in the traditional sense that we discussed earlier, since managers are probably well aware of what they are doing and the written rating is at odds with what the manager really believes about employee performance.

PERFORMANCE APPRAISAL METHODS

Since the early years of their use by the federal government, methods of evaluating personnel have evolved considerably. Old systems have been replaced by new methods that represent technical improvements and are more consistent with the purposes of appraisal. In the discussion that follows, we will examine in some detail those methods that have found widespread use, and we will briefly touch on other methods that are used less frequently.

Performance appraisal methods can be broadly classified as either *relative-judgment* methods, such as individual rating scales and comparison methods, or *outcome-oriented* approaches, such as MBO systems. Rating scales continue to be the more popular systems despite their inherent subjectivity. The outcome-oriented approaches are gaining popularity because they focus on the measurable contributions that employees make to the organization.

Rating Scales

Rating scales are a very common method of performance appraisal. In one research study almost 60 percent of respondents reported using some sort of rating scale.[28] In the **rating scale method,** each trait or characteristic to be rated is represented by a scale on which a rater indicates the degree to which an employee possesses that trait or characteristic. An example of this type of scale is shown in Figure 9–2 on page 275. There are many variations of the rating scale. The differences are to be found in (1) the characteristics or dimensions on which individuals are rated, (2) the degree to which the performance dimension is defined for the rater, and (3) how clearly the points on the scale are defined. In Figure 9–2 the dimensions are defined briefly, and some attempt is made to define the points on the scale. Subjectivity is reduced when the dimensions on the scale and the scale points are defined as exactly as possible. This can be achieved by training raters and by including descriptive appraisal guidelines in a performance appraisal reference book developed by the organization.

Also, the rating form should provide sufficient space for comments on the behavior associated with each scale. These comments improve the accuracy of the appraisal since they require the rater to think in terms of observable employee behaviors while providing specific examples to discuss with the employee during the appraisal interview.

GLOBAL RATING While a rating scale with several relevant dimensions is preferable, many organizations simply use a single rating of overall job performance, for example, appraising an employee's total performance as "average." Such a rating, commonly referred to as a **global rating,** is useful for making some HRM decisions, such as those concerning salary increases or promotions. It is, however, of little value to employees in understanding whether their specific job performance has been successful, and it is likely to be viewed as discriminatory.

Global ratings should therefore be used only to supplement ratings on specific characteristics.

MIXED STANDARD SCALE **Mixed standard scales** are a modification of the basic rating scale. Rather than evaluate a trait according to a scale, the rater is given three specific behavioral descriptions relevant to each trait. For example, for the trait of cooperation, the descriptions might be as follows:

a. Employee is extremely cooperative. Can be expected to take the lead in developing cooperation among employees. Completes job tasks with a positive attitude.
b. Employee is generally agreeable. However, at times becomes argumentative when given job assignments. Cooperates with other employees as expected.
c. Employee normally displays an argumentative or defensive attitude toward fellow employees and job assignments.

The descriptions for the trait should reflect three types of performance—superior, average, or inferior. After the three descriptions for each trait are written, they are randomly sequenced to form the mixed standard scale.[29] Supervisors then evaluate employees by indicating that their performance is better than, equal to, or worse than the standard for each behavior.

BEHAVIORALLY ANCHORED RATING SCALE (BARS) We mentioned earlier that one way to improve a rating scale is to have descriptions of behavior along a scale, or continuum. These descriptions permit the rater to readily identify the point where a particular employee falls on the scale. An appraisal procedure has been developed that attempts to identify many dimensions of performance in terms of specific behaviors. It utilizes a device known as the **behaviorally anchored rating scale (BARS).**

Patrol officers may be rated against a BARS.

The BARS consists of a series of five to ten vertical scales—one for each important dimension of job performance anchored by the incidents judged to be critical. A *critical incident* occurs when employee behavior results in unusual success or unusual failure on some part of the job. The critical incidents are placed along the scale and are assigned points according to the opinions of experts. A BARS for the job of patrol officer is shown in Figure 9–3. Note that this particular scale is for the dimension described as "Awareness of procedures, laws, and court rulings, and changes in them."

A BARS is typically developed by a committee that includes both subordinates and managers.[30] The committee's task is to identify all the relevant characteristics or dimensions of the job. Behavioral anchors in the form of statements are then established for each of the job dimensions. Several participants are asked to review the anchor statements and indicate which job dimension each anchor illustrates. The only anchors retained are those which at least 70 percent of the group agree belong with a particular dimension. Finally, anchors are attached to their job dimensions and placed on the appropriate scales according to values that the group assigns to them.

FIGURE 9–3

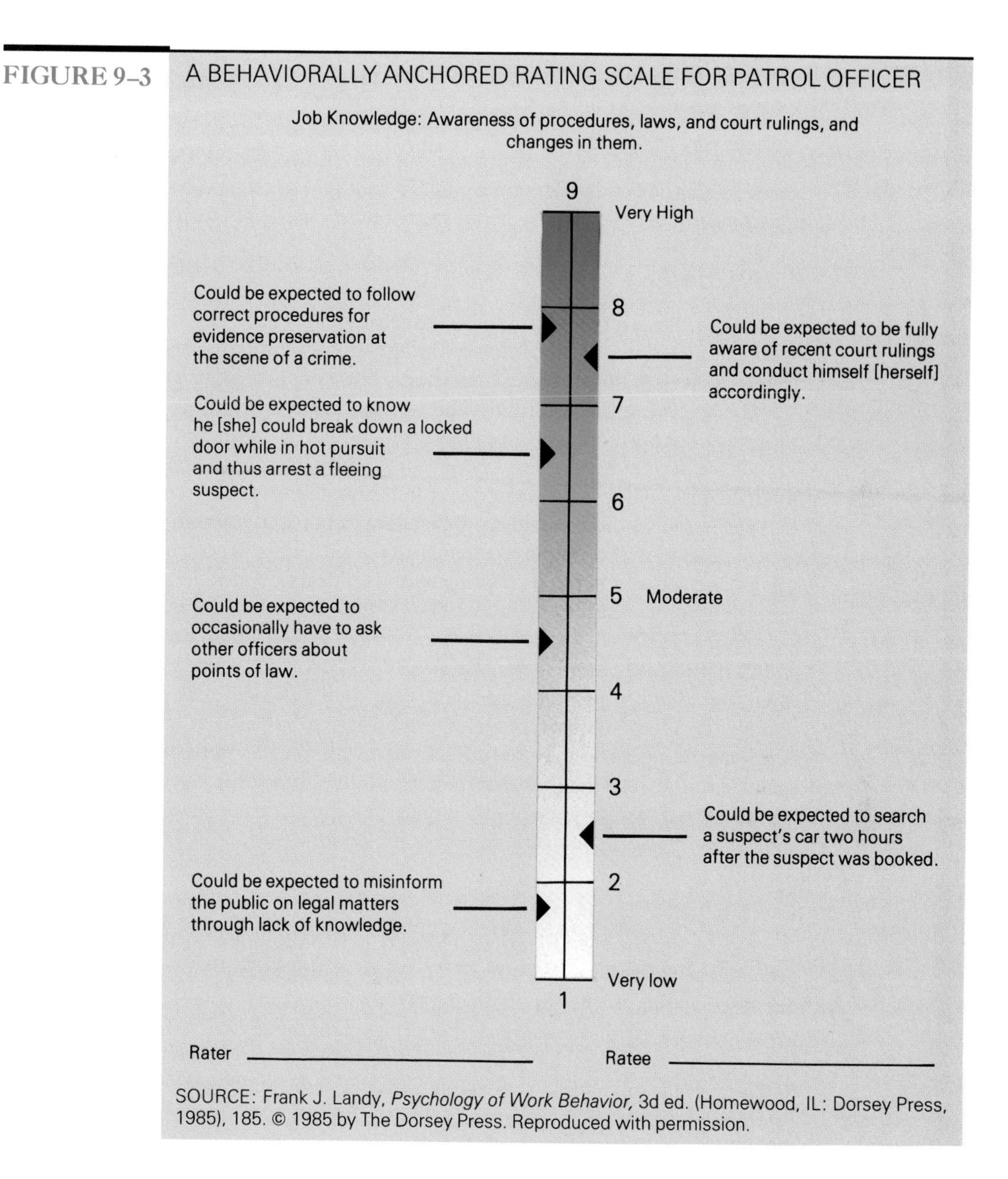

SOURCE: Frank J. Landy, *Psychology of Work Behavior,* 3d ed. (Homewood, IL: Dorsey Press, 1985), 185. © 1985 by The Dorsey Press. Reproduced with permission.

At present there is no strong evidence that a BARS reduces *all* of the rating errors mentioned previously.[31] However, some studies have shown that scales of this type can yield more accurate ratings.[32] One major advantage of a BARS is that personnel outside of the HR department participate with HR staff in its development. Employee participation can lead to greater acceptance of the performance appraisal process and of the performance measures that it uses.

The procedures followed in developing a BARS also result in scales that have a high degree of content validity. The main disadvantage of a BARS is that it requires considerable time and effort to develop. In addition, because the scales are specific to particular jobs, a scale designed for one job may not apply to another.

Essay Method

Unlike the rating scale method, which provides a highly structured form of appraisal, the **essay method** requires the appraiser to compose a statement that best describes the employee being appraised. The appraiser is usually instructed to describe the employee's strengths and weaknesses and to make recommendations for his or her development. Often the essay method is combined with other rating methods. Essays may provide additional descriptive information on performance not obtained with a structured rating scale, for example.

The essay method provides an excellent opportunity to point out the unique characteristics of the employee being appraised. This aspect of the method is heightened when a supervisor is instructed to describe specific points about the employee's promotability, special talents, skills, strengths, or weaknesses. A major limitation of the essay method is that composing an essay that attempts to cover all of an employee's essential characteristics is a very time-consuming task; though when combined with other methods, this method does not require a lengthy statement. Another disadvantage of the essay method is that the quality of the performance appraisal may be influenced by the supervisor's writing skills and composition style. Good writers may simply be able to produce more-favorable appraisals. A final drawback of this appraisal method is that it tends to be subjective and may not focus on relevant aspects of job performance.

Management-by-Objectives Method

Management by objectives (MBO) is a philosophy of management first proposed by Peter Drucker in 1954.[33] It seeks to judge the performance of employees based on their success in achieving the objectives they have established through consultation with their superiors. Performance-improvement efforts under MBO focus on the *goals* to be achieved by employees rather than the activities they perform or the traits they exhibit in connection with their assigned duties.

MBO is a system involving a cycle (see Figure 9–4) that begins with setting the organization's common goals and objectives and ultimately returns to that step. The system acts as a goal-setting process whereby objectives are established for the organization, individual departments, and individual managers and employees.

As Figure 9–4 illustrates, a significant feature of the cycle is the establishment of specific goals by the employee (step 3) using a broad statement of employee responsibilities prepared by the supervisor. Employee-established goals are discussed with the supervisor and jointly reviewed and modified until both parties are

FIGURE 9–4 PERFORMANCE APPRAISAL UNDER AN MBO PROGRAM

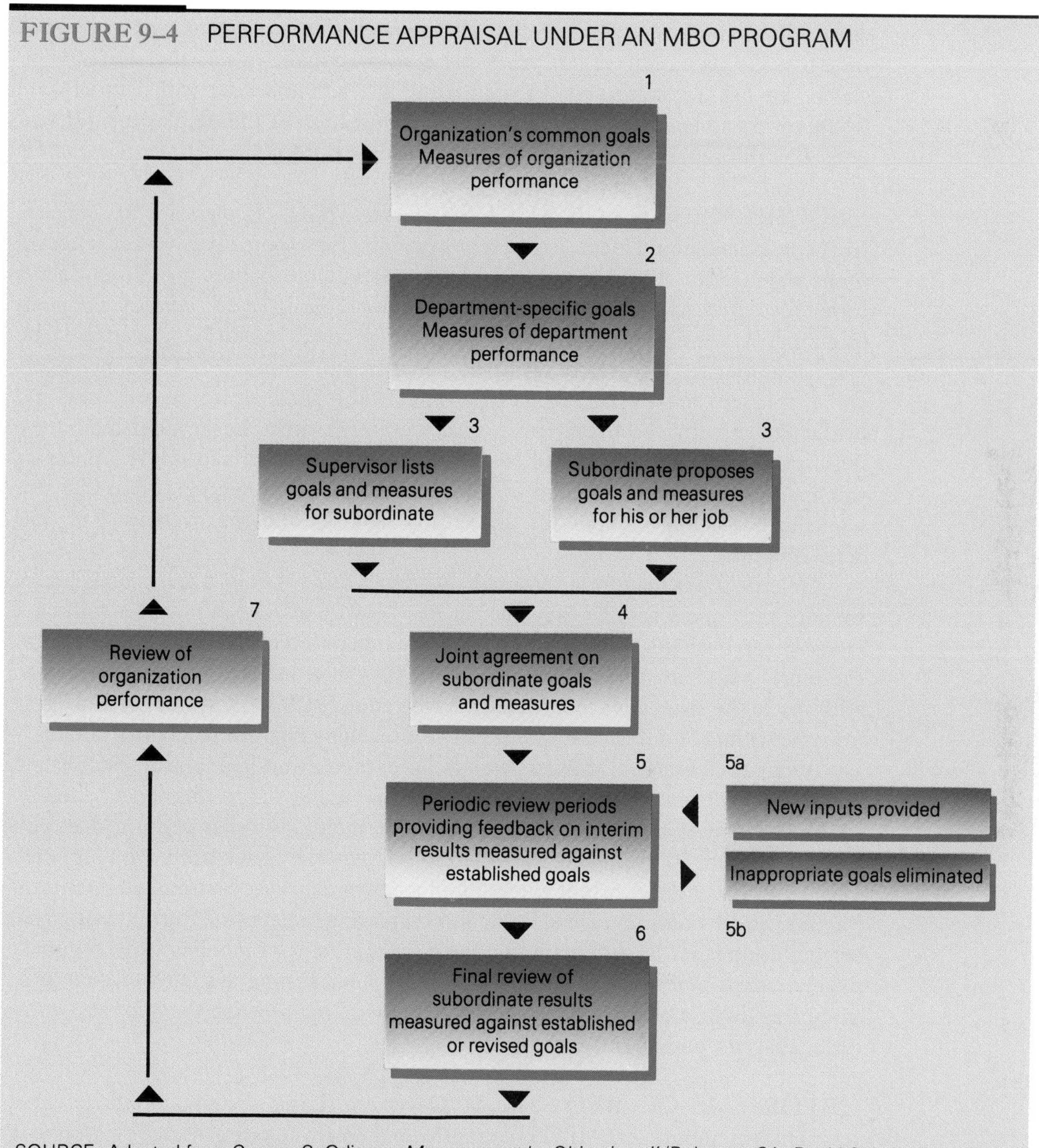

SOURCE: Adapted from George S. Odiorne, *Management by Objectives II* (Belmont, CA: David S. Lake Publishers, 1979). Copyright © 1979. Reproduced with permission.

satisfied with them (step 4). The goal statements are accompanied by a detailed account of the actions the employee proposes to take in order to reach the goals. During periodic reviews, as objective data are made available, the progress that the employee is making toward the goals is then assessed (step 5). Goals may be changed at this time as new or additional data are received. At the conclusion of a period of time (usually six months or one year), the employee makes a self-appraisal of what she or he has accomplished, substantiating the self-appraisal with factual data wherever possible. The "interview" is an examination of the employee's self-appraisal by the supervisor and the employee together (step 6).

REQUIREMENTS FOR SUCCESSFUL MBO If they are to succeed, MBO programs should meet several requirements. First, objectives set at each level of the organization should be quantifiable and measurable for both the long and short term. Second, the expected results must be under the employee's control, and goals (e.g., profit, cost of product made, sales per product, quality control) must be consistent for each level (top executive, manager, and employee). Third, managers and employees must establish specific times when goals are to be reviewed and evaluated. Finally, each employee goal statement must be accompanied by a description of how that goal will be accomplished. Highlights in HRM 2 presents the goal-setting worksheet used by Universal Service Corporation. Note that this worksheet contains sections for the setting of goals and the evaluation of goal achievement.

Odiorne states that the success of MBO depends heavily on a behavioral change by both the supervisor and the subordinate.[34] Both individuals must be willing to *mutually* establish goals and measurable standards for employee performance. Furthermore, MBO must be viewed as part of a system of managing, not as merely an addition to the manager's job. Managers who adopt MBO as a system of managing must be willing to delegate responsibility for reaching goals to their subordinates.

A major advantage of MBO is that it requires the setting of employee-established goals. Goal setting has been shown to improve employee performance, thereby leading to increased productivity.[35] Measurable increases in job performance typically range from 10 to 25 percent, and in some cases they have been even higher.[36] Goal setting works because it allows employees to focus their efforts on important job tasks and makes them accountable for completing these tasks. Furthermore, goal setting establishes an automatic feedback system, since employees can regularly evaluate their performance against their goals. Goal setting has been of benefit to groups as diverse as clerical personnel, scientists, maintenance employees, computer analysts, and engineers.

CRITICISMS OF MBO The MBO system is not without its critics. One researcher contends that MBO is a lengthy and costly appraisal system with only a moderate impact on organizational success.[37] Another criticism of MBO is that performance data are designed to measure results on a short-term rather than a long-term basis. Thus, line supervisors, for example, may let their equipment suffer to reduce maintenance costs. In fact, in any job involving interaction with others, it is not enough to meet certain production or sales objectives. Factors such as cooperation, adaptability, initiative, and concern for human relations may be important to job success. If these factors are important job standards, they should be added

HIGHLIGHTS IN HRM

2 EXAMPLE OF A GOAL-SETTING WORKSHEET

UNIVERSAL SERVICE CORPORATION

Employee's Rating Record

Name ______________________ Date ______________________

Job Title ______________________ Department ______________________

Appraised by ______________________ Date Started ______________________

Summary of Appraisal

Development Needs

Major Responsibilities and Period Goals	**Evaluation of Attainment of Goals**
Responsibility	
Goal	
Responsibility	
Goal	
Responsibility	
Goal	

to the appraisal review. Thus, to be realistic, both the results *and* the method used to achieve them should be considered.

Other Methods of Performance Appraisal

Several other methods of performance appraisal are used, though they are not as common as those already discussed. These methods are sometimes mentioned as ways to avoid various rater error or to reduce problems with the construction of appraisal forms. While each method has its unique advantages and disadvantages, none of them has found universal acceptance among HR professionals.

One of the oldest appraisal techniques is the checklist method. It consists of having the rater check those statements on a list that the rater believes are characteristic of the employee's performance or behavior. A checklist developed for computer salespersons might include a large number of statements such as the following:

____ Is able to explain equipment clearly.
____ Tends to be a steady worker.
____ Is receptive to customer needs.
____ Processes orders correctly.

A more sophisticated form of the checklist employs the forced-choice method. The rater chooses from statements, often in pairs, that appear equally favorable or equally unfavorable. The statements, however, are designed to distinguish between successful and unsuccessful performance. The rater selects one statement from the pair without knowing which statement correctly describes successful job behavior. For example, forced-choice pairs might include the following:

1a. works hard
1b. works quickly

2a. is responsive to customers
2b. shows initiative

3a. produces poor quality
3b. lacks good work habits

The forced-choice method is not without limitations, the primary one being the cost of establishing and maintaining its validity. The fact that it has been a source of frustration to many raters has sometimes caused the method to be eliminated from appraisal programs. In addition, it cannot be used as effectively as some of the other methods to help achieve the commonly held objective of using appraisals as a tool for developing employees by such means as the appraisal interview.

Among other methods that at one time enjoyed some degree of popularity are the comparison method and the ranking method. These techniques require the rater to make relative comparisons between the employees they are appraising. In the ranking method, raters are required to arrange employees in order from the best to the poorest. Employees are evaluated against one another, usually based on some organizational standard or guideline. For example, they may be compared on the basis of their ability to meet production standards or their "overall" ability to perform their job. The employees can then be ordered by rank or by forced distribution as desired (see Figure 9–5).

Managers appraising employees under a forced-distribution system would be required to place a certain percentage of employees into various performance categories. Since employees are usually compared only in terms of overall suitability, this method may result in a legal challenge (see *Albemarle Paper Company* v. *Moody*, discussed in Chapter 3).

The critical-incident method, described earlier in connection with the BARS, has been used as a method of appraisal. Unless both favorable and unfavorable incidents are discussed, however, employees who are appraised may have negative feelings about this method. Some employees have been known to refer to it as the "little black book" approach. Perhaps its greatest contribution is in developing job specifications and in constructing other types of appraisal procedures such as the BARS.

A favorable critical incident is illustrated by the janitor who observed that a file cabinet containing classified documents had been left unlocked at the close of business. The janitor called the security officer, who took the necessary action to correct the problem. An unfavorable incident would be illustrated by a mail clerk who failed to deliver an Express Mail package immediately, instead putting it in with the regular mail routed two hours later.

Which Performance Appraisal Method to Use?

The choice of method should be based largely on the purpose of the appraisal. Figure 9–6 lists six approaches to performance appraisal that were evaluated by Steers. Note that the simplest and least expensive techniques often yield the least accurate information. However, research has not always supported the evaluations reached by Steers. For example, results from a study comparing the relative advantages of the BARS and global rating scales in terms of rating dispersion, test/retest reliability, halo effect, and criterion-related validity showed that the BARS was not superior to global ratings in the scale properties examined.[38] While researchers and HR managers generally believe that the more sophisticated and more time-consum-

FIGURE 9–5 FORCED DISTRIBUTION OF EMPLOYEES IN A WORK GROUP

PERFORMANCE CATEGORIES				
Superior	**Above Average**	**Average**	**Below Average**	**Poor**
10% of Employees	20% of Employees	40% of Employees	20% of Employees	10% of Employees

FIGURE 9–6 MAJOR STRENGTHS AND WEAKNESSES OF VARIOUS APPRAISAL TECHNIQUES

	RATINGS	RANKINGS	CRITICAL INCIDENTS	BARS	MBO	ASSESSMENT CENTERS*
Meaningful dimensions	Sometimes	Seldom	Sometimes	Usually	Usually	Usually
Amount of time required	Low	Low	Medium	High	High	High
Developmental costs	Low	Low	Low	High	Medium	High
Potential for rating errors	High	High	Medium	Low	Low	Low
Acceptability to subordinates	Low	Low	Medium	High	High	High
Acceptability to superiors	Low	Low	Medium	High	High	High
Usefulness for allocating rewards	Poor	Poor	Fair	Good	Good	Fair
Usefulness for employee counseling	Poor	Poor	Fair	Good	Good	Good
Usefulness for identifying promotion potential	Poor	Poor	Fair	Fair	Fair	Good

*Assessment centers are discussed in Chapter 8.

SOURCE: From Richard M. Steers, *Introduction to Organizational Behavior,* 3d ed. (Glenview, IL: Scott, Foresman, 1988). Copyright © 1988 by Scott, Foresman and Company. Reprinted by permission.

ing methods offer more useful information, this may not always be the case. Managers must make cost-benefit decisions about which methods to use.

Review of an Evaluator's Appraisal

In over 90 percent of performance appraisal programs, an employee's immediate supervisor has the responsibility to appraise the employee's performance.[39] Where a supervisor appraises employees independently, provision is often made for a review of the appraisals by the supervisor's superior. Having appraisals reviewed by a supervisor's superior reduces the chance of superficial or biased evaluations. Reviews by superiors generally are more objective and provide a broader perspective of employee performance than do appraisals by immediate supervisors. Some organizations use a review system that requires supervisors to substantiate their appraisals before a committee composed of peer supervisors.

APPRAISAL INTERVIEWS

The appraisal interview gives a manager the opportunity to discuss a subordinate's performance record and to explore areas of possible improvement and growth. It also provides an opportunity to identify the subordinate's attitudes and feelings more thoroughly and thus to improve communication.

The format for the appraisal interview will be determined in large part by the purpose of the interview, the type of appraisal system used, and the organization of the interview form. Most appraisal interviews attempt to give feedback to employees on how well they are performing their jobs and to make plans for their future development. Interviews should be scheduled far enough in advance to allow the interviewee, as well as the interviewer, to prepare for the discussion. Usually ten days to two weeks is a sufficient amount of lead time.

Areas of Emphasis

Since a major purpose of the appraisal interview is to make plans for improvement, it is important to focus the interviewee's attention on the future rather than the past. The interviewer should observe the following points:

1. Emphasize strengths on which the employee can build rather than weaknesses to overcome.
2. Avoid suggestions about personal traits to change; instead suggest more acceptable ways of performing.
3. Concentrate on opportunities for growth that exist within the framework of the employee's present position.
4. Limit plans for growth to a few important items that can be accomplished within a reasonable period of time.

The appraisal interview is perhaps the most important part of the entire performance appraisal process. Unfortunately, the interviewer can become overburdened by attempting to discuss too much, such as the employee's past performance *and* future development goals. Dividing the appraisal interview into two sessions, one for the performance review and the other for the employee's growth plans, can alleviate time pressures. Moreover, by separating the interview into two sessions, the interviewer can give each session the proper attention it deserves. It can be difficult for a supervisor to perform the role of both evaluator and counselor in the same review period. Dividing the sessions also may improve communication between the parties, thereby reducing stress.[40]

Procedural Guidelines

Many of the principles of effective interviewing discussed in Chapter 6 apply to performance appraisal interviews as well. Here are some other guidelines that should also be considered.

LISTEN MORE THAN YOU TALK The more the interviewer talks, the less effective the interview will be. As a rule of thumb, supervisors should spend only about 30–35 percent of the time talking during the interview. The rest of the time they should be listening to employees respond to questions.

VARY THE QUESTIONS Questions are meant to get an employee thinking and talking. Interviewers should minimize the number of questions that call for a yes or no answer and instead vary their questions, particularly those of an open-ended nature. For example, "Why do you believe your sales performance went down this quarter?" requires a detailed response by the employee. Straight open-ended questions such as "What could we do to improve customer satisfaction?" can also be effective. A useful variation to this type of questioning might be to pose a hypothetical problem for the employee to solve on the spot.

USE FOLLOW-UP QUESTIONS If the employee is nervous, seems critical, or gives only short answers, follow-up questions should be asked. These questions can immediately follow the employee's response, or they may be asked at a later time when pursuing the point seems more appropriate. Spacing out follow-up questions may help to determine the consistency of the information provided.

REFLECT FEELINGS The skillful interviewer makes use of a technique employed by clinicians. It is to recognize the feelings that are being expressed and reflect them back to the employee. Note the following exchange:

Subordinate: The worst part of my job is having to take a lot of guff from angry customers.
Supervisor: You find some customers almost too much to take.
Subordinate: Yes, I sure do. But usually only a few of them.

The feeling expressed is reflected back to the subordinate in the form of a restatement. This lets subordinates know that their feelings are important and that the supervisor is listening carefully and with understanding.

AVOID THE "SANDWICH TECHNIQUE" Many supervisors use the "sandwich technique," in which praise serves to cushion criticism. That is, positive statements are followed by negative ones, which are then followed by positive

In an appraisal interview, a supervisor should allow time for an employee to respond.

statements. This approach may not work for several reasons. Praise often alerts the employee that criticism will be coming. Positive comments following the criticism then suggest to the employee that no more negative comments will come for a while. Also, even the most stoic employees can absorb only so much criticism before they start to get defensive. HR managers note that if the rater follows an appraisal form, this will avoid the problem of the sandwich technique. Furthermore, if employees are kept informed of their behavior on a regular basis, there will be no need for this appraisal technique to be used.

Three Types of Appraisal Interviews

The individual who has probably studied different approaches to performance appraisal interviews most thoroughly is Norman R. F. Maier. In his classic book *The Appraisal Interview,* he analyzes the cause-and-effect relationships in three types of appraisal interviews: tell-and-sell, tell-and-listen, and problem-solving.

TELL-AND-SELL METHOD The skills required in the **tell-and-sell method** include the ability to persuade an employee to change in a prescribed manner. This may require the development of new behaviors in the employee, as well as a knowledge of how to make use of the kinds of incentives that motivate each individual employee.

TELL-AND-LISTEN METHOD In the **tell-and-listen method** the skills required include the ability to communicate the strong and weak points of an employee's job performance during the first part of the interview. During the second part of the interview, the employee's feelings about the appraisal are thoroughly explored. The supervisor is still in the role of appraiser, but the method requires listening to disagreement and coping with defensive behavior without attempting to refute any statements. The tell-and-listen method assumes that the opportunity to release frustrated feelings will help to reduce or remove them.

PROBLEM-SOLVING METHOD The skills associated with the **problem-solving method** are consistent with the nondirective procedures of the tell-and-listen method in that listening, accepting, and responding to feelings are essential. However, the problem-solving method goes beyond an interest in the employee's feelings. It seeks to stimulate growth and development in the employee by discussing the problems, needs, innovations, satisfactions, and dissatisfactions the employee has encountered on the job since the last appraisal interview. Maier recommends this method, since the objective of appraisal is normally to stimulate growth and development in the employee.[41]

Managers should not assume that only one type of appraisal interview is appropriate for every review session. Rather, they should be able to use one or more of the interview types depending on the topic being discussed or the behavior of the employee being appraised. The interview should be seen as requiring a flexible approach.[42]

IMPROVING PERFORMANCE

In many instances the appraisal interview will provide the basis for noting deficiencies in employee performance and for making plans for improvement. Unless these deficiencies are brought to the employee's attention, they are likely to continue until they become quite serious. Sometimes, underperformers may not understand exactly what is expected of them. However, once their responsibilities are clarified, they are in a position to take the corrective action needed to improve their performance.

Sources of Ineffective Performance

There are many reasons why an employee's performance might not meet the standards. First, each individual has a unique pattern of strengths and weaknesses that play a part. In addition, other factors—such as the work environment, the external environment including home and community, and personal problems—have an impact on job performance. To provide a better understanding of possible sources of ineffective performance related to these environments, we have devised the comprehensive list shown in Figure 9–7.

It is recommended that a diagnosis of poor employee performance focus on three interactive elements: skill, effort, and external conditions. For example, if an employee's performance is not up to standards, the cause could be a skill problem (knowledge, abilities, technical competencies), an effort problem (motivation to get the job done), and/or some problem in the external conditions of work (poor economic conditions, supply shortages, difficult sales territories).[43] If any one of the three elements is deficient or unfavorable, performance will suffer.

Managing Ineffective Performance

The first step in managing ineffective performance is to determine its source. Once the source is known, a course of action can be planned. This action may lie in providing training in areas that would increase the knowledge and/or skills needed for effective performance. A transfer to another job or department might give an employee a chance to become a more effective member of the organization. In other instances, greater attention may have to be focused on ways to motivate the individual.[44]

If ineffective performance persists, it may be necessary to demote the employee, take disciplinary action, or discharge the person from the organization. Whatever action is taken to cope with ineffective performance, it should be done with objectivity, fairness, and a recognition of the feelings of the individual involved.

FIGURE 9–7 SOURCES OF INEFFECTIVE PERFORMANCE

ORGANIZATION POLICIES AND PRACTICES

- Ineffective job placement
- Insufficient job training
- Ineffectual employment practices
- Permissiveness with enforcing policies or job standards
- Heavy-handed management
- Lack of attention to employee needs or concerns
- Inadequate communication within organization
- Unclear reporting relationships

JOB CONCERNS

- Unclear or constantly changing work requirements
- Boredom with job
- Lack of job growth or advancement opportunities
- Management–employee conflict
- Problems with fellow employees
- Unsafe working conditions
- Unavailable or inadequate equipment or materials
- Inability to perform the job
- Excessive workload
- Lack of job skills

PERSONAL PROBLEMS

- Marital problems
- Financial worries
- Emotional disorders (including depression, guilt, anxiety, fear)
- Conflict between work demands and family demands
- Physical limitations including handicaps
- Low work ethic
- Other family problems
- Lack of effort
- Immaturity

EXTERNAL FACTORS

- Industry decline or extreme competition
- Legal constraints
- Conflict between ethical standards and job demands
- Union–management conflict

SUMMARY

The success of an organization depends largely on the performance of its human resources. To determine the contributions of each individual, it is necessary to have a formal appraisal program with clearly stated objectives. Carefully defined performance standards that are relevant and reliable are essential foundations for evaluation.

If appraisal interviews and any corrective actions are to be based on valid information, managers and supervisors should be thoroughly trained in the particular methods they will use in evaluating their subordinates. Participation in developing rating scales, such as a BARS, automatically provides such training. Whatever methods are used should meet the objectives of the performance appraisal.

The degree to which the performance appraisal program benefits the organization and its members is directly related to the quality of the appraisal interviews that are conducted. Interviewing skills are best developed through instruction and supervised practice. In the interview, deficiencies in employee performance can be discussed and plans for improvement can be made.

DISCUSSION QUESTIONS

1. What are the major purposes of performance appraisal, and in what ways might they be contradictory?
2. Describe the relationships among performance appraisal and selection, compensation management, and training and development.
3. Describe the characteristics of the ideal appraiser.
4. What performance standards could be used to evaluate the performance of people working in the following jobs?
   a. sales representative
   b. TV repairer
   c. director of nursing in a hospital
   d. HR manager
   e. air-traffic controller
5. Discuss the guidelines that performance appraisals should meet in order to be legally defensible.
6. In many organizations, evaluators submit ratings to their immediate superiors for review before discussing them with the individual employees they have rated. What advantages are there to this procedure?
7. Three types of appraisal interviews are described in this chapter.
   a. What different skills are required for each of the types of appraisal interviews? What reactions can one expect from using these different skills?
   b. How can one develop the skills needed for the problem-solving type of interview?
   c. Which method do you feel is the least desirable? Why?
8. Discuss how you would diagnose poor performance, and list several factors to consider.

MINI-CASE 9–1 Setting Performance Standards at General Telephone Company of California*

Raymond Sanchez, a new college graduate with a degree in human resources, was recently hired by General Telephone Company of California. His first job assignment was

*While the case is factual, employee names are fictitious.

as college recruiter, with the responsibility to fill entry-level supervisory positions and staff assignments in accounting, finance, data processing, and marketing. This full-time position required Raymond to have effective interviewing and public-relations skills. Raymond was in charge of a recruiting schedule that included 12 colleges and universities. Six of the schools were located in California, three in Arizona, two in Oregon, and one in Nevada.

The annual HR planning schedule for the company was completed by December of each year. This enabled Raymond to know the types and numbers of college graduates needed by each department and operating area for the coming year. Managers requesting new graduates also stated on the employment requisition form the date by which these positions were to be filled.

Over the past two years, the company has made a concerted effort to develop a comprehensive and effective college recruiting program. It was decided that part of this effort should be devoted to creating a positive and continuing relationship with the college placement offices, as well as with certain professors who would be in a position to refer students for job openings. Establishing this relationship with the schools was viewed as critical for identifying and selecting high-potential employees.

Daniel Turner, manager of the HR department, established yearly performance standards for each of his subordinates. Company guidelines indicated that, where possible, observable and measurable performance standards should be set. Since Raymond has now been with GT&E for three months, he and Mr. Turner agreed to set his performance standards for the upcoming recruitment period. Both acknowledged that setting measurable standards for Raymond's job might be somewhat difficult because of the subjective nature of college recruiting. His current job description states only that Raymond should develop and maintain rapport with the colleges and universities, that openings should be filled in a timely manner, and that college graduates selected for company interviews should be of high quality. Mr. Turner has asked Raymond to come up with four to six observable and measurable performance standards that would capture the duties and responsibilities of the college recruiter's job.

QUESTIONS

1. Develop four to six observable and measurable performance standards suitable to Raymond's position as college recruiter.
2. Discuss any obstacles that might make this task difficult.

MINI-CASE 9–2 Here, Just Sign the Form

"John," said supervisor Mark Krause, "would you stop by my office about 15 minutes before you clock out? I want to give you your annual performance appraisal. It won't take long, and I know you'll want to leave by five o'clock."

John had forgotten that it was "that time of year" again, but he was looking forward to the meeting because he wanted to discuss some new performance standards for his job. Also, he was slightly worried about the appraisal because he didn't think his performance had been up to par over the past year.

Promptly at 4:45 John knocked on Mark's office door and was asked to come in. As he entered, John found his supervisor rushing to get some last-minute orders dated so they could be filled by the late shift. As John sat down, Mark began, "I've filled out your performance appraisal, so why don't you look it over and sign it. You'll see that I've given you excellent ratings on all the factors, but everyone in the crew got excellent ratings this year. I was really impressed with how everyone pitched in to get the Seattle order out this month. That order was really important to the company. I don't have anything else to add; just keep up the good work, and I'll get you a good raise."

John looked the appraisal over and signed it. He could tell Mark was really busy, so he thought he had better leave. Besides, he didn't want to ruin his chances for a salary increase. However, as he left Mark's office, he felt disappointed with the interview.

QUESTIONS

1. Discuss Mark's handling of John's performance appraisal interview.
2. Place yourself in John's position, and develop a checklist to conduct the interview effectively.

NOTES AND REFERENCES

1. Alan H. Locher and Kenneth S. Teel, "Appraisal Trends," *Personnel Journal* 67, no. 9 (September 1988): 139.
2. G. Stephen Taylor, Carol M. Lehman, and Connie M. Forde, "How Employee Self-Appraisals Can Help," *Supervisory Management* 34, no. 8 (August 1989): 32. See also David A. Waldman and Ron S. Kent, "Improve Performance by Appraisal," *HR Magazine* 35, no. 7 (July 1990): 66–69.
3. H. John Bernardin and Richard W. Beatty, *Performance Appraisal: Assessing Human Behavior at Work* (Boston: Kent, 1984), 3–9.
4. *Your Guide to Performance Appraisal*, The Travelers, revised September 1978, p. 2.
5. Locher and Teel, 140.
6. Mark R. Edwards, "Team Evaluation and Management System" (Presented at Ninth Annual HRSP Conference, Houston, Texas, April 17–19, 1989), 1.
7. Mark R. Edwards, "Measuring Creativity at Work: Developing a Reward-for-Creativity Policy," *The Journal of Creative Behavior* 23, no. 1 (First quarter, 1989): 26–37. See also Mark Edwards, "Joint-Appraisal Efforts," *Personnel Journal* 69, no. 6 (June 1990): 122–128.
8. Glenn M. McEvoy and Paul F. Buller, "User Acceptance of Peer Appraisals in an Industrial Setting," *Personnel Psychology* 40, no. 4 (Winter 1987): 785–797.
9. John W. Lawrie, "Your Performance: Appraise It Yourself," *Personnel* 66, no. 1 (January 1989): 21–23. See also Len Sandler, "Two-Sided Performance Reviews," *Personnel Journal* 69, no. 1 (January 1990): 75–78.
10. Shaul Fox and Yossi Dinur, "Validity of Self-Assessment: A Field Evaluation," *Personnel Psychology* 41, no. 3 (Autumn 1988): 582.
11. Jiing-Lih Farh, James D. Werbel, and Arthur G. Bedeian, "An Empirical Investigation of Self-Appraisal–Based Performance Evaluation," *Personnel Psychology* 41, no. 1 (Spring 1988): 141–156.
12. Glenn M. McEvoy, "Evaluating the Boss," *Personnel Administrator* 33, no. 9 (September 1988): 115–120.
13. Rick Jacobs and Steve W. J. Kozlowski, "A Closer Look at Halo Error in Performance Ratings," *Academy of Management Journal* 28, no. 1 (March 1985): 210–212.

14. Beverly Geber, "The Hidden Agenda of Performance Appraisals," *Training* 25, no. 6 (June 1988): 42–46.

15. Robert A. Gacalone, "Image Control: The Strategies of Impression Management," *Personnel* 66, no. 5 (May 1989): 52–55.

16. Gregory H. Dobbins, Robert L. Cardy, and Donald M. Truxillo, "The Effects of Purpose of Appraisal and Individual Differences in Stereotypes of Women on Sex Differences in Performance Ratings: A Laboratory and Field Study," *Journal of Applied Psychology* 73, no. 3 (August 1988): 551–558.

17. Gary P. Latham and Kenneth N. Wexley, *Increasing Productivity Through Performance Appraisal* (Reading, MA: Addison-Wesley, 1981), 116.

18. Stephen B. Wehrenberg, "Train Supervisors to Measure and Evaluate Performance," *Training* 67, no. 2 (February 1988): 77–79.

19. Frank J. Landy and James L. Farr, "Performance Ratings," *Psychological Bulletin* 87, no. 1 (January–February 1980). See also Loren Falkenberg, "Improving the Accuracy of Stereotypes," *Journal of Management* 16, no. 1 (March 1990): 107–118.

20. Stephenie Overman, "Best Appraisals Measure Goals, Not Traits," *Resource* 8, no. 2 (February 1989): 16.

21. John Lawrie, "Steps Toward an Objective Appraisal," *Supervisory Management* 34, no. 5 (May 1989): 17–24.

22. Ernest J. McCormick and Daniel R. Ilgen, *Industrial Psychology,* 7th ed. (Englewood Cliffs, NJ: Prentice-Hall, 1980), 52–55.

23. *Albemarle Paper Company* v. *Moody,* 422 U.S. 405 (1975).

24. Edmund J. Metz, "Designing Legally Defensible Performance Appraisal Systems," *Training and Development Journal* 42, no. 7 (July 1988): 47.

25. For a review of performance appraisal court cases see Robert W. Goddard, "Is Your Appraisal System Headed for Court?" *Personnel Journal* 68, no. 1 (January 1989): 114–118.

26. Gerald V. Barrett and Mary C. Kernan, "Performance Appraisal and Terminations: A Review of Court Decisions Since *Brito* v. *Zia* with Implications for Personnel Practice," *Personnel Psychology* 40, no. 3 (Autumn 1987): 501.

27. Dave Day, "Performance Management Year-Round," *Personnel* 66, no. 8 (August 1989): 43–45.

28. Locher and Teel, 140.

29. Philip G. Benson, M. Ronald Buckley, and Sid Hall, "The Impact of Rating Scale Format on Rater Accuracy: An Evaluation of the Mixed Standard Scale," *Journal of Management* 14, no. 3 (September 1988): 415–423.

30. Margaret E. Griffin, "Personnel Research in Testing, Selection, and Performance Appraisal," *Public Personnel Management* 18, no. 2 (Summer 1989): 130.

31. Brendan D. Bannister, Angelo J. Kinicki, Angelo S. Dinisi, and Peter Hom, "A New Method for the Statistical Control of Rating Error in Performance Ratings," *Educational and Psychological Measurement* 47, no. 3 (Autumn 1987): 583–596.

32. For a comprehensive review of the research on BARS, see Bernardin and Beatty, Chapter 6.

33. Peter F. Drucker, *The Practice of Management* (New York: Harper & Brothers, 1954).

34. George S. Odiorne, *Management by Objectives* (New York: Pitman, 1965), 77–79.

35. E. A. Locke, "Toward a Theory of Task Motivation and Incentives," *Organizational Behavior and Human Performance* 3, no. 2 (May 1968): 157–189.

36. Robert D. Pritchard, Philip L. Roth, Steven D. Jones, Patricia J. Galgay, and Margaret D. Watson, "Designing a Goal-Setting System to Enhance Performance: A Practical Guide," *Organizational Dynamics* 17, no. 1 (Summer 1988): 70.

37. Dennis Daley, "Performance Appraisal and Organizational Success: Public Employee Perceptions in an MBO-based Appraisal System," *Review of Public Personnel Administration* 9, no. 1 (Fall 1988): 17–27.

38. Luis R. Gomez-Mejia, "Evaluating Employee Performance: Does the Appraisal Instrument Make a Difference?" *Journal of Organizational Behavior Management* 9, no. 2 (Fall 1988): 155–172.

39. Locher and Teel, 140.

40. Paul D. Slattery, "Performance Appraisal Without Stress," *Personnel Journal* 64, no. 2 (February 1985): 49–51.

41. Norman R. F. Maier, *The Appraisal Interview* (New York: John Wiley & Sons, 1958); and Maier, *The Appraisal Interview—Three Basic Approaches* (San Diego: University Associates, 1976).
42. Howard J. Klein, Scott A. Snell, and Kenneth N. Wexley, "Systems Model of the Performance Appraisal Interview Process," *Industrial Relations* 26, no. 3 (Fall 1987): 267–279.
43. Scott A. Snell and Kenneth N. Wexley, "Performance Diagnosis: Identifying the Causes of Poor Performance," *Personnel Administrator* 30, no. 4 (April 1985): 117–127.
44. Dorri Jacobs, "Coaching to Reverse Poor Performance," *Supervisory Management* 10, no. 2 (July 1989): 21–28.

PART FOUR

Implementing Compensation and Security

The four chapters in Part Four focus on employee compensation and security issues. Chapter 10 deals with evaluating organizational jobs and establishing monetary rates for these jobs based on both internal and external influences. Also discussed in this chapter are the legal requirements of compensation management. Chapter 11 looks at incentive payment plans for nonmanagerial, managerial, and executive employees. Chapter 12 completes the discussion of compensation administration by reviewing the myriad of benefit programs offered by organizations to their employees. Included here is a relevant discussion of employee benefit costs and various cost-containment programs. Chapter 13 is concerned with the issues pertaining to employee safety and health. It contains discussions related to employee workplace stress, alcoholism, and substance abuse. When managers pay attention to the compensation and security needs of employees, they provide a work environment that contributes to both employee job satisfaction and organizational success.

CHAPTER 10

Managing Compensation

After reading this chapter you will be able to:

1. *Identify the various factors that influence the setting of wages.*
2. *Discuss the mechanics of each of the major job evaluation systems.*
3. *Explain the purpose of a wage survey.*
4. *Develop a wage curve and discuss the effect that the degree of its slope can have on wage rates and labor costs.*
5. *Describe the wage structure with ranges for each job class.*
6. *Explain the major provisions of the federal laws affecting compensation.*
7. *Discuss the current issues concerning equal pay for comparable work.*
8. *Define the key terms in the chapter.*

TERMS TO IDENTIFY

pay-for-performance standard *(305)*
pay equity *(308)*
hourly or day work *(310)*
piecework *(310)*
nonexempt/exempt employees *(310)*
escalator clauses *(312)*
consumer price index (CPI) *(312)*
real wages *(313)*
job evaluation *(315)*
job ranking system *(315)*
job grade or classification system *(317)*
point system *(317)*
factor comparison system *(319)*
Hay profile method *(322)*
wage and salary survey *(324)*
wage curve or conversion line *(325)*
wage classes or grades *(325)*
skill-based pay *(327)*
wage-rate compression *(328)*
two-tier wage system *(330)*
comparable worth *(336)*

An extensive review of the literature indicates that important work-related variables leading to job satisfaction include challenging work, interesting job assignments, equitable rewards, competent supervision, and rewarding careers.[1] In Chapter 2 we emphasized that employees currently in the work force are more concerned than their predecessors with the quality of their work life and with the psychological rewards to be derived from their employment. It is doubtful, however, whether many of them would continue working were it not for the money they earn. Employees desire compensation systems that they perceive as being fair and commensurate with their skills and expectations. Pay, therefore, is a major consideration in HRM because it provides employees with a tangible reward for their services, as well as a source of recognition and livelihood.

Both HR professionals and scholars agree that the way compensation is allocated among employees sends a message about what the organization feels is important and the types of activities it encourages. Furthermore, for an employer, the payroll constitutes a sizable operating cost. In manufacturing firms compensation is seldom as low as 20 percent of total expenditures, and in service enterprises it often exceeds 80 percent.[2] A sound compensation program, therefore, is essential so that pay can serve to motivate employee production sufficiently to keep labor costs at an acceptable level. This chapter will be concerned with the management of a compensation program, job evaluation systems, and pay structures for determining compensation payments. Included will be a discussion of federal regulations that affect wage and salary rates. The current controversial issues involving equal pay for comparable work will also be considered. Chapter 11 will review financial incentive plans for employees.

Employee benefits that are part of the compensation package are discussed in Chapter 12.

THE COMPENSATION PROGRAM

A significant interaction occurs between compensation management and the other functions of the HR program. For example, in the recruitment of new employees, the rate of pay for jobs can increase or limit the supply of applicants. Many fast-food restaurants, traditionally low-wage employers, have needed to raise their starting wages to attract a sufficient number of job applicants to meet staffing requirements. If rates of pay are high, creating a large applicant pool, then organizations may choose to raise their selection standards and hire better-qualified employees. This in turn can reduce employer training costs. Of course, the opposite may occur when low rates of pay attract unskilled workers who require extensive training to perform satisfactorily. When employees perform at exceptional levels, their performance appraisals may justify an increased pay rate. Also, as we will discuss in Chapter 17, if employees believe their rates of pay are low or the employer's compensation policies are unfair, they may unionize or simply leave the organization. For all of these reasons, an organization should develop a formal HR program to manage employee compensation. This program establishes both the objectives it is intended to achieve and the policies for determining compensation payments and how they will be disbursed. Included as part of the program should be the communication of information concerning wages and benefits to employees.

Compensation Objectives and Policies

Fast-food jobs may pay more than the minimum wage.

The objectives of a compensation program, like those pertaining to other HR functions, should facilitate the effective utilization and management of an organization's human resources. Compensation objectives should also contribute to the overall objectives of the organization. A compensation program, therefore, must be tailored to the needs of an organization and its employees.[3]

It is not uncommon for organizations to establish very specific goals for their compensation program. Formalized compensation goals serve as guidelines for HR managers to ensure that wage and benefit policies achieve their intended purpose. The more common goals of compensation policy include the following:

1. To reward employees' past performance.
2. To remain competitive in the labor market.
3. To maintain salary equity among employees.
4. To motivate employees' future performance.
5. To maintain the budget.
6. To attract new employees.
7. To reduce unnecessary turnover.[4]

To achieve these goals, policies must be established to guide management in making decisions. Compensation policies typically include the following:

1. The rate of pay within the organization and whether it is to be above, below, or at the prevailing community rate.
2. The ability of the pay program to gain employee acceptance while motivating employees to perform to the best of their abilities.
3. The pay level at which employees may be recruited and the pay differential between new and more senior employees.
4. The intervals at which pay raises are to be granted and the extent to which merit and/or seniority will influence the raises.
5. The pay levels needed to facilitate the achievement of a sound financial position in relation to the products or services offered.

When setting these compensation policies, organizations must ensure that their pay practices comply with federal and state laws and regulations. These regulations will be covered later in this chapter.

Pay-for-Performance Standard

To raise productivity and lower labor costs in today's competitive economic environment, organizations are increasingly setting compensation objectives based on a **pay-for-performance standard.**[5] It is agreed that managers must tie at least some reward to employee effort and performance. Without this standard, motivation to perform with greater effort will be low, resulting in higher wage costs to the organization.[6] While a pay-for-performance standard has most often applied to salaried or managerial personnel, today its importance extends to hourly employees.

The term pay-for-performance refers to a wide range of compensation options including merit pay, cash bonuses, incentive pay, and various gainsharing plans (gainsharing plans are discussed in Chapter 11). Each of these compensation systems seeks to differentiate between the pay of average and outstanding performers. Bank managers at Comerica, Inc., note that "good workers aren't rewarded when everyone gets the same boost. Differentiating performance is a process that improves an organization's performance."[7] Interestingly, productivity studies show that employees will increase their output by 15 to 35 percent when an organization installs a pay-for-performance program.[8] In addition, the results of one study of hospital employees showed a positive relationship between pay-for-performance perceptions and pay satisfaction even after controlling for salary level, performance rating, and job tenure.[9] Clearly, both organizations and their employees benefit when pay-for-performance programs are successfully implemented.

Unfortunately, designing a sound pay-for-performance system is not easy. Considerations must be given to how employee performance will be measured, the monies to be allocated for compensation increases, which employees to cover, the payout method, and the periods when payments will be made.[10] Each of these concerns was faced by Eastern Michigan University when it implemented its pay-for-performance program for athletic-department administrators and team coaches, as described in Highlights in HRM 1.

The Motivating Value of Compensation

Pay constitutes a quantitative measure of an employee's relative worth. For most employees, pay has a direct bearing not only on their standard of living, but also on the status and recognition they may be able to achieve both on and off the job. Since pay represents a reward received in exchange for an employee's contributions, it is essential, according to the equity theory discussed in Chapter 14, that the pay be equitable in terms of those contributions. It is essential also that an employee's pay be equitable in terms of what other employees are receiving for their contributions.

PAY EQUITY Equity can be defined as anything of value earned through the investment of something of value. Wallace and Fay report that "fairness is achieved

Pay-for-performance incentives for coaches have been successful at Eastern Michigan University.

HIGHLIGHTS IN HRM

1 PAY-FOR-PERFORMANCE AT EASTERN MICHIGAN UNIVERSITY

In 1988 Eastern Michigan University implemented a rigorous pay-for-performance program for athletic coaches and athletic-department administrators. The primary purpose of the program was to raise the school's expectations for each of 22 sports and its athletic department. All sports were expected to reach a level of competitiveness equal to the top third of the school's athletic conference. A second objective of the pay-for-performance program was to differentiate in the salary increases between successful and unsuccessful coaches. Prior to the new salary program, all coaches received the same annual salary adjustment regardless of team performance.

The pay-for-performance program is based on an objective performance appraisal system that provides clear indicators of job success. At the end of each athletic season, coaches are evaluated according to preestablished criteria (i.e., adherence to budget, adherence to NCAA rules, graduation rate of athletes, attainment of fund-raising goals, etc.), plus their win/loss record, conference placement, conference record, and improvement in team record. A total point score is calculated for each coach, and coaches attaining a score of at least 150 points qualify for a salary increase (see Exhibit 1). Exhibit 2 illustrates the salary increases coaches can receive, depending on their evaluation level and total evaluation score. The primary advantage of the pay system is that coaches understand what is expected of them and that achieving or exceeding objectives merits an individual salary reward. Since implementation of the pay-for-performance program, Eastern Michigan has won five conference championships, placed second in four other sports, and received its first invitation to the NCAA basketball tournament.

EXHIBIT 1
POINTS ASSIGNED TO PERFORMANCE LEVELS

Performance Level	Total Score
Exceeds expectations	250–300
Meets expectations	150–249
Below expectations	100–149
Unsatisfactory	0–99

EXHIBIT 2
1987–88 MERIT PAY INCREASE GUIDELINES
MATRIX FOR COACHES' PAY-FOR-PERFORMANCE PLAN

Evaluation Level	Range Penetration Goal	Evaluation Total Score
Mid-American Conference (MAC) or comparable championship	4th Quartile	250–300 + championship
Exceeds expectations	3rd Quartile	250–300

EXHIBIT 2 *Continued*

Evaluation Level	Range Penetration Goal	Evaluation Total Score
Meets expectations	Midpoint	150–249
Below expectations	1st Quartile	100–149
Unsatisfactory	Minimum	0–99

Performance Evaluation	Current Range Penetration: 1st Quartile	2nd Quartile	3rd Quartile	4th Quartile
Championship (5%)	9%–13% + Bonus	8%–10% + Bonus	6%–9% + Bonus	3%–8% + Bonus
Exceeds expectations (15%)	8%–10%	7%–9%	5%–8%	3%–7%
Meets expectations (60%)	7%–9%	6%–8%	4%–6%	3%–6%
Below expectations (15%)	0%	0%	0%	0%
Unsatisfactory (5%)	0%	0%	0%	0%

NOTE: Maximum 13% increase. Minimum 3% increase if "meets expectations" or above. Base salary not to exceed maximum range unless approved by vice-president in cases of continuous championship performance.

SOURCE: James R. Laatsch, Cindy Klann, and Roy Wilbanks, "Pay-for-Performance in Action: A Case Study," *Personnel* 66, no. 6 (June 1989): 11. Reproduced with permission.

when the return on equity is equivalent to the investment made."[11] For employees, **pay equity** is achieved when the compensation received is equal to the value of the work performed.

Not only must pay be equitable, but it must also be perceived as such by employees. Research clearly demonstrates that employees' perceptions of pay equity, or inequity, can have dramatic effects on their motivation for both work behavior and productivity. HR managers must therefore develop pay practices that are both internally and externally equitable. Employees must believe that wage rates for jobs within the organization approximate the job's worth to the organization. Also, the employer's wage rates must correspond closely to prevailing market rates for the employee's occupation.

PAY EXPECTANCY The expectancy theory of motivation predicts that one's level of motivation depends on the attractiveness of the reward sought (see Chapter 14). Therefore, the theory holds that employees should exert greater work effort if they have reason to expect that it will result in a reward that is valued. To motivate this effort, the attractiveness of any valued monetary reward should be high. Employees also must believe that good performance is valued by their employer and will result in their receiving the expected reward.

Figure 10–1 illustrates the relationship between pay-for-performance and the expectancy theory of motivation. The model predicts that high effort will lead to high performance (expectancy), and high performance in turn will lead to monetary rewards that are appreciated (valued). Since we previously stated that pay-for-performance leads to a feeling of pay satisfaction, this feeling should reinforce one's high level of effort.

Thus, how employees view compensation can be an important factor in determining the motivational value of compensation. Furthermore, the effective communication of pay information together with an organizational environment that elicits employee trust in management can contribute to employees having more accurate perceptions of their pay. The perceptions employees develop concerning their pay are influenced by the accuracy of their knowledge and understanding of the compensation program.

THE IMPACT OF PAY SECRECY Misperceptions by employees concerning the equity of their pay and its relationship to performance can be created by secrecy about the pay that others receive. According to Lawler, there is reason to believe that secrecy can generate distrust in the compensation system, reduce employee motivation, and inhibit organizational effectiveness. Yet pay secrecy seems to be an accepted practice in many organizations in both the private and the public sector.

Managers may justify secrecy on the grounds that most employees prefer to have their own pay kept secret. Furthermore, research by Lawler indicates that where secrecy prevails, there is no great demand for pay rates to be publicized; but where pay has been made public, employees tend to favor this practice.[12] Probably one of the reasons for pay secrecy that managers may be unwilling to admit is that it gives

FIGURE 10–1 RELATIONSHIP BETWEEN PAY-FOR-PERFORMANCE AND EXPECTANCY THEORY

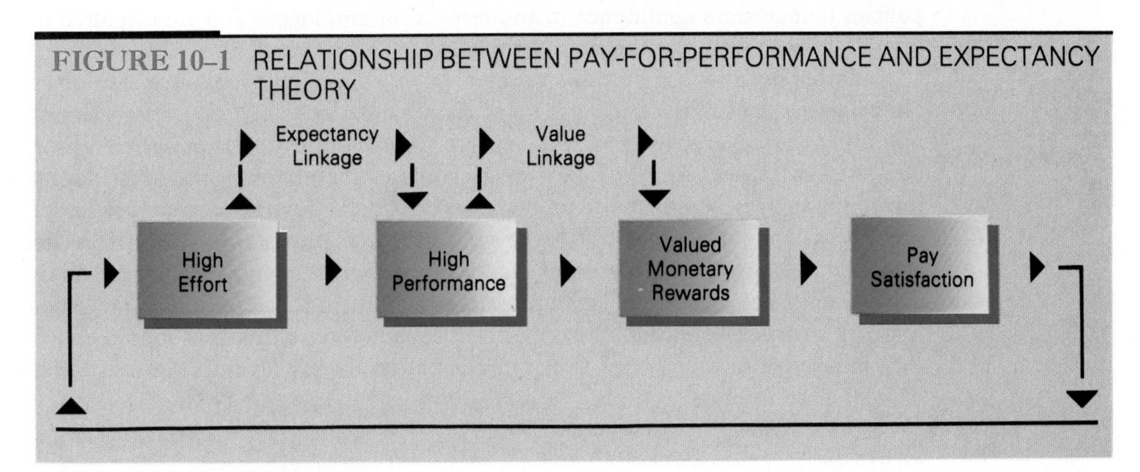

them greater freedom in compensation management, since pay decisions are not disclosed and there is less need to justify or defend them. Employees who are not supposed to know what others are being paid have no objective basis for pursuing grievances about their own pay.[13]

Secrecy also serves to cover up inequities existing within the pay structure. Before the veil of secrecy can be lifted in such situations, however, managers first must move toward the creation of an objective and defensible salary structure. Otherwise the disclosure of pay rates could prove disastrous to employee performance and morale.

The Bases for Compensation

Work performed in most private, public, and not-for-profit organizations has traditionally been compensated on an hourly basis. It is referred to as **hourly** or **day work,** in contrast to **piecework,** in which employees are paid according to the number of units they produce. Hourly work, however, is far more prevalent than piecework as a basis for compensating employees.

Employees compensated on an hourly basis are classified as *hourly employees,* or wage earners. Those whose compensation is computed on the basis of weekly, biweekly, or monthly pay periods are classified as *salaried employees.* Hourly employees are normally paid only for the time they work. Salaried employees, by contrast, are generally paid the same for each pay period even though they occasionally may work more or fewer than the regular number of hours in a period. They also usually receive certain benefits not provided to hourly employees.

The distinction between hourly and salaried employee classifications has been reduced considerably as hourly employees have acquired additional benefits in the areas of paid time off and medical coverage. Some companies, such as IBM and Polaroid, have gone so far as to establish a universal system in which all employees are paid a salary. Pay is guaranteed even though, on a particular day, employees may be tardy or fail to report to work. Compensation policies of this type assume that employees are mature and responsible people who should be treated as such. These policies demonstrate confidence in and respect for employees and are intended to invite favorable reciprocation from them.

Another basis for compensation centers on whether employees are classified as either *nonexempt* or *exempt* under the Fair Labor Standards Act (FLSA). **Nonexempt employees** are covered by the Act and must be paid at a rate of $1^1/_2$ times their *regular* pay rate for time worked in excess of 40 hours in their workweek. Most hourly workers employed in interstate commerce are considered nonexempt workers under the FLSA. Employees not covered by the overtime provision of the FLSA are classified as **exempt.** Managers and supervisors as well as a large number of white-collar employees are in the exempt category. The U.S. Department of Labor imposes a narrow definition of exempt status; therefore, employers should check the exact terms and conditions of exemption before classifying employees as either exempt or nonexempt.

COMPONENTS OF THE WAGE MIX

A combination of *external* and *internal* factors can influence, directly or indirectly, the rates at which employees are paid.[14] Through their interaction these factors constitute the wage mix, as shown in Figure 10–2. For example, the area wage rate for stenographers might be $8.50 per hour. However, one employer may elect to pay its stenographers $10.25 per hour because of their excellent performance. The influence of government legislation on the wage mix will be discussed later in the chapter.

External Factors

The major external factors that influence wage rates include labor market conditions, area wage rates, cost of living, and collective bargaining if the employer is unionized.

LABOR MARKET CONDITIONS The labor market reflects the forces of supply and demand for qualified labor within an area. These forces help to influence the wage rates required to recruit or retain competent employees. It must be recognized, however, that counterforces can reduce the full impact of supply and demand on the labor market. The economic power of unions, for example, may prevent employers from lowering wage rates even when unemployment is high among union members. Government regulations also may prevent an employer from paying at a market rate less than an established minimum.

FIGURE 10–2 EXTERNAL AND INTERNAL FACTORS AFFECTING THE WAGE MIX

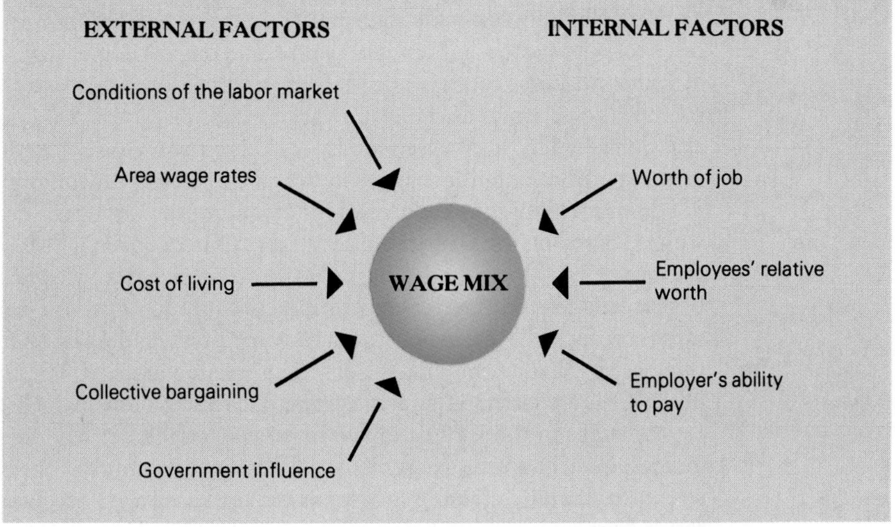

AREA WAGE RATES A formal wage structure should provide rates that are in line with those being paid by other employers for comparable jobs within the area. Data pertaining to area wage rates may be obtained from local wage surveys. For example, the Arizona Department of Economic Security conducts an annual wage survey for both large and small employers in various cities throughout the state. Wage-survey data also may be obtained from a variety of sources including the American Management Association, Administrative Management Society, U.S. Department of Labor, and Federal Reserve Banks. Many organizations, like the City of New York, Northwest Airlines, and Wang Laboratories, conduct their own surveys. Others engage in a cooperative exchange of wage information or rely on various professional associations for these data.

Data from area wage surveys can be used to prevent the rates for certain jobs from drifting too far above or below those of other employers in the region. When rates rise above existing area levels, an employer's labor costs may become excessive. Conversely, if they drop too far below area levels, it may be difficult to recruit and retain competent personnel. Wage-survey data must also take into account indirect wages paid in the form of benefits.

COST OF LIVING Because of inflation, compensation rates have had to be adjusted upward periodically to help employees maintain their purchasing power. This can be achieved through **escalator clauses** found in various labor agreements. These clauses provide for quarterly cost-of-living adjustments (COLA) in wages based on changes in the **consumer price index (CPI).** The CPI is a measure of the average change in prices over time in a fixed "market basket" of goods and services.[15] The most common adjustments are one cent per hour for each 0.3- or 0.4-point change in the CPI.

The CPI is largely used to set wages. The index is based on prices of food, clothing, shelter, and fuels; transportation fares; charges for medical services; and prices of other goods and services that people buy for day-to-day living. The Bureau of Labor Statistics collects price information on a monthly basis and calculates the CPI for the nation as a whole and various U.S. city averages. Separate indexes are also published by size of city and by region of the country. Employers in a number of communities monitor changes in the CPI as a basis for compensation decisions.

Increases in wages and in benefit payments for social security, retirement, and welfare based on the CPI are under attack. One criticism is that the CPI overstates the cost of living because the market basket on which it is based is fixed. This market basket fails to reflect reductions in the consumption of those items hit hardest by inflation, and it fails to reflect accurately the downgrading of quality in items being purchased. In addition, critics claim that housing costs, which are the largest item in the CPI, are based on high mortgage rates and on unusually high home prices.

Changes in the CPI can have important effects on pay rates. Granting wage increases solely on the basis of the CPI helps to compress pay rates within a pay structure, thereby creating inequities among those who receive them. Inequities result from adjustments being made on a cent-per-hour rather than a percentage basis. For example, a cost-of-living adjustment of 50 cents represents a 10 percent increase for an employee earning $5 per hour, but only a 5 percent increase for one earning $10 per hour. Unless adjustments are made periodically in employee base rates, the desired differential between higher- and lower-paying jobs will gradually be reduced. The incentive to accept more-demanding jobs will also be reduced.

Unfortunately, the inequities created by tying wage increases to the CPI are difficult to eliminate. Efforts to change the way the CPI is calculated inevitably evoke vigorous political opposition from those groups likely to be affected adversely by the change. People whose incomes do not rise with inflation are forced to bear the burden of inflation that tying wage increases to the CPI helps to create. Regardless of these problems, wage setters—whether labor or management—consider the CPI extremely important in establishing wages.

COLLECTIVE BARGAINING One of the primary functions of a labor union, as emphasized in Chapter 17, is to bargain collectively over conditions of employment, the most important of which is compensation. The union's goal in each new agreement is to achieve increases in **real wages**—wage increases larger than the increase in the CPI—thereby improving the purchasing power and standard of living of its members. This goal includes gaining wage settlements that equal if not exceed the pattern established by other unions within the area.

In obtaining a settlement, union negotiators focus on those elements of the wage mix that support their demands and attempt to play down those elements that may favor the employer's position. The agreements negotiated by unions tend to establish rate patterns within the labor market. As a result, wages are generally higher in areas where organized labor is strong. To recruit and retain competent personnel and avoid unionization, nonunion employers must either meet or exceed these rates. The "union scale" also becomes the prevailing rate that all employers must pay for work performed under government contract. The impact of collective bargaining, therefore, extends beyond that segment of the labor force which is unionized.

Internal Factors

The internal factors that influence wage rates are the worth of a job, an employee's relative worth in meeting job requirements, and an employer's ability to pay.

WORTH OF A JOB Organizations without a formal compensation program generally base the worth of jobs on the subjective opinions of people familiar with them.[16] In such instances, pay rates may be influenced heavily by the labor market or, in the case of unionized employers, by collective bargaining. Organizations with formal compensation programs, however, are more likely to rely on a system of *job evaluation* to aid in rate determination. Even when rates are subject to collective bargaining, job evaluation can assist the organization in maintaining some degree of control over its wage structure.

The use of job evaluation is widespread in both the public and the private sector. The cities of Chicago and Miami use job evaluation in establishing wage structures, as do Levi Strauss and J. C. Penney. The jobs covered most frequently by job evaluation comprise clerical, technical, and various blue-collar groups, whereas those jobs covered least frequently are managerial and top-executive positions.

EMPLOYEE'S RELATIVE WORTH It is common practice in some industries, notably construction, for unions to negotiate a single rate for jobs in a particular occupation. This egalitarian practice is based on the argument that employees who possess the same qualifications should receive the same rate of pay. Furthermore, the itinerant nature of work in the construction industry usually prevents the accumulation of employment seniority on which pay differentials might be based. Even so, it is not uncommon for employers in the trades to seek to retain their most competent employees by paying them more than the union scale.

In industrial and office jobs, differences in employee performance can be recognized and rewarded through promotion and with various incentive systems. (The incentive systems used most often will be discussed in the next chapter.) Superior performance can also be rewarded by granting merit raises on the basis of steps within a rate range established for a job class. If merit raises are to have their intended value, however, they must be determined by an effective performance appraisal system that differentiates between those employees who deserve the raises and those who do not.[17] This system, moreover, must provide a visible and credible relationship between performance and any raises received. Unfortunately, too many so-called merit systems provide for raises to be granted automatically. As a result, employees tend to be rewarded more for merely being present than for being productive on the job.

Striking flight attendants carry signs attesting to wage concessions.

EMPLOYER'S ABILITY TO PAY In the public sector, the amount of pay and benefits employees can receive is limited by the funds budgeted for this purpose and by the willingness of taxpayers to provide them. In the private sector, pay levels are limited by the profits that employers can derive from the goods and services their employees produce. Thus, an organization's ability to pay is determined in part by the productivity of its employees. This productivity is a result not only of their performance, but also of the amount of capital the organization has invested in labor-saving equipment. Generally, increases in capital investment reduce the number of employees required to perform the work and increase an employer's ability to provide higher pay for those it employs.

Economic conditions and competition faced by employers can also significantly affect the rates they are able to pay. Competition and recessions can force prices down and reduce the income from which compensation payments are derived. In such situations, employers have little choice but to reduce wages and/or lay off employees, or, even worse, to go out of business. Employers and workers in the trucking and airline industries, for example, can attest to the competitive effects of deregulation and its influence on wage levels and job security. Likewise, companies such as Ford, USX (formerly U.S. Steel), Goodyear, and Phelps Dodge have had their ability to pay large wage increases severely limited by growing competition from the international market.

JOB EVALUATION SYSTEMS

As we discussed earlier, one important component of the wage mix is the worth of the job. Organizations formally determine the value of jobs through the process of job evaluation. **Job evaluation** is the systematic process of determining the *relative* worth of jobs in order to establish which jobs should be paid more than others within the organization. Job evaluation helps to establish internal equity between various jobs.[18] The relative worth of a job may be determined by comparing it with others within the organization or by comparing it with a scale that has been constructed for this purpose. Each method of comparison, furthermore, may be made on the basis of the jobs as a whole or on the basis of the parts that constitute the jobs.

Four methods of comparison are shown in Figure 10–3. They provide the basis for the principal systems of job evaluation. We will begin by discussing the simpler, nonquantitative approaches and conclude by reviewing the more popular, quantitative systems. Regardless of the methodology used, it is important to remember that all job evaluation methods require varying degrees of managerial judgment.[19]

Job Ranking System

The simplest and oldest system of job evaluation is the **job ranking system,** which arrays jobs on the basis of their relative worth. One technique used to rank jobs consists of having the raters arrange cards listing the duties and responsibilities of each job in order of the importance of the jobs.

Another common approach to job ranking is the paired-comparison method. Raters compare each job to all other jobs by means of a paired-comparison ranking table that lists the jobs in both rows and columns, as shown in Figure 10–4. To use the table, raters compare a job from a row with the jobs from each of the columns. If the row job is ranked higher than a column job, an "x" is placed in the appropriate

FIGURE 10–3 DIFFERENT JOB EVALUATION SYSTEMS

	SCOPE OF COMPARISON	
BASIS FOR COMPARISON	JOB AS A WHOLE (NONQUANTITATIVE)	JOB PARTS OR FACTORS (QUANTITATIVE)
Job versus Job	Job Ranking System	Factor Comparison System
Job versus Scale	Job Grade System	Point System

FIGURE 10–4 PAIRED-COMPARISON JOB RANKING TABLE

Row Jobs \ Column Jobs	Senior Administrative Secretary	Data-Entry Operator	Data Processing Director	File Clerk	Systems Analyst	Programmer	Total
Senior Administrative Secretary	—	X		X		X	3
Data-Entry Operator		—		X			1
Data Processing Director	X	X	—	X	X	X	5
File Clerk				—			0
Systems Analyst	X	X		X	—	X	4
Programmer		X		X		—	2

Directions: Place an X in cell where the value of a row job is higher than that of a column job.

cell. After all the jobs have been compared, raters total the x's for row jobs. The total number of x's for a row job will establish its worth relative to other jobs.[20] Differences in rankings should then be reconciled into a single rating for all jobs. After jobs are evaluated, wage rates can be assigned to them through use of the salary survey discussed later in the chapter.

The basic weakness of the job ranking system is that it does not provide a very refined measure of each job's worth. Since the comparisons are normally made on the basis of the job as a whole, it is quite easy for one or more of the factors of a job to bias the ranking given to a job, particularly if the job is complex. This drawback can be partially eliminated by having the raters—prior to the evaluation process—agree on one or two important factors with which to evaluate jobs and the weights to be assigned these factors. Another disadvantage of the job ranking system is that the final ranking of jobs merely indicates the relative importance of the jobs, not the differences in the degree of importance that may exist between jobs. A final limitation of the job ranking method is that it should only be used with a small number of jobs, probably no more than fifteen.

Job Grade System

In the **job grade,** or **classification, system,** jobs are classified and grouped according to a series of predetermined wage classes or grades. Successive grades require increasing amounts of job responsibility, skill, knowledge, ability, or other factors selected to compare jobs. For example, Grade GS-1 from the federal government grade descriptions reads as follows:

> GS-1 includes those classes of positions the duties of which are to perform, under immediate supervision, with little or no latitude for the exercise of independent judgment—(A) the simplest routine work in office, business, or fiscal operations; or (B) elementary work of a subordinate technical character in a professional, scientific, or technical field.

The descriptions of each of the job classes constitute the scale against which the specifications for the various jobs are compared. Managers then evaluate jobs by comparing job descriptions with the different wage grades in order to "slot" the job into the appropriate grade. While this system has the advantage of simplicity, it is less precise than the point and factor comparison systems (discussed in the next sections) because the job is evaluated as a whole. The federal civil service job classification system is probably the best-known system of this type. The job grade system is widely used by municipal and state governments.

Point System

The **point system** is a quantitative job evaluation procedure that determines a job's relative value by calculating the total points assigned to it. It has been successfully used by the USX Corporation, the Johnson Wax Company, and many other public and private organizations both large and small. Although point systems are rather complicated to establish, once in place they are relatively simple to understand and use. The principal advantage of the point system is that it provides a more refined basis for making judgments than either the ranking or grade systems and thereby can produce results that are more valid and less easy to manipulate.

The point system permits jobs to be evaluated quantitatively on the basis of factors or elements—commonly called *compensable factors*—that constitute the job. The skills, efforts, responsibilities, and working conditions that a job usually entails are the more common major compensable factors that serve to make one job more or less important than another.[21] The major compensable factors are further subdivided into subfactors and degrees. The number of compensable factors an organization uses depends on the nature of the organization and the jobs to be evaluated. This also applies to the number of degrees assigned to each compensable factor.

The point system requires the use of a *point manual.* The point manual is, in effect, a handbook that contains a description of the factors and the degrees to which these factors may exist within the jobs. A manual also will indicate—usually by means of a table (see Highlights in HRM 2)—the number of points allocated to each factor and to each of the degrees into which these factors are divided. The point value assigned to a job represents the sum of the numerical degree values of each compensable factor that the job possesses.

DEVELOPING A POINT MANUAL A variety of point manuals have been developed by organizations, trade associations, and management consultants. An organization that seeks to use one of these existing manuals should make certain that the manual is suited to its particular jobs and conditions of operation. If necessary, the organization should modify the manual or develop its own to suit its needs.

The job factors and subfactors that are illustrated in Highlights in HRM 2 represent those covered by the National Metal Trades Association point manual. Each of the factors listed in this manual has been divided into five degrees. The number of degrees into which the factors in a manual are to be divided, however, can be greater or smaller than this number, depending on the relative weight assigned to each factor and the ease with which the individual degrees can be defined or distinguished.[22]

After the job factors in the point manual have been divided into degrees, a statement must be prepared defining each of these degrees, as well as each factor as a whole. The definitions should be concise and yet distinguish the factors and each of their degrees. Highlights in HRM 3 represents another portion of the point manual used by the National Metal Trades Association to describe each of the degrees for the knowledge factor. These descriptions enable those conducting a job evaluation to determine the degree to which the factors exist in each job being evaluated.

The final step in developing a point manual is to determine the number of points to be assigned to each factor and to each degree within these factors. Although the total number of points is arbitrary, 500 points is often the maximum.

USING THE POINT MANUAL Job evaluation under the point system is accomplished by comparing the job specifications, factor by factor, against the various factor degree descriptions contained in the manual. Each factor within the job being evaluated is then assigned the number of points specified in the manual. When the points for each factor (or subfactor) have been determined from the manual, the total point value for the job as a whole can be calculated. The relative worth of the job is then determined from the total points that have been assigned to that job.[23]

HIGHLIGHTS IN HRM

2 POINT VALUES FOR JOB FACTORS OF THE NATIONAL METAL TRADES ASSOCIATION

FACTORS	1ST DEGREE	2ND DEGREE	3RD DEGREE	4TH DEGREE	5TH DEGREE
Skill					
1. Job knowledge	14	28	42	56	70
2. Experience	22	44	66	88	110
3. Initiative and ingenuity	14	28	42	56	70
Effort					
4. Physical demand	10	20	30	40	50
5. Mental or visual demand	5	10	15	20	25
Responsibility					
6. Equipment or process	5	10	15	20	25
7. Material or product	5	10	15	20	25
8. Safety of others	5	10	15	20	25
9. Work of others	5	10	15	20	25
Job Conditions					
10. Working conditions	10	20	30	40	50
11. Hazards	5	10	15	20	25

SOURCE: Developed by the National Metal Trades Association. Reproduced with permission of the American Association of Industrial Management, Springfield, MA.

Factor Comparison System

The **factor comparison system,** like the point system, permits the job evaluation process to be accomplished on a factor-by-factor basis. It differs from the point system, however, in that the compensable factors of the jobs to be evaluated are compared against the compensable factors of *key jobs* within the organization that serve as the job evaluation scale. Thus, instead of beginning with an established point scale, the factor comparison system requires a scale to be developed as part of the job evaluation process.

DEVELOPING A FACTOR COMPARISON SCALE There are four basic steps in developing and using a factor comparison scale: (1) selecting and ranking key jobs, (2) allocating wage rates for key jobs across compensable factors, (3) setting up the factor comparison scale, and (4) evaluating non-key jobs.

HIGHLIGHTS IN HRM

3 DESCRIPTION OF KNOWLEDGE FACTOR AND DEGREES OF THE NATIONAL METAL TRADES ASSOCIATION

1. Knowledge

This factor measures the knowledge or equivalent training required to perform the position duties.

1st Degree

Use of reading and writing, adding and subtracting of whole numbers; following of instructions; use of fixed gauges, direct reading instruments, and similar devices where interpretation is not required.

2nd Degree

Use of addition, subtraction, multiplication, and division of numbers including decimals and fractions; simple use of formulas, charts, tables, drawings, specifications, schedules, wiring diagrams; use of adjustable measuring instruments; checking of reports, forms, records, and comparable data where interpretation is required.

3rd Degree

Use of mathematics together with the use of complicated drawings, specifications, charts, tables; various types of precision measuring instruments. Equivalent to one to three years applied trades training in a particular or specialized occupation.

4th Degree

Use of advanced trades mathematics, together with the use of complicated drawings, specifications, charts, tables, handbook formulas; all varieties of precision measuring instruments. Equivalent to complete accredited apprenticeship in a recognized trade, craft or occupation; or equivalent to a two-year technical college education.

5th Degree

Use of higher mathematics involved in the application of engineering principles and their performance of related practical operations, together with a comprehensive knowledge of the theories and practices of mechanical, electrical, chemical, civil, or like engineering field. Equivalent to complete four years of technical college or university education.

SOURCE: Developed by the National Metal Trades Association. Reproduced with permission of the American Association of Industrial Management, Springfield, MA.

Step 1. The first step in the development of a factor comparison scale is to select and rank key jobs on the basis of compensable factors. *Key jobs* can be defined as those jobs that are important for wage-setting purposes and are widely known in the labor market. Key jobs have the following characteristics:

1. They are important to employees and the organization.
2. They vary in terms of job requirements.
3. They have relatively stable job content.
4. They are used in salary surveys for wage determination.

Key jobs are normally ranked against five factors—skill, mental effort, physical effort, responsibility, and working conditions. It is normal for the ranking of each key job to be different because of the different requirements of jobs. The ranking of three key jobs is shown in Figure 10–5, although usually 15 to 20 key jobs will constitute a factor comparison scale.

Step 2. The next step is to determine the proportion of the current wage being paid on a key job to each of the factors composing the job. Thus, the proportion of a key job's wage rate that is allocated to the skill factor will depend on the importance of skill in comparison with mental effort, physical effort, responsibility, and working conditions. It is important that the factor rankings in step 1 be consistent with the wage-apportionment rankings in step 2. Figure 10–6 illustrates how the rate for three key jobs has been allocated according to the relative importance of the basic factors that make up these jobs.

Step 3. After the wages for each key job have been apportioned across the factors, the data are displayed on a factor comparison scale as shown in Figure 10–7. The location of the key jobs on the scale and the compensable factors for these jobs provide the benchmarks against which other jobs are evaluated.

Step 4. We are now ready to compare the non-key jobs against the key jobs in the columns of Figure 10–7. As an example of how the scale is used, let's assume that the job of screw machine operator is to be evaluated through the use of the factor comparison scale. By comparing the skill factor for screw machine operator with the skill factors of the key jobs on the table, it was decided that the skill demand of the job placed it about halfway between those of storekeeper and punch press operator. The job, therefore, was placed at the $5.55 point on the scale. The same procedure was used to place the job at the appropriate point on the scale for the remaining factors.

FIGURE 10–5 RANKING KEY JOBS BY COMPENSABLE FACTORS

JOB	SKILL	MENTAL EFFORT	PHYSICAL EFFORT	RESPONSIBILITY	WORKING CONDITIONS
Machinist Planner	1	1	3	1	3
Punch Press Operator	2	2	1	3	2
Storekeeper	3	3	2	2	1

FIGURE 10–6 WAGE APPORTIONMENT FOR EACH FACTOR

JOB	TOTAL	SKILL	MENTAL EFFORT	PHYSICAL EFFORT	RESPON-SIBILITY	WORKING CONDITIONS
Machinist Planner	$13.00	$6.50 (1)	$3.50 (1)	$0.50 (3)	$1.60 (1)	$0.90 (3)
Punch Press Operator	11.30	6.20 (2)	1.60 (2)	1.00 (1)	0.80 (3)	1.70 (2)
Storekeeper	9.85	4.90 (3)	1.30 (3)	0.70 (2)	1.20 (2)	1.75 (1)

USING THE FACTOR COMPARISON SCALE The evaluated worth of the jobs added to the scale is computed by adding up the money values for each factor as determined by where the job has been placed on the scale for each factor. Thus, the evaluated worth of screw machine operator of $9.72 would be determined by totaling the monetary value for each factor as follows:

Skill	$5.55
Mental effort	1.35
Physical effort	0.82
Responsibility	0.60
Working conditions	1.40
	$9.72

Job Evaluation for Management Positions

Because management positions are more difficult to evaluate and involve certain demands not found in jobs at the lower levels, some organizations do not attempt to include them in their job evaluation programs. Those that do evaluate these positions, however, may extend their regular system of evaluation to include such positions, or they may develop a separate evaluation system for management positions.

Several systems have been developed especially for the evaluation of executive, managerial, and professional positions. One of the better-known is the **Hay profile method,** developed by Edward N. Hay. The three broad factors that constitute the evaluation in the "profile" include knowledge (or know-how), mental activity (or problem solving), and accountability.[24] The Hay method uses only three factors because it is assumed that these factors represent the most important aspects of all executive and managerial positions. The profile for each position is developed by determining the percentage value to be assigned to each of the three factors. Jobs are then ranked on the basis of each factor, and point values that make up the profile are then assigned to each job on the basis of the percentage-value level at which the job is ranked.

FIGURE 10–7 FACTOR COMPARISON SCALE

HOURLY RATE	SKILL	MENTAL EFFORT	PHYSICAL EFFORT	RESPONSIBILITY	WORKING CONDITIONS
6.50	• Machinist Planner				
6.25	• Punch Press Operator				
6.00					
5.75					
5.50	• *Screw Mach. Operator*				
5.25					
5.00	• Storekeeper				
4.75					
4.50					
4.25					
4.00					
3.75					
3.50		• Machinist Planner			
3.25					
3.00					
2.75					
2.50					
2.25					
2.00					• Storekeeper
1.75					• Punch Press Operator
1.50		• Punch Press Operator		• Machinist Planner	• *Screw Mach. Operator*
1.25		• *Screw Mach. Operator*		• Storekeeper	
1.00		• Storekeeper	• Punch Press Operator	• Punch Press Operator	• Machinist Planner
0.75			• *Screw Mach. Operator*		
0.50			• Storekeeper • Machinist Planner	• *Screw Mach. Operator*	

NOTE: If this scale contained the 15 to 20 key jobs that typically constitute a factor comparison scale, the gaps between jobs on the scale would be reduced substantially.

THE COMPENSATION STRUCTURE

Job evaluation systems provide for internal equity and serve as the basis for wage-rate determination. They do not determine the wage rate. The evaluated worth of each job in terms of its rank, class, points, or monetary worth must be converted into an hourly, daily, weekly, or monthly wage rate. The compensation tool used to help set wages is the wage and salary survey.

Wage and Salary Surveys

The **wage and salary survey** is a survey of the wages paid by employers in an organization's relevant labor market—local, regional, or national, depending on the job. The *labor market* is frequently defined as that area from which employers obtain certain types of workers. The labor market for clerical personnel would be local, whereas the labor market for engineers would be national. It is the wage and salary survey that permits an organization to maintain external equity, that is, to pay its employees wages equivalent to the wages similar employees earn in other establishments. Although surveys are primarily conducted to gather competitive wage data, surveys can also collect information on employee benefits or organizational pay practices (e.g., overtime rates or shift differentials).

COLLECTING SURVEY DATA While many organizations conduct their own wage and salary surveys, a variety of "preconducted" pay surveys are available to satisfy the requirements of most public and not-for-profit or private employers.[25] The Bureau of Labor Statistics (BLS) is the major publisher of wage and salary data, putting out three major surveys—area wage surveys, industry wage surveys, and the National Survey of Professional, Administrative, Technical, and Clerical Pay.

Many states conduct surveys on either a municipal or county basis that are available to employers. Besides these government surveys, trade groups such as the Dallas Personnel Association, the Society for Human Resource Management, the American Management Association, and the National Society of Professional Engineers conduct special surveys tailored to their members' needs. While all of these third-party surveys provide certain benefits to their users, they also have various limitations. Two problems with all published surveys are that (1) they are not always compatible with the user's jobs, and (2) the user cannot specify what specific data to collect. To overcome these problems, organizations may collect their own compensation data.

A national labor market exists for engineers.

EMPLOYER-INITIATED SURVEYS Employers wishing to conduct their own wage and salary survey must first select the jobs to be used in the survey and identify the organizations with whom they actually compete for employees. Since it is not feasible to survey all the jobs in an organization, normally only key jobs are used. The survey of key jobs will usually be sent to 10 or 15 organizations that represent a valid sample of other employers likely to compete for the employees of the surveying organization. A diversity of organizations should be selected—large and small, public and private, new and established, and union and nonunion—since each classification of employer is likely to pay different wage rates for surveyed jobs.

After the key jobs and the employers to be surveyed have been identified, the surveying organization must decide what information to gather on wages, benefit types, and pay policies. For example, when requesting pay data, it is important to specify whether hourly, daily, or weekly pay figures are needed. In addition, those conducting surveys must state if the wage data are needed for new hires or senior employees. Precisely defining the compensation data needed will greatly increase the accuracy of the information received and the number of purposes for which it can be used. Once the survey data are tabulated, the compensation structure can be completed.

The Wage Curve

The relationship between the relative worth of jobs and their wage rates can be represented by means of a **wage curve** or **conversion line.** This curve may indicate the rates currently paid for jobs within an organization, the new rates resulting from job evaluation, or the rates for similar jobs currently being paid by other organizations within the labor market. A curve may be constructed graphically by preparing a scattergram consisting of a series of dots that represent the current wage rates. A freehand curve is then drawn through the cluster of dots in such a manner as to leave approximately an equal number of dots above and below the curve, as illustrated by Figure 10–8. The wage curve can be relatively straight or curved. This curve can then be used to determine the relationship between the value of a job and its wage rate at any given point on the line.

Wage Classes

From an administrative standpoint, it is generally preferable to group jobs into **wage classes** or **grades,** and to pay all jobs within a particular class the same rate or rate range. When the grade or classification system of job evaluation is used, jobs are grouped into classes as part of the evaluation process. When the point and factor comparison systems are used, however, wage classes must be established at selected intervals representing either the point or evaluated monetary value of these jobs. The graph in Figure 10–9 illustrates a series of wage classes designated along the horizontal axis at 50-point intervals.

The rates for wage classes may also be determined by means of a conversion table similar to the one illustrated in Figure 10–10. The classes within a wage structure may vary in number. The number is determined by such factors as the slope of the wage curve, the number and distribution of the jobs within the structure, and the organization's wage administration and promotion policies. The number utilized should be sufficient to permit difficulty levels to be distinguished, but not so great as to make the distinction between two adjoining classes insignificant.

FIGURE 10–8 FREEHAND WAGE CURVE

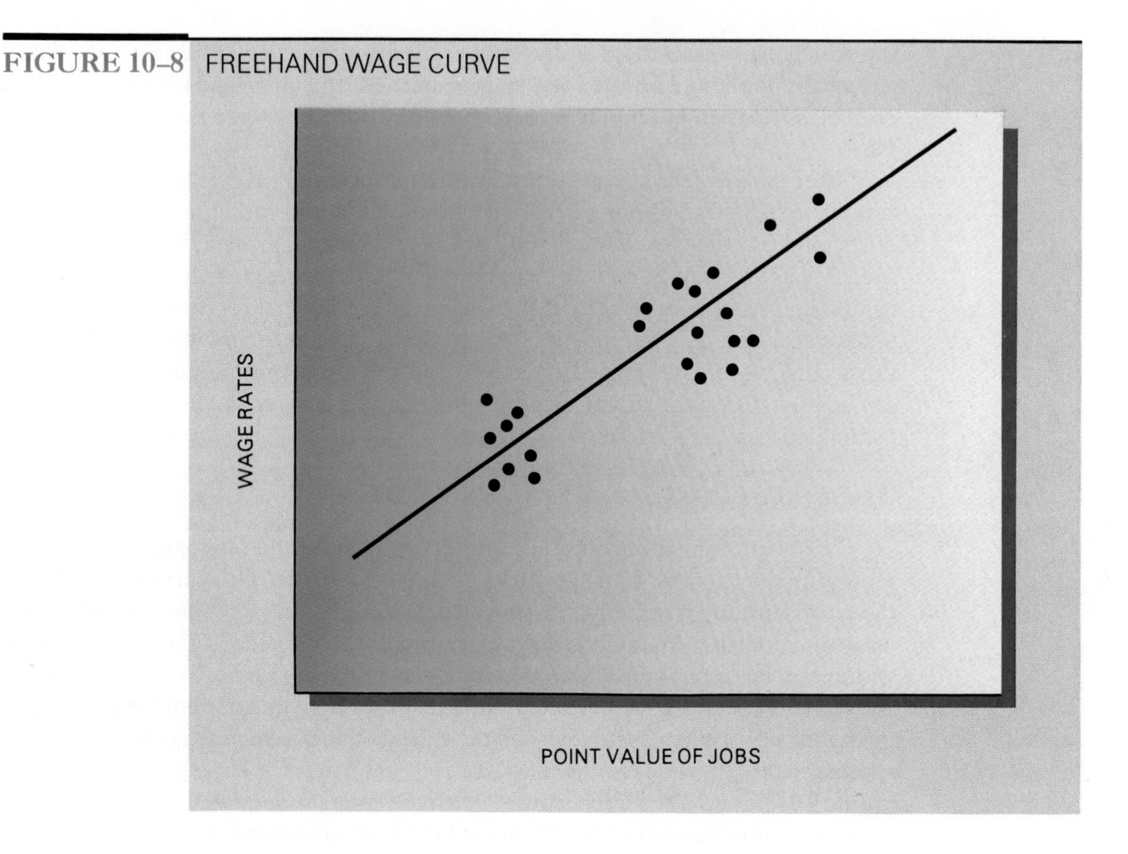

Rate Ranges

Although a single rate may be created for each wage class, as shown in Figure 10–9, it is more common to provide a range of rates for each of them. The rate ranges may be the same for each class or proportionately greater for each successive class, as shown in Figure 10–11. Rate ranges constructed on the latter basis provide a greater incentive for employees to accept a promotion to a job in a higher class.[26]

Rate ranges generally are divided into a series of steps that permit employees to receive increases up to the maximum rate for the range on the basis of merit or seniority or a combination of the two. Most salary structures provide for the ranges of adjoining wage classes to overlap. The purpose of the overlap is to permit an employee with experience to earn as much as or more than a person with less experience in the next-higher job classification.

Classification of Jobs

The final step in setting up a wage structure is to determine the appropriate wage class into which each job should be placed on the basis of its evaluated worth. Traditionally, this worth is determined on the basis of job requirements without

FIGURE 10–9 SINGLE RATE STRUCTURE

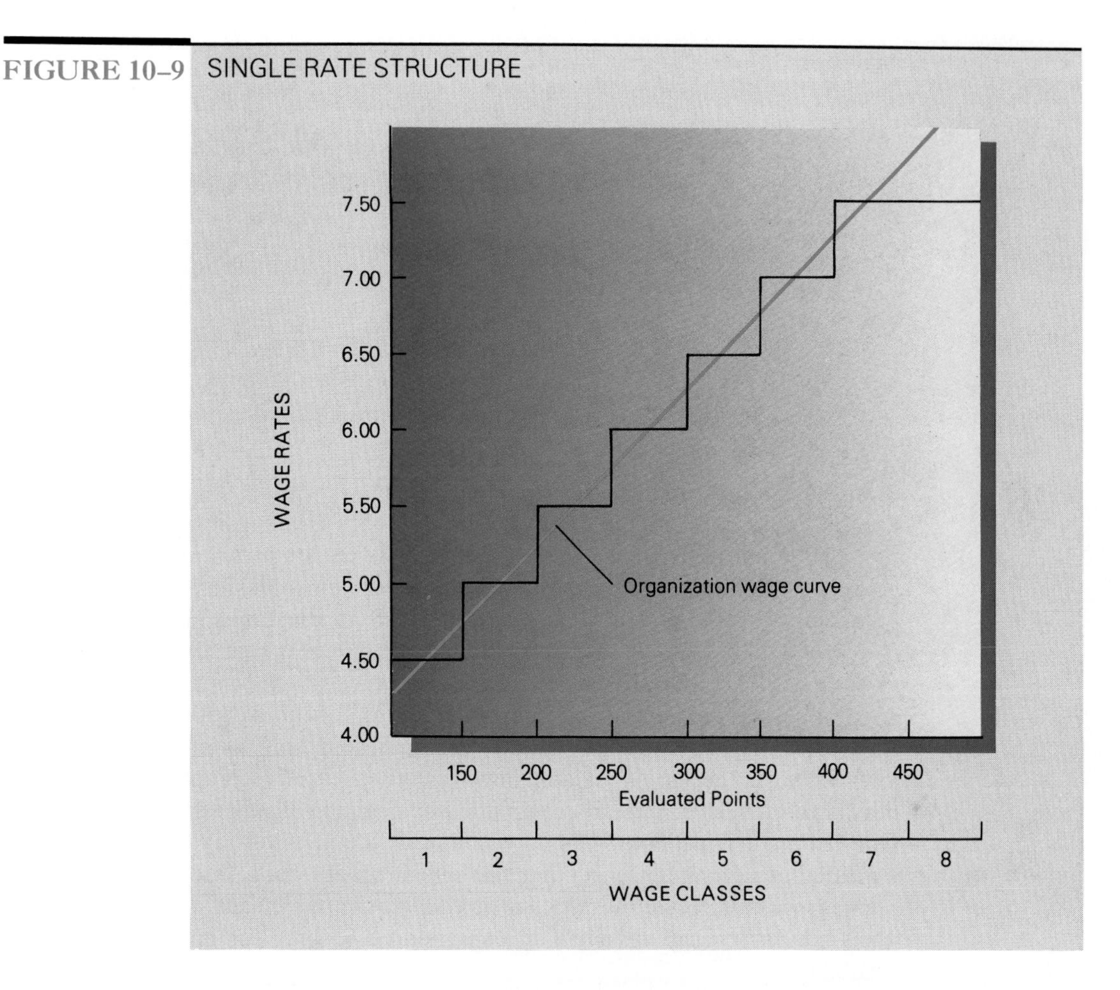

regard to the performance of the person in that job. Under this system, the performance of those who exceed the requirements of a job may be acknowledged by merit increases within the class range or by promotion to a job in the next-higher wage class.

Unfortunately, such a system often fails to reward employees for the skills or knowledge they possess or to encourage them to learn new job-related skills. It tends to consider employees as jobholders rather than as individuals. To correct these weaknesses, organizations such as Frito-Lay, Sherwin-Williams, Shell Oil, and Cummins Engine have introduced **skill-based pay** plans. Also referred to as multi-skill-based, knowledge-based, or pay-for-knowledge plans, these programs compensate employees for the skills and knowledge they possess rather than for the jobs they hold in a designated job category.[27]

Although the types of skill-based plans are sometimes thought to be interchangeable, there are important technical differences between them. Organizations

FIGURE 10–10 POINT CONVERSION TABLE

WAGE CLASS	POINT RANGE	HOURLY RATE RANGE
1	101–150	$ 4.25– 5.50
2	151–200	5.25– 6.50
3	201–250	6.25– 7.50
4	251–300	7.25– 8.50
5	301–350	8.25– 9.50
6	351–400	9.25–10.50
7	401–450	10.25–11.50
8	451–500	11.25–12.50

using multiskill-based pay systems compensate employees for the number of different skills they learn and can apply to different jobs in the organization. Multiskill-based pay plans are frequently used where employees are part of autonomous work groups or work teams. As team members master new job skills, they advance to higher pay levels; so it is clear that pay levels in the multiskill plans directly correspond to the number of different jobs an employee is capable of performing.[28] In contrast, knowledge-based pay plans, also called pay-for-knowledge plans, reward employees for gaining new knowledge and skills within the same job category. Employees increase their pay as they become "experts" by acquiring new job knowledge. Either pay program, however, encourages employees to grow and develop their talents, thereby contributing to increased organizational productivity. One HR professional notes, "In a few companies, skill-based pay stands by itself as a nontraditional strategy in an otherwise conventional setting, but typically it is one element in a multifaceted approach to productivity improvement."[29] Skill-based pay plans are particularly attractive to organizations looking for greater job-staffing flexibility.

Unfortunately, skill-based pay plans may encounter some long-term difficulties. Some plans limit the amount of compensation employees can earn regardless of the new skills or knowledge they acquire. Thus, after achieving the top wage, employees may be reluctant to continue their educational training. Furthermore, employees can become discouraged when they acquire new abilities but find there are no higher-rated jobs to which they can transfer. Finally, unless all employees have the opportunity to increase their pay through the attainment of new skills, employees who are not given this opportunity may feel disgruntled.

Wage-Rate Compression

The primary purpose of the pay differentials between the wage classes is to provide an incentive for employees to prepare for and accept more-demanding jobs. Unfortunately, this incentive is being significantly reduced by **wage-rate compression**—the reduction of differences between job classes. Wage-rate compression is

FIGURE 10–11 WAGE STRUCTURE WITH INCREASING RATE RANGES

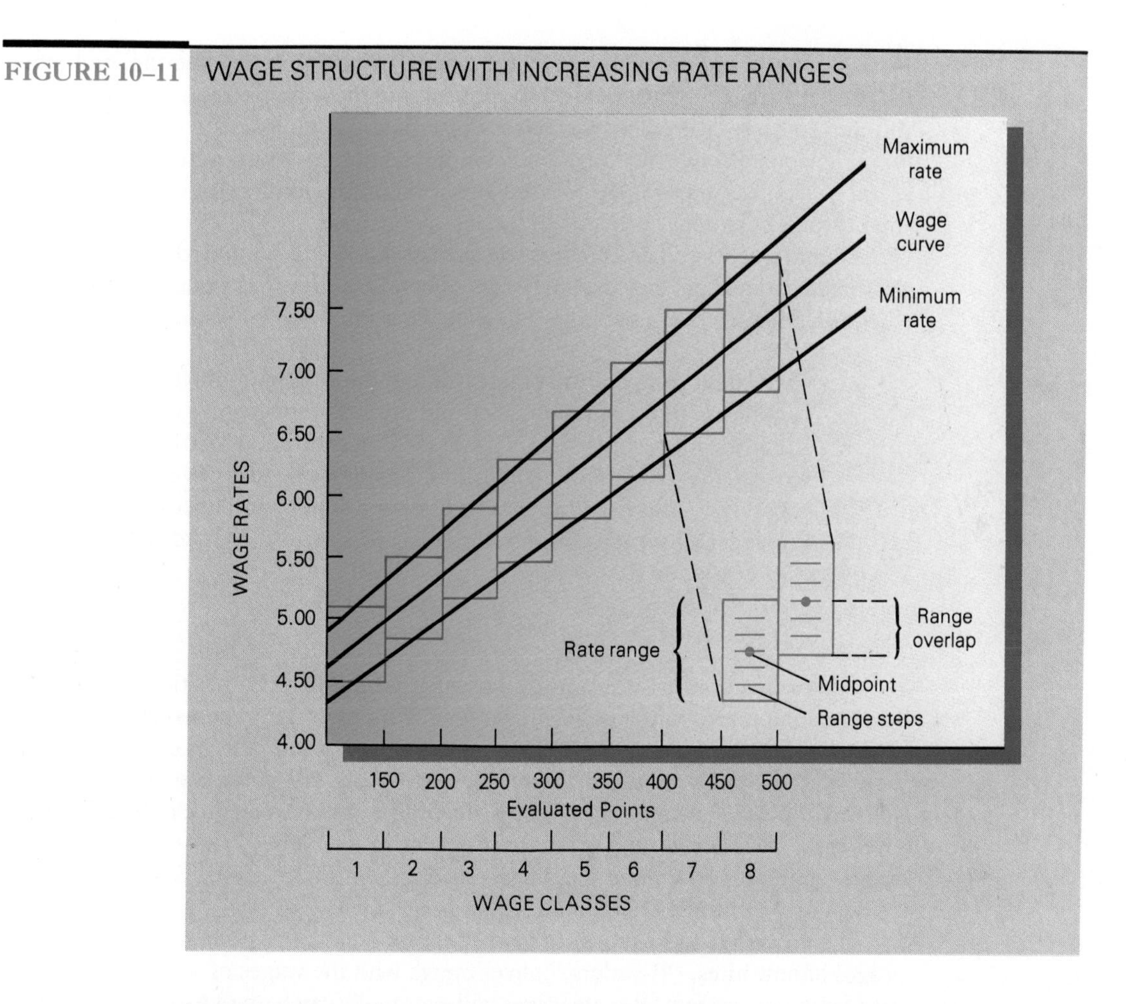

largely an internal pay-equity concern. The problem occurs when employees perceive that there is too narrow a difference between their compensation and that of colleagues in lower-rated jobs.[30] Because of the trend toward an egalitarian pay structure, getting ahead may no longer mean getting more pay.

HR professionals acknowledge that wage-rate compression is a widespread organizational problem affecting diverse occupational groups: white-collar and blue-collar workers, technical and professional employees, and managerial personnel. It can cause low employee morale, leading to issues of reduced employee performance, higher absenteeism and turnover, and even delinquent behavior such as employee theft.

There is no single cause of wage-rate compression. For example, it can occur when unions negotiate across-the-board increases for hourly employees but supervisory personnel are not granted corresponding wage differentials. Such increases can result in part from COLAs provided for in labor agreements. Other inequities have resulted from the scarcity of applicants in computers, engineering, and other professional and technical fields. Job applicants in these fields frequently have been offered starting salaries not far below those paid to employees with considerable experience and seniority. Wage-rate compression often occurs when organizations grant pay adjustments for lower-rated jobs without providing commensurate adjustments for occupations at the top of the job hierarchy.

Identifying wage-rate compression and its causes is far simpler than implementing organizational policies to alleviate its effect. Organizations wishing to minimize the problem may incorporate the following ideas into their pay policies:

1. Give larger compensation increases to more-senior employees.
2. Emphasize pay-for-performance and reward merit-worthy employees.
3. Limit the hiring of new applicants seeking exorbitant salaries.
4. Design the pay structure to allow a wider spread between hourly and supervisory jobs or between new hires and senior employees.
5. Provide equity adjustments for selected employees hardest hit by pay compression.

Two-Tier Wage Systems

Many organizations affected by deregulation, foreign competition, and aggressive nonunionized competitors implement two-tier wage systems as a means of lowering their labor costs. A **two-tier wage system** is a compensation plan that pays newly hired employees less than present employees performing the same or similar jobs. With some two-tier wage systems, new employees may receive reduced benefit packages. Two-tier wage systems are popular in the airline, aerospace, trucking, retail food, copper, and automobile industries. The U.S. Postal Service operates under a two-tier wage structure.

There are two basic types of two-tier wage systems. In a permanent system, the wages of new hires, "B-scalers," never merge with the wages of senior employees. In a temporary system, B-scale wages will eventually catch up to A-scale wages after a specified period of time. For example, employees on the B-scale at American Airlines achieve pay parity with senior employees after ten years of service. Unfortunately, lower-paid employees can have feelings of pay inequity when working under either of these wage systems. There is a perceived lack of fairness when new hires and senior employees perform the same job but receive different wages. Feelings of inequity can, in turn, lead to low levels of job commitment, work attendance problems, reduced productivity, and employee resentment.

Two-tier wage systems are commonly used in unionized organizations. Union leaders accept these pay schemes as a concession to employers plagued by high labor costs. In return for lower wages for new employees, union employees receive job-security provisions in the labor agreement. While historically opposed to wage systems that deny equal pay for equal work, union representatives can claim that they have avoided wage cuts or layoffs for their members.

GOVERNMENTAL REGULATION OF COMPENSATION

Compensation management, like the other areas of HRM, is subject to state and federal regulations. A majority of states have minimum wage laws or wage boards that fix minimum wage rates on an industry-by-industry basis. Most of them also regulate hours of work and overtime payments.

The three principal federal laws affecting wages are the Davis-Bacon Act, the Walsh-Healy Act, and the Fair Labor Standards Act. These laws were enacted during the 1930s to prevent the payment of abnormally low wage rates and to encourage the spreading of work among a greater number of workers. The latter objective was accomplished by forcing organizations to pay a premium rate for overtime work (all hours worked in excess of a prescribed number).

Davis-Bacon Act of 1931

The Davis-Bacon Act, also referred to as the Prevailing Wage Law, was passed in 1931 and is the oldest of the three federal wage laws. It requires that the minimum wage rates paid to persons employed on federal public works projects worth more than $2,000 be at least equal to the prevailing rates and that overtime be paid at $1^1/_2$ times this rate.

There have been efforts in Congress to repeal the Davis-Bacon Act on the grounds that the situation it was designed to alleviate at the time of its passage no longer exists. The Act is also criticized for contributing to inflation because the minimum pay can be based on the rate paid to only 30 percent of the workers in an area. This "30 percent rule" usually results in forcing contractors on federal construction projects to pay rates negotiated by unions (union scale), as long as their workers represent at least 30 percent of workers within the area. These rates are often higher than the average rate prevailing within the area. Failing to have the Act repealed, its opponents have sought to eliminate the 30 percent rule as a basis for establishing the prevailing rate on federal public works projects.

Walsh-Healy Act of 1936

The Walsh-Healy Act, which is officially called the Public Contracts Act, was passed in 1936 and covers workers employed on government contract work for supplies, equipment, and materials worth in excess of $10,000. The Act requires contractors to pay employees at least the prevailing wage rates established by the Secretary of Labor for the area, and overtime of $1^1/_2$ times the regular rate for all work performed in excess of 8 hours in one day or 40 hours in one week, depending on which basis provides the larger premium. For example, an employee working 4 days of 12 hours each during a given week would be entitled to receive 16 hours of overtime and 32 hours of regular time for the week. In computing overtime payments under the Walsh-Healy Act, as under the Fair Labor Standards Act, the wage rate used must include any bonuses or incentive payments that may be a part of the employee's total earnings. The Walsh-Healy Act also contains restrictions covering the use of child and convict labor.

Fair Labor Standards Act of 1938, As Amended

The Fair Labor Standards Act (FLSA), commonly referred to as the Wage and Hour Act, was passed in 1938 and since then has been amended many times. It covers those employees who are engaged in the production of goods for interstate and foreign commerce, including those whose work is closely related to or directly essential to such production. The coverage of the Act also includes agricultural workers, as well as employees of certain retail and service establishments whose sales volume exceeds a prescribed amount. The major provisions of the FLSA are concerned with minimum wage rates and overtime payments, child labor, and equal rights.[31]

WAGE AND HOUR PROVISIONS The minimum wage prescribed by federal law has been raised many times, from an original figure of 25 cents per hour to $3.80 per hour in April 1990 and then to $4.25 per hour in April 1991 (see Highlights in HRM 4 for the federal minimum wage poster that employers are required to display). This minimum rate applies to the actual earning rate before any overtime premiums have been added. An overtime rate of 1½ times the base rate must be paid for all hours worked in excess of 40 during a given week. The base wage rate from which the overtime rate is computed must include incentive payments or bonuses that are received during the period.[32] For example, if a person employed at a base rate of $6 an hour works a total of 45 hours in a given week and receives a bonus of $90, that person is actually working at the rate of $8 an hour. (The $90 bonus divided by the 45 hours required to earn it equals $2 per hour, which, when added to the base rate of $6 per hour, increases the employee's earning rate to $8 per hour for the week.) Earnings for the week would total $380, computed as follows:

Regular time	40 × $ 8 = $320
Overtime	5 × $12 = 60
Total earnings	$380

If the bonus is paid on a monthly or quarterly basis, earnings for the period must be recalculated to include this bonus in the hourly rate for overtime payments. When employees are given time off in return for overtime work, it must be granted at 1½ times the number of hours that were worked as overtime. Employees who are paid on a piece-rate basis also must receive a premium for overtime work. The hourly rate on which overtime is to be based is computed by dividing earnings from piecework by the total number of hours of work required to earn this amount. For

HIGHLIGHTS IN HRM

4 THE FEDERAL MINIMUM WAGE

NOTICE TO EMPLOYEES

Federal Minimum Wage

$3.80 per hour
Effective April 1, 1990

$4.25 per hour
Effective April 1, 1991

Most employees in the United States qualify for both minimum wage and overtime pay under THE FAIR LABOR STANDARDS ACT. Overtime pay may not be less than 1 1/2 times the employee's regular rate of pay for hours worked over 40 in one workweek.

Certain full-time students, student learners, apprentices, and workers with disabilities may be paid less than the minimum wage under special certificates issued by the Department of Labor.

Covered Employees

- Employees engaged in interstate commerce or in the production of goods for interstate commerce (i.e., goods that travel across state lines), regardless of the employer's annual volume of business.
- Employees who work for enterprises that have an annual gross volume of sales made or business done of over $500,000.
- Employees of hospitals, residential facilities that care for those who are physically or mentally ill or disabled, or aged, schools for children who are mentally or physically disabled or gifted, pre-schools, elementary and secondary schools, and institutions of higher education, regardless of the annual volume of business.
- Employees of public agencies.

Child Labor

An Employee must be at least 16 years old to work in most non-farm jobs and at least 18 to work in non-farm jobs declared hazardous by the Secretary of Labor. Youths 14 and 15 years old may work outside school hours in various non-manufacturing, non-mining, non-hazardous jobs under the following conditions:
No more than —

3 hours on a school day or 18 hours in a school week;
8 hours on a non-school day or 40 hours in a non-school week.

Also work may not begin before 7 a.m. or end after 7 p.m. except from June 1 through Labor Day, when evening hours are extended to 9 p.m. Different rules apply in agricultural employment.

Training Wage

A training wage of $3.35 per hour, or 85 percent of the applicable minimum wage, which ever is greater, may be paid to most employees under 20 years of age for up to 90 days under certain conditions. Individuals may be employed at this training wage for a second 90 day period by a different employer if certain additional requirements are met. No individual may be employed at the training wage, in any number of jobs, for more than a total of 180 days. Employers may not displace regular employees in order to hire those eligible for the training wage.

Tipped Employees

A tipped employee is one who regularly receives more than $30 a month in tips. Tips received by such employees may be counted as wages up to a certain percentage of the minimum wage. The minimum cash wage that employers must pay (from their own pockets) to tipped employees is $2.09 an hour effective April 1, 1990. It will rise to $2.13 an hour effective April 1, 1991. If an employee's hourly tip earnings (averaged weekly) added to this hourly wage do not equal the minimum wage, the employer is responsible for paying the balance.

Enforcement

The Department of Labor may recover back wages either administratively or through court action, for the employees that have been underpaid in violation of the law. Violations may result in civil or criminal action.

Civil money penalties of up to $1,000 per violation may be assessed against employers who violate the child labor provisions of the law or who willfully or repeatedly violate the minimum wage or overtime pay provisions. This law *prohibits* discriminating against or discharging workers who file a complaint or participate in any proceedings under the Act.

Note: Certain occupations and establishments are exempt from the minimum wage and /or overtime pay provisions.

Special provisions apply to workers in Puerto Rico and American Samoa.

Where state law requires a higher minimum wage the higher standard applies.

FOR ADDITIONAL INFORMATION CONTACT the Wage and Hour Division office nearest you - - listed in your telephone directory under United States Government, Labor Department.

The law requires employers to display this poster where employees can readily see it.

U.S. Department of Labor
Employment Standards Administration
Wage and Hour Division
Washington, D.C. 20210

WH Publication 1088
Revised April 1990

☆ U.S.G.P.O. 1990 257-453/00539

example, if an employee produced 1,250 units of work at 20 cents per unit during a 50-hour week, the earning rate would be $5 per hour, computed as follows:

$$\frac{1{,}250 \text{ units} \times 20 \text{ cents}}{50 \text{ hours}} = \$5 \text{ per hour}$$

Since the 10 hours in excess of a 40-hour week constitute overtime at $1\frac{1}{2}$ times the regular rate, total earnings for the week would be $275, computed as follows:

Regular time	40 × $5.00	= $200
Overtime	10 × $7.50	= 75
Total earnings		$275

Furthermore, under the FLSA, an employer must pay an employee for whatever work the employer "suffers or permits" the employee to perform, even if the work is done away from the workplace and even if it is not specifically expected or requested. Accordingly, under the FLSA it doesn't matter that the supervisor never asked the employee to work extra time; all that matters is that the supervisor knew the employee was putting in the time and did nothing to prevent it. This rule, as well as the overtime and bonus rules discussed earlier, applies only to nonexempt employees.

CHILD LABOR PROVISIONS The FLSA forbids the employment of minors between 16 and 18 years of age in hazardous occupations such as mining, logging, woodworking, meat-packing, and certain types of manufacturing. Minors under 16 cannot be employed in any work destined for interstate commerce except that which is performed in a nonhazardous occupation for a parent or guardian or for an employer under a temporary work permit issued by the Department of Labor.

THE TRAINING WAGE Some argue that the "floor" imposed by the minimum wage makes it more difficult for high school students and young adults to find jobs. Many employers who might otherwise be willing to hire these individuals are unwilling to pay them the same rate as adults because of their lack of experience. In addition, civil rights advocates point out that the minimum wage particularly harms black youth, who traditionally have a higher unemployment rate compared to white youth.

In an effort to reduce chronically high unemployment in this wage group, the FLSA was amended in 1990 to include a training wage that can be paid to most employees under 20 years of age. The training wage is fixed at $3.35 per hour, or 85 percent of the applicable minimum wage, whichever is greater. This wage can be paid for up to 90 days or for 180 days if the individual is hired by a second employer. Employers are prohibited from discharging regular employees in order to employ those eligible for the training wage. The training wage provisions expire March 31, 1993.

A young worker in an Iowa coal mine before child labor was illegal (circa 1912).

EXEMPTIONS UNDER THE ACT The feature of the FLSA that perhaps creates the most confusion is the exemption of certain groups of employees from coverage by the Act or from certain of its provisions. The Act now provides more than 40 separate exemptions, some of which apply only to a certain group of personnel or to certain provisions of the Act, such as those relating to child labor or to overtime.[33] One of the most common exemptions concerns the overtime provisions of the Act. Four employee groups—executives, administrators, professionals, and outside salespersons—are specifically excluded from the overtime provisions. However, persons performing jobs in these groups must meet specific job requirements as stated under the law. For example, a manager is defined as someone whose *primary* duty is the direction of two or more other employees. "Primary duty" means the manager generally devotes more than 50 percent of his or her time to supervising others. Because exemptions are generally narrowly defined under FLSA, an employer should carefully check the exact terms and conditions for each. Detailed information is available from local wage-hour offices.

EQUAL RIGHTS PROVISIONS One of the most significant amendments to the FLSA was the Equal Pay Act passed in 1963 (see Chapter 3). The federal Age Discrimination Act of 1967, as amended, extends the equal rights provisions by forbidding wage discrimination based on age for employees 40 years of age and older.

Neither of these acts, however, prohibits wage differentials based on factors other than age or sex such as seniority, merit, or individual incentive plans.

In spite of the Equal Pay Act, the achievement of parity by women in the labor market has been slow in coming. In 1989, the median earnings level of all women workers in the United States was 72 percent of the median for all working men. This figure is about 10 percentage points higher than in 1979, with little change since 1986.[34] Fortunately, the 1989 median earnings of young women (ages 16 to 24) are 90 percent of those of similar-age men—up from 77 percent in 1979. As Janet Norwood, Bureau of Labor Statistics commissioner, notes, "If this trend toward greater comparability in earnings continues as these women become older, this age cohort may set the stage for more equitable treatment in the future."[35] However, it is still important to remember that young women, and young men as well, typically work in low-paying, entry-level jobs. For women, these are often clerical or sales positions.

Because of the continued differences in pay for women and men, some HR professionals are suggesting that the wage differences could be reduced if women were paid on the basis of equal pay for comparable work.

THE ISSUE OF EQUAL PAY FOR COMPARABLE WORK

One of the most important compensation issues of the 1990s is equal pay for comparable work. The issue stems from the fact that jobs performed predominantly by women are paid less than those performed by men. This practice results in what critics term *institutionalized sex discrimination*, causing women to receive less pay for jobs that may be different from but comparable in worth to those performed by men. The issue of **comparable worth** goes beyond providing equal pay for jobs that involve the same duties for women as for men. It is not concerned with whether a female secretary should receive the same pay as a male secretary. Rather, the argument for comparable worth is that jobs held by women are not compensated the same as those held by men, even though both job types may contribute equally to organizational success.[36]

Problem of Measuring Comparability

Advocates of comparable worth argue that the difference in wage rates for predominantly male and female occupations rests in the undervaluing of traditional female occupations. To remedy this situation, they propose that wages should be equal for jobs that are "somehow" equivalent in total worth or compensation to the organization.[37] Unfortunately, there is no consensus on a comparable worth standard by which to evaluate jobs, nor is there agreement on the ability of present job evaluation techniques to remedy the problem. Indeed, organizations may skirt the comparable worth issue by using one job evaluation system for clerical and secretarial jobs and another system for other jobs.[38] Furthermore, the advocates of comparable worth argue that current job evaluation techniques simply serve to continue the differences in pay between the sexes.

The argument over comparable worth is likely to remain an important HR issue for many years to come. Unanswered questions such as the following will serve to keep the issue alive:

1. If comparable worth is adopted, who would determine the worth of jobs, and by what means?
2. How much would comparable worth cost employers?
3. Would comparable worth reduce the wage gap between men and women caused by labor market supply and demand forces?
4. Would comparable worth reduce the number of employment opportunities for women?

Impact of the Labor Market and Collective Bargaining

Even if an acceptable comparable worth standard can eventually be established, consideration must also be given to the labor market and collective bargaining forces that are a part of our economic system. We know that a shortage of applicants for certain jobs can help to increase the compensation rates for these jobs and, in turn, reduce their shortage. To eliminate the impact of the labor market, wage rates would have to be determined by the courts or by commissions established for this purpose. It is doubtful, however, whether those making the determination of comparable worth would be better qualified than those currently performing the task. Nor would the judgments of courts or commissions be any less free of bias.

Collective bargaining that affects the labor market can be a source of many pay inequities. To prevent these inequities, wage determination based on comparable worth would also have to be subject to government control, which some would see as conflicting with the tenets of our free economic society.

Position of Congress and the Courts

When the Equal Pay Act was being debated, proponents of comparable worth attempted to have equal pay based on this criterion rather than on equal work. A majority in Congress, however, deliberately chose to avoid using the comparable worth criterion. Thus, as Supreme Court Justice Rehnquist concluded in a dissenting opinion involving a suit by matrons working at the county jail in Washington County, Oregon,

> Congress realized that the adoption of the comparable worth doctrine would ignore the economic relations of supply and demand, and would involve both government agencies and the courts in the impossible task of ascertaining the worth of comparable work in an area in which they have little expertise.[39]

In the Oregon case, however, the majority opinion held that the jail matrons who performed similar but not identical work to that performed by male jailers could sue for equal pay.[40] (The county settled out of court by paying each matron $3,500, after which it abolished the job of jail matron.) This leading court case and others, such as *AFSCME* v. *State of Washington*, have given encouragement to supporters of comparable worth.[41] Nevertheless, court decisions are traditionally extremely slow in effecting sweeping changes. In addition, some believe that comparable worth is a societal problem, not just a legal one.[42] Nonjudicial determination of comparable worth through collective bargaining and pressure-group action may be a better way to achieve gender-based pay equity. Currently, organizations like Tektronix and Motorola are adhering closely to internal comparisons, as are BankAmerica Corporation and Northwestern Bell Telephone.[43] These organizations are showing corporate responsibility by providing a positive response to a societal concern.

Finally, organizations implementing comparable worth policies have raised women's wages. In one public-sector study of the impact of comparable worth legislation on men's and women's earnings, the researcher concluded that "women would earn an average of 17 percent more if a comparable worth policy were implemented and men would earn an average of 1 percent more."[44] The compensation gap between men and women will not disappear overnight, but the persistence of comparable worth advocates will help shrink it.

SUMMARY

Compensation is a key function of HRM. The basis on which compensation payments are determined and the way they are administered can have a significant impact on employee productivity and the achievement of organizational goals. While the worth of the job and the performance of the jobholder are major factors in determining an employee's rate of pay, this rate may also be affected by other factors, such as labor market conditions, area wage rates, cost of living, employer's ability to pay, and collective bargaining.

Rate structures based on the relative worth of the jobs within organizations can be developed through job evaluation systems. Data obtained through these systems provide the basis for establishing wage classes in which jobs can be grouped according to their relative worth. Rate ranges can then be constructed for jobs in each class to recognize differences in performance and/or seniority among employees in these jobs.

Understanding compensation management requires attention to both technical and legal matters. Managers involved in compensation decisions must be aware of the legal requirements of the Davis-Bacon Act, the Walsh-Healy Act, the Fair Labor Standards Act, and individual state compensation laws in order to compensate employees correctly. Managers also need to be familiar with the requirements of the Equal Pay Act, as discussed in Chapter 3. Failure to abide by wage and salary laws can invite legal charges from employees and can weaken employee morale.

Two important compensation issues are wage-rate compression and equal pay for comparable work. Wage-rate compression largely affects managerial and senior employees as the pay given to new employees or the wage increases gained through union agreements erodes the pay differences between these groups. Comparable worth involves the concept that jobs historically held by women are compensated at a lower rate than those performed by men. This happens even though both types of jobs may contribute equally to organizational productivity. The magnitude of wage-rate compression and comparable worth problems suggests that they will not be eliminated by stopgap policies.

DISCUSSION QUESTIONS

1. What are the disadvantages of pay secrecy? Despite its disadvantages, why do some managers prefer pay secrecy?
2. Since employees may differ in terms of their job performance, would it not be more feasible to determine the wage rate for each employee on the basis of his or her relative worth to the organization?
3. What are some of the criticisms being raised concerning COLA and the CPI on which COLA is based?
4. During collective bargaining, unions have sometimes responded to a company claim of inability to pay with the statement that the union should not be expected to

subsidize inefficient management. To what extent do you feel that a response of this type has or does not have merit?

5. Describe the basic steps in conducting a wage and salary survey. What are some factors to consider?
6. One of the objections to granting wage increases on a percentage basis is that the lowest-paid employees, who are having the most trouble making ends meet, get the smallest increase, while the highest-paid employees get the largest increase. Is this objection a valid one?
7. An employee covered by the FLSA earns $5 per hour, works 50 hours during a given week, and receives a production bonus of $20. What are this employee's gross earnings for the week?
8. What are some of the problems of developing a pay system based on equal pay for comparable work?

MINI-CASE 10–1 Making Up for Time Lost

Ethel Perkins was the owner of a small business that she chose to operate in a rather informal manner without too much concern for "red tape originating in Washington." Her employees, who were treated like members of the family, were paid on a weekly basis. If they were absent during a week because work was slow, because they were ill, or because they had to attend to personal business, they would still receive their full pay. The employees made up for their absences by working a few extra hours when their services were needed. One employee even accumulated extra hours in advance to cover the week he took off each year during the deer-hunting season. Because this informal time-off arrangement accommodated the employees' personal needs, they appeared happy with it.

Everything was fine until Richard Gross, a Department of Labor representative, paid a visit and requested the opportunity to make what Ms. Perkins perceived to be a routine inspection of her payroll records. Upon completion of this inspection, Ms. Perkins was informed that she owed five employees a total of about $5,000 in back wages for the overtime they had worked. Mr. Gross informed her that, under FLSA guidelines, any time worked to make up for hours lost during a week had to be worked the same week. Three employees who were due overtime pay stated that they would refuse to accept payment. The other two had quit, owing money to Ms. Perkins on personal loans that were greater than the amount of overtime alleged to be due them.

QUESTIONS

1. How should the problem involving overtime be resolved?
2. What dilemma do problems such as this create for law enforcement agencies? For owners of small businesses?

MINI-CASE 10–2 Two-Tier Wage Schedules

Two-tier wage schedules became a popular compensation strategy during the early and mid-1980s. Under these pay plans, new hires performing the same jobs as senior employees are paid at lower wage rates. In some cases, new employees—"B-scalers"—also receive fewer benefits, including reduced insurance coverage, less vacation time, and lower pension allotments. Organizations implementing these compensation plans sought to cut or maintain labor costs in the face of deregulation and growing nonunion and foreign competition. Two-tier pay plans continued to be popular, since between 1984 and 1989 more than 650 negotiated labor contracts found new hires on lower pay scales than their senior co-workers. These contracts have been negotiated in a variety of industries, including airlines, retail food, metal fabrication, and wood products. Both union and nonunion employees accept two-tier pay schedules in order to secure their own jobs and maintain existing wage levels instead of accepting across-the-board wage cuts.

While some employee groups, such as Lockheed Corporation machinists and Northwest Airlines pilots, have recently accepted two-tier contracts, there is growing evidence that these pay plans may be losing favor with both managers and employees. A 1989 study reported by the Bureau of National Affairs showed that only 6 percent of the 962 nonconstruction contracts negotiated in 1989 contained two-tier pay schedules, down from a high of 11 percent in 1985. Furthermore, in many of the earlier plans the wages of the A- and B-scale employees never merged. Currently, there is a move to eliminate the B-scale by having it "catch up" to the A-scale after a specified number of years. This can be accomplished by granting larger wage increases to B-scale employees than to A-scale employees. While HR professionals predict that two-tier wage schedules will always be around, the current business environment will likely curtail their use.

SOURCE: "Employers and Unions Feeling Pressure to Eliminate Two-Tier Labor Contracts," *Wall Street Journal* (April 20, 1990): B1.

QUESTIONS

1. What do you see as the advantages and disadvantages of two-tier wage schedules?
2. What factor may be leading to their lack of growth in the early 1990s?

NOTES AND REFERENCES

1. Robert Kreitner and Angelo Kinicki, *Organizational Behavior* (Homewood, IL: BPI/Irwin, 1989), Chapter 15.

2. David W. Belcher and Thomas J. Atchison, *Compensation Management,* 2d ed. (Englewood Cliffs, NJ: Prentice-Hall, 1987), 4.

3. Thomas A. Mahoney, "Employment Compensation Planning and Strategy," in *Compensation and Benefits,* ed. Luis R. Gomez-Mejia (Washington, DC: American Society for Personnel Administra-

tion/Bureau of National Affairs, 1989), 3-1 to 3-28. See also Edward E. Lawler, *Strategic Pay* (San Francisco: Jossey-Bass, 1990); and Caroline L. Weber and Sara L. Rymes, "Effects of Compensation Strategy on Job Pay Decisions," *Academy of Management Journal* 34, no. 1 (March 1991): 86–109.

4. Sara M. Freedman, Robert T. Keller, and John R. Montanari, "The Compensation Program: Balancing Organizational and Employee Needs," *Compensation Review* 14, no. 2 (Second Quarter 1982): 50. See also Bruce R. Ellig, "The Compensation Function: From the Chief Personnel Officer's Perspective," *Compensation and Benefits Review* 22, no. 1 (January–February 1990): 20–35.

5. Thomas Rollins, "Pay for Performance: Is It Worth the Trouble?" *Personnel Administrator* 33, no. 5 (May 1988): 42–46.

6. James L. Whitney, "Pay Concepts for the 1990s, Part 2," *Compensation and Benefits Review* 20, no. 3 (May–June 1988): 45.

7. "Matching Pay Raises to Inflation Seems a Policy That Has Seen Its Day," *Wall Street Journal* (March 6, 1990): 1.

8. Edward E. Lawler III, "Pay-for-Performance: A Strategic Analysis," in *Compensation and Benefits*, ed. Luis R. Gomez-Mejia (Washington, DC: American Society for Personnel Administration/Bureau of National Affairs, 1989), 3–136.

9. Robert L. Neheman, David B. Greenberger, and Stephen Strasser, "The Relationship Between Pay-for-Performance Perceptions and Pay Satisfaction," *Personnel Psychology* 41, no. 4 (Winter 1988): 745.

10. Edward E. Lawler III, "Pay-for-Performance: Making It Work," *Personnel* 65, no. 10 (October 1988): 68–71.

11. Marc J. Wallace, Jr., and Charles H. Fay, *Compensation Theory and Practice*, 2d ed. (Boston: PWS-Kent, 1988), 14.

12. Edward E. Lawler III, *Pay and Organizational Development* (Reading, MA: Addison-Wesley, 1981), 44–45.

13. Julio D. Burroughs, "Pay Secrecy and Performance: The Psychological Research," *Compensation Review* 14, no. 3 (Third Quarter 1982): 47–49.

14. William L. White and Douglas O. Jensen, "Pressure Points: Factors Influencing Total Compensation," *Compensation Review* 6, no. 2 (Second Quarter 1984): 63–70.

15. *CPI Detailed Report October 1988* (U.S. Department of Labor, Bureau of Labor Statistics, December 1989), 106.

16. Robert J. Greene, "Determinants of Occupational Worth," *Personnel Administrator* 34, no. 8 (August 1989): 78–82.

17. Gary P. Latham and Kenneth N. Wexley, *Increasing Productivity Through Performance Appraisal* (Reading, MA: Addison-Wesley, 1981), Chapter 7.

18. C. Terrence Walker, "The Use of Job Evaluation Plans in Salary Administration," *Personnel* 64, no. 3 (March 1987): 28–31.

19. Gundars E. Kaupins, "Lies, Damn Lies, and Job Evaluation," *Personnel* 66, no. 11 (November 1989): 62–65. See also Chad T. Lewis, "Assessing the Validity of Job Evaluation," *Public Personnel Management* 18, no. 1 (Spring 1989): 45–58.

20. Frederick S. Hills, *Compensation Decision Making* (Chicago: Dryden Press, 1987), 176.

21. Howard W. Risher, "Job Evaluation: Validity and Reliability," *Compensation and Benefits Review* 21, no. 1 (January/February 1989): 32–33.

22. Leonard R. Burgess, *Compensation Administration*, 2d ed. (Columbus, OH: Merrill, 1989), 166.

23. For an expanded discussion of both the point system and the factor comparison system, see George T. Milkovich and Jerry M. Newman, *Compensation*, 3d ed. (Plano, TX: Business Publications, 1990), 114–127.

24. Alvin O. Bellak, "The Hay Guide Chart-Profile Method of Job Evaluation," in *Handbook of Wage and Salary Administration*, 2d ed., ed. Milton L. Rock (New York: McGraw-Hill, 1984), Chapter 15.

25. Michael A. Camuso, "Keep Competitive with the Right Salary Survey," *Personnel Journal* 64, no. 10 (October 1985): 86–91. See also Michael A. Conway, "Salary Surveys: Avoid the Pitfalls," *Personnel Journal* 63, no. 6 (June 1984): 62–65.

26. E. James Brennan, "Everything You Need to Know About Salary Ranges," *Personnel Journal* 63, no. 3 (March 1984): 10–16.

27. Jerry Franklin, "For Technical Professionals: Pay for Skill and Pay for Performance," *Personnel* 65, no. 5 (May 1988): 20–28.

28. Fred Luthans and Marilyn L. Fox, "Update on Skill-Based Pay," *Personnel* 66, no. 3 (March 1989): 26–31.

29. Dale Feuer, "Paying for Knowledge," *Training* 24, no. 5 (May 1987): 58.

30. Wendell C. Lawther, "Ways to Monitor (and Solve) the Pay-Compression Problem," *Personnel* 66, no. 3 (March 1989): 84–87.

31. Because the FLSA is always subject to future amendments, an employer should consult the appropriate publications of one of the labor services previously mentioned or the Wage and Hour Division of the U.S. Department of Labor in order to obtain the latest information regarding its current provisions, particularly the minimum wage rate.

32. Gina Ameci, "Overtime Pay: Avoiding FLSA Violations," *Personnel Administrator* 32, no. 2 (February 1987): 117–118.

33. Robert M. Pattison, "Fine Tuning Wage and Hour Practices," *Personnel Journal* 66, no. 9 (September 1987): 166–168.

34. "Earnings Gap Narrowing Faster Between Young Men and Women," *Employee Relations Weekly* (Bureau of National Affairs, November 20, 1989), 1451.

35. Ibid.

36. Doug Grider and Mike Shurden, "The Gathering Storm of Comparable Worth," *Business Horizons* 30, no. 4 (July–August 1987): 81–86.

37. Larry S. Luton and Suzanne Thompson, "Progress in Comparable Worth: Moving Toward Non-Judicial Determination—Problems and Prospects," *Review of Public Personnel Administration* 9, no. 2 (Spring 1989): 78–85.

38. Edward Ost, "Comparable Worth: A Response for the 80's," *Personnel Journal* 64, no. 2 (February 1985): 64–69.

39. "Review and Outlook: Pandora's Worth," *Wall Street Journal* (June 16, 1981): 1.

40. *Washington County* v. *Gunther,* 101 Sup. Ct. 2242 (1981), 452 U.S. 161.

41. *AFSCME* v. *State of Washington,* 578 F. Supp. 846 (W.D. Wash. 1983).

42. Luton and Thompson, 79.

43. "Comparable Worth: It's Already Happening," *Business Week* (April 28, 1986): 52.

44. Elaine Sorensen, "Effect of Comparable Worth Policies on Earnings," *Industrial Relations* 26, no. 3 (Fall 1987): 227–239.

CHAPTER 11

Incentive Compensation

After reading this chapter you will be able to:

1. *Describe the characteristics of piecework and the advantages and disadvantages of using it to motivate employees.*
2. *Explain why merit raises may fail to motivate employees adequately and discuss ways to increase their motivational value.*
3. *Identify the principal methods for compensating salespersons and the advantages of each method.*
4. *Describe the different methods by which executive bonuses may be determined and paid.*
5. *List the different gainsharing programs and describe the methods by which these gains may be shared with employees.*
6. *Discuss the objectives of employee stock ownership plans, the reasons for their growth, and possible abuses in adopting them.*
7. *Define the key terms in the chapter.*

TERMS TO IDENTIFY

straight piecework *(350)*
differential piece rate *(350)*
bonus *(352)*
standard hour plan *(353)*
merit guidelines *(355)*
lump-sum merit program *(356)*
straight salary plan *(357)*
straight commission plan *(358)*
combination salary and commission plan *(358)*
career curves or maturity curves *(359)*
perquisites *(364)*
gainsharing plans *(366)*
profit sharing *(366)*
Scanlon Plan *(368)*
Rucker Plan *(370)*
Improshare *(371)*
employee stock ownership plans (ESOPs) *(372)*

In the previous chapter we emphasized that the worth of a job is a significant factor in determining the pay rate for that job. However, pay based solely on this measure may fail to motivate employees to perform to their full capacity. Unmotivated employees are likely to meet only minimum performance standards. Recognizing this fact, nearly half of all companies offer some form of incentive to workers below top-executive ranks.[1] These organizations are attempting to get more motivational mileage out of employee compensation by tying it more clearly to employee performance. Managers at Grumman Corporation note that incentives linked with output "encourage people to work smarter, work together as a group." One executive remarked, "If we increase production, we can produce things for less cost and that makes us more competitive."[2] In their attempt to raise productivity, managers are focusing on the many variables that help to determine the effectiveness of pay as a motivator. Based on the knowledge that researchers and HR practitioners are acquiring, financial incentive plans are being developed to meet the needs of both employees and employers more satisfactorily.[3]

In this chapter we will discuss incentive plans in terms of the objectives they hope to achieve and the various factors that may affect their success. We will also attempt to identify the plans that are most effective in motivating different categories of employees to achieve these objectives. For discussion purposes, incentive plans have been grouped into two broad categories, individual incentive plans and group incentive plans, as shown in Figure 11–1.

FIGURE 11–1 INCENTIVE COMPENSATION PLANS

INDIVIDUAL	GROUP
Hourly:	*Hourly and Managerial:*
Piecework	Scanlon Plan
Bonuses	Rucker Plan
Standard Hour Plan	Improshare
Managerial:	Profit Sharing
Merit Raises	
Sales Personnel:	
Sales Incentive Plans	
Professional:	
Maturity Curves	
Executive:	
Bonuses	
Stock Options	

REASONS AND REQUIREMENTS FOR INCENTIVE PLANS

Over the years, organizations have implemented incentive plans for a variety of reasons: high labor costs, competitive product markets, slow technological advances, and high potential for production bottlenecks.[4] While these reasons are still cited, contemporary arguments for incentive plans focus on pay-for-performance and improved organizational productivity.[5] By linking compensation to employee effort, organizations believe that employees will improve their job performance. Incentives are designed to encourage employees to put out more effort to complete their job tasks—effort they might not be motivated to expend under hourly and/or seniority-based compensation systems. Financial incentives, therefore, are offered to improve or maintain high levels of productivity, which in turn improves the market for U.S. goods and services in a global economy.

Do incentive plans work? Various studies have demonstrated a measurable relationship between incentive plans and improved organizational performance. In the area of manufacturing, productivity will often improve by as much as 20 percent after the adoption of incentive plans.[6] Improvements, however, are not limited to goods-producing industries. Service organizations also show productivity gains when incentives are linked to organizational goals. For example, after beginning an incentive pay program, Domino's Pizza boasted of an increase in sales, and Avis Inc. found that customer complaints dropped 35 percent in the first year after it began distributing stock to employees.[7]

Because of the benefits organizations have derived from incentive pay programs, these programs are predicted to increase in popularity. The results of one compensation study showed that "service firms expect to nearly triple the number of gainsharing plans in effect and to double the number of small group incentive plans."[8] Figure 11–2 shows both the current and the projected use of selected incentive pay programs. Interestingly, while the use of all forms of incentive plans will increase, small-group incentives and gainsharing (group plans) will grow the most.

However, incentive plans have not always led to organizational improvement, for two main reasons. First, incentive plans sometimes fail to satisfy employee needs.

FIGURE 11–2 CURRENT AND PROJECTED USE OF INCENTIVE PAY PLANS

CURRENT USE OF SELECTED INCENTIVES

Type of Incentive	Percentage of Firms
Individual incentives	28
Small-group incentives	14
Gainsharing	13

PERCENTAGE OF PLANS IMPLEMENTED IN LAST FIVE YEARS

Type of Incentive	Percentage of Plans
Individual incentives	42
Small-group incentives	62
Gainsharing	73

PROJECTED INCREASE IN THE NUMBER OF FIRMS USING SELECTED INCENTIVES

Type of Incentive	Percentage of Firms
Individual incentives	31
Small-group incentives	70
Gainsharing	68

SOURCE: From *People, Performance, and Pay* (American Productivity & Quality Center and the American Compensation Association, 1987), reflecting responses from 1,598 organizations employing more than 9 million people (about 10 percent of the U.S. civilian working population). The sample included 40 different industry groups, 741 goods-producing firms, 741 service firms, and 116 government or unclassified organizations. The survey covered both exempt and nonexempt employees. Reprinted, by permission of the publisher, from William E. Buhl, "Compensation Management in Practice: Keeping Incentives Simple for Nonexempt Employees," *Compensation and Benefits Review* 21, no. 2 (March–April 1989): 15. © 1989. American Management Association, New York. All rights reserved.

Second, management may have failed to give adequate attention to the design and implementation of the program.[9] Furthermore, the success of an incentive plan will depend on the environment that exists within an organization. A plan is more likely to work in an organization where morale is high, employees believe they are being treated fairly, and there is harmony between employees and management.

Employee Acceptance of the Plan

For an incentive plan to succeed, employees must have some desire for the plan. This desire can be influenced in part by how successful management is in introducing the plan and convincing employees of its benefits. Encouraging employees to participate in administering the plan is likely to increase their willingness to accept it.

Employees must be able to see a clear connection between the incentive payments they receive and their job performance. This connection is more visible if there are objective standards by which they can judge their performance.[10] Commitment by employees to meet these standards is also essential for incentive plans to succeed. This requires mutual understanding and confidence between employees and their supervisors, which only open channels of two-way communication can provide. Incentive payments must never be permitted to be seen as a guarantee. Instead, they should be viewed as a reward that must be earned through effort. This perception can be strengthened if the incentive money is distributed to employees in a separate check.

Recognition of Differences in Employee Needs

Employees differ in their need for money and in their willingness to put in the time and effort necessary to earn it. Their attitudes toward money may be affected by their level of income, the size of their family, and their life-style. When some employees have sufficient income to satisfy their economic needs, they would rather devote their time and energy to recreational or other pursuits than to additional work. Furthermore, as income levels rise, so does the amount of tax that must be paid on these incomes. As a result, the value of incentive pay is reduced.

How much extra pay an employee can earn under an incentive plan will also affect the motivational value of the incentives. Generally, and not surprisingly, the higher the extra pay, the more willing employees will be to put forth the effort to earn it. So, if we remember our discussion of compensation in Chapter 10, it seems only logical to assume that if incentive payments are small, employees are unlikely to be motivated to increase their effort. Another factor is the probability of earning incentive payments. If it is either too high or too low, the plan may provide less inducement for employees to work hard.

Incentive Plan Administration

While incentive plans based on productivity can reduce direct labor costs, to achieve their full benefit they must be carefully thought out, implemented, and maintained. A cardinal rule is that thorough planning combined with a "proceed with caution" approach will help ensure success. Compensation managers repeatedly discuss a number of points related to the effective administration of incentive plans. Four of the more important points are as follows:

1. Incentive systems are effective only when managers are willing to grant incentives based on differences in individual performance. Allowing incentive payments to become pay guarantees defeats the motivational intent of the incentive. The primary purpose of an incentive compensation plan is not to pay off under almost all circumstances, but rather to motivate performance. Thus, if the plan is to succeed, poor performance must go unrewarded.[11]
2. Annual salary budgets must be large enough to reward and reinforce exceptional performance. When compensation budgets are set to ensure that pay increases do not exceed certain limits (often established as a percentage of payroll or sales), these constraints may prohibit rewarding outstanding individual or group performance.[12]
3. Incentive systems must be based on clearly defined and accepted performance standards effectively communicated to employees. Then organizational appraisal systems can objectively measure individual or group output against standards in order to establish the pay-for-performance linkage.
4. The overhead costs associated with plan implementation and administration must be determined. These may include the cost of establishing performance standards and the added cost of recordkeeping. The time consumed in communicating the plan to employees, answering questions, and resolving any complaints about it must also be included in these costs.

INCENTIVES FOR NONMANAGEMENT PERSONNEL

Many factors influence the design of incentive plans for nonmanagement personnel. For example, incentive plans for this group are designed with consideration for the type of work these employees do and the technology they use. Also, when employees work in groups, a group incentive plan may be preferred since individual effort may not be distinguishable from group effort. Organizations may also use group incentives in cases where some employees are likely to try to maximize their output at the expense of their co-workers. One report stated that "group incentives may reduce rivalry and promote cooperation and concern for the unit's overall performance."[13] In addition, in highly competitive industries such as retail foods and retailing, low profit margins will affect the availability of monies for incentive payouts. All these considerations suggest that tradition and philosophy, as well as economics and technology, help to govern the design of nonmanagement incentive systems. The various gainsharing plans discussed later in the chapter are typically offered to both nonmanagement and management personnel.

Incentives for Hourly Personnel

Incentive payments for hourly employees may be determined by the number of units produced, by the achievement of specific performance goals, or by productivity improvements in the organization as a whole. In the majority of incentive plans, incentive payments serve to supplement the employee's basic wage.

PIECEWORK One of the oldest incentive plans is piecework. Under **straight piecework,** employees receive a certain rate for each unit produced. Their compensation is determined by the number of units they produce during a pay period. At Steelcase, an office furniture maker, employees can earn more than their base pay, often as much as 35 percent, through piecework for each slab of metal they cut or chair they upholster.[14] An advocate of piecework, Frederick W. Taylor, whose contributions to scientific management were discussed in Chapter 1, devised a **differential piece rate.** Under this rate, employees whose production exceeds the

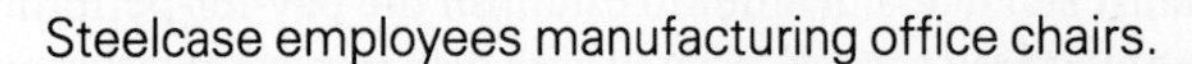
Steelcase employees manufacturing office chairs.

standard output receive a higher rate for *all* of their work than the rate paid to those who do not exceed the standard.

Piecework can provide financial motivation for employees who have a strong desire to increase their earnings, because the wages they receive are directly proportional to their output. The wage payment for each employee is simple to compute; and the plan permits an organization to predict its labor costs with considerable accuracy since these costs are the same for each unit of output. The piecework system is more likely to succeed when units of output can be measured readily, when the quality of the product is less critical, when the job is fairly standardized, and when a constant flow of work can be maintained.

Employees normally are not paid for the time they are idle unless the idleness is due to conditions for which the organization is responsible, such as delays in work flow, defective materials, inoperative equipment, or power failures. When the delay is not the fault of employees, they are paid for the time they are idle.

COMPUTING THE PIECE RATE Although time standards establish the time required to perform a given amount of work, they do not by themselves determine what the incentive rate should be. The incentive rates must be based on hourly wage rates that would otherwise be paid for the type of work being performed. Say, for example, the standard time for producing one unit of work in a job paying $6.50 per hour was set at 12 minutes. The piece rate would be $1.30 per unit, computed as follows:

$$\frac{60 \text{ (minutes per hour)}}{12 \text{ (standard time per unit)}} = 5 \text{ units per hour}$$

$$\frac{\$6.50 \text{ (hourly rate)}}{5 \text{ (units per hour)}} = \$1.30 \text{ per unit}$$

LIMITED USE OF PIECEWORK In spite of its incentive value, the use of piecework is limited. One reason is that production standards on which piecework must be based can be difficult to develop for many types of jobs. In some instances the cost of determining and maintaining this standard may exceed the benefits gained from the system. Jobs in which individual contributions are difficult to distinguish or measure, or in which the work is mechanized to the point that the employee exercises very little control over output, also may be unsuited to piecework. The same is true of jobs in which employees are learning the work or in which high standards of quality are paramount.

One of the most significant weaknesses of piecework, as well as other incentive plans based on individual effort, is that it may not always be an effective motivator. If employees believe that an increase in their output will provoke disapproval from fellow workers, they may avoid exerting maximum effort because their desire for peer approval outweighs their desire for more money. Over a period of time, the standards on which piece rates are based tend to loosen, either because of peer pressure to relax the standards or because employees discover ways to do the work in less than standard time. In either case, employees are not required to exert as much effort to receive the same amount of incentive pay, so the incentive value is reduced.

NEGATIVE REACTION TO PIECEWORK Despite the opportunity to earn additional pay, employees, especially those belonging to unions, have held negative attitudes toward piecework plans. Some union leaders have feared that management will use piecework or similar systems to try to speed up production, getting more work from employees for the same amount of money. Another fear is that the system may induce employees to compete against one another, thereby taking jobs away from workers who are shown to be less productive. There is also the belief that the system will cause some employees to lose their jobs as productivity increases or cause craft standards of workmanship to suffer.

INDIVIDUAL BONUSES A **bonus,** as Highlights in HRM 1 illustrates, is an incentive payment that is supplemental to the basic wage. It has the advantage of providing employees with more pay for exerting greater effort, while at the same time they still have the security of a basic wage. A bonus payment may be based on the number of units that an individual produces, as in the case of piecework. For example, at the basic wage rate of $7 an hour plus a bonus of 15 cents per unit, an employee who produces 100 units during an 8-hour period is paid $71, computed as follows:

(hours × wage rate) + (number of units × unit rate) = wages
(8 × $7) + (100 × 15¢) = $71

Bonuses may also be determined on the basis of cost reduction, quality-improvement goals, or performance criteria established by the organization.

GROUP BONUSES Group bonuses are most desirable to use when the contributions of individual employees either are difficult to distinguish or depend on group cooperation.[15] Thus, as production has become more automated, as teamwork and coordination among workers have become more important, and as the contribution of those engaged indirectly in production work has increased, group bonuses have grown more popular. Most group bonus plans developed in recent years, furthermore, base incentive payments on such factors as increases in company profits, improvements in efficiency, or reductions in labor costs. Group bonuses, unlike incentive plans based solely on output, can broaden the scope of the contributions that employees are motivated to make.

For example, if labor costs represent 30 percent of an organization's sales dollars and the organization is willing to pay a bonus to employees, then whenever employee labor costs represent less than 30 percent of sales dollars, those savings are put into

HIGHLIGHTS IN HRM

1 COMPUTING THE BONUS AT PROCTER & GAMBLE

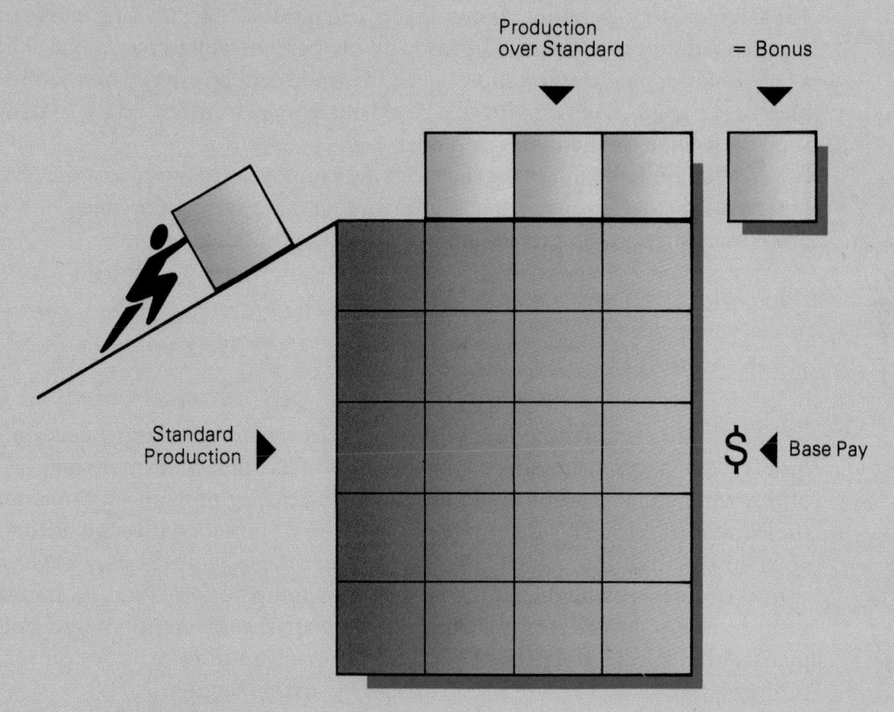

SOURCE: Reproduced with permission of the Procter & Gamble Company.

a bonus pool for employees. Information on the status of the pool is reported to employees on a weekly or monthly basis, explaining why a bonus was or was not earned. The group bonus may be distributed to employees equally, in proportion to their base pay, or on the basis of their relative contribution to the group.

Standard Hour Plan

Another common incentive technique is the **standard hour plan,** which sets incentive rates based on a predetermined "standard time" for completing a job. If employees finish the work in less than the expected time, they are still paid based on the standard time for the job multiplied by their hourly rate. For example, if the standard time to install an engine in a half-ton truck is five hours and the mechanic completes the job in four and a half hours, the payment would be the mechanic's hourly rate times five hours. Standard hour plans are particularly suited to long-cycle operations or those jobs or tasks that are nonrepetitive and require a variety of skills.[16]

The Wood Products Southern Division of Potlatch Corporation has successfully used a standard hour plan for the production of numerous wood products. The incentive payment is based on the standard hours calculated to produce and package 1,000 feet of wood paneling. If employees can produce the paneling in less time than the standard, incentives are paid based on the percentage improvement. Thus, with a 1,000-hour standard and completion of the wood paneling in 900 hours, a 10 percent incentive is paid. Each employee's base hourly wage is increased by 10 percent and then multiplied by the hours worked.[17]

While standard hour plans can motivate employees to produce more, employers must ensure that equipment maintenance or product quality does not suffer as employees strive to do their work faster to earn additional income.

INCENTIVES FOR MANAGEMENT EMPLOYEES

Merit raises constitute one of the financial incentive systems used most commonly for managerial employees. In one study of pay practices, more than 80 percent of responding organizations reported having merit pay programs for one or more of their employee groups.[18] Incentive pay may also be provided through different types of bonuses. Like those for hourly employees, these bonuses may be based on a variety of criteria involving either individual or group performance. As stated earlier, managerial employees are also usually included in the different types of gainsharing plans. Although they may not technically manage employees, sales personnel and professional employees will also be discussed in this section.

Merit Raises

Merit raises can serve to motivate managerial, sales, and professional employees if they perceive the raises to be related to the performance required to earn them. Furthermore, theories of motivation, in addition to behavioral science research, provide justification for merit pay plans as well as other pay-for-performance programs.[19] For employees to see the link between pay and performance, however, their performance must be evaluated in light of objective criteria. If this evaluation also includes the use of subjective judgment by their superiors, employees must have confidence in the validity of this judgment. Most important, any increases granted on the basis of merit should be distinguishable from employees' regular pay and from any cost-of-living or other general increases. Where merit increases are based on pay-for-performance, merit pay should be withheld when performance is seen to decline.[20]

Problems with Merit Raises

Merit raises may not always achieve their intended purpose. Unlike a bonus, a merit raise may be perpetuated year after year even when performance declines. When this happens, employees come to expect the increase and see it as being unrelated to their performance. Furthermore, employees in some organizations are opposed to merit raises because, among other reasons, they do not really trust management. What are referred to as merit raises often turn out to be increases based on seniority or favoritism, or raises to accommodate increases in cost of living or in area wage rates. Even when merit raises are determined by performance, the employee's gains may be offset by inflation and higher income taxes. Compensation specialists also recognize the following problems with merit pay plans:

1. Merit increases may be inadequate to raise employees' base pay.
2. Employees may not believe that their compensation is tied to effort and performance.
3. There may be a lack of honesty and cooperation between management and employees.[21]

Probably one of the major weaknesses of merit raises lies in the performance appraisal system on which the increases are based. Even with an effective system, performance may be difficult to measure. Furthermore, any deficiencies in the performance appraisal program (these were discussed in Chapter 9) can impair the operation of a merit pay plan. Moreover, the performance appraisal objectives of employees and their superiors are often at odds. Employees typically want to maximize their pay increases, whereas superiors may seek to reward employees in an equitable manner based on their performance. In some instances, employee pressures for pay increases actually may have a harmful effect on their performance appraisal.

While there are no easy solutions to these problems, organizations using a true merit pay plan often base the percentage pay raise on **merit guidelines** tied to performance appraisals. For example, Figure 11–3 illustrates a merit guideline chart

FIGURE 11–3 MERIT GUIDELINE CHART

	RATING				
	Outstanding	Above Average	Good	Adequate	Unacceptable
Percentage increase	14–12	11–9	8–6	5–3	0

NOTE: Percentage may change annually based on such factors as annual inflation rate, profitability or ability to pay, job market rates, and/or compensation policy.

for awarding merit raises. The percentages may change each year depending on various internal or external concerns, such as profit levels or national economic conditions as indicated by changes in the consumer price index. Under the illustrated merit plan, to prevent all employees from being rated outstanding or above average, managers may be required to distribute the performance rating according to some preestablished formula (e.g., only 10 percent can be rated outstanding). Furthermore, when setting the merit percentages, organizations should consider how personnel will perceive the size of the merit increase. The results of one study showed that it is important to consider the smallest amount of pay increase that an individual finds meaningful. Therefore, when setting merit percentage guidelines, organizations should consider individual performance along with such factors as training, experience, and current earnings.[22]

Lump-Sum Merit Pay

To make merit increases more flexible and visible, organizations such as B. F. Goodrich, Timex, and Westinghouse have implemented a **lump-sum merit program.** Under this type of plan, employees receive a single lump-sum increase at the time of their review—an increase that is not added to their base salary. Unless management takes further steps to compensate employees, their base salary is essentially frozen until they receive a promotion.[23]

Lump-sum merit programs offer several advantages. For employers, this innovative approach provides financial control by maintaining annual salary expenses. Merit increases granted on a lump-sum basis do not contribute to escalating base

salary levels. In addition, organizations can contain employee benefit costs, since the levels of benefits are normally calculated from current salary levels. For employees, an advantage is that receiving a single lump-sum merit payment can provide a clear link between pay and performance. For example, a 6 percent merit increase granted to an employee earning $20,000 a year translates into a weekly increase of $23.07—a figure that looks small compared to a lump-sum payment of $1,200.

Organizations using a lump-sum merit program will want to adjust base salaries upward after a certain number of years. These adjustments should keep pace with the rising cost of living and increases in the general market wage.

Incentives for Sales Personnel

The enthusiasm and drive required in most types of sales work demand that sales personnel be highly motivated. This fact, as well as the competitive nature of selling, explains why financial incentives for salespeople are widely used. These incentive plans must provide a source of motivation that will enlist cooperation and trust. Motivation is particularly important for personnel out in the field who cannot be supervised closely and who, as a result, must exercise a high degree of self-discipline.

UNIQUE NEEDS OF SALES INCENTIVE PLANS Incentive systems for salespeople are complicated by the wide differences in the types of sales jobs. These range from department store clerks ringing up customer purchases to industrial salespersons from McGraw-Edison providing consultation and other highly technical services. Salespersons' performance may be measured by the dollar volume of their sales and by their ability to establish new accounts. Other measures are the ability to promote new products or services and to provide various forms of customer service and assistance that do not produce immediate sales revenues.

Performance standards for sales personnel are difficult to develop, however, because their performance is often affected by external factors beyond their control. Economic and seasonal fluctuations, sales competition, changes in demand, and the nature of the sales territory can all affect an individual's sales record. Sales volume alone, therefore, may not be an accurate indicator of the effort salespeople have expended.

In developing incentive plans for salespeople, employers are also confronted with the problem of how to reward extra sales effort and at the same time compensate for activities that do not contribute directly or immediately to sales. Furthermore, sales personnel must be able to enjoy some degree of income stability.

Sales volume is but one measure of selling performance.

TYPES OF SALES INCENTIVE PLANS Compensation plans for sales personnel may consist of a straight salary plan, a straight commission plan, or a combination salary and commission plan.[24] A **straight salary plan** permits salespeople to be paid for performing various duties not reflected immediately in their sales volume. It enables them to devote more time to providing services and building up the goodwill of customers without jeopardizing their income. The principal limitation of the straight salary plan is that it may not motivate salespeople to exert sufficient effort in maximizing their sales volume.

On the other hand, the **straight commission plan,** based on a percentage of sales, provides maximum incentive and is easy to compute and understand. For example, organizations that pay a straight commission based on total volume may use the following simple formulas:[25]

$$2\% \times \text{total volume} = \text{total cash compensation}$$

or

$$2\% \times \text{total volume up to quota} + 4\% \times \text{volume over quota} = \text{total cash compensation}$$

However, the straight commission plan is limited by the following disadvantages:

1. Emphasis is on sales volume rather than on profits (except in those rare cases where the commission rate is a percentage of the profit on the sale).
2. Territories tend to be milked rather than worked.
3. Customer service after the sale is likely to be neglected.
4. Earnings tend to fluctuate widely between good and poor periods of business, and turnover of trained sales personnel tends to increase in poor periods.
5. Salespeople are tempted to grant price concessions.
6. Salespeople are tempted to overload their wholesale customers with inventory.

When a **combination salary and commission plan** is used, the percentage of cash compensation paid out in commissions (i.e., incentives) is called *leverage*. Leverage is usually expressed as a ratio of base salary to commission.[26] For example, a salesperson working under a 70/30 combination plan would receive total cash compensation paid out as 70 percent base salary and 30 percent commission. The amount of leverage will be determined after considering the constraining factors affecting performance discussed earlier and the sales objectives of the organization. The following advantages indicate why the combination salary and commission plan is so widely used:

1. The right kind of incentive compensation, if linked to salary in the right proportion, has most of the advantages of both the straight salary and the straight commission forms of compensation.
2. A salary-plus-incentive compensation plan offers greater design flexibility and, therefore, can be more readily set up to help maximize company profits.
3. The plan can develop the most favorable ratio of selling expense to sales.
4. The field sales force can be motivated to achieve specific company marketing objectives in addition to sales volume.

Incentives for Professional Personnel

Like other salaried workers, professional personnel—engineers, scientists, lawyers, etc.—may be motivated through bonuses and merit increases. In some organizations, unfortunately, professional employees cannot advance beyond a certain point in the salary structure unless they are willing to take an administrative assignment. When they are promoted, their professional talents are no longer utilized fully. In the process, the organization may lose a good professional employee and gain a poor administrator. To avoid this situation, some organizations have extended the salary range for professional positions to equal or nearly equal that for administrative positions. The extension of this range provides a double-track wage system whereby professionals who do not aspire to become administrators still have an opportunity to earn comparable salaries.

Organizations also use **career curves** or **maturity curves** as a basis for providing salary increases to professional personnel. These curves, such as the ones shown in Figure 11–4, provide for the annual salary rate to be based on experience and performance. Separate curves are established to reflect different levels of performance and to provide for annual increases. The curves representing higher levels of performance tend to rise to a higher level and at a faster rate than the curves representing lower performance levels.

INCENTIVES FOR EXECUTIVE PERSONNEL

A major function of incentive plans for executives is to motivate them to develop and use their abilities and contribute their energies to the fullest possible extent. Incentive plans should also facilitate the recruitment and retention of competent executive personnel. This can be accomplished with plans that will enable them to accumulate a financial estate and to shelter a portion of their compensation from current income taxes.

Components of Executive Compensation

Organizations commonly have more than one compensation plan for executives in order to meet various organizational goals and executive needs. For example, chief executive officers (CEOs) may have their compensation packages heavily weighted toward long-term incentives, because CEOs should be more concerned about the long-term impact of their decisions than the short-term implications. Group vice-presidents, on the other hand, may receive more short-term incentives since their decisions affect operations on a 6- to 12-month basis.[27] Regardless of the compensation mix, executive compensation plans consist of five basic components: (1) base salary, (2) short-term incentives or bonuses, (3) long-term incentives or stock plans, (4) employee benefits, and (5) perquisites.

FIGURE 11–4 MATURITY CURVES FOR PROFESSIONALS

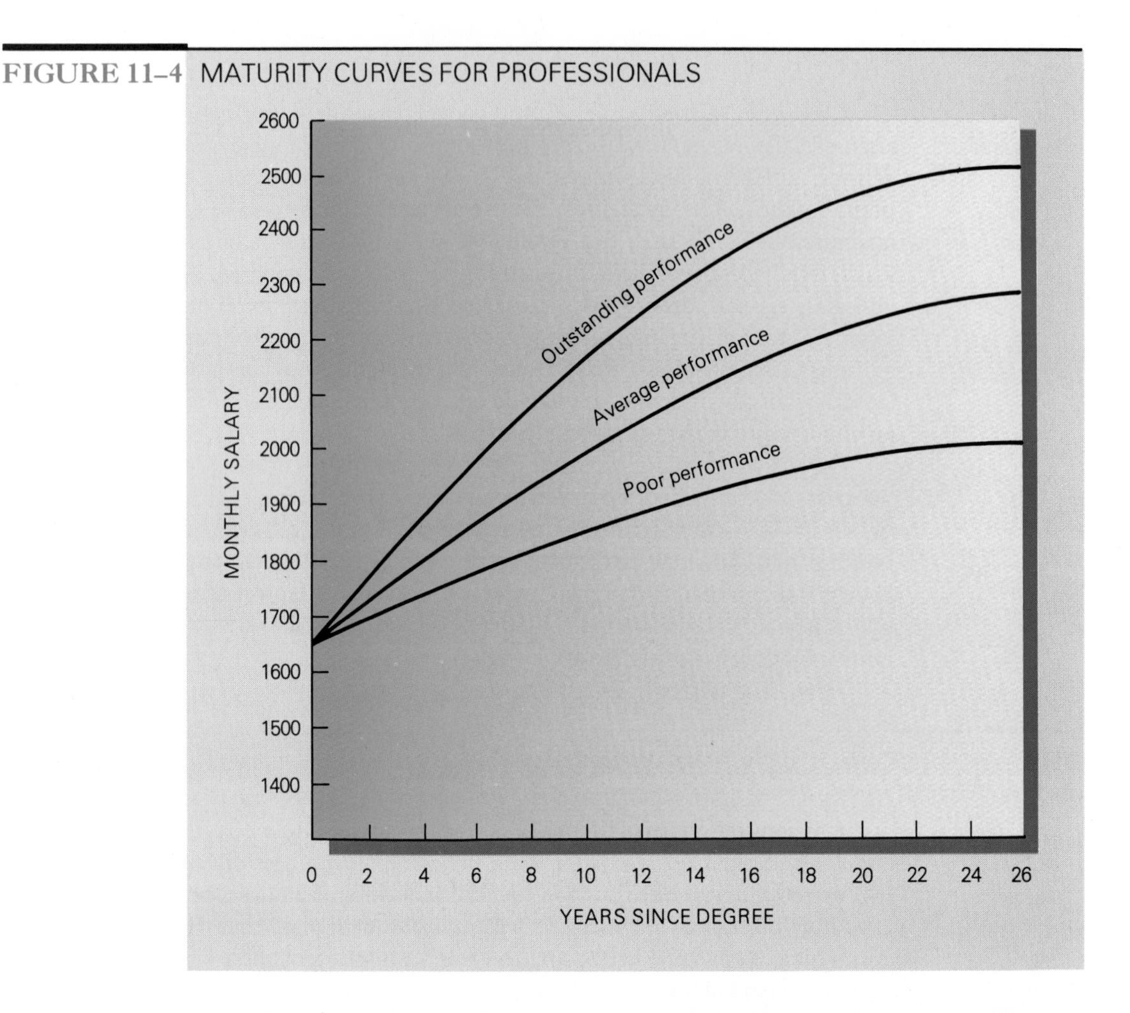

COVERAGE OF THE PLAN Theoretically, the incentive plan should cover key executives whose duties and responsibilities make them substantial contributors to the organization. Because responsibilities overlap between executive positions, however, these contributions may be difficult to determine exactly. Although there may be pressure to expand the number of positions covered by a plan, coverage should be restricted to those positions that demonstrably contribute to organizational performance. Incentives for the executives who are not covered may be provided through merit raises or gainsharing plans.

BASES FOR EXECUTIVE SALARIES The levels of competitive salaries in the job market exert perhaps the greatest influence on executive base salaries. An organization's compensation committee—normally members of the board of directors—will order a salary survey to find out what executives earn in comparable enterprises. Comparisons may be based on organization size, sales volume, or

Paul Fireman of Reebok International was one of the highest-paid chief executives in 1989.

industry grouping. By analyzing the survey data, the committee can determine the equity of the compensation package outside the organization.

Job evaluation will allow the organization to establish internal equity between top managers and executives. For executives, the Hay profile method (see Chapter 10) is probably the most widely used method of job evaluation. Finally, base pay will be influenced by the performance of the executive. Most organizations evaluate their executives against a set of predetermined goals or objectives.

BASES FOR EXECUTIVE SHORT-TERM INCENTIVES Incentive bonuses for executives should be based on the contribution the individual makes to the organization. A variety of formulas have been developed for this purpose. Incentive bonuses may be based on a percentage of a company's total profits or a percentage of profits in excess of a specific return on stockholders' investments. Some formulas also seek to adjust the payments to reflect an organization's performance within the industry. In other instances the payments may be tied to an annual profit plan whereby the amount is determined by the extent to which an agreed-upon profit level is exceeded. Payments may also be based on performance ratings or the achievement of specific objectives established with the agreement of executives and the board of directors.[28]

Top corporate executives have the opportunity to earn large sums of money. Frequently, a significant part of their total compensation comes from incentive bonuses. When long-term compensation is added to annual base salary increases and bonuses, the total compensation of some executives may well reach into the millions of dollars. Highlights in HRM 2 shows the compensation received by the nation's 20 highest-paid executives in 1989.

PRO'S AND CONS OF EXECUTIVE BONUSES Are top executives worth the salaries and bonuses they receive? The answer may depend largely on whom you ask. Corporate compensation committees justify big bonuses as a way to reward superior performance. Other reasons for defending high levels of compensation include the following:

1. Executives are responsible for large amounts of capital.
2. Business competition is fierce and demanding.
3. Executive talent is in great demand.
4. Executives create shareholder wealth.[29]

Others justify high compensation as a "fact of business life" reflecting market compensation trends.

Nevertheless, strong criticism is heard regarding high salaries and bonuses awarded to senior executives. Some critics attack the size of incentive bonuses and the often vague criteria on which bonuses are based. Others point out that some executives receive record bonuses while their organizations are in financial trouble and employees are asked to make wage and benefits concessions. Large bonuses can also serve to raise prices, ultimately leading to inflation and higher unemployment.

HIGHLIGHTS IN HRM

2 THE 20 HIGHEST-PAID CHIEF EXECUTIVES...

		COMPANY	1989 SALARY AND BONUS	LONG-TERM COMPENSATION	TOTAL PAY
			(Thousands of dollars)		
1.	Craig O. McCaw	McCaw Cellular	$ 289	$53,655	$53,944
2.	Steven J. Ross	Time Warner	4,800	29,400	34,200
3.	Donald A. Pels	Lin Broadcasting	1,363	21,428	22,791
4.	Jim P. Manzi	Lotus Development	991	15,372	16,363
5.	Paul Fireman	Reebok International	14,606	—	14,606
6.	Ronald K. Richey	Torchmark	1,078	11,588	12,666
7.	Martin S. Davis	Paramount	4,095	7,540	11,635
8.	Roberto C. Goizueta	Coca-Cola	2,542	8,173	10,715
9.	Michael D. Eisner	Walt Disney	9,589	—	9,589
10.	August A. Busch III	Anheuser-Busch	1,464	7,397	8,861
11.	William G. McGowan	MCI	1,325	7,341	8,666
12.	James R. Moffett	Freeport McMoRan	1,350	5,950	7,300
13.	Donald E. Petersen	Ford Motor	3,050	4,097	7,147
14.	P. Roy Vagelos	Merck	2,340	4,423	6,764
15.	W. Michael Blumenthal	Unisys	725	5,786	6,511
16.	S. Parker Gilbert	Morgan Stanley	5,475	35	5,510
17.	Harry A. Merlo	Louisiana-Pacific	575	4,739	5,314
18.	Reuben Mark	Colgate-Palmolive	1,407	3,597	5,004
19.	Robert J. Pfeiffer	Alexander & Baldwin	1,467	3,476	4,943
20.	William P. Stiritz	Ralston Purina	1,064	3,790	4,854

SOURCE: From "Pay Stubs of the Rich and Corporate," *Business Week* (May 7, 1990): 57. Reprinted from May 7, 1990 issue of *Business Week* by special permission, copyright © 1990 by McGraw-Hill, Inc.

Another criticism of some executive incentive plans is that the time period for which executive performance is measured is often too short and the rewards are too large. This encourages executives to focus on short-term items such as quarterly earnings growth and to neglect longer-term items such as research and development and market share.[30] In the long run, therefore, stockholders may not receive a return equal to what they might have earned from other investments, and they might look for a better investment with a different organization.

FORM OF BONUS PAYMENT A bonus payment may take the form of cash or stock. Also, the timing of the payment may vary. Payment can be immediate (which is frequently the case), deferred for a short term, or deferred until retirement.[31]

Most organizations pay their short-term incentive bonuses in cash (in the form of a supplemental check), in keeping with their pay-for-performance philosophy. By providing a reward soon after the performance, and thus linking it to the effort on which it is based, they can use cash bonuses as a significant motivator. Cash payment also best serves those executives who must satisfy immediate financial needs. If the money is not needed right away, the executive can invest it elsewhere and receive a greater return than would otherwise be earned in a deferred plan.

USE OF DEFERRED BONUSES A deferred bonus can be used to provide the sole source of retirement benefits or to supplement a regular pension plan. If they are in a lower tax bracket when the deferred benefits are ultimately received—which is not always the case—executives can realize income tax savings. In addition, interest on the deferred amount can allow it to appreciate without being taxed until it is received. To the organization's advantage, deferred bonuses are not subject to the reporting requirement of the Employee Retirement Income Security Act (ERISA). Moreover, the organization can have the use of the money during this period. However, deferred income funds also become a part of the company's indebtedness—a part or all of which might be lost should the company become insolvent. If these funds do not appreciate with inflation, participants also stand to suffer a loss from inflation.

When an organization requires bonus payments to be deferred, the bonuses can provide the "golden handcuffs" with which to retain valuable executives. To receive the bonus, executives must remain with the organization for a certain number of years—frequently until retirement. However, such practices can work against an organization. Highly competent executives are likely to have other employers seeking their services promise to reimburse them for the loss of any bonus that the move might cause them to suffer. Thus, the golden handcuffs may allow the organization to retain only its less competent executives, who are unable to obtain such reimbursements. The recognition of this fact, together with competitive pressures to offer cash bonuses, is causing fewer organizations to require that executive bonuses be deferred.

Bases for Executive Long-Term Incentives

Short-term incentive bonuses are criticized for causing top executives to focus on quarterly profit goals to the detriment of long-term survival and growth objectives.[32] Emhart Corporation faced this problem when deciding whether to update and expand a profitable facility that manufactured industrial hardware. At one time, Emhart would have opted not to expand, since the executives making this decision received their incentive bonuses primarily on the basis of profit growth. Expansion of the hardware plant would not increase short-term profit growth and thus would cut into their bonuses. But Emhart revamped its compensation plan, deciding to link executive bonuses with the long-term price of stock. Consequently, according to Emhart Chairman T. Mitchell Ford, the company okayed the expansion. "The plan lets us manage with a long-term view of the business," said Sherman B. Carpenter, vice-president for administration.[33]

Sears, Combustion Engineering, and Borden, like Emhart, have adopted compensation plans that tie executive pay to long-term performance measures. Each of these organizations recognizes that, while incentive payments for executives may be based on the achievement of specific goals relating to their positions, the plans must also take into account the performance of the organization as a whole. Important to stockholders are such performance results as growth in earnings per share, return on stockholders' equity, and, ultimately, stock price appreciation. A variety of incentive plans, therefore, have been developed to tie rewards to these performance results, particularly over the long term.

Stock options are the primary long-term incentive offered to executives. The basic principle behind stock options is that executives should have a stake in the business so that they have the same perspective as owners—i.e., stockholders. The major long-term incentives fall into three broad categories:

1. Stock price appreciation grants
2. Restricted stock and restricted cash grants
3. Performance-based grants[34]

Each of these broad categories includes various stock grants or cash incentives for the payment of executive compensation; see Figure 11–5 for definitions of the different grant types. Often, as one observer notes, organizations "combine stock options with tandem stock appreciation rights plus performance-based grants to balance market performance and internal, strategic performance."[35] Interestingly, the use of long-term incentives as a part of total executive compensation has increased significantly—from 15 percent of organizations in 1978 to 42 percent in 1988.[36] The granting of stock options contributes substantially to executives' million-dollar compensation packages, as Highlights in HRM 2 demonstrated.

Executive Perquisites

In addition to incentive programs, executive personnel are often given special benefits and perquisites. **Perquisites,** or "perks," are a means of demonstrating the executives' importance to the organization while giving them an incentive to improve their performance. Furthermore, perks serve as a status symbol both inside and outside the organization. Perquisites can also provide a tax saving to executives, since some are not taxed as income. Some of the more common perquisites include assigned chauffeurs, country club memberships, special vacation policies, executive physical exams, use of an executive dining room, liability insurance, and financial counseling.[37]

FIGURE 11–5 DEFINITIONS OF TYPES OF LONG-TERM INCENTIVE PLANS

Stock Price Appreciation

Stock options. Rights granted to executives to purchase shares of their company's stock at a fixed price (usually market value at the time the option is granted) for a fixed period of time (most often ten years).

Stock appreciation rights (SARs). Rights attached to options that enable executives to receive direct payment for the related option's appreciation during the option term without exercising the option.

Stock purchases. Opportunities for executives to purchase shares of their company's stock valued at market at full value or a discount price, often with the company providing financing assistance.

Restricted Stock/Cash

Restricted stock. Grants to executives of stock or stock units subject to restrictions on transfer and risk of forfeiture until earned by continued employment.

Restricted cash. Grants of fixed-dollar amounts (not tied to stock price) subject to transfer and forfeiture restrictions until earned by continued employment.

Performance-Based

Performance shares/units. Grants of stock, stock units, or contingent cash amounts—the full payment of which is contingent upon the company's achieving certain long-term performance goals.

Formula-value grants. Rights to receive units or the gain in value of units determined by a formula rather than market value.

Dividend units. Rights to receive the equivalent of the dividends paid on a specified number of company shares.

SOURCE: Reprinted, by permission of the publisher, from "Long-Term Incentives for Management: An Overview," by George B. Paulin, *Compensation and Benefits Review* 21, no. 4 (July–August 1989): 38.

Compensating Overseas Managers and Executives

With the growth of multinational organizations, HR managers have had to develop compensation packages for managers and executives involved in overseas assignments. While those assigned to foreign positions may still participate in the traditional pay practices of their organizations—merit raises, bonuses, and stock options—they may also receive compensation payments unique to a post overseas. For example, managers and executives asked to go abroad are sometimes given a financial incentive to accept these assignments, to compensate them for any reluctance to relocate. Furthermore, they may be provided with supplemental living allowances to compensate for the high costs of overseas living. In addition, they are often provided with financial assistance covering such items as moving costs, storage payments, and children's educational expenses. Because of the importance of compensation to international HRM, we will elaborate on this topic in Chapter 19.

GAINSHARING INCENTIVE PLANS

The quest for greater productivity has led many organizations to implement a variety of gainsharing plans.[38] **Gainsharing plans** enable employees to share in the benefits of improved efficiency realized by the organization or major units within it. Many of these plans cover managers and executives as well as hourly workers. The plans encourage teamwork among all employees and reward them for their total contribution to the organization. Such features are particularly desirable when working conditions make individual performance difficult if not impossible to measure. One authority on productivity improvement and incentives defines gainsharing plans as

> programs designed to involve employees in improving productivity through more effective use of labor, capital, and raw materials. Both the employees and the company share the financial gains according to a predetermined formula that reflects improved productivity and profitability. The emphasis is upon group plans as opposed to individual incentives.[39]

The more common gainsharing plans include profit-sharing plans, the Scanlon and Rucker Plans, and Improshare.

Profit-Sharing Plans

Lincoln Electric has instituted a highly successful incentive program for its employees.

Probably no incentive plan has been the subject of more widespread interest, attention, and misunderstanding than profit sharing. **Profit sharing** is any procedure by which an employer pays, or makes available to all regular employees, special current or deferred sums based on the organization's profits. As defined here, profit sharing represents cash payments made to eligible employees at designated time periods, as distinct from profit sharing in the form of contributions to employee pension funds.

Profit-sharing plans are intended to give employees the opportunity to increase their earnings by contributing to the growth of their organization's profits. These contributions may be directed toward improving product quality, reducing operating costs, improving work methods, and building goodwill rather than just increasing rates of production. Profit sharing can help to stimulate employees to think and feel more like partners in the enterprise and thus to concern themselves with the welfare of the organization as a whole. Its purpose, therefore, is to motivate a total commitment from employees rather than simply to have them contribute in specific areas.[40]

A popular example of a highly successful profit-sharing plan is the one in use at Lincoln Electric Company, a manufacturer of arc welding equipment and supplies.

This plan was started in 1934 by J. F. Lincoln, president of the company. Each year the company distributes a large percentage of its profits to employees in accordance with their salary level and merit ratings. In recent years the annual bonus has ranged from a low of 55 percent to a high of 115 percent of annual wages.[41] In addition, Lincoln's program includes a piecework plan with a guarantee, cash awards for employee suggestions, a guarantee of employment for 30 hours of the 40-hour workweek, and an employee stock purchase plan.

The success of Lincoln Electric's incentive system depends on a high level of contribution by each employee. The performance evaluations employees receive twice a year are based on four factors—dependability, quality, output, and ideas and cooperation. There is a high degree of respect among employees and management for Lincoln's organizational goals and for the profit-sharing program.

VARIATIONS IN PROFIT-SHARING PLANS Profit-sharing plans differ in the proportion of profits shared with employees and in the distribution and form of payment. The amount shared with employees may range from 5 to 50 percent of the net profit. In most plans, however, about 20 to 25 percent of the net profit is shared. Profit distributions may be made to all employees on an equal basis, or they may be based on regular salaries or some formula that takes into account seniority and/or merit. The payments may be disbursed in cash, deferred, or made on the basis of combining the two forms of payment.

REQUIREMENTS FOR SUCCESSFUL PROFIT-SHARING PLANS Most authorities in the field agree that to have a successful profit-sharing program, an organization must first have a sound HR program, good labor relations, and the trust and confidence of its employees. Profit sharing thus is a refinement of a good HR program and a supplement to an adequate wage scale rather than a substitute for either one. As with all incentive plans, it is the underlying philosophy of management, rather than the mechanics of the plan, that may determine its success. Particularly important to the success of a profit-sharing plan are the provisions that enable employees to participate in decisions affecting their jobs and their performance.

WEAKNESSES OF PROFIT-SHARING PLANS In spite of their potential advantages, profit-sharing plans are also prone to certain weaknesses. The profits shared with employees may be the result of inventory speculation, climatic factors, economic conditions, national emergencies, or other factors over which employees have no control. Conversely, losses may occur during years when employee contributions have been at a maximum.[42] The fact that profit-sharing payments are made only once a year or deferred until retirement may reduce their motivational value. If a plan fails to pay off for several years in a row, this can have an adverse effect on productivity and employee morale.

Scanlon and Rucker Plans

To provide employees with bonuses that encourage maximum effort and cooperation but are not tied to profit fluctuation, two unique plans have been developed. These plans, which bear the names of their originators, Joe Scanlon and Alan W. Rucker, are similar in their philosophy. Both plans emphasize participative management. Both encourage cost reduction by sharing with employees any savings resulting from these reductions. The formulas on which the bonuses are based, however, are somewhat different.

THE SCANLON PLAN The philosophy behind the **Scanlon Plan** is that employees should offer ideas and suggestions to improve productivity and, in turn, be rewarded for their constructive efforts. The plan requires good management, leadership, trust and respect between employees and managers, and a work force dedicated to responsible decision making. When correctly implemented, the Scanlon Plan can result in improved efficiency and profitability for the organization and steady employment and high compensation for employees.

According to one of Scanlon's associates, effective employee participation, which includes the use of committees on which employees are represented, is the most significant feature of the Scanlon Plan.[43] This gives employees the opportunity to communicate their ideas and opinions and to exercise some degree of influence over decisions affecting their work and their welfare within the organization. Employees have an opportunity to become managers of their time and energy, equipment usage, the quality and quantity of their production, and other factors relating to their work. They accept changes in production methods more readily and volunteer new ideas. The Scanlon Plan encourages greater teamwork and sharing of knowledge at the lower levels.[44] It demands more efficient management and better planning as workers try to reduce overtime and to work smarter rather than harder or faster.

The primary mechanisms for employee participation in the Scanlon Plan are the shop committees established in each department (see Figure 11–6 for an illustration of the Scanlon Plan suggestion process). These committees consider production problems and make suggestions for improvement within their respective departments to an organization-wide screening committee. The function of the screening committee is to oversee the operation of the plan, to act on suggestions received from the shop committees, and to review the data on which monthly bonuses are to be based. The screening committee is also responsible for consulting with and advising top management, which retains decision-making authority. Both the shop committees and the screening committee are composed of equal numbers of employees and managers.

Financial incentives under the Scanlon Plan are ordinarily offered to all employees (a significant feature of the plan) on the basis of an established formula. This formula is based on increases in employee productivity as determined by a norm that has been established for labor costs. The norm, which is subject to review, reflects

FIGURE 11–6 SCANLON PLAN SUGGESTION PROCESS

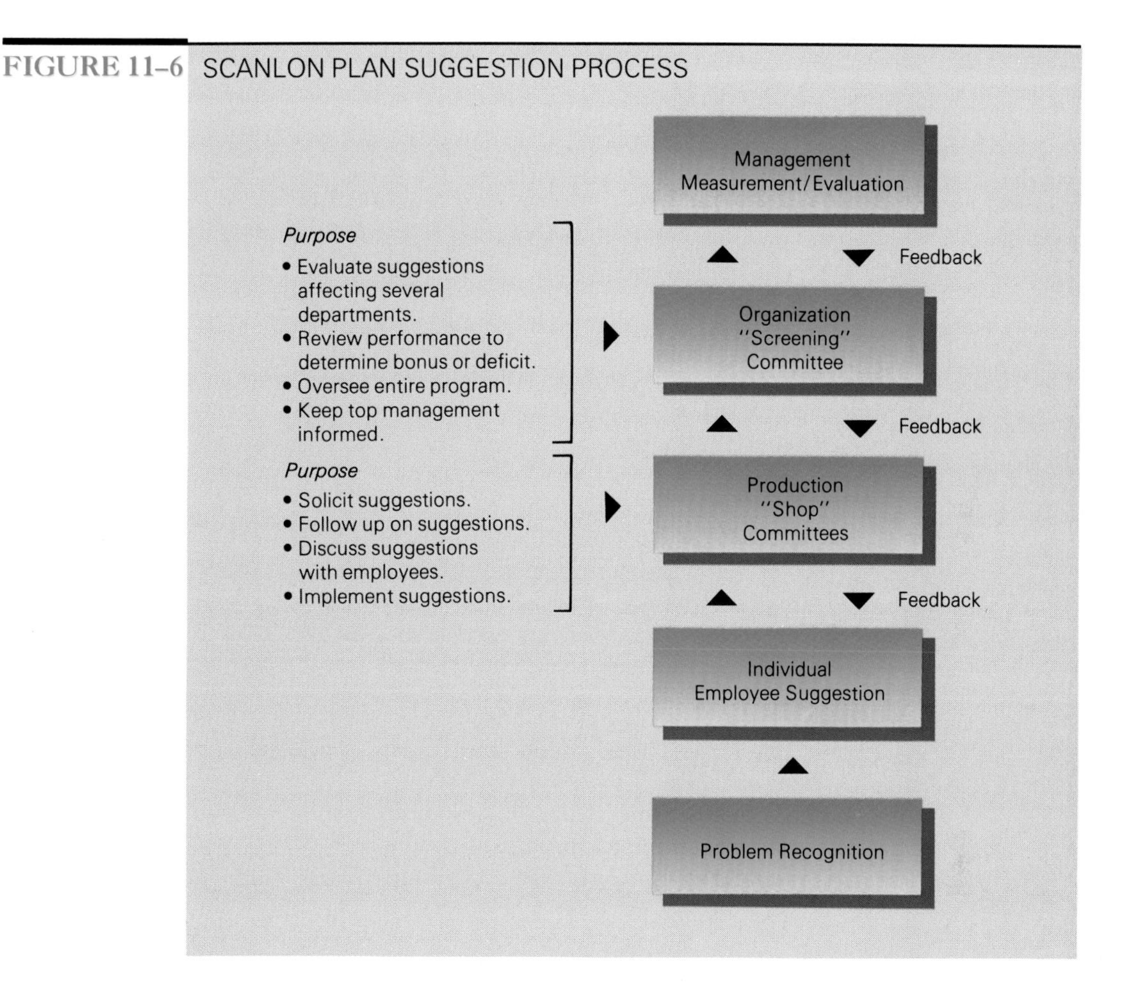

the relationship between labor costs and the sales value of production (SVOP). The SVOP includes sales revenue and the value of goods in inventory. Figure 11–7 illustrates how the two figures are used to determine the Scanlon Plan incentive bonus.

The plan also provides for the establishment of a reserve fund into which 25 percent of any earned bonus is paid to cover deficits during the months when labor costs exceed the norm. After the reserve portion has been deducted, the remainder of the bonus is distributed, with 25 percent going to the organization and 75 percent to the employees. At the end of the year, any surplus that has been accumulated in the reserve fund is distributed to employees according to the same formula.

The Scanlon Plan (and variations of it) has become a fundamental way of managing, if not a way of life, in organizations such as American Value Company, TRW, and Weyerhaeuser. The Trans-Matic Manufacturing Company uses a Scanlon program based on the following three objectives:

FIGURE 11–7 DETERMINING THE SCANLON PLAN INCENTIVE BONUS

1990 ANNUAL BASE YEAR FIGURES

Sales value of production (SVOP)		=	$15,000,000
Total wage bill		=	$ 4,750,000

$$\frac{\text{Total wage bill}}{\text{SVOP}} \quad \text{(Norm)} \quad = \frac{4{,}750{,}000}{15{,}000{,}000}$$
$$= 0.316 = 31.6\%$$

CURRENT PRODUCTION MONTH

SVOP		$1,600,000
Allowable wage bill	.316 × $1,600,000 =	$505,600
Monthly wage bill		$ 450,000
Labor cost savings		$ 55,600
Scanlon Plan bonus available for distribution		$ 55,600

SOURCE: Adapted from George T. Milkovich and Jerry M. Newman, *Compensation,* 3d ed. (Homewood, IL: BPI/Irwin, 1990), 347. Used with permission.

1. To provide a clearly defined participative management system within the organization.
2. To facilitate the sharing of responsibility for improved productivity by everyone in the company.
3. To offer all employees the opportunity to earn a bonus based on company performance.

The Scanlon Plan at Trans-Matic pays a bonus on profits above 12 percent. These profits are split 50-50 between employees and the company. Bonuses are paid quarterly and are distributed as a percentage of each employee's compensation.[45]

THE RUCKER PLAN The share of production plan (SOP), or **Rucker Plan,** normally covers just production workers but may be expanded to cover all employees. As with the Scanlon Plan, committees are formed to elicit and evaluate employee suggestions. The Rucker Plan, however, uses a far less elaborate participatory structure. As one authority noted, "It commonly represents a type of program that is used as an alternative to the Scanlon Plan in firms attempting to move from a traditional style of management toward a higher level of employee involvement."[46]

The financial incentive of the Rucker Plan is based on the historic relationship between the total earnings of hourly employees and the production value that employees create. The bonus is based on any improvement in this relationship that employees are able to realize. Thus, for every 1 percent increase in production value that is achieved, workers receive a bonus of 1 percent of their total payroll costs.[47]

LESSONS FROM THE SCANLON AND RUCKER PLANS Perhaps the most important lesson to be learned from the Scanlon and Rucker plans is that any management expecting to gain the cooperation of its employees in improving efficiency must permit them to become involved psychologically as well as financially in the organization. If employees are to contribute maximum effort, they must have a feeling of involvement and identification with their organization, which does not come out of the traditional manager–subordinate relationship. Consequently, it is important for organizations to realize that while employee cooperation is essential to the successful administration of the Scanlon and Rucker plans, the plans themselves do not necessarily stimulate this cooperation.

The attitude of management is of paramount importance to the success of either plan. For example, where managers show little confidence and trust in their employees, the plans tend to fail. HR managers further note that Scanlon and Rucker plans are successful when the following are true:

- Bonus formulas are clearly understood and can be reviewed by employees.
- Management is highly committed to making the plan succeed.
- Adequate training is given to both employees and supervisors.
- Adequate potential exists for employee rewards.[48]

Like any other incentive plan, the Scanlon and Rucker plans are no better than the organizational environment in which they are used.

Improshare

Improshare—improved productivity through sharing—is a gainsharing program developed by Mitchell Fain, an industrial engineer with experience in traditional individual incentive systems. Whereas individual production bonuses are typically based on how much an employee produces above some standard amount, Improshare bonuses are based on the overall productivity of the *work group*. Improshare output is measured by the number of finished products that a work group produces in a given period. Both production (direct) employees and nonproduction (indirect) employees are included in the determination of the bonus.[49] Since a cooperative environment benefits all, Improshare promotes increased interaction and support between employees and management.

The bonus is based not on dollar savings, as in the Scanlon and Rucker plans, but on productivity gains that result from reducing the time it takes to produce a finished product. Bonuses are determined monthly by calculating the difference between standard hours (Improshare hours) and actual hours, and dividing the result by actual hours. The employees and the company each receive payment for 50 percent of the improvement. Companies such as Hinderliter Energy Equipment Corporation pay the bonus as a separate check to emphasize that it is extra income.

Stock Ownership

Stock ownership plans for employees have existed in some organizations for many years. These programs are sometimes implemented as part of an employee benefit plan. However, organizations that offer stock ownership programs to employees do so with the belief that there is some incentive value to the systems. By allowing employees to purchase stock, the organization hopes they will increase their productivity and thus cause the stock price to rise.

Not uncommon are plans for purchasing stock on an installment basis through payroll deductions and without the payment of brokerage fees. Over the years, the stock of some of the larger blue-chip companies such as Sears, General Telephone and Electronic, Warner Communications, and Ralston Purina has proved to be a good investment for their employees. Furthermore, stock ownership programs have become a popular way to salvage a failing organization, thereby saving employee jobs.

Employee Stock Ownership Plans (ESOPs)

Employee stock ownership plans (ESOPs) grew steadily during the 1980s, adding 600 to 800 new plans a year covering a total of 500,000 to 1 million employees.[50] The Chicago Tribune Company, Southwest Airlines, Roadway Services, and Cincinnati Bell are organizations with recently established ESOPs. Companies such as Weirton Steel and Hyatt Clark Industries have been rescued by ESOP-financed employee buyouts, and Polaroid and Chevron have used ESOPs to fight hostile takeover bids.[51] ESOPs can be used to generate funds used to purchase an organization's stock that is available to outside raiders.

These Chevron employees own part of their company through an ESOP plan.

Employee stock ownership plans take two primary forms—a stock bonus plan and a leveraged plan. With either plan, the public or private employer establishes an ESOP trust that qualifies as a tax-exempt employee trust under Section 401(a) of the Internal Revenue Code. With a stock bonus plan, each year the organization gives stock to the ESOP or gives cash to the ESOP to buy outstanding stock. The ESOP holds the stock for employees, and they are routinely informed of the value of their accounts. Stock allocations can be based on employee wages or seniority. When employees leave the organization or retire, they can sell their stock back to the organization, or they can sell it on the open market if it is traded publicly. Leveraged ESOPs work in much the same way as stock bonus plans, except that the ESOP borrows money from a bank or other financial institution to purchase stock. The organization then makes annual tax-deductible payments to the ESOP, which in turn repays the lending institution. Organizations may also use the stock placed in an ESOP trust as collateral for a bank loan. As the loan is repaid, the stock used as collateral is allocated to employee accounts. Payments of both the principal and interest can be deducted from the organization's income tax liability.

ADVANTAGES OF ESOPs Encouraged by favorable federal income tax provisions, employers utilize ESOPs as a means of providing retirement benefits for their employees. Favorable tax incentives permit a portion of earnings to be excluded from taxation if that portion is assigned to employees in the form of shares of stock.[52] Therefore, employers can provide retirement benefits for their employees at relatively low cost because stock contributions are in effect subsidized by the federal government.[53] ESOPs can also increase employees' pride of ownership in the organization, providing an incentive for them to increase productivity and help the organization prosper and grow. Enthusiastic promoters of ESOPs go so far as to claim that these plans will make U.S. organizations more competitive in world markets. The plans, they maintain, will increase productivity, improve employee–management relations, and promote economic justice.[54]

PROBLEMS WITH ESOPs Generally, ESOPs are more likely to serve their intended purposes in publicly held companies than in closely held ones. A major problem with the closely held company is its potential inability to buy back the stock of employees when they retire. Unfortunately, these employees do not have the alternative of disposing of their stock on the open market. Requiring organizations to establish a sinking fund to be used exclusively for repurchasing stock could eliminate this problem.

Another criticism of ESOPs is that they cost the country a tremendous amount in lost taxes. If Congress determines that employers are abusing ESOP advantages, or if national budget pressures intensify, it could change the tax rules. A growing problem with ESOPs is that as more retirement income comes from these plans, the more dependent a pensioner becomes on the price of company stock. Future retirees are vulnerable to stock market fluctuations as well as to management mistakes. Finally, although studies show that productivity improves when ESOPs are implemented, these gains are not guaranteed. ESOPs help little unless managers are willing to involve employees in organizational decision making. Unfortunately, ESOPs are sometimes set up in ways that restrict employee decision making and expose the ESOP to risk, though providing investors with large potential gains.

SUMMARY

In an effort to tie the pay of employees more closely to their performance, a variety of financial incentive plans are in use today. The success of a particular plan often depends more on the organizational climate in which it must operate, employee confidence in it, and its suitability to organizational needs than on the mechanics of the plan. Most important, employees must view their incentive pay as being equitable and related to their performance.

A variety of financial incentive plans have been developed to motivate nonmanagement employees working in different types and levels of jobs. These plans differ in terms of the areas of performance they are intended to motivate, the criteria by which performance is measured, and the form in which rewards are paid to employees. Incentive payments may be based on individual or group performance or on the organization's overall performance. The performance of the organization may be measured in terms of earnings, profits, return on stockholder investment, or the market performance of its stock.

Incentive plans at the executive level provide for bonus payments on either a cash or a deferred basis. Bonuses may also be in the form of either stock or options to purchase stock.

Gainsharing plans, particularly those covering personnel below the executive level, are becoming quite prevalent. Favorable tax concessions offered to employers have spurred the growth of employee stock ownership plans. While these plans have some motivational value, they serve primarily to provide employees with a source of retirement benefits. However, these plans may pose some disadvantage to future retirees if the price of the stock in their accounts should fall.

DISCUSSION QUESTIONS

1. A company that paid its production employees entirely on a piece-rate system pointed with pride to the fact that it permitted its employees "to go into business for themselves." To what extent do you feel this claim is true or untrue?
2. The standard time for producing one unit of a product is 4 minutes. What would the piece rate per unit be if the rate for this particular type of work was $3 an hour?
3. Suggest ways in which the motivating value of merit raises may be increased.
4. What are the reasons for the different payment methods for sales personnel?
5. What are some of the primary objectives of financial incentive plans for managers, and how do these plans differ from those for nonmanagement personnel?
6. What are some of the advantages and disadvantages to employees of a deferred, as opposed to a cash, bonus plan?

7. What are the reasons for the success of the Scanlon and Rucker plans?
8. What are some of the reasons for the rapid growth of ESOPs? Cite some of the potential problems concerning their use.

MINI-CASE 11–1 Financial Incentive for Nurses

In January 1984, the Samaritan Memorial Hospital implemented a formal performance appraisal program for its 78 staff nurses. The program originally met with some resistance from a few nurses and supervisors, but generally the system was welcomed as an objective way to appraise nursing performance. Nursing supervisors are required to appraise employee performance annually and to forward to the HR department a copy of each appraisal form.

In July 1986, Thomas Tittle, HR manager for the hospital, reviewed all nurses' appraisals on file since the beginning of the program. From this study he concluded that the large majority (82 percent) of nurses were evaluated as performing at an "average level," as indicated by a global rating at the bottom of the form. As a response to this finding, Mr. Tittle decided to base the annual raise for all nurses on the consumer price index for the hospital's metropolitan area. This, he concluded, would allow the nurses to maintain their standard of living while guaranteeing all nurses a yearly raise. For the past three years, nurses have received their annual wage increase according to this policy.

As part of the hospital's employee involvement program, Mr. Tittle holds quarterly meetings with groups of employees to solicit their feelings regarding hospital policy and their jobs. Both positive and negative opinions are expressed at these gatherings. These opinions are used to change or modify hospital policy. At meetings in the past year, a number of both junior and senior nurses have expressed dissatisfaction with the "across-the-board" pay policy for annual raises. The biggest complaint concerns the lack of motivation to increase output, since all nurses are paid the same regardless of individual performance. These comments have been numerous enough that Mr. Tittle has considered changing the nurses' compensation policy. During the past seven months, nine of the better nurses have quit to take jobs with area hospitals that award annual increases on a merit or pay-for-performance basis.

QUESTIONS

1. What are the advantages of adopting a merit pay plan for hospital nurses? Are there any disadvantages of starting a merit pay program?
2. What problems might arise with supervisors' appraisals of nurses?

MINI-CASE 11–2 Employee Ownership at Whitman Corporation

Effective January 1, 1989, Whitman Corporation, formerly IC Industries, implemented a corporate restructuring plan. Karl D. Bays, the firm's CEO and chairman, noted that "empowerment of employees" was the motivating force behind the restructuring effort.

A quality-improvement program that Bays calls "organized common sense" was begun to increase productivity and efficiency. The results of this effort have been a marked change in employee attitudes and a shortened production cycle time, from 19 days to 11 days, after a series of group meetings at the company's St. Louis plant.

Whitman Corporation combined the quality-improvement program with an ESOP. This move encouraged employees to develop personal responsibility and an entrepreneurial spirit, qualities required for global competitiveness. The ESOP granted about 15 percent of the publicly traded company stock to approximately 5,000 active salaried employees—up from just under 2 percent previously held just by managers. Whitman is considering ways of extending corporate ownership to its 20,000 unionized hourly employees.

The ESOP investment is $500 million in convertible preferred stock allocated to individual employee accounts over a 12-year period. Employees are fully vested (guaranteed their accrued benefits) after five years of service. Under provisions of the ESOP, the value of the stock will be guaranteed not to fall below 20 percent of annual compensation. There is no upper limit to share value. The ESOP will replace the corporate pension and retiree medical plan for active employees. Retired employees will continue to receive the company's traditional pension and medical benefits program.

SOURCE: Adapted from "Executive Praise Plans as Key to Entrepreneurship, Competitiveness." Reprinted with permission from *BNA's Employee Relations Weekly* 7, no. 43 (October 30, 1989): 1359–1360. Copyright 1989 by The Bureau of National Affairs, Inc.

QUESTIONS

1. Discuss several advantages of the ESOP as established by the Whitman Corporation.
2. Explain why the company would eliminate the retiree medical plan as part of granting the ESOP.

NOTES AND REFERENCES

1. "Worker Incentives Proliferate. Now Let's See Them Work," *Wall Street Journal* (December 12, 1989): 1.

2. Ibid.

3. Richard L. Bunning, "Rewarding a Job Well Done," *Personnel Administrator* 34, no. 1 (January 1989): 60–63.

4. George T. Milkovich and Jerry M. Newman, *Compensation*, 3d ed. (Homewood, IL: BPI/Irwin, 1990), 325–326.

5. Victoria A. Hoevemeyer, "Performance-based Compensation: Miracle or Waste?" *Personnel Journal* 68, no. 7 (July 1989): 64.

6. Robert E. Sibson, *Increasing Employee Productivity* (New York: AMACOM, 1976), 170–185. See also Gary W. Florkowski, "Analyzing Group Incentive Plans," *HR Magazine* 35, no. 1 (January 1990): 36–38.

7. "Worker Incentives Proliferate."

8. This study is reported in William E. Buhl, "Compensation Management in Practice: Keeping Incentives Simple for Nonexempt Employees," *Compensation and Benefits Review* 21, no. 2 (March–April 1989): 14.

9. Robert D. Pritchard, Philip L. Roth, Patricia Galgay Roth, Margaret D. Watson, and Steven D. Jones, "Incentive Systems: Success by Design," *Personnel* 66, no. 5 (May 1989): 63–68.

10. Daniel C. Rowland and Bob Green, "Incentive Pay: Productivity's Own Reward," *Personnel Journal* 66, no. 3 (March 1987): 48–57.

11. Graef S. Crystal, "To the Rescue of Pay for Performance," *Personnel* 62, no. 1 (January 1985): 8–11.

12. E. James Brennan, "The Myth and the Reality of Pay for Performance," *Personnel Journal* 64, no. 3 (March 1985): 73–75.

13. Pritchard et al., 66.

14. Bob Cohn, "A Glimpse of the 'Flex' Future," *Newsweek* (August 1, 1988): 38.

15. David W. Belcher and Thomas J. Atchinson, *Compensation Administration*, 2d ed. (Englewood Cliffs, NJ: Prentice-Hall, 1987), 285. See also James E. Nickel and Sandra O'Neal, "Small Group Incentives: Gain Sharing in the Microcosm," *Compensation and Benefits Review* 22, no. 2 (March–April 1990): 22–29.

16. Milkovich and Newman, 341.

17. American Productivity Center, Houston, Texas, Case Study 20: Potlatch Corporation, 1981.

18. Frederick S. Hills, K. Dow Scott, Steven E. Markham, and Michael J. West, "Merit Pay: Just or Unjust Desserts," *Personnel Administrator* 32, no. 9 (September 1987): 53.

19. John F. Sullivan, "The Future of Merit Pay Programs," *Compensation and Benefits Review* 20, no. 3 (May–June 1988): 23.

20. Barry L. Wisdom, "Before Implementing a Merit System . . . Know the Environments and Situations That Demand Caution," *Personnel Administrator* 34, no. 10 (October 1989): 46–49.

21. Robert L. McGinty and John Hanke, "Compensation Management in Practice: Merit Pay Plans—Are They Truly Tied to Performance?" *Compensation and Benefits Review* 21, no. 5 (September–October 1989): 12–16.

22. Poonoi Varadarajan and Charles Futrell, "Factors Affecting Perceptions of Smallest Meaningful Pay Increase," *Industrial Relations* 23, no. 2 (Spring 1984): 278–285.

23. Suzanne L. Minken, "Does Lump-Sum Pay Merit Attention?" *Personnel Journal* 67, no. 6 (June 1988): 77–78.

24. To promote higher sales efforts, organizations may also offer special cash incentives and noncash incentives such as merchandise, travel awards, and status and recognition awards. One study showed that the majority of responding organizations use noncash incentives in addition to their standard compensation plan. See Jerry McAdams, "Rewarding Sales and Marketing Performance," *Personnel* 64, no. 10 (October 1987): 8–16; and Alfred J. Candrilli, "Success Through a Quality-based Sales Incentive Program," *Compensation and Benefits Review* 22, no. 5 (September–October 1990): 54–59.

25. Matt S. Walton III, "How to Draft a Sales Compensation Plan," *Personnel* 62, no. 6 (June 1985): 71–74.

26. John S. Rogers and Robert J. Davenport, Jr., "Designing Effective Sales Incentives," in *Handbook of Wage and Salary Administration*, 2d ed., ed. Milton L. Rock (New York: McGraw-Hill, 1984), Chapter 29, 1–12.

27. Paul S. Bradley, "Justify Executive Bonuses to the Board," *Personnel Journal* 67, no. 9 (September 1988): 120.

28. Graef S. Crystal, "Executive Compensation: Challenges in the Year Ahead," *Personnel* 65, no. 1 (January 1988): 34.

29. Louis J. Brindisi, Jr., "The Compelling Case for Executive Compensation," *Management Review* 77, no. 3 (March 1988): 61.

30. Sheldon Friedman, "The Compelling Case for Cutting Executive Compensation," *Management Review* 77, no. 3 (March 1988): 61–62. See also "It's Not How Much You Pay CEOs: But How," *Wall Street Journal* (May 17, 1990): A16.

31. Leonard R. Burgess, *Compensation Administration*, 2d ed. (Columbus, OH: Merrill, 1989), 343.

32. Jane R. Goodson, Gail W. McGee, and Peter M. Ginter, "Stock Options," *Personnel Administrator* 33, no. 8 (August 1988): 71–75.

33. "Rewarding Executives for Taking the Long View," *Business Week* (April 1, 1984): 99–100. See also Jeffrey M. Kanter and Matthew P. Ward, "Long-Term Incentives for Management, Part 4," *Compensation and Benefits Review* 22, no. 1 (January–February 1990): 36–49.

34. George B. Paulin, "Long-Term Incentives for Management: An Overview," *Compensation and Benefits Review* 21, no. 4 (July–August 1989): 37. See also Lawrence C. Bickford and Leslie A. Lucania, "Long-Term Incentives for Management, Part 6: Plan Administration and Grant Usage," *Compensation and Benefits Review* 22, no. 3 (May–June 1990): 56–67.

35. Paulin, 38.

36. Amanda Bennett, "A Great Leap Forward for Executive Pay," *Wall Street Journal* (April 24, 1989): B1.

37. Milton Moskowitz, "Companies That Put Perks in Every Pot," *Business and Society Review*, no 69 (Spring 1989): 26–29.

38. Thomas Rollins, "Productivity-based Group Incentive Plans: Powerful, but Use with Caution," *Compensation and Benefits Review* 21, no. 3 (May–June 1989): 39–50. See also Kevin M. Paulsen, "Gain Sharing: A Group Motivator," *Management World* 18, no. 3 (May–June 1989): 23–25.

39. Carla S. O'Dell, *Gainsharing: Involvement, Incentives, and Productivity* (New York: AMACOM, 1981), 8. See also Larry L. Hatcher and Timothy L. Ross, "Organizational Development Through Productivity Gainsharing," *Personnel* 62, no. 10 (October 1985): 42–50.

40. Theresa M. Welbourne and Luis R. Gomez-Mejia, "Gainsharing Revisited," *Compensation and Benefits Review* 20, no. 4 (July–August 1988): 19–28.

41. Richard I. Henderson, *Compensation Management: Rewarding Performance*, 5th ed. (Englewood Cliffs, NJ: Prentice-Hall, 1989), 353. Lincoln Electric's profits are divided three ways. The company retains a certain portion for capital improvements and financial security. Stockholders receive a dividend of approximately 6 to 8 percent of book value of company stock. Employees receive their year-end bonus based on all remaining profits.

42. Edward Ost, "Gain Sharing's Potential," *Personnel Administrator* 34, no. 7 (July 1989): 94.

43. Linda S. Tyler and Bob Fisher, "The Scanlon Concept: A Philosophy As Much As a System," *Personnel Administrator* 29, no 7 (July 1983): 33–37.

44. Frederick G. Lesieur, *The Scanlon Plan: A Frontier in Labor-Management Cooperation* (Cambridge, MA: M.I.T. Press, 1975), 30.

45. American Productivity Center, Houston, Texas, Case Study 19: Trans-Matic Manufacturing Company, 1981.

46. Ost, 92.

47. The Rucker Plan uses a somewhat more complex formula for determining employee bonuses. For a detailed example of the Rucker bonus, see Milkovich and Newman, 346.

48. Jeffrey C. Ewing, "Gainsharing Plans: Two Key Factors," *Compensation and Benefits Review* 21, no. 1 (January–February 1989): 49–53. See also Barry W. Thomas and Madeline Hess Olson, "Gain Sharing: The Design Guarantees Success," *Personnel Journal* 67, no. 5 (May 1988): 73–79.

49. The basis of Improshare's measurement system is the base productivity factor (BPF), which is the ratio of standard direct labor hours produced to total actual hours worked in a base period. The productivity of subsequent periods is then measured by enlarging standard direct labor hours earned by the BPF ratio to establish Improshare hours (IH). The IH is then compared with actual hours worked in the same period. If earned hours exceeded actual hours, 50 percent of the gain is divided by actual hours worked in order to establish a bonus percentage for all employees in the plan.

50. Corey Rosen, "Forum," *Employee Relations Weekly* 7 (Bureau of National Affairs, July 31, 1989): 975.

51. "How to Keep Raiders at Bay—on the Cheap," *Business Week* (January 29, 1990): 59.

52. Edward M. Bixler, "ESOPs: Seven Myths Dispelled," *Compensation and Benefits Review* 21, no. 2 (March–April 1989): 31–37.

53. "ESOPs: Are They Good for You?" *Business Week* (May 15, 1989): 116.

54. Corey Rosen, "Using ESOPs to Boost Corporate Performance," *Management Review* 7, no. 3 (March 1988): 30–34. See also William Smith, Harold Lazarus, and Harold Murray Kalkstein, "Employee Stock Ownership Plans: Motivation and Morale Issues," *Compensation and Benefits Review* 22, no. 5 (September–October 1990): 37–47.

CHAPTER 12

Employee Benefits

After reading this chapter you will be able to:

1. *Explain the growth of employee benefits and the changing philosophy regarding them.*
2. *Outline the requirements for a sound benefits program.*
3. *Identify the categories and relative costs of employee benefits.*
4. *Describe the major types of pension plan funding.*
5. *Explain the effects of social and economic conditions as well as federal legislation on pension programs.*
6. *List the various types of service benefits that employers typically provide.*
7. *Discuss the recent trends in retirement policies and retirement programs.*
8. *Define the key terms in the chapter.*

TERMS TO IDENTIFY

total compensation *(380)*

flexible benefit plans (or cafeteria plans, self-designated plans, employee choice plans) *(384)*

Employment Retirement Income Security Act (ERISA) *(385)*

Consolidated Omnibus Budget Reconciliation Act of 1986 (COBRA) *(388)*

contributory plan *(391)*

noncontributory plan *(391)*

defined-benefit plan *(392)*

defined-contribution plan *(392)*

vesting *(393)*

unemployment insurance benefits *(397)*

supplemental unemployment benefits (SUBs) *(398)*

workers' compensation insurance *(398)*

health maintenance organization (HMO) *(401)*

preferred provider organization (PPO) *(401)*

employee assistance program (EAP) *(404)*

elder care *(406)*

silver handshake *(410)*

In the previous chapter we discussed the different types of incentive compensation plans that organizations use to motivate employees. As we noted, some of those plans provide for deferred payment of compensation, thereby serving as a source of retirement income. Because this deferment reduces the incentive value of these compensation plans, some companies classify profit sharing, stock ownership, and similar deferred incentive plans as *employee benefits plans*. Whether or not they offer these particular plans, virtually all employers provide a variety of benefits to supplement the cash payments of wages or salaries to their employees. These benefits, some of which are required by law, must be considered a part of their total compensation. Like the money that goes directly into the paycheck, employee benefits are a growing labor cost. This is why some organizations now use the term **total compensation** to emphasize that employee benefits are part of an employee's actual income.

In this chapter we will examine the characteristics of employee benefits programs, the major benefits that employers offer, the types of services provided, and the kinds of retirement programs in use.

EMPLOYEE BENEFITS PROGRAMS

Employee benefits constitute an indirect form of compensation that is intended to improve the quality of work life for an organization's labor force. In return, employers generally expect employees to be loyal to the organization and to be productive. Since employees have come to expect an increasing number of benefits, the motivational value of these benefits depends on how the benefits program is designed and communicated. Once viewed as a gift from the employer, benefits are now considered rights to which all employees are entitled, and have become one of the fastest-growing areas of employment law and litigation. This trend has required many employers to have a professionally staffed division in the HR department to develop and manage a wide variety of benefits and services.

Growth of Employee Benefits

Not until the 1920s were employee benefits offered by more than just a few employers. Because these benefits were supplemental to the paycheck and were of minor value, they were referred to initially as *fringe benefits*. From this rather meager beginning, benefits programs have expanded in terms of both the types of benefits offered and their cost.

FACTORS CONTRIBUTING TO GROWTH Initially, employee benefits were introduced by some employers to promote and reward employee loyalty and to discourage unionization. The paternalistic belief that employees were incapable of providing for their personal welfare and managing their private affairs was another reason for offering certain benefits. In either case, the benefits were provided in a spirit of benevolence without much input from the recipients.

As unions acquired power during the 1930s, their leaders were able to use collective bargaining to obtain additional benefits along with higher wages. During World War II, a wage freeze further stimulated the growth of employee benefits. Wishing to retain their employees but prohibited by the freeze from raising wages, employers provided special inducements in the form of nonwage supplements such as pensions, paid vacations, sick leave, and health and life insurance. Most employers then found themselves obligated to continue these benefits after the war because employees were unwilling to give them up.

When the war ended, so did the wage freeze, and union leaders concentrated their efforts on obtaining wage increases. As the cost of living began to level off around 1948, union wage demands began to meet with public disfavor. However, the public still generally accepted that employees should have better standards of health and welfare than they were enjoying. Thus, employee benefits became a bargaining goal that the unions could pursue realistically. Interpretations by the National Labor Relations Board and the Supreme Court to the effect that employers were obligated to bargain for pensions were also major factors stimulating the growth of these particular benefits. Demands for supplemental unemployment insurance, company-paid medical insurance, and other benefits were soon to follow. Another factor in the growth of employee benefits was the exemption from personal income tax on benefits paid for by the employer.

BENEFITS VERSUS RIGHTS With the growth of employee benefits came a change in the concept of what actually constitutes a benefit. Such items as food services, parking, and counseling, once considered to be fringe benefits, are regarded by most employers today as an integral part of the HR compensation package. Furthermore, employees no longer view benefits as something being given to them, but rather as earned compensation. Past union successes in bargaining for more benefits and the exemption of these benefits from income tax served to encourage the expansion of benefits programs. However, as benefits provide a larger share of an employee's total compensation and as some of them are being made taxable, they may be growing less attractive than cash compensation.

It is difficult to predict specifically what employees in the future will expect in the way of benefits. Despite the threat of increased taxation, the long-term growth of employee benefits over several decades has maintained most of its momentum. Prominent among newer benefits are corporate-sponsored diet programs, health club memberships, child care, preretirement assistance, personal financial counseling, and others to be discussed later.[1]

Requirements for a Sound Benefits Program

Too often a particular benefit is provided because other employers are doing it, because someone in authority believes it is a good idea, or because there is union pressure. However, the contributions that benefits will make to the HR program will depend on how much attention is paid to certain basic considerations.

ESTABLISHING SPECIFIC OBJECTIVES Like any other component of the HR program, an employee benefits program should be based on specific objectives. The objectives an organization establishes will depend on many factors, including size, location, degree of unionization, profitability, and industry patterns. Most important, these aims must be compatible with the philosophy and policies of the organization. The chief objectives of most benefits programs are to improve employee satisfaction, to meet employee health and security requirements, to attract and motivate employees, to reduce turnover, to keep the union out, and to maintain a favorable competitive position. Further, these objectives must be considered within the framework of cost containment—a major issue in today's programs.[2]

Unless an organization has a flexible benefits plan (to be discussed later), an optimum combination or mix of benefits should be developed into a package. This involves careful consideration of the various benefits that can be offered, the relative preference shown for each benefit by management and the employees, the estimated cost of each benefit, and the total amount of money available for the entire benefits package.

ALLOWING FOR EMPLOYEE INPUT Before a new benefit is introduced, the need for it should first be determined through consultation with employees. Many organizations establish committees composed of managers and employees to administer, interpret, and oversee their benefits policies.[3] Opinion surveys are also used to obtain employee input. Having employees participate in designing benefits programs helps to ensure that management is moving in the direction of satisfying employee wants. It also provides a basis for exchanging information about any problems associated with the benefits.

MODIFYING EMPLOYEE BENEFITS To serve their intended purpose, employee benefits programs must reflect the changes that are continually occurring within our society. Particularly significant are changes in the composition and life-styles of the work force. These changes make it necessary to develop new types of benefits to meet shifting needs. Traditionally, employee benefits were designed to suit the "typical employee." Not long ago there *was* a typical employee—a middle-aged man who worked full time, supported 2.5 children, and had a wife who stayed at home. Today the vast majority of employees are anything but typical.[4] For example, as we indicated in Chapter 2, the number of women in the work force is continuing to grow. Which benefits are most valuable to them (and to men) will be

Society has changed dramatically to include a much broader spectrum of life-styles than the once "typical" work force did.

determined largely by whether they have dependent children and whether they have a spouse who has benefit coverage.

Many benefits plans create an environment of disincentives for the young and healthy, limiting the organization's ability to attract and retain such employees. For example, many employers provide extra compensation in the form of dependent coverage to their workers with families, but the principle of equal pay for equal work suggests that all employees doing the same job should receive the same total compensation regardless of family status. Similarly, the employer's contribution to the pension plan for a 30-year-old employee is approximately one-fourth the contribution for a 50-year-old employee for the same amount of pension commencing at age 65. This difference discriminates against the younger worker, although legally it is not regarded as discriminatory.[5] These examples illustrate the need for benefits programs that take into account the differing needs of a variety of workers in order to attract a highly capable work force.

PROVIDING FOR FLEXIBILITY To accommodate the individual needs of employees, there is a trend toward **flexible benefits plans,** also known as **cafeteria plans, self-designated plans,** or **employee choice plans.** These plans enable individual employees to choose the benefits that are best suited to their particular needs. They also prevent certain benefits from being wasted on employees who have no need for them. Typically, employees are offered a basic or core benefits package of life and health insurance, sick leave, and vacation, plus a specified number of credits they may use to "buy" whatever other benefits they need. Thus, rather than choosing a child care plan as an additional benefit, some employees may prefer to use their credits to select vacations, personal holidays, or thrift plans. The three most common flexible features are life insurance, dental care, and a choice of two or more basic health plans. Employees generally consider the medical plan their most important option.[6]

The Educational Testing Service, one of the pioneers in flexible benefits, began a program in 1974 tailored to the individual needs of its 2,500 employees. In 1978, American Can introduced a sophisticated flexible benefits program that even today gives its employees the greatest degree of choice of any work force in the country.[7] Satisfaction with employee benefits at American Can was found to be 50 to 100 percent higher than that of a national sample of employers with traditional benefits plans. One author observes that "by accommodating the diverse life-styles of their employees, they attract and keep good workers, lift company morale, and wring more efficiency out of every dollar spent on benefits."[8]

The ability of flexible benefits plans to manage costs and increase the level of employee satisfaction has stimulated interest in this kind of program. Yet in a 1989 survey of 943 firms, the Foster Higgins benefits consulting organization found only 23 percent of employers offering flexible plans. A since-repealed nondiscrimination rule and other IRS proposals slowed progress, according to Foster Higgins. However, an additional 28 percent of respondents plan to start new programs, with cost-cutting as their chief motive.[9]

Benefits programs must be flexible enough to accommodate the constant flow of new legislation and IRS regulations that affect them. A number of benefits consulting firms are available to help HR managers keep up with changes in all phases of the programs they oversee. There is also an abundance of computer software for processing employee benefits records that incorporates the latest legislative and regulatory changes.

COMMUNICATING EMPLOYEE BENEFITS INFORMATION

The true measure of a successful benefits program is the degree of trust, understanding, and appreciation it earns from the employees. In communicating with employees about benefits, employers should clarify information about complicated insurance and pension plans so that there will be no misunderstanding about what the plans will and will not provide.

The communication of employee benefits information was aided significantly by the passage of the **Employee Retirement Income Security Act (ERISA)** in 1974. The Act requires that employees be informed about their pension and certain other benefits in a manner calculated to be understood by the average employee. A widely used method of communication is in-house publications, including employee benefits handbooks and organization newsletters. To ensure that employees are familiar with the benefits program, benefits administrators should be allowed sufficient time in new hire orientation and other training classes to present information regarding benefits and to answer questions.[10]

In addition to having general information, it is important for each employee to have a current statement of the status of her or his benefits. A popular means is the personalized computer-generated statement of benefits. As Highlights in HRM 1 shows, this statement can be one of the best ways of slicing through a maze of benefit technicalities to provide concise data to employees about the status of their personal benefits.[11] Coopers & Lybrand offers a Benefits Information Line that allows employers to provide employees with instant access to a wide variety of benefits and HR information from any touch-tone telephone. Individual account information is available upon entering a personal identification number. Some employers summarize benefit information on a paycheck stub as a reminder to employees of their total compensation.

Computerized data also enable management to keep accurate records of the cost of each benefit for purposes of maintaining a cost-effective program. To assist employers with the administrative and communication functions, the International Foundation of Employee Benefit Plans in Brookfield, Wisconsin, maintains an extensive library of employee benefits publications. It also prepares publications on this subject. The foundation has developed an on-line database that members can use to get immediate, comprehensive responses to questions about employee benefits. In co-sponsorship with the Wharton School at the University of Pennsylvania and with Dalhousie University in Canada, the foundation offers a college-level program leading to the Certified Employee Benefit Specialist (CEBS) designation. Over 30,000 individuals are now pursuing this certification.[12]

HIGHLIGHTS IN HRM

1 PERSONALIZED STATEMENT OF BENEFITS

Highlights of Your Neles-Jamesbury, Inc. Benefits Program

This report is based on various Company records as of January 1, 1990. Please notify Human Resources if any of the following data is incorrect:

Date of Birth: 1/16/51
Date of Hire: 12/12/83
Social Security Number: 123-45-6789

Individually prepared for:

J. J. DOE
NELES-JAMESBURY
640 LINCOLN STREET
WORCESTER, MA 01615

Dear Neles-Jamesbury Employee:

It is our pleasure to provide you with this personalized 1990 statement of benefits.

Neles-Jamesbury's benefit plans are an important part of your total compensation. They help provide for the financial security of you and your family both now and in the future.

After reading this statement, we hope you will better understand and appreciate the importance of your benefits package, and that you will share this information with your family.

You are an important part of Neles-Jamesbury. Our benefits program is just one more way in which we can express our appreciation for your continuing contributions toward the goals of our company.

Sincerely,

Daniel L. DeSantis

Daniel L. DeSantis
President and Chief Executive Officer

Health Care

Hospital Benefits
All of our medical plans pay the following benefits for you and your family:

100% of eligible expenses for semi-private room and board, hospital expenses and covered physicians' services.

100% of eligible maternity benefits including covered physicians' services for normal delivery, Caesarian section, or miscarriage.

Please consult your medical plan comparison booklet for more details on the Health Care options available to you and the services they provide.

After retirement, at age 65, you may choose personal coverage for yourself under Medex III or the Fallon Senior Plan.

Non-Hospital Benefits
100% of eligible office visits, laboratory, and x-ray services, minus $2 to $5 co-pay charges.

100% of eligible outpatient psychiatric services, minus $2 to $5 co-pay charges up to a maximum of $500 per person per calendar year.

100% of eligible therapy visits, minus $2 to $25 co-pay charges.

100% of eligible prescription drugs, minus $1 to $4 co-pay charges.

YOU HAVE FAMILY COVERAGE
WITH BLUE CROSS/BLUE SHIELD.

Dental Insurance
The Plan pays 70% of expenses for covered services up to a $750 calendar year maximum for employees.

Survivors' Security

Lump Sum Benefits
In the event of your death while an active employee, your beneficiaries may receive the following payments:

$50,000	Basic Group Life Insurance
N/A	Supplemental Life Insurance
$13,855	Thrift-Investment Plan
$255	Social Security for an eligible dependent

In addition, if death were due to an accident, your beneficiaries might also receive:

$50,000	Basic Accident Insurance
N/A	Supplemental Accident Insurance

If death should occur as a result of an accident while traveling on Company business, your survivors may also receive an additional amount of Business Travel Accident Insurance.

Are your beneficiary designations up to date?

Monthly Income Payments
Social Security survivors' benefits are payable to unmarried dependent children under 18, surviving spouses caring for children under 16, and widows or widowers over age 60. Presently, these benefits are estimated to be:

$682	for each eligible child under 18
$682	for a spouse caring for children under 16
$650	for a spouse, age 60
$1,592	is the maximum monthly benefit per family

Post Retirement Benefits
After you retire from the Company, $2,000 of Life Insurance Coverage is continued at no cost to you.

Dependent Life and Accident Insurance

YOU HAVE $50,000 LIFE COVERAGE
FOR YOUR SPOUSE.

IF YOU PURCHASE SUPPLEMENTAL ACCIDENT INSURANCE, YOU MAY ALSO INSURE YOUR SPOUSE AND CHILDREN BY ELECTING THE FAMILY PLAN.

Sickness and Disability Benefits

Short Term Disability

IF YOU ARE ILL OR INJURED AND UNABLE TO WORK, YOU ARE ELIGIBLE FOR FULL PAY FOR UP TO 13 WEEKS. IF YOU ARE STILL UNABLE TO WORK AFTER 13 WEEKS, YOU WILL BE PAID 75% OF YOUR REGULAR PAY FOR UP TO 13 ADDITIONAL WEEKS.

Long Term Disability

If you remain disabled beyond 26 weeks, you will be eligible to receive $2,777 monthly from the Long Term Disability Plan until you are able to return to work in some capacity or to age 65, whichever occurs first.

This benefit would be reduced by the amount of other sources of income for which you are eligible such as Social Security.

In the event of your total disability you would be eligible to receive the balance of your Thrift-Investment Account in a lump sum.

Employee Thrift-Investment Plan

You are eligible to participate in the Thrift-Investment Plan on the first day of the month following your date of employment.

You may elect to contribute from 1%-15% of your base pay to the Thrift-Investment Plan allowing you to save for your short or long term goals.

Tax Savings Account

Contributions to the Tax Savings Account are limited to 1%-12% of your base pay and are made with pre-tax dollars. These contributions will reduce your current taxable income while providing for long term savings. (Withdrawals from this account are not allowed until age 59½.)

Thrift Account

Contributions to the Thrift Account are limited to 1%-12% of your base pay and are made with after-tax dollars. Withdrawals from this account can be made at the end of any quarter. Distribution takes place approximately 6 to 8 weeks after the end of each quarter.

Matching Company Contributions

The Company adds $.50 to your account for every $1 you save up to the first 6% of your pay.

As of January 1, 1990 $13,855 is the value of your Thrift-Investment Account.

Please refer to your quarterly Thrift-Investment statements for a more detailed explanation of your account.

Your Future Security

Projected Retirement Income

Your Normal Retirement Date (at age 65) is 02/01/2016.

At that time, based on your current salary and assuming continuous service until retirement, you would be eligible for an estimated monthly income of:

$3,394	from the Retirement Plan
$850	from Social Security
$4,244	estimated total monthly retirement income at age 65

If you choose to retire earlier (at age 62) we estimate the following payments:

$2,279	from the Retirement Plan
$877	from Social Security
$3,156	estimated total monthly retirement income at age 62

Vesting

Effective December 1, 1989, participants in the Retirement Plan will become vested after 5 years of service. Prior to this amendment, the service requirement for vesting was ten years.

Social Security

In addition to your benefit shown to the left, your spouse may also qualify for monthly Social Security based on either his or her own working career, or for being your dependent. This estimated benefit would be $425 starting at age 65.

Employee Thrift-Investment Plan

If you are a participant in the Thrift-Investment Plan, you may receive your account balance at retirement in either a lump sum or installments. If you elect the installment method, we will assist you in arranging a tax-deferred annuity.

Your Benefits Cost

In addition to the benefits described above, there are other valuable benefits you enjoy as an employee of Neles-Jamesbury, such as paid Vacation and Holidays, Sick/Emergency pay, Bereavement pay, Workers' Compensation, Unemployment Insurance, Bonus Plan, Tuition Reimbursement/Advancement, and Recreational programs.

You and your family have available the security and protection provided by the benefits described above:

$13,544	is the total estimated annual cost of your benefits program.
$2,270	is your cost including $2,088 for Social Security.
$11,274	is the balance paid by Neles-Jamesbury to provide these benefits.

SOURCE: Jamesbury Corp. and Godwins Inc. Reproduced with permission.

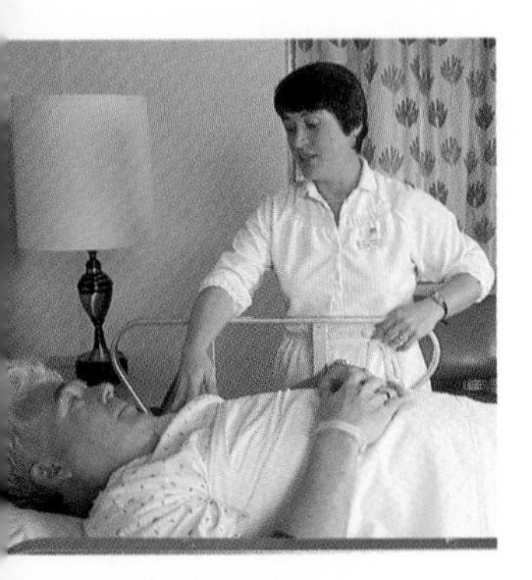

COBRA assures employees of continued medical coverage at the organizational rate upon termination of their employment.

Concerns of Management

Managing an employee benefits program requires close attention to the many forces that must be kept in balance if the program is to succeed. In attempting to have a program that provides the optimum benefits for each individual, management must consider union demands, the benefits other employers are offering, tax consequences, costs, and legal ramifications. We will briefly examine the last two concerns.

RISING COSTS According to a 1988 U.S. Chamber of Commerce study of 932 companies, the costs of employee benefits in that year averaged 37 percent of payroll. The average distribution of these benefits was $10,750 per employee per year. Costs varied widely among industries, and larger firms tended to pay higher benefits than smaller firms. Costs of benefits were higher in manufacturing than in nonmanufacturing industries.[13] Figure 12–1 provides a detailed description of benefits categories and a breakdown of the 1988 percentage by category.

CONTROLLING COSTS Since many benefits represent a fixed rather than a variable cost, management must decide whether or not it can afford this cost under less favorable economic conditions. It is generally recognized that if an organization is forced to discontinue a benefit, the negative effects of cutting it may outweigh any positive effects that may have accrued from providing it.

Besides the actual costs of employee benefits, there are costs of administering them. The federal reporting requirements under ERISA require a considerable amount of paperwork for employers. In addition, new requirements, such as those mandated by the **Consolidated Omnibus Budget Reconciliation Act of 1986 (COBRA),** now require employers to make health coverage—at the same rate the employer would pay—available to employees, their spouses, and their dependents upon termination of employment, death, or divorce. Thus, former employees and their families benefit by paying a lower premium for health coverage than is available to individual policyholders.

SALLY FORTH. Reprinted with special permission of North America Syndicate.

FIGURE 12–1 EMPLOYEE BENEFIT COSTS

TYPES OF BENEFITS	TOTAL PERCENTAGE, ALL COMPANIES
Payments for vacations, sick leave, holidays, etc.	10.6
Legally required payments	8.9
Medical and medically related benefit payments	8.7
Retirement and savings (employer's share)	5.0
Paid rest periods, lunch periods, etc.	2.3
Miscellaneous benefits	0.9
Life insurance and death benefits (employer's share)	0.6
Total employee benefits as percent of payroll	37.0

SOURCE: Adapted from *Employee Benefits, 1988* (Washington, DC: U.S. Chamber of Commerce, 1989), 5. Reprinted with the permission of the Chamber of Commerce of the United States from *Employee Benefits* © 1989.

To meet this requirement, employers have to establish procedures to collect premiums and to keep track of former employees, their spouses, and their dependents. Because of government intrusion in benefits, one consultant writes that the following shifts could occur in employee benefits:

- Retrenchment in employer-sponsored plans.
- Government mandating of private plans and a growing conflict with flexible benefits plans.
- Government control over benefits and the providers of benefits services.
- Increased government-imposed rigidity in benefits.
- Increased provision of benefits by government, possibly including a national health plan.

He advises employers to stay informed about legislative developments and to be prepared to communicate their concerns to Congress.[14]

The cost of health care benefits has long been of concern to all employers. The employer's share of private health insurance premiums has been increasing every year. As shown in Figure 12–2, the cost of the average annual health plan per employee went from $1,645 in 1984 to $2,748 in 1989. Saving money on health care is important, but employers must be careful to recognize the importance of health care plans to their workers. According to one consultant, "Employees are willing to go on strike rather than have their health benefits reduced."[15] Competitive alternatives to traditional health care appear to be the fastest-growing sector of the health care market. We will discuss some of these alternatives later, in the context of health care benefits.

FIGURE 12–2 HEALTH PLAN COSTS CLIMB

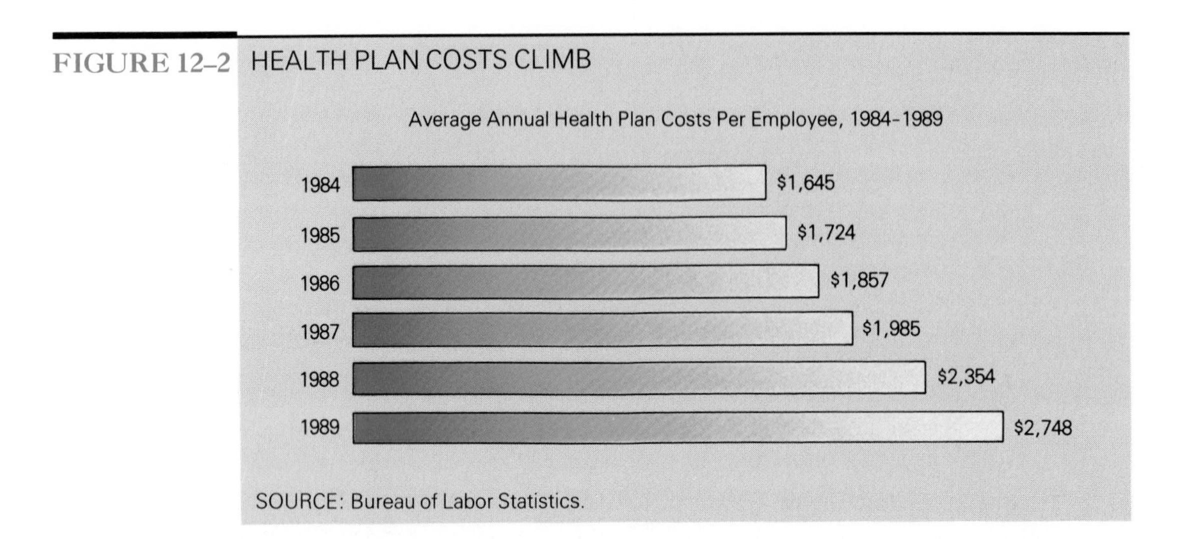

SOURCE: Bureau of Labor Statistics.

LEGAL CONCERNS Benefits can become a source of union grievances, employee complaints, even legal actions. Food services, parking, and similar facilities can become a magnet for complaints. An extreme example may be lawsuits by employees over injuries in organization-sponsored recreational activities and during or following organizational social functions.

Benefits can also be a source of discrimination complaints. For example, the EEOC ruled that it is unlawful for an employer to make benefits available to the wives and families of male employees where the same benefits are not made available to the husbands and families of female employees. Subsequently, in 1983, the Supreme Court ruled in *Newport News Shipbuilding and Drydock Company* v. *EEOC* that employers must treat male and female employees equally in providing health insurance for their spouses. As noted in Chapter 3, the Pregnancy Discrimination Act of 1978 requires that employers must give pregnant workers the same group health insurance or disability benefits they give other workers with medical conditions or disabilities. As a result of these and other laws and court decisions, inequities that often gave rise to grievances and legal actions have been eliminated.

MAJOR EMPLOYEE BENEFITS

Employee benefits may be categorized in different ways. In the preceding section we saw the categories of benefits that have been used by the U.S. Chamber of Commerce in studies of benefits since 1951. In the discussion that follows, we will use a somewhat different but compatible grouping of benefits to highlight the important issues and trends in managing an employee benefits program.

Pension Plans

Employer-sponsored pension plans have existed since 1875, when the first-known plan was initiated by the American Express Company. A few years later, the Baltimore & Ohio Railroad developed a pension plan for its employees. Other railroads followed suit, until the majority of workers in this industry were covered by some form of plan. Personnel in the civil and military services of the federal government were also among the first groups to receive pension benefits.

Originally, pensions were based on a *reward philosophy,* which viewed pensions primarily as a way to retain personnel by rewarding them for staying with the organization until they retired. Those employees who quit or who were terminated before retirement were not considered deserving of such rewards. Because of the vesting requirements negotiated into most union contracts and more recently required by law, pensions are now based on an *earnings philosophy*. This philosophy regards a pension as deferred income that employees accumulate during their working lives and that belongs to them after a specified number of years of service, whether or not they remain with the employer until retirement. The earnings philosophy was supported by the 1948 U.S. Court of Appeals (7th Circuit) decision in *Inland Steel Company* v. *NLRB*, upheld by the Supreme Court in 1949.

Since the passage of the Social Security Act in 1935, pension plans have been used to supplement the floor of protection provided by social security. The majority of private pension plans and a significant number of public plans integrate their benefits with social security benefits.

The decision whether or not to offer a pension plan is up to the employer. Only 46 percent of the nation's privately employed, full-time workers are currently covered by a private pension plan—a drop of 4 percent since 1979. For younger workers the drop is much sharper. In 1979, 46 percent of men under age 35 were covered by employer-financed pension plans, whereas in 1988 only 37 percent were covered, in large part because they were not finding unionized manufacturing jobs anymore and were forced into industries where pensions are scarce. Young women, on the other hand, have about the same coverage today as they did in 1979. Only 40 million of the 76 million workers these plans cover have their pensions insured by the federal government's Pension Benefit Guaranty Corporation. Pensions in offices or shops with fewer than 25 employees are not insured by the government.[16]

TYPES OF PENSION PLANS There are two major ways to categorize pension plans: (1) according to contributions made by the employer, and (2) according to the amount of pension benefits to be paid. In a **contributory plan,** contributions to a pension plan are made jointly by employees and employers. In a **noncontributory plan,** the contributions are made solely by the employer. Most of the plans existing in industry are of the noncontributory type, whereas those in government are of the contributory type.

When pension plans are classified by the amount of pension benefits to be paid, there are two basic types: the defined-benefit plan and the defined-contribution plan. Under a **defined-benefit plan,** the amount an employee is to receive upon retirement is specifically set forth. This amount may be based on such factors as the employee's years of service, average earnings during a specific period of time, and age at time of retirement. While a variety of formulas exist for determining pension benefits, the one used most often is based on the employee's average earnings (usually over a three- to five-year period immediately preceding retirement), multiplied by the number of years of service with the organization.

The **defined-contribution plan** establishes the basis on which an employer will contribute to the pension fund. The contributions may be made through profit sharing, thrift plans, employer-sponsored Individual Retirement Accounts (IRAs), and various other means. The amount of benefits employees are to receive upon retirement is then determined by the funds accumulated in their behalf at the time of retirement and what retirement benefits these funds will purchase. These plans, however, do not offer the benefit-security predictability that is highly desirable to employees; although even under defined-benefit plans, retired employees may not receive the benefits promised them if the plan has not been adequately funded.

More employers are pulling back from using defined-benefit plans, with their fixed payouts, in favor of defined-contribution plans. Fewer than 70 percent of U.S. employees in pension plans in 1990 had defined-benefit coverage, compared with 80 percent in 1980. Defined-benefit plans have become less popular with employers because they cost more and because they require compliance with complicated government rules.[17]

While there have been great strides made in expanding pension coverage, employees in small businesses (fewer than 100 employees) and highly mobile workers still find it difficult to qualify for a pension. A plan known as the salary reduction plan, or 401(k) plan—after section 401(k) of the Internal Revenue Code—offers employees an opportunity to save through payroll deduction and to have their contributions matched by the employer. Employees' taxable income is reduced, and they pay no income taxes on these funds until after retirement. For the majority of such plans, full vesting either is immediate or comes within five years. Once vested, participants can roll over their account into a qualified plan such as an IRA. Primarily because of the widespread employee participation in 401(k) plans and the resulting decrease in tax revenues, the Tax Reform Act of 1986 substantially reduced the maximum permissible annual 401(k) deferral and established greater restrictions on the proportion of "highly compensated employees" in an organization who could participate.[18]

FEDERAL REGULATION OF PENSION PLANS Private pension plans are subject to federal regulations under ERISA. Although the Act does not require employers to establish a pension plan, it provides certain standards and controls for pension plans. It requires minimum funding standards to ensure that benefits will be available when an employee retires. It also requires that the soundness of the actuarial assumptions on which the funding is based be certified by an actuary at least every three years. Of special concern to the individual employee is the matter of vesting.

Vesting is a guarantee of accrued benefits to participants at retirement age regardless of their employment status at that time. Vested benefits that have been earned by an employee cannot be revoked by an employer. Under ERISA, all pension plans must provide that employees will have vested rights in their accrued benefits after certain minimum requirements have been met.

Legislation passed since ERISA has changed the vesting rules. The Tax Equity and Fiscal Responsibility Act of 1982 (TEFRA) introduced the concept of a top-heavy plan and provided for accelerated vesting for such plans. A top-heavy plan is one in which, as of the "determination date," the present value of the accrued benefits of "key employees" exceeds 60 percent of the present value of the benefits accrued to all employees. The Tax Reform Act of 1986 provided for employees to be able to become vested sooner, and its provisions were generally effective for plan years beginning after December 31, 1988. The general vesting provisions and top-heavy vesting provisions are shown in Figure 12–3.

FIGURE 12–3 VESTING PROVISIONS (GENERAL AND TOP-HEAVY PLANS)

General Provisions*

1. *5-Year Vesting:* An employee must receive nonforfeitable rights after five years of service to all accrued benefits derived from employer contributions.
2. *3- to 7-Year Vesting:* An employee must receive nonforfeitable rights after three years of service to 20 percent of accrued benefits derived from employer contributions. Nonforfeitable rights increase 20 percent each year until the employee is 100 percent vested in the employer-derived accrued benefits after seven years of service.
3. *Multiemployer Plans:* An employee covered pursuant to a collective bargaining agreement must receive nonforfeitable rights after ten years of service to all accrued benefits derived from employer contributions.

Top-Heavy Vesting**

1. *3-Year Vesting:* An employee must receive nonforfeitable rights after three years of service to all accrued benefits derived from employer contributions.
2. *6-Year Graded Vesting:* An employee must receive nonforfeitable rights after two years of service to 20 percent of accrued benefits derived from employer contributions. Nonforfeitable rights increase 20 percent each year until the employee is 100 percent vested in the employer-derived accrued benefit after six years of service.

*Internal Revenue Code, Section 411(a).
**Internal Revenue Code, Section 416(b).

Three government agencies administer ERISA: the Internal Revenue Service (IRS), the Department of Labor (DOL), and the Pension Benefit Guaranty Corporation (PBGC). The IRS is concerned primarily with qualified retirement plans—those that offer employers and employees favorable income tax treatment under a special section of the tax law. The DOL's main responsibility is to protect participants' rights. The PBGC ensures that if a plan is terminated, *guaranteed* benefits are paid to participants. The PBGC is supported by premiums paid by employers.[19] It has become apparent, however, that employer contributions are inadequate to cover the increased use of Chapter 11 bankruptcy, which passes pension liabilities of organizations on to the PBGC.

In 1984 the Retirement Equity Act (REA) amended ERISA. REA is intended to provide greater equity under private pension plans for workers and their spouses by taking into account changes in work patterns, the status of marriage as an economic partnership, and the substantial contributions made by both spouses. All qualified pension plans are affected by the Act, which brought major changes in eligibility and vesting provisions, parental leave, spouse survivor benefits, assignments of benefits in divorce cases, and other areas.[20] Where employees decline to elect survivors' benefits, employers are required to inform prospective beneficiaries of this fact.

The Tax Equity and Fiscal Responsibility Act of 1982 (TEFRA) did not have as much impact as ERISA, but it did impose many restrictions and benefits and establish rules for group life insurance and medical plans. The Deficit Reduction Act of 1984 (DEFRA) has had a significant impact on employee benefits, such as pension and group insurance plans, in determining what is taxable and nontaxable to employees.[21]

PENSION PORTABILITY A weakness in most private pension plans of the past was that they lacked the portability to enable employees who changed employment to maintain equity in a single pension. Before ERISA, unions had sought to address this problem by encouraging the development of multiemployer plans that cover the employees of two or more unrelated organizations in accordance with a collective bargaining agreement. Such plans are governed by employer and union representatives who constitute the plan's board of trustees. Multiemployer plans tend to be found in industries where the typical company has too few employees to justify an individual plan. They are also found more frequently in industries where there is seasonal or irregular employment. The manufacturing industries where these plans commonly exist include apparel, printing, furniture, leather, and metalworking. They are common in such nonmanufacturing industries as mining, construction, services, entertainment, communications, and public utilities.

Employees also have the opportunity to establish their own IRAs as a source of retirement benefits. In the past, Congress had encouraged the use of IRAs by permitting an employee to shelter from income tax the amount contributed to an IRA up to an annual maximum of $2,000, or $2,250 where the employee's spouse was not employed outside the home. The Tax Reform Act of 1986 curtailed or eliminated deductible IRA contributions for highly compensated employees covered by employer-sponsored pension plans.

PENSION FUNDS Pension funds may be administered through either a trusteed or an insured plan. In a trusteed pension plan, pension contributions are placed in a trust fund. The investment and administration of the fund are handled by trustees appointed by the employer or, if the employees are unionized, by either the employer or the union. Contributions to an insured pension plan are used to purchase insurance annuities. The responsibility for administering these funds rests with the insurance company providing the annuities.

Pension funds constitute the largest pool of investible capital in the world, with $2.6 trillion in assets. They have made possible the stock market boom of the 1980s and the explosion of hostile takeovers, management buyouts, employee stock ownership plans, and investments using venture capital. According to one estimate, pension plans have $600 million more than they will need to pay retirees. More than 80 percent of pension plans are overfunded.[22] In spite of the present surplus of pension funds, one cannot be complacent about the future. Social security will be stretched thin as baby boomers age, and pensions will be vulnerable to poorly performing investments. It should also be noted that the pension funds of some organizations are not adequate to cover their obligations. This has been most apparent in the steel industry. Such deficiencies present legal and ethical problems that must be addressed.

Current pension fund difficulties have been caused in part by the fact that the wages on which pensions are based today drastically exceed the wages on which pension fund contributions were based in earlier years. Furthermore, those drawing pensions are also exceeding the life expectancies on which their pension benefits were calculated.

While fund managers are supposed to invest funds where the return will be most profitable, employees have demanded a greater voice in determining where pension funds will be invested. There is also a movement to have more pension funds diverted to investments that employees consider "socially desirable," such as in home mortgages, health centers, child care centers, hospitals, and similar investments in areas where members live.

Any policy of investing in socially desirable projects must give consideration to the provisions of ERISA. The Act requires that fiduciaries (fund managers) act solely in the interest of the participants and beneficiaries—for the exclusive purpose of providing benefits. It does, however, permit a consideration of incidental features of investments, provided they are equal in economic terms.

PROBLEMS WITH PENSION PROGRAMS Two significant types of problems are associated with the pension benefits themselves. One is related to inflation, and the other has its basis in sex discrimination.

The purchasing power that pension benefits provide is continually being eroded by inflation. What might have been an adequate retirement annuity 20 years ago, for example, very likely would be inadequate in terms of today's living costs. Employers, therefore, are finding themselves under employee and union, as well as societal, pressure to provide supplemental benefits to workers who retired a few years ago and whose pensions are now inadequate. Many employers have granted periodic increases in the absence of a provision for indexing pensions to some cost-of-living standard.

As in other areas of HRM, sex discrimination has become an issue that must be addressed in the area of pension benefits. This issue stems from the actuarial reality that life expectancy after retirement age, on average, is greater for women than for men. Therefore, the cost of providing the same pension benefits is greater for women than for men. Similarly, an equal amount of money in a pension fund at the time of retirement will provide smaller pension payments for a woman than for a man of the same age. In the landmark *Arizona* v. *Norris* decision in 1983, the Supreme Court ruled that women and men must be paid equal pension benefits for equal contributions, thus overturning the traditional practice of paying women smaller benefits based on their longer life expectancy.[23]

Employee Benefits Required by Law

Legally required employee benefits constitute nearly a quarter of the benefits package that employers provide. These benefits include employer contributions to social security, unemployment insurance, workers' compensation insurance, and state disability insurance.

This Amtrak employee is exempted from social security benefits, but is covered by the Railroad Retirement Act.

SOCIAL SECURITY INSURANCE Passed in 1935, the Social Security Act provides an insurance plan designed to indemnify covered individuals against loss of earnings resulting from various causes. These causes may include retirement, unemployment, disability, or, in the case of dependents, the death of the person supporting them. Thus, as with any type of casualty insurance, social security does not pay off except in the case where a loss of income is actually incurred through loss of employment.

To be eligible for old-age and survivors' insurance (OASI) as well as disability and unemployment insurance under the Social Security Act, an individual must have been engaged in employment covered by the Act. Most employment in private enterprise, most types of self-employment, active military service after 1956, and employment in certain nonprofit organizations and governmental agencies are subject to coverage under the Act.[24] Railroad workers and civil service employees who are covered by their own systems and some occupational groups, under certain conditions, are exempted from the Act.[25]

The social security program is supported by means of a tax levied against an employee's earnings that must be matched by the employer in each pay period. Social security taxes collected from employers and employees are used to pay three major types of benefits: (1) old-age insurance benefits, (2) disability benefits, and (3) survivors' insurance benefits. Because of the continual changes that result from legislation and administrative rulings, as well as the complexities of making determinations of an individual's rights under social security, we will describe these benefits only in general terms.

To qualify for old-age insurance benefits, a person must have reached retirement age and be fully insured. A *fully insured person* is one who has earned 40 credits (a maximum of four credits a year for ten years, based on annual earnings of $2,000 or more). Having enough credits to be fully insured makes one eligible for retirement benefits, but it does not determine the amount. The amount of monthly social security retirement benefits is based on earnings, adjusted for inflation, over the years an individual is covered by social security.

To receive old-age insurance benefits, covered individuals must also meet the *retirement earnings test.* Persons under 70 years of age cannot be earning more than the established annual exempt amount through gainful employment without a reduction in benefits. This limitation on earnings does not include income from sources other than gainful employment, such as investments or pensions.

Social security retirement benefits consist of those benefits which individuals are entitled to receive in their own behalf, called the primary insurance amount (PIA), plus supplemental benefits for eligible dependents. These benefits can be determined from a prepared table. There are also both minimum and maximum limits to the amount that individuals and their dependents can receive.

The social security program provides disability benefits to workers too severely disabled to engage in "substantial gainful work." To be eligible for such benefits, however, an individual's disability must have existed for at least 6 months and must be expected to continue for at least 12 months or be expected to result in death. After receiving disability payments for 24 months, a disabled person receives Medicare protection. Those eligible for disability benefits, furthermore, must have worked under social security long enough and recently enough before becoming disabled. Disability benefits, which include auxiliary benefits for dependents, are computed on the same basis as retirement benefits and are converted to retirement benefits when the individual reaches the age of 65.

Survivors' insurance benefits represent a form of life insurance paid to members of a deceased person's family who meet the eligibility requirements. As with life insurance, the benefits that the survivors of a covered individual receive may greatly exceed their cost to this individual. Survivors' benefits can be paid only if the deceased worker had credit for a certain amount of time spent in work covered by social security. The exact amount of work credit needed depends on the worker's age at death. Generally, older workers need more years of social security work credit than younger workers for benefits to be payable to their survivors, but never more than 40 credits. As with other benefits discussed earlier, the *amount* of benefit is based on the worker's lifetime earnings in work covered by social security.

UNEMPLOYMENT INSURANCE Employees who have been working in employment covered by the Social Security Act and who are laid off may be eligible for **unemployment insurance benefits** during their unemployment for a period up to 26 weeks. Eligible persons must submit an application for unemployment compensation with their state employment agency, register for available work, and be willing to accept any suitable employment that may be offered to them. However, the term *suitable* gives individuals considerable discretion in accepting or rejecting job offers.

The amount of compensation that workers are eligible to receive, which varies among states, is determined by their previous wage rate and previous period of employment. Funds for unemployment compensation are derived from a federal payroll tax based on the wages paid to each employee, up to an established maximum. The major portion of this tax is refunded to the individual states, which in turn operate their unemployment compensation programs in accordance with minimum standards prescribed by the federal government.

While *not* required by law, in some industries unemployment compensation is augmented by **supplemental unemployment benefits (SUBs)** financed by the employer. These benefits were introduced in 1955 when the United Auto Workers successfully negotiated a SUB plan with automobile manufacturers, establishing a pattern for other industries. This plan enables an employee who is laid off to draw, in addition to state unemployment compensation, weekly benefits from the employer that are paid from a fund created for this purpose. Many SUB plans in recent years have been liberalized to permit employees to receive weekly benefits when the length of their workweek is reduced and to receive a lump-sum payment if their employment is terminated permanently. The amount of benefits is determined by length of service and wage rate. Employer liability under the plan is limited to the amount of money that has been accumulated within the fund from employer contributions based on the total hours of work performed by employees.

WORKERS' COMPENSATION INSURANCE Both state and federal **workers' compensation insurance** are based on the theory that the cost of work-related accidents and illnesses should be considered one of the costs of doing business and should ultimately be passed on to the consumer. Individual employees should not be required to bear the cost of their treatment or loss of income, nor should they be subjected to complicated, delaying, and expensive legal procedures.

In most states, workers' compensation insurance is compulsory. Only in New Jersey, South Carolina, and Texas is it elective. When compulsory, every employer subject to it is required to comply with the law's provisions for the compensation of work-related injuries. The law is compulsory for the employee also. When elective, the employers have the option of either accepting or rejecting the law. If they reject it, however, they lose the customary common-law defenses—assumed risk of employment, negligence of a fellow employee, and contributory negligence.[26]

Two methods of providing for workers' compensation risks are commonly used. One method is for the state to operate an insurance system that employers may join and, in some states, are required to join. Another method is for the states to permit employers to insure with private companies, and in some states, employers may be certified by the commission handling workers' compensation to handle their own risks without any type of insurance. Under most state and private insurance plans, it is to the advantage of the employer and the employee to maintain good safety and health records.

Workers' compensation laws typically provide that employees will be paid a disability benefit that is usually based on a percentage of their wages. Each state also specifies the length of the period of payment and usually indicates a maximum amount that may be paid. Benefits, which vary from state to state, are generally provided for four types of disability: (1) permanent partial disability, (2) permanent total disability, (3) temporary partial disability, and (4) temporary total disability. Disabilities may result from injuries or accidents, as well as from occupational diseases such as "black lung," radiation illness, and asbestosis. Before any workers' compensation claim will be allowed, the work-relatedness of the disability must be established. Also, the evaluation of a claimant by an occupational physician is an essential part of the claim process. To provide the reader with an awareness of the various injuries and diseases for which workers' compensation claims are filed, excerpts from actual records are cited in Highlights in HRM 2. These excerpts are necessarily brief and do not reflect the comprehensive nature of the typical medical examination report. Other types of work-related injuries and illnesses will be covered in the next chapter, which focuses on safety and health.

In addition to the disability benefits, provision is made for payment of medical and hospitalization expenses up to certain limits, and in all states, death benefits are paid to survivors of the employee. Commissions are established to adjudicate claims at little or no expense to the claimant.

Health Care Benefits

The benefits that receive the most attention from employers today because of sharply rising costs and employee concern are health care benefits. In the past, health plans covered only medical, surgical, and hospital expenses. Today employers are under pressure to include prescription drugs, as well as dental, optical, and mental health care, in the package they offer their workers.

ESCALATING COSTS According to a U.S. Chamber of Commerce study, medical and medically related benefit payments average 8.7 percent of payroll costs. Other studies cite much higher figures, up to 13 percent of payroll costs.[28] The United States currently spends 11.4 percent of the GNP on health care—over $500 billion a year. Employers bear most of these costs, because approximately 85 to 90 percent of all health insurance is purchased through group plans that HR departments will manage. Increases in health care premiums are estimated to be three times the inflation rate.[29]

Excessive health care costs have been attributed to a number of factors. They include federal legislation, increased costs of retirement benefits, changes in Medicare pricing, the greater need for health care by an aging population, the costs of technological advances in medicine, skyrocketing malpractice insurance rates, rising

HIGHLIGHTS IN HRM

2 EXCERPTS FROM WORKERS' COMPENSATION MEDICAL EXAMINATIONS

Case 1

Claimant states that he was trying to pull a battery out of a high lift when he developed a dull aching pain in the shoulder blades. He went to the plant nurse and was later treated by a chiropractor. He has lost no time from this accident.

Impression from medical examination: Healed strain of the cervical and thoracic spine.

Conclusion: His condition has reached maximum medical improvement. According to AMA guidelines, he has a permanent partial impairment of 0 percent. He may resume his previous occupation in the Maintenance Department. He does not have any limitations.

Case 2

While throwing a switch, claimant slipped on pellets in the steel mill, hurting his low back, head, and right wrist. He was taken to the emergency room, where X-rays were done, and he was then sent home. After being off work for a period of several months, during which time he received treatment, he went on pension and retirement disability.

Impression from medical examination: Old healed strain, lumbar spine; healed contusion of the head and right wrist.

Conclusion: It is my opinion that the permanent partial impairment has decreased by 15 percent, from the previous PPI award of 20 percent down to 5 percent.

Case 3

Claimant states that she was injured using a grinder while working on a coal pipe in the power plant. The grinder disintegrated, broke off, and cut her right forearm and chin. She was taken to the medical center emergency room, where the doctor put stitches in her right forearm. After an appropriate interval the stitches were removed and she went back to work. She now works in the kitchen of the power plant.

Impression from medical examination: Well-healed laceration, right forearm.

Conclusion: As a result of the claimant's occupational injury, she has a permanent partial impairment of 1 percent.

Case 4

Claimant stated that he developed pain when he lifted a dock platform in a tractor-trailer. He states that he tried to work after that and then later went off work. He was under the care of a back specialist, and now that he is working, he has only an occasional twinge of pain in the right back.

Impression from medical examination: Healed strained lumbar spine.

Conclusion: Claimant has reached maximum medical improvement and has returned to work. He has a permanent partial impairment of 0 percent. His complaints are not a direct result of his accident but are more directly related to underlying degenerative changes of the lumbar spine. These changes existed prior to the cited accident. At this time he can continue performing his work as a truck driver. He does not have an unstable back.

SOURCE: Alexander J. Kavic, M.D., President and CEO, Tri-State Industrial Medical Consultants, Inc., 3427-C Route 151, Aliquippa, PA 15001.

costs of health care labor, overutilization of health care services, and the high costs of transplants and AIDS treatment.

COST CONTAINMENT The approaches most frequently taken to contain the costs of health care benefits include reduction in coverages, increased coordination of benefits, increased deductibles or co-payments, use of health maintenance organizations and preferred providers, incentives for outpatient surgery and testing, and mandatory second opinions where surgery has been indicated. Employee assistance programs and wellness programs may also contribute to an organization's ability to cut the costs of its health care benefits.

As just noted, a **health maintenance organization (HMO)** is sometimes offered to employees as a way to contain the costs of employee health care. HMOs are organizations of physicians and other health care professionals who provide a wide range of services to subscribers and their dependents on a prepaid basis. They generally emphasize preventive care and early intervention. Because they are contractually obligated to provide all covered services for a fixed dollar amount, HMOs have an incentive to provide care early. Since 1980, HMOs have increased enrollment by over 200 percent and now have more than 30 million members.[30] The HMO Act of 1973 was instrumental in encouraging employers to offer HMOs as a health care option. The approximately 400 HMOs in the United States are patterned after the one first established by industrialist Henry Kaiser, which bears his name.

Preferred provider organizations, which are fairly new to the health care field, have also helped to contain costs. The **preferred provider organization (PPO)** is a hospital or group of physicians who establish an organization that guarantees cost efficiency to the employer, usually by covering a higher percentage of their bills than if they go elsewhere. The employer reciprocates by steering workers to the PPO. The acceptance by General Motors employees of HMOs and PPOs was given as one of the major reasons for GM's reduction in health care costs in 1985—the first time in 25 years that the company experienced a reduction.[31] In an effort to have more control over medical costs, many insurance companies have become active in organizing PPOs. Since employees and the federal government will continue to push for improved health care, employers will find it necessary to have an active program for cost containment.

OTHER BENEFITS Dental care as an employee benefit has grown very rapidly in the past two decades. A study conducted in 1973 showed that 8 percent of employers provided some type of dental insurance. A 1986 *Personnel Journal* study reported that 77 percent of employers offered a dental plan.[32]

Dental plans are designed to help pay for dental care costs and to encourage employees to receive regular dental attention. Like medical plans, dental care plans may be operated by insurance companies, dental service corporations, those administering Blue Cross/Blue Shield plans, HMOs, and groups of dental care providers. Typically, the plan pays a portion of the charges, and the subscriber pays the remainder.

"You'll hate it here. The pay is low, conditions are fairly chaotic, and I myself am quite impossible. Nevertheless, we have a pretty good dental plan."

Reprinted with permission of J. B. Handelsman.

Optical care is another, relatively new benefit that many employers are offering. Coverage can include visual examinations and a percentage of the costs of lenses and frames.

Payment for Time Not Worked

The "payment for time not worked" category of benefits includes paid vacations, bonuses given in lieu of paid vacations, payments for holidays not worked, paid sick leave, military and jury duty, and payments for absence due to a death in the family or other personal reasons. As Figure 12–1 showed, they account for the largest portion of payroll costs—10.6 percent.

VACATIONS WITH PAY It is generally agreed that vacations are essential to the well-being of an employee. Eligibility for vacations varies by industry, locale, and organization size. Ordinarily, hourly employees have to wait longer than salaried workers before they qualify for one- and two-week vacations. To qualify for longer vacations of 3, 4, or 5 weeks, one may expect to work for 7, 15, and 20 years, respectively.

PAID HOLIDAYS Both hourly and salaried workers can usually expect to be paid for ten or more holidays a year. The type of business tends to influence both the number and observance of holidays. Virtually all employers in the United States, however, observe and pay their employees for New Year's Day, Memorial Day, Independence Day, Labor Day, Thanksgiving Day, and Christmas Day. An increasing number of employers give workers an additional two or three personal days off.

SICK LEAVE There are several ways in which employees may be compensated during periods when they are unable to work because of illness or injury. Most public employees, as well as many in private industry, particularly in white-collar jobs, receive a set number of sick-leave days each year to cover such absences. Where permitted, sick leave that employees do not use can generally be accumulated up to at least a sufficient amount to cover prolonged absences. Accumulated vacation leave may sometimes be used as a source of income when sick-leave benefits have been exhausted. Group insurance that provides for income protection is also becoming more common. Loss of income during absences resulting from job-related injuries can be reimbursed, at least partially, by means of workers' compensation insurance.

Another recent trend is the development of sick-leave banks. A *sick-leave bank* allows employees to pool some of their compensated sick-leave days in a common fund. They may then draw on the fund if extensive illness uses up their remaining time off. Sick-leave banks are fairly common among teachers, police, and firefighters.

SEVERANCE PAY A one-time payment is normally given to employees who are being terminated. Known as *severance pay*, it may cover only a few days' wages or wages for several months, usually depending on the employee's length of service. Employers that are down-sizing their organizations often use severance pay as a means of lessening the negative effects of unexpected termination on employees.

Leaves Without Pay

The birth of a baby requires a leave of absence for the mother, and in some states employers must grant leaves for the fathers as well.

Most employers grant leaves of absence (LOA) to their employees for personal reasons. These leaves are usually taken without pay, but there is no loss of seniority or benefits. An unpaid leave may be granted for a variety of reasons, including extended illness, illness in the family, pregnancy, the birth or adoption of a child, educational or political activities, and social service activities. The topic of LOA is "hot and getting hotter," according to one specialist in employment law. As growing numbers of women have continued to enter the work force and remain there after having children, the issue of LOA has taken on new importance.[33]

As we discussed in Chapter 3, the Pregnancy Discrimination Act of 1978 requires employers to treat women needing time off because of pregnancy, childbirth, or related medical conditions just as it treats employees who need time off for medical reasons unrelated to pregnancy. In recent years there has been an increase in state legislation regarding LOAs. Several states have granted pregnant employees preferential treatment, while other states have enacted laws mandating that employees be given LOAs for any type of disability. Some states have gone further, enacting laws that require employers to grant LOAs for paternity, the adoption of a child, or serious illness in the family.[34]

Several employers have taken the initiative in developing LOA programs. Recognizing that family concerns adversely affect employee productivity, Johnson & Johnson implemented a comprehensive program in 1989. The program allows

J & J employees up to one year of unpaid leave to care for a newborn or newly adopted child, or a sick child, spouse, or elderly parent, with a guarantee of reinstatement to the prior job if they return to work within three months and to a comparable job for leaves longer than three months.[35]

It is essential for an organization to have a clear LOA policy that is applied consistently to all employees. Such a policy, which typically covers length of LOAs and reinstatement rights, must be in accordance with federal and state laws. Employers can expect that parental leave will be a congressional topic discussed as much in the future as it has been in the past (e.g., in 1987 and 1990).

Life and Disability Insurance

One of the oldest and most popular employee benefits is group term life insurance, which provides death benefits to beneficiaries and may also provide accidental death and dismemberment benefits. It is nearly universal in the United States, with over $2.8 trillion worth of employee and dependent coverage under group life insurance in force at the end of 1986. Group protection amounted to 40 percent of life insurance in force in the United States at the end of 1986.[36]

EMPLOYEE SERVICES

The variety of benefits in the miscellaneous category includes paid rest periods, lunch periods, travel time, and get-ready time. Altogether they account for about 3.2 percent of payroll costs. Employee services provided by employers are generally not included in the data compiled by the U.S. Chamber of Commerce. These services, like other benefits, also represent a cost to the employer. The benefits that employees and employers derive from them, however, can far exceed their cost. In recent years there has been an increase in the types of services that are being used to make life at work more rewarding and to enhance the well-being of employees.

Employee Assistance Programs

To help workers cope with a wide variety of problems that interfere with the way they perform their jobs, organizations have developed employee assistance programs. An **employee assistance program (EAP)** typically provides diagnosis, counseling, and referral for advice or treatment when necessary for problems related to alcohol or drug abuse, emotional difficulties, and marital or family difficulties. The main intent is to help employees solve their personal problems or at least to prevent problems from turning into crises that affect their ability to work productively. To handle crises, many EAPs offer 24-hour hotlines. A 1989 SHRM survey showed that 79 percent of employers provide some type of EAP and one-half of the remaining organizations plan to establish a program.[37] The ways in which specific problems are handled will be examined more thoroughly in the next chapter. It should be recognized at this point, however, that organizations providing EAPs as an employee benefit find that the costs are easily justified. The EAP can be seen as an investment in HR designed to maintain and enhance workers' productive capacities.[38]

Counseling Services

An important part of an EAP is the counseling services it provides to employees. While most organizations expect supervisors to counsel subordinates, some employees may have problems that require the services of professional counselors. A large percentage of organizations refer such individuals to outside counseling services such as religious organizations, family counseling services or marriage counselors, and mental health clinics. Some organizations have a qualified person on staff, such as a clinical psychologist, counselor, or comparable specialist, to whom employees may be referred. The methods used by professionals to counsel employees will be described in detail in Chapter 15. Managers and supervisors should also learn the techniques of counseling so they may be as effective as possible in their relationships with subordinates. Since they interact with their subordinates frequently, managers and supervisors are usually in the best position to observe changes in behavior and to assist in identifying and resolving problems. They should also know how to make referrals and should be ready to assume responsibility for providing help when and where it is needed.

Educational Assistance Plans

One of the benefits most frequently mentioned in literature for employees is the educational assistance plan. The primary purpose of this plan is to help employees keep up-to-date with advances in their fields and to help them get ahead in the organization. Usually the employer covers the costs of tuition and fees, and the employee is required to pay for books, meals, transportation, and other expenses.

Child Care

The increased employment of women with dependent children has created an unprecedented demand for child care arrangements. For many decades, working parents typically had to make their own arrangements with sitters or with nursery schools for preschool children. Today benefits include financial assistance, alternative work schedules, family leave, and on-site child care centers. A few companies, including Honeywell, have instituted programs that give employees the option of staying home when their children are mildly ill.[39]

It is not uncommon to find community centers established for the benefit of working parents by unions and nonprofit organizations, and even child care centers set up on company premises. Hoffman-LaRoche opened a child care center only one block from its Nutley, New Jersey, plant. The facility includes several classrooms, a playground, and a nearby park. The company subsidizes the program, but parents pay as well.[40] Among other companies with on-site facilities are Stride-Rite Corporation, Campbell Soup Company, and Wang Laboratories. Government agencies have also established on-site child care facilities. The California State Department of Transportation and the Department of Motor Vehicles have set up child care centers in Sacramento. The Pentagon has elaborate facilities for over 200 children. While there are approximately 800 employers that have developed on- or near-site centers, a high percentage of them prefer other options, such as promoting community centers and helping employees find suitable facilities.[41]

Already plagued by labor shortages, however, many employers are using child care benefits in an attempt to retain their female employees. The benefits may also help recruitment, since a large percentage of those entering the labor force in the next decade will be women. While it is a costly service, one employer whose child care center accounted for $60,000 in red ink in a year remarked, "On paper it looks like a real loser, but the benefits—reduced turnover, absenteeism, and retraining costs—are not quantifiable."[42]

Elder Care

Responsibility for the care of aging parents and other relatives is another fact of life for increasing numbers of employees. The term **elder care,** as used in the context of employment, refers to the circumstance where an employee provides volunteer care to an elderly relative or friend while remaining actively at work. The majority of caregivers are women. A BNA survey conducted in 1988 revealed that less than half (44 percent) of responding HR directors are aware of employees in their organization with elder care responsibilities. Half of those who were aware indicated that their organization had experienced problems as a result of the employees' responsibilities; the problems they identified are shown in Figure 12–4. About two-thirds of responding organizations said they offer some type of assistance to employees who are caregivers for elderly relatives, including personal leave benefits, work schedule adjustments, financial benefits, information and referral services, and counseling and support services.[43]

Because the topic of elder care is relatively new to employers, many are focusing on information gathering and distribution. Elder care counseling, educational fairs or seminars, and distribution of printed resource materials are types of employee assistance offered by such firms as Marriott Corporation, American Security Bank, Pepsi Company, Pitney Bowes, Florida Power & Light, and Mobil Corporation.[44]

Other Services

The variety of benefits and services that employers offer today could not have been imagined a few years ago. Some are fairly standard, and we will cover them briefly. Some are unique and obviously grew out of specific concerns, needs, and interests. Among the less common benefits are free taxi rides home after working nights at Time, Inc.; Fridays off in May and employee vegetable gardens at Reader's Digest; a free home computer at Apple Computer; and adoption aid at Leo Bur-

FIGURE 12–4 PROBLEMS AMONG EMPLOYEES WITH ELDER CARE RESPONSIBILITIES

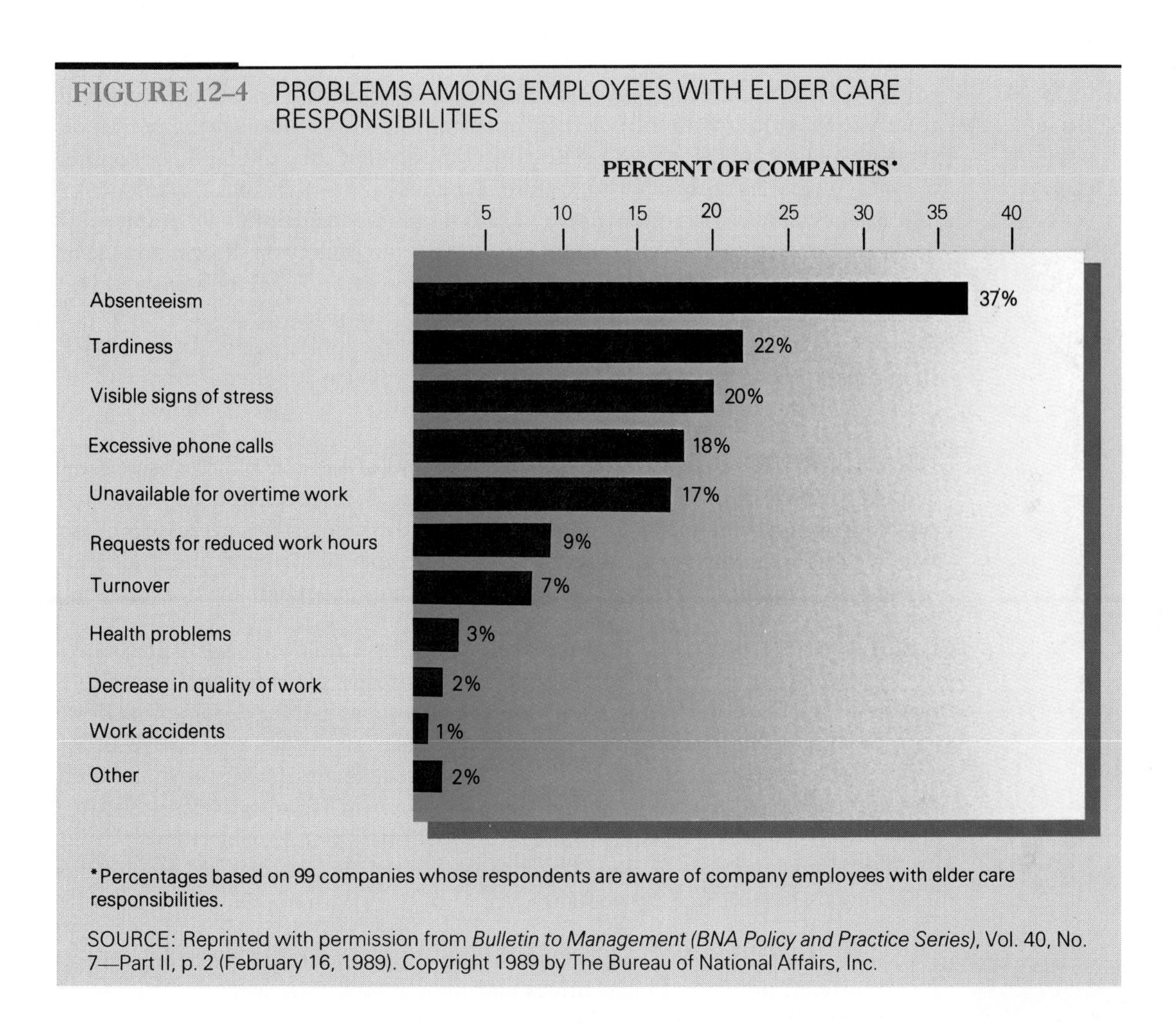

*Percentages based on 99 companies whose respondents are aware of company employees with elder care responsibilities.

SOURCE: Reprinted with permission from *Bulletin to Management (BNA Policy and Practice Series)*, Vol. 40, No. 7—Part II, p. 2 (February 16, 1989). Copyright 1989 by The Bureau of National Affairs, Inc.

nett.[45] These examples represent only a few of the possibilities for benefits that go beyond those typically offered.

FOOD SERVICES Vending machines represent the most prevalent form of food service program (87 percent of organizations), with cafeterias second (57 percent), according to a survey of organizational subscribers to the *Personnel Journal*. Coffee trucks and lunch wagons rank third (15 percent). To provide these services, most employers (81 percent) contract with an outside firm. Although $4.5 billion is spent on employee food service, only 51 percent of the organizations indicated that a manager was employed to oversee this function. The HR department manages the program in 43 percent of the organizations, and it has the responsibility for one or more decisions in this area in 32 percent of the organizations.[46]

The HR staff's degree of participation in food service arrangements would appear to provide it with an excellent opportunity to upgrade the quality of food service. A major problem with vending machines is that they often do not include the most nutritious types of foods. Cafeteria menus prepared by outside contractors may be appealing but are often prepared with minimal consideration for employees' health and energy needs. The current emphasis in our society on the importance of fresh fruits and vegetables and a diet lower in fat, cholesterol, and sodium should be reflected in the food served under an employer's direction. Obviously, there is a payoff for everyone in improved health, energy, and productivity. Food service should be a key component in an organization's wellness program—a topic to be discussed in the next chapter.

HEALTH SERVICES Almost all organizations of any size provide some form of on-site health services. The extent of these services varies considerably, but they are generally designed to handle minor illnesses and injuries. They may also include alcohol- and drug-abuse referral services, in-house counseling programs, and wellness clinics. We will discuss these and related programs in detail in the next chapter.

LEGAL SERVICES One of the fastest-growing employee benefits has been the legal service plan. There are two general types: access plans and comprehensive plans. *Access plans* provide free telephone or office consultation, document review, and discounts on legal fees for more complex matters. *Comprehensive plans* cover other services such as representation in divorce cases, real estate transactions, and civil and criminal trials. According to the American Prepaid Legal Services Institute, about 6 million workers are covered under employer-paid plans, such as those offered by Hyatt Legal Services, one of 30 companies that offer such plans to employers. The annual fee is about $140 per employee.[47]

FINANCIAL PLANNING One of the newer benefits is financial planning. As yet offered primarily to executives and middle-level managers, it is likely to become available to more employees through flexible benefits programs. Such programs cover investments, tax planning and management, estate planning, and related topics.

Most organizations provide a full range of services to assist employees with relocation.

HOUSING AND MOVING EXPENSES The days of "company houses" are now past, except in mining or logging operations, construction projects in remote areas, or the armed forces. However, a variety of housing services are provided by nearly all organizations that move employees from one office or plant to another in connection with a transfer, promotion, or plant relocation. These services include helping employees find living quarters, paying for travel and moving expenses, and protecting transferred employees from loss in selling their homes.

TRANSPORTATION POOLING Daily transportation to and from work is often a major concern of employees and employers that results in considerable time and energy being devoted to organizing car pools and scrambling for parking spaces.

Many employers have attempted to ease conditions by offering transportation in vans. Employer-organized van pooling was started by 3M in 1973 and has since been adopted by other organizations.[48] Many employers report that tardiness and absenteeism are reduced by van pooling.

PURCHASING ASSISTANCE Organizations may use various methods to assist their employees in purchasing merchandise more conveniently and at a savings. One type of enterprise is the "company store" or commissary. In its present form it represents a real service to the employees, especially in remote areas where the community or a substantial part of it is owned by the organization. Most firms sell their own products at a discount to their employees, and in some instances they procure certain items of other manufacturers that they then offer to employees at a discount.

CREDIT UNIONS Credit unions have been established in many organizations to serve the financial needs of employees. Like commercial banks, they offer interest or dividends on deposits and make loans to their members. Many of the larger credit unions have expanded their services in recent years by offering checking accounts, automated teller services, and credit cards such as Visa and MasterCard. While some employers may provide office space and a payroll deduction service for the credit union, credit unions are operated by employees under federal and state legislation and supervision. Their popularity is reflected by the fact that in 1990 there were 15,008 credit unions in the United States with 60.9 million members and combined assets of $214.7 billion. Deposits are insured up to $100,000 per account by the National Credit Union Share Insurance Fund, a U.S. government agency, in approximately 90 percent of the credit unions.[49]

SOCIAL AND RECREATIONAL SERVICES Most organizations offer some type of sports program in which personnel may participate on a voluntary basis. Bowling, handball, racquetball, golf, baseball, and tennis are quite often included in an intramural program. In addition to intramurals, many organizations have teams that represent them in competitions with other local organizations. Health clubs and fitness centers are also popular offerings (see Chapter 13).

Many social functions are organized for employees and their spouses or entire families. Employees should have a major part in planning such programs and events if these functions are to be successful. However, the employer should retain control of all events associated with the organization because of possible legal liability.

AWARDS Awards are often used to recognize productivity, special contributions, and service to an organization. Typically they are presented by executives at special meetings, banquets, and other functions where the honored employees will receive wide recognition. While cash awards are usually given for cost-saving suggestions from employees, a noncash gift is often more appropriate to recognize special achievement. For example, incentive travel has emerged as an important part of many sales programs. It has been suggested that an all-expense-paid trip for two to

Paris is likely to be a unique and more memorable experience than a cash gift.[50] An extensive discussion of awards is included in Chapter 14.

RETIREMENT PROGRAMS

Retirement is an important part of life for which there should be sufficient and careful preparation. In convincing job applicants that theirs is a good organization to work for, employers usually emphasize the retirement benefits that can be expected after a certain number of years of employment. After being hired, as we observed earlier in the chapter, employees are typically given a statement of benefits that contains personalized information about projected retirement income from pensions, social security, and employee investment plans.

Retirement Policy

Prior to 1979, employers were permitted to determine the age (usually 65) at which their employees would be required to retire. A 1978 amendment to the Age Discrimination in Employment Act of 1967 prohibited mandatory retirement under the age of 70 in private employment and at any age in federal employment. The 1986 amendment removes the ceiling age of 70 and prohibits age-based employment discrimination for *ages 40 and older.* Despite the law's provision for continued employment past 70 (with exceptions for some groups), there have not been an overwhelming number of older persons desiring to remain on the job. In fact, a growing number of workers are retiring before age 65. Others choose partial retirement or work part-time for a period preceding complete retirement.

Early Retirement

To avoid layoffs, particularly of the more recently hired members of protected classes, and to reduce HR costs, organizations in the public sector and many corporations such as U.S. West and Tektronix Corporation have encouraged early retirement.[51] This encouragement has been in the form of increased pension benefits for several years or cash bonuses, sometimes referred to as the **silver handshake.** The cost of these retirement incentives can frequently be offset by the lower compensation paid to replacements and/or by a reduction in the work force.

One of the major factors affecting the decision to retire early and the satisfaction to be gained from doing so is the individual's personal financial condition. Consequently, a major obstacle to early retirement today is inflation, which over the long term threatens to seriously erode the purchasing power of an employee's income following retirement. In spite of this deterrent and laws guaranteeing them the right to work longer, a growing number of older workers are choosing to retire early. The Bureau of Labor Statistics reports that 29 percent of men age 60 were no longer in the labor force in 1985, compared with 16 percent in 1970 and 12 percent in 1963.

Sixteen percent of men age 55 reported being out of the labor force in 1985, compared with 8 percent and 7 percent in 1970 and 1963, respectively. Women do not follow the same pattern. In 1963 just over half of the women age 55 were no longer in the work force; by 1985 that figure had fallen to only 44 percent.[52] Possibility of future layoffs, failing health, and inability to meet the demands of their jobs, together with attractive pension benefits, are among the reasons individuals choose to retire early.

Preretirement Programs

While most people eagerly anticipate retirement, many are bitterly disappointed once they reach this stage of life. Preretirement planning programs, therefore, should help make employees aware of the kinds of adjustments they may need to make when they retire. These adjustments may include learning to live on a reduced, fixed income and having to cope with the problems of lost prestige, marital friction, and idleness that retirement may create. Unfortunately, if left to their own resources, most employees spend more time planning a two-week vacation than they do planning for their retirement.

Those who have enjoyed and have been absorbed in their work often have the greatest difficulty in adjusting to retirement. It was their work that enabled them to feel "worth something"—a feeling that helped them to face the challenges of daily life. Unfortunately, most employees must face retirement without the benefit of prior experience or the chance for a second time around. All they can do is try to

Preretirement programs help people adjust to their new life-style, allowing them to lead more fulfilling lives.

profit from the knowledge and experience of others made available to them through preretirement programs.

Preretirement programs include seminars, booklets and other informational materials, and even retirement rehearsals. The National Council on Aging has developed a retirement planning program for employers. Atlantic Richfield, Travelers Insurance, and Alcoa are among the more than 75 organizations using this program. In many communities, hospitals are developing resource centers for health and retirement planning. To help older workers get used to the idea of retirement, some organizations experiment with retirement rehearsal. Polaroid, for example, offers employees an opportunity to try out retirement through an unpaid three-month leave program. They also offer a program that permits employees to gradually cut their hours before retirement. Employees are paid only for hours worked, but they receive full medical insurance and prorated pension credits. Most experts agree that preretirement planning is a much-needed, cost-effective employee benefit.[53]

The types of information presented in such programs are shown in Figure 12–5. Note that pension plans are a topic of major importance in such programs.

Many organizations have developed a large body of "alumni" who play an important part in the organization's public image. There are, for example, fewer

FIGURE 12–5 TYPES OF RETIREMENT PREPARATION INFORMATION PRESENTED

TYPE OF INFORMATION	PERCENTAGE OF FIRMS PRESENTING
Company pension plans	93.6
Social security/Medicare	78.4
Corporate health insurance	60.2
Adjustment to retirement	48.0
Personal financial planning	42.4
Estate planning	36.3
Health prevention	32.5
Legal concerns	32.5
Investments	31.3
Volunteering	28.1
Part-time employment	25.7
Second careers	25.7
Psychological problems	23.1
Educational opportunities	22.5
Housing options	22.2
Widows/widowers	21.3
Relocation	20.2

SOURCE: Malcolm H. Morrison and M. Kathryn Jedriewski, "Retirement Planning: Everybody Benefits," *Personnel Administrator* 33, no. 1 (January 1988): 74–78. Reproduced with permission.

than two employees for every retiree at the Aluminum Company of America (Alcoa). In 1985 the annual shareholders meeting was moved from Pittsburgh to Atlanta so that a large number of people who helped build the company and who now lived in Atlanta could attend the meeting. A special retiree dinner was held the night before the meeting.[54]

SUMMARY

Employees receive a sizable portion of their compensation in the form of benefits rather than cash payments. There is every indication that this practice will continue because of employee demands and the need for employers to be competitive in the labor market, as well as increased pressure from Congress to provide additional benefits. Employees continue to view benefits as something they have earned and to which they are entitled. Furthermore, employees want their own personal choice of benefits. This has given rise to flexible benefits plans that enable employers to control costs while making employees more aware of the value of the benefits. Employers that previously did not have flexible benefits are planning to introduce them, as a tailored way to meet employee needs. Increased attention is being given to communicating benefits information to employees.

The rising costs of health care benefits have posed a major challenge to employers that recognize the high value employees place on them. Various alternatives to traditional health care are being explored intensively. A large percentage of employers are attempting to reduce the costs of benefits by switching their pension plans from defined-benefit to defined-contribution plans. ERISA, as amended by REA, has forced employers to comply with standards concerning the administration and the actuarial soundness of their pension plans. It requires that employees be provided with a vested right in their pension funds. Federal legislation has provided for more-rapid vesting for plan years beginning in 1989. Court decisions also caution employers to avoid sex discrimination in determining pension benefits.

Payments for time not worked and legally required payments for social security, unemployment insurance, and workers' compensation constitute a sizable portion of the costs of benefits to the employer. While cost data for employee services are not readily available, it is generally agreed that such services as employee assistance plans, educational assistance plans, child care, food service, and transportation pooling benefit both the employees and the organization.

Restrictions on mandatory retirement, which have affected retention and retirement policies, have had a definite impact on HR planning. A majority of the larger employers offer or plan to offer preretirement programs to help employees prepare for the social and emotional, as well as the financial, aspects of retirement.

DISCUSSION QUESTIONS

1. Many organizations are concerned about the rising cost of employee benefits and question their value to the organization and to the employees.
   a. In your opinion, what benefits are of greatest value to employees? To the organization? Why?

   b. What can management do to increase the value to the organization of the benefits provided to employees?
2. Employee benefits were found to cost over $10,750 a year per employee in United States organizations surveyed by the U.S. Chamber of Commerce.
   a. What would you think of a plan that called for removing all benefits except those required by law, and giving the employees this amount in cash as part of wages?
   b. Discuss the advantages and disadvantages of such a plan.
3. What are some of the reasons for the greater attention organizations are devoting to the communication of benefits information to employees?
4. Some organizations offer their employees a choice of certain benefits in a self-designated benefits plan. What are the advantages and disadvantages of this type of plan to the employee? To the employer?
5. What effect is further government intrusion in the area of employee benefits likely to have on benefits programs?
6. Why are the costs of health care benefits escalating? What steps can employers take to contain these costs?
7. We observed that prior to 1979, all employers could prescribe a mandatory retirement age—usually 65 years. What would you think are the advantages and disadvantages of a mandatory retirement age?
8. What factors may affect an individual's decision to retire at a particular time and his or her ability to adjust to retirement?

MINI-CASE 12–1 Keeping the Corporate Connection

Although various community organizations recruit retiree volunteers and promote and coordinate volunteer activities, company-sponsored programs have proven to be uniquely productive. There was a time when employees who retired were completely separated from their former employers except for a monthly pension check. But this is no longer the case. A company-sponsored retiree volunteer program provides a valuable link between a retiree and the company that benefits the community in which both reside. A company knows its retirees, how to reach them, and something about what they can do. It also provides the retiree with an environment of familiarity—familiar faces and past shared experiences—an esprit de corps—an extension of the workplace that is so important to many retirees. Community organizations do not have this advantage.

An outstanding example of company/retiree partnership is the highly successful Honeywell Retiree Volunteer Project (HRVP), the first formally organized corporate retiree volunteer program in the Twin Cities area, and possibly in the nation. Honeywell initiated this organization in 1979 as part of a program to expand its role with the Minneapolis-St. Paul area nonprofit community service agencies. Since then, HRVP has placed more than 1,600 retirees in responsible volunteer positions at more than 335 volunteer and nonprofit agencies. It is estimated that in 1990 these active seniors contributed more than 350,000 hours to the community. At a nominal $6 an hour, this would be about $2.1 million in-kind contributions.

Although the program has top Honeywell support, it is managed entirely by the retirees themselves, who even share the management responsibilities. Each retiree manager contributes one or two days a week to the project recruiting volunteers and interfacing with the various community nonprofit agencies, and managing the day-to-day routine of the project. In addition, each day manager is responsible for certain ongoing projects and interest areas, and for referring matters concerning other special projects to the responsible day manager. When a special project becomes too large to be handled as part of the daily routine, a project manager is appointed to oversee its activities and growth. The status of these projects is reviewed at monthly staff meetings.

Every attempt is made to involve retirees in community work that is rewarding, interesting, and challenging. An important step in this process is HRVP's one-on-one interview of each new prospective retiree volunteer to determine individual interest, ability, desire, and motivation. These are then matched, as closely as possible, to an agency's needs according to their job descriptions. A prospective volunteer is then interviewed by the agency so that both parties can determine if a match can be made. As a result of this careful interviewing and matching, the turnover rate of HRVP's volunteers after placement is only 6 percent.

Most volunteers work on their own terms, ranging from half a day a week to as much as five days a week. Honeywell retirees are engaged in a variety of community activities: youth and adult educational programs, technical services, rehabilitation services, health services, and recreation and civic organizational projects. These diverse activities meet the needs of the retirees, and also of the company and the community. According to Elmer Frykman, HRVP's first manager, "The volunteers like the work because they keep up with their skills and feel useful, and because they maintain the camaraderie established during their working years."

SOURCE: Mr. Bernard L. Mooney, Manager, Promotional Projects, Honeywell Retiree Volunteer Project. Reproduced with permission.

QUESTIONS

1. How does a volunteer program like this one benefit the company?
2. In what ways can an HR department assist the staff that manages the program?
3. Why would some retirees choose to serve as volunteers rather than seek employment in the community?

MINI-CASE 12–2 Benefits Tradeoffs Prove Attractive

Ex-Cell-O Corporation, a diversified Fortune 500 company with 41 plant locations in the United States, found its costs for medical benefits tripling over a period of six years. Management had to bring these costs under control without penalizing employees. To achieve these goals, Ex-Cell-O management decided to use a flexible benefits plan to give employees new advantages and attractive tradeoffs in return for reductions in their medical benefits. It launched its new program with salaried employees and later extended it to hourly workers.

In announcing the reasons for the new plan, management found a responsive awareness of rising medical costs among employees. Explaining the company goal—to cut costs, not cut benefits—management offered a broad choice of medical options together with new benefits and improvements in other areas. One such improvement was a new 401(k) plan giving employees an opportunity for tax deferment on a generous level of long-term savings—up to 15 percent of pretax pay. The company would match employee contributions dollar for dollar up to 2.5 percent of pay. This capital-accumulation plan replaced Ex-Cell-O's former, more expensive plan that had not covered employees in more recently acquired units. In effect, the 401(k) option made a deferred compensation plan available to all, while reducing the company's total commitment. Another benefits plan enhancement was a health care reimbursement account that would allow pretax salary dollars to be used to pay for a wide range of health care expenses.

Ex-Cell-O provided every employee with a personalized workbook describing each benefit option in detail. Compiled using data generated in the enrollment process, the attractively printed workbooks contained individually computer-posted benefit credits and option price tags. Thus, employees had all the information they needed as they completed their enrollment forms.

The health care reimbursement account proved to be popular, with 26.8 percent of employees choosing to participate. The critical medical plan elections resulted in 16.3 percent opting to reduce their coverage and 8.1 percent opting for HMOs. Acceptance of the new 401(k) plan was strong, as management had hoped. More than 78 percent of eligible employees chose to participate. Overall, 98.2 percent of Ex-Cell-O employees elected to make changes in their benefits.

SOURCE: Adapted, by permission of the publisher, from "Guidelines to Successful Flex Plans: Four Companies' Experiences," Lance D. Tane, *Compensation and Benefits Review* (July–August 1985): 41–42.

QUESTIONS

1. How do you account for the individual changes in medical plan coverage?
2. What changes have occurred in the last 20 years that require employers to consider flexible benefits plans and to make individualized plans feasible?
3. In what ways can a workbook contribute to the success of a program?

NOTES AND REFERENCES

1. J. H. Foegen, "Update on Benefits: Health, Home, Help, Fun, Taxes," *Personnel Administrator* 30, no. 11 (November 1985): 87–91.

2. David E. Bowen and Christopher A. Wadley, "Designing a Strategic Benefits Program," *Compensation and Benefits Review* 21, no. 5 (September–October 1989): 44–56; and Robert M. McCaffery, *Managing the Employee Benefits Program*, rev. ed. (New York: AMACOM, 1983), 14.

3. *BNA Bulletin to Management* 37, no. 6 (Washington, DC: Bureau of National Affairs, February 6, 1986): 47.

4. John A. Haslinger, "Flexible Compensation: Getting a Return on Benefit Dollars," *Personnel Administrator* 30, no. 6 (June 1985): 39–46, 224. See also William J. Wiatrowski, "Family-related Benefits in the Workplace," *Monthly Labor Review* 13, no. 3 (March 1990): 28–33.

5. Bowen and Wadley.

6. For a detailed explanation of the various approaches to flexible benefits, see Carolyn A. Baker, "Flex Your Benefits," *Personnel Journal* 67, no. 5 (May 1988): 54–61; and Betty A. Iseri and Robert R. Cangemi, "Flexible Benefits: A Growing Option," *Personnel* 67, no. 3 (March 1990): 30–32.

7. Haslinger.

8. *Resource* (October 1985): 1. See also Melissa Famulari and Marilyn E. Manser, "Employer-provided Benefits: Employer Cost Versus Employee Value," *Monthly Labor Review* 112, no. 12 (December 1989): 24–30.

9. Labor Letter, *Wall Street Journal* (March 27, 1990): A1.

10. Deborah L. Davies, "Benefits—How to Bridge the Communication Gap," *Personnel Journal* 65, no. 1 (January 1986): 83–85.

11. Detailed recommendations for preparing benefits statements are presented in James F. White, "Preparing Benefit Statements," *Personnel* 63, no. 5 (May 1986): 13–18. See also the following articles by the same author: "Communications: Electronic Printing Increases Flexibility of Employee Communications," *Journal of Compensation and Benefits* 21, no. 6 (November–December 1989): 172–174; and "Scope of Personalized Communication Is Expanding," *Journal of Compensation and Benefits* 21, no. 5 (September–October 1989): 118–119.

12. *Our Numbers Speak for Us* (Brookfield, WI: International Foundation of Employee Benefit Plans, September 1988).

13. *Employee Benefits, 1988* (Washington, DC: U.S. Chamber of Commerce, 1989), 2.

14. Carson E. Beadle, "The Future of Employee Benefits: More Mandates Ahead," *Compensation and Benefits Review* 20, no. 6 (November–December 1988): 36–44.

15. *The Sacramento Bee,* April 29, 1990.

16. Associated Press release, November 16, 1989; and Aaron Bernstein, "In Search of the Vanishing Nest Egg," *Business Week* (July 30, 1990): 46.

17. Larry Light, "The Power of the Pension Funds," *Business Week* (November 6, 1989): 154–158.

18. Stuart J. Brahs, "What's the Fate of 401(k)s?" *Pension World* 22, no. 5 (May 1986): 28, 30. See also Jack H. Schechter, "Tax Reform Act of 1986: Its Impact on Compensation and Benefits, Part 1," *Personnel* 63, no. 12 (December 1986): 61–67, and Part 2, *Personnel* 64, no. 1 (January 1987): 72–75.

19. *Fundamentals of Employee Benefit Programs,* 2d ed. (Washington, DC: Employee Benefit Research Institute, 1985), 26–27.

20. Jack H. Schechter, "The Retirement Equity Act: Meeting Women's Pension Needs," *Compensation Review* 17, no. 1 (First Quarter, 1985): 11–13. See also Judith F. Mazo, "Another Compliance Challenge for Employers: The Retirement Equity Act," *Personnel* 62, no. 2 (February 1985): 43–49.

21. Henry Saveth, "Benefit Programs After Tax Reform," *Personnel Journal* 63, no. 10 (October 1984): 28–35. See also *Fundamentals of Employee Benefit Programs,* 221.

22. Light.

23. *City of Los Angeles, Department of Water and Power et al.* v. *Manhart et al.*, 435 U.S. 702 (U.S. S. Ct., 1978), 16 EPD 8250. See also Norma Nielsen, "Pension Plans—Basic Factors," Chapter 29 in *The Handbook of Employee Benefits—Design, Funding, and Administration,* ed. Jerry S. Rosenbloom (Homewood, IL: Dow Jones–Irwin, 1984), 427.

24. Active military service completed between 1940 and 1956 inclusive was granted social security credit gratuitously based on monthly earnings of $160 per month. If this credit is used for social security benefits, however, it cannot be counted toward any other federal service pension. Since the Social Security Act is continually subject to amendment, readers should refer to the literature provided by the nearest social security office for the most current details pertaining to the tax rates and benefit provisions of the Act. A long-time publication, *Your Social Security,* has been superseded by a series of pamphlets, *Retirement, Disability, Survivors, Medicare, SSI,* published by the Social Security Administration, U.S. Department of Health and Human Services. The October 1990 editions of these publications were used as the basis for this discussion.

25. For a more detailed account of exempted groups, see the current edition of *Labor Course* or *Tax Course* (Englewood Cliffs, NJ: Prentice-Hall).

26. *BNA Policy and Practice Series—Compensation* (Washington, DC: Bureau of National Affairs, 1988), 365: 2. LaVerne C. Tinsley, "State Workers' Compensation: Significant Legislation in 1989," *Monthly Labor Review* 113, no. 1 (January 1990): 57–63. The three defenses are defined as follows: (1) the *doctrine of the assumption of risk* holds that when employees accept a job, they assume the ordinary risks of the job; (2) the *fellow-servant rule* provides that if the employee was injured as a result of the negligence of a fellow employee, the employer would not be liable for the injury; and (3) the *doctrine of contributory negligence* states that the employer would not be liable if the injury of the employee was due wholly or in part to negligence.

27. For comprehensive coverage of workers' compensation policies and procedures, see Jeffrey V. Nackley, *Primer on Workers' Compensation* (Washington, DC: Bureau of National Affairs, 1987); and *Occupational Health Law—A Guide for Industry,* ed. Joseph LaDou (New York: Marcel Dekker, 1981).

28. Fred Luthans and Elaine Davis, "The Healthcare Cost Crisis: Causes and Containment," *Personnel* 67, no. 2 (February 1990): 24–30.

29. Ibid.

30. David L. Brenneman, "New Rx to Cure Health Care Cost Increases," *Pension World* 25, no. 11 (November 1989): 12–16. See also John F. Sheridan and Jonathan S. Newpol, "The Mystique and Method of HMOs as Employee Benefits," *Pension World* 26, no. 6 (June 1990): 10–12.

31. *Bulletin to Management* (Washington, DC: Bureau of National Affairs, April 3, 1986), 115. See also Frederic R. Curtiss, "How Managed Care Works," *Personnel Journal* 68, no. 7 (July 1989): 38–53.

32. Mitchell Meyer, *Profile of Employee Benefits: 1981 Edition,* Report no. 813 (New York: The Conference Board, 1981), 13; and Morton E. Grossman and Margaret Magnus, "Benefits: Costs and Coverage," *Personnel Journal* 65, no. 5 (May 1986): 74–79.

33. Robert J. Nobile, "Leaving No Doubt About Employee Leaves," *Personnel* 67, no. 5 (May 1990): 54–60.

34. Ibid.

35. *BNA's Employee Relations Weekly* (November 20, 1989), 1453.

36. *Life Insurance Fact Book Update* (Washington, DC: American Council of Life Insurance, 1987), 14.

37. *Resource* (April 1989): 2.

38. For an expanded discussion of the policies for an EAP and their implementation, see Stanley J. Smits, Larry A. Pace, and William J. Perryman, "The Business of EAPs," *Personnel Journal* 68, no. 6 (June 1989): 96–106.

39. *BNA Employee Relations Weekly* (November 20, 1989), 1453.

40. "Management in Practice," *Management Review* 73, no. 8 (August 1984): 39–40. See also Jan Mason, "Corporate Kids," *Life* 9, no. 4 (April 1986): 67–72.

41. Toni A. Campbell and David E. Campbell, "71% of Employers Say They Could Be Part of the Child Care Solution," *Personnel Journal* 67, no. 4 (April 1988): 84–86. See also Jaclyn Fierman, "Child Care: What Works—and Doesn't," *Fortune* 118, no. 12 (November 21, 1988): 163–176.

42. Beth Brophy, "Companies Responding to the Cry for Child Care," *USA Today* (September 4, 1985): 28.

43. "Special Survey Report—Elder Care and the Work Place," *BNA Policy and Practice Series—Bulletin to Management* 40, no. 7—Part II (February 16, 1989). See also Andrew E. Scharlach, Beverly F. Lowe, and Edward L. Schneider, *Elder Care and the Work Force* (Lexington, MA: Lexington Books, 1990).

44. Kathleen Glynn, "Providing for Our Aging Society," *Personnel Administrator* 33, no. 11 (November 1988): 56–59.

45. Robert Levering, Milton Moskowitz, and Michael Katz, *The 100 Best Companies to Work for in America* (New York: New American Library, 1985), 66, 366.

46. Morton E. Grossman and Margaret Magnus, "Order Up Food Services," *Personnel Journal* 68, no. 3 (March 1989): 70–72.

47. *Wall Street Journal* (January 13, 1989): B3.

48. "Van Pooling Takes U.S. by Storm," *San Francisco Sunday Examiner and Chronicle* (September 26, 1982): D–12.

49. Data obtained from Mr. Jerry Karbon of the Credit Union National Association, Madison, WI, June 5, 1990.

50. William H. Wagel, "Make Their Day—the Noncash Way!" *Personnel* 67, no. 5 (May 1990): 41–44.

51. "Bank America to Reduce Costs with Early Retirement," *Employee Benefit Plan Review* 38, no. 9 (March 1984): 77–83.

52. "Retirement Before Age 62: Growth, Reasons Explored," *Employee Benefit Plan Review* 44, no. 1 (July 1989): 16–18.

53. Catherine D. Fyock, "Crafting Secure Retirements," *HR Magazine* 35, no. 7 (July 1990): 30–33. For information on retirement counseling programs see Harold Geist, *Manual for Retirement Counselors* (San Diego, CA: Libra Publishers, 1988); this book contains a valuable bibliography.

54. "Alcoa Aids in Preparing for Retirement, and After," *Employee Benefit Plan Review* 40, no. 7 (January 1986): 12–13.

CHAPTER 13

Safety and Health

After reading this chapter you will be able to:

1. *Summarize the general provisions of the Occupational Safety and Health Act (OSHA).*
2. *Explain how OSHA standards are developed.*
3. *Describe what management can do to create a safe work environment.*
4. *Cite the measures that should be taken to control and eliminate health hazards.*
5. *Describe the characteristics of organization wellness programs.*
6. *Explain the role of employee assistance programs in HRM.*
7. *Summarize the sources of job stress and the possible remedies for them.*
8. *Define the key terms in the chapter.*

TERMS TO IDENTIFY

voluntary protection programs (VPPs) *(423)*
employee right-to-know laws *(424)*
Material Safety Data Sheets (MSDSs) *(426)*
recordable case *(431)*
cumulative trauma disorders *(435)*
clinical ecology *(442)*
stress *(446)*
eustress *(446)*
distress *(446)*
alarm reaction *(446)*
organizational stressors *(447)*
burnout *(448)*

In the preceding chapters we examined the various compensation and benefit programs that are designed to meet the needs of employees for economic security. Their needs for physical and emotional security demand equal attention. Employers are required by law to provide working conditions that do not impair the safety or health of their employees. Therefore, employers must ensure a work environment that protects employees from physical hazards, unhealthy conditions, and unsafe acts of other personnel. Through effective safety and health programs, the physical and emotional well-being, as well as the economic security, of employees may be preserved and even enhanced.

While the laws safeguarding employees' physical and emotional well-being are certainly an incentive, many employers are motivated to provide desirable working conditions by virtue of their sensitivity to human needs and rights. The more cost-oriented employer recognizes the importance of avoiding accidents and illnesses wherever possible. Costs associated with sick leave, disability payments, replacement of employees who are injured or killed, and workers' compensation far exceed the costs of maintaining a safety and health program. Accidents and illnesses attributable to the workplace may also have pronounced effects on employee morale and on the goodwill that the organization enjoys in the community and in the business world. Thus, there are many reasons for management to create a working environment and establish a program that will protect employee safety and health.

LEGAL REQUIREMENTS FOR SAFETY AND HEALTH

In the late 1960s, Congress became increasingly concerned that each year, job-related accidents were accounting for more than 14,000 worker deaths and nearly

2.5 million worker disabilities. Also in the late 1960s, estimated new cases of occupational diseases totaled 300,000 annually. As a result of lost productivity and wages, medical expenses, and disability compensation, the burden on the nation's commerce was staggering. There was no way to calculate human suffering. These conditions led to the passage of the Occupational Safety and Health Act (OSHA) in 1970. The Act, which was designed *"to assure so far as possible every working man and woman in the Nation safe and healthful working conditions and to preserve our human resources,"* has been very effective in reducing the number of injuries and illnesses resulting in lost work time, as well as the number of job-related deaths.[1] A comparison of the late 1960s with the late 1980s reveals the improvement that has taken place under OSHA. In 1988, with almost twice as many workers as in the 1960s, there were 10,600 fatalities and 1.8 million disabling injuries. The estimated cases of occupational disease recognized or diagnosed in 1987 fell to 190,200. The death rate (i.e., deaths per 100,000 workers) dropped from 19 in 1967 to 9 in 1988.[2]

In general, the Act extends to all employers and their employees, with only a few exceptions including the federal government and any state or political subdivision of a state. Each federal agency, however, is required to establish and maintain a safety and health program that is monitored by the Occupational Safety and Health Administration. Likewise, a state seeking OSHA approval of its safety and health program for the private sector must provide a similar program that covers its state and local government employees and is at least as effective as its program for private employers. Where state programs for the private sector have been approved by the federal government as meeting federal standards, the state carries out the enforcement functions that would otherwise be performed by the federal government. Approximately one-half of the states currently have their own OSHA-approved programs.[3]

OSHA Standards

One of the responsibilities of the Occupational Safety and Health Administration is to develop and enforce mandatory job safety and health standards. OSHA standards fall into four major categories: general industry, maritime, construction, and agriculture. These standards cover the workplace, machinery and equipment, material, power sources, processing, protective clothing, first aid, and administrative requirements. It is the responsibility of employers to become familiar with those standards that are applicable to their establishments and to ensure that their employees use personal protective gear and equipment when required for safety. The *Federal Register* is the principal source of information on proposed, adopted, amended, and deleted OSHA standards. Large and small employers often subscribe to it and/or the OSHA Subscription Service.

The Occupational Safety and Health Administration can begin standards-setting procedures on its own initiative or on petition from other parties, including the Secretary of Health and Human Services (HHS) and the National Institute for Occupational Safety and Health (NIOSH). Other bodies that may also initiate

To ensure compliance with safety laws, OSHA officers carefully inspect work sites and report any violations.

standards-setting procedures are state and local governments and any nationally recognized standards-producing organization, employer, or labor representative. NIOSH, however, is a major source of standards. As an agency of the Department of Health and Human Services, it is responsible for conducting research on various safety and health problems, including the psychological factors involved.[4]

Employer Compliance with OSHA

The Secretary of Labor is authorized by the Occupational Safety and Health Act to conduct workplace inspections, to issue citations, and to impose penalties on employers. Inspections have been delegated to the Occupational Safety and Health Administration of the U.S. Department of Labor.

WORKPLACE INSPECTIONS Under the Act, "upon presenting appropriate credentials to the owner, operator, or agent in charge," an OSHA compliance officer is authorized to do the following:

- "Enter without delay and at reasonable times any factory, plant, establishment, construction site or other areas, workplace, or environment where work is performed by an employee of an employer; and to
- "Inspect and investigate during regular working hours, and at other reasonable times, and within reasonable limits and in a reasonable manner, any such place of employment and all pertinent conditions, structures, machines, apparatus, devices, equipment and materials therein, and to question privately any such employer, owner, operator, agent, or employee."[5]

Typically, OSHA inspectors will arrive at a work site unannounced and ask for a meeting with a representative of the employer. At the meeting the inspectors will explain the purpose of the visit, describe the procedure for the inspection, and ask to review the employer's safety and health records. An employer may either agree voluntarily to the inspection or require the inspectors to obtain a search warrant.

The Act gives both the employer and the employees the right to accompany inspectors on their tour of the work site. After the tour the OSHA officials will conduct a closing conference to inform the employer and employee representatives, if any, of the results of their inspection. They will point out conditions or practices that appear to be hazardous and issue a written citation if warranted.

Obviously, not all of the 5 million workplaces covered by the Act can be inspected at the same time. The worst situations need attention first. Therefore, OSHA has established a system of inspection priorities, listed in Figure 13–1.

CITATIONS AND PENALTIES Citations may be issued immediately following the inspection or later by mail. Citations tell the employer and employees which regulations and standards are alleged to have been violated and the amount of time allowed for their correction. The employer must post a copy of each citation at or near the place the violation occurred for three days or until the violation is abated, whichever is longer.

FIGURE 13–1 OSHA PRIORITIES FOR WORKPLACE INSPECTIONS

1. Inspection of imminent-danger situations.
2. Investigation of catastrophes, fatalities, and accidents resulting in hospitalization of five or more employees.
3. Investigation of valid employee complaints of alleged violation of standards or of unsafe or unhealthful working conditions.
4. Special-emphasis inspections aimed at specific high-hazard industries, occupations, or substances that are injurious to health.
5. Follow-up inspections to determine if previously cited violations have been corrected.

SOURCE: U.S. Department of Labor, Occupational Safety and Health Administration, *All About OSHA*, rev. ed. (Washington, DC: U.S. Government Printing Office, 1985), 19–23.

OSHA has a wide range of penalties for violations. Fines of as much as $1,000 are imposed for serious violations, including violations of posting requirements. For willful or repeated violations, OSHA can assess penalties of up to $10,000 for each violation. The law provides for appeal by employers and by employees under specified circumstances.[6]

ON-SITE CONSULTATION OSHA provides a free on-site consultation service. Consultants from the state government or private contractors help employers identify hazardous conditions and determine corrective measures. A clear separation is maintained between consultative and enforcement staffs. No citations are issued in connection with a consultation, and the consultant's files cannot be used to trigger an OSHA inspection. However, in accepting a consultation visit, employers must agree to eliminate any hazardous condition that the consultants warn could result in death or serious physical harm.

VOLUNTARY PROTECTION PROGRAMS The **voluntary protection programs (VPPs)** represent one component of OSHA's effort to extend worker protection beyond the minimum required by OSHA standards. There are three of these programs which, when coupled with an effective enforcement program, expand worker protection to help meet the goals of the 1970 Act. The three VPPs are designed to do the following:

1. Recognize outstanding achievement of those who have successfully incorporated comprehensive safety and health programs into their total management system;
2. Motivate others to achieve excellent safety and health results in the same outstanding way; and
3. Establish a relationship among employers, employees, and OSHA based on cooperation rather than coercion.

The Star Program is the most demanding and the most prestigious VPP. The Try Program and the Praise Program are stepping-stones to the Star Program. Once it has been approved for a VPP, an organization is then taken off OSHA's list for routine inspections. However, any employee complaints, serious accidents, or fatalities in these organizations are handled according to regular enforcement procedures.[7]

Responsibilities and Rights Under OSHA

Both employers and employees have certain responsibilities and rights under OSHA. We will discuss only those that relate directly to the management of human resources.

EMPLOYERS' RESPONSIBILITIES AND RIGHTS In addition to providing a hazard-free workplace and complying with the applicable standards, employers must inform all of their employees about the safety and health requirements of OSHA. Employers are also required to display the OSHA poster that lists employees' rights and responsibilities (see Figure 13–2), to keep certain records, and to compile and post an annual summary of work-related injuries and illnesses. It is the employer's responsibility to make sure employees use protective equipment when necessary. Employers, therefore, must engage in safety training and be prepared to discipline employees for failing to comply with safety rules.

Employers must not discriminate against employees who exercise their rights under the Act by filing complaints. Employers are afforded many rights under the law, most of which pertain to receiving information, applying for variances in standards, and contesting citations.

EMPLOYEES' RESPONSIBILITIES AND RIGHTS Employees are required to comply with all applicable OSHA standards, to report hazardous conditions, and to follow all employer safety and health rules and regulations, including those prescribing the use of protective equipment. Workers have a right to demand safe and healthy conditions on the job without fear of punishment. They also have many rights that pertain to requesting and receiving information about safety and health conditions.

Right-to-Know Laws

While the preamble to the original OSHA standards specified that the rights of workers or their designated representatives would include broad access to relevant environmental exposure and medical records, failure of the federal government in this area led to the passage of **employee right-to-know laws** in several states. These statutes address such issues as the definition of toxic or hazardous substance, the duties of employers and manufacturers to provide health-risk information to employees, trade-secret protection, and enforcement provisions.[8]

FIGURE 13–2 JOB SAFETY AND HEALTH PROTECTION

The Occupational Safety and Health Act of 1970 provides job safety and health protection for workers by promoting safe and healthful working conditions throughout the Nation. Provisions of the Act include the following:

Employers

All employers must furnish to employees employment and a place of employment free from recognized hazards that are causing or are likely to cause death or serious harm to employees. Employers must comply with occupational safety and health standards issued under the Act.

Employees

Employees must comply with all occupational safety and health standards, rules, regulations and orders issued under the Act that apply to their own actions and conduct on the job.

The Occupational Safety and Health Administration (OSHA) of the U.S. Department of Labor has the primary responsibility for administering the Act. OSHA issues occupational safety and health standards, and its Compliance Safety and Health Officers conduct jobsite inspections to help ensure compliance with the Act.

Inspection

The Act requires that a representative of the employer and a representative authorized by the employees be given an opportunity to accompany the OSHA inspector for the purpose of aiding the inspection.

Where there is no authorized employee representative, the OSHA Compliance Officer must consult with a reasonable number of employees concerning safety and health conditions in the workplace.

Complaint

Employees or their representatives have the right to file a complaint with the nearest OSHA office requesting an inspection if they believe unsafe or unhealthful conditions exist in their workplace. OSHA will withhold, on request, names of employees complaining.

The Act provides that employees may not be discharged or discriminated against in any way for filing safety and health complaints or for otherwise exercising their rights under the Act.

Employees who believe they have been discriminated against may file a complaint with their nearest OSHA office within 30 days of the alleged discriminatory action.

Citation

If upon inspection OSHA believes an employer has violated the Act, a citation alleging such violations will be issued to the employer. Each citation will specify a time period within which the alleged violation must be corrected.

The OSHA citation must be prominently displayed at or near the place of alleged violation for three days, or until it is corrected, whichever is later, to warn employees of dangers that may exist there.

Proposed Penalty

The Act provides for mandatory penalties against employers of up to $1,000 for each serious violation and for optional penalties of up to $1,000 for each nonserious violation. Penalties of up to $1,000 per day may be proposed for failure to correct violations within the proposed time period. Also, any employer who willfully or repeatedly violates the Act may be assessed penalties of up to $10,000 for each such violation.

There are also provisions for criminal penalties. Any willful violation resulting in death of an employee, upon conviction, is punishable by a fine of up to $250,000 (or $500,000 if the employer is a corporation), or by imprisonment for up to six months, or both. A second conviction of an employer doubles the possible term of imprisonment.

Voluntary Activity

While providing penalties for violations, the Act also encourages efforts by labor and management, before an OSHA inspection, to reduce workplace hazards voluntarily and to develop and improve safety and health programs in all workplaces and industries. OSHA's Voluntary Protection Programs recognize outstanding efforts of this nature.

OSHA has published Safety and Health Program Management Guidelines to assist employers in establishing or perfecting programs to prevent or control employee exposure to workplace hazards. There are many public and private organizations that can provide information and assistance in this effort, if requested. Also, your local OSHA office can provide considerable help and advice on solving safety and health problems or can refer you to other sources for help such as training.

Consultation

Free assistance in identifying and correcting hazards and in improving safety and health management is available to employers, without citation or penalty, through OSHA-supported programs in each State. These programs are usually administered by the State Labor or Health department or a State university.

Posting Instructions

Employers in States operating OSHA approved State Plans should obtain and post the State's equivalent poster.

Under provisions of Title 29,Code of Federal Regulations, Part 1903.2(a)(1) employers must post this notice (or facsimile) in a conspicuous place where notices to employees are customarily posted.

More Information

Additional information and copies of the Act, specific OSHA safety and health standards, and other applicable regulations may be obtained from your employer or from the nearest OSHA Regional Office in the following locations:

Atlanta	(404) 347-3573
Boston	(617) 565-7164
Chicago	(312) 353-2220
Dallas	(214) 767-4731
Denver	(303) 844-3061
Kansas City	(816) 426-5861
New York	(212) 337-2325
Philadelphia	(215) 596-1201
San Francisco	(415) 995-5672
Seattle	(206) 442-5930

Elizabeth Dole

Elizabeth Dole, Secretary of Labor

Washington, D.C.
1989 (Revised)
OSHA 2203

U.S. Department of Labor

Occupational Safety and Health Administration

Eventually, OSHA published the federal worker "right-to-know" regulation, known as the Hazard Communication Standard (HCS), which applies to all employers and preempts state worker right-to-know laws. The HCS prescribes a system for communicating data on health hazards to employees. It includes a format for **Material Safety Data Sheets (MSDSs).** MSDSs should include the chemical name of a hazardous substance; all of the risks involved in using it, including potential health risks; safe handling practices; personal protective equipment needed; first aid in the event of an accident; and information identifying the manufacturer.

Enforcement Efforts

As with any law, enforcement efforts will vary from one administration to the next. Under the Carter administration, OSHA inspectors were viewed as being unduly strict on relatively minor infractions, whereas under the Reagan administration OSHA enforcement efforts were seen as virtually nonexistent. The Bush administration has been described as striking a balance between regulatory zealousness and a hands-off approach. Still, unions and safety groups continue to worry that OSHA is lax in monitoring its agreements with organizations, and they prefer mandatory standards instead of voluntary guidelines for problems such as injuries related to jobs involving repetitive motion.

In recent years OSHA has imposed more-substantial fines for safety, health, and recordkeeping violations. The OSHA leadership favors legislation that would stiffen criminal penalties—to as much as ten years in prison—for violations that lead to a worker's death. New York's state court of appeals has also ruled that the federal act does not preempt criminal actions against employers that put the safety and health of their workers at risk. In the case where this ruling was made, the defendants face up to 15 years in prison.[9] It is reasonably safe to assume that penalties for willful violations of safety and health laws and regulations will become more severe.

CREATING A SAFE WORK ENVIRONMENT

We have seen that employers are required by law to provide safe working conditions for their employees. In a survey by the Bureau of National Affairs, over 80 percent of the organizations reported having a formal safety program to meet this requirement.[10] In almost half of these organizations, the HR department or the industrial relations department was reported to be responsible for the safety program. One-third of the respondents have a separate department for administering the safety program. Where there is a separate department, 26 percent of the safety directors report to the top HR officer. In 78 percent of the organizations, the safety officer has the authority to stop operations considered to be hazardous. While the success of a safety program depends largely on managers and supervisors of operating departments, the HR department typically coordinates the safety communication and training programs, maintains safety records required by OSHA, and works closely with managers and supervisors in a cooperative effort to make the program a success.

The BNA survey also showed that nine out of ten organizations with formal safety programs have a safety committee which includes representatives from each department or manufacturing unit. In some of the organizations, union representatives are on the safety committee. Committees are generally involved in investigating accidents and helping to publicize the importance of safety rules and their enforcement.

Safety Motivation and Knowledge

Probably the most important role of a safety program is motivating managers, supervisors, and subordinates to be aware of safety considerations. If managers and supervisors fail to demonstrate this awareness, their subordinates can hardly be expected to do so. Unfortunately, as one expert notes, most managers and supervisors wear their "safety hat" far less often than their "production, quality control, and methods improvement hats." Just as important as safety motivation are a knowledge of safety and an understanding of where to place safety efforts. Training can help personnel on all levels understand the organization's policy on safety, its safety procedures, and its system of establishing accountability.[11]

In recent years it has become increasingly clear that while today's workplace is notably more productive, it is also becoming more dangerous. Safety and labor officials are concerned about recent injury rate increases that appear to be tied to such factors as merger mania and competition. They contend that employees are becoming victims of smaller work crews, more overtime, and faster assembly lines. They caution organizations to be particularly mindful of "Safety First" when they enter heavy production periods.[12]

Safety Awareness Programs

Most organizations have a safety awareness program that entails the use of several different media. Safety lectures, commercially produced films, specially developed videocassettes to meet the specific needs of an organization, and other media such as pamphlets are useful for teaching and motivating employees to follow safe work procedures. A page from one of these pamphlets is shown in Highlights in HRM 1. Posters have been found very effective because they can be displayed in strategic locations where workers will be sure to see them. For example, a shipyard found that placing posters at the work site helped reduce accidents by making employees more conscious of the hazards of using scaffolds.[13]

Safety awareness efforts are usually coordinated by a safety director whose primary function is to enlist the interest and cooperation of all personnel. However, the safety director depends a great deal on managerial and supervisory personnel for the success of the program. It is essential that these personnel set safety goals and

HIGHLIGHTS IN HRM

1 A SAFETY PAMPHLET

SOURCE: National Safety Council. Reproduced with permission.

provide subordinates with feedback concerning their department's performance in meeting these goals.

COMMUNICATION ROLE OF THE SUPERVISOR One of a supervisor's major responsibilities is to communicate to an employee the need to work safely. Beginning with new employee orientation, safety should be emphasized continually. Proper work procedures, the use of protective clothing and devices, and potential hazards should be explained thoroughly. Furthermore, employees' understanding of all these considerations should be verified during training sessions, and employees should be encouraged to take some initiative in maintaining a concern for safety.[14] Since training alone does not ensure continual adherence to safe work practices, supervisors must observe employees at work and reinforce safe practices. Where unsafe acts are detected, supervisors should take immediate action to find the cause. Supervisors should also foster a team spirit of safety among the work group.

SAFETY TRAINING PROGRAMS The safety training programs found in many organizations include first aid, defensive driving, accident prevention techniques, handling of hazardous equipment, and emergency procedures. These programs emphasize the use of emergency first-aid equipment and personal safety equipment. The most common types of personal safety equipment are safety glasses and goggles, face protectors, safety shoes, hard hats, hair protectors, and safety belts. There are also a variety of devices used in many jobs to protect hearing and respiration. Furthermore, many organizations provide training in off-the-job safety—at home, on the highway, etc.—as well as in first aid. Injuries and fatalities away from the job occur much more frequently than those on the job and are reflected in employer costs for insurance premiums, wage continuation, and interrupted production.

SAFETY INCENTIVES For safety training programs to reach their objectives, special attention must be given to the incentives that managers and supervisors use to motivate safe behavior in their subordinates. The goal of every safety incentive program is to reduce accidents and make the workplace safer. Too often, however, an incentive program is based more on penalties and punishments than rewards. Two researchers recently looked at 24 studies where positive reinforcement and feedback were used to reinforce safe behavior. In all of the studies, they found these incentives successful in improving safety conditions or reducing accidents. The incentives included praise, public recognition, cash awards, and certificates that could be exchanged for company products. Every study emphasized the use of feedback.[15]

SAFETY CAMPAIGNS In addition to organizing the regular safety training programs, safety directors often plan special safety campaigns. These campaigns typically emphasize competition among departments or plants, with the department

Safety campaigns remind employees of safe work procedures to be followed.

or plant having the best safety record receiving some type of award or trophy. In some organizations, cash bonuses are given to employees who have outstanding safety records.

Enforcement of Safety Rules

Specific rules and regulations concerning safety are found in 93 percent of the organizations surveyed by the Bureau of National Affairs. Of those surveyed, 77 percent communicate these rules primarily through supervisors; 73 percent, through bulletin-board notices; and 65 percent, through employee handbooks. Safety rules are also emphasized in regular safety meetings, at new employee orientations, and in manuals of standard operating procedures. Such rules typically refer to the following types of employee behaviors:

- Using proper safety devices.
- Using proper work procedures.
- Following good housekeeping practices.
- Complying with accident-and-injury reporting procedures.
- Wearing required safety clothing and equipment.
- Avoiding carelessness or horseplay.

Penalties for violation of safety rules are usually stated in the employee handbook. In a large percentage of organizations, the penalties imposed on violators are the same as those for violations of other rules. They include an oral or written warning for the first violation, suspension or disciplinary layoff for repeated violations, and, as a last resort, dismissal. However, for serious violations—such as smoking around volatile substances—even the first offense may be cause for termination.

Accident Investigations and Records

Every accident, even those considered minor, should be investigated by the supervisor and a member of the safety committee. Such an investigation may determine the factors contributing to the accident and may reveal what corrections are needed to prevent it from happening again. Correction may require rearranging workstations, installing safety guards or controls, or, more often, giving employees additional safety training and reassessing their motivation for safety. Research shows that more than 90 percent of all job-related injuries and accidents are caused by unsafe acts. This is as true in the office as it is in the factory.[16]

OSHA requires that a Log and Summary of Occupational Injuries and Illnesses (OSHA Form 200) be maintained by the organization. All recordable cases are to be entered in the log. A **recordable case** is any occupational death, occupational illness, or occupational injury (except those involving only first aid).[17] Each year the Summary portion of the log is to be posted for one month where employee notices are customarily posted. For every recordable case written in the log, a Supplementary Record of Occupational Injuries and Illnesses (OSHA Form 101) is to be completed. OSHA Form 101 requires answers to questions about the case.

CREATING A HEALTHY WORK ENVIRONMENT

From its title alone, the Occupational Safety and Health Act was clearly designed to protect the health, as well as the safety, of employees. Because of the dramatic impact of workplace accidents, however, managers and employees alike may pay more attention to these kinds of immediate safety concerns than to job conditions that are dangerous to their health. It is essential, therefore, that health hazards be identified and controlled. Attention should also be given to non-work-related illnesses and injuries and their impact on the organization and its members. Special health programs may also be developed to provide assistance to employees with health problems.

Largely because of the growing public awareness of the efforts of environmentalists, factors in the work environment affecting health are receiving greater attention. Air and water pollution on an unprecedented scale throughout the world has made all of us more conscious of the immediate environment in which we live and work. Articles about workers who have been exposed to potential dangers at work can frequently be found in the newspapers. Pressure from the federal government and unions, as well as increased public concern, has given employers a definite incentive to provide the safest and healthiest work environment possible.

Health Hazards and Issues

The scope of possible hazards—chemical, physical, safety, and psychological—and examples of typical work sites where they may occur are shown in the overview in Figure 13–3. Note that the examples given in the right-hand column cover a wide range of jobs and industries.

At one time health hazards were associated primarily with jobs found in industrial processing operations. In recent years, however, hazards in jobs outside the plant, such as in offices, health care facilities, and airports, have been recognized and preventive methods adopted. Substituting materials, altering processes, enclosing or isolating a process, issuing protective equipment, and improving ventilation are some of the common preventions. General conditions of health with respect to sanitation, housekeeping, cleanliness, ventilation, water supply, pest control, and food handling are also important to monitor.

PROLIFERATING CHEMICALS It is estimated that there are more than 65,000 different chemicals currently in use in the United States with which humans may come into contact. No toxicity data are available for about 80 percent of those used commercially.[18] Many of these chemicals are harmful, lurking for years in the body with no outward symptoms until the disease they cause is well established. Cancer, for example, may develop 20 to 40 years after the original exposure to a carcinogen. This time-bomb effect can embroil government, industry, labor, and ultimately the public in controversy over how to care for victims of past exposure and how to develop preventive controls. Specialists in HRM inevitably must participate in helping to solve many specific problems that arise as a result of this controversy.

With the passage of the Toxic Substances Control Act of 1976, the 700-plus new chemicals that are marketed each year must be pretested for safety. Since 1977, OSHA has been giving greater attention to setting standards for toxic conditions created by hazardous chemicals. Until that time, toxic substances had been a neglected area despite the fact that their effects showed up in OSHA statistics. As of 1987, skin diseases and disorders (54,200 cases) and respiratory conditions due to toxic agents (14,300 cases) were outnumbered only by disorders associated with repeated trauma to the wrists and arms. Of increasing concern are the reproductive health hazards faced by employees.

Employers must make the workplace as safe as possible and should warn employees—male and female—of possible hazards. However, some employers, including at least 15 major corporations, have gone beyond warnings to the adoption of *fetal protection* policies in some of their plants. Among those having such policies are General Motors, DuPont, Olin, Monsanto, and B. F. Goodrich. While fetal protection policies appear to many to provide reasonable precautions to fetal injury, they have often been viewed as an excuse for denying women equal employment opportunities.

Since 1982 Johnson Controls, Inc., the largest maker of automobile batteries, had a policy that excluded all women capable of bearing children from its battery factories because they could be exposed to lead—a known danger to a developing fetus. A lawsuit filed by women working in the Johnson Controls plant in Fullerton, California, finally resulted in a U.S. Supreme Court decision (6–3 vote). In *Interna-*

FIGURE 13–3 OVERVIEW OF OCCUPATIONAL HEALTH HAZARDS AND EXAMPLES OF ASSOCIATED WORK SETTINGS

HAZARDS	EXAMPLES OF TYPICAL WORK SITES
Chemical hazards	
Carcinogens (e.g., asbestos, benzene, radon, nickel)	Chemical industry, hospitals, metal mining and smelting, welding, agriculture
Pulmonary toxins (e.g., cotton dust, silica, cigarette smoke, indoor air pesticides)	Textile industry, chemical industry, coal miners, construction workers, office workers
Reproductive hazards (e.g., solvents, lead pesticides)	Health care workers, chemical workers, textile workers, laboratory technicians, agricultural workers, microelectronics industry
Skin irritants and sensitizers (e.g., formaldehyde, spices, dyes, metals, photographic chemicals)	Food handlers, health care workers, office workers, household workers
Physical hazards	
Ionizing radiation (e.g., X-rays, alpha, beta, and gamma rays)	Health care workers, nuclear power plant workers, airline flight crews
Non-ionizing radiations (e.g., microwaves)	Radar operators, diathermy machine operators, food processors
Noise and vibration	Airport workers, factory workers, computer operators, woodworkers, power tool operators
Heat and cold	Meat handlers, bakery workers, glassworkers, smelter and mill workers
Safety hazards	
Electrical hazards	Electricians; health care workers, office workers
Fire	All workers
Biomechanical stressors (e.g., lifting, uncomfortable working position)	Video display terminal operators, health care workers, truck drivers, hand tool operators
Slipping and falling hazards	Construction workers, cleaners, and maintenance workers
Psychological hazards (e.g., work overload, organizational structure, job insecurity, interpersonal relationships)	All workers

SOURCE: Jeanne M. Stellman and Barry R. Snow, "Occupational Safety and Health Hazards and the Psychological Health and Well-Being of Workers," in *Health and Industry—A Behavioral Medicine Perspective,* ed. Michael F. Cataldo and Thomas J. Coates (New York: Wiley, 1986), 272. Reprinted with permission.

tional Union v. *Johnson Controls*, the Court ruled in 1991 that employers may not bar women of childbearing age from certain jobs because of potential risk to their fetuses. The Court said that such policies are a form of sex bias that is prohibited by federal civil rights law. The decision will make it important for employers to inform and to warn women workers about fetal health risks on the job.[19]

OFFICE HAZARDS In the first book written for a general readership about the hazards of office environments, the author warns that, among all of the hazards, air pollution may be the most severe.[20] He lists 20 major air pollutants that come from building materials, furniture and furnishings, duplicating fluids, typewriter cleaners, tobacco smoke, photocopier toners, rubber cement, correction fluids, and other items commonly found in an office. Chemicals used in an office can also cause a variety of skin problems. Like factory workers, office workers are subject to hazards such as cuts, trips, falls, electrical shock, fires, and noise.

VIDEO DISPLAY TERMINALS The expanding use of computers and video display terminals (VDTs) in the workplace has generated intense debate over the possible hazards to which VDT users may be exposed. Many fears about VDT use have been shown to be unfounded, but serious health complaints remain an issue drawing attention to the need for more information, education, and positive action. Problems that HR managers have to confront in this area fall into four major groups:

1. *Visual Difficulties.* VDT operators frequently complain of blurred vision, sore eyes, burning and itching eyes, and glare.
2. *Radiation Hazards.* Cataract formation and reproductive problems, including miscarriages and birth defects, have been attributed to VDT use. The risks of exposure to VDT radiation have yet to be determined.
3. *Muscular Aches and Pains.* Pains in the back, neck, and shoulders are common complaints of VDT operators.
4. *Job Stress.* Eye strain, postural problems, noise, insufficient training, excessive workloads, and monotonous work are complaints reported by three-quarters of VDT users.[21]

To capitalize on the benefits of VDTs while safeguarding employee health, organizations are advised to consider several strategies. These include educating employees in proper use of VDTs; involving employees in system design; encouraging open-door communication with management so that concerns may be voiced and solutions found; using rest periods and job rotation; using ergonomically designed equipment; and ensuring that workstations have appropriate lighting. It should be recognized that many employees feel threatened by the new technology, and some are apprehensive about "blowing" the system. As a result, HR managers should plan for VDT operators to receive training in how the computer system as a whole works, and they should understand that they will not crash the system by pushing the wrong button.[22] This understanding can help to reduce the stress that

VDT operators experience. Other ways of reducing stress will be discussed later in this chapter.

It is interesting to note how one company handles one type of VDT concern. While IBM does not have a written policy of reassigning pregnant VDT operators to jobs not involving use of VDTs, when such requests are made, the company does everything it can to accommodate these employees.[23]

CUMULATIVE TRAUMA DISORDERS Meat cutters, fish filleters, dental hygienists, textile workers, violinists, flight attendants, office workers at computer terminals, and others whose jobs require repetitive motion of the fingers, hands, or arms are reporting injuries in growing percentages. Known as **cumulative trauma disorders**, these injuries involve tendons that become inflamed from repeated stresses and strains. One of the more common conditions is carpal tunnel syndrome, which is characterized by tingling or numbness in the fingers occurring when a tunnel of bones and ligaments in the wrist narrows and pinches nerves that reach the fingers and base of the thumb. To prevent repetitive-motion injuries, minibreaks involving exercises, properly designed workstations, the changing of positions, and improvement in tool design have been found helpful. These kinds of injuries often go away if they are caught early. If they are not, they may require months or years of treatment or even surgical correction.[24]

According to a 1984 estimate, lost earnings and costs of medical treatment for repetitive-motion injuries amount to more than $27 billion each year. Recognizing that the problem is growing, OSHA is attacking it aggressively. The levying of OSHA fines has prompted employers to take action to prevent these injuries. Unfortunately, many physicians do not see a connection between employees' symptoms and their work environments, and they tell patients that the problem is psychosomatic. Such reports lead employers to believe that workers are malingering. Gradually, however, more physicians are realizing that work is the origin for these disorders.[25] While HRM personnel are not expected to play the role of doctor, they should be alert to injuries that occur among employees who perform similar tasks under similar conditions.

TOBACCO SMOKE Probably the most heated workplace health issue of the 1980s was smoking. Nonsmokers, fueled by studies linking "passive smoking" (inhaling other people's smoke) with disease and death, and irritated by smoke getting in their eyes, noses, throats, clothes, etc., have been extremely vocal in demanding a smoke-free environment. At least 42 states and the District of Columbia, as well as numerous cities, towns, and counties, have passed laws restricting smoking in offices and other public places. Often, as in California, the local ordinances are broader and more stringent than the state law and frequently mandate stiffer fines for violators.

The number of employers with policies on workplace smoking has increased almost fourfold since the early 1980s, according to an Administrative Management

Where laws do not require it, organizations often institute their own no-smoking policies.

survey of 283 managers in 1989. Sixty percent of the respondents said their organizations have a smoking policy—up from just 16 percent in 1980. A 1987 ASPA/BNA survey of 623 organizations showed that 54 percent had smoking policies. Large organizations are somewhat more likely than small employers to have such policies. There are also significant regional differences, with 73 percent in the West, 58 percent in the Northeast, 55 percent in north central states, and 44 percent in the South having smoking policies.[26]

Organizational policies on smoking in the workplace typically explain the reason for the policy, specify where employees can and cannot smoke, and state the penalties for violations. Procedures for resolving disputes between smokers and nonsmokers are frequently included. A model policy for smoking in the workplace developed by BNA is shown in Highlights in HRM 2.

Efforts to help employees quit smoking are being promoted by many employers. The two most popular steps taken are to distribute quit-smoking literature and to sponsor employee wellness programs that encourage workers to stop smoking. Employer-sponsored quit-smoking clinics are found in such organizations as Sandia Laboratories in Albuquerque, the Iowa Methodist Medical Center, Alcoa, and Control Data Corporation, as well as in Johnson & Johnson's Live for Life Program.[27] Other employers have been more direct in their approach. In 1985, Pacific Northwest Bell Telephone put its 15,000 employees on notice: In three months there would be no smoking allowed at work—anywhere, anytime. It is interesting to note that a poll at Texas Instruments found that 90 percent of all employees favored policies to protect nonsmokers.[28]

Because of documented higher health care costs for smokers, some employers are charging smokers more for health insurance or are reducing their benefits. Many employers, however, prefer positive reinforcement through wellness programs to encourage their employees to stop smoking.[29]

AIDS In recent years, few workplace issues have received as much attention as AIDS (acquired immune deficiency syndrome). Many legal and medical questions have arisen that have made it imperative for employers to provide answers to everyone concerned.

As we observed in Chapter 3, AIDS is a handicap covered by federal, state, and local protective statutes. Employers subject to statutes under which AIDS victims are likely to be considered handicapped are required to hire or retain an AIDS victim qualified to perform the essential functions of his or her job. The federal Rehabilitation Act, the Americans with Disabilities Act, and statutes of several states also require employers to give reasonable accommodation to the person through job restructuring, modified work schedules, less rigid physical requirements, etc.[30]

While there is still no evidence that AIDS can be spread through casual contact in the typical workplace, one of the major problems employers face is the concern that many people have about contracting it. Employers have found it important to have programs to educate managers about the transmission of AIDS and to educate the entire work force about AIDS through newsletters, posters, and seminars. The

HIGHLIGHTS IN HRM

2 A SMOKING POLICY

Sample Policy

Subject: Workplace Smoking

Purpose: To protect the health of all employees, avoid conflicts between smoking and nonsmoking workers, and ensure accommodations for nonsmokers' preferences when necessary.

Guidelines:

1. Smoking is permitted outdoors or in designated sections of the cafeteria and employee lounges and break areas.
2. Smoking is prohibited in all meeting rooms, classrooms, restrooms, hallways, elevators, and other common-access areas.
3. Employees who do not smoke have the right to post a no-smoking sign on their desk or at their work station and co-workers who smoke must honor these requests. Employees who have objections to smoke in their work area must submit a written statement to their supervisor outlining the basic reasons for their objections along with possible solutions to the problem.
4. Work units or departments may formulate smoking policies for their work areas designed to accommodate the preferences of smokers and nonsmokers. All employees in a unit shall be allowed to vote on any such policy. If differences cannot be resolved, the manager of the unit or department will be responsible for trying to fashion a reasonable accommodation, such as ventilation modifications, the use of filtering devices such as air purifiers or cleaners, or the relocation of work stations. The cost of purchasing filtering devices will be borne by employees who request them.
5. Supervisors who receive a written statement of objections to smoking from a worker will meet with the employee to discuss possible accommodations. Employees should be asked if devices such as air purifiers or filters would satisfy their objections. The supervisor should consider the feasibility of separating the work stations of smokers and nonsmokers if this would resolve the problem. If no mutually acceptable solution can be found, the supervisor must accommodate the nonsmoker by designating the work area as a no-smoking zone.
6. Employees may enroll in either a worksite smoking-cessation program or outside programs sponsored by local agencies and organizations. The worksite program will be free of charge to participants and one-half of the time spent in the sessions will be paid time. The company will reimburse employees for three-quarters of the cost of participating in an off-site smoking-cessation program. Employees who successfully quit smoking for a one-year period will be eligible for a one-time $50 bonus.
7. The company will be responsible for supplying all no-smoking signs, notices, and postings used on the premises.

8. Violators of the smoking restrictions set forth in this policy will be subject to the standard disciplinary penalties, i.e., first offenses will elicit an oral warning, second offenses a written warning, etc.
9. These guidelines will be effective 90 days from the date they are issued.

SOURCE: Reprinted with permission from *Employment Guide,* p. 50:84. Copyright 1991 by The Bureau of National Affairs, Inc.

American Management Association has prepared a briefing book on AIDS for managers that contains chapters on how to handle AIDS in the workplace, including legal issues, insurance concerns, and medical considerations.[31] The managers' job of communicating AIDS information has also been assisted by the Surgeon General's Report on AIDS, which has been distributed widely by various health organizations, many government offices, and members of Congress.

The Bureau of National Affairs reports that as of 1989, U.S. employers have generally taken a low-key approach to dealing with AIDS. A BNA survey revealed that only 2 percent had issued formal, written policies; 21 percent said they were considering such policies.[32] BankAmerica and Wells Fargo were among the first to establish policy guidelines. BankAmerica's policy may be found in Chapter 3, Highlights in HRM 1. (It would be a good idea to review this policy now. Note that it refers to assisting employees with any life-threatening illness, including AIDS.)

Because of the controversial nature of AIDS, employers have found that managers and HR personnel must be carefully briefed on all aspects of the issue so they may act in the best interests of all concerned. HR journals, as well as health journals, have published numerous articles in the past several years that can be useful in developing reading files for the HR staff and for managerial and supervisory personnel.[33]

Building Better Health

Along with improving working conditions that are hazardous to employee health, many employers provide health services and have programs that encourage employees to improve their health habits. It is recognized that better health not only benefits the individual, but also pays off for the organization in reduced absenteeism, increased efficiency, better morale, and other savings. An increased understanding of the close relationship between physical/emotional health and job performance has made broad health-building programs attractive to employers, as well as to employees.

HEALTH SERVICES The type of health services employers provide is primarily related to the size of the organization and the importance of such services. Some organizations have only limited facilities, such as those needed to handle first-aid cases, while others offer complete medical diagnostic, treatment, and emergency surgical services. Since employers are required to provide medical services after an injury, they usually have nursing personnel on full-time duty and physicians on call. Medium-sized and larger organizations have one or more physicians on duty as regular employees. Typically, HR personnel work closely with them in the performance of their job functions.

We noted in Chapter 6 that about one-half of all employers give preemployment medical examinations to prospective employees. Generally, these examinations are required to assure employers that the health of applicants is adequate for the job. The preemployment examination should include a medical history with special reference to previous hazardous exposures. Exposure to hazards whose effects may be cumulative, such as noise, lead, and radiation, are especially relevant. For jobs involving unusual physical demands, the applicant's muscular development, flexibility, agility, range of motion, and cardiac and respiratory functions should be evaluated. The preemployment medical examination that includes laboratory analyses can help screen those applicants who abuse drugs. Many organizations also give periodic examinations on either a required or a voluntary basis. Such examinations are useful in determining the effects of potential hazards in the workplace, as well as detecting any health problems to which an employee's particular life-style or health habits may contribute.

WELLNESS PROGRAMS Many organizations have developed programs that emphasize regular exercise, proper nutrition, weight control, and avoidance of substances harmful to health. For example, the employee health management program at Xerox includes cardiovascular fitness through aerobic exercises such as jogging, skipping rope, and racquet sports. The company gives its employees a *Fitbook* that provides instructions and illustrations for a variety of exercises. The book also includes chapters on the hazards of smoking and the effects of alcohol and drug abuse, facts on nutrition and weight control, and guidelines for managing stress and learning to relax.[34] Smaller organizations may distribute booklets available from services specializing in employee communication materials. Highlights in HRM 3 is a page from such a booklet, *What Everyone Should Know About Wellness*.

Tenneco, with headquarters in Houston, has one of the finest fitness centers in corporate America. It includes racquetball courts, exercise rooms, saunas, and a one-fifth-mile indoor jogging track. The center has its own computer program to help employees monitor their progress. Employees of ROLM Corporation in California's Silicon Valley enjoy a million-dollar recreation facility, where in midafternoon it is common to see them swimming, playing racquetball, or working out in an aerobics class.[35] Some employers have inaugurated plans that provide monetary rewards for individuals who follow certain health rules or who reach goals established for healthful living.

There is mounting evidence to support the link between certain nutritional deficiencies and various physiological and psychological disorders, including alcoholism, depression, nervousness, low energy level, perceptual inaccuracy, and lack of reasonability. In fact, a person's mental and emotional states are affected by the foods he or she consumes. It has been suggested that the potential return on a minimal investment in a sound nutritional plan is great, in terms of both dollars and

HIGHLIGHTS IN HRM

3 EMPLOYEE PUBLICATIONS ON WELLNESS

SOURCE: Reproduced from "About Wellness" with permission, © 1988, Channing L. Bete Co., South Deerfield, MA 01373.

morale, because human behavior might be more easily and quickly modified by dietary changes than by more sophisticated organizational modification techniques.[36] Lotus Development Corporation organized a nutrition education program where employees can choose to spend one lunch hour a week in class. After completing the program, 81 percent of the participants attribute feeling better to an improved diet, and 69 percent report being more productive on the job.[37]

SPECIAL HEALTH PROGRAMS FOR EXECUTIVES Long before fitness programs for the public became popular, attention was being given to the health of executive personnel. For an executive health program to be effective, it should include more than just a periodic physical examination. It should provide services that deal with the whole person—intellect, emotions, physical well-being—and the individual's life-style. Physicians who use a preventive approach with emphasis on nutrition, exercise, and healthful living are frequently affiliated with executive health programs.

Special programs, such as those offered by the Longevity Research Center of Santa Monica, California, provide training in proper diet and exercise, primarily walking. The late Nathan Pritikin and his colleagues developed a plan known as the "2100 Program" that has been successful in helping people overcome degenerative diseases. The scientific basis for the diet is given in Pritikin's books.[38] It involves avoiding fats, oils, sugar, salt, cholesterol, and caffeine—dietary items linked to heart attacks, diabetes, strokes, and other diseases associated with aging. By participating in special health programs designed for them, executives can learn how to change their life-styles to reduce the risk of strokes and heart attacks.

Employee Assistance Programs

A broad view of health includes the emotional, as well as the physical, aspects of one's life. While emotional problems, personal crises, alcoholism, and drug abuse are considered to be personal matters, they become organizational problems when they affect behavior at work and interfere with job performance. To be able to handle such problems, 87 percent of all employers with 5,000 or more workers offer an employee assistance program (EAP).[39] Typically, such a program refers employees in need of assistance to in-house counselors or outside professionals, usually psychologists or psychiatrists. Supervisors are often given training and policy guidance in the type of help they can offer their subordinates. In contracting with professional counselors outside the organization, the HR department needs to give special attention to their credentials, liability and confidentiality, cost, accountability, and service capabilities.

PERSONAL CRISES The most prevalent problems among employees are personal crises involving marital, family, financial, or legal matters. Such problems often come to a supervisor's attention. In most instances, the supervisor can usually provide the best help simply by being understanding and supportive and by helping the individual find the type of assistance he or she needs. In many cases, in-house counseling or referral to an outside professional is recommended. In recent years, crisis hot lines have been set up in many communities to provide counseling by telephone for those too distraught to wait for an appointment with a counselor.

EMOTIONAL PROBLEMS While personal crises are typically fraught with emotion, most of them are resolved in a reasonable period of time and the troubled individual's equilibrium is restored. There will, however, be a small percentage of employees—roughly 3 percent on average—who have emotional problems serious enough to require professional treatment. Whether such individuals will be able to perform their jobs must be determined on an individual basis. In reviewing such cases, the organization should pay particular attention to workplace safety factors, since there is general agreement that emotional disturbances are primary or secondary factors in a large proportion of industrial accidents.

Managers should also be aware that the behavior of some individuals is adversely affected by substances in the workplace that apparently do not affect others, or at least not as severely. Such individuals are, in fact, allergic to these substances. They may simply need to be reassigned to a different work environment rather than sent to a physician. Physicians who work in this area, called **clinical ecology,** report numerous cases of individuals whose behavior on and off the job is affected by petrochemicals, molds, cleaning substances, cosmetics and toiletries, plastics, tobacco smoke—in fact, virtually anything that can be found in the environment. Those who are allergic to such items may exhibit behavioral symptoms ranging from severe depression to extreme hyperactivity that interfere with job performance. Remove the substance, or get the individuals away from the substance, and the symptoms disappear. Dr. Theron Randolph, a Chicago allergist, was among the first to write about the importance of environmental chemicals, in addition to foods, as the cause of many physical and emotional illnesses.[40] His work has stimulated other allergists, as well as mental health practitioners, to study the phenomenon further.

ALCOHOLISM Business and industry lose an estimated $20.6 billion each year because of alcoholism, according to The Conference Board. The National Council for Alcoholism reports that in this country alone there are more than 10.5 million alcoholics. Alcoholism affects workers in every occupational category—blue-collar, white-collar, and managerial.[41]

In confronting the problem, employers must recognize that alcoholism is a disease that follows a rather predictable course. Because of this fact, they can take specific actions to deal with employees showing symptoms of the disease at particular stages of its progression. Alcoholism typically begins with social drinking getting out of control. As the disease progresses, the alcoholic loses control over how much to drink and eventually cannot keep from drinking even at inappropriate times. The person uses denial to avoid facing the problems created by the abuse of alcohol and often blames others for these problems. A U.S. Air Force counselor states that the first step in helping the alcoholic is to awaken the person to the reality of his or her situation.[42]

To identify alcoholism as early as possible, it is essential that supervisors monitor the performance of all personnel regularly and systematically. A supervisor should carefully document evidence of declining performance on the job and then confront the employee with unequivocal proof that the job is suffering. The employee should be assured that help will be made available without penalty. Since the evaluations are made solely in terms of lagging job performance, a supervisor can avoid any mention of alcoholism and allow such employees to seek aid as they would for any other problem. Disciplinary action may be taken against employees who refuse to take advantage of such assistance or whose performance does not improve with repeated warnings. Between 70 and 80 percent of the employees accept the offer to get help and resolve their problems. It is important for employers to recognize, however, that in discharge cases brought by alcoholic employees, arbitrators look at on-the-job alcoholism as a sickness, not as a disciplinary matter.

EAPs typically provide assistance to the alcoholic employee. Rehabilitation is generally conducted by referral agencies. A large percentage of medical insurance now covers part of the treatment costs for alcoholism, making it possible to receive treatment at reasonable costs.

DRUG ABUSE The abuse of drugs by employees is one of the major employment issues today. Once confined to a small segment of the population, drug abuse is now a growing national problem that has spread to every industry and occupation as well as employee level. Executives and federal officials say that the use of cocaine and crack in the workplace is growing rapidly. Estimates of the costs of substance abuse by employees vary considerably. The federal government estimates in one report that alcohol and drug abuse cost the economy $177 billion a year, including $99 billion for lost productivity.[43] In addition to lost productivity, there are the costs of increased numbers of accidents and injuries, higher medical insurance costs, and rising rates of employee theft. The costs of substance abuse are having a dramatic impact on the bottom line.

A poster such as this is usually found in the employment office.

In the past, most efforts to curb workplace drug abuse have been voluntary actions on the part of management. Now, however, a wide range of employers, including federal contractors and private and public transportation firms, are subject to new regulations aimed at eliminating the use of illegal drugs on the job. The new federal anti-drug initiatives are as follows:

1. Drug-Free Workplace Act of 1988, which requires federal contractors and recipients of federal grants to take specific steps to ensure a drug-free work environment. One of the main provisions of the Act is the preparation and distribution of an anti-drug policy statement, a sample of which is shown in Highlights in HRM 4.
2. Department of Defense (DOD) Contract Rules, which specify that employers entering into contracts with the DOD must agree to a clause certifying their intention to maintain a drug-free workplace.

HIGHLIGHTS IN HRM

4 POLICY ON DRUG-FREE WORKPLACE

Sample Policy Statement

To: All Employees
From: [Company President]
Re: Policy on Drug-Free Workplace

This is to reiterate, and state in a more formal way, our policy regarding the work-related effects of drug use and the unlawful possession of controlled substances on company premises. Our policy is as follows:

- Employees are expected and required to report to work on time and in appropriate mental and physical condition for work. It is our intent and obligation to provide a drug-free, healthful, safe, and secure work environment.
- The unlawful manufacture, distribution, dispensation, possession, or use of a controlled substance on company premises or while conducting company business off company premises is absolutely prohibited. Violations of this policy will result in disciplinary action, up to and including termination, and may have legal consequences.
- The company recognizes drug dependency as an illness and a major health problem. The company also recognizes drug abuse as a potential health, safety, and security problem. Employees needing help in dealing with such problems are encouraged to use our employee assistance program and health insurance plans, as appropriate. Conscientious efforts to seek such help will not jeopardize any employee's job, and will not be noted in any personnel record.
- Employees must, as a condition of employment, abide by the terms of the above policy and report any conviction under a criminal drug statute for violations occurring on or off company premises while conducting company business. A report of a conviction must be made within five (5) days after the conviction. (This requirement is mandated by the Drug-Free Workplace Act of 1988.)

SOURCE: Reprinted with permission from *Personnel Management (BNA Policy and Practice Series)*, p. 247:553. Copyright 1990 by The Bureau of National Affairs, Inc.

3. Department of Transportation (DOT) regulations, which require that employees whose jobs include safety or security-related duties be tested for illegal drug use under DOT rules.[44]

We observed in Chapter 6 that a number of employers test for substance abuse in the final stages of the employee selection process. At this point it is often easy to screen out applicants who may become problem employees. Once an applicant is accepted, however, the employer is faced with the problem of controlling drug abuse. For this reason, an increasing number of employers are instituting testing programs.

As noted earlier, employers operating under the new federal requirements are required to test for drug use under certain specified conditions. However, employers that are exempt from the federal requirement may operate under state or local laws restricting or prohibiting drug tests. Issues related to drug testing under state or local laws are discussed in Chapter 16 in the context of employee rights.

While our discussion has focused primarily on the abuse of illegal drugs, it should be noted that the abuse of legal drugs can also pose a problem for employers. Employees who abuse legal drugs—i.e., those prescribed by physicians—often do not realize they have become addicted or how their behavior has changed as a result of their addiction. Often such individuals have prescriptions from more than one physician and may be cross-medicating with drugs that fall under the general headings of sedatives, narcotics, and stimulants. Others may not have advised their physician of their drug dependency even if they are aware of it. Also, HR personnel should be aware that some employees may be taking legal sedatives or stimulants as part of their medical treatment and that their behavior at work may be affected by their use of these drugs.[45]

Various approaches are used in EAPs to assist individuals with a chemical dependency, ranging from outpatient treatment to an extended stay in a specialized hospital unit. One approach that has proved successful and less expensive is known as a day treatment program. United Technologies has developed an intensive program in which the average treatment lasts two weeks. Participants report each day for a structured program that avoids the costs of a residential program with bed and board. Employees prefer this form of treatment because it enables them to stay in touch with their job and to avoid painful separation from their families while receiving treatment.[46]

THE MANAGEMENT OF STRESS

Many jobs require employees to adjust to conditions that place unusual demands on them. In time these demands create stresses that can affect the health of employees as well as their productivity and satisfaction. Fortunately, increasing attention is being given to ways of identifying and preventing undue stress on the job. Even greater attention must be given to identifying and removing sources of stress to protect the well-being of employees and to reduce the costs to organizations. The costs of stress in health insurance claims, disability claims, and lost productivity alone are between $50 billion and $150 billion per year. Looking to the mid-1990s and beyond, NIOSH has predicted a need for greater emphasis on ways to reduce stress in the workplace.[47]

What Is Stress?

Stress is any demand on the individual that requires coping behavior. Stress comes from two basic sources: physical activity and mental or emotional activity. The physical reaction of the body to both sources is the same. According to the late Hans Selye, human beings thrive on stress because "stress is the spice of life."[48] Selye uses two separate terms to distinguish between positive and negative life consequences of stress for the individual, even though reactions to the two forms of stress are the same biochemically. **Eustress** is positive stress that accompanies achievement and exhilaration. Eustress is the stress of meeting challenges such as those found in a managerial job or physical activity. Selye regards eustress as a beneficial force that helps us to forge ahead against obstacles. He is of the opinion that what is harmful is **distress.** Stress becomes distress when we begin to sense a loss of our feelings of security and adequacy. Helplessness, desperation, and disappointment turn stress into distress.

The stress reaction is a coordinated chemical mobilization of the entire body to meet the requirements of fight-or-flight in a situation perceived to be stressful. The sympathetic nervous system activates the secretion of hormones from the endocrine glands that places the body on a "war footing." This response, commonly referred to as the **alarm reaction,** basically involves an elevated heart rate, increased respiration, elevated levels of adrenaline in the blood, and increased blood pressure. It persists until one's estimate of the relative threat to well-being has been reevalu-

ated. While the alarm reaction may have made life safer for our ancestors who were confronted daily with physical peril, it lacks value for most of the invisible enemies of contemporary life.

If distress persists long enough, it can result in fatigue, exhaustion, and even physical and/or emotional breakdown. When Selye first published his experimental findings more than half a century ago, many medical practitioners failed to recognize the role of stress in a wide range of illnesses for which there is no specific cause. Some research has suggested a link between stress and heart disease. A recent study is the first to show a connection between chronic stress and hypertension (high blood pressure). High blood pressure, the most common cause of strokes, contributes to heart disease.[49]

Job-related Stress

Although the body experiences a certain degree of stress (either eustress or distress) in all situations, here we are primarily concerned with the stress related to the work setting. It is in this setting that management can use some preventive approaches.

SOURCES OF JOB-RELATED STRESS James and Jonathan Quick have made a careful study of stress in organizational settings. In Figure 13–4, taken from their article, we observe that the major sources of stress in organizations—**organizational stressors**—involve role factors, job factors, physical factors, and interpersonal factors. These stressors give rise to either the fight or flight reaction described previously. The effects of distress are usually expressed in terms of individual costs and organizational costs. In their article, the Quicks recommend some preventive methods that will be examined later in this discussion.

EXAMPLES OF JOB-RELATED DISTRESS Disagreements with supervisors or fellow employees are a common cause of distress. A myriad of other events may also prove distressful. One individual, for example, remembers the time in the armed forces when he was made to rewrite a letter 13 times. "I couldn't walk off the job," he recalls, "so I went to the men's room and hit the wall so hard my co-workers came in to see what was wrong." Feeling trapped in a job for which a person is ill-suited can be equally distressing. An airline attendant said that she was sick of "smiling when I don't want to smile" and "making excuses for the airline to furious passengers," but she did not consider herself qualified for other jobs with similar pay and benefits.[50]

Many minor irritations can also be sources of distress. Lack of privacy in offices, unappealing music, excessive smoke, and other conditions can be distressful to one person or another. There are even more serious conditions related to the management of personnel. Potentially distressful factors include having little to say about how a job is performed, overspecialization, lack of communication on the job, and lack of recognition for a job well done.

FIGURE 13–4 STRESS IN ORGANIZATIONAL SETTINGS

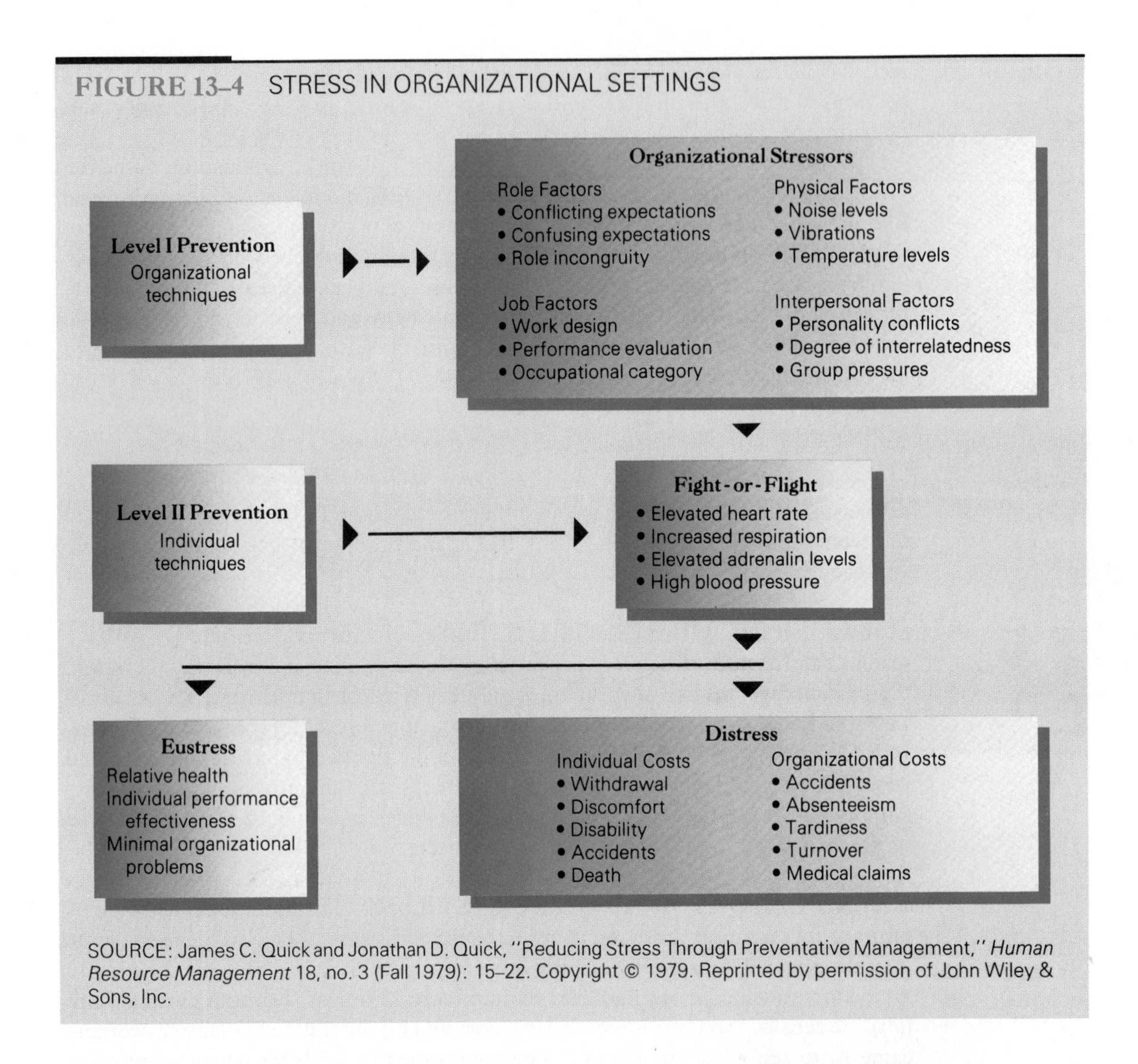

SOURCE: James C. Quick and Jonathan D. Quick, "Reducing Stress Through Preventative Management," *Human Resource Management* 18, no. 3 (Fall 1979): 15–22. Copyright © 1979. Reprinted by permission of John Wiley & Sons, Inc.

Burnout is the most severe stage of distress. Career burnout generally occurs when a person begins questioning his or her own personal values. Quite simply, one no longer feels that what he or she is doing is important. Depression, frustration, and a loss of productivity are all symptoms of burnout. Burnout is due primarily to a lack of personal fulfillment in the job or a lack of positive feedback about performance.

EMPLOYER RESPONSIBILITY FOR JOB-RELATED DISTRESS

The issue of stress on the job has received considerable publicity in the various media. As a result, employees have begun to recognize that stress may have caused them psychological harm and have responded by striking back in the courts. Employers that once gave minimal attention to stress on the job are now required to take positive steps to identify specific sources of organizational stressors and to take corrective action.

According to a 1988 study, stress accounts for about 14 percent of occupational disease claims, up from less than 5 percent in 1980. In California alone the number of mental-stress claims grew more than fivefold between 1980 and 1986. Claims have mushroomed because of (1) the growing number of employees in service jobs where the work is more mental than manual, (2) the repetitive nature of tasks, (3) the trend toward seeking compensation for mental as well as physical injuries, and (4) the receptivity of the courts to such cases.[51]

Awareness of the legal implications of workplace stressors will help managers to initiate programs. Citing landmark cases that have provided compensation for psychological injuries resulting from emotional stress, several experts recommend the following five-step program:

1. Formulate a preventive legal strategy through analysis and forecasting of trends that indicate the direction of new legislation.
2. Develop a stress diagnostic system to increase awareness and sensitivity to employee concerns.
3. Involve top-level management in developing priorities and procedures for correcting problem areas.
4. Evaluate current programs by determining if stress-related problems still remain.
5. Document what has been done to correct situations that result in stress, but be prepared to do something about them.[52]

Training managers to recognize the symptoms of stress, to refer employees who may need professional help, and to implement programs for monitoring and treating problems is an important responsibility of the HR department. It is generally agreed that stress-management programs usually result in a net savings rather than a cost. The Equitable Life Assurance Society, for example, estimates that for every dollar it spends on its program, it saves $5.52.[53]

Stress-Management Programs

Many employers have developed stress-management programs to teach employees how to minimize the negative effects of job-related stress. A typical program might include relaxation techniques, coping skills, listening skills, methods of dealing with difficult people, time management, and assertion. All of these techniques are designed to break the pattern of tension that accompanies stress situations and to help participants achieve greater control of their lives. Organizational techniques, such as clarifying the employee's work role, redesigning and enriching jobs, correcting physical factors in the environment, and effectively handling interpersonal factors, should not be overlooked in the process of teaching employees how to handle stress. A recent review of research on work-site stress-management programs reveals that organizational stressors have not received the attention they should. There has been too much emphasis on helping individuals adjust to undesirable working conditions rather than on changing the conditions themselves.[54]

Even though the number and severity of organizational stressors can be reduced, everyone encounters situations that may be described as distressful. Those in good physical health are generally better able to cope with the stressors they encounter in their everyday lives. For those who wish to improve their power to cope with stress, one group of researchers that worked with 300 managers from 12 companies in London, Ontario, recommends the following coping techniques:

1. Building resistance by regular sleep and good health habits.
2. Keeping work and nonwork life separate.
3. Getting exercise.
4. Talking things through with on-the-job peers.
5. Withdrawing physically from a situation when necessary.[55]

Many organizations also remind their employees through various publications and posters that stress can be reduced by the employee's own behavior.

Employees should be made aware that some of the popular rituals that are supposed to relieve stress, such as the "coffee break," may be counterproductive if they lead to overconsumption of beverages containing caffeine. Many individuals develop anxiety symptoms from overdoses of caffeine. Their condition, which is often misdiagnosed as a psychological ailment, may well affect their behavior and

Exercise instead of coffee at break time may help reduce stress more effectively.

their productivity on the job. Instead of coffee breaks, many organizations are encouraging their employees to take exercise breaks.

Before concluding this discussion, we should observe that stress which is harmful to some employees may be healthy for others. Most executives learn to handle distress effectively and find that it actually stimulates better performance. However, there will always be those who are unable to handle stress and need assistance in learning to cope with it. The increased interest of young and old alike in developing habits that will enable them to lead happier and more productive lives will undoubtedly be beneficial to them as individuals, to the organizations where they work, and to a society where people are becoming more and more interdependent.

SUMMARY

The Occupational Safety and Health Act of 1970 has provided considerable impetus for the improvement of safety and health on the job. Both employers and employees have responsibilities and rights under the Act; however, employers have the major burden. In recent years, government administrators have simplified regulations and emphasized their enforcement for the most serious safety and health problems. The need to meet the equipment and environmental requirements of OSHA standards has caused employers to overlook the behavioral aspects of safety. Having well-publicized rules, motivating supervisors and employees to observe safety, and creating a work climate that is conducive to safety are essential components of any safety program.

Many processes and materials that may be hazardous to health are found in the workplace. Among these health hazards are chemicals, video display terminals, cumulative trauma disorders, and tobacco smoke. Not all of the hazards are acute or easily identified. As a result, the onset of illnesses that may become chronic is often unnoticed. It is the responsibility of employers to identify, control, and eliminate the source of these illnesses.

The emotional, as well as the physical, aspects of an employee's life are now recognized as management concerns. Employee assistance programs have been given increased attention in an effort to assist workers who have emotional problems or who need assistance for alcohol or drug abuse. Growing attention is being given to the prevention of all kinds of health problems through physical fitness and health programs of various types. Creating less stressful work environments and helping employees cope with stress are preventive steps that are receiving increased attention from employers.

DISCUSSION QUESTIONS

1. When OSHA was enacted in 1970, it was heralded as the most important new source of protection for the American worker in this half of the 20th century. What opinions about the effectiveness or the ineffectiveness of the Act or its implementation have you heard from acquaintances who have been affected by it?
2. What steps should be taken by management to increase motivation for safety?

3. Many occupational health hazards that once existed no longer do. However, industry has to remain vigilant to the possibility of new hazards.
   a. What are some of the occupational health hazards that were once common but are seldom found today? What factors contributed to their elimination?
   b. What are some possible present and future hazards that did not exist in the past?
   c. What role should periodic medical examinations play in the detection and elimination of occupational hazards?
4. What approaches can be used to provide work areas free from tobacco smoke? How far should management go in restricting smoking at work?
5. What value would periodic consultations with a psychiatrist or clinical psychologist have for an executive? Who should pay for this service?
6. We observed that the field of clinical ecology relates directly to work situations.
   a. Have you noticed any chemicals that appear to affect how you feel or your behavior?
   b. On what jobs are these chemicals likely to be found?
   c. How can specialists in HRM use this information?
7. In several states employers can require an employee to take a drug test only if there is a "reasonable cause" for testing. What are some behaviors that would indicate that a worker may be under the influence of drugs?
8. Identify the sources of stress in an organization.
   a. In what ways do they affect the individual employee? The organization?
   b. What can managers and supervisors do to make the workplace less stressful?

MINI-CASE 13–1 Too Much Stress

Donald Knolls was a supervisor for TGK Systems. In 1986, he began to experience depression and depression-related problems due in great part to stresses on the job. In 1988, he requested and was granted an unpaid disability leave for treatment of his depression. After eight months, his physician and a licensed consulting psychologist agreed that he was sufficiently improved to return to his former position. TGK sent Donald to the physician it had used when Donald had first requested his disability leave. The doctor concluded that Donald, while he had made considerable strides in overcoming his problems, should not be returned to his former supervisory position because the conditions of the job had not changed and Donald was apt to find the stress too great. Instead, he recommended that Donald be returned to a nonsupervisory position on a trial basis. TGK followed the advice of its doctor and did not return Donald to a supervisory position, so Donald filed a grievance that went to arbitration.

The employer argued that it had the right to rely on the medical opinion of "a fair and impartial" doctor who had determined that Donald should not be returned to the position that was the cause of his original stress-related emotional problems. "The arbitrator," the company lawyer said, "need not review management's decision in this matter. The disability-leave provision states that an employer 'may require appropriate medical documentation . . . if it has reason to believe the supervisor is not fit to return to work.' "

The union representative argued that the disability-leave provision and the nondiscrimination-leave provision were violated. "According to the union, TGK does not have the right to select a doctor of 'its choice,' then claim that its adherence to that doctor's recommendations, in the face of conflicting evidence from other medical sources, is reasonable. The arbitrator should arrive at a decision after reviewing the medical evidence as presented. Since the greater medical evidence is in the grievant's favor, such evidence overcomes the negative evaluation of the employer's doctor."

The union representative also contended that Donald was the victim of discrimination based on his disability. "What happened to Donald would not have happened if his disability had been of a more conventionally accepted variety," the rep concluded.

SOURCE: Reprinted by permission of publisher, from *Supervisory Management,* July 1989 © 1989. American Management Association, New York. All rights reserved.

QUESTION

How would you decide this case? For the union? For the company? Compromise? If so, how?

MINI-CASE 13–2 Safety Squabble

Ray Walsh hurt his right wrist on the job. A doctor who examined him told him to keep the arm elevated and apply ice packs to it for 24 hours. The employer's policy in such cases was to try to get injured workers back on the job as soon as possible, if necessary assigning them light duty that did not entail any undue strain.

About 19 hours after the accident, Walsh reported for work wearing tennis shoes rather than his customary work shoes. His supervisor, Doug Williams, told him to change into work shoes. Walsh complied, although he needed the help of another employee to lace up the shoes. Williams then ordered Walsh to perform a routine equipment inspection of the department. However, Walsh refused to carry out part of this assignment that would have required him to descend a flight of stairs and inspect an area that was dimly lit and contained moving equipment. According to Walsh, his injured wrist deprived him of the use of his right arm, which made him fear for his safety in the event that he fell during the inspection.

Williams then made an appointment for Walsh to be examined by a doctor. The doctor cleared Walsh for return to work, but told him not to use his right arm for six days. When Walsh returned to the job site, Williams again ordered him to perform the inspection task, and again Walsh refused.

"No way I'm going to do that job—it's plain unsafe, especially with my arm out of commission," Walsh said. "I might be able to do a little bit of it, but you're going to have to find somebody else to do the rest."

"That job's well within your capabilities and you know it," retorted Williams. "Since you're refusing an order, you can consider yourself suspended."

With the help of the union steward, Walsh filed a grievance that ultimately went to arbitration.

SOURCE: Adapted and reprinted with permission from *Bulletin to Management (BNA Policy and Practice Series),* Vol. 37, no. 10, p. 75 (March 6, 1986). Copyright 1986 by The Bureau of National Affairs, Inc.

QUESTIONS

1. Do you believe that the company policy for such situations is sound? Why or why not?
2. If you were the HR manager of this organization, what would you consider to be the implications of this incident for your safety training program for supervisory personnel?
3. If you were the arbitrator, how would you rule in this case?

NOTES AND REFERENCES

1. U.S. Department of Labor, Occupational Safety and Health Administration, *All About OSHA*, rev. ed. (Washington, DC: U.S. Government Printing Office, 1985), 1. For a historical view of job hazards from the experiences of an early industrial physician, see the autobiography of Alice Hamilton, M.D., *Exploring the Dangerous Trades*, copyright 1943 by Little, Brown. Reprinted 1985 by Northeastern University Press, Boston. See also David Rosner and Gerald Markowitz, *Dying for Work: Workers' Safety and Health in Twentieth Century America* (Bloomington, IN: Indiana University Press, 1989). Authors from several disciplines illuminate interrelationships between industrial and social organization and workers' health.
2. *Accident Facts—1989 Edition* (Chicago: National Safety Council, 1989), 32, 35, 46.
3. The states with OSHA-approved state programs are: Alaska, Arizona, California, Connecticut, Hawaii, Indiana, Iowa, Kentucky, Maryland, Michigan, Minnesota, Nevada, New Mexico, New York, North Carolina, Oregon, South Carolina, Tennessee, Utah, Vermont, Virginia, Washington, and Wyoming; also Puerto Rico and the Virgin Islands. Programs in Connecticut and New York cover public employees only.
4. *All About OSHA*, 5–6.
5. Ibid., 18.
6. Ibid., 37–42.
7. Ibid., 36–38.
8. Matthew M. Carmel and Michael F. Dolan, "An Introduction to Employee Right-to-Know Laws," *Personnel Administrator* 29, no. 9 (September 1984): 117–121.
9. Susan B. Garland, "A New Chief Has OSHA Growling Again," *Business Week* (August 20, 1990): 57; Amy Dockser Marcus and Jose de Cordoba, "Employers Can Be Charged in Injury Cases," *Wall Street Journal* (October 17, 1990): B7; and "Scannell Brings New Look to OSHA," *Occupational Health and Safety* 59, no. 1 (January 1990): 18–20, 34.
10. *Safety Policies and the Impact of OSHA*, Personnel Policies Forum Survey no. 117 (Washington, DC: Bureau of National Affairs, May 1977), 4. (This appears to be the most recent information.)
11. Dan Petersen, *Safety Management—A Human Approach*, 2d ed. (Rivervale, NJ: Aloray, 1988), 33–36.
12. Clare Ansberry, "Workplace Injuries Proliferate As Concerns Push People to Produce," *Wall Street Journal* (June 16, 1989): A1.
13. Kaija Leena Saarela, "A Poster Campaign for Improving Safety on Shipyard Scaffolds," *Journal of Safety Research* 20 (1989): 177–185.
14. Robert A. Reber and Jerry A. Wallin, "The Effects of Training, Goal Setting, and Knowledge of Results on Safe Behavior: A Component Analysis," *Academy of Management Journal* 27, no. 3 (September 1984): 544–560; and John A. Jenkins, "Self-directed Work Force Promotes Safety," *HR Magazine* 35, no. 2 (February 1990): 54–56.
15. R. Bruce McAffee and Ashley R. Winn, "The Use of Incentives/Feedback to Enhance Work Place Safety: A Critique of the Literature," *Journal of Safety Research* 20 (1989): 7–19. See also Thomas R. Krause, John H. Hidley, and Stanley J. Hodson, "Broad-based Changes in Behavior Key to Improving Safety Culture," *Occupational Health and Safety* 59, no. 7 (July 1990): 31–37, 50.
16. Dwight Monk, "Conducting a Safety Audit in Your Workplace," *Management Solutions* 33, no. 9 (September 1988): 16–19.

17. OSHA defines an *occupational injury* as any injury, such as a cut, fracture, sprain, or amputation, that results from a work accident or from an exposure involving a single accident in the work environment. An *occupational illness* is any abnormal condition or disorder, other than one resulting from an occupational injury, caused by exposure to environmental factors associated with employment. It includes acute and chronic illnesses or diseases that may be caused by inhalation, absorption, ingestion, or direct contact. Not recordable are first-aid cases that involve one-time treatment and subsequent observation of minor scratches, cuts, burns, splinters, etc., that do not ordinarily require medical care, even though such treatment is provided by a physician or registered professional personnel.

18. Tina Adler, "Experts Urge Control of Aerospace Toxics," *APA Monitor* (American Psychological Association, May 1989): 1. For coverage of other health issues, see David H. Wegman and Lawrence J. Fine, "Occupational Health in the 1990s," *Annual Review of Public Health* (Palo Alto, CA: Annual Reviews, Inc., May 1990).

19. *Accident Facts*, 46. *Mesa (Arizona Tribune* (March 21, 1991): A1; and Stephen Wermiel, "Justices Bar 'Fetal Protection' Policies," *Wall Street Journal* (March 21, 1991): B1. The Supreme Court decision in *International Union* v. *Johnson Controls* may be found in 59 *U.S. Law Week* 4029.

20. Joel Makower, *Office Hazards—How Your Job Can Make You Sick* (Washington, DC: Tilden Press, 1981), 14–24.

21. *BNA Policy and Practice Series—Personnel Management* (Washington, DC: Bureau of National Affairs, 1988), 247: 164.

22. Robert C. Miljus and Brian W. Sholly, "The Work Environment: How Safe Are Video Display Terminals?" *Personnel Journal* 64, no. 3 (March 1985): 27–31.

23. Yvette Debow, "Just How Dangerous *Are* VDTs?" *Management Review* 77, no. 8 (August 1988): 44–46.

24. Gina Kolata, "New Scrutiny for Arm Injuries," *New York Times*, as reprinted in the *Sacramento Bee* (January 1, 1989): F3; and Maria Mallory and Naomi Freundlich, "An Invisible Workplace Hazard Gets Harder to Ignore," *Business Week* (January 30, 1989): 92–93.

25. Mallory and Freundlich. See also Marilyn Joyce and Ulrika Wallersteiner, *Ergonomics—Humanizing the Automated Office* (Cincinnati: South-Western, 1989), 85.

26. *BNA Policy and Practice Series* (1989), 247: 72–74. See also Steve Allen and Bill Adler, Jr., *The Passionate Nonsmoker's Bill of Rights* (New York: Morrow, 1989). This book contains a no-punches-pulled approach to smoking. The appendixes provide valuable information, including names and addresses of individuals and organizations active in the nonsmokers' rights movement.

27. *BNA Policy and Practice Series.*

28. " 'No Smoking' Sweeps America" *Business Week* (July 27, 1987): 40–52. See also Robert J. Nobile, "Putting Out Fires with No-Smoking Policy," *Personnel* 67, no. 3 (March 1990): 6–7, 10.

29. Ron Winslow, "Some Firms Put a Price on Smoking," *Wall Street Journal* (March 6, 1990): B1.

30. Robert S. Letchinger, "AIDS: An Employer's Dilemma," *Personnel* 63, no. 2 (February 1986): 58–63; and Linda C. Kramer, "Legal and Ethical Issues Affect Conduct Toward AIDS Sufferers," *Occupational Health and Safety* 59, no. 1 (January 1990): 49–50, 57.

31. *BNA Policy and Practice Series—Personnel Management* (Washington, DC: Bureau of National Affairs, 1989), 247: 162 c,d,e,f.

32. Ibid., 247: 162.

33. *BNA Policy and Practice Series* (1989), 247: 143–162; *BNA Bulletin to Management* 40, no. 19 (May 11, 1989): 145–146; George E. Stevens, "Understanding AIDS," *Personnel Administrator* 33, no. 8 (August 1988): 84–88; Marilyn Chase, "Corporations Urge Peers to Adopt Humane Policies for AIDS Victims," *Wall Street Journal* (January 20, 1988): 29; and *BNA Fair Employment Practices* 25, no. 9 (April 27, 1989): 51. Also, *Personnel Journal* periodically publishes a Guide to Services and Information about AIDS. See *Personnel Journal* 67, no. 2 (February 1988): 101–111.

34. Kenneth R. Pelletier, *Healthy People in Unhealthy Places: Stress and Fitness at Work* (New York: Dell, 1984), 140–141. See also Marjorie Blanchard, "Wellness Programs Produce Positive Results," *Personnel Journal* 68, no. 5 (May 1989): 30; and Shari Caudron and Mike Rozek, "The Wellness Payoff," *Personnel Journal* 69, no. 7 (July 1990): 54–60.

35. Robert Levering, Milton Moskowitz, and Michael Katz, *The 100 Best Companies to Work for in America* (New York: New American Library, 1985), 324, 364.

36. Stuart Murray and Jim Francis, "Nutrition and Decision Making," *Business Horizons* 23, no. 4 (August 1980): 7–14.

37. Allan Halcrow, "For Your Information: A Nutritious Plan for Improved Productivity," *Personnel Journal* 64, no. 8 (August 1985): 17.

38. The "2100 Program" is described in Jon N. Leonard, J. L. Hofer, and N. Pritikin, *Live Longer Now* (New York: Grosset & Dunlap, 1976); in Nathan Pritikin with Patrick M. McGrady, Jr., *The Pritikin Program for Diet and Exercise* (New York: Grosset & Dunlap, 1979); in Nathan Pritikin, *The Pritikin Promise: 28 Days to a Longer, Healthier Life* (New York: Simon & Schuster, 1983); and in Robert Pritikin, *The New Pritikin Program* (New York: Simon & Schuster, 1990).

39. *BNA Bulletin to Management* 40, no. 6 (February 9, 1989): 44. See also Jerry Beilinson, "Are EAPs the Answer?" *Personnel* 68, no. 1 (January 1991): 3–4.

40. Theron G. Randolph, *Human Ecology and Susceptibility to the Chemical Environment* (Springfield, IL: Charles C. Thomas, 1962); and Theron G. Randolph and Ralph W. Moss, *An Alternative Approach to Allergies* (New York: Lippincott & Crowell, 1980). See also *Clinical Ecology,* ed. Lawrence D. Dickey (Springfield, IL: Charles C. Thomas, 1976).

41. "Dealing with Alcoholism on the Job," *Management Review* 74, no. 7 (July 1985): 4–5; Delores A. Rumpel, "Motivating Alcoholic Workers to Seek Help," *Management Review* 78, no. 7 (July 1989): 37–39; and Jim Castelli, "Addiction," *HR Magazine* 35, no. 4 (April 1990): 55–58.

42. Rumpel. See also Dianna L. Stone and Debra A. Kotch, "Individuals' Attitudes Toward Organizational Drug Testing Policies and Practices," *Journal of Applied Psychology* 74, no. 3 (June 1989), 518–521. See also Joseph G. Rosse, Deborah F. Crown, and Howard D. Feldman, "Alternative Solutions to the Workplace Drug Problem: Results of a Survey of Personnel Managers," *Journal of Employment Counseling* 27, no. 2 (June 1990): 60–75.

43. Milt Freudenheim, "Business Pays Heavy Price As Substance Abuse Grows," *New York Times,* as reprinted in the *Sacramento Bee* (December 18, 1988): I3.

44. *BNA Bulletin to Management* 40, no. 6—Part II (February 9, 1989): 1. See also Drusilla Campbell and Marilyn Graham, *Drugs and Alcoholism in the Workplace: A Guide for Managers* (New York: Facts on File Publications, 1988).

45. Michael E. Cavanagh, "Abuse of Legal Drugs," *Personnel Journal* 69, no. 3 (March 1990): 124–128.

46. Ann Bensinger and Charles F. Pilkington, "Treating Chemically Dependent Employees in a Non-Hospital Setting," *Personnel Administrator* 30, no. 8 (August 1985): 45–52. The following books are recommended: Tia Schneider Denenberg and R. V. Denenberg, *Alcohol and Drugs—Issues in the Workplace* (Washington, DC: Bureau of National Affairs, 1983); Marc A. Schuckit, *Drug and Alcohol Abuse: A Clinical Guide to Diagnosis and Treatment* (New York: Plenum Press, 1984); and Michael D. Newcomb, *Drug Use in the Workplace: Risk Factors for Disruptive Substance Use Among Young Adults* (Dover, MA: Auburn House, 1988). For details of one company's drug rehabilitation program, see Cheryl Thieme, "Better-Bilt Builds a Substance Abuse Program That Works," *Personnel Journal* 69, no. 8 (August 1990): 52–58.

47. Mark O. Hatfield, "Stress and the American Worker," *American Psychologist* 45, no. 10 (October 1990): 1162–1164.

48. Hans Selye, *Stress Without Distress* (Philadelphia: Lippincott, 1974; Signet Books reprint, 1975), 83.

49. *USA Today* (April 11, 1990): 1A.

50. "How to Deal with Stress on the Job," *U.S. News and World Report* (March 13, 1978): 80–81.

51. Michael J. McCarthy, "Stressed Employees Look for Relief in Workers' Compensation Claims," *Wall Street Journal* (April 7, 1988): 27; and "Stress on the Job," *Newsweek* (April 25, 1988): 40–45.

52. John M. Ivancevich, Michael T. Matteson, and Edward P. Richards III, "Who's Liable for Stress on the Job?" *Harvard Business Review* 85, no. 2 (March–April 1985): 60–72; and Matteson and Ivancevich, *Controlling Work Stress: Effective Human Resource and Management Strategies* (San Francisco: Jossey-Bass, 1987).

53. *Bulletin to Management* 37, no. 17 (Washington, DC: Bureau of National Affairs, April 24, 1986): 134.

54. John M. Ivancevich, Michael T. Matteson, Sara M. Freedman, and James F. Phillips, "Worksite Stress Management Interventions," *American Psychologist* 45, no. 2 (February 1990): 252–261.

55. "Coping with Stress," *Human Behavior* 5, no. 5 (May 1976): 38.

PART FIVE

Creating a Productive Work Environment

Part Five deals with issues pertaining to the direct supervision of employees. In Chapter 14 the important topics of employee motivation and leadership are discussed. Chapter 15 discusses employee–management communication, highlighting the role played by the HR department in communicating with employees. Chapter 16 is concerned with issues of employee rights and the corresponding responsibilities of managers to provide employees with workplace justice. This chapter concludes with a discussion of disciplinary practices used by managers when employees disregard organizational rules. When these HR activities are performed correctly, employees and managers interact in a productive manner based on mutual understanding and respect.

CHAPTER 14

Motivating Employees

After reading this chapter you will be able to:

1. *Describe how rewards and award systems are used to increase the productivity of employees.*
2. *Discuss the demotivating effects of inequity in the workplace.*
3. *Explain suggestion systems such as the employee involvement group.*
4. *Describe how to structure the workplace to increase job involvement and commitment.*
5. *Explain how leader profiles are used in selecting, training, and appraising leaders.*
6. *Identify the behavioral and situational theories of leadership, which seek to describe and thus to improve the leadership skills of managers.*
7. *Discuss emerging leadership theories that HR managers may use to develop training programs.*
8. *Define the key terms in the chapter.*

TERMS TO IDENTIFY

hierarchy of needs *(461)*
equity *(464)*
employee involvement *(469)*
employee involvement groups (EIs) *(470)*
job involvement *(472)*
two-factor theory *(472)*
work team *(472)*
Scandinavian management *(473)*
commitment *(475)*
traits of leaders *(477)*
needs for achievement, power, and affiliation *(478)*
motive to manage *(479)*
leader behavior *(480)*
path-goal theory *(482)*
expectancy theory *(482)*
situational leadership theory *(482)*
social influence model *(484)*
self-leadership theory *(484)*
transformational leadership *(485)*

Many managers believe they can increase productivity by adding robots, introducing information systems, or modifying production procedures. However, as Adrian Gozzard, group personnel director for the United Kingdom's Cadbury Schweppes, makes clear, productivity and the achievement of strategic goals are a matter not of computers and production systems, but of people: "In the company you have one resource; it's people and the management of those people. . . . it is motivation [of those people] that makes the difference between mediocrity and excellence. It is the glue that holds together the objectives and strategies of the organization. . . ."[1]

Recent data suggest that some industrialized countries, particularly the United States and Italy, have fallen far behind other nations in one measure of productivity, growth in output per worker (see Figure 14–1). One way to address productivity problems is to focus on the impact of human resources management on productivity. This approach has been shown to be useful by a recent study of five innovative HRM practices: flexible reward systems, production bonus plans, goal-oriented performance appraisal, alternative work schedules, and organizational development. The study concluded that these practices made a difference in the financial performance (return on equity) of the organization.[2]

Before HR managers can address problems of organizational productivity, however, they must first understand the motivational bases of performance as well as the leadership skills required to motivate employees to increase their output. In this chapter we will examine selected approaches to motivation and leadership that

---

This chapter was prepared by Dr. Larry E. Penley, Professor of Management, Arizona State University, Tempe, Arizona.

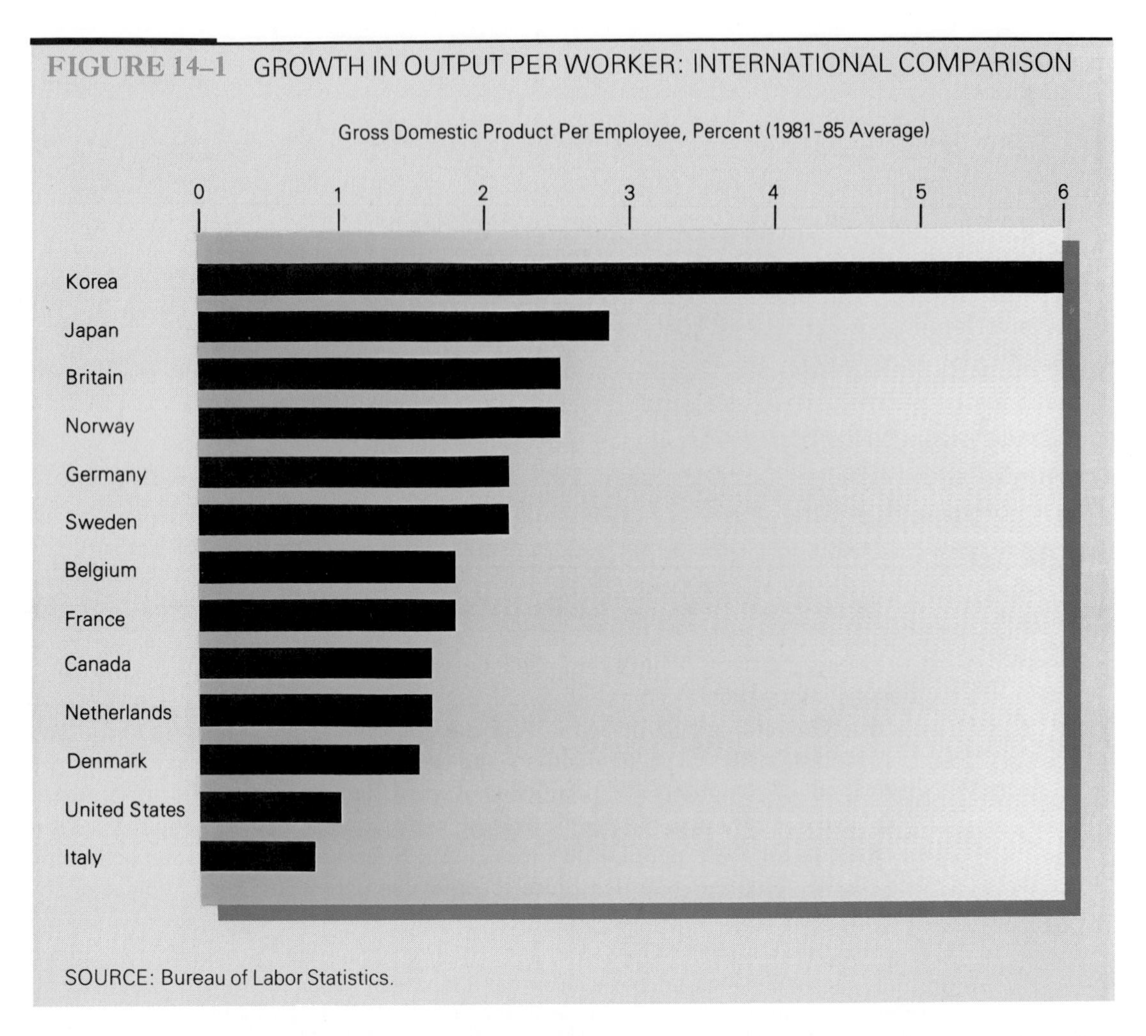

FIGURE 14–1 GROWTH IN OUTPUT PER WORKER: INTERNATIONAL COMPARISON

SOURCE: Bureau of Labor Statistics.

research and practice suggest can help managers improve employee productivity. We begin by discussing motivation, including employee rewards, managing employee perceptions of equity, and various employee involvement programs. Later we will focus on various theories of leadership, including trait leadership, situational leadership, social influence, self-leadership, and transformational leadership.

USING REWARDS TO MOTIVATE EMPLOYEES

HR managers have numerous choices of how to motivate employees to be productive. Quite often, a combination of strategies works best. In this first section we will discuss several approaches to motivation—reward, equity, and involvement strategies—with a focus on how HR managers use these motivational techniques.

A special vacation may improve employee motivation if it is given in recognition for superior performance.

Rewards: The Key to Performance

Rewards are an important motivational tool for any organization. Although they may include a wide range of incentives—paychecks, productivity bonuses, five-year pins, certificates, special vacations, etc.—rewards are not always effectively used to enhance productivity. For example, if pay raises are given simply for "showing up" for work rather than for increasing output, they will do little to motivate employees to work harder. In the language of the behavioral scientist, rewards such as these are not "performance-contingent."

According to two noted experts in this field, Fred Luthans and Robert Kreitner, whether employees maintain high productivity depends on how they perceive the consequences of their efforts. If they believe high productivity will be rewarded, they will be more likely to work to achieve it. For this reason, organizations should place considerable emphasis on rewards that employees perceive as desirable.[3]

Using Pay as a Reward

One rather obvious reward for performance is pay and the various forms of incentive pay systems that we discussed in Chapter 11. Since pay can be a powerful incentive, those whose job includes establishing pay systems need to understand the effect of pay on motivation. HR managers who understand this relationship are in a much better position to implement effective pay-for-performance systems.

Foremost, pay is something that employees value, and its value may be best understood in terms of the different needs employees have. Abraham Maslow developed the **hierarchy of needs,** a theory of motivation that arranges five universal needs in order of priority: (1) *physiological* needs for food, water, etc.; (2) *safety* needs for physical and psychological security; (3) *belongingness* needs for love and

"My advice to you, Hawkins, is to take the pins out of the map and stick them into the salesmen."

Reprinted with permission of Chon Day.

inclusion; (4) *esteem* needs for self-respect; and (5) *self-actualization* needs, or the need to reach one's potential.[4] (See Figure 14–2.) Pay is an important reward in part because it may satisfy several of these needs. It provides employees with the means to purchase food to satisfy their physiological needs; it allows them to afford shelter to satisfy their need for safety; and it enables them to meet their esteem needs, since pay is one measure of relative worth.

In addition, there are four other important reasons for HR managers to implement effective pay-for-performance systems. First, pay serves to differentiate among employees. High-performing employees usually resent systems that reward everyone equally, and they may feel that there is no reason to stay with an organization that allows the less competent to "beat the system" by receiving the same reward with less effort or ability. By serving to differentiate among employees, pay strengthens feelings of equity, a topic discussed later in the chapter.

Second, using pay as a reward makes the formal performance appraisal a significant event. Where there is no link between pay and performance, employees may see appraisals as nothing more than a perfunctory requirement of the HR department. Where pay is clearly based on performance, however, it is seen as an important consequence of effective performance, thus underscoring the importance of the appraisal process.

FIGURE 14–2 PRIORITY OF HUMAN NEEDS

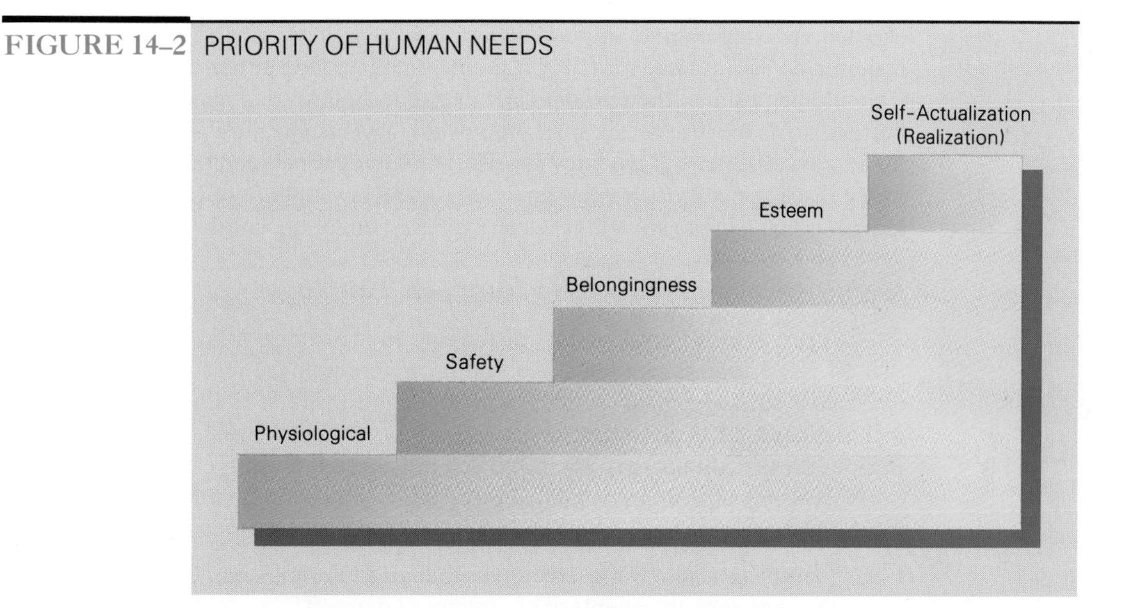

Third, pay-for-performance can be an important means of allocating scarce compensation dollars. Even in difficult financial circumstances, organizations are well advised to retain merit pay for their high-performing employees. Not only will rewarding outstanding performance help retain the superior employees, but it may also encourage the poorer-performing employees to leave the organization.

Finally, pay-for-performance can be used to encourage a culture of high productivity in the organization. Transforming an apathetic culture into one where productivity is highly valued can be a very difficult task. Effective motivational strategies, including using pay as a performance reward, can help to move the organizational culture in the direction of better performance. After all, pay affects every employee in the organization, so it has considerable potential to change the entire culture, one employee at a time.[5]

For example, Sola Ophthalmics changed its traditional reward system from one based on the job's sophistication and difficulty to one in which employees were paid based on the number of skills they possessed (see Chapter 10 for a more complete description of skill-based pay). Employees were thus rewarded for acquiring a greater variety of skills, the plant gained flexibility in assigning work to employees, and supervision requirements decreased because workers were more knowledgeable about their jobs.[6]

Using Other Rewards

There are a variety of other rewards that are very important to employees and quite useful as means of motivating performance. Simple feedback from managers serves as a valued reward. A survey by the Houston-based American Productivity Center found that 91 percent of its members believe recognition for a job well done

A handwritten letter of thanks will show employees that their efforts are appreciated.

is either very important or important.[7] For feedback to be most effective, however, it should be face to face. Certainly it should be immediate rather than delayed, and it should be positive, though some HR managers believe that negative feedback is better than no feedback at all, since employees may mistake the absence of feedback for approval (no news is good news). Also, the survey concluded that a high amount of feedback is better than a low amount, since a low amount of feedback conveys low confidence in the subordinate and may even anger the employee.[8]

Using Award Programs to Motivate Employees

In a survey of 171 organizations by the Bureau of National Affairs, results showed that 94 percent of respondents had one or more employee awards programs. An example of such a program is provided in Highlights in HRM 1. These programs can include many different awards, such as jewelry, crystal, blazers, and certificates. Besides these traditional awards, novel and unexpected rewards can be offered. For example, some organizations may find the following useful for encouraging higher levels of performance:

- Workplace visits by top executives to high-performing employees.
- Surprise announcements of afternoons or days off.
- Trophies, wall plaques, certificates, and pins for exceptional performance.
- Letters to spouses commending the employee's performance.
- Personal handwritten notes of thanks accompanying paychecks.
- High performers invited to lunch by managers.
- Achievement decals for hats or cloth badges for jackets.
- Small cash awards.
- Telephone calls by top executives to employees at home.[9]

It should be remembered that, if award systems are to be effective, they must recognize only those employees who have performed well. In other words, they must differentiate the mediocre performer from the high performer. Furthermore, to be effective, such systems must ensure that the award is valued by the employee. Finally, awards have less effect when they are given as part of a regular meeting or sandwiched between departmental activities. Special occasions—annual dinners and award meetings—are required if awards are to be perceived as anything more than an afterthought. Figure 14–3 provides additional suggestions for ensuring an effective award system.

ENSURING EQUITY TO MOTIVATE EMPLOYEES

A basic principle in HR management is **equity.** Employees expect that what they give to the organization will be equivalent to what they receive from it. When things are out of balance, employees will take actions to bring them back into

HIGHLIGHTS IN HRM

1 RECOGNITION AT BANK OF AMERICA

Although the San Francisco–based Bank of America has long used recognition programs as part of its reward system, it has placed renewed emphasis on these programs to communicate to employees the value it places on their performance. Alex Reyes, the manager of the special recognition program, described Bank of America's philosophy this way: "The bank is strongly committed to recognition as a key part of our corporate values. Service awards have been given for many years. We have a strong program, but intend to make strategic improvements to let employees know that their efforts and commitment to our company, particularly during the past five years or so, are genuinely appreciated."

The bank began its efforts to improve its performance recognition program by reviewing current practices concerning its service awards, comparing its service award program with those of other major employers in the area, and surveying 660 bank employees selected at random. Using these perspectives, Bank of America modified its award program in the following ways.

Employees wanted a wider selection of gifts for service awards, so the bank has moved to expand their choices, particularly to include more items for business use such as a leather portfolio case. Employees did not previously feel that the different levels of awards were meaningful, so the bank has chosen a new set of higher-quality awards with recognizable brand names and clear distinctions among the various levels.

Perhaps the greatest change to the award program has been in the role played by management. In the old system, employees were sent a card prior to their service anniversary date. They simply selected a gift and returned the card to the vendor without their manager's involvement. One discovery the bank made was that employees wanted managers to be more involved. Now the managers receive notification of the service anniversary, and they inform the employee. This gives them a chance to thank the employee personally for service to the bank and to comment on specific parts of the employee's performance for which he or she deserves recognition. In addition to being involved in the notification, managers have been given guidelines for making award presentations so that the awards are more meaningful to the employee. Bank of America's former CEO (now Executive Committee Chairman), A. W. (Tom) Clausen, has also spoken with managers about the importance of employee recognition, and a variety of written materials have been distributed to managers about their role in the process.

Bob Beck, the executive vice-president of corporate human resources, said of the recognition program, "All of our approaches to compensation, ranging from all employees on merit pay to those covered by our more than 30 specialized incentive plans, emphasize and reward individual achievement. The service awards program supports that philosophy by recognizing sustained contributions and achievement. . . ."

SOURCE: Adapted from Holly Rawlinson, "Renewed Recognition at Bank of America," *Personnel Journal* 5, no. 10 (October 1988): 142–146. Reprinted with the permission of *Personnel Journal*, Costa Mesa, California; all rights reserved.

FIGURE 14–3 MAKING AWARDS COUNT FOR EMPLOYEES

1. Tie awards to employees' needs. Managers must get to know their employees well enough to understand their needs.
2. Make sure an award is large enough to have symbolic value. A $25 increase in the monthly paycheck may go unnoticed. A $300 bonus check is more likely to get an employee's attention.
3. Proper timing is important. Schedule the presentation of the award close to the time the award was announced.
4. Attend the awards presentation. The manager's presence shows the importance of an awards ceremony and thus of the awards themselves.
5. Talk up the value of an award. Pointing out the benefits of the award helps to make it seem more meaningful.
6. Make certain the presenter is someone the employees respect.
7. Use a public forum for the presentation. Schedule a special event to highlight the importance of the award.
8. Set high standards for the awards, and make them contingent upon meeting or exceeding those standards.
9. Increase the exclusiveness of an award. Awards received by fewer employees are valued more highly.
10. Do not oversell the award. Attempting to make a weekly sales bonus seem tremendously valuable only makes the award look meaningless.

SOURCE: Adapted from Philip C. Grant, "Rewards: The Pizzazz Is the Package, Not the Prize," *Personnel Journal* 67, no. 3 (March 1988): 76–81. Reprinted with the permission of *Personnel Journal*, Costa Mesa, California; all rights reserved.

balance. Equity theory is the motivational theory that explains how employees respond to situations in which they feel they have received less—or more—than they deserve. The theory states that feelings of inequity will motivate a person to reduce inequity.

Theory of Inequity

Adams's version of equity theory is perhaps the most extensive and explicit.[10] It is a general theory of social inequity. Central to the theory is the role of perception in motivation and the fact that individuals make comparisons. It states that individuals form a ratio of their inputs in a situation to their outcomes in that situation. They then compare the value of that ratio with the value of the input/outcome ratio for other individuals in a similar class of jobs. If the value of their ratio equals the value of another's, they perceive the situation as equitable and no tension exists. However, if they perceive their input/outcome ratio as inequitable relative to others', this creates tension and motivates them to eliminate or reduce it. The strength of their motivation is proportional to the magnitude of the perceived inequity.

Perceived Inequity

Employees may develop feelings of inequity for a variety of reasons, the most obvious of which is pay. If employees believe they give more effort, but know they are paid less, than the person with whom they compare themselves, they will feel that the organization is treating them inequitably. Older, more experienced employees who believe that younger employees are receiving more than their fair share of compensation will feel that they are being treated inequitably. An employee who believes it is her turn to have the day off may resent it and perceive inequity when the day off is given to another employee.

Reactions to Inequity

When faced with perceptions of inequity, employees handle it in a variety of ways. They may do one or more of the following:

- Sabotage the work process.
- Reduce the amount of effort they put into their work.
- Seek more pay to achieve equity because of their perceived larger contribution.
- Quit their job or increase their absenteeism, thereby avoiding the situation or the person that is the source of their feelings of inequity.
- Try to persuade their fellow employees to reduce their effort.

Employees may also decide to compare themselves with yet another person, thus reducing the perceived inequity of the earlier comparison. Some of these means of reducing inequity can be particularly damaging to an organization. One way for an employer to minimize feelings of inequity in its employees is through a fair compensation plan. Such plans are discussed in detail in Chapter 10 on compensation.

Managers who understand that some employees can react more than others to inequity are better able to deal with these perceptions. Some employees, referred to as "sensitives" (see Figure 14–4), respond in one of the ways just described. Other employees see themselves as "entitled" to whatever rewards they can get. They are willing to tolerate a great deal of perceived inequity as long as the inequity results in their receiving more outcomes (O) than are warranted given their inputs (I). Still other employees may be described as "benevolents." These individuals are willing to put more into their work than they receive in comparison with others.[11] Not surprisingly, the largest group of employees falls into the category of equity "sensitives," although some HR managers believe that the work force of the future may include more employees classified as "entitleds."

Managing Equity

That inequity can lead to productivity problems for the organization is ample reason for HR professionals to address perceptions of inequity and unfairness, beyond the usual compensation plans. Recognizing the need to address unfairness in a variety of managerial settings, one senior vice-president of a Fortune 500 firm

FIGURE 14–4 THE EQUITY SENSITIVITY CONTINUUM

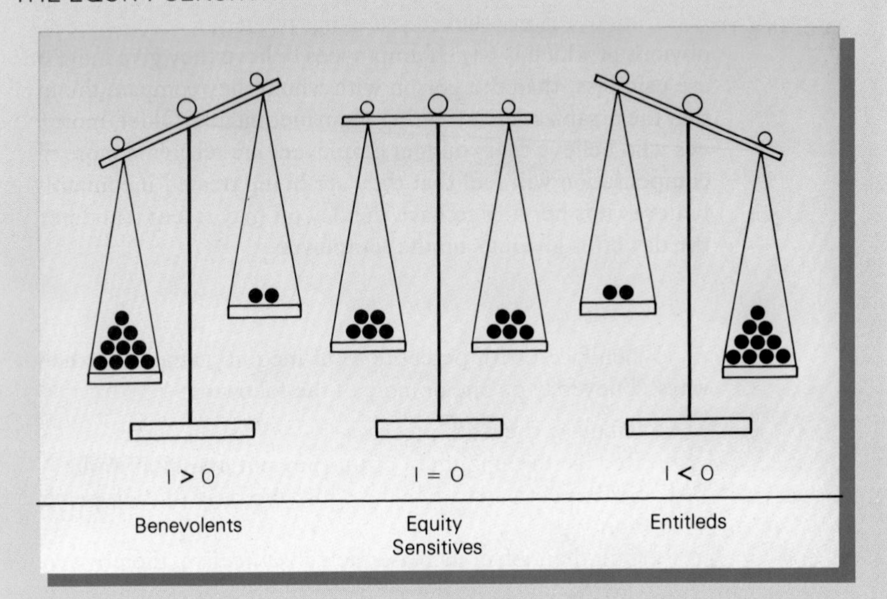

SOURCE: From *Managing the Equity Factor* by Richard C. Huseman and John D. Hatfield, copyright © 1989 by Richard C. Huseman and John D. Hatfield. Reprinted by permission of Houghton Mifflin Co.

stated, "What's fair is whatever the workers think is fair. My job is to convince them that what's good for the company is fair for them as individuals." Figure 14–5, which highlights the results of a nationwide survey of managers, reveals the techniques managers use to ensure equity in the workplace. Specific means of addressing inequity and unfairness include the following:

- Emphasizing equitable rewards for employees.
- Recognizing that the basis for perceived inequity is comparison with others.
- Listening carefully to employees to understand the basis of comparisons.
- Responding to employees individually.
- Letting employees know of the contributions of others.
- Describing employees' current accomplishments in relation to their earlier accomplishments.
- Accurately describing the outcomes for specific levels of performance.
- Using public meetings to recognize employees.[12]

DESIGNING WORK FOR EMPLOYEE INVOLVEMENT

Providing rewards based on performance and equitably distributing them are only two of the important tools organizations can use to elicit high performance from

FIGURE 14–5 MANAGERS' REPORTS OF WHAT THEY DO TO APPEAR FAIR

RESPONSE	FREQUENCY
Announce all pay raises and promotions.	81%
Explain how pay raises are determined.	76%
Allow workers to participate in decisions.	55%
Explain why work assignments are made.	43%

SOURCE: Adapted from Jerald Greenberg, "Cultivating an Image of Justice: Looking Fair on the Job," *Academy of Management Executive* 2, no. 2 (May 1988): 156. Reprinted with permission.

their employees. Another is enhancing **employee involvement.** Increased employee involvement in organizations has become the charge of many HR managers and the hope of numerous self-motivated employees. Although a variety of programs have been developed to involve employees more fully in their organizations, all of these programs have one common ingredient: participation. They increase the degree to which employees participate in making critical job or organizational decisions.

Increased employee participation in decision making offers a number of advantages, including stronger commitment to the organization's goals, better understanding of the decisions made in the organization, and improvement in the quality of the decisions themselves. A more extensive list of the advantages of greater employee participation is provided in Figure 14–6. To achieve these advantages, three general ways to increase employee involvement and participation are proposed: (1) adopting suggestion systems, (2) increasing job involvement through work teams, and (3) building individual commitment to the organization.[13]

Suggestion Systems

The oldest and still most widely used employee involvement system is the suggestion system, which can take various forms. The traditional suggestion system, discussed in Chapter 15, is one of the ways to ensure upward communication in organizations. However, suggestion systems are also an important means of motivating employees by involving them in the decision-making and reward systems of the organization, assuming that management takes its employees' suggestions seriously.

GAINSHARING SUGGESTION SYSTEMS Programs that reward employees for their suggestions are a part of organizational gainsharing systems, so called because employees share in the gains that result from their suggestions. Such systems can have considerable impact on organizational productivity. In its pursuit of market leadership, Herman Miller, Inc., a manufacturer of office furniture, realized $36 million in productivity gains and cost savings from its gainsharing suggestion system.[14] Gainsharing plans are discussed fully in Chapter 11.

FIGURE 14–6 ADVANTAGES OF INCREASED EMPLOYEE PARTICIPATION

1. Increased understanding of decisions and acceptance by subordinates.
2. More commitment to decisions.
3. Increased understanding of organizational objectives.
4. Greater ability to meet the psychological needs of employees (e.g., belongingness, esteem, self-actualization).
5. Greater social pressure on employees to comply with decisions made through participation.
6. Increased identification with the work team.
7. Availability of more constructive means of conflict resolution.
8. Better decisions.

SOURCE: Adapted from Gary A. Yukl, *Leadership in Organizations,* 2d ed. (Englewood Cliffs, NJ: Prentice-Hall, 1989), 83. Adapted by permission of Prentice-Hall, Inc., Englewood Cliffs, New Jersey.

EMPLOYEE INVOLVEMENT GROUPS Groups of five to ten employees doing similar or related work who meet together regularly to identify, analyze, and suggest solutions to shared problems are often referred to as **employee involvement groups (EIs).** Also widely known as quality circles (QCs), EIs are used principally as a means of involving employees in the larger goals of the organization through their suggestions for improving work flow, cutting costs, and so on. Growth of EIs in the United States started slowly, with only about 25 organizations using them in 1978. Just seven years later, however, 90 percent of Fortune 500 companies reported having some form of EI. Generally, EIs recommend their solutions to management, which decides whether or not to implement them.

The employee involvement group process, illustrated in Figure 14–7, begins with EI members brainstorming job-related problems or concerns and gathering data about these issues. The process continues through the generation of solutions and recommendations that are then communicated to management. If the solutions are implemented, results are measured, and the EI and its members are usually recognized for the contributions they have made. EIs typically meet four or more hours per month, and the meetings are chaired by a group leader chosen from the group. The leader does not hold an authority position, but instead serves as a discussion facilitator.

Organizations must do considerable planning to ensure the effective performance of employee involvement groups. Implementing the EI process usually requires the appointment of a project manager. Though this role is sometimes filled by an outside consultant, a better choice may be an insider from the HR department who understands the organizational culture and knows which employees are good candidates for membership in the group. Successful users of EIs have also found it necessary to appoint an advisory committee, composed of managers, to coordinate the EI process across departments, evaluate recommendations, manage implemen-

FIGURE 14–7 THE EMPLOYEE INVOLVEMENT GROUP

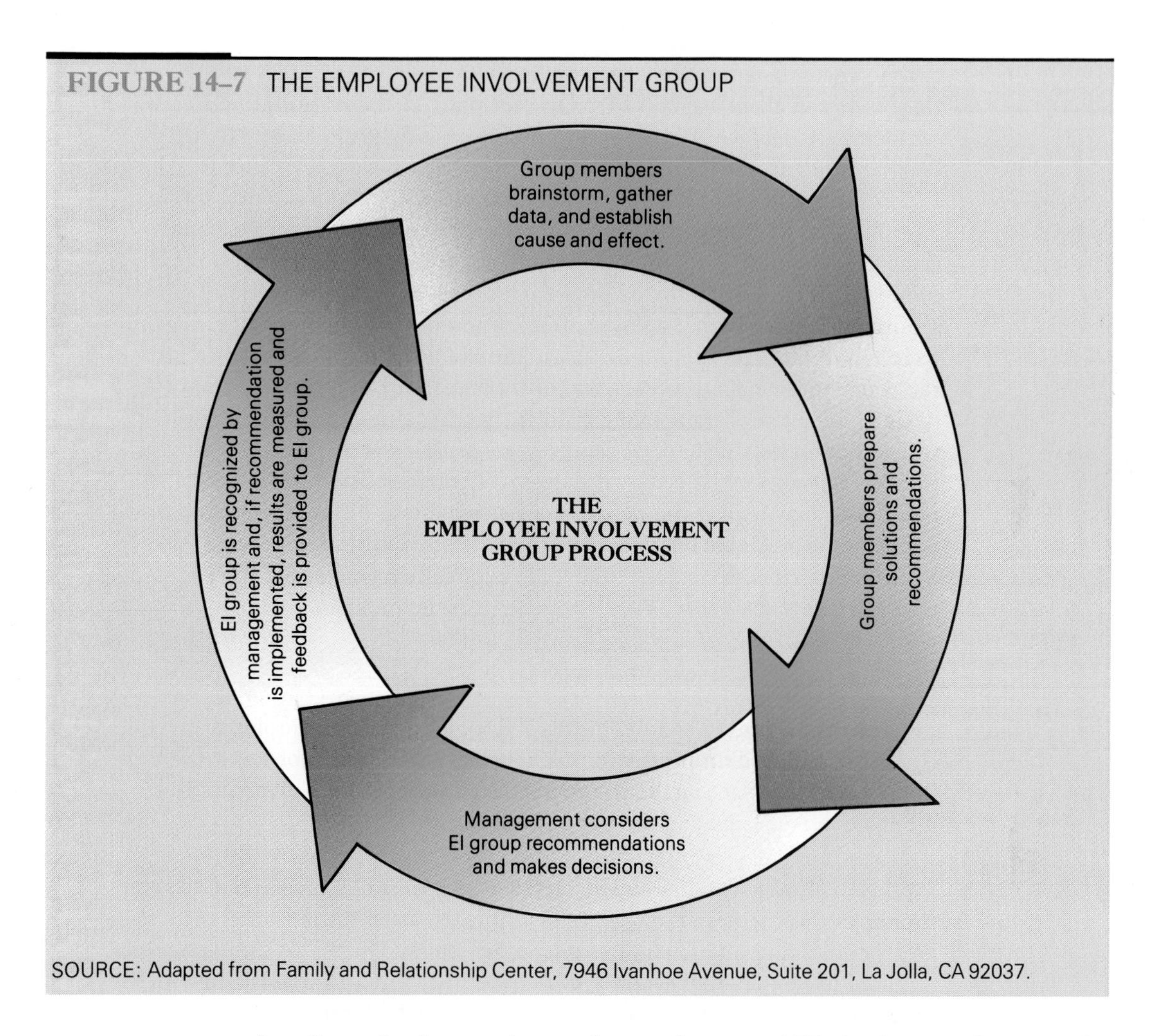

SOURCE: Adapted from Family and Relationship Center, 7946 Ivanhoe Avenue, Suite 201, La Jolla, CA 92037.

tation of contributions, and recognize employees and EIs that have made successful contributions. In addition to the advisory committee, EI support staff (usually from the HR department) must provide training to EI members in problem solving, statistical quality control, and group processes.

Although EIs have become an important organizational suggestion system, they are not without their problems and their critics. For example, EIs can go stale. Barbara Connellee of Los Alamos National Laboratory suggests several ways to keep EIs fresh and revive them when needed. First, managers should recognize the group when a recommendation is made, regardless of whether the recommendation is adopted. This approach encourages the group to continue coming up with ideas even when they are not all implemented by management. Second, periodic recesses should be planned. After a group has spent weeks wrestling with a particularly complex and difficult problem, its members can be exhausted. A recess is needed to rejuvenate the group. In some cases this break can be used for retraining. Third, field trips can allow a group to visit other parts of the organization, learning how problems are dealt with there and gaining new insight into old problems the group faces in its own area.

Organizations that have used EIs have often needed to modify the traditional EI process to fit their particular organizational needs. For example, some organizations have found that voluntary EIs have not always proven successful. They have found that the results of the EI program process are best achieved with natural work groups rather than with employees from different work groups. Other organizations have found that EIs run out of ideas, and management must feed them ideas for them to continue the process. Still other objections to EIs come from their basic design. Some critics argue that EIs do not fundamentally change the organization in which they are established. As a form of suggestion system, they may work well, but they do not alter organizational culture. Therefore, they argue, employees who participate may realize the benefits of participation, but most employees who are not included in EIs are unaffected by their efforts. Furthermore, some organizations have found that management's failure to adopt all suggestions of EIs can sometimes result in loss of the participants' confidence in the program.

Increasing Job Involvement

Job involvement, another means of designing work for employee involvement, is the degree of identification employees have with their jobs and the degree of importance they place on them. Among the approaches used to increase job involvement are job redesign and the use of work teams.

JOB REDESIGN The aim of job redesign is to enrich a job so that the employee is more motivated to do the work. This approach usually builds increased autonomy and feedback into the job, adds tasks to the job, and increases the number of skills required to complete the work. One of the earliest theories associated with such job redesign was Herzberg's **two-factor theory,** which identified two sets of factors in organizations: extrinsic factors like pay and working conditions, which he called *hygiene factors,* and intrinsic factors like job challenge and responsibility, which he called *motivators.*[15] Herzberg's motivators have a parallel in Maslow's self-actualization needs, and it is these factors that bring about the kind of improvement in performance that management seeks. Despite lingering questions about the validity of the two-factor theory,[16] it did become the stimulus for considerable concern with job design, discussed fully in Chapter 4.

WORK TEAMS Another approach to increasing employee job involvement—the **work team**—focuses on the work group as the primary unit of involvement. It creates group goals, and it compensates employees, at least in part, based on group accomplishment of these goals. The approach also seeks to make all members of the work group share responsibility for the group's performance. Furthermore, decisions are decentralized to the level of the work team. For example, a work team at a Procter & Gamble manufacturing plant may be partly responsible for deciding how many units to produce, making decisions about assignment of tasks, setting prices if working as a product team, making its own quality-control checks, and also setting inventory levels.[17] In contrast with gainsharing and EIs, work teams involve changes in job design and organizational design, thereby affecting more employees and making a longer-lasting impact on the organizational culture and the employees.

A description of the use of work teams is provided in Highlights in HRM 2. At General Foods, as well as Procter & Gamble and some other organizations, the benefits of work teams have included more integration of individual skills, better performance in terms of quantity and quality, reduced turnover and absenteeism, and a growing sense of confidence and accomplishment among team members.[18]

In recent years, Scandinavian organizations have received growing attention, because a central part of the **Scandinavian management** system is the use of work teams. Among the most successful team approaches has been that used at the Volvo automobile production facilities in Sweden. In 1974, Volvo introduced work teams consisting of about 20 workers to replace the long-line assembly process at its Kalmar plant. Since the adoption of work teams, production improvements have been dramatic. For example, faults discovered in final inspection have dropped by 39 percent, labor hours per car have been reduced by 40 percent, and absenteeism and turnover have also been modestly reduced. Because of this success, Volvo built another plant based on work teams at Uddevalla, Sweden. Work teams at the new plant were reduced to about ten people rather than the 20 at Kalmar, and work cycles increased to 60 minutes from 20 minutes at Kalmar. An additional change is that all team members receive training on all stages of the car's production so that work is less monotonous and employees perceive their jobs more in terms of craftsmanship.[19]

Despite successes in the use of work teams, there are difficulties, including substantial startup costs. As in the Volvo example, whole plants must be built from scratch or significantly redesigned for the efficient use of the work-team approach. Furthermore, the technology of the organization may make the use of work teams very difficult or even impossible. For successful implementation of this approach, the work should be of the kind that no one individual can do alone or do as well as a team. For example, teams are appropriate in process production facilities such as chemical plants, and they are appropriate to some activities in service areas such as airlines. America West Airlines has adopted a procedure whereby employees are cross-trained so that they can perform a variety of the tasks required of the service crew. Another difficulty with work teams is that they alter the traditional manager–employee relationship. Managers often find it hard to adapt to the role of leader rather than supervisor and sometimes feel threatened by the growing power of the team and the reduced power of management. Furthermore, some employees may also have difficulty adapting to a role that includes traditional supervisory responsibilities. A final difficulty with work teams is that they must be incorporated into the organization's strategic planning process. Since work teams do alter the organization

HIGHLIGHTS IN HRM

2 TEAMWORK AT GENERAL FOODS FOR PEAK PERFORMANCE

General Foods adopted work teams as a strategic approach to maximizing productivity and promoting high performance among its employees. It called the groups "interfunctional work teams." Achieving peak performance is based on (1) a strong commitment to goals of high levels of performance, (2) collaboration and support among group members, and (3) a strong sense of ownership and responsibility for the results of the team effort. Team members are expected to go beyond the functional contribution they normally make as accountants, marketing specialists, etc. For example, the financial member of the Minute Rice team is expected to contribute to advertising, strategic planning, package design, product quality, and financial structure of the product. General Foods has sought to encourage five characteristics in its teams to achieve its intended results:

1. *Goals.* Team members must collaborate to set clear goals based on the mission of the strategic business unit.
2. *Roles.* Individuals bring diverse roles to the group, but must recognize that interdependence is essential. Team members must develop a common vision of the expected accomplishments of the team.
3. *Leadership.* The team leader must retain a multifunctional outlook, establish a positive working climate for team members, and obtain resources for the team.
4. *Team Relations.* Emphasis is placed on open communication of team members' expectations for one another. In addition to goal accomplishment, there is an emphasis on ensuring that the interpersonal team processes are addressed.
5. *Rewards.* Rewards are provided for team members as a group, and the team is encouraged to celebrate its accomplishments during the life of the project.

General Foods has addressed several obstacles to effective team function, including expectations, compensation, continuity, career movement, and power. New team members must be retrained to work outside their primary functional areas. Compensation systems must be constructed that reward individuals for team accomplishments. Because of the integration of the team members, continuity in membership is critical. Thus, employees may be asked to make a three- to five-year commitment before joining a team, or team members may be chosen from older, less mobile employees. Since team membership demands more-general skills, and it moves an employee out of the historical career path, new career paths to general management must be created from team experience. Finally, the members become capable of carrying out functions such as strategic planning that were previously restricted to higher levels of management. Managers must be prepared to use this newfound expertise.

SOURCE: Adapted from Marc Bassin, "Teamwork at General Foods: New & Improved," *Personnel Journal* 67, no. 5 (May 1988): 62–70. Reprinted with the permission of *Personnel Journal,* Costa Mesa, California; all rights reserved.

These America West employees are trained to perform in-flight and reservation services as well.

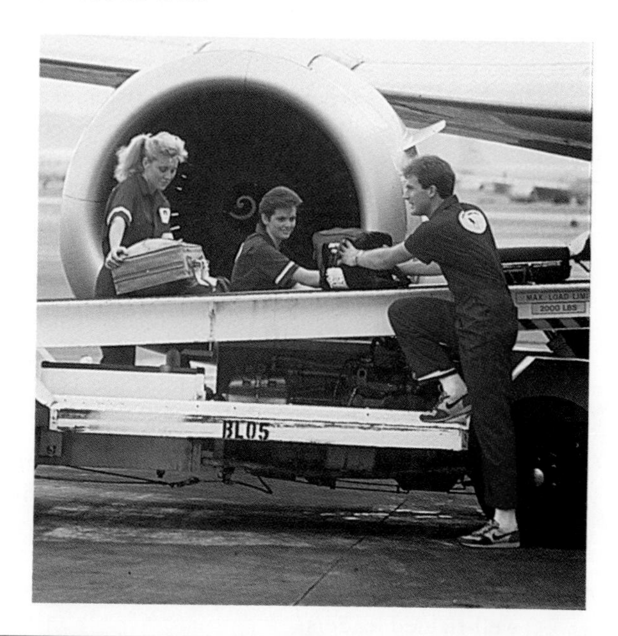

structurally, they must be taken into account when organizational strategies and tactics are being established. HR managers can play an active role in the strategic planning for work-team implementation by incorporating work-team changes into managerial career ladders, introducing relevant organizational development tactics, and planning for necessary managerial and team-member training.

Creating Employee Commitment

The final means of increasing employee involvement in the organization is through the creation of **commitment,** a kind of high-intensity attachment to the organization.[20] Like job involvement, commitment encourages employees to communicate, and it involves them in their jobs in ways that give them more control. However, employee commitment goes beyond improved communication or greater job control. Building commitment to organizations means that employees acquire a feeling that their personal goals are congruent with the organization's goals. Their level of involvement must be high so that they see personal rewards as attainable through the success of the organization. In describing this type of "high involvement," one management scholar differentiated it from the previous employee involvement strategies in the following way:

> Employees are not only asked to make decisions about their work activities, they are also asked to play a role in organizational decisions having to do with strategy, investment, and other major areas. Rewards are based on the performance of the organization. . . .[21]

Dina Nemeroff, corporate director of customer affairs for Citicorp, described her organization's philosophy of obtaining employee commitment while also satisfying employee needs: "A company must set standards of excellence and professionalism for employees. . . . But more importantly, while employees are aiming for those standards, they must feel their own needs are being met."[22]

At Citicorp, building employee commitment is seen as a way to obtain higher levels of customer service from employees. Furthermore, HR managers have learned, and research has demonstrated, that commitment reduces turnover, enhances satisfaction, and increases the likelihood of career advancement.[23] To achieve these results, however, organizations must use a wide range of strategies, including the following:

- Having realistic expectations in the selection process.
- Increasing job challenge by enriching jobs with more autonomy, feedback, and responsibility.
- Using work teams where appropriate.
- Clarifying job responsibilities through effective communication programs and well-trained leaders.
- Providing long-term opportunities with multifaceted career ladders that emphasize the long-run opportunities with the organization.
- Focusing on the realization of individuals' needs.
- Providing employees with a sense of power and control over their jobs by encouraging participation in all levels of organizational decisions.

Strategies such as these are organization-wide. Interestingly, however, most of these activities are associated with HR functions. Achieving the positive benefits of commitment in employees depends on active programs from the HR department.

MOTIVATING EMPLOYEES THROUGH EFFECTIVE LEADERSHIP

The word "leader" may be traced back about 700 years, and the concept may be found in the earliest writings of the Greeks and their predecessors. However, "leadership" did not exist in the English language until less than 200 years ago.[24] Leadership has been defined in numerous ways, but it is usually seen as the influence exerted by one individual on a group of persons to accomplish some goal. In organizations, leadership is usually associated with the influence that a manager exerts in the accomplishment of goals associated with the productivity of the organization. Thus, effective leadership among managers may be viewed as a means of motivating employees to improve their performance. Since a major concern of HR managers is to improve employee performance, it is not surprising that the study of leadership has been of such interest to them.

The sources of three types of leaders' power are listed in Figure 14–8. Position power is derived from such structural sources as formal authority and control over resources, rewards, and punishments. In designing managerial jobs, HR professionals can enhance the power of managers by ensuring that control over these areas is decentralized to the leader. Personal power is derived from personal characteristics such as expertise, need for affiliation, and charisma. To enhance the personal power of leaders, HR professionals can focus on selecting managers with technical expertise as well as a moderate need for affiliation, a need discussed later in the chapter. Finally, political power is derived from control over decisions and sensitivity to the use of political alliances. Again, HR managers can influence the political power of the leader by decentralizing decisions with the work group. They can also focus on selecting managers with the interpersonal skills to build coalitions and relationships among key organizational employees.

Identification of Effective Leader Traits

In the first half of this century, more than 100 studies attempted to identify **traits of leaders.** These studies undertook to verify the belief that certain characteristics

FIGURE 14–8 SOURCES OF LEADERS' POWER

TYPE OF POWER	SOURCE
Position Power	Formal authority Control over resources Control over rewards and punishments Control of information Control of physical surroundings
Personal Power	Expertise Moderate need for affiliation Charisma
Political Power	Control over decision processes Development of coalitions Use of co-optation

SOURCE: Adapted from Gary A. Yukl, *Leadership in Organizations,* 2d ed. (Englewood Cliffs, NJ: Prentice-Hall, 1989), 14. Adapted by permission of Prentice-Hall, Inc., Englewood Cliffs, New Jersey.

possessed by leaders are not possessed by nonleaders. Such research has held great interest for HR professionals, since identification of specific leadership traits could facilitate the selection and training functions of HRM. Managers could be selected who possessed certain leadership traits, or managers lacking such traits might be able to develop them. Early trait research studied such traits as intelligence, initiative, persistence, self-confidence, and desire for control. In his 1948 review of these studies, Stogdill found a consistent pattern of support for only five traits: (1) intelligence, (2) scholarship, (3) dependability, (4) social participation, and (5) socioeconomic status. Therefore, he concluded, "A person does not become a leader by virtue of the possession of some combination of traits. . . ."[25]

Despite the failure of early studies to identify a broad range or consistent set of traits that effective leaders possess, the research has continued. However, behavioral scientists today use a greater variety of measurement procedures to focus more directly on organizational managers rather than other types of leaders, such as military leaders. Furthermore, today's research looks at traits of leaders in terms of the process of leading.

McCLELLAND'S MANAGERIAL MOTIVATION One modern approach to explaining the traits of leaders has focused on the motivations that managers must possess to be successful. This research has used the *Thematic Apperception Test* (TAT), a projective test, to reveal the strength of three motivations, or needs, in particular: **needs for achievement, power, and affiliation.**

The need for achievement is prominent among successful executives. These individuals generally perceive themselves to be hard-working persons who need solid accomplishments in order to feel satisfied. Executive positions typically give them the challenge they need. Some of the characteristics of those with high achievement motivation are preference for moderate risk, persistence, personal responsibility for performance, need for performance feedback, and innovativeness.[26] Studies have shown that achievement-motivated people prefer tasks of moderate levels of difficulty. Thus, a supervisor must structure jobs and assign people to them so that they see their chances of job performance as neither too low nor too high.[27]

A moderate affiliation between managers and employees will facilitate task accomplishment and employee motivation.

Needs for power and affiliation also characterize those who are successful managers. The need for power is important to managers since they must exercise control and influence over their subordinates, peers, and superiors. McClelland has been careful to describe the need for power among leaders as a need that must be constrained. That is, the need for power must be such that it is satisfied through accomplishments associated with reaching organizational goals. Thus, power is important for leaders as a means of achievement rather than as an end in itself. The need for affiliation must also be constrained. A moderate need for affiliation will enable managers to socialize sufficiently to accomplish their tasks, and it will orient them toward the needs of their subordinates, thereby facilitating the motivation of employees.

MINER'S MOTIVE TO MANAGE In another approach to leader-trait identification, John Miner has drawn attention to the **motive to manage** as he has focused on the skills and traits a person must have to function effectively as a manager. Among these traits are the following:

1. Willingness to develop positive relationships with superiors.
2. Willingness to compete with peers for resources and power.
3. Desire to be assertive and take charge.
4. Willingness to exercise power over and apply sanctions to others.
5. Willingness to take positions that draw attention and produce conflict.
6. Willingness to meet routine role requirements associated with the bureaucracy.[28]

Despite its intuitive appeal, research on the motive to manage has been inconsistent. One study reported that there were significant correlations between this motive and managerial advancement to higher levels in large bureaucratic organizations, but that managerial success in small firms was not related to the motive to manage.[29] Perhaps HR managers should recognize that the motive to manage is less a set of leadership traits than a set of managerial characteristics. To the extent that it is associated with managerial success in large organizations, the motive gives HR managers direction for recruitment and selection.

OTHER TRAIT RESEARCH In addition to the work of McClelland and Miner, useful trait research has come from assessment centers (see Chapter 8). Assessment centers use projective tests, in-basket exercises, and leaderless groups to assess managerial success. An overall evaluation of the participant's performance is made by observers who review the performance of the manager in the exercises and examine test results. The observers are looking for leadership traits that predict the advancement potential of managers. Therefore the traits identified in assessment centers may be substantially different from those noted in the earlier trait leadership studies.

Cadbury Schweppes, a long-time user of assessment centers, has developed a trait profile of the competent manager for its operations. The traits include vision, drive, sociability, persuasion skill, delegation skills, teamwork skills, analytical ability, organizing skill, and personal factors such as integrity and ambition. Interestingly, social science research has provided results that are somewhat consistent with Cadbury's experience. Social scientists have identified four traits—emotional stability, action orientation, interpersonal skills, and cognitive skills—as consistently associated with organizational leaders.[30] These research findings, as well as Cadbury's experience, provide considerable opportunity for HR professionals. For example, this information may be used as a starting point in any organization for developing an organization-specific leader profile that can be used as a basis for selection, training, and employee appraisal.

Leader Behavior

Despite some recent success with the trait approach to leadership, early dissatisfaction with it had led to the study of the behavior of managers. Rather than focusing on the traits of successful managers, this approach emphasized the behavior that facilitates effective interaction of work-group members.

EMPLOYEE-CENTERED AND PRODUCTION-CENTERED LEADERSHIP In the late 1940s, the Survey Research Center of the University of Michigan embarked on a program to determine how **leader behavior** affected work-group performance and employee satisfaction. One of the major findings of these early studies was that production-centered supervisors, those concerned primarily with production, are less effective in terms of measurable productivity than employee-centered supervisors, those who give their attention to the people who do the work. Even in these early studies, employee-centered supervisors also exhibited concern for high performance goals and enthusiasm for achieving them. The third type of leadership under investigation by the Michigan researchers was participative leadership. As in early studies at the university, subordinates who had participative leaders exhibited higher work-related satisfaction and performance.[31]

STRUCTURE AND CONSIDERATION At the same time as the Michigan studies, researchers at Ohio State University were studying two major dimensions of supervisory behavior—*consideration* and *initiating structure*. Consideration, like employee orientation in the Michigan research, includes leader behaviors that encourage mutual trust, respect, and warmth between leaders and their work-group members. Initiating structure, like production orientation in the Michigan studies, includes leader behaviors such as organizing activities, defining the role of work-group members, and assigning tasks to get the work done.[32]

Considerable research has examined the effect of the task and relationship orientations of leaders. Results of questionnaire-based as well as case-based research have demonstrated that at least a moderate degree of *both* orientations is desirable in a leader. Therefore, it is important in developing more satisfied and productive employees that HR managers focus on training that encourages both behavioral dimensions of leadership.[33]

THE MANAGERIAL GRID A model known as the Managerial Grid has been popular as a basis for training managers and supervisors.[34] The grid, shown in Figure 14–9, expresses the relationship between concern for people and concern for production. By referring to the grid and identifying their behavior in the two areas of concern, managers and supervisors are better able to understand the approach they use with their subordinates. The grid itself, however, only provides the conceptual framework. It must be implemented through participation in seminars if it is to be effective. In the Managerial Grid seminars, managers and supervisors learn to identify personal and organizational changes that are necessary and to become more effective in their interpersonal relationships and their work groups.

FIGURE 14–9 THE MANAGERIAL GRID®

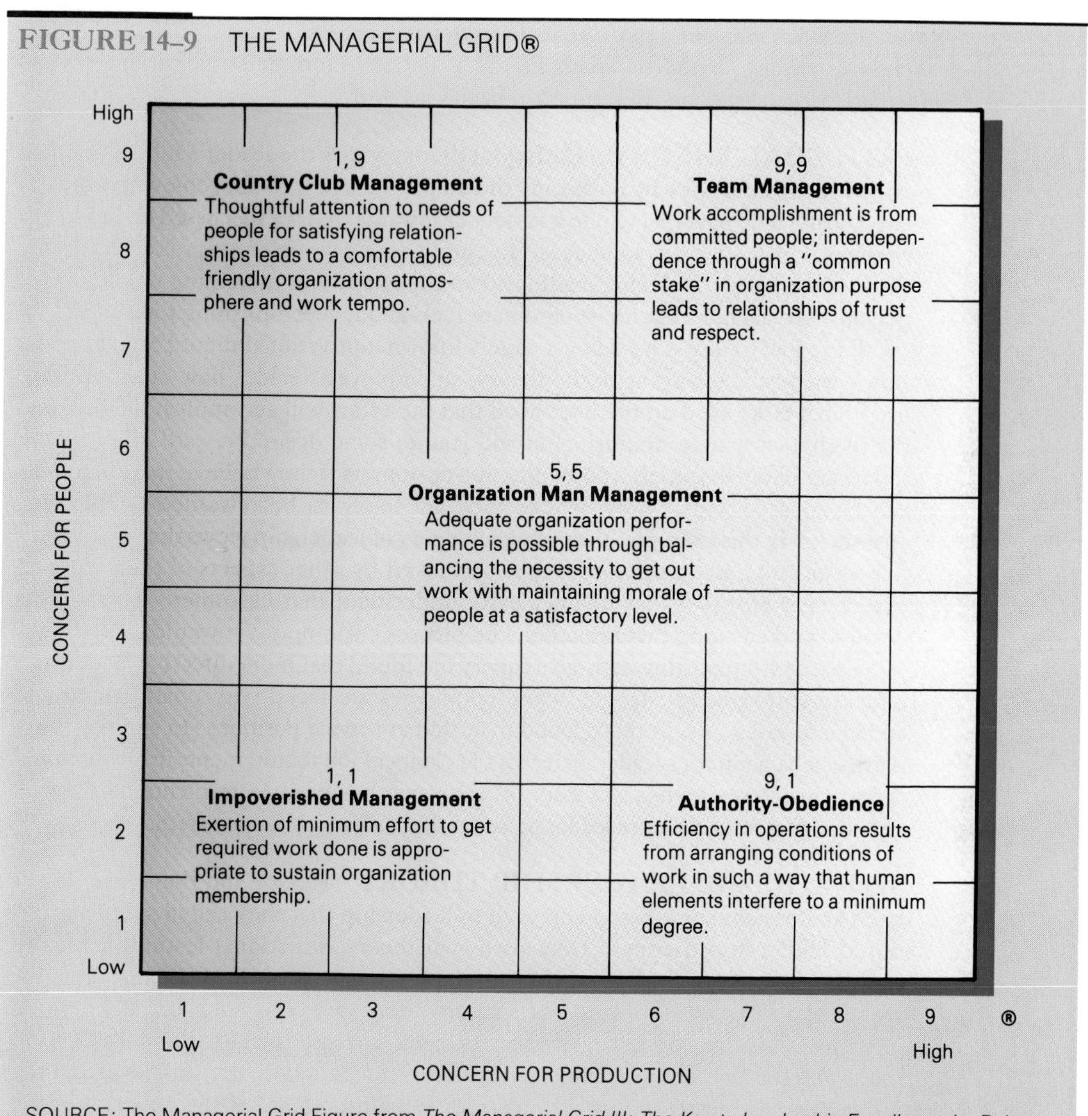

SOURCE: The Managerial Grid Figure from *The Managerial Grid III: The Key to Leadership Excellence*, by Robert R. Blake and Jane Srygley Mouton. Houston: Gulf Publishing Company, Copyright © 1985, page 12. Reproduced by permission.

Situation-based Theories of Leadership

Despite some support for the revised trait leadership approach and the behavioral leadership approach, the research has proved inconsistent and inadequate. While leaders may possess certain traits such as achievement motivation and may be more successful if they have both a production-centered and an employee-centered orientation, there was a growing realization that successful leaders behaved differently according to the demands of the situation. From this realization, several situation-based theories of leadership have emerged.

PATH-GOAL THEORY **Path-goal theory** views the leader's role as being to motivate the employee by increasing the employee's payoffs for achieving work-related goals. The payoffs include a variety of rewards that we discussed earlier in the chapter. The leader acts to increase an employee's payoffs or rewards by clarifying work-related goals, reducing roadblocks to the goals, and increasing the degree of personal satisfaction that the subordinate feels about accomplishing the goals.[35]

Path-goal theory is based on a widely known motivational theory called **expectancy theory.**[36] According to the theory, an employee decides how much effort to invest in a task based on the likelihood that the effort will accomplish the task and the likelihood that accomplishment will lead to some desired reward. Thus, bank tellers are likely to put effort into pleasing customers if they believe that customers can be pleased and if they believe they are likely to be rewarded for pleasing customers. In this example, the path-goal theory of leadership views the supervisor's role as ensuring that customers are not annoyed by other aspects of their banking experience, ensuring that tellers clearly understand that customer satisfaction is desired, and ensuring that the teller who pleases customers is rewarded.

Research supporting path-goal theory has found that more directive leaders can increase employee satisfaction when employees are faced with unstructured and ambiguous tasks such as those found in customer-service positions. In addition, supportive behavior from a leader increases the clarity of job requirements in unstructured tasks. Finally, the path-goal theory of leadership has been instrumental in drawing attention to the variations in leader behavior that different situations require.

SITUATIONAL LEADERSHIP THEORY Hersey and Blanchard developed another situation-based approach to leadership that they called simply **situational leadership theory.**[37] Like path-goal theory, situational leadership theory assumes that leaders vary their behaviors depending on what the situation demands. However, in Hersey and Blanchard's theory, the leader behavior is broadly defined in terms of relationship behavior and task behavior, and the situation is defined in terms of follower readiness. Follower readiness refers to both the skill level and the self-confidence possessed by the subordinate, and both affect the behavior of the leader. For example, as employee readiness increases, the leader's task behavior decreases (see Figure 14–10). In other words, employees with greater self-confidence and better skills require less supervision from their manager. The contribution the situational leadership theory makes to management is that it appreciates the complexity of the manager's situation.

Emerging Theories of Leadership

Leadership is such a complex phenomenon that no single approach has offered managers a full understanding of what is required to lead employees to higher levels

FIGURE 14–10 SITUATIONAL LEADERSHIP

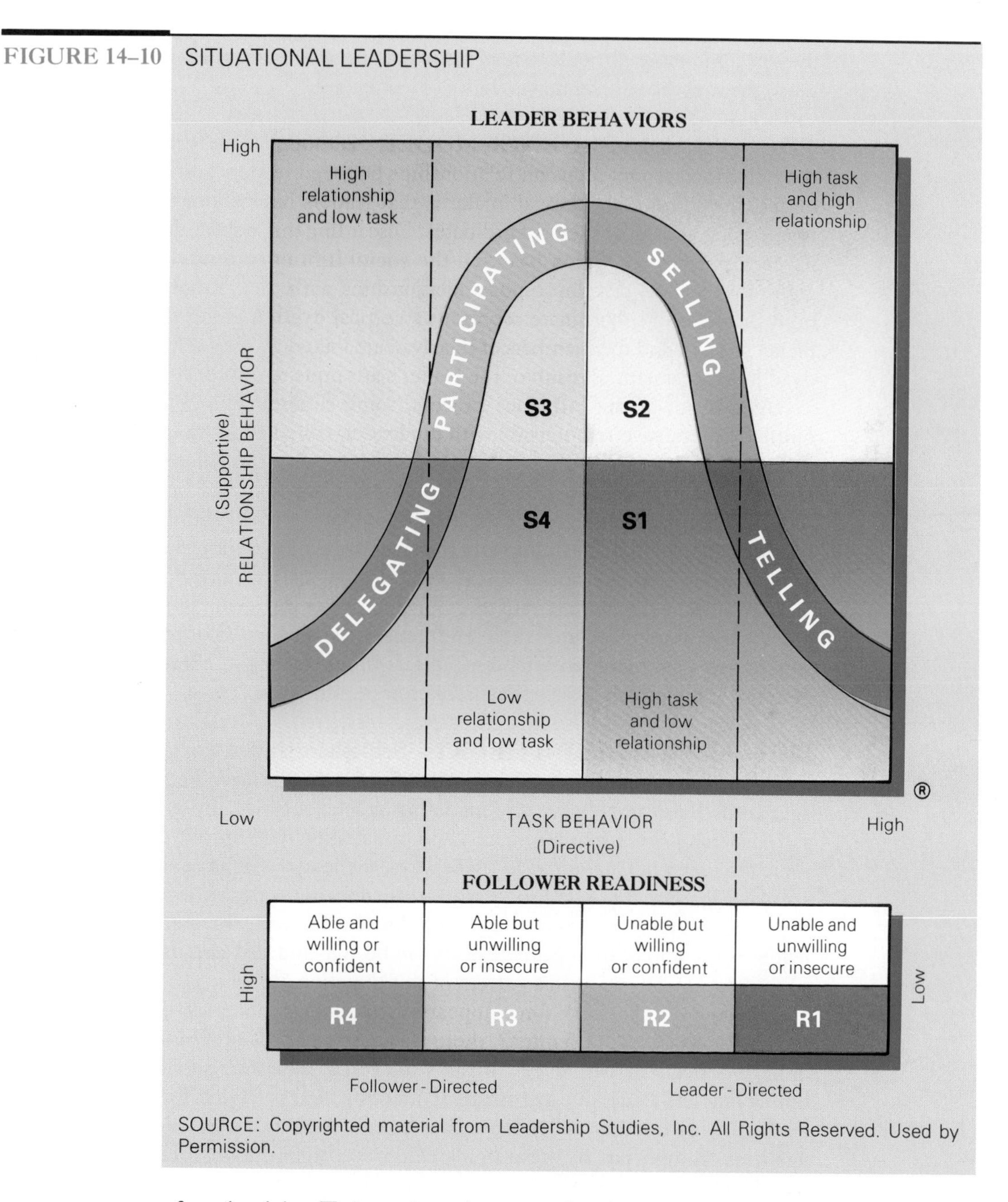

SOURCE: Copyrighted material from Leadership Studies, Inc. All Rights Reserved. Used by Permission.

of productivity. Traits such as those associated with McClelland's managerial motivation or Miner's motive to manage offer some insight, and the situational theories provide HR managers with some practical advice. Unfortunately, as these theories become more complex in order to address the phenomenon of leadership thoroughly, they become more difficult to test. Growing out of somewhat limited success with these theories are several newer views of leadership.

THE SOCIAL INFLUENCE MODEL Although leadership models such as the behavioral model focus on relationships between leaders and subordinates, an underlying assumption they all make is that leaders have about the same type of relationship with all of their subordinates. Discarding this assumption, the industrial psychologist George Graen has used the **social influence model** of leadership to argue that leaders develop unique relationships with their subordinates. Accordingly, leader and subordinate represent a vertical dyad (a group of two, separated hierarchically), and the members of this dyad are linked by their relationship. Vertical dyad links are a natural result of the leader's attempts to influence subordinates.[38]

As a result of the influence process, some subordinates develop a positive, mutually supportive relationship with the leader, called an *in-group exchange*. Other subordinates fail to develop trusting relationships with the leader, resulting in an *out-group exchange*. The in-group exchange has been found to be associated with higher performance and greater job satisfaction, along with other positive work-related outcomes.[39] The best time for a manager to develop an in-group exchange with an employee is at the outset of the relationship. HR managers can assist other managers in the development of in-group exchanges by encouraging them to get to know their employees and their preferences. Managers who get to know their subordinates are more likely to develop in-group exchanges, thereby realizing the benefits of higher job satisfaction and better performance.[40]

SELF-LEADERSHIP THEORY **Self-leadership theory** focuses on encouraging subordinates to exercise leadership for themselves. The successful manager leads by example (i.e., by modeling self-leadership), by giving rewards for self-leadership among subordinates, and by assisting with employee goal setting, a topic discussed in Chapter 9. In these ways, the leader teaches employees to act as their own leaders. Thus, the successful leader does not appear to lead by influencing, directing, coercing, and punishing subordinates. Instead, the mark of a successful leader is the ability to encourage others to be self-directed and to offer rewards to subordinates who establish a pattern of self-direction.[41]

Changes in the work force appear to support the potential of self-leadership theory. As we noted in Chapter 2, there are growing numbers of better-educated and more independent employees in the work force, and they should be capable of employing self-leadership as a means of directing their behavior. Furthermore, there are a growing number of service organizations, such as community mental health agencies. Employees in these kinds of service organizations perform their tasks largely outside the view of their supervisors. In addition, more-sophisticated information systems permit decentralization of decision making. Where employees act on their own, encouraging self-leadership seems to be the most effective means of ensuring that their behavior is consistent with the organization's mission and goals.

Reprinted by permission of *Supervision* magazine, © 1977 The National Research Bureau, Inc. 424 North Third Street, Burlington, Iowa 52601–5224.

Even in the more structured and traditional organizational setting, self-leadership may have merit in that it allows employees autonomy and responsibility for their own performance and satisfaction. Because the work force is so diverse, managers should recognize that some employees may be better suited to self-leadership than others.

TRANSFORMATIONAL LEADERSHIP With the success of such leaders as Steven Jobs at both Apple Computer and Next and Lee Iacocca at Chrysler, public attention has been drawn to the transformational leader. **Transformational leadership** refers to a leader's success in changing an organization by building enthusiasm and commitment to the leader's vision of the organizational mission. The role of the transformational leader may be described in the following way:

Lee Iacocca's enthusiasm and commitment to changing the direction of Chrysler Corp. make him a transformational leader.

> The transformational leader motivates followers to do more than originally expected. Such transformation can be achieved by (a) raising an awareness of the importance and value of designated outcomes, (b) getting followers to transcend their own self-interests, or (c) altering or expanding followers' needs on Maslow's hierarchy of needs.[42]

Transformational leaders do not abandon traditional leader behaviors such as providing appropriate rewards or controlling the actions of subordinates in order to accomplish goals. Rather, they go beyond these traditional leader behaviors, behaving charismatically by sensing what is important and communicating that vision in the form of an organizational mission. They also stimulate the development of individuals by assigning projects and coaching employees in a way that recognizes the individual's capabilities. Finally, transformational leaders provide intellectual stimulation by encouraging followers to think in new ways.[43]

Behavioral science research concerning transformational leadership is encouraging. First, it appears that transformational leaders may be found in a variety of organizational levels, not just at the top. Second, transformational leadership produces positive responses from followers, and it appears to make a difference in their performance.[44] Third, and perhaps its greatest contribution, transformational leadership helps to improve the culture of an organization. Transformational leaders develop a vision for a changed, more successful, higher-performing organization. They then develop commitment for that vision by implementing strategies for institutionalizing the vision among employees as well as in external constituencies of the organization.[45]

SUMMARY

More organizations are looking at their HRM activities as a key means to improve organizational productivity. In doing so they turn to a variety of strategies that are founded in motivational and leadership theory. Among those strategies is the use of appropriate and novel rewards for employees. Pay is a particularly important reward that is used as a performance-contingent means of enhancing performance. A variety of other rewards and organizational award programs are also being implemented by HR departments. Another means of motivating employees is derived from equity theory. From this perspective, HR managers develop tactics based on employees' perceived equity and their reactions to perceptions of inequity. An alternative to these approaches to motivating employees is the use of various means of enhancing employee involvement in the organization. Involvement approaches include suggestion systems such as employee involvement groups, job involvement tactics such as work teams, and various means for encouraging employee commitment to their organizations.

Analyzing effective leadership is another means by which HR managers may develop strategies for improving organizational productivity. Although the study of leader traits was once considered of little value, the work of McClelland, Miner's motive to manage, and various leader profiles derived from assessment centers have been useful in identifying traits on which selection, appraisal, and training decisions can be made. Other leadership theories that have proved useful in improving organizational productivity are the behavioral theories and situational theories, such as path-goal theory and Hersey and Blanchard's situational leadership theory. Also of use may be several emerging leadership theories, including social influence theory, self-leadership theory, and transformational leadership theory.

DISCUSSION QUESTIONS

1. What is motivation? How is it related to performance?
2. How can rewards be used effectively to increase employee performance? What role can organizational award programs play in motivating performance?
3. Describe the relationship of employee involvement groups to suggestion systems, and explain the limitations of employee involvement groups in obtaining employee commitment.
4. How could you increase the commitment of employees working for you?
5. Which of the theories of leadership discussed in the chapter do you feel would be the most useful in the management of personnel? Why does it appeal to you?
6. How are self-leadership theory and transformational leadership theory inconsistent with one another? What relationship does transformational leadership theory have with the behavioral theories?
7. Why is it necessary to provide managers with leadership training?
8. Consider the approaches used by different instructors under whom you have studied to motivate and lead class discussions. Which approaches were most and least effective? Why?

MINI-CASE 14–1 Quality—The Goal at Pepsi

Among more than 200 bottlers in the United States, the Pepsi-Cola bottler in Springfield, Missouri, is particularly proud of its performance, and justifiably so: it has won the award for highest quality among Pepsi bottlers for ten consecutive years. In addition to its outstanding record of quality, this bottler has other characteristics worth noting. Turnover is almost nonexistent, with most employees having worked there for 15 years; no one has worked there for less than 8 years. Employees exhibit a high degree of loyalty and pride in their organization. There is a sense of family, with everyone calling each other by first name.

Several qualities seem to make the difference at this bottler. One of the most important is its adherence to standards of quality that exceed Pepsi's corporate standards. Springfield performs all of Pepsi's required tests, but it does so more frequently than other bottlers. If any employee notices any problem on the line, production is halted immediately until management determines that the problem has been solved. In one instance, employees discovered that a shipment of plastic bottles had tiny black specks embedded in them, although they were still entirely sanitary. This discovery was made after 300 cases had already been filled with the imperfect bottles. Nevertheless, all 300 cases were poured out. Customers expect the product to appear exactly as promised, and Springfield employees will not renege on that promise.

In addition, there are no time constraints on quality tests. If repeated tests are required, they are performed until the employee conducting the test is satisfied with the results. Records of the performance of route salespersons are kept on a daily basis, and these workers are given daily feedback on their performance and recognized for outstanding performance.

Managers are expected to know the various jobs in the organization and to be capable of taking over not only a production or route job but other managerial jobs as well. Every manager started out as a member of the production line or as a route salesperson. Managers are expected to lead and motivate by example, and a great deal of emphasis is placed on teamwork. General staff meetings discuss all aspects of the business, including production, finance, and marketing. Managers are expected to communicate regularly with employees and with managers in other departments. Thus the sales manager is expected to work closely with the comptroller concerning sales expectations.

SOURCE: Adapted from D. Keith Denton, "Quality Is Pepsi's Challenge," *Personnel Journal* 67, no. 6 (June 1988): 143–147. Reprinted with the permission of *Personnel Journal,* Costa Mesa, California;

QUESTIONS

1. Explain how the Springfield Pepsi bottler is successful in terms of the various motivation theories discussed in this chapter.
2. How does this organization virtually eliminate turnover, and what role does the low turnover play in the overall strategy for motivating employees in this organization?

MINI-CASE 14–2 Leadership at Delta Air Lines

Russell Heil is senior vice-president of HR at Delta Air Lines in Atlanta, Georgia. He started working for Delta as an aircraft performance engineer after leaving the military service, where he had served a tour of duty in Vietnam. Prior to joining the military, Heil had attended Georgia State University for his engineering degree. After joining Delta, he obtained an MBA at Georgia State and took a position as administrative assistant when the opportunity arose. When Delta merged with Northeast Airlines in 1972, there was a great deal to be done in the HR department, and Heil was asked to provide assistance. He liked the department so much that he eventually took a permanent position there and rose to the top.

Heil endorses the strict policy of no layoffs for employees. Even during periods when business was slow, pilots and others were reassigned to other jobs to avoid laying anyone off. Heil believes that employees are willing to work harder because of the loyalty the organization shows to them. One of Heil's subordinates commented that Heil has an enthusiastic vision for Delta that he readily conveys to others. The same employee added that Heil is willing to work as hard as anyone. Heil feels strongly about the need to communicate effectively why decisions are made, and he emphasizes that Delta employees are a special group of people in whom he has great confidence and for whom he has great respect.

SOURCE: Adapted from Bill Leonard, "Making the Message Clear," *Personnel Administrator* 34, no. 11 (November 1989): 46–49. Reprinted with the permission from *HRMagazine* (formerly *Personnel Administrator*), published by the Society for Human Resource Management, Alexandria, VA.

QUESTIONS

1. In what ways does Russell Heil exhibit the characteristics of the various leadership models?
2. How does Delta maintain the high commitment of its employees?

NOTES AND REFERENCES

1. J. Richards, "Adrian Gozzard," *Personnel Management* 21, no. 1 (January 1989): 34–35.
2. Fredrick E. Shuster, "Reviving Productivity in America," *Personnel Administrator* 33, no. 7 (July 1988): 65–68.
3. Fred Luthans and Robert Kreitner, *Organizational Behavior Modification and Beyond: An Operant and Social Learning Approach* (Glenview, IL: Scott, Foresman, 1985).
4. These needs are adapted from Abraham H. Maslow, *Motivation and Personality*, 2d ed. (New York: Harper & Brothers, 1970).
5. These four reasons for instituting pay-for-performance systems are included in a list of pro's and cons of developing such systems by Thomas Rollins, "Pay for Performance: Is It Worth the Trouble?" *Personnel Administrator* 33, no. 5 (May 1988): 42–46.
6. Richard L. Bunning, "Skill-based Pay," *Personnel Administrator* 34, no. 6 (June 1989): 65–70.
7. Holly Rawlinson, "Make Awards Count," *Personnel Journal* 67, no. 10 (October 1988): 139–146; and Jennifer Koch, "Perpetual Thanks: Its Assets," *Personnel Journal* 69, no. 1 (January 1990): 72–73.
8. Priscilla Diffie-Couch, "How to Give Feedback," *Supervisory Management* 28, no. 8 (August 1983): 27–31.
9. These novel awards are adapted from the suggestions of Richard C. Huseman and John D. Hatfield, *Managing the Equity Factor: "After All I've Done For You . . ."* (Boston: Houghton Mifflin, 1989), 94–100.
10. J. Stacey Adams, "Inequity in Social Exchange," in *Advances in Experimental Social Psychology*, ed. L. Berkowitz (New York: Academic Press, 1965), 276–299.
11. Richard C. Huseman, John D. Hatfield, and Edward W. Miles, "A New Perspective on Equity Theory: The Equity Sensitivity Construct," *Academy of Management Review* 12, no. 2 (June 1987): 222–234. For another view of equity sensitivity, see Huseman and Hatfield, *Managing the Equity Factor*, 22–26.
12. There are a variety of practical, work-related, and nonwork-related suggestions for managing equity and ensuring fairness in Huseman and Hatfield, *Managing the Equity Factor*, 56–101.
13. These three approaches are adapted from Professor Lawler's three approaches to involvement: (1) parallel suggestions involvement, (2) job involvement, and (3) high involvement. For more information about his three approaches, see Edward E. Lawler, "Choosing an Involvement Strategy," *Academy of Management Executive* 2, no. 3 (August 1988): 197–204.
14. "HRM Update," *Personnel Administrator* 34, no. 8 (August 1989): 20.
15. Among the classic references to the work of Herzberg and his colleagues are the following: Frederick Herzberg, Bernard Mausner, and Barbara B. Snyderman, *The Motivation to Work*, 2d ed. (New York: Wiley, 1959), 113–114; and Frederick Herzberg, *Work and the Nature of Man* (Cleveland: World, 1966).

16. Herzberg provided considerable empirical support for his theory; however, research using other methods failed to provide this support. For a discussion of the research criticizing the two-factor theory, see Nathan King, "Clarification and Evaluation of the Two-Factor Theory of Job Satisfaction," *Psychological Bulletin* 74, no. 1 (July 1970): 18–31. Reviews supporting the two-factor theory are also available; for example, see Ben Grigaliunas and Yoash Wiener, "Has the Research Challenge to Motivation-Hygiene Theory Been Conclusive? An Analysis of Critical Studies," *Human Relations* 27, no. 9 (December 1974): 839–871.

17. A description of how plants are organized around work teams appears in Edward E. Lawler, "The New Plant Revolution," *Organizational Dynamics* 6, no. 3 (Winter 1978): 2–12. An example of work team organization at Sola is available in Richard L. Bunning and Ralph Althisar, "Modules: A Team Model for Manufacturing," *Personnel Journal* 69, no. 3 (March 1990): 90–96.

18. Marc Bassin, "Teamwork at General Foods: New & Improved," *Personnel Administrator* 33, no. 5 (May 1988): 62–70.

19. Phil Farish, "HRM Update," *Personnel Administrator* 34, no. 1 (January 1989): 14.

20. For additional information about this high-intensity type of commitment, see Larry E. Penley and Sam Gould, "Etzioni's Model of Organizational Involvement: A Perspective for Understanding Commitment to Organizations," *Journal of Organizational Behavior* 9, no. 7 (January 1988): 43–59.

21. Lawler, 201.

22. These and other comments were made by leading corporate executives of service organizations as they described how high standards of customer service are maintained by their company. See James Fraze, "CEOs Stress Employee Link in Quality Service," *Resource* 8, no. 1 (January 1989): 5–6.

23. The type of high-intensity involvement referred to here as commitment is called moral commitment by some and affective commitment by others. Its impact on employee performance and satisfaction is best described by John P. Meyer, Sampo V. Paunonen, Ian R. Gellatly, Richard D. Goffin, and Douglas N. Jackson, "Organizational Commitment and Job Performance: It's the Nature of Commitment that Counts," *Journal of Applied Psychology* 74, no. 1 (February 1989): 152–156.

24. Although one of the classic references on leadership is Ralph M. Stogdill, *Handbook of Leadership: A Survey of the Literature* (New York: Free Press, 1974), readers may also wish to consult Bernard M. Bass and Ralph M. Stogdill, *Bass and Stogdill's Handbook of Leadership: Theory, Research, and Managerial Applications*, 3d ed. (New York: Free Press, 1990).

25. Ralph M. Stogdill, "Personal Factors Associated with Leadership: A Survey of the Literature," *Journal of Psychology* 25 (1948): 64.

26. Craig C. Pinder, *Work Motivation: Theories, Issues, and Applications* (Glenview, IL: Scott, Foresman, 1984), 63; and David C. McClelland, *Human Motivation* (Glenview, IL: Scott, Foresman, 1985), 595–596.

27. Pinder, 63–65.

28. John B. Miner and Norman R. Smith, "Decline and Stabilization of Managerial Motivation Over a 20-Year Period," *Journal of Applied Psychology* 67, no. 3 (June 1982): 297–305.

29. Gary A. Yukl, *Leadership in Organizations*, 2d ed. (Englewood Cliffs, NJ: Prentice-Hall, 1989), 183–184.

30. These and other traits of leaders are summarized from a large body of research in Yukl, 176–194.

31. The results of the University of Michigan studies were summarized in two books by Rensis Likert: *New Patterns of Management* (New York: McGraw-Hill, 1961), and *The Human Organization: Its Management and Value* (New York: McGraw-Hill, 1967).

32. This research is described in Stogdill, 1974.

33. Yukl, 74–97.

34. Robert R. Blake and Jane S. Mouton, *The Versatile Manager* (Homewood, IL: Irwin, 1981). Earlier books about the grid by these authors were published in 1964 and 1978.

35. Robert J. House, "A Path-Goal Theory of Leader Effectiveness," *Administrative Science Quarterly* 16, no. 3 (September 1971): 321–339.

36. Victor H. Vroom, *Work and Motivation* (New York: Wiley, 1964).

37. A relatively recent formulation of situational leadership theory is provided in Paul Hersey and Kenneth H. Blanchard, *Management of Organizational Behavior: Utilizing Human Resources*, 5th ed. (Englewood Cliffs, NJ: Prentice-Hall, 1988). Unfortunately, the complexity of situational leadership theory has limited the research into it. To date, only a few tests of the theory have been published; one of these studies provides support for the theory, particularly for employees with low readiness (called *maturity* in earlier formulations of the theory). See Robert P. Vecchio, "Situational Leadership Theory: An Examination of a Prescriptive Theory," *Journal of Applied Psychology* 72, no. 3 (August 1987): 444–451.

38. For a description of the vertical dyad linkage model, see Fred Dansereau, Jr., George Graen, and William Haga, "A Vertical Dyad Linkage Approach to Leadership Within Formal Organizations," *Organizational Behavior and Human Performance* 13, no. 1 (February 1975): 46–78.

39. Robert P. Vecchio and Bruce C. Godbel, "The Vertical Dyad Linkage Model of Leadership: Problems and Prospects," *Organizational Behavior and Human Performance* 34, no. 1 (August 1984): 5–20.

40. Both empirical research and practical managerial suggestions with regard to the social influence model are available in the work of Professor Vecchio and his colleagues. See Robert P. Vecchio and Mario Sussman, "Preferences for Forms of Supervisory Social Influence," *Journal of Organizational Behavior* 10, no. 2 (1989): 135–143; and Vecchio, "Are You In or Out with Your Boss?" *Business Horizons* 29, no. 6 (November–December 1986): 76–78.

41. The leader capable of producing self-leadership is described as a super leader in Manz and Sims' overview of the development and encouragement of self-leadership. See Charles C. Manz and Henry P. Sims, *Super-Leadership: Leading Others to Lead Themselves* (Englewood Cliffs, NJ: Prentice-Hall, 1989).

42. John J. Hater and Bernard M. Bass, "Superiors' Evaluations and Subordinates' Perceptions of Transformational and Transactional Leadership," *Journal of Applied Psychology* 73, no. 4 (November 1988): 695.

43. More complete descriptions of transformational leadership are available in Bernard M. Bass, *Leadership and Performance Beyond Expectations* (New York: Free Press, 1985); and James M. Burns, *Leadership* (New York: Harper & Row, 1978).

44. Hater and Bass, 695–702.

45. Noel M. Tichy and Mary Anne Devanna, *The Transformational Leader* (New York: Wiley, 1986).

CHAPTER 15

The Role of Communication in HRM

After reading this chapter you will be able to:

1. *Explain the role of communication in HRM.*
2. *Describe the rationale for careful choice of verbal and nonverbal symbols.*
3. *Explain how to reduce the impact of false assumptions on communication-related misunderstandings.*
4. *Discuss effective downward and upward communication systems.*
5. *List ways to improve managerial communication competency.*
6. *Explain the major techniques used in counseling.*
7. *Define the key terms in the chapter.*

TERMS TO IDENTIFY

verbal and nonverbal symbols *(495)*
inference *(496)*
active listening *(498)*
downward communication *(499)*
upward communication *(507)*
grapevine *(512)*
communication competency *(513)*
media sensitivity *(513)*
cross-cultural communication *(514)*
counseling *(516)*
directive counseling *(520)*
nondirective counseling *(520)*
participative counseling *(521)*

No aspect of HRM is so pervasive as communication. Communication provides the means of gathering and disseminating information in the employee selection process. Through communication, managers give feedback and counsel to employees in the performance appraisal process. Compensation programs depend on the communication skills of those who gather information for setting wage rates; labor relations are affected by negotiation skills, counseling skills, and presentation skills; and successful training programs depend on how effectively trainers, videotapes, and written materials can communicate. Moreover, HR managers are frequently charged with ensuring that their employer has an effective program of organizational communication. HR managers must therefore understand how to manage communication as well as how to communicate effectively with employees at all levels of the organization.[1]

In this chapter we address each of these communication responsibilities. We will identify the communication skills that effective HR managers need and discuss the communication systems that must be managed by HR departments. Finally, we will devote special attention to the communication skills required for counseling, which is widely used by managers in disciplining and appraising, as well as assisting, their employees.

THE VITAL ROLE OF COMMUNICATION

Every manager depends on communication to carry out the tasks of the organization. In his study of the work of managers, Henry Mintzberg identified ten

This chapter was prepared by Dr. Larry E. Penley, Professor of Management, Arizona State University, Tempe, Arizona.

managerial roles, five of which are explicitly communication-related: liaison, monitor, disseminator, spokesperson, and negotiator.[2] The remaining five roles, though not as explicitly, still demand skillful communication. One managerial consultant described the relationship of communication to managing this way:

> We all learn in school that management is supposed to link levels vertically and departments horizontally through planning, leadership, organizing, and controlling. In practice, these things cannot be done without constant attention to good communication. It isn't an adjunct to the manager's job, it is the manager's job.[3]

Effective managers are effective communicators.[4] Their communication skills can affect the satisfaction of those who work for them, the effectiveness of the work unit, and their subordinates' understanding of their duties.[5]

To be effective communicators, managers must respond to specific needs that employees have for information. Since employees may distort what they communicate upward to their managers, determining these needs and then responding to them can be difficult. One nationwide poll of 3,500 working Americans found that more than half rated their employer as only average or poor in providing information on such topics as "the way pay is determined," "personnel policies and procedures," "grievance procedures," and "job openings."[6] Figure 15–1 presents more of the results of this poll.

Considerable time in communicating is required to do a good job in providing information about these topics. An effective manager's day must be consumed with communicating—with subordinates, with other managers, with consumers, with regulators, and so on. Managers spend the largest amount of their time (45 percent) communicating with subordinates. About 25 percent of their time is spent talking with persons outside the organization, and the remaining 30 percent of their time is

FIGURE 15–1 HOW WELL EMPLOYEES BELIEVE THEIR EMPLOYERS COMMUNICATE

TOPIC	PERCENT RATING EMPLOYER AS GOOD/VERY GOOD*
Benefits	58%
Personnel policies and procedures	50%
How pay is determined	48%
Job openings	45%
Grievance procedures	37%

*The remaining employees rated their employers as average or poor in providing information about each topic.

SOURCE: Adapted from Wyatt WorkAmerica Study, The Wyatt Company, 1989.

divided about equally between their superiors and others within the organization. Not surprisingly, managers use face-to-face communication as the predominant medium. In fact, when one-on-one communication is considered together with meetings, more than 80 percent of managers' communication may be classified as face-to-face as opposed to written or telephone communication.[7]

In seminars conducted by the authors, managers consistently note the importance of communication with employees, and most agree that their organizations need to improve communication between employees and management. Supporting this observation was a Coopers & Lybrand poll of manufacturing executives and plant managers; 99 percent of the executives agreed that improving communication between management and workers was important, and 59 percent believed that their organizations had not done enough to improve employee–management communication.

THE NATURE OF COMMUNICATION

HR managers must first understand the process of communication before they can successfully address any problems that result from poor communication. Communication is a process in which a sender and a receiver of a message interact in order to give the message meaning. This complex process has often been oversimplified in traditional communication models: A sender delivers a message that is captured by a receiver, who in turn provides feedback to the sender indicating that the message has been received. This simplistic model of communication ignores communication difficulties created by an interaction process that relies on individual perceptions of complex verbal and nonverbal messages. Traditional descriptions of communication also create false expectations about what a manager must do to communicate effectively.[8]

Communicating with Symbols

We are able to communicate with one another because we can manipulate a broad range of **verbal and nonverbal symbols** that stand for objects and abstractions. For example, if we tell someone to "lay the pen on the table," selecting symbols (i.e., words) such as "table" and "pen" to communicate our message, we only have to agree with that person on the general meaning of the symbols for the communication to succeed. However, in the complex world of organizational communication, a variety of words can be used to refer to the same object, practice, or idea, so the choice of a particular word often implies bias in communicators' evaluations and perceptions.[9] For example, managers may choose to call those who report to them subordinates, workers, supervisees, staff, crew, the gang, my people, hired hands, etc. Employees will perceive a certain kind of relationship with their manager depending on which word is used to describe them. Therefore, managers face the challenge of choosing the right words to communicate with employees, since this choice can have a significant influence on their relationship.

Furthermore, the words a manager chooses when communicating convey a message themselves—about the manager, about the person the manager is communicating with, and about the situation. One linguist described words as loaded weapons: when used improperly, they can be dangerous.[10] For example, certain words can convey racial or sex bias on the part of the communicator, and managers must recognize this danger if they are to communicate effectively with diverse groups of employees.

Problems of False Assumptions

The effective communicator must also recognize the role that assumptions play in communication. The perceptions of communicators are based on certain assumptions they have about one another, about the situation, and about other persons and places they have in common. Whenever senders and receivers have conflicting assumptions, the quality of their communication deteriorates. Highlights in HRM 1 provides an illustration of the effect of different perceived assumptions as a manager and employee discuss a job opportunity. This account demonstrates why managers must take the time to adapt their messages to the intended receiver. Some of the assumptions that led to the communication problem between these two managers were as follows:

- The source of the new training program.
- The use of a written medium for the initial message when an oral or less formal medium would have conveyed more information.
- The lack of openness and honesty between the two managers.
- The usual reluctance of subordinates to communicate their negative reactions and feelings to their managers.
- The failure of the manager to solicit the subordinate's reactions and feelings.
- The failure of the manager to communicate her own reactions and feelings about the subordinate's messages.

There are two primary ways to improve communication and reduce the impact of false assumptions: separating fact from inference and active listening.

SEPARATING FACT FROM INFERENCE A fact is a verifiable statement to which many people can agree. An **inference** is a conclusion that is based on fact but depends on the assumptions that are made.[11] An example of an inference may be seen in the illustration in Highlights in HRM 1: Sharon *inferred* that Laura was displeased with her performance because Laura recommended the new managerial training program. Communication can be improved by differentiating facts from inferences. By training oneself to separate factual information from the inferences made from those facts, it is possible to develop an awareness of the distinction in a variety of settings. A supervisor might infer, for example, that the employee

HIGHLIGHTS IN HRM

1 A PROBLEM OF MISUNDERSTANDING

Laura Alvarez moved from California to East Tennessee as the training director for a division of a large electronic manufacturing company. When her company had opened the division, it had created a relatively large training staff in order to provide three types of training: (1) technical training, (2) managerial training, and (3) remedial, basic education. These three areas of training were headed by unit managers who reported to Laura. One of these managers, Sharon Watson, headed the managerial training unit. Laura had hired Sharon as a trainer when the division had first opened, and her satisfaction with Sharon's performance and demonstrated potential had led to Sharon's promotion to manager of the managerial training unit.

One day Laura received a report from one of her counterparts at the home office in California. The report described impressive improvements in productivity that might be attributed to some new concepts that had been introduced in the California office's managerial training program. She scribbled a note to Sharon that said, "Why aren't we doing this?" Attaching the report to her note, she gave it to her new secretary, who, rather than sending the handwritten note, typed it and sent it to Sharon. Knowing Laura's preference for "no secrets" in the training area, the secretary also sent a copy of the note and report to the other unit directors in training, but she failed to list them as copy recipients on the typed memorandum.

When Sharon received the memorandum, she was surprised at the curtness of the note and the unusual formality of its having been typed. Why, she wondered, had Laura sent the report with the note? Was she implying that Sharon was unable to implement training programs that really made a difference? She also found herself particularly annoyed at Laura's having blind copied the memorandum and report.

Sharon requested a meeting with Laura, an unusual event since they usually met informally rather than at scheduled meetings. The meeting went poorly. Sharon had assumed, prior to receiving Laura's memorandum, that she was an excellent manager and a favorite of Laura's. Laura, prior to this meeting, assumed that Sharon thought well of her and trusted her. Not understanding the purpose of the meeting and immediately noticing Sharon's cool demeanor, Laura felt herself becoming defensive. Sharon was anxious and spoke with more formality than usual as she showed Laura the report and asked what Laura's expectations were. Thinking that she had merely passed on some potentially useful information, Laura defensively suggested that her expectations were that Sharon would read the material and use it. Sharon replied, "Then you don't think we're doing all we can in my area." Again not really understanding, Laura responded, "Of course I don't think we're doing all we can. There are always new ways to do things with new people."

By this time, Sharon had revised her assumptions about Laura's perception of her. She now assumed that Laura was disappointed in her and was looking for someone new to manage her unit. Laura, too, had revised her assumptions about Sharon. She now saw Sharon as unpredictable and more difficult to work with than she had thought. From that point on, Laura found it difficult to talk with Sharon. She noticed that Sharon avoided her and that Sharon's contributions at staff meetings were minimal. It was only a few weeks before she received Sharon's notice that she was leaving the company.

To think this employee is very interested in her job because she works late is an inference.

who works late every day is extremely interested in the job. Or a manager looking at résumés might infer that an applicant who sings in a church choir is of the highest moral character. While these inferences may be reasonably sound, they are still just inferences, not facts. Both facts and inferences are indispensable to communication, but managers must take care to remember that one person's inference may not be the same as another's, despite their being derived from the same set of facts.

ACTIVE LISTENING All of us have a natural tendency to judge, to evaluate, to approve or disapprove. Sometimes we engage in these judgments prematurely, based on our preconceived assumptions, thereby reducing our ability to communicate effectively. One way to limit these premature judgments is through a counseling technique called **active listening.**[12] As a means of reducing assumptions that interfere with day-to-day communication, active listening depends on allowing others to explain their perspective more fully. Active listening by Laura could have made a difference in the situation discussed in Highlights in HRM 1. Active listening is most appropriate in the following circumstances:

1. When we do not understand how the other person feels and we need to understand the person's perspective.
2. When we believe that what is being said is not as important as what is *not* being said.
3. When the other person is so confused that a clear message cannot be communicated.[13]

In using the technique of active listening, it is important to remember that, while it has the potential to improve communication, it is not always appropriate in organizational situations. For example, active listening is inappropriate in the following instances:

1. When someone asks us for advice and expects that we will respond.
2. When someone asks for direction or for specific information.
3. When the purpose is to debate an issue, presenting both sides of a question.
4. When we hold such strong views of what the other person has said that it would only be honest to express those views rather than attempt to understand the other person's assumptions.[14]

Active listening will be discussed more fully later in the chapter.

DOWNWARD COMMUNICATION SYSTEMS

Like other managers, HR professionals have a responsibility to be effective communicators. In addition, they are often responsible for developing effective communication systems for the organization, many of which are designed to convey information from management to employees. This type of communication is usually referred to as **downward communication.** Downward communication systems are one way organizations maintain links between management and employees.

The success of downward communication systems is affected by the general communication philosophy and policy of the organization. Organizations have recognized that communication policies are essential to both downward and upward communication. Thus organizations such as Federal Express and Allstate Insurance have developed strong policies that encourage management to communicate with employees. These policies emanate from general philosophies of how employees should be treated and the ideal relationship that should exist between employees and management.

One organization, Nashville-based Aladdin Industries, has focused its attention on increasing the total amount of communication managers have with their employees.[15] Aladdin produces thermos bottles and other containers that keep food and beverages hot or cold. After a difficult six-month strike, the HR staff developed a program to provide more information about the organization and its products to employees. This desire grew out of two goals: improved industrial relations and improved productivity. One tactic for improving communication was having managers take production employees to industry trade shows. Workers could then compare Aladdin's products with those of its competitors, thus giving them a better understanding of their employer's market situation. Aladdin's strategy of improving employees' knowledge of products and the market is similar to some Japanese firms' practice of reading production figures to their employees each morning.

Aladdin has also added other programs to improve downward communication. When a section of the organization has to be closed down, employees are given notice—and an explanation—prior to the closing. Aladdin then retrains displaced employees for new jobs. The results of these and other downward communication programs have been increased employee understanding and commitment to organizational goals.

Along with programs such as those initiated by Aladdin, creating a successful downward communication system involves a variety of approaches. They include employee handbooks and policy manuals, company newspapers, bulletin boards, videos for training and safety purposes, benefits reports, and timely informational notices.

Employee Handbooks and Policy Manuals

One of the important means of training and socializing new employees is the employee handbook. It provides information about organizational benefits; it describes the rights and responsibilities of employees; and it often explains the organization's disciplinary system.

Managers today have also become concerned with developing a limited set of policies that are critical to the functioning of the organization and consistent with the philosophy and culture of senior management. These policies are frequently compiled in a formal document called a policy manual. Policy manuals help to ensure that policies are enforced. Written but unenforced policies have been the basis of many court actions by employees against present or former employers, and employers have thus been given an incentive to make their actions correspond to their policies. Figure 15–2 lists several important guidelines for effectively communicating organizational policies.

Organizations must be constantly attentive to the need to update policy manuals as a result of changes in benefits, social concerns, and employee rights, as well as the adoption of such programs as employee involvement groups and flextime. To make policy manuals a useful addition to their downward communication systems,

FIGURE 15–2 GUIDELINES FOR COMMUNICATING ORGANIZATIONAL POLICIES

1. Policies should cover only areas where employees and managers need guidance.
2. Policies must be communicated by means other than just the policy manual (e.g., management training, orientation programs).
3. Policies should help to communicate the organizational culture and philosophy; they should thus be evaluated against this culture and philosophy.
4. Policies should be written in the detail required to convey the message—no more, no less.
5. The policy manual should include statements to the effect that the manual does not constitute a contract between the organization and the employee.
6. Training should accompany communication of any change in policy.
7. Policies should be reviewed periodically and irrelevant ones discarded.

SOURCE: Adapted from Thomas M. Hestwood, "Make Policy Manuals Useful and Relevant," *Personnel Journal* 67, no. 4 (April 1988): 44. Reprinted with the permission of *Personnel Journal,* Costa Mesa, California; all rights reserved.

organizations must communicate policy changes through several channels, including HR-developed training programs. The recent U.S. District Court ruling in *Kalwecz* v. *AM International, Inc.*, made it clear that employees must receive proper notice of changes in policy manuals and the employee handbook. Kalwecz, an employee of AM International, was awarded $130,000 as a result of the company's failure to notify him properly of a disclaimer in the employee handbook. The disclaimer concerned a previous policy of finding another position in the company for employees of ten years or longer tenure whose jobs were being eliminated.[16]

Organizational Newspapers

Organizational newspapers serve a variety of purposes for management. First, they provide a convenient means for announcing changes in organizational policy and procedure. Second, they may be used to publish notices of job openings for the organization's in-house job posting program. Third, they are a way to convey the organization's mission and long-term goals, and fourth, they offer management a means of responding to questions. Some organizations have also found that they can use their newspapers to encourage upward communication by running a routine column that encourages employees to ask questions. In providing answers to these questions, organizations satisfy employees' need to know and contribute to the general knowledge that employees have about the organization.

Bulletin Boards

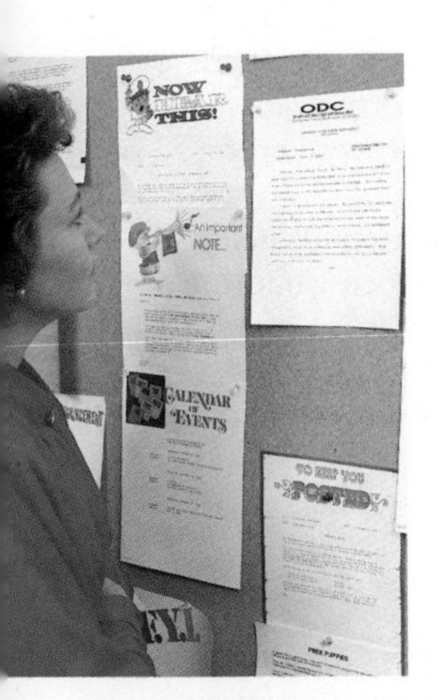

Bulletin boards provide the basis for communicating with a wide audience.

Bulletin boards are used for a variety of types of messages that must be communicated to a broad audience. Job openings are posted there, as well as safety information, and announcements of a broad range of organization- or department-wide events including meetings, picnics, and baseball games.

Using bulletin boards effectively means placing them where employees are likely to pause in the course of their day—for example, near water fountains, time clocks, or reception areas. Getting employees to read posted messages requires that the bulletin boards be routinely monitored, with notices arranged neatly for easy reading and dated postings removed. Many organizations that are geographically dispersed use fax machines to provide their employees with timely notices for their bulletin boards.

One of the newest approaches to handling notices is the electronic bulletin board. Ciba-Geigy uses a computerized job posting system instead of tacking up its monthly list of job openings on bulletin boards. This system allows the company to list jobs immediately when they open up and to delete them as soon as they are filled. Organizations that use electronic mail heavily have three additional electronic options for posting announcements. First, notices can be flashed on videotext screens as users sign onto the electronic mail system, forcing the employee to at least "pass by" the notices. Second, special electronic bulletin systems can be designed to enable users to access a special screen for current notices. A third option is the ability of some systems to flash notices to each of the videotext screens currently being used in conjunction with the electronic mail system.

Videos

Nearly everyone is accustomed to receiving a considerable amount of information from television. The use of videos in the workplace is thus a natural extension of a very common means of communicating. The potential for using video messages in organizations is unlimited, but so far the most frequent uses have been for orientation programs, specialized training programs, safety procedures, and special messages from senior executives. Organizations may also use video messages to describe benefits such as medical plans or retirement options or to provide realistic job previews, mentioned earlier in Chapter 5 and illustrated here in Highlights in HRM 2. The advantages of video include employees' familiarity with the medium, the medium's ability to demonstrate something visually, and the savings associated with videos when training must be repeated many times or provided in distant locations.

One variation on videos that is becoming increasingly useful to organizations is the interactive video.[17] Interactive videos combine the use of computers, video images, and touch-sensitive screens. They allow employees to ask questions and receive information geared specifically to the topic of immediate interest. For example, employees contemplating retirement can examine the long-term results of various retirement plans offered by the organization. The interactive format allows retirement information to be adapted to the employee in terms of the individual's age, time with the company, and projected income. Other possible topics for interactive videos include medical benefits, managerial training, organizational history, current news from senior management, or information about special events such as parties or stress-management classes.

UNNUM, a Maine-based life insurance company, has gone one step further in its use of interactive video technology. The company created a video game for workers to learn about employee benefits. The game challenges employees to test their knowledge of their benefits. As a series of questions are asked, the users watch as Flex, a cartoon character, attempts to lift a pair of dumbbells; Flex succeeds if the worker responds correctly to the question. Employees reported that the game was fun, and UNNUM's HR staff concluded that employees learned a great deal about the benefits program.[18]

Benefits Reports

Employee benefits now represent about 37 percent of their earnings. Organizations offer the benefits they believe make them competitive with other organizations in recruiting employees. They also offer benefits that will increase the organizational commitment of employees and reduce their turnover. However, achieving these goals depends on getting employees to recognize the nature and extent of their

HIGHLIGHTS IN HRM

2 USING VIDEO RECORDED MESSAGES FOR THE REALISTIC JOB PREVIEW

The use of video recorded messages of realistic job previews (RJPs) is receiving more and more attention from HR professionals. RJPs are designed to give recruits organizational information that is likely to be dissatisfying when discovered and therefore may result in turnover. The Canadian Armed Forces use short, five-minute videos for each of their military specialties (rifleman, tank crew member, etc.). Each video highlights critical issues that may lead to dissatisfaction on the job.

Businesses have found that RJPs can save them from 6 to 12 percent of their replacement costs, depending on their turnover rates. To realize these savings, organizations must develop effective RJPs. These RJPs may include written documents, the selection interview, and, of course, the video version, discussed in this chapter. For the video to be effective, it must have the following characteristics:

1. The people used in the video should be real employees, not actors.
2. The employees in the video should go beyond merely describing aspects of the organization; they must express their opinions. For example, in discussing the realities of working in a public accounting firm, the employees in the video should mention the unpleasant aspects of having to rearrange family schedules to meet a client's unexpected request.
3. An effective RJP video should provide negative information, but the degree of negativity should be moderate rather than high. Topics of moderate negativity might include hours of work required, lack of opportunity for praise, or having to stand long hours while working. Topics of high negativity, such as the possibility of serious injury or exposure to potential health hazards, should not be given too much attention.

SOURCE: Adapted from John P. Wanous, "Installing a Realistic Job Preview: Ten Tough Choices," *Personnel Psychology* 42, no. 1 (Spring 1989): 117–134. Reprinted with permission.

benefits, and this is one of the greatest communication challenges faced by HR professionals. One survey found that about one-half of the employees questioned thought benefits represented less than 10 percent of their earnings.[19] Employees must know and understand the benefits offered if organizations are to receive any return for these expensive labor costs.

The need for effective communication of benefits has led to the use of extended benefits reports, such as those described in Chapter 12. These reports derive their impact from the personalization of information, the layout and organization of the material presented, and their timeliness. Benefits reports can be prepared using many human resources information systems, which allow the report to be individualized to specify the exact amount of medical coverage and life insurance provided for each employee. Benefits reports can be generated at almost any time, depending on the needs of the employee and the goals of the organization. Furthermore, these reports may be organized so that the most expensive benefits or the benefits of greatest interest to employees can be placed at the upper left of the report, where they are most likely to be seen.

Effective communication of benefits involves more than videos and benefits reports, however. It requires the development of an overall plan for such communication. An example of this type of plan is presented in Highlights in HRM 3.

Meetings

None of us like to attend useless meetings, particularly those where we have to sit quietly while the speaker drones on about an uninteresting topic. Yet there are times when the most expedient way to communicate information is at one time to a group of employees. Such meetings are a worthwhile part of the organization's downward communication program. In fact, failure to hold informational meetings will probably lead employees to feel alienated from the organization.

Typically in these meetings the division head, the departmental manager, or other senior managers give an overview of some major change in the organization's long-term goals. For example, USAA, a major life insurance firm for U.S. military officers and their dependents, has found that large employee meetings have been especially helpful in obtaining employees' commitment to its goals. Another, somewhat different use of large meetings is to announce reductions in the work force. HR managers have found that negative information, such as layoff announcements, should be communicated promptly and openly. Reporting bad news quickly will help the organization get past difficult times in a shorter period by letting employees vent their anger and frustration. Furthermore, it will reduce the amount of time employees spend needlessly discussing partially accurate information, and because it is honest communication, it will gain the respect of employees.[20]

One modern variation on the company meeting has been introduced by James McElwain, vice-president for HR services at NCR Corporation. McElwain and his staff have developed S-Net, a satellite network with 140 downlinks to 90 percent of NCR's employees. S-Net's interactive video format permits NCR's employees to meet by teleconference. NCR intends to spread its S-Net to its international locations in Europe as the member countries of the European Economic Community (EEC) develop a uniform set of regulations in conjunction with their 1992 target for reducing international trade barriers. Not surprisingly, S-Net is used for a variety of purposes beyond company meetings. In fact, NCR publishes a weekly program guide with about 30 hours of weekly programming.

Through periodic conferences to which individuals in certain positions are invited, department managers, including HR managers, can communicate information and ideas and obtain feedback from the participants. In the larger organizations with operations widely separated, conferences that utilize telephone circuits, known as teleconferences, may be held. Teleconferences may be restricted to voice trans-

HIGHLIGHTS IN HRM

3 EFFECTIVE COMMUNICATION OF BENEFITS INFORMATION

Aetna Life and Casualty Company faced three problems in implementing its new benefits program: (1) getting large numbers of employees to enroll in the programs offered, thereby cutting enrollment costs; (2) overcoming resistance to change in benefits programs; and (3) communicating program information to 38,000 employees in 400 locations.

To deal with these problems, Aetna's HR department developed a four-step benefits communication program called "Portfolio." First, brochures describing benefits were mailed to the homes of employees. These brochures included profiles of various categories of employees, such as a young couple with small children. Printed on the back of the profile were examples of the benefits that were particularly useful to that category of employee. Second, posters continuing this theme were used to draw attention to changes in benefits. Third, a video was produced to describe the program; and fourth, benefits meetings were held. Because of the earlier communication attempts, attendance at the benefits meetings was 85 percent. Furthermore, nearly 90 percent of employees enrolled on the basis of these initial meetings.

SOURCE: From Tim Chauran, "Benefits Communication," *Personnel Journal* 68, no. 1 (January 1989): 70–77. Reprinted with the permission of *Personnel Journal,* Costa Mesa, California;

Teleconferences allow groups to communicate over a long distance inexpensively.

mission or may include videoconferencing, as illustrated in the photo. Here we see a group in one city communicating face to face with a group in another city. Teleconferencing facilitates the interaction of participants and avoids the inconvenience and expense associated with travel.

If informational meetings are to succeed, the manager who makes the presentation must do so skillfully. Effective presentations require audience analysis, careful preparation, and a positive, employee-oriented attitude. Figure 15–3 presents several useful suggestions for developing an effective presentation.[21]

In making an effective presentation, the presenter should also consider the value that can be derived from visuals appropriate to the presentation. Studies have clearly shown that visuals increase the effectiveness of presentations. One study demonstrated that employee attention can be increased by about 10 percent with visuals and the persuasive impact can be increased by about 43 percent. When using visuals, however, these guidelines should be followed:

1. Use only one idea per visual.
2. Use only one illustration per visual.
3. Present no more than six or seven lines per visual.

FIGURE 15–3 MAKING EFFECTIVE PRESENTATIONS

1. Understand your motives for making the presentation, and avoid using the presentation as a statement of your authority.
2. Prepare the presentation by writing down the most important ideas to be communicated.
3. Develop visuals that will allow the audience to follow the presentation easily.
4. If the presentation is intended to be persuasive rather than informational, tell the audience that you are giving them your point of view.
5. Recognize the audience's attitudes and biases.
6. Set realistic time limits that consider the disposition of the audience (e.g., frustrated) and the time of day (e.g., late afternoon).
7. Dress and act as if the presentation begins the moment you walk into the room.
8. Avoid appearing casual, threatening, or defensive.
9. After you have been introduced, reintroduce yourself and include helpful information about yourself and an overview of the presentation.
10. Address individuals in the audience by talking directly to them.
11. Listen carefully to the comments and questions of the audience and respond to both the emotion and the content of an employee's remark.
12. Remain about ten minutes after the presentation so that individuals may talk to you informally.

SOURCE: Adapted from Michael E. Cavanaugh, "Communication: Make Effective Speeches," *Personnel Journal* 67, no. 3 (March 1988): 51–55. Reprinted with the permission of *Personnel Journal,* Costa Mesa, California; all rights reserved.

4. Use no more than seven words per line.
5. Hold lettering sizes to three or fewer per visual.
6. Include no more than four colors.[22]

UPWARD COMMUNICATION SYSTEMS

Through **upward communication,** organizations obtain useful ideas, resolve problems, and motivate and encourage organizational commitment. Fortunately, both managers and employees agree that the upward flow of information is important for organizational success. Unfortunately, they often disagree on how much opportunity there is for this type of communication.

One survey of employees found that 40 percent believed they had no opportunity for upward communication.[23] However, these same employees identified three ways that managers can promote upward communication. First, managers should venture out and meet employees to give employees a chance to communicate face to face. Second, management can give employees the opportunity to participate in decisions affecting their own jobs. Third, managers can use feedback systems so that employees know their messages are being heard. These systems can include a forum for questions *and answers* in the organizational newspaper and special meetings in which the employees ask questions and managers respond. Furthermore, employees must feel free from reprisal for communicating negative information; some upward communication systems must guarantee anonymity to senders of this sort of message.

Complaint Procedures

No matter how hard managers try to manage effectively, problems will come up that lead to employee complaints about supervisors, the job, or the organization. As a result, a growing number of organizations have gone beyond the traditional upward communication systems and have introduced whistle-blowing policies and investigative procedures to allow employees to report wrongdoing before harm comes to the organization.[24] Problems are magnified when supervisors are not receptive to the problems their employees face, and sometimes the supervisors themselves can be the source of the problem. When this happens, employees need to be able to communicate their complaints or observations of wrongdoing to management anonymously. In response to these needs, organizations have developed a variety of complaint systems that are usually managed by the HR department. Some use voice-mail technology, enabling employees to dial into a computerized telephone system and describe problems or make complaints. Others use special counselors or ombudsmen within the HR department (see Chapter 16). Other complaint systems, such as the "Speak Up!" program at IBM, use specially designed forms on which employees can write a complaint and submit it to management. At IBM, only the administrator of the program knows the identity of the writer. By serving as a focal point, the administrator can direct an employee's question or concern to an appropriate executive and obtain a written, confidential response. " 'Speak Up!' lets us respond directly yet anonymously to employees' concerns," explains Norm Koestline, director of information at IBM's U.S. headquarters. "It's a highly effective two-way communication channel that also gives management a 'finger on the pulse' of employees' attitudes and opinions on a broad range of issues."

Suggestion Programs

The suggestion program is a type of upward communication that is widely used to stimulate participation by rewarding employees for their suggestions. The suggestions may cover such areas as work methods and procedures, equipment design, safety devices, and other matters related to the effectiveness of the organization. For the program to succeed, it must have the support of managers and supervisors. Supervisors, however, sometimes feel that such programs infringe on their time, and they fear adverse effects if employees make suggestions they themselves should have proposed.

The present-day suggestion program is quite different from the early suggestion boxes that date back to the mid-1800s when the Yale and Towne Manufacturing Company nailed up an idea box. For decades, suggestion boxes were used primarily to let employees blow off steam. Today suggestion programs encourage employees to submit ideas that will contribute to increased productivity, quality, safety, and other important outcomes.

Most firms pay employees a percentage of the net savings, up to a maximum amount, that result from their suggestions. In 1989, the more than 1,000 member organizations of the National Association of Suggestion Systems (NASS) adopted over 322,000 suggestions resulting in a total savings of approximately $2 billion.[25] Along with cost-cutting advantages are intangible benefits such as improved communication between employees and managers; increased team spirit; and prompting employees to think about productivity, product quality, and workplace safety.

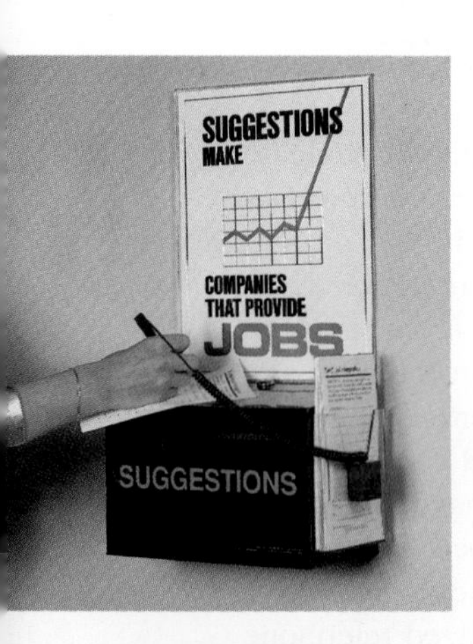

Suggestion programs encourage employees to share their ideas and concerns with management.

Attitude Surveys

The employee attitude survey is another method designed to help employees communicate with management. The survey is best accomplished through the use of questionnaires that are completed anonymously. From responses to the questionnaires, management can learn how employees view their jobs, their supervisors, their wages and benefits, their working conditions, and other aspects of their employment. Among the newest versions of the attitude survey is IBM's computerized employee opinion survey. It is faster, more flexible, easier to analyze than traditional surveys, and preferred by employees.[26]

Before conducting a survey, an organization should be able to answer yes to three specific questions:

1. Is the organization willing to invest the time and money to conduct the survey properly?
2. Is management willing to report the major findings of the survey to employees?
3. Is management willing to take action on the basis of the survey's results?

The support of top management for the survey needs to be conveyed through a cover letter to all employees, signed by the CEO or president. Steps should be taken to assure employees that the anonymity of their responses will be preserved and that the survey results will be acted on.[27] The organization must enlist the participation of as many employees as possible to ensure an accurate assessment of their attitudes. Also, management must report the survey results to employees even when those results are negative or show the organization in an unfavorable light. Finally, management must work to develop an action plan for dealing with the responses it receives from the survey.[28] At ARCO Transportation Co., one of the action plans that came from an attitude survey was the creation of an anonymous employee feedback system in which a third party, a "processor," solicits feedback from the manager's subordinates and shares the results with the manager to preserve the anonymity of the subordinates.[29] More information about attitude surveys may be found in Chapter 20.

Committees

Although committees may be used to make decisions, provide suggestions, and represent other employees, their primary purpose is to facilitate upward communi-

cation. This role becomes clear from the variety of assignments that organizations give to their committees—evaluating employee suggestions, resolving grievances, evaluating jobs and employee performance, selecting candidates for promotion, and administering recreation and benefits programs. Some organizations also use committees to consider compensation issues as well as employment policies and work practices. In addition to benefiting organizations by facilitating upward communication, there is even some evidence that organizations with advisory committees are more likely to remain nonunion.[30]

For several decades, Pitney Bowes has had a personnel council—a monthly forum where representatives of management and employees sit down to discuss mutual problems and opportunities. This is done on a sectional, departmental, and divisional level with the main council serving as the top tribunal.[31] This use of committees enhances downward communication as well as upward communication.

For a committee to make the maximum possible contribution, its goal should be stated as clearly as possible. The employees who should sit on the committee can then be identified. Persons who will be affected by the committee's decision should be included, but it may be unwise to include those who are likely to stall the efforts of the committee unless their perspective is essential to the decision. The size of the committee is another important consideration. If there are more than 11 members, not all of them are likely to participate in discussions, and the committee will change from an interacting group to an audience for a few of the most vocal members. The leader of the committee should establish an agenda, and members should come prepared to address the issues slated for discussion. At times the leader will need to summarize and clarify issues for the committee, and often he or she will need to encourage reluctant contributors and rein in those who monopolize the discussion. At the close of each meeting, it is essential for the leader to review the committee's goal in light of its discussion in that session.[32]

Electronic Mail

Electronic mail is becoming an increasingly useful tool for upward communication. Organizations with electronic mail systems usually make "address lists" of all users available to any employee with access to the system. Communicating with the CEO or the vice-president for human resources is thus as easy as communicating with a colleague. Furthermore, messages from all employees, whether managers or not, appear in similar form. Rapid access and the greater consistency of messages have encouraged the use of electronic mail as a means of upward communication.

Organizations that successfully use electronic mail have identified certain qualities that contribute to its growing use. One is access to the system by nearly all employees. Another is wide acceptance and usage of electronic mail by managers. A third quality is the responsiveness of managers to employees' messages. When senior managers respond quickly to messages, employees are encouraged to send additional messages.

THE INFORMAL COMMUNICATION SYSTEM

In addition to the formal systems of upward and downward communication in organizations, there is also an informal system. Sometimes called the **grapevine,** this system can convey messages upward, downward, laterally, and externally. It can foster employee motivation, encourage commitment, and create job and organizational satisfaction. Unfortunately, it can also distort information, create resentment, and work against management plans and objectives. Communication experts note that the grapevine is a generally accurate means of communication that employees rely on more heavily when they feel threatened or insecure.[33] Recently, electronic transmission of messages by facsimile (fax) and electronic mail have added to the speed with which the grapevine functions.[34]

Patterns of Informal Communication

Although the grapevine's structure may be influenced by formal organizational relationships, it is more likely to be influenced by a variety of other factors, such as the setup of the workplace. The placement of building entrances, elevators, even restrooms affects employees' ability to exchange information. Lunches and coffee breaks provide time for talking with co-workers or friends. Friendships at work lead to after-hours get-togethers at the health club or local hangout. These opportunities and relationships serve to facilitate communication across work groups and lines of management.[35]

Using the Informal Communication System

The informal communication system provides a great deal of useful information to employees. Because employees value it and because it grows out of such natural relationships as friendships between co-workers, this network cannot be controlled or eliminated by management, nor should it be. Attempts by management to control the informal communication of employees will only create resentment and will probably not succeed anyway.

Since they cannot control the grapevine, managers must learn to accept it and use it effectively. For example, HR managers know that the grapevine can transmit accurate information much faster than the formal communication system. Therefore, those willing to listen to the grapevine will be able to identify employee concerns or organizational problems more quickly. The grapevine can also provide meaningful supplemental information to standard employee feedback from attitude surveys.

Besides using the grapevine as a source of information, HR managers can also use it to communicate information to employees, though this requires some knowledge of how the grapevine works. In particular, it is helpful for managers to know which employees have the widest range of contacts in the organization.

Despite the grapevine's numerous advantages, some managers object strongly to it. Their objections may arise in part because of the system's tendency to distort information or convey it before it is complete. However, the realities of the grapevine will not change, and management must accept this. What can change is how the organization deals with this system of communication. Also, if management takes steps to ensure open, candid communication, the formal system will carry most of the same messages as the informal system. With an open system of communication, therefore, there will be less need for managers and employees to rely on the grapevine.

IMPROVING ORGANIZATIONAL COMMUNICATION

Experience has shown that putting upward and downward communication systems into place and managing the grapevine effectively will not solve all of an organization's communication problems, nor will it guarantee effective communication. HR managers must champion communication as their responsibility and, at the same time, as the responsibility of all organizational managers. In describing the challenges for management at Levi Strauss, Donna Goya, senior vice-president for personnel, focused almost exclusively on the single issue of communication:

> [The challenges ahead for managers are] to communicate with their employees, to give regular feedback, not just once-a-year appraisals, so there are no surprises. To give recognition, not just when merit increase time rolls around but to continually say thank you, and have some fun and make people feel appreciated. To allow diverse opinions and not to be so control-oriented as to deny you don't have all the answers.[36]

A study of the communication behavior of leaders confirms the accuracy of these remarks. Managers who are effective leaders provide task information so employees are aware of job requirements and performance information so employees know how well they are doing. In addition to these types of communication, the study also identified two other specific types that are important for effective leadership. First, day-to-day, non-task-related communication such as personal greetings and inquiries about the employee's well-being helps to establish a basis for a good working relationship between manager and employee. Second, communication about the career development of the employee is also critical.[37]

Communication Competency

HR managers can improve their ability to provide task-related, performance-related, career-related, and personal communication by focusing on specific communication skills or competencies that are known to affect managerial performance. **Communication competency** refers to a manager's oral communication skills (speaking and listening), written communication skills (reading and writing), and ability to choose the appropriate medium for communication. Managers who are

Toastmasters International provides members with a forum for practicing their communication skills.

more competent communicators are more successful in their careers and perform better in their jobs.[38]

SPEAKING AND LISTENING SKILLS Managers must be able to deliver an oral message competently, and they must have good listening skills. There are a variety of options for improving managers' skill at speaking. HR managers can hire specialists to teach public speaking skills. Local community colleges and universities offer courses in communication, and most cities have Toastmasters' clubs for assistance in developing oral presentation skills. For managers who are particularly apprehensive about speaking, special programs are available that focus on reducing public speaking anxiety.[39]

Despite a willingness to improve their speaking skills, too frequently managers have the feeling that there is little that can be done to improve listening skills. In fact, trainers also teach listening skills. Moreover, there are a variety of things managers can do on their own to improve their listening skills.

First, managers can force themselves to talk less and listen more during conversations with employees. By doing so, they can focus on what they can learn from a discussion, and talking less will encourage them to search for new information. Next, managers can learn to use the three following types of questions that facilitate listening:

1. "Will you tell me about the remaining issue?" (helps to move the speaker on to the next point)
2. "Are you saying that this process will never allow us to cut scrap by 50 percent?" (invites the speaker to sum up or draw a conclusion)
3. "Could you summarize the critical problems for me?" (reminds the speaker to summarize at the close of the discussion)

Finally, managers should try to make sense of what the speaker is saying by fitting it into a context that is meaningful for them.[40]

READING AND WRITING SKILLS The performance of managers is directly related to their competency in handling written communication, including message-writing ability and reading comprehension. HR departments can help to improve the reading and writing skills of managers by suggesting communications courses offered at local colleges, as well as through training programs developed by the department itself. Often the first step in improving written communication competency is an evaluation of managers that is sponsored by the HR department. The link between this competency and managerial performance provides a sound argument for such evaluation.

MEDIA SENSITIVITY Another important communication skill is **media sensitivity,** the ability to select an appropriate medium for sending a message. It will come as no surprise that higher-performing managers have greater media-sensitivity.[41] Among the choices of media are the face-to-face meeting, the telephone, the electronic mail system, and the written memorandum. Some of these media are "richer" than others, in that they can convey more information. Face-to-face communication is the richest medium since it permits immediate feedback, it includes both verbal and nonverbal messages, and it is the most personal. The written letter or memorandum is much less rich; feedback is slow, the medium is strictly visual, and it is formal and impersonal. Other media such as the telephone or electronic mail have a richness somewhere between these two extremes.

It is important for managers to understand the relative richness of a medium, since messages vary in their difficulty of transmission or translation. For example, informing employees about the loss of a major contract is a difficult task that may result in much misunderstanding if the right medium is not used. The message has a high potential for distortion (i.e., considerable translation difficulty) and therefore requires a very rich medium, such as a face-to-face meeting. However, a message reminding a subordinate of a meeting with a client is much simpler and is not as likely to be distorted. This type of message contains little transmission or translation difficulty, and a medium such as a written note or electronic mail will serve very well for its transmission.[42]

Communicating with Diverse Groups

As we discussed in early chapters of this book, the work force in the United States, Canada, and elsewhere is undergoing tremendous changes as a result of immigration, increased numbers of working women, and greater opportunities for minorities. While just over 50 percent of the U.S. work force is currently made up of minorities and women, demographers predict that this will rise to 80 percent by the year 2000. Further adding to the demands of communicating with diverse and multicultural workers are the changes that are occurring internationally. As we will discuss in Chapter 19, the internationalization of business makes U.S. managers more likely to find themselves interacting with managers from Europe, Asia, Africa, and Latin America. At the same time, American businesses wishing to stay competitive are likely to increase their activities in international markets. The internationalization of business and changes in the demography of the labor pool will increase the **cross-cultural communication** demands on HR managers. By necessity they will have to communicate effectively with very diverse cultural groups.

COMMUNICATION BETWEEN MEN AND WOMEN Behavioral scientists have identified some differences in the communication styles of men and women. The fact that the workplace has been traditionally dominated by men has meant that the language found there is more reflective of the way men communicate. It does not mean, however, that there is some inherent reason that this should be the preferred form of business communication.

Some studies have shown that women tend to use tag questions such as "This is the way we do it, isn't it?" more often than men. While this is an accepted form of speech, such questions may make women *seem* less decisive than men. Also, some research has documented that men's speech is less grammatical than women's, which may lead to the perception that women are more formal than men. While there is some disagreement among social scientists about these and other research findings, researchers do conclude that there are real differences between the communication styles of men and women.[43]

LANGUAGE DIFFERENCES Special communication problems also originate from cultural and language differences. For example, European managers working in the United States, Canada, and Latin America usually make a relatively easy transition to the languages found there. Asian and Middle Eastern managers, however, often face a more considerable language barrier in the Americas, because of the fundamentally greater differences in the languages.[44] All managers in cross-cultural positions therefore need to be sensitive to the language difficulties they and their foreign counterparts are likely to encounter.

Although less troublesome than language differences, unfamiliar accents can sometimes create communication difficulties. A manager whose subordinate is not a native English speaker, for example, must be careful to distinguish the person's ability to do the job from his or her ability to use English fluently. Though communicating with such employees may be difficult, managers should not let this influence their judgment of an employee's other capabilities.

NONVERBAL CULTURAL DIFFERENCES Cross-cultural communication difficulties go beyond language. They also include differences in nonverbal communication. For example, in appraisal interviews and in work-group meetings, foreign-born employees may not openly communicate their perceptions and ideas. These employees may be reluctant to express their thoughts for fear of showing their limited language skills. Or their culture may have taught them to respect authority even when they believe that the authority is wrong. Addressing these and other communication problems that come from managing a multicultural and diverse work force requires the attention of the HR department. Managerial training in communication and cultural differences is needed in all types of organizations.

Figure 15–4 provides some suggestions for training programs for managers who must deal with diverse groups of employees.

COUNSELING

In a discussion of organizational communication that focuses on HRM, the role of counseling in the achievement of individual and organizational objectives deserves special attention. Managers and supervisors, HR department personnel, those responsible for various employee assistance programs, and other staff members find that their job responsibilities require them to serve in a counseling role. Depending on their position, the amount of time they must spend in this activity will vary.

FIGURE 15–4 TRAINING MANAGERS TO DEAL WITH EMPLOYEES WHO ARE DIFFERENT

1. Managers must recognize that communicating effectively with different types of employees is valuable because of the wider range of skills and perspectives that these workers bring to the workplace.
2. Managers may need to be reminded that their own cultural and ethnic backgrounds may lead them to certain preferences in food, housing, entertainment, etc.
3. Managers can play imagination games that ask them to imagine what it would be like to speak with an accent that is difficult for their fellow workers to understand, etc.
4. Managers may identify the particular characteristics of a group that makes it different, including language and social differences.
5. Managers can rely on more experienced work-group members who are similar to the new, "different" employee.
6. Managers can talk to employees with cultural differences about their own concerns about being fair and communicating effectively with them.

SOURCE: Adapted from Bob Abramms-Mezoff and Diane Johns, "Managing a Culturally Diverse Work Force," *Supervisory Management* (February 1989): 34–38; and Steve Hanamura, "Working with People Who Are Different," *Training & Development Journal* 42, no. 6 (June 1989): 110–114. Reprinted, by permission of publisher, from *Supervisory Management,* February 1989. © 1989 American Management Association, New York. All rights reserved. Also reprinted with the permission of *Training & Development Journal.*

In many organizations, especially the large ones, there are positions that include "counselor" in the title. There are other jobs where counseling is specified as a duty or where it is assumed that the person will at times serve in a counseling role. Thus, counseling should be approached as a communication skill that one must acquire to carry out the responsibilities of a line or staff position.

Since counseling is important in meeting many of the objectives of an HRM program, it will be discussed here as well as in other chapters. In this chapter the focus will be on the counseling process as it is applied in a wide variety of situations. General principles and procedures will be discussed here. Specific applications of these principles are examined in other chapters, especially in career counseling (Chapter 8), in performance appraisal (Chapter 9), in working with problem employees (Chapter 16), in assisting with personal problems, alcoholism, and drug abuse (Chapter 13), and in retirement counseling (Chapter 12).

The Counseling Process

Unlike an interview, which is often restricted to obtaining and giving information, **counseling** is a process involving a dynamic relationship between two parties in which a person is free to discuss needs, feelings, and problems of concern for the purpose of obtaining help. As shown in Figure 15–5, it involves many variables on

Reprinted by permission of United Feature Syndicate, Inc.

the side of the helper as well as the helpee. The relationship is the chief means of meshing the helpee's problems with the counsel of the helper.[45] The relationship is constantly changing at verbal and nonverbal levels. It typically involves an expression of emotions and feelings that goes beyond that of the ordinary interview.

PURPOSE OF COUNSELING The purpose of counseling is to allow the person seeking help to achieve four kinds of outcomes. A typical counseling session is likely to involve a combination of these outcomes.

1. *Changes in feeling states,* especially negative feeling states, including frustration, depression, anger, and jealousy. This can be accomplished by helping a person clarify underlying values and assumptions.
2. *Increased understanding.* The type of understanding that is lacking is usually understanding about oneself, others, and circumstances. It can be caused by incomplete or inaccurate information and misperception.
3. *Decisions.* Helping people to clarify their concerns and assisting them in learning decision-making skills are important uses of counseling.
4. *Implementing decisions.* Helping to plan action necessary to carry through with what one has decided is another critical function of counseling.[46]

NATURE OF THE RELATIONSHIP Counseling does not take place in a vacuum. The basic relationship between the two parties is the context in which counseling occurs. Whether an employee is counseled by a supervisor, a career counselor, a psychologist in the HR department, or a professional outside the organization, the context will affect the counseling relationship. In organizations, authority affects the nature of the relationship between the two parties. An employee, for example, is not free to ignore a supervisor's help in matters related to the

FIGURE 15–5 DEVELOPING THE COUNSELING RELATIONSHIP

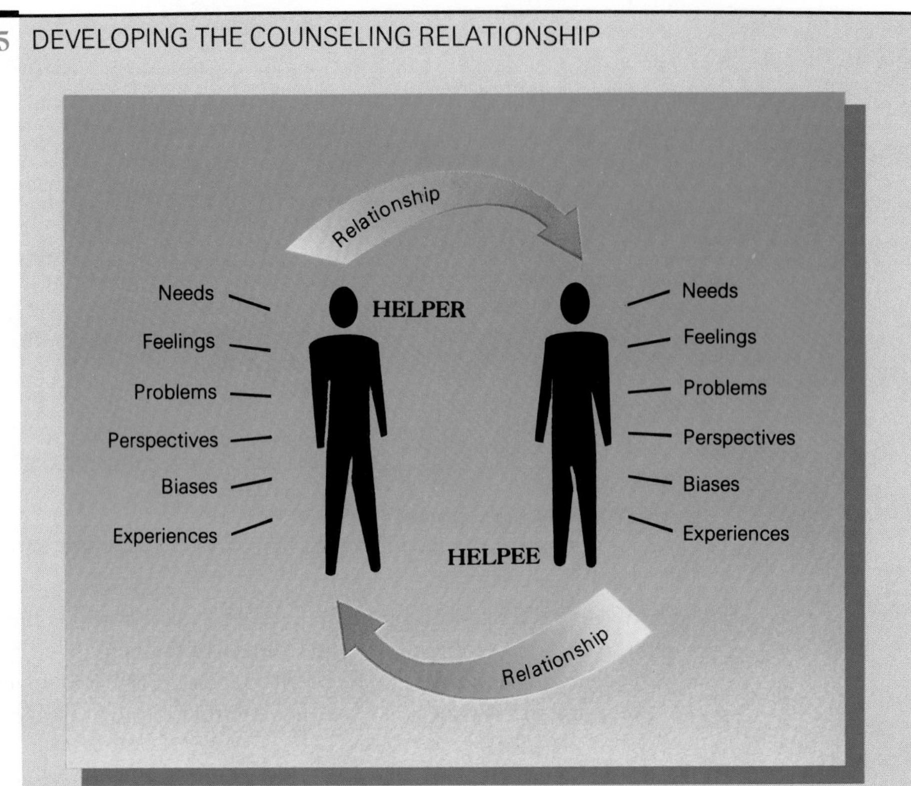

job. Another factor in the counseling relationship is confidentiality. Generally, what takes place in a counseling relationship is expected *not* to go beyond the two parties involved. There are times, however, when it is necessary to report certain types of information that may result in serious harm to others if not reported. Another factor that can affect the relationship is the counselor's degree of commitment to be of assistance.

THE COUNSELOR'S ATTITUDE The counselor's attitude toward the counselee is a major factor in determining the outcomes of counseling. It is essential that the counselor convey *acceptance* of the counselee as a person and of what the counselee has to say. Acceptance does not imply agreement, but rather accepting the counselee's right to have opinions and feelings. Certainly, a desire to help and to provide whatever information, assistance, or reassurance is necessary is basic and should be conveyed both verbally and nonverbally to the counselee.

COUNSELING TECHNIQUES Like other communication skills, counseling techniques can be learned. At first these techniques often seem strange, but with experience they become a comfortable and customary way of interacting with others in a counseling situation.

The important technique of *active listening* involves trying to understand what the other person is thinking and why. Active listening was discussed earlier as a communication technique that is very useful in reducing the problem of false assumptions. When counseling, or when using this technique to make communication more effective, counselors listen so they can assist the counselee in self-understanding. In the process of active listening, they should follow these guidelines:

1. Establish *contact* by looking at the counselee when he or she talks.
2. Maintain a *natural relaxed posture* which indicates interest.
3. Use *natural gestures* that communicate the intended messages.
4. Use *verbal statements* that relate to the counselee's statements without interruptions, questions, or new topics.[47]

The technique of reflecting feelings involves expressing in somewhat different words the counselee's feelings, either stated or strongly implied. The purpose of this technique is to focus on feelings rather than content, to bring vaguely expressed feelings into clearer focus, and to assist the person in talking about his or her feelings.

Examples of reflected feelings are: "You resent the way the boss treats you," and "You feel that you deserve more recognition from the company." The technique of reflecting feelings is especially useful in the early stages of counseling to bring out the counselee's feelings. It is the standard procedure in *nondirective counseling,* a type of counseling to be discussed later.

Very often a counselee is confused and needs assistance in determining what the problem really is. Rather than trying to make a diagnosis or questioning the counselee like a trial lawyer, the professional counselor uses techniques to assist the counselee in identifying the problem. One approach is *restatement.* By restating in their own words what the counselee has said, counselors provide feedback that helps to clarify the problem. *Paraphrasing,* in which counselors restate in their own words what the counselee has said, is another clarification technique that is used.

Another way to assist the counselee is to ask questions that will help that person understand his or her problem. Generally, the questions should be open-ended questions, i.e., those that cannot be answered with a yes or no (for example, "Tell me more about your experiences with Mr. Jones"). They should be questions that lead to clarification for the counselee rather than information for the counselor. Open-ended questions leave the counselee free to take the interview in the direction that will do the most for him or her.

Counseling Approaches

In attempting to help an employee who has a problem, a variety of counseling approaches are used. All of these approaches, however, depend on active listening. Sometimes the mere furnishing of information or advice may be the solution to what at first appeared to be a knotty problem. More frequently, however, the problem cannot be solved easily because of frustrations or conflicts that are accompanied by strong feelings such as fear, confusion, or hostility. A counselor, therefore, needs to learn to use whatever approach appears to be suitable at the time. Because counseling is a dynamic process, the effective counselor is one who is flexible in the use of approaches.

DIRECTIVE COUNSELING In **directive counseling,** the counselor attempts to control, directly or indirectly, the topics the counselee is talking about, describes the choices that face the counselee, and/or advises the counselee what to do. While directive counseling has its place in professionally trained hands, it is not recommended as an approach to be used indiscriminately by the lay person. There are many instances in job counseling and contacts when it is appropriate to furnish information and advice in areas where the counselor is knowledgeable and experienced, especially where information and/or advice is sought. However, where there are choices to be made and frustration and/or conflict are apparent, the use of the directive approach is to be avoided.

NONDIRECTIVE COUNSELING In **nondirective counseling,** the counselee is permitted to have maximum freedom in determining the course of the interview. The importance of nonevaluative listening as a communication skill was described earlier. It is also a primary technique used in nondirective counseling. Fundamentally, the approach is to listen, with understanding and without criticism or appraisal, to the problem as it is described by the counselee. The counselee is encouraged, through the counselor's attitude and reaction to what is said or not said, to express feelings without fear of shame, embarrassment, or reprisal.

As the counseling session progresses, the counselor should strive to reflect the counselee's feelings by restating them. For example, if the counselee has discussed several situations that indicate feelings of being treated unfairly, the counselor at the conclusion of this particular statement would probably say, "You feel that you have been treated unfairly." While questions may be used at appropriate places in the counseling session, the counselor should use general questions that stimulate the counselee to pursue those areas that are troublesome. Questions that call for yes or no answers by the counselee should be avoided.[48]

The free expression that is encouraged in the nondirective approach tends to reduce tensions and frustrations. The counselee who has had an opportunity to release pent-up feelings is usually in a better position to view the problem more objectively and with a problem-solving attitude. The permissive atmosphere allows the counselee to try to work through the entanglements of the problem and to see it in a clearer perspective, often to reach a more desirable solution. There are times, however, when a directive approach will be more suitable, such as when counselees ask for specific information or when it is essential that counselors express their opinions or inform counselees of rules that may have been violated.

PARTICIPATIVE COUNSELING The directive and nondirective approaches that have just been described are obviously at the extremes of a continuum.

While a particular professional counselor may tend to be at one end of the continuum or the other, most of them vary their approach during the course of a session and/or in subsequent sessions. Overall, many choose to emphasize a middle-of-the-road approach in which both parties work together in planning how a particular problem will be analyzed and solved. This approach, which may be thought of as **participative counseling,** is particularly suitable for use in work organizations.

Many of the problems that managers and supervisors are concerned with require not only that the subordinates' feelings be recognized, but also that subordinates be made aware of and adhere to management's expectations for them to be productive, responsible, and cooperative. On the other side of the coin, most people with problems would prefer to be actively involved in the solution once they see that there is a positive course of action available. In many of the work situations where counseling will be used, the participative approach is recommended in working with an individual over a period of time. At times, in the course of a single session, it will be advisable to be directive and/or nondirective.

Success and Failure in Counseling

Counseling as a helping relationship has been discussed in order to present techniques that facilitate communication and help solve problems that affect the well-being of employees and the organization. It should be recognized, however, that counseling by managers will not always be successful in achieving this goal. Nevertheless, some progress can often be made by using counseling techniques where this type of action is appropriate. In cases where counseling apparently fails to yield results, it will often be necessary to take other measures, such as discipline or a transfer.

SUMMARY

Communication is essential to HRM functions, including selection, appraisal, compensation, training, discipline, and labor relations. Although HR managers perform tasks that are essentially communication tasks, they also often retain responsibility for overall organizational communication programs. To fulfill their role as managers and their responsibility for organizational communication, HR managers must understand how to communicate effectively. Because of the nature of communication, HR managers must learn to manipulate verbal and nonverbal symbols effectively to convey the desired meaning. They must be able to cut through false assumptions that cause misunderstandings and impede effective communication.

Downward communication systems include the following: employee handbooks and policy manuals, organizational newspapers, traditional and electronic bulletin boards, presentation and interactive videos, benefits reports, and both traditional meetings and electronic meetings such as teleconferences. Upward communication systems include the development of complaint procedures for employees, suggestion programs, attitude surveys, and electronic mail. Organizations do not rely only on formal systems of upward and downward communication; they may also effectively use the informal system, or grapevine.

Improving an organization's communication goes beyond developing and managing formal and informal systems of communication. It also includes developing communication competency among managers. Communication competency includes effective speaking and listening skills, reading and writing skills, and a sensitivity to what communication medium is most appropriate for a particular message.

In addition to their other communication responsibilities, HR managers as well as other organizational managers are expected to play a counseling role on various occasions. Their understanding of counseling techniques and their skills in using them can enable them to help employees achieve greater productivity and satisfaction in their jobs.

DISCUSSION QUESTIONS

1. Explain why effective communication is so critical to HRM.
2. In our everyday language, especially when we talk about people, we use labels such as "businessman," "union leader," "good-looking secretary," and "blue-collar worker." What effect does this have on communication? Does the use of these labels facilitate or hinder communication? Explain.
3. Many people are not good listeners.
   a. How do you account for this fact?
   b. What effect may this deficiency have on an individual's progress in a job and in other areas of life?
   c. How can listening ability be improved?
4. What problems have you experienced in your attempts to communicate with individuals who are younger or older than you? Have you been able to make any improvement in such communication? What approaches have you used?
5. We observed that suggestion programs in which cash awards are paid are used to improve efficiency and safety and to reduce costs.
   a. In your opinion, what procedures should be followed in soliciting and processing suggestions?
   b. What role should supervisors have in a suggestion program?
   c. Are there any problems that may arise in the administration of a suggestion program? Explain.
   d. In what ways can a suggestion program contribute to the objectives of the HR program?
6. What are the advantages of conducting periodic employee attitude surveys? Are any problems likely to arise over a survey? Explain.
7. What are the major differences among the three counseling approaches described in the chapter? How should one decide which approach to use at a particular time with a counselee?
8. How is the internal communication of an organization related to its communication with customers and the community?

MINI-CASE 15–1 Working with a Different Employee

Tran, a Vietnamese-born employee, has been an effective employee in the produce warehouse of a large grocery chain in Seattle, Washington. His managers have noticed his skills, his ability to work with others (especially persons of Vietnamese and Mexican origin), and his willingness to put extra effort into his work. As a result of encouragement from those around him, he has applied for the position of supervisor.

Sandra, the human resources specialist in charge of recruitment, has read Tran's résumé and was favorably impressed. She has also received excellent references from several people who have worked around him. She calls Tran to her office for an interview. When she asks him to elaborate on his work experience and his education, Tran has little to say. He does point out to her that all of this information is stated on his résumé. Sandra is surprised by his reluctance and concludes that he must lack confidence in his abilities. After all, he should be willing to describe his strengths.

Sandra is also surprised by the thickness of Tran's accent. English skills are essential for the position, and she begins to question Tran's language skills and his education. As a result of this interview, Sandra decides to recommend another applicant for the position of supervisor.

SOURCE: Adapted from S. Thiederman, "Overcoming Cultural and Language Barriers," *Personnel Journal* 67, no. 12 (December 1988): 34–40. Reprinted with the permission of *Personnel Journal,* Costa Mesa, California; all rights reserved.

QUESTIONS

1. For what possible reasons would Tran be reluctant to describe his own strengths?
2. How can HR managers do an effective job of assessing the qualifications of foreign-born applicants?

MINI-CASE 15–2 Buyout at Research Associates

Research Associates was a product testing firm that had operated independently in Texas for more than 15 years. Its employees were predominantly locally born and a large proportion of them were Hispanic. Because of its success in winning contracts with the major auto makers, it was purchased by a larger, nationwide research firm headquartered in Michigan. The new owners quickly sent in their own managers to fill a few key positions. Most of the engineers, technicians, and clerical staff remained with the firm at first, but after 18 months, turnover increased substantially among the technicians and the younger engineers.

To address these turnover problems, the senior managers conducted an attitude survey of the employees. The results revealed that employees felt cut off from management. They described the key managers who had been transferred in as "aloof," and they even described managers who had been with Research Associates for many years as being more difficult to talk with since the changeover. In response to open-ended questions, employees commented that they had once known who to go to with a problem or a suggestion. Now they had no one to turn to with their ideas or complaints. When asked during the interview phase of the attitude survey about her job-related tasks, one employee described them as calculating a set of statistics for the engineers. When she was asked about the purpose of her work, she explained curtly that she had been told to complete the calculations and not ask questions.

QUESTIONS

1. What are the possible sources of the problems identified in the survey?
2. What changes in the communication systems would you recommend for Research Associates?

NOTES AND REFERENCES

1. A description of an organization's communication system is available in Leslie Lamkin and Emily W. Carmain, "Crisis Communication at Georgia Power," *Personnel Journal* 70, no. 1 (January 1991): 35–37.
2. For a detailed description of these five roles as well as the managerial roles of figurehead, leader, entrepreneur, disturbance handler, and resource allocator, see Henry Mintzberg, *The Nature of Managerial Work* (New York: Harper & Row, 1973).
3. Len Sandler, "Rules for Management Communication," *Personnel Journal* 67, no. 9 (September 1988): 40.
4. Fred Luthans, Stuart A. Rosenkrantz, and Henry W. Hennessey, "What Do Successful Managers Really Do? An Observation Study of Managerial Activities," *Journal of Applied Behavioral Science* 21, no. 3 (September 1985): 255–270.
5. Lynda R. Willer and Linda S. Henderson, "Traditional Management Versus Communication Competence Behaviors: An Exploratory Study" (Paper presented at the annual meeting of the Academy of Management, Anaheim, CA, 1988).
6. "Wyatt WorkAmerica" (The Wyatt Company, 1989).
7. Fred Luthans and Janet K. Larsen, "How Managers Really Communicate," *Human Relations* 39, no. 2 (February 1986): 161–178.
8. Stephen R. Axley, "Managerial and Organizational Communication in Terms of the Conduit Metaphor," *Academy of Management Review* 9, no. 3 (July 1984): 428–437.
9. Beverly Sherman, "Evaluation of Articles Based on the Physical Attractiveness and Biographical Descriptions of Female Authors" (Master's thesis, California State University, Sacramento, CA, 1978), 35–36.
10. Dwight Bolinger, *Language: The Loaded Weapon* (London: Longman, 1980), 89–104.
11. S. I. Hayakawa, *Language in Thought and Action* (New York: Harcourt, Brace & World, 1949).
12. Carl R. Rogers and Fritz J. Roethlisberger, "Barriers and Gateways to Communication," *Harvard Business Review* 30, no. 4 (July–August 1952): 46–52.
13. For a detailed description of the role of active listening in effective communication, see Anthony G. Athos and John H. Gabarro, *Interpersonal Behavior: Communication and Understanding in Interpersonal Relationships* (Englewood Cliffs, NJ: Prentice-Hall, 1978), 448–449.
14. Ibid., 450–451.
15. "HRM Update," *Personnel Administrator* 34, no. 5 (May 1989): 19.
16. N. C. Baker, "The Need for Caution in Handbook Changes," *Resource* 7, no. 12 (December 1988): 6.
17. Elizabeth Minich, Michael A. DiBattista, and Brian Raila, "Are You Game for Video Information?" *Personnel Journal* 67, no. 4 (April 1988): 57–63.
18. Ibid., 57–59.

19. Louis C. Kleber, "Give Your Employees Individual Statements," *Personnel Administrator* 34, no. 4 (April 1989): 64–68.

20. Jeffrey P. Davidson and Anthony Alessandra, "Why Employees Should Be Told Bad News," *Supervisory Management* 34, no. 3 (March 1989): 12–13.

21. Michael E. Cavanaugh, "Communication: Make Effective Speeches," *Personnel Journal* 67, no. 3 (March 1988): 51–55.

22. Virginia Johnson, "Picture-Perfect Presentations," *Training & Development Journal* 43, no. 5 (May 1989): 45–47.

23. Valorie A. McClelland, "Upward Communication: Is Anyone Listening?" *Personnel Journal* 67, no. 6 (June 1988): 124–130.

24. Timothy R. Barnett and Daniel S. Cochran, "Making Room for the Whistleblower," *HR Magazine* 36, no. 1 (January 1991): 58–61.

25. Carol Baker of the National Association of Suggestion Systems (Chicago, IL) provided the 1989 data in a telephone conversation in March 1991.

26. Walter H. Read, "Gathering Opinion On-line," *HR Magazine* 36, no. 1 (January 1991): 51–53.

27. David R. York, "Attitude Surveying," *Personnel Journal* 64, no. 5 (May 1985): 70–73.

28. Louis E. Tagliaferri, "Taking Note of Employee Attitudes," *Personnel Administrator* 33, no. 4 (April 1988): 96–102.

29. "HRM Update," *Personnel Administrator* 34, no. 7 (July 1989): 19.

30. Dennis J. Francecki, Ralph F. Catalanello, and Curtiss K. Behrens, "Employee Committees: What Effect Are They Having?" *Personnel* 61, no. 4 (July–August 1984): 67–73. See also Norman B. Sigband, "Meetings with Success," *Personnel Journal* 64, no. 5 (May 1985): 48–55.

31. Fred T. Allen, "Ways to Improve Employee Communications," *Nation's Business* 63, no. 9 (September 1975): 54–56.

32. For information on committee management see Dave Day, "Make the Most of Meetings," *Personnel Journal* 69, no. 3 (March 1990): 34–39; or Sandra E. O'Connell, *The Manager as Communicator* (San Francisco: Harper & Row, 1979), 28–64.

33. Keith Davis, "Management Communication and the Grapevine," *Harvard Business Review* 31, no. 5 (September–October 1953): 43–49.

34. Both authorized, intended use and unintended use of facsimiles are discussed in Jerry Jakubovics, "Companies Hop Aboard the Fax Express," *Supervisory Management* 35, no. 2 (February 1990): 5.

35. Alan Zaremba, "Working with the Organizational Grapevine," *Personnel Journal* 67, no. 7 (July 1988): 38–42.

36. Holly Rawlinson, "Homegrown for HRM," *Personnel Administrator* 34, no. 8 (August 1989): 53.

37. Larry E. Penley and Brian Hawkins, "Studying Interpersonal Communication in Organizations: A Leadership Application," *Academy of Management Journal* 28, no. 2 (June 1985): 309–326.

38. Several studies have investigated the relationship between aspects of communication competence and managerial performance. One study examined the relationship of communication competence to upward mobility; see Beverly D. Sypher and Theodore E. Zorn, "Communication-related Abilities and Upward Mobility: A Longitudinal Investigation," *Human Communication Research* 12, no. 3 (September 1986): 420–431. Another study examined the relationship of various oral and written skills to managerial performance; see Larry E. Penley, Elmore R. Alexander, I. Edward Jernigan, and Katherine Henwood, "Communication Abilities of Managers: The Relationship to Performance," *Journal of Management*, forthcoming.

39. Lynne Kelly, "Implementing a Skills Training Program for Reticent Communicators," *Communication Education* 38, no. 2 (April 1989): 85–101.

40. Glenn C. Pearce, "Doing Something About Your Listening Ability," *Supervisory Management* 34, no. 3 (March 1989): 29–34.

41. Richard L. Daft, Robert H. Lengel, and Linda K. Trevino, "The Relationship Among Message Equivocality, Media Selection, and Manager Performance: Implications for Information Support Systems," *MIS Quarterly* 11, no. 3 (September 1987): 355.

42. A complete discussion of information richness and the contingency model of media choice is available in Richard L. Daft and Robert H. Lengel, "Information Richness: A New Approach to Managerial Behavior and Organization Design," in *Research in Organizational Behavior*, ed. Barry M. Staw and Larry L. Cummings (Greenwich, CT: JAI Press, 1984), 191–233.

43. Christopher J. Zajn, "The Bases for Differing Evaluations of Male and Female Speech: Evidence from Ratings of Transcribed Conversation," *Communication Monographs* 56, no. 1 (March 1989): 59–74.

44. Sondra Thiederman, "Overcoming Cultural and Language Barriers," *Personnel Journal* 67, no. 12 (December 1988): 35–40.

45. Lawrence M. Brammer, *The Helping Relationship: Process and Skills*, 4th ed. (Englewood Cliffs, NJ: Prentice-Hall, 1988). For an expanded discussion of counseling techniques, see Brammer, *Therapeutic Psychology*, 5th ed. (Englewood Cliffs, NJ: Prentice-Hall, 1989).

46. John W. Loughary and Theresa M. Ripley, *Helping Others Help Themselves: A Guide to Counseling Skills* (New York: McGraw-Hill, 1979), 9–16.

47. Brammer, *The Helping Relationship*.

48. For a detailed description of nondirective techniques as applied to work situations, see Norman R. F. Maier and Gertrude Casselman Verser, *Psychology in Industrial Organizations*, 5th ed. (Houghton Mifflin, 1982), Chapter 18.

CHAPTER 16

Employee Rights and Discipline

After reading this chapter you will be able to:

1. *Explain the job-as-property doctrine, the employment-at-will principle, and the implied contract concept.*
2. *Identify the job expectancy rights of employees.*
3. *Describe the proper implementation of organizational rules and regulations.*
4. *Discuss the meaning of discipline when applied to employee misconduct.*
5. *Discuss how to proceed with the investigation of a disciplinary problem.*
6. *Explain two approaches to disciplinary action.*
7. *Identify the different types of nonunion appeal procedures.*
8. *Define the key terms in the chapter.*

TERMS TO IDENTIFY

employee rights (529)
job-as-property doctrine (530)
employment-at-will principle (530)
hot-stove rule (541)
discipline (541)
progressive discipline (545)
positive, or nonpunitive, discipline (546)
outplacement (551)
step-review system (552)
peer-review system, complaint committee, or tribunal (553)
hearing officer (554)
open-door policy (554)
ombudsman (555)

In this chapter we discuss the important HR topics of employee rights, workplace privacy, and employee discipline. HR managers believe that in the future these topics will have a major influence on the activities of both employees and supervisors. Eric H. Joss, a corporate attorney, notes that employee rights and workplace privacy will be "the hottest employment law topic of the 1990s."[1] Managers are discovering that the right to discipline and discharge employees—a traditional responsibility of management—is more difficult to exercise in light of the growing attention to employee rights. Furthermore, disciplining employees is a difficult and unpleasant task for most managers and supervisors; many of them report that taking disciplinary action against an employee is the most stressful duty they perform. Balancing employee rights and employee discipline may not be easy, but it is a universal requirement of organizational life and a critical aspect of good management.

Because the growth of employee rights issues has led to an increase in the number of lawsuits filed by employees, we conclude this chapter with a discussion of organizational nonunion appeal procedures as a way to foster organizational justice. Since disciplinary actions are subject to challenge and possible reversal through governmental agencies or the courts, management should make a positive effort to prevent the need for such action. When disciplinary action becomes impossible to avoid, however, it should be taken in accordance with carefully developed HR policies and practices.

EMPLOYEE RIGHTS

Until recently, employee rights focused on protecting the individual in the workplace. Various antidiscrimination laws, wage and hour statutes, and safety and

Legislation has been passed in several states for advance notice of a plant closing.

health legislation brought numerous job improvements. Currently, however, employee rights litigation is shifting from litigation over getting a job to litigation over keeping the job and winning job improvements.[2] For example, new workplace issues have forced HR managers to consider the rights of employees to protest unfair disciplinary action, have access to their personnel files, refuse to take a drug test, and receive advance notice of a plant closing.

The current emphasis on employee rights is a natural result of the evolution of societal, business, and employee interests. Society continues to define its work values through the courts and legislatures, and it is in the employment relationship that many of these issues take shape. Pat Choate, vice-president of policy analysis at TRW, Inc., notes, "Today's trend in employee rights is a harbinger of the future's employee/employer relationship. The development of employee rights is really the way for society to evolve and survive."[3]

Employee rights can be defined as the guarantees that employees expect from an employer to protect their employment status through fair treatment. These expectations become rights when they are granted to employees by the courts, legislatures, or employers. Unfortunately, the distinction between rights and benefits or entitlements is not always clear, and both benefits and entitlements are often included under the general heading of employee rights.

Balanced against employee rights is the employer's responsibility to provide a safe workplace for employees while guaranteeing safe and quality goods and services to consumers. Furthermore, an employer has the right to expect responsible conduct and reasonable productivity from its employees. An employee who uses drugs may exercise his or her privacy right and refuse to submit to a drug test; but should that employee produce a faulty product as a result of drug impairment, the employer can be held liable for any harm caused by that product. It is here that employee rights and employer responsibilities come most pointedly into conflict. The failure of employers to honor employee rights can result in costly lawsuits, damage the organization's reputation, and hurt employee morale. But the failure of organizations to protect the safety and welfare of employees or consumer interests can invite litigation from both groups. In the remainder of this section we will discuss various employee rights topics from the perspective of employees—employment protection and the expectation of fair treatment by the employer.

Employment Protection Rights

We noted in Chapter 4 that jobs are the primary source of income for employees. Therefore, it is not surprising that employees should regard their jobs as an established right—a right that should not be taken away without just cause and fair treatment.[4] This line of reasoning has led to the emergence of three legal considerations regarding the security of one's job: the job-as-property doctrine, the employment-at-will principle, and the concept of the implied contract.

JOB-AS-PROPERTY DOCTRINE Management has traditionally possessed the right to direct employees and to take corrective action when needed. Nevertheless, many individuals also believe that a job should be the property right of an employee. The **job-as-property doctrine** states that the loss of employment has such serious consequences that employees should not lose their jobs without the protection of *due process* as afforded under the Fourteenth Amendment to the Constitution. The amendment states, "Nor shall any state deprive any person of life, liberty, or property, without due process of law." While HR managers may differ in how they interpret due process, the following principles—or rights—should be part of all interpretations of the concept:

1. The right to know job expectations and the consequences of not fulfilling those expectations.
2. The right to consistent and predictable management action for the violation of rules.
3. The right to fair discipline based on facts, the right to question those facts, and the right to present a defense.
4. The right to appeal disciplinary action.
5. The right to progressive discipline.[5]

In general, the job-as-property doctrine does *not* guarantee employees a permanent right to their jobs. It does, however, obligate management to act in a consistent manner that is fair and equitable to all employees.

EMPLOYMENT-AT-WILL The employment relationship has traditionally followed the common-law doctrine of employment-at-will. The **employment-at-will principle** assumes that an employee has a right to sever the employment relationship for a better job opportunity or for other personal reasons. Employers, likewise, are free to terminate the employment relationship at any time—and without notice—for any reason, no reason, or even a bad reason.[6] Therefore, employees are said to work "at the will" of the employer.

The employment-at-will relationship is created when an employee agrees to work for an employer for an unspecified period of time. Since the employment is of an indefinite duration, it can, in general, be terminated at the whim of either party. This freedom includes the right of management to unilaterally determine the conditions of employment and to make personnel decisions. In 1908, the Supreme Court upheld the employment-at-will doctrine in *Adair* v. *United States,* and this principle continues to be the basic rule governing the private-sector employment relationship.[7]

Employees in the public sector enjoy additional constitutional protection of their employment rights. One author writes that while both public- and private-sector employees have various constitutional protection of their job rights—under the Fifth and Fourteenth Amendments to the Constitution—these amendments have "acted to limit the methods and reasons that may be utilized to dismiss an incumbent employee in the public sector."[8] The clauses of the Fifth Amendment that prohibit denial of either life, liberty, or property without due process of law, as well as the Fourteenth Amendment, provide the principal constitutional protection afforded public-sector employees.

WRONGFUL DISCHARGE SUITS In recent years, a substantial number of employees have sued their former employers for "wrongful or unjust discharge." In their suits, these employees have sought to establish exceptions to the employment-at-will doctrine, as well as to obtain awards for damages suffered. One study shows that the typical jury verdict in such suits awarded damages in excess of $500,000 and that the employees were victorious in 70 percent of the jury trials.[9]

By 1989, courts in 39 states recognized the following three important exceptions to the employment-at-will doctrine:

1. *Violation of Public Policy.* This exception occurs in instances where an employee is terminated for refusing to commit a crime; for reporting criminal activity to government authorities; for disclosing illegal, unethical, or unsafe practices of the employer; or for exercising employment rights.[10] (See Figure 16–1.)
2. *Implied Contract.* This exception occurs when employees are discharged despite the employer's promise (expressed or implied) of job security or contrary to established termination procedures. An employer's oral or written statements may constitute a contractual obligation if they are communicated to employees and employees rely on them as conditions of employment.
3. *Implied Covenant.* This exception occurs where a lack of good faith and fair dealing by the employer has been suggested. By inflicting harm without

FIGURE 16–1 DISCHARGES THAT VIOLATE PUBLIC POLICY

Firing an employee for:

- Refusing to commit perjury in court on the employer's behalf.
- Cooperating with a government agency in the investigation of a charge or giving testimony.
- Refusing to violate a professional code of conduct.
- Reporting Occupational Safety and Health Administration (OSHA) infractions.
- Refusing to support a law or political candidate favored by the employer.
- "Whistle-blowing," or reporting illegal conduct by the employer.
- Informing a customer that the employer has stolen property from the customer.
- Complying with summons to jury duty.

justification, the employer violates the implied covenant.[11] Discharged employees may seek tort damages for mental distress or defamation.

At the present time the confusion and conflict between the traditional right of employers to terminate at will and the right of employees to be protected from unjust discharges are far from resolved. However, in 1988, some important principles for the employment-at-will doctrine were established by *Foley* v. *Interactive Data Corporation.*[12] In this landmark California case, the court endorsed violations of public policy, breach of implied contract, and breach of covenant of good faith and fair dealing as exceptions to the employment-at-will doctrine. The court held, however,

"I'm sensing confidence, boldness and moral sensibility. You're not going to turn out to be a whistle-blower are you?"

From the *Wall Street Journal*—Permission, Cartoon Features Syndicate.

that costly tort remedies were generally not available to employees suing for breach of implied covenant. The *Foley* decision can help employees prove their wrongful discharge claims, since the court ruled that an implied covenant of good faith and fair dealing constitutes a part of every employment relationship as a matter of contract law.[13] The decision also provides relief to employers by eliminating most tort actions, punitive damages, and costly jury trials.[14] Employees can generally seek only compensatory damages, such as lost wages, when suing their employer for wrongful discharge.

IMPLIED CONTRACT Although it is estimated that 70 percent of employees in the United States work without benefit of an employment contract,[15] under certain conditions these employees may be granted contractual employment rights. This can occur when an implied promise by the employer suggests some form of job security to the employee. These implied contractual rights can be based on either oral or written statements made during the preemployment process or subsequent to hiring. Often these promises are contained in employee handbooks, HR manuals, or employment applications or are made during the selection interview.[16] Once these explicit or implicit promises of job security have been made, courts have generally prohibited the employer from terminating the employee without first exhausting the conditions of the contract. For example, a leading case, *Toussaint* v. *Blue Cross and Blue Shield of Michigan*, found an employee handbook enforceable as a unilateral contract.[17] The following are some examples of how an implied contract may become binding:

- Telling employees their jobs are secure as long as they perform satisfactorily and are loyal to the organization.
- Stating in the employee handbook that employees will not be terminated without the right of defense or access to an appeal procedure.
- Urging an employee to leave another organization by promising higher wages and benefits, then denying those promises after the person has been hired.

Fortunately, employers may lessen their vulnerability to implied contract lawsuits by prudent managerial practices, training, and HR policies. HR experts recommend the following approaches:

1. Training supervisors and managers not to imply contract benefits in conversations with new or present employees.
2. Including in employment offers a statement that an employee may voluntarily terminate employment with proper notice and the employee may be dismissed by the employer at any time and for a justified reason. The language in this statement must be appropriate, clear, and easily understood.
3. Including employment-at-will statements in all employment documents (e.g., employee handbooks, employment applications, and letters of employment).

4. Having written proof that employees have read and understood the employment-at-will disclaimers.[18]

Job Expectancy Rights

Once hired, employees expect certain rights associated with fair and equitable employment. Employee rights on the job include those regarding substance abuse and drug testing, privacy, plant closing notification, and just-cause disciplinary and discharge procedures.

SUBSTANCE ABUSE AND DRUG TESTING The impact of employee drug abuse on employers is staggering. Drug abuse by employees costs U.S. employers nearly $50 billion a year in absenteeism and turnover.[19] Also, in these litigious times, the failure of an employer to ensure a safe and drug-free workplace can result in astronomical liability claims when consumers are injured because of a negligent employee or faulty product.[20] In response to the workplace drug problem, close to one-third of all companies with 5,000 or more employees use some form of drug testing for job applicants or employees, according to a 1988 study by the National Institute on Drug Abuse (NIDA).[21]

Drug testing is most prevalent among employees in "sensitive positions" within the public sector, in organizations doing business with the federal government, and in public and private transportation concerns.[22] While the definition of sensitive position is still being formulated by the courts, employees holding positions requiring top-secret national security clearance (*Harmon* v. *Thornburgh*), those working in the interdiction of dangerous drugs (*Treasury Employees Union* v. *Von Raab*), uniformed police officers and firefighters (*City of Annapolis* v. *United Food and Commercial Workers Local 400*), and employees in transportation safety positions (*Skinner* v. *Railway Labor Executives Association*) can be required to submit to a drug test even without an "individualized suspicion" of drug usage.[23] The courts in these cases have held that an employer's interest in maintaining a drug-free workplace outweighs any privacy interest the employee may have. At the federal level, the Drug-Free Workplace Act of 1988 requires, among other things, that organizations with government contracts of $25,000 or more publish and furnish a policy statement to employees prohibiting drug usage at work, establish awareness programs, and notify the federal contracting agency of any employees who have been convicted of a drug-related criminal offense. (See Chapter 13 for a sample policy statement.)

These urine samples have tested positive for drugs.

Legislation on drug testing in the private sector is still in its formative stage. Unless state or local laws either restrict or prohibit drug testing, private employers have a right to require employees to submit to a urinalysis or blood test where "probable cause" exists. Probable cause could include observable safety, conduct, or performance problems. Employers wishing to implement mandatory or random drug testing programs may face more stringent state court restrictions.[24]

Some of the sharpest criticism of drug testing is aimed at the technology and standards with which the tests are conducted. Although the technology is advanced, drug testing involves a number of different steps in which human error can occur. Machines can be miscalibrated or insufficiently cleaned, samples can become contaminated or confused, and other accidents can occur. To overcome these problems, employers are establishing drug testing standards, such as the two-step process of an immunoassay screen followed by a gas chromatography/mass spectrometry confirmation. J. Michael Walsh, director of NIDA's Division of Applied Research, notes that many large organizations are now using a medical review officer as a safeguard in the testing procedure.[25] TWA and 3M believe that medical review officers help both managers and employees to understand the complexities of drug testing. NIDA has established mandatory guidelines for federal workplace drug testing (see Highlights in HRM 1).

EMPLOYEE SEARCHES AND SURVEILLANCE Sabotage, theft, drug dealing, and other illegal employee acts in the workplace drain organizational resources. To help fight these employee crimes, the courts have allowed random searches of lockers, desks, suitcases, toolboxes, and general work areas where adequate justification exists and employees have received proper notification beforehand. As two attorneys have noted, "Employees have no reasonable expectation of privacy in places where work rules that provide for inspections have been put into effect."[26] Employees are obligated to comply with the probable-cause searches of employers, and they can be appropriately disciplined—normally for insubordination—for refusing to comply with search requests.

Managers must be diligent when conducting employee searches. Improper searches can lead to employee lawsuits charging the employer with invasion of privacy, defamation of character, and negligent infliction of emotional distress. Employers are advised to develop an HR search policy based on the following guidelines:

Telephone surveillance monitors customer service and prevents theft.

1. The search policy should be widely publicized and should advocate a probable or compelling reason for the search.
2. The search policy should be applied in a reasonable, evenhanded manner.
3. Where possible, searches should be conducted in private.
4. The employer should attempt to obtain the employee's consent prior to the search.
5. The search should be conducted in a humane and discreet manner to avoid infliction of emotional distress.[27]

It is not uncommon for employers to monitor the conduct of employees through surveillance techniques. General Electric uses tiny fisheye lenses installed behind pinholes in walls and ceilings to observe employees suspected of crimes. DuPont employs long-distance cameras to monitor its loading docks.[28] One of the most common means of electronic surveillance by employers is telephone surveillance to ensure that customer requests are handled properly or to prevent theft. Employers have the right to monitor employees provided they are doing it for compelling business reasons. Employees can sue for invasion of privacy, but courts have held

HIGHLIGHTS IN HRM

1 DRUG TESTING AT THE DEPARTMENT OF HEALTH AND HUMAN SERVICES

Under drug testing guidelines issued by the Department of Health and Human Services (HHS), employees are tested for five classes of drugs: marijuana, cocaine, opiates (heroin, morphine, etc.), phencyclidine (PCP), and amphetamines (speed). Before taking a drug test, employees must present accurate photo identification and remove "any unnecessary outer garments . . . that might conceal items or substances that could be used to tamper with or adulterate the individual's urine specimen." Urination must be performed at a toilet bowl into which a bluing agent has been poured to color the water and prevent adulteration of the sample. Four minutes after the sample has been collected, the sample's temperature must be taken. The sample will be rejected if the temperature is not between 90.5 and 99.8 degrees Fahrenheit. Positive urine samples are confirmed by the gas chromatography/mass spectrometry technique. HHS drug testing guidelines developed by the National Institute of Drug Abuse constitute a "reasonable search" according to the Supreme Court decision in *Treasury Employees Union* v. *Von Raab.*

SOURCE: *BNA's Employee Relations Weekly* 7 (August 7, 1989): 1008.

that to win damages, the employees' reasonable expectations of privacy must outweigh the organization's reason for surveillance.

PLANT CLOSING NOTIFICATION Sixteen million jobs were lost in the United States between 1976 and 1982 as a result of the closing of large firms. Between January 1981 and January 1986, the BLS reported that about 11 million employees were released from employment because of plant closings or permanent layoffs.[29] Approximately two-thirds of all employees laid off did not receive advance notice. Plant closings have a tragic impact on the lives of employees and their communities. It is estimated that for every 100 jobs lost from a plant closing, the local community loses 200 to 300 jobs through a ripple effect.[30]

Because of statistics such as these, several states, local bodies, and the federal government have passed legislation restricting the unilateral right of employers to close or relocate their facilities. Maine, Wisconsin, Connecticut, and Massachusetts have adopted plant closing legislation that includes prenotification or severance provisions. Wisconsin's law requires 60 days' notification for plant closings and major layoffs. In 1988, Congress passed the Plant Closing Act, which requires organizations with more than 100 employees to give employees and their communities 60 days' written notice of any closure or layoff affecting 50 or more full-time employees. The Act allows several employer exemptions, including "unforeseeable circumstances" and the need to acquire private capital to maintain the facility.

PERSONNEL FILES The information kept in an employee's personnel file can have a significant impact—positive or negative—on career development. The personnel file, typically kept by the HR department, can contain medical records, performance appraisals, salary notices, investigatory reports, credit checks, criminal records, test scores, and family data. Unfortunately, errors and/or omissions in these files, or access to the files by unauthorized persons, can create employment or personal hardships. The growth of HR information systems (HRIS) can complicate personnel file problems by making personnel information more accessible to those with prying eyes or those who might use the information inappropriately.[31]

Legislation at the federal level (see Figure 16–2) and, in several instances at the state level, permits employees to inspect their own personnel files. The states that grant employees this privilege generally provide the following privacy rights:

- The right to know of the existence of one's personnel file.
- The right to inspect one's own personnel file.
- The right to correct inaccurate data in the file.[32]

Even in the absence of specific legislation, most employers give their employees access to their personnel files. According to a study by the Society for Human Resource Management, 96 percent of 520 responding organizations permit such access. Many employer policies, however, include restrictions on access. For example, 92 percent require that a member of the HR department be present during the review; 52 percent either disallow or limit the copying of files; and 49 percent specify designated viewing hours or require appointments.[33]

FIGURE 16–2 RIGHT-TO-PRIVACY LAWS

Crime Control and Safe Streets Act (1968)
Prohibits employers from intercepting or listening to an employee's confidential communication without the employee's prior consent.

Fair Credit Reporting Act (1970)
Permits job applicants and employees to know of the existence and context of any credit files maintained on them. Employees have the right to know of the existence and nature of an investigative consumer report compiled by the employer.

Privacy Act (1974)
Applies to federal agencies and to organizations supplying goods or services to the federal government. Gives individuals the right to examine references regarding employment decisions. Allows employees to review their personnel records for accuracy. Employers who willfully violate the act are subject to civil suits.

Family Education Rights and Privacy Act—The Buckley Amendment (1974)
Educational institutions are prohibited from supplying information about students without prior consent. Students have the right to inspect their educational records.

Our discussion of employee rights has touched on the major employee rights issues currently affecting HR management. Other areas of growing concern include sexual harassment (Chapter 3), discriminatory treatment (Chapter 3), smoking in the workplace (Chapter 13), sexual preference, personal relationships, and conduct away from the workplace. In the future we can expect state courts and legislative bodies to give these concerns even more attention.

DISCIPLINARY POLICIES AND PROCEDURES

As the preceding discussion illustrates, the right of managers to discipline and discharge employees is constantly being limited. There is thus an even greater need for managers at all levels of the organization to understand discipline procedures. When disciplinary action is taken against an employee, it must be for justifiable reasons and there must be effective policies and procedures to govern its use. Such policies and procedures serve to assist those responsible for taking disciplinary action and to help ensure that employees will receive fair and constructive treatment. Equally important, these guidelines help to prevent disciplinary action from being voided or from being reversed through the appeal system.

Disciplinary policies and procedures should cover a number of important areas to ensure thorough coverage. Figure 16–3 presents a disciplinary model that illustrates the areas where provisions should be established. The model also shows the logical sequence in which disciplinary steps must be carried out to ensure enforceable decisions.

FIGURE 16–3 THE DISCIPLINARY MODEL

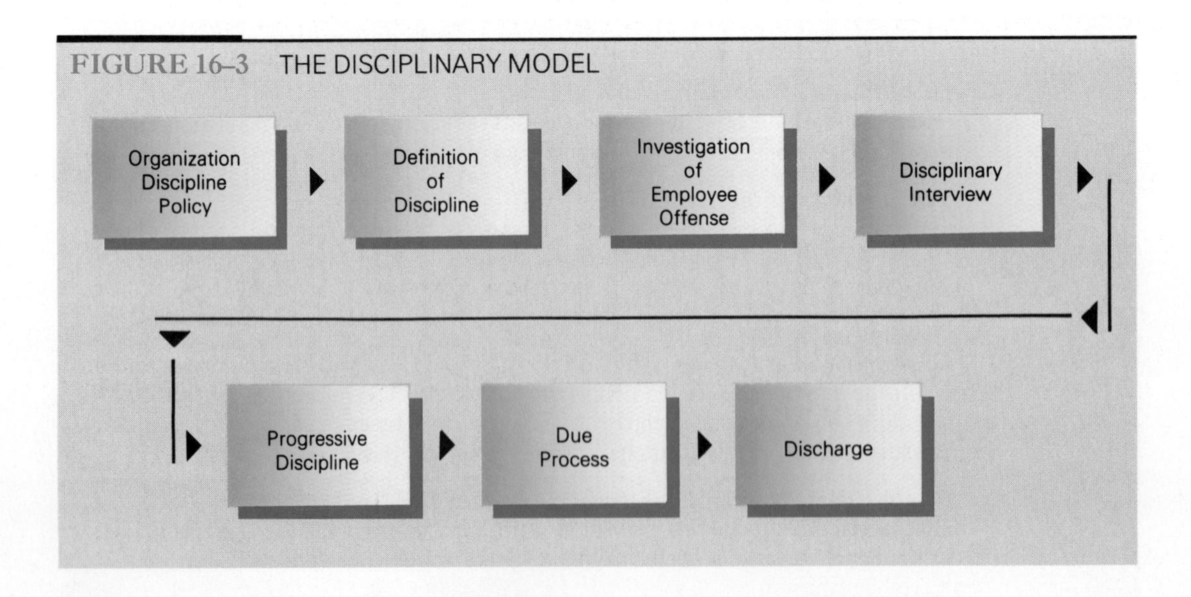

A major responsibility of the HR department is to develop, and to have top management approve, its disciplinary policies and procedures. Such development, however, must involve the participation of the supervisors and managers who must carry out these policies. Their experience can contribute to more effective coordination and consistency in the use of disciplinary action throughout the organization. The HR department is also responsible for ensuring that disciplinary policies, as well as any disciplinary action taken against employees, are consistent with the labor agreement (if one exists) and conform with current law.

The primary responsibility for preventing or correcting disciplinary problems rests with an employee's immediate supervisor. The supervisor is the person best able to observe evidence of unsatisfactory behavior or performance and to discuss the matter with the employee. Such discussions are frequently all that is needed to correct the problem, so that disciplinary action becomes unnecessary. However, when disciplinary action is needed, the supervisor should attempt to use a problem-solving approach. The causes underlying the problem are as important as the problem itself, and any attempt to prevent recurrence will require an understanding of these causes. Admittedly, it is often difficult for supervisors to maintain an objective attitude toward employee infractions. But if supervisors can approach these infractions with a problem-solving attitude, they are likely to come up with a diagnosis that is nearer the truth than would be possible were they to use the approach of a trial lawyer.

The Results of Inaction

Figure 16–4 lists the more common disciplinary problems noted by HR managers. Failure to take disciplinary action in any of these areas only serves to aggravate a problem that eventually must be resolved. Such failure implies that the performance of the employee concerned has been satisfactory. If disciplinary action is eventually taken, the delay will make it more difficult to justify the action if appealed. In defending against such an appeal, the employer is likely to be asked why an employee who had not been performing or behaving satisfactorily was kept on the payroll. Or an even more damaging question might be, "Why did that employee receive satisfactory performance ratings (or perhaps even merit raises)?"

Such contradictions in HR practice can only aid employees in successfully challenging management's corrective actions. Unfortunately, there are supervisors who try to build a case to justify their corrective actions only *after* they have decided that a particular employee should be discharged. In one study, the following were the five most common reasons given by supervisors for their failure to impose a disciplinary penalty:

1. The supervisor had failed to document earlier actions, so no record existed on which to base subsequent disciplinary action.
2. Supervisors believed they would receive little or no support from higher management for the disciplinary action.

FIGURE 16–4 COMMON DISCIPLINARY PROBLEMS

ATTENDANCE PROBLEMS

- Unexcused absence
- Chronic absenteeism
- Unexcused/excessive tardiness
- Leaving without permission

DISHONESTY AND RELATED PROBLEMS

- Theft
- Falsifying employment application
- Willfully damaging organizational property
- Punching another employee's time card
- Falsifying work records

WORK PERFORMANCE PROBLEMS

- Failure to complete work assignments
- Producing substandard products or services
- Failure to meet established production requirements

ON-THE-JOB BEHAVIOR PROBLEMS

- Intoxication at work
- Insubordination
- Horseplay
- Smoking in unauthorized places
- Fighting
- Gambling
- Failure to use safety devices
- Failure to report injuries
- Carelessness
- Sleeping on the job
- Using abusive or threatening language with supervisors
- Possession of narcotics or alcohol
- Possession of firearms or other weapons
- Sexual harassment

3. The supervisor was uncertain of the facts underlying the situation requiring disciplinary action.
4. Failure by the supervisor to discipline employees in the past for a certain infraction caused the supervisor to forgo current disciplinary action in order to appear consistent.
5. The supervisor wanted to be seen as a good guy.[34]

Setting Organizational Rules

Figure 16–3 showed that the discipline model begins when the organization develops disciplinary policies and procedures to govern the type of behavior expected of employees. Organizations as diverse as Gerber Products, Union Pacific, Monsanto, and Bristol-Myers Squibb have written policies explaining the type of conduct required of employees. Since employee behavior standards are established through the setting of organizational rules and regulations, the following suggestions may help reduce problems in this area:

1. Rules should be widely disseminated and known to all employees. It should not be assumed that employees know all the rules.
2. Rules should be reviewed periodically—perhaps annually—especially those rules critical to work success.
3. The reasons for a rule should always be explained. Acceptance of an organizational rule is greater when employees understand the reasons behind it.
4. Rules should always be written. Ambiguity should be avoided, since this can result in different interpretations of the rules by different supervisors.
5. Rules must be reasonable and relate to the safe and efficient operation of the organization. Rules should not be made simply because of personal likes or dislikes.
6. If management has been lax in the enforcement of a rule, the rule must be restated, along with the consequences for its violation, before disciplinary action can begin.

In attempting to uncover reasons for unsatisfactory behavior, supervisors must keep in mind the fact that employees may not be aware of certain work rules. Before initiating any disciplinary action, therefore, it is essential that supervisors consider whether or not they have given their employees careful and thorough orientation in the rules and regulations relating to their jobs. In fact, the proper communication of organizational rules and regulations is so important that labor arbitrators cite the neglect of communicating rules as a major reason for reversing the disciplinary action taken against an employee.[35]

The Hot-Stove Approach to Rule Enforcement

Regardless of the reason for the disciplinary action, it should be taken as soon as possible after the infraction has occurred and a complete investigation has been conducted. HR professionals often use the **hot-stove rule** to explain the correct application of discipline. A hot stove gives *warning* that it should not be touched. Those who ignore the warning and touch it are assured of being burned. The punishment is *immediate* and a direct consequence of breaking the rule never to touch a hot stove. Likewise, a work rule should apply to all employees and should be enforced consistently and in an *impersonal* and unbiased way. Employees should know the consequences of violating the rule, so that the rule will have preventive value.

Defining Discipline

In management seminars conducted by the authors of this text, when managers are asked to define the word *discipline,* their most frequent response is that discipline means punishment. Although this answer is not incorrect, it is only one of three possible meanings. As normally defined, **discipline** has these meanings:

1. Treatment that punishes.
2. Orderly behavior in an organizational setting.
3. Training that molds, strengthens, or corrects undesirable conduct and encourages development of self-control.

To some managers, discipline is synonymous with force. They equate the term with the punishment of employees who violate rules or regulations. Other managers think of discipline as a general state of affairs—a condition of orderliness where employees conduct themselves according to standards of acceptable behavior. Discipline viewed in this manner can be considered positive when employees willingly practice self-control and respect organizational rules.

The third definition considers discipline a management tool used to correct undesirable employee behavior. Discipline is applied as a constructive means of getting employees to conform to acceptable standards of performance. Many organizations, such as Goodyear Aerospace and Arizona State University, define the term discipline in their policy manual as "training that corrects, molds, or perfects knowledge, attitudes, behavior, or conduct." Discipline is thus viewed as a way to correct poor employee performance rather than simply as punishment for an offense. As these organizations emphasize, discipline should be seen as a method of training employees to perform better or to improve their job attitudes or work behavior. It is also interesting to note that the word *discipline* is derived from the word *disciple*, which means follower or pupil. Mosley, Megginson, and Pietri believe that the implication of this meaning is that good discipline is based on good supervisory leadership.[36]

When taken against employees, disciplinary action should never be thought of as punishment. Discipline can embody a penalty as a means of obtaining a desired result; however, punishment should not be the intent of disciplinary action. Rather, discipline must have as its goal the improvement of the employee's future behavior. To apply discipline in any other way—as punishment or as a way of getting even with employees—can only invite problems for management, including possible wrongful discharge suits.

Investigating the Disciplinary Problem

Managers frequently have an intuitive sense of how to investigate employee misconduct. Unfortunately, the investigation may be conducted in a haphazard manner; or worse, the investigation may omit one or more investigative concerns. Figure 16–5 lists seven questions to consider in investigating an employee offense. Attending to each question will help ensure a full and fair investigation while providing reliable information free from personal prejudice. In conducting an employee investigation, it is important to be objective and to avoid the assumptions, suppositions, and biases that often surround discipline cases.

DOCUMENTATION OF EMPLOYEE MISCONDUCT "It's too complicated"; "I just didn't take time to do it"; "I have more important things to do." These are some of the frequent excuses used by managers who have failed to docu-

FIGURE 16–5 QUESTIONS TO CONSIDER IN DISCIPLINARY INVESTIGATIONS

1. *In very specific terms, what is the offense charged?*
   - Is management sure it fully understands the charge against the employee?
   - Was the employee really terminated for insubordination, or did the employee merely refuse a request by management?
2. *Did the employee know he or she was doing something wrong?*
   - What rule or provision was violated?
   - How would the employee know of the existence of the rule?
   - Was the employee warned of the consequence?
3. *Is the employee guilty?*
   - What are the sources of facts?
   - Is there direct or only indirect evidence of guilt?
   - Has anyone talked to the employee to hear his or her side of the situation?
4. *Are there extenuating circumstances?*
   - Were there conflicting orders given by different supervisors?
   - Does anybody have reason to want to "get" this employee?
   - Was the employee provoked by a manager or another employee?
5. *Has the rule been uniformly enforced?*
   - Have all managers applied the rule consistently?
   - What punishment have previous offenders received?
   - Were any other employees involved in this offense and possibly guilty?
6. *Is the offense related to the workplace?*
   - Is there evidence that the offense hurt the organization?
   - Is management making a moral judgment or a business judgment?
7. *What is the employee's past work record?*
   - Years of service?
   - Years or months in present job?
   - Personnel record as a whole, especially disciplinary record?

ment cases of employee misconduct. The most significant cause of inadequate documentation, however, is that managers have no idea of what constitutes good documentation.[37] Unfortunately, the failure of managers to record employee misconduct accurately can result in the reversal of any subsequent disciplinary action. The maintenance of *accurate* and *complete* work records, therefore, is an essential part of an effective disciplinary system. For documentation to be complete, the following eight items should be included:

1. Date, time, and location of the incident(s).
2. Negative performance or behavior exhibited by the employee—the problem.
3. Consequences of that action or behavior on the employee's overall work performance and/or the operation of the employee's work unit.
4. Prior discussion(s) with the employee about the problem.
5. Disciplinary action to be taken and specific improvement expected.
6. Consequences if improvement is not made, and a follow-up date.

The maintenance of accurate and complete work records is essential to an effective disciplinary system.

7. The employee's reaction to the supervisor's attempt to change behavior.
8. The names of witnesses to the incident (if appropriate).

When preparing documentation, it is important for a manager to record the incident immediately after the infraction takes place, when the memory of it is still fresh, and to ensure that the record is complete and accurate.[38] Documentation need not be lengthy, but it must include the eight points in the preceding list. Remember, a manager's records of employee misconduct are considered business documents, and as such they are admissible as evidence in arbitration hearings, administrative proceedings, and courts of law.

THE INVESTIGATIVE INTERVIEW Before any disciplinary action is initiated, an investigative interview should be conducted to make sure employees are fully aware of the offense. This interview is necessary because the supervisor's perceptions of the employee's behavior may not be entirely accurate. The interview should concentrate on how the offense violated the performance and behavior standards of the job. It should avoid getting into personalities or areas unrelated to job performance. Most important, the employee must be given a full opportunity to explain his or her side of the issue so that any deficiencies for which the organization may be responsible are revealed.

In the leading case *NLRB* v. *Weingarten, Inc.*, the Supreme Court upheld a National Labor Relations Board ruling in favor of the employee's right to representation during an investigative interview in a unionized organization.[39] The Court reasoned that the presence of a union representative would serve the beneficial purpose of balancing the power between labor and management, since the union representative could aid an employee who was "too fearful or inarticulate to relate accurately the incident being investigated, or too ignorant to raise extenuating factors."[40] In the *Weingarten* case, the Court decided that since the employee had reason to believe that the investigative interview might result in action jeopardizing her job security, she had the right to representation. The *Weingarten* decision does not apply to nonunion employers, however. In the 1985 *Sears Roebuck and Company* case, the NLRB decided that when no union is present, an employer is entirely free to choose how it will deal with its employees regarding actual or potential disciplinary action.[41]

It is important to note also that an employee's right to representation in a unionized organization does not extend to all interviews with management. The *Weingarten* case places some carefully defined limits on an employee's representation rights. The rules limiting these rights are as follows:

1. Representation rights apply only to *investigative interviews*, not to run-of-the-mill shop-floor discussions.
2. The rights arise only in incidents where the employee *requests* representation and where the employee *reasonably believes that discipline may result* from the interview.
3. Management has *no obligation to bargain* with the employee's representative.[42]

Even if employees and management comply with these rules, managers are still not required to hold an investigative interview. The *Weingarten* decision does not guarantee an employee an investigative interview; it only grants the right to representation *if requested*. The law does permit employers to cancel the interview if a representative is requested, and management may then continue the investigation by other appropriate means. Where employers violate the law, however, the NLRB can impose remedies including cease-and-desist orders, reinstatement and back pay for discharged employees, and the removal of the record of disciplinary action.

Approaches to Disciplinary Action

If a thorough investigation shows that an employee has violated some organization rule, disciplinary action must be imposed. Two approaches to disciplinary action are progressive discipline and positive discipline.

PROGRESSIVE DISCIPLINE Generally, discipline is imposed in a progressive manner. By definition, **progressive discipline** is the application of corrective measures by increasing degrees. Progressive discipline is designed to motivate an employee to correct his or her misconduct voluntarily. The technique is aimed at nipping the problem in the bud, using only enough corrective action to remedy the shortcoming. However, the sequence and severity of the disciplinary action vary with the type of offense and the circumstances surrounding it. Since each situation is unique, a number of factors must be considered in determining how severe a disciplinary action should be. Some of the factors to consider were listed in Figure 16–5.[43]

The typical progressive discipline procedure includes four steps. From an oral warning (or counseling) that subsequent unsatisfactory behavior or performance will not be tolerated, the action may progress to a written warning, to a suspension without pay, and ultimately to discharge.

A slightly different progressive-discipline procedure, used by the Northwestern Mutual Life Insurance Company, is shown in Highlights in HRM 2. In the traditional progressive-discipline system and in the insurance company example, the focus of discipline is on doing everything possible to retain employees by encouraging and helping them to correct their deficiencies. The "capital punishment" of discharge is utilized only as a last resort. Organizations normally use lower forms of disciplinary action for less severe performance problems. It is important for managers to remember that three important things occur when progressive discipline is applied properly:

1. Employees always know where they stand regarding offenses.
2. Employees know what improvement is expected of them.
3. Employees understand what will happen next if improvement is not made.

POSITIVE DISCIPLINE Although progressive discipline is the most popular approach to correcting employee misconduct, recently some managers have questioned its logic. They have noted that it has certain flaws, including its intimidating and adversarial nature, which prevent it from achieving the intended purpose.[44] For these reasons, organizations such as Tampa Electric Company, the Texas Department of Mental Health and Mental Retardation, Union Carbide, the Liberty National Bank of Oklahoma, and General Electric are using an approach called **positive,** or **nonpunitive, discipline.** Positive discipline is based on the concept that employees must assume responsibility for their personal conduct and job performance.

Positive discipline requires a cooperative environment where the employee and the supervisor engage in joint discussion and problem solving to resolve incidents of employee irresponsibility.[45] The approach focuses on the early correction of misconduct, with the employee taking total responsibility for resolving the problem. Nothing is imposed by management; all solutions and affirmations are jointly reached. As Redeker states, "Nonpunitive discipline replaces threats and punishment with encouragement."[46]

Figure 16–6 illustrates the procedure for implementing positive discipline. While positive discipline appears similar to progressive discipline, its emphasis is on giving employees reminders rather than reprimands as a way to improve performance.[47] The technique is implemented in three steps.[48] The first is a conference between the employee and the supervisor. The purpose of this meeting is to find a solution to the problem through discussion, with oral agreement by the employee to improve his or her performance. The supervisor refrains from reprimanding or threatening the employee with further disciplinary action. Supervisors may document this conference, but a written record of this meeting is not placed in the employee's file unless the misconduct arises again.

HIGHLIGHTS IN HRM

2 NORTHWESTERN MUTUAL LIFE'S PROGRESSIVE LADDER OF DISCIPLINE

LEVEL OF DISCIPLINE	WHERE AND WHO	DOCUMENTATION
Discharge	In privacy. Employee may request union representative.	Written documentation to manager's and Human Resources Dept.'s files, Dept. Head, Human Resources Officer and Admin. Officer. Notice to union president, same day.
Final written warning (Warn & Watch)	In privacy. Employee may request union representative.	Written W & W to employee; denote length of W & W period. Copies to manager's and Human Resources Dept.'s files, Dept. Head, Human Resources Officer, Admin. Officer and union president.
Formal discussion and written summary (a "pre-warning")	In privacy. Employee may request union representative.	Written admonishment to employee. Copy to manager's and Human Resources Dept.'s files, Dept. Head, Human Resources Officer and Administrative Officer.
Formal discussion(s)	At manager's desk or in more private place.	Summarize discussion in writing to employee. Copy to manager's file; blind copy to Human Resources Officer and Administrative Officer.
Semi-formal discussion(s)	At manager's desk.	Memo in manager's file. Blind copy to Human Resources Officer and Administrative Officer.
Informal reminder(s)	At workstation.	Note in manager's file.

"Discipline" is supervisory action necessary to bring about employee self-discipline; it is not to be punishment.

Always use the *lowest* ladder rung necessary to achieve the desired performance/attendance change. Climbing the ladder too quickly might cause antagonism and failure—the goal is success.

The supervisor can get on the ladder on any rung; he/she may stay on any rung, repeating the action at that level; he/she may skip rungs, except for written warning.

Final written warning *must* be given prior to discharge (except where it is not practicable).

When performance/attendance improves as desired, tell employee and place documentation in file to reflect current performance/attendance progress.

SOURCE: Used with permission of Northwestern Mutual Life Insurance Company.

If improvement is not made after this first step, the supervisor holds a second conference with the employee to determine why the solution agreed to in the first conference did not work. At this stage, however, a written reminder is given to the employee. This document states the new or repeated solution to the problem, with an affirmation that improvement is the responsibility of the employee and a condition of continued employment.

When both conferences fail to produce the desired results, the third step is to give the employee a one-day *decision-making leave* (a paid leave). The purpose of this paid leave is for the employee to decide whether he or she wishes to continue working for the organization. The organization pays for this leave to demonstrate its desire to retain the person. Also, paying for the leave eliminates the negative effects for the employee of losing a day's pay. Employees given a decision-making leave are instructed to return the following day with a decision either to make a total commitment to improve performance or to quit the organization. If a commitment is not made, the employee is dismissed with the assumption that he or she lacked responsibility toward the organization.

Compiling a Disciplinary Record

In applying either progressive or positive discipline, it is important for managers to maintain complete records at each step of the procedure. When employees fail to meet the obligation of a disciplinary step, they should be given a warning, and the warning should be documented by their manager. A copy of this warning is usually placed in the employee's personnel file. After an established period—frequently six months—the warning is usually removed, provided that it has served its purpose. Otherwise it remains in the file to serve as evidence should a more severe penalty become necessary later.

An employee's personnel file contains the employee's complete work history. It serves as a basis for determining and supporting disciplinary action and for evaluating the organization's disciplinary policies and procedures. Maintenance of

FIGURE 16–6 POSITIVE DISCIPLINE PROCEDURE

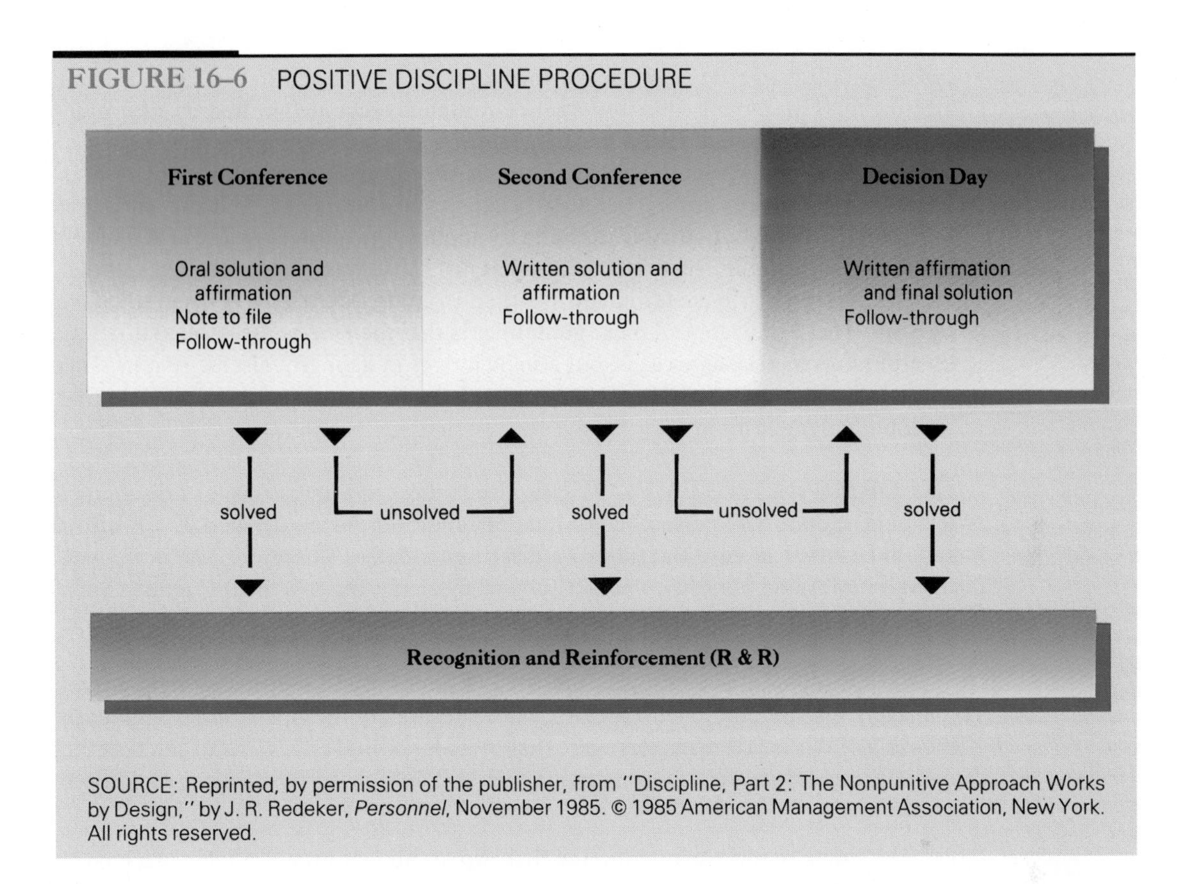

SOURCE: Reprinted, by permission of the publisher, from "Discipline, Part 2: The Nonpunitive Approach Works by Design," by J. R. Redeker, *Personnel*, November 1985. © 1985 American Management Association, New York. All rights reserved.

proper records also provides management with valuable information about the soundness of its rules and regulations. Those rules that are violated most frequently should receive particular attention, because the need for them may no longer exist or some change might be required to facilitate their enforcement. If the rule is shown to have little or no value, it should be revised or rescinded. Otherwise employees are likely to feel they are being restricted unnecessarily.

Discharging Employees

When employees fail to conform to organizational rules and regulations, the final disciplinary action in many cases is discharge. Since discharge has such serious consequences for the employee—and possibly for the organization—it should be undertaken only after a deliberate and thoughtful review of the case.[49] If an employee is fired, he or she may file a wrongful discharge suit claiming the termination was "without just or sufficient cause," implying a lack of fair treatment by management.

If an employee termination is to be upheld for good cause, what constitutes fair employee treatment? This question is not easily answered, but standards governing just-cause discharge do exist, in the form of rules developed in the field of labor arbitration. These rules consist of a set of guidelines that are applied by arbitrators to dismissal cases to determine if management had just cause for the termination.[50] These guidelines are normally set forth in the form of questions, provided in Figure 16–7. For example, before discharging an employee, did the manager forewarn the person of possible disciplinary action? A no answer to any of the seven questions in the figure generally means that just cause was not established and that management's decision to terminate included arbitrary, capricious, or discriminatory reasons. The significance of these guidelines is that they are being applied not only by arbitrators in discharge cases, but also by judges in wrongful discharge suits. It is critical that managers at all levels understand the just-cause guidelines, including their proper application.

INFORMING THE EMPLOYEE Regardless of the reasons for a discharge, it should be done with personal consideration for the employee affected. Every effort should be made to ease the trauma a discharge creates. Therefore, the employee must be informed honestly, yet tactfully, of the exact reasons for the action. Such candor can help the employee face the problem and adjust to it in a constructive manner.

In a study of how employees are fired, Fulmer found that many higher-level managers discuss, and even rehearse, with their peers the upcoming termination meeting.[51] While HR managers agree that there is no single right way to conduct the discharge meeting, the following guidelines will help to make the discussion more effective:

1. Come to the point within the first two or three minutes, and list in a logical order all reasons for the termination.

FIGURE 16–7 "JUST-CAUSE" DISCHARGE GUIDELINES

1. Did the organization forewarn the employee of the possible disciplinary consequences of his or her action?
2. Were management's requirements of the employee reasonable in relation to the orderly, efficient, and safe operation of the organization's business?
3. Did management, before discharging the employee, make a reasonable effort to establish that the employee's performance was unsatisfactory?
4. Was the organization's investigation conducted in a fair and objective manner?
5. Did the investigation produce sufficient evidence or proof of guilt as charged?
6. Has management treated this employee under its rules, orders, and penalties as it has other employees in similar circumstances?
7. Did the discharge fit the misconduct, considering the seriousness of the proven offense, the employee's service record, and any mitigating circumstances?

2. Be straightforward and firm, yet tactful, and remain resolute in your decision.
3. Make the discussion private, businesslike, and fairly brief.
4. Avoid making accusations against the employee and injecting personal feelings into the discussion.
5. Avoid bringing up any personality differences between you and the employee.
6. Provide any information concerning severance pay and the status of benefits and coverage.
7. Explain how you will handle employment inquiries from future employers.[52]

Termination meetings should be held in a neutral location, such as a conference room, so that the manager can leave if the meeting gets out of control. Finally, the prudent manager will have determined, prior to the termination decision, that the dismissal does not violate any legal rights the employee may have. Certain federal and state laws limit an employer's freedom to discharge employees. As we will discuss in Chapter 17, the Taft-Hartley Act makes it illegal for an employer to discharge or otherwise discriminate against employees because of their union activities. As we noted in Chapter 3, state fair employment practice laws, Title VII of the Civil Rights Act, and other statutes prohibit discrimination in personnel decisions on the basis of race, religion, color, sex, national origin, or age. Also prohibited are reprisals against employees who exercise their rights under these laws. The antidiscrimination laws make it essential that managers review their discharge decisions carefully to ensure that there is no evidence of bias or prejudice on the part of supervisors who have made the decisions.

UTILIZING OUTPLACEMENT ASSISTANCE Some employers use employment agencies to assist in locating jobs for employees who are being discharged. This assistance is more likely to be provided for managers of long tenure or for executives being terminated because of organizational down-sizing or restructuring or because they don't fit a changed corporate identity.[53] Rather than being called a discharge, a termination under such conditions is often referred to as **outplacement.**

Human resources vice-presidents who were asked to list the primary reasons for providing outplacement services gave the following responses: concern for the well-being of employees; the need for the organization to protect itself against age-discrimination and fair employment practice lawsuits; competition from other organizations offering such services; and the psychological effect on remaining employees.[54] The study also showed that outplacement consultants assist employees being terminated in a variety of ways. In addition to helping reduce their anger and grief, outplacement consultants can help these persons regain self-confidence and begin searching in earnest for a new job. Since many terminated workers have been out of the job market for some time, they may lack the knowledge and skill needed to look for a job. Outplacement specialists can coach them in how to develop contacts, how to probe for job openings through systematic letter writing and telephone campaigns, and how to handle employment interviews and salary negotiations.

APPEALING DISCIPLINARY ACTIONS

With growing frequency, organizations are taking steps to protect employees from arbitrary and inequitable treatment by their supervisors. These organizations are placing particular emphasis on creating a climate in which employees are assured that they can voice their dissatisfaction with their superiors without fear of reprisal. This safeguard can be provided through the implementation of a formal procedure for appealing disciplinary actions.

Complaint Procedures in Nonunion Organizations

In organizations that are unionized, grievance procedures are stated in virtually all labor agreements. In nonunion organizations, however, employee complaint procedures are a relatively recent development. Employers' interest in these programs stems from their desire to meet employees' expectations for fair treatment in the workplace while guaranteeing them due process, in the hope of minimizing wrongful discharge suits. Some organizations champion these procedures as an avenue for upward communication for employees and as a way to gauge the temperament of the work force. Others view these systems as a way to resolve minor problems before they mushroom into major issues, thus leading to improved employee morale and productivity.[55]

The appeal procedures that will be described in this chapter are the step-review system, the peer-review system, the use of a hearing officer, the open-door policy, and the use of an ombudsman.

STEP-REVIEW SYSTEMS As Figure 16–8 illustrates, a **step-review system** is based on a preestablished set of steps—normally four—for the review of an employee complaint by successively higher levels of management. These procedures are patterned after the union grievance systems we will discuss in Chapter 18. For example, they normally require that the employee's complaint be formalized as a written statement, and managers at each step are required to provide a full response to the complaint within a specified time period, perhaps three to five working days.

An employee is sometimes allowed to bypass the meeting with his or her immediate supervisor if the employee fears reprisal from this person. Unlike appeal systems in unionized organizations, however, nonunion appeal procedures ordinarily do not provide for a neutral third party—such as an arbitrator—to serve as the judge of last resort.[56] In the majority of step-review systems, the organization's president, chief executive officer, vice-president, or HR director acts as the final

FIGURE 16–8 CONVENTIONAL STEP-REVIEW APPEAL PROCEDURE

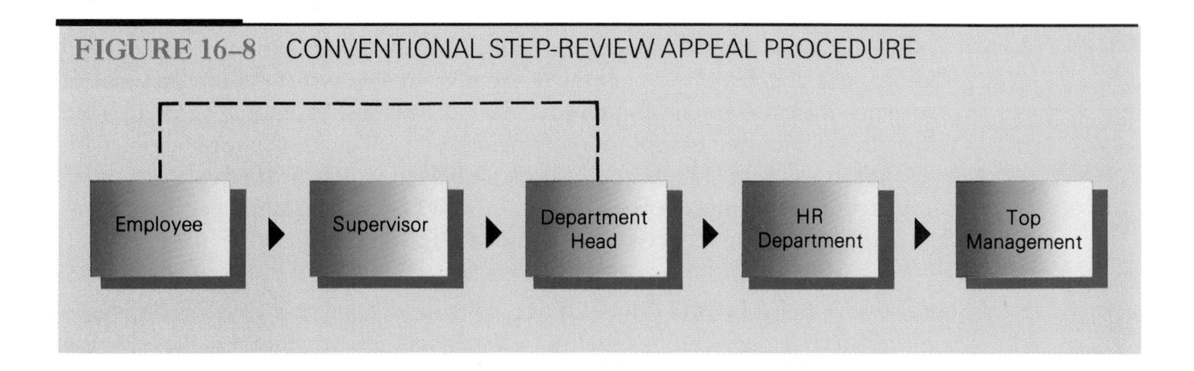

authority, and this person's decision is not appealable. Some organizations give employees assistance in preparing their complaint cases. For example, an employee who desires it may be able to get advice and counsel from a designated person in the HR department before discussing the issue with management.

Unfortunately, step-review systems may not yield their intended benefits. Employees can have negative attitudes toward the system adopted in their organization. They may believe that management is slow in responding to complaints and that management's response often does not solve the problem. Furthermore, employees may believe that, regardless of organization policy forbidding reprisal, supervisors would still hold it against them if they exercised their rights as spelled out in the step-review system. All these concerns do not lead to the conclusion that all step-review systems are ineffective, but rather that management must take special precautions to ensure the systems work and provide the benefits intended. We offer the following suggestions to employers to make their step-review systems successful:

1. Consult employees when designing the complaint system. Commitment to the process is enhanced when employees participate in its design.
2. Train supervisors in handling complaints.
3. Handle complaints in a timely manner.
4. Make sure that all employees know how to use the complaint procedure, and *encourage* them to use the system when they feel aggrieved.
5. Handle cases in a fair manner, and assure employees that they need not fear reprisal for filing complaints.

PEER-REVIEW SYSTEMS A **peer-review system,** also called a **complaint committee** or **tribunal,** is composed of equal numbers of employee representatives and management appointees. Employee representatives are normally elected by secret ballot by their co-workers for a rotating term, whereas management representatives are assigned, also on a rotating basis. A peer-review system functions as a jury since its members weigh evidence, consider arguments, and, after deliberation, vote independently to render a final decision.[57]

Organizations such as Federal Express, Northrop Corporation, Polaroid, and Citicorp consider one of the benefits of the peer-review system to be the sense of justice that it creates among employees. The peer-review system can be used as the sole method for resolving employee complaints, or it can be used in conjunction with a step-review system. For example, if an employee is not satisfied with management's action at step one or two in the step-review system, the employee can submit the complaint to the peer-review committee for final resolution.

USE OF A HEARING OFFICER The use of a hearing officer is ordinarily confined to large organizations, such as a state government, where employees may be represented by unions. The **hearing officer** holds a full-time position with an organization but assumes a neutral role when deciding cases between an aggrieved employee and management. Hearing officers are technically a part of and paid by the organization; however, they function independently from other managers and occupy a special place in the organizational hierarchy. Their success rests on their being perceived as neutral, highly competent, and completely unbiased in handling employee complaints. They hear cases upon request, almost always made by the employee. After considering the evidence and facts presented, they render decisions or awards that are normally final and binding on both sides. Like the peer-review system, the hearing-officer system can be used by itself or as part of a step-review procedure.

OPEN-DOOR POLICY The **open-door policy** is an old standby for settling employee complaints. In fact, most managers, regardless of whether their organization has adopted a formal open-door policy, profess to maintain one for their employees. The traditional open-door policy identifies various levels of management above the immediate supervisor that an aggrieved employee may contact, and the levels may extend as high as a vice-president, president, or chief executive officer. Typically the person who acts as "the court of last resort" is the HR director or a senior staff official.

The problems with an open-door policy are well documented. Two of its major weaknesses are the unwillingness of managers to listen honestly to employee complaints, and employees' reluctance to approach managers with their complaints. As an employee once told the authors of this text, "My manager has an open-door policy but the door is only open one inch." Obviously this employee felt he had little opportunity to get through to his manager. Other problems are attributed to this system as well. The open-door policy generally fails to guarantee consistent decision making since what is fair to one manager may seem unfair to another. Higher-level managers tend to support supervisors for fear of undermining the latter's authority. And, as a system of justice, open-door policies lack credibility with employees.[58] Still, the open-door policy is likely to be successful where it is supported by all levels of management and where management works to establish a reputation for being fair and open-minded.

OMBUDSMAN SYSTEM An **ombudsman** is a designated individual from whom employees may seek counsel for the resolution of their complaints.[59] The ombudsman listens to an employee's complaint and attempts to resolve it by mediating a solution between the employee and the supervisor. This individual works cooperatively with both sides to reach a settlement, often employing a clinical approach to problem solving. Since the ombudsman has no authority to finalize a solution to the problem, compromises are highly possible and all concerned tend to feel satisfied with the outcome.

The use of an ombudsman to resolve complaints has received increased acceptance. While ombudsmen have been used more commonly to protect individuals from abuses by government agencies, they are also being used more in educational and other nonprofit organizations to assist employees in resolving their problems. Ombudsmen are found in some private corporations, too. Xerox and General Electric are examples of two corporations that have had considerable success with them.

To function successfully, ombudsmen must be able to operate in an atmosphere of confidentiality that does not threaten the security of the managers or subordinates who are involved in a complaint. While ombudsmen do not have power to overrule the decision made by an employee's supervisor, they should be able to appeal the decision up the line if they believe an employee is not being treated fairly. Apart from helping to achieve equity for employees, ombudsmen can help to provide management with a check on itself.

Complaint Procedures in Government Organizations

Public organizations have traditionally offered as many as three appeals procedures by which employees can seek redress for their complaints. First, an employee might appeal a disciplinary action to a civil service board or merit commission. A decision by this body may be appealed to the courts. Second, public agencies that have collective bargaining contracts with unions or employee associations have formalized grievance procedures specified in the labor agreement. As a third option, public agencies have implemented nonunion complaint procedures for the adjudication of specific employee complaints.

In a study examining nonunion complaint procedures in 22 public-sector organizations, the predominant method of complaint adjustment was the step-review system used either alone or in combination with a peer-review committee.[60] In a city agency, for example, the step-review procedure preceded the peer-review committee where "the Grievance Committee is a neutral administrative hearing board and shall be composed of four city employees (two supervisory employees and two non-supervisory employees) to be randomly selected. A separate committee will normally be designated for each grievance."[61] Decisions resulting in a tie or based on a majority vote are reviewable by a final agency representative—an agency head, HR officer, or city manager. Interestingly, government agencies are careful to exempt specific issues from the complaint procedure, including employment status, position classification, salaries and benefits, civil service examination and results, and employee performance ratings. Employees with complaints in these areas may use other governmental appeal procedures to seek redress.

REDUCING COMPLAINTS

The most effective way to reduce complaints is to encourage them to be brought out into the open. Once expressed, they should be resolved quickly in a mutually satisfactory manner. The HR department may uncover evidence of dissatisfaction through the analysis of statistical data that it compiles or through its direct communication with employees. However, immediate supervisors who are in continual contact with employees are in a better position to draw out and listen to complaints. For this reason it is important for supervisors to create the type of climate and rapport that will encourage their subordinates to speak up and discuss anything that may be bothering them without fear of provoking resentment.

Symptoms of Complaints

Usually the complaints that are the most difficult for managers to resolve are those that employees are unable or unwilling to express. These complaints may be evidenced by such symptoms as sullenness, moodiness, tardiness, indifference, insubordination, or a decline in quality and quantity of work. The manager who can interpret these symptoms correctly will be more successful in resolving complaints. Such results can be achieved with an approach aimed at diagnosing the causes underlying the symptoms. With many complaints, the symptoms may represent only the tip of the iceberg.

Causes of Complaints

The fact that complaints may be the result of more than one cause can make them difficult to diagnose and handle. Some of the causes of complaints include those relating to the labor agreement, to the employee's job, and to problems of a personal nature.

CAUSES RELATING TO THE LABOR AGREEMENT Many grievances related to the labor agreement result from omissions or ambiguities in its provisions (also see Chapter 18). The grievances may also result from union attempts to make changes in the agreement that it was unable to win at the bargaining table. At times, union representatives may solicit grievances simply to demonstrate to employees what the union can do for them or to divert the attention of members from union weaknesses or leadership deficiencies. Court decisions, as we have noted, also have made union officers more likely to process grievances that previously might have been dropped.

CAUSES RELATING TO THE JOB Job-related complaints may stem from the failure of employees either to meet the demands of their jobs or to gain satisfaction from performing them. Employees who are placed in the wrong job or who lack adequate orientation, training, or supervision are more likely to perform unsatisfactorily. This can cause them to become dissatisfied with their employment and be a problem to their supervisors. Job-related complaints, therefore, often are a result of how well individuals are able to meet the demands of their jobs. The supervisor's attitude and behavior toward individual workers and the union may also be a cause for job-related complaints. Supervisors who play favorites, who fail to live up to promises, or who are too demanding are likely to encounter many complaints from workers.

CAUSES RELATING TO PERSONAL PROBLEMS Poor health, drug or alcohol abuse, family illness, marital discord, or financial difficulties are typical personal problems that employees may bring with them to the job. The frustration resulting from these problems may cause employees to find fault with their jobs or with others around them. Their expressed complaints thus may not accurately reflect the real cause of their dissatisfactions.

Complaints stemming from personal problems frequently cannot be resolved by changing jobs or employment conditions. Since the cause of these problems is not job-related, corrective action requires the individual to make the necessary personal adjustments. Therefore, an important part of every manager's job is to counsel troubled subordinates and to help them to recognize and to work out solutions to their personal problems. This can be done through the counseling process, which was discussed in Chapter 15.

SUMMARY

Employees have rights and expectations in the employment relationship. Their rights may include safeguards for keeping their job, and their expectations may include those of being treated fairly and equitably by their employer. Employers, too, have rights and responsibilities relating to employee conduct. Managers have the right to expect employees to perform effectively, to respond to direction, and to obey organizational rules and regulations. When either party disregards the rights of the other, problems may arise that may lead to employer-imposed discipline or employee complaints and lawsuits. When employees make a formal complaint, government agencies, the courts, or managers may grant them additional job rights that may restrict management's freedom to act in the future.

Restrictions on management's authority have forced organizations to take greater precautions and a more constructive approach in disciplinary actions. Greater emphasis has also been placed on the correct use of progressive discipline or newer positive-discipline procedures. The focus is on coping with the unsatisfactory performance and dissatisfactions of employees before the problems become major. In taking HR actions, management should be aware of the basis on which its actions may be reversed by other managers through appeal systems or by a court of law. Any action it takes, therefore, must be in accordance with organizational and legal jurisprudence, as well as sound principles of human relations.

DISCUSSION QUESTIONS

1. Define the employment-at-will doctrine. What are the three major court exceptions to the doctrine?
2. What are the legislative and court restrictions to employer drug testing in both the private and the public sector?
3. If you were asked to develop a policy on discipline, what topics would you believe should be covered in the policy?
4. What should be the purpose of an investigative interview, and what approach should be taken in conducting it?
5. Discuss why documentation is so important to the disciplinary process. What constitutes correct documentation?
6. Why are some employers making use of outplacement consultants to assist them with terminations?
7. What do you think would constitute an effective nonunion appeal system? What benefits would you expect from such a system?
8. If you were asked to rule on a discharge case, what facts would you analyze in deciding whether to uphold or reverse the employer's action?

MINI-CASE 16–1 The Whistle-Blower's Dilemma

Tom Corbin has worked as a manager at Harbor Electric for 11 years. Shortly after being promoted to director of the electric generator division, Tom made a discovery that dramatically changed his managerial career. While cleaning out some old files, he stumbled across a seven-year-old report that clearly documented some design flaws in the company's large industrial R-1 electric generator. While these flaws presented no safety hazards, they held the potential to increase construction costs, creating cost overruns for the purchaser. Also, though breakdowns would probably not be immediate, the flaws made the units more susceptible to mechanical failure. If breakdowns occurred after the warranty period had expired, the costly repairs would be paid for by the purchasing organization. The R-1 generators were sold mainly to utility companies, so cost overruns or the cost of mechanical failures would ultimately be passed on to consumers.

Tom was genuinely upset by the report and quickly decided to show it to Robert Medlock, the vice-president of manufacturing. Their meeting was brief and to the point. Mr. Medlock expressed surprise and dismay at the report but seemed to express no great desire to correct the problems. While not denying the design flaws, Mr. Medlock explained that the R-1 generator was basically a well-designed unit that offered an excellent value to purchasers. He further noted that the success of the company rested largely on sales of the generator and to admit any design flaws at this time would be catastrophic to future sales. Public exposure could lead to complaints from consumer groups and government regulators while providing competitors with damaging product information. When Tom argued that Harbor was essentially "ripping off" utility companies and consumers, he was told to cool down and to forget he ever saw the report. Tom replied that the report made him sick and that he couldn't believe Harbor would risk its reputation by selling generators with potentially costly design flaws. He concluded the meeting by saying that he had joined the company because of its honesty and dedication to responsible customer relations, but now he had serious doubts.

Tom stormed out of Mr. Medlock's office. On his way back to the generator division, he considered calling the state utility commission to report the design flaws. He clearly realized what public knowledge of the problems would do to sales of the R-1 generator. He also considered the consequences of reporting the design flaws for his career with Harbor Electric.

QUESTIONS

1. Discuss all the possible consequences of reporting the design flaws to the state utility commission.
2. What do you think would be a proper course of action to correct the design flaws in the R-1 generator?

MINI-CASE 16–2 The Absent Employee

Ever since she was hired by Beach Mining Company, Mary Schwartz had been an absenteeism problem. According to HR department records, in no year since 1982 had Mary been absent less than 3 percent of her total working hours. In 1985 and in 1986 she was absent 17 percent and 22 percent of the time, respectively. Her worst year was 1988, when she was absent 37.6 percent of the time. However, unlike other absent employees, Mary was always absent because of genuine and verifiable illnesses or work-related accidents. Mary's supervisor had talked to her periodically about her attendance problem, but she was never given an official warning notice—oral or written—that she would be fired if her attendance record did not improve.

Finally, on July 19, 1990, her supervisor, with concurrence from the department manager, terminated her employment for "unsatisfactory attendance." Mary did not dispute the attendance record; however, she filed a grievance through the company's nonunion complaint procedure alleging that management did not discharge her according to the organization's published disciplinary policy. She pointed to the section in the policy manual which states, "Employees will be warned for absenteeism before they are terminated." Mary maintained that she was never officially warned as required. Management replied that Mary was well aware of her absentee problem but that warning her would have served no purpose since she was unable to prevent her continued illnesses from occurring.

SOURCE: Based on an arbitration case heard by George W. Bohlander. Names have been changed.

QUESTIONS

1. Evaluate the arguments of Mary Schwartz and management in this case.
2. If you were a member of the company's peer-review complaint committee, how would you vote in this case? What facts would cause you to vote this way?

NOTES AND REFERENCES

1. "Is Your Boss Spying on You?" *Business Week* (January 15, 1990): 71. See also Michael B. Bixby, "Was It an Accident or Murder? New Thrusts in Corporate Criminal Liability for Workplace Deaths," *Labor Law Journal* 41, no. 7 (July 1990): 417–424.
2. Jonathan S. Leonard, "The Changing Face of Employees and Employment Regulation," *California Management Review* 31, no. 2 (Winter 1989): 38.
3. Martha I. Finney, "A Game of Skill or Chance?" *Personnel Administrator* 33, no. 3 (March 1988): 40.
4. James R. Redeker, *Employee Discipline: Policies and Practices* (Washington, DC: Bureau of National Affairs, 1989), 21. This book gives an excellent discussion of the rights and responsibilities of employers and employees in the employment relationship while also providing a comprehensive discussion of employee discipline.
5. Ibid., 25–38.
6. Sandra Perry Henry, "Can You Recognize the Wrongful Discharge?" *Labor Law Journal* 40, no. 3 (March 1989): 168–176.
7. *Adair* v. *United States,* 2078 U.S. 161 (1908).
8. Gary L. Tidwell, "Employment at Will: Limitations in the Public Sector," *Public Personnel Management* 13, no. 3 (Fall 1984): 293–300.
9. David L. Beacon and Angel Gomez III, "How to Prevent Wrongful Termination Lawsuits," *Personnel* 65, no. 2 (February 1988): 71.
10. James L. Payne and Kevin M. Smith, "Establishing the Boundaries of Wrongful Discharge: California's *Foley* Decision," *Employee Relations Law Journal* 16, no. 1 (Summer 1989): 39.
11. Daniel J. Koys, Steven Briggs, and Jay Grenig, "State Court Disparity on Employment-at-Will," *Personnel Psychology* 40, no. 3 (Autumn 1987): 565–576.
12. *Foley* v. *Interactive Data Corporation,* 47 Cal. 3d 654, 254 Cal. Rptr. 211 (1988).
13. "Management Attorney Says *Foley* Will Aid Discharged Employees," *BNA's Employee Relations Weekly* 7 (October 23, 1989): 1323.
14. Ibid., 1323.
15. M. Ronald Buckley and William Weitzel, "Employing at Will," *Personnel Administrator* 33, no. 8 (August 1988): 78.
16. Raymond L. Hogler, *The Employment Relationship: Law and Policy* (New York: Ardsley House, 1989), 6.
17. *Toussaint* v. *Blue Cross and Blue Shield of Michigan,* 408 Mich. 579, 292 N.W. 2d 880 (1980).
18. Philip R. Voluck and Michael J. Hanlon, "Contract Disclaimers in Policy Documents," *Personnel Journal* 66, no. 8 (August 1987): 123–131.
19. "Privacy," *Business Week* (March 28, 1988): 61.
20. Ibid., 61.
21. "Workplace Drug Testing Evolves As Courts, Government Define Limits," *BNA's Employee Relations Weekly* 7, no. 32 (August 7, 1989): 5.
22. Ibid., 6.
23. *Harmon* v. *Thornburgh,* CA, DC No. 88-5265 (July 30, 1989); *Treasury Employees Union* v. *Von Raab,* US SupCt No. 86-18796 (March 21, 1989); *City of Annapolis* v. *United Food and Commercial Workers Local 400,* Md. CtApp No. 38 (November 6, 1989); and *Skinner* v. *Railway Labor Executives Association,* US SupCt No. 87-1555 (March 21, 1989).
24. Robert M. Preer, Jr., "The Impact of Drug Testing," *Labor Law Journal* 40, no. 1 (January 1989): 50–57.

25. "Drug Testing 'Here to Stay,' Says NIDA Applied Research Director," *BNA's Employee Relations Weekly* 7 (August 7, 1989): 1007.

26. Susan R. Mendelsohn and Kathryn K. Morrison, "Employee Searches," *Personnel* 65, no. 7 (July 1988): 24.

27. Ibid., 20–27.

28. "Is Your Boss Spying on You?" 74.

29. Denis Collins, "Plant Closings: Establishing Legal Obligations," *Labor Law Journal* 40, no. 2 (February 1989): 67.

30. Ibid., 68.

31. Joe Pasqualetto, "Staffing, Privacy, and Security Issues," *Personnel Journal* 67, no. 9 (September 1988): 84.

32. Suzanne Cook, "Privacy Rights: Whose Life Is It Anyway?" *Personnel Administrator* 32, no. 4 (April 1987): 64.

33. "Most Employers Surveyed Give Employees Restricted Access to Personnel Files," *BNA's Employee Relations Weekly* 7, no. 30 (July 24, 1989): 936.

34. Edward L. Harrison, "Why Supervisors Fail to Discipline," *Supervisory Management* 30, no. 4 (April 1985): 18–22.

35. Caleb S. Atwood, "Discharge Now, Pay Later? Establishing Reasonable Rules Can Keep You Out of Hot Water," *Personnel Administrator* 34, no. 8 (August 1989): 92–93.

36. Donald C. Mosley, Leon C. Megginson, and Paul H. Pietri, *Supervisory Management: The Art of Working With and Through People,* 2d ed. (Cincinnati: South-Western, 1989), 319.

37. Ira G. Asherman and Sandra Lee Vance, "Documentation: A Tool for Effective Management," *Personnel Journal* 60, no. 8 (August 1981): 641–643.

38. Karen L. Vinton, "Documentation That Gets Results," *Personnel* 67, no. 2 (February 1990): 42–46. See also Daniel M. Shideler, "Documenting Disciplinary Situations," *Supervisory Management* 10, no. 2 (July 1989): 15–20.

39. *NLRB* v. *Weingarten, Inc.*, 95 S. Ct. 959 (1975) 402 U.S. 251, 43 L. Ed. 2nd 171.

40. Ibid.

41. 274 NLRB No. 55 (February 22, 1985).

42. John G. Kruchko and Lawrence E. Dube, Jr., "New Rights for Non-Union Workers," *Personnel* 60, no. 6 (November–December 1983): 59–64. See also Dave Israel, "The Weingarten Case Sets Precedent for Co-Employee Representation," *Personnel Administrator* 28, no. 2 (February 1983): 23–26.

43. Dan Cameron, "The When, Why, and How of Discipline," *Personnel Journal* 23, no. 7 (July 1984): 37–39. See also Brian S. Klars and Hoyt N. Wheeler, "Managerial Decision Making About Employee Discipline: A Policy-Capturing Approach," *Personnel Psychology* 43, no. 1 (Spring 1990): 117–134.

44. James R. Redeker, "Discipline, Part 1: Progressive Systems Work Only by Accident," *Personnel* 62, no. 10 (October 1985): 8–12.

45. Redeker, "Discipline, Part 2: The Nonpunitive Approach Works by Design," *Personnel* 62, no. 11 (November 1985): 7–14. See also Alan W. Bryant, "Replacing Punitive Disciplines with a Positive Approach," *Personnel Administrator* 29, no. 2 (February 1984): 79–87.

46. Redeker, "Discipline, Part 2," 8.

47. "Punishing Workers with a Day Off," *Business Week* (June 16, 1986): 80.

48. David N. Campbell, R. L. Fleming, and Richard C. Grote, "Discipline Without Punishment—At Last," *Harvard Business Review* 63, no. 4 (July–August 1985): 162–174. See also Redeker, "Discipline, Part 2," 9–14.

49. Lawrence E. Dube, Jr., "Planning for the Defensible Discharges," *Management Review* 75, no. 3 (March 1986): 44–48.

50. For an expanded discussion of just cause, see Frank Elkouri and Edna Asher Elkouri, *How Arbitration Works*, 4th ed. (Washington, DC: Bureau of National Affairs, 1985), 650–654.

51. William E. Fulmer, "How Do You Say, 'You're Fired'?" *Business Horizons* 29, no. 1 (January–February 1986): 31–38. See also Steve Buck, "To Fire or Not to Fire," *Supervisory Management* 31, no. 2 (February 1986): 30–33.

52. Cecil G. Howard, "Strategic Guidelines for Terminating Employees," *Personnel Administrator* 33, no. 4 (April 1988): 106–109.

53. Lewis Newman, "Outplacement the Right Way," *Personnel Administrator* 34, no. 2 (February 1989): 83–86.

54. Edmund B. Piccolino, "Outplacement: The View from HR," *Personnel* 65, no. 3 (March 1988): 24–27.

55. George W. Bohlander and Harold C. White, "Building Bridges: Nonunion Employee Grievance Systems," *Personnel* 65, no. 7 (July 1988): 62–66.

56. Douglas M. McCabe, "Corporate Nonunion Grievance Arbitration Systems: A Procedural Analysis," *Labor Law Journal* 40, no. 7 (July 1989): 432–437.

57. Douglas M. McCabe, *Corporate Nonunion Complaint Procedures and Systems* (New York: Praeger, 1988), 79.

58. Steve Ventura and Eric Harvey, "Peer Review: Trusting Employees to Solve Problems," *Management Review* 77, no. 2 (January 1988): 48.

59. James T. Ziegehfoss, Mary Rowe, Lee Robbins, and Robert Munzenrider, "Corporate Ombudsmen," *Personnel Journal* 68, no. 3 (March 1989): 76–79.

60. George W. Bohlander, "Public Sector Independent Grievance Systems: Methods and Procedures," *Public Personnel Management* 18, no. 3 (Fall 1989): 339–354. See also George W. Bohlander and Ken Behringer, "Public Sector Nonunion Complaint Procedures: Current Research," *Labor Law Journal* 41, no. 8 (August 1990): 563–568.

61. Ibid., 349.

PART SIX

Strengthening Employee-Management Relations

The two chapters in Part Six discuss employee representation by labor unions. Chapter 17 focuses on issues involved in the unionization of employees, including the legal statutes governing this very specific area of HR management. Included in Chapter 17 is a discussion of the many challenges that currently face the union movement. Chapter 18 explores the relationship between labor and management once employees elect to unionize and a labor agreement is negotiated between the two parties. Recent trends in collective bargaining are reviewed, as are programs to enhance labor–management cooperation. An understanding of labor relations and its processes will improve the supervisory skills of managers in both union and nonunion enterprises.

CHAPTER 17

The Dynamics of Labor Relations

After reading this chapter you will be able to:

1. *Identify the key elements of the labor relations process.*
2. *Cite the reasons why employees join unions.*
3. *Describe the process by which unions organize employees and gain recognition as their bargaining agent.*
4. *Describe the composition of organized labor and the functions labor unions perform at the national and local levels.*
5. *Identify the principal federal laws that provide the framework for labor relations.*
6. *Identify the differences between private-sector and public-sector labor relations.*
7. *Discuss some of the effects that changing conditions are having on labor organizations.*
8. *Define the key terms in the chapter.*

TERMS TO IDENTIFY

Mention the word ***union*** and most people will have some opinion—positive or negative—regarding U.S. labor organizations. To some, the word evokes images of labor–management unrest—grievances, violence, picketing, or boycotts. To others, the word represents industrial democracy, fairness, opportunity, or equal representation. Many think of the word as simply a synonym for *strike*.

Regardless of one's attitudes toward them, since the early industrialization of the United States unions have been an important force shaping organizational practices, legislation, and political thought. Today, unions continue to be of interest because of their influence on organizational productivity, U.S. competitiveness, the development of labor law, and HR policies and practices. Like business organizations themselves, unions are undergoing changes in both operation and philosophy. Labor–management cooperative programs, union company buyouts, and union representation on an organization's board of directors are illustrative of labor's new role in society.

In spite of the long history and continuing importance of unions, however, the intricacies of labor relations remain a mystery to many individuals. Therefore, this chapter will be concerned with describing the labor relations process, the reasons why workers join labor organizations, the structure and leadership of labor unions, government regulation of labor relations, and contemporary challenges to labor organizations.

Unions and other labor organizations can affect significantly the ability of managers to direct and control the various functions of HRM. For example, union seniority provisions in the labor contract may influence who is selected for job promotions or training programs. Pay rates may be determined through union negotiations, or unions may impose restrictions on management's employee appraisal methods. Therefore, it is essential that managers understand how unions operate and be thoroughly familiar with the growing body of law governing labor relations. Labor relations is thus a highly specialized function of HRM to which employers must give appropriate consideration.

THE LABOR RELATIONS PROCESS

Individually, employees may be able to exercise relatively little power in their relations with employers. The treatment and benefits they receive depend in large part on how their employers view their worth to the organization. Of course, if they believe they are not being treated fairly, they have the option of quitting. However, another way to correct the situation is to organize and bargain with the employer collectively. When employees pursue this direction, the labor relations process begins. As Figure 17–1 illustrates, the **labor relations process** consists of a logical sequence of four events: (1) workers desiring collective representation, (2) union organizing campaigns, (3) collective negotiations, and (4) contract administration. Laws and administrative rulings influence each of the separate events by granting special privileges to or imposing defined constraints on workers, managers, and union officials.[1]

Why Employees Unionize

The majority of research on why employees unionize comes from the study of blue-collar employees in the private sector. These studies generally conclude that employees unionize because of economic needs, because of a general dissatisfaction with managerial policies and practices, and/or as a way to fulfill social and status needs.[2] They see unionism as a way to achieve results they cannot achieve acting individually.

It should be pointed out that some employees join unions because of the union-shop provisions of the labor agreement. In states where it is permitted, a **union shop** is a provision of the labor agreement that requires employees to join as a condition of employment. Even when compelled to join, however, many employees accept the concept of unionism once they become involved in the union as a member.

ECONOMIC NEEDS Whether or not a union can become the bargaining agent for a group of employees will be influenced by the employees' degree of dissatisfaction, if any, with their employment conditions. It will depend also on whether the employees perceive the union as likely to be effective in improving these conditions. Dissatisfaction with wages, benefits, and working conditions appears to provide the strongest reason to join a union. This point is supported by several research studies which found that both union members and non-members have their highest expectations of union performance regarding the "bread and butter" issues of collective

FIGURE 17–1 THE LABOR RELATIONS PROCESS

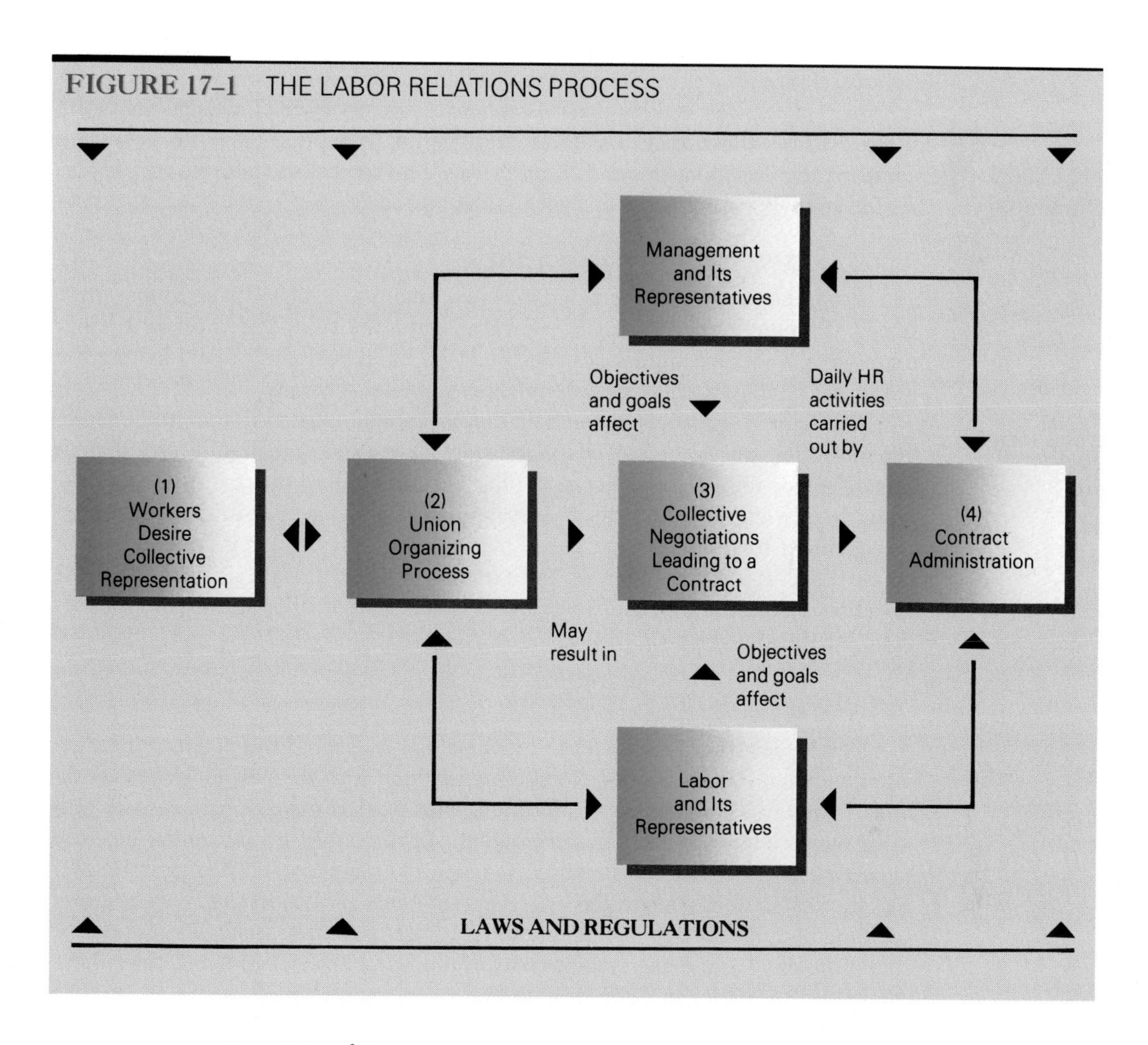

bargaining.[3] It is these traditional issues of wages and benefits on which unions are built.

DISSATISFACTION WITH MANAGEMENT Employees may seek unionization when they perceive that managerial practices regarding promotion, transfer, shift assignment, or other job-related policies are administered in an unfair or biased manner. Employees cite favoritism shown by supervisors as a major reason for joining unions. This is particularly true when the favoritism concerns the HR areas of discipline, promotion, and wage increases.

The failure of employers to give employees an opportunity to participate in decisions affecting their welfare may also encourage union membership. In a highly publicized organizing effort by the United Auto Workers at the Nissan plant in

Management meets employees' needs when it allows them an active role in resolving work issues.

Smyrna, Tennessee, the union lost the election because workers were satisfied with the voice in decision making that Nissan's participatory style of management gave them. Nissan's director of human resources noted, "We pride ourselves in being a company that functions in a participatory way. The vote was a statement of support for the strongly participatory management at Nissan."[4]

SOCIAL AND STATUS CONCERNS Employees whose needs for status and recognition are being frustrated may join unions as a means of satisfying these needs. Through their union, they have an opportunity to fraternize with other employees who have similar desires, interests, problems, and gripes. Joining the union also enables them to put latent leadership talents to use.

The limited studies conducted on employee unionization in the public sector generally find public employees unionizing for reasons similar to those of their private-sector counterparts. For example, one study found that extrinsic factors—higher wages and benefits, job security, and protection against arbitrary and unfair management treatment—were the primary motives for unionization among state employees.[5] In the final analysis, the extent to which employees perceive that the benefits of joining a union outweigh the costs associated with membership is likely to be the deciding factor.[6]

Maintaining Nonunion Status

Employees who do not wish to unionize may be spared this action if management works to minimize employees' dissatisfaction with their employment conditions.[7] Effective two-way communication helps to alert management to problems when they occur and to take corrective action.[8] Furthermore, it enables management to become aware of any outside efforts to unionize employees. Highlights in HRM 1 lists the key strategies identified by HR practitioners and academicians as means of avoiding unionization. It is important to recognize that these strategies address the conditions cited as the main reasons why workers unionize. In addition, since these conditions are under the direct control of management, they can be unilaterally changed to help prevent unionism.[9]

Organizing Campaigns

Once employees desire to unionize, a formal organizing campaign may be started either by a union organizer or by employees acting on their own behalf. Contrary to popular belief, most organizing campaigns are begun by employees rather than union organizers. Large national unions like the United Auto Workers, the United Brotherhood of Carpenters, the United Steelworkers, and the Teamsters, however, have formal organizing departments whose purpose is to identify organizing opportunities and launch organizing campaigns.

Since such campaigns can be expensive, union leaders carefully evaluate their chances of success and the possible benefits to be gained from their efforts. Important in this evaluation is the employer's vulnerability to unionization.[10] Union

HIGHLIGHTS IN HRM

1 UNION AVOIDANCE STRATEGIES

- Competitive wages and benefits based on labor market comparisons and salary and benefit surveys.
- Supervisors trained in progressive human relations skills, including employee motivation, job design, and employment law.
- Formal procedures to resolve employee complaints and grievances. These may include peer-review committees, step-review complaint systems, or open-door policies.
- Employee involvement in work decisions affecting job performance or the quality or quantity of the product or service provided.
- Attention to employee growth and development needs. Recognition of a work force that is growing older, more female, more militant, better educated, less patient, and more demanding.
- HR policies reflecting legal safeguards and the application of fairness and equity in employment conditions such as discipline, promotions, training, and layoffs.

leaders also consider the effect that allowing an employer to remain nonunion may have on the strength of their union within the area. A nonunion employer can impair a union's efforts to standardize employment conditions within an industry or geographic area, as well as weaken the union's bargaining power with employers it has unionized.

ORGANIZING STEPS Terry Moser, a Teamster organizer, once told the authors that the typical organizing campaign follows a series of progressive steps that can lead to employee representation. The organizing process as described by Moser normally includes the following steps:

1. Employee/union contact
2. Initial organizational meeting
3. Formation of in-house organizing committee
4. Election petition and voting preparation

Step 1. The first step begins when employees and union officials make contact to explore the possibility of unionization. During these discussions, employees will investigate the advantages of labor representation, and union officials will begin to gather information on employee needs, problems, and grievances. Labor organizers will also seek specific information about the employer's financial health, supervisory styles, and organizational policies and practices. To win employee support, labor organizers must build a case *against* the employer and *for* the union.

Step 2. As an organizing campaign gathers momentum, the organizer will schedule an initial union meeting to attract more supporters. The organizer will use the information gathered in Step 1 to address employee needs and explain how the union can secure these goals. Two additional purposes of organizational meetings are (1) to identify employees who can help the organizer direct the campaign and (2) to establish communication chains that reach all employees.

Step 3. The third important step in the organizing drive is to form an in-house organizing committee composed of employees willing to provide leadership to the campaign. The committee's role is to interest other employees in joining the union and in supporting its campaign. An important task of the committee is to have employees sign an **authorization card** (see Figure 17–2) indicating their willingness to be represented by a labor union in collective bargaining with their employer. The number of signed authorization cards demonstrates the potential strength of the labor union.[11] At least 30 percent of the employees must sign authorization cards before the National Labor Relations Board (NLRB) will hold a representation election.

Step 4. If a sufficient number of employees support the union drive, the organizer will proceed to the final step of the campaign. A representation petition will be filed with the NLRB, asking that a secret-ballot election be held to determine

FIGURE 17–2 A UNION AUTHORIZATION CARD

United Food & Commercial Workers International Union

Affiliated with AFL-CIO-CLC

AUTHORIZATION FOR REPRESENTATION

I hereby authorize the United Food & Commercial Workers International Union, AFL-CIO-CLC, or its chartered Local Union(s) to represent me for the purpose of collective bargaining.

(Print Name) (Date)

(Signature) (Home Phone)

(Home Address) (City) (State) (Zip)

(Employer's Name) (Address)

(Hire Date) (Type Work Performed) (Department)

Day Shift ____ Night Shift ____ Full Time ____ Part-Time ____

(Hourly Rate) (Day Off)

Would you participate in an organizing committee? Yes ____ No ____ if employees actually desire unionization. Before the election, a large publicity campaign will be directed toward employees, seeking their support and election votes. This is a period of intense emotions for the employees, the labor organization, and the employer.

EMPLOYER TACTICS In counteracting a union campaign, employers must not threaten employees with the loss of their jobs or with other dire consequences if they vote to unionize. However, within the limits permitted by the Taft-Hartley Act, employers can express their views about the disadvantages of being represented by a union. When possible, employers will stress the favorable employer–employee relationship they have experienced in the past without a union. Employers may emphasize any advantages in wages, benefits, or working conditions the employees may enjoy in comparison with those provided by organizations that are already unionized. "While you have a right to join a union," the employers may remind their employees, "you also have a right not to join one and to deal directly with the organization free from outside interference."

Employers may also emphasize any unfavorable publicity the organizing union has received with respect to corruption or the abuse of members' legal rights. Employers may use government statistics to show that unions commit large numbers of unfair labor practices. For example, 10,813 unfair labor practices were charged against unions in 1989; the majority (7,575) alleged illegal restraint and coercion of employees.[12]

If the union has engaged in a number of strikes, employers may stress this fact to warn employees about possible work disruption and loss of income.[13] Also, employers are not likely to fail to point out the cost to employees of union dues and special assessments, along with any false promises made by the union in the course of its campaign. Furthermore, employers may initiate legal action should union members and/or their leaders engage in any unfair labor practices during the organizing effort.

Employees working for the same organization often have different interests when negotiating labor agreements.

How Employees Become Unionized

The employees to be organized constitute the bargaining unit to be covered by the labor agreement. The NLRB defines a **bargaining unit** as a group of two or more employees who have common employment interests and conditions and may reasonably be grouped together for purposes of collective bargaining.[14] If an employer and a union cannot agree on who should be in the bargaining unit, an "appropriate" bargaining unit will be determined by the NLRB based on a community of interest among employees within the unit. For example, in hospitals, the NLRB has designated separate units for nurses, technicians, doctors, maintenance employees, office clerical personnel, all other nonprofessionals, and guards.

EMPLOYER RECOGNITION Once a union has succeeded in signing up the required number of employees within the bargaining unit, the union may request recognition by the employer.[15] Typically, evidence is produced in the form of authorization cards signed by employees. If no other union is competing to represent the employees, the employer at this point can simply agree to recognize the union and negotiate an agreement with it. However, if the employer believes that a majority of its employees do not want to belong to the union or if more than one union is attempting to gain recognition, the employer can insist that a representation election be held. This election will determine which union, if any, will represent the employees. The petition to hold representation elections usually is initiated by the union although employers, under certain conditions, have the right to petition for one.

TYPES OF NLRB REPRESENTATION ELECTIONS The NLRB offers two election options. The first option, called a **consent election**, is used when the petition to hold a representation election is not contested. Here there are no disagreements between the union and the employer; therefore, no preelection hearing is needed. The NLRB sets a date to hold the election, and voting is conducted by secret ballot. Should the request for representation be contested by the employer or should more than one union be seeking recognition, then *preelection hearings* must be held. This second option is called a **stipulation election**. At the preelection hearings several important issues will be discussed, including the NLRB's jurisdiction to hold the election, determination of the bargaining unit (if contested by the parties), and the voting choice(s) to appear on the ballot. The ballot lists the names of the unions that are seeking recognition and also provides for the choice of "no union."

After the election is held, the winning party will be determined based on the number of actual votes, *not* on the number of members of the bargaining unit. For example, suppose the bargaining unit at XYZ Corporation comprised 100 employees, but only 27 employees voted in the election. The union receiving 14 "yes" votes among the 27 voting (a majority) would be declared the winner, and the union would bargain for all 100 employees.

If none of the available choices receives a majority of the votes, a runoff election must be conducted between the two top choices. Unless the majority votes "no union," the union that receives a majority of the votes in the initial or the runoff election is the one certified by the NLRB as the bargaining agent for a period of at least a year, or for the duration of the labor agreement. Once the union is certified, the employer is obligated to begin negotiations leading toward a labor agreement.

An important statistic in labor relations is the win/loss record of unions in certification elections. This statistic is often regarded as an indication of the general vitality of the union movement. As Figure 17–3 shows, from 1984 through 1988 unions consistently lost more than 50 percent of elections held by the NLRB. This contrasts sharply with the union win rate of 74.5 percent in 1950 and 60.2 percent in 1965. The conclusion can be drawn from Figure 17–3 that unions have lost much of their ability to unionize employers. However, as one study showed, when more

FIGURE 17–3 NLRB ELECTIONS—SELECTED YEARS

YEAR	ELECTIONS HELD	UNIONS WON	UNION PERCENTAGE WINS
1950	5,619	4,186	74.5
1955	4,215	2,849	67.6
1965	7,775	4,880	60.2
1975	8,577	4,134	48.2
1984	4,436	1,861	42.0
1985	4,614	1,956	42.4
1986	4,520	1,951	43.2
1987	4,069	1,788	43.9
1988	4,153	1,921	46.3
1989	4,413	2,059	46.7

SOURCE: Annual Reports of the National Labor Relations Board, U.S. Government Printing Office, Washington, DC.

than one union appears on the election ballot, unions are much more successful, with win rates as high as 90 percent in certain years.[16]

Impact on HRM

The unionization of employees can affect HRM in several ways. Perhaps most significant is the effect it can have on the prerogatives exercised by management in making decisions about employees. Furthermore, unionization restricts the freedom of management to formulate HR policy unilaterally and can challenge the authority of supervisors.

CHALLENGES TO MANAGEMENT PREROGATIVES Unions typically attempt to achieve greater participation in management decisions that affect their members. Specifically, these decisions may involve such issues as the subcontracting of work, work standards, and job content. Employers quite naturally seek to claim many of these decisions as their exclusive **management prerogatives**—decisions over which management claims exclusive rights. However, these prerogatives increasingly are subject to challenge and erosion by the union. They may be challenged at the bargaining table, through the grievance procedure, and through strikes.

BILATERAL FORMULATION OF HR POLICIES Some HR policies, such as those covering wages, work hours, work rules, and benefits, must be consistent with the terms of the labor agreement. When formulating these policies, management should consult with the union to gain the union's acceptance of them as well as its cooperation in administering them. Because unions are on the lookout for inconsistencies in the treatment of employees, a more centralized coordination in the enforcement of HR policies may be required. Such coordination provides a greater role for the HR staff.

POSSIBLE DILUTION OF SUPERVISORY AUTHORITY The focal point of the union's impact is at the operating level, where supervisors administer the terms of the labor agreement. These terms can determine what corrective action is to be taken in directing and in disciplining employees. When disciplining employees, supervisors must be certain they can demonstrate *just cause* for their actions, because these actions can be challenged by the union and the supervisor called as defendant during a grievance hearing. If the challenge is upheld, the supervisor's effectiveness in coping with subsequent disciplinary problems may be impaired.

STRUCTURES, FUNCTIONS, AND LEADERSHIP OF LABOR UNIONS

Unions that represent skilled craft workers, such as carpenters or masons, are called **craft unions.** Craft unions include the International Association of Iron Workers, the United Brotherhood of Carpenters, and the Plumbers. Unions that represent unskilled and semiskilled workers employed along industry lines are known as **industrial unions**. The American Union of Postal Workers is an industrial union, as is the United Auto Workers, the United Steelworkers, the United Rubber Workers, and the Office and Professional Employees International Union. While this distinction still exists, technological changes and competition among unions for members have helped to reduce it. Today skilled and unskilled workers, white-collar and blue-collar workers, and professional groups are being represented by both types of union.

Besides unions, there are also **employee associations** representing various groups of professional and white-collar employees. Examples of employee associations include the National Education Association, the Michigan State Employees Association, the American Nurses' Association, and the Air Line Pilots Association. In competing with unions, these associations, for all purposes, may function as unions and become just as aggressive as unions in representing members.

Regardless of their type, labor organizations are diverse organizations, each with its own method of governance and objectives. Furthermore, they have their own structures that serve to bind them together. For example, when describing labor organizations, most researchers divide them into three levels: (1) the American Federation of Labor and Congress of Industrial Organizations (AFL-CIO), (2) national unions, and (3) local unions belonging to a parent national union. Each level has its own purpose for existence, as well as its own operating policies and procedures.

Structure and Functions of the AFL-CIO

In 1955, the American Federation of Labor—composed largely of craft unions—and the Congress of Industrial Organizations—made up mainly of industrial unions—merged to form the AFL-CIO. The AFL-CIO is a federation of 83 autonomous national and international unions. Because the interests and organizing activities of these autonomous unions in the AFL-CIO do not always coincide, a chief advantage of belonging to the AFL-CIO is a provision that affords protection to member unions against "raiding" by other unions within the federation. A violation of this "no raiding" provision can lead to expulsion from the federation.

In effect, the AFL-CIO is the "House of Labor" that serves to present a united front on behalf of organized labor. Most major unions belong to this federation. The AFL-CIO claims a membership of almost 13.5 million members, or about 75 percent of all union members.[17] As Figure 17–4 shows, the AFL-CIO is composed of different trades and industrial departments that reflect the diversity of labor's objectives. Specifically, the AFL-CIO serves its members by:

1. Lobbying before legislative bodies on subjects of interest to labor.
2. Coordinating organizing efforts among its affiliated unions.
3. Publicizing the concerns and benefits of unionization to the public.
4. Resolving disputes between different unions as they occur.

Besides offering these services, the AFL-CIO maintains an interest in international trade and domestic economic issues as well as foreign policy matters. On the staff of the AFL-CIO are researchers, economists, and quality-of-work-life experts.

The federation is governed by its constitution and various policies set at its biennial conventions. National unions send a number of delegates to the convention based on the size of the unions. Thus, larger unions have greater voting power on the resolutions adopted at the convention. Between conventions, the AFL-CIO is run by its Executive Council and executive officers. The affiliated unions pay per capita dues (currently 13 cents per member per month) to support federation activities.

Structure and Functions of National Unions

The center of power in the labor movement resides with national and international unions. It is these organizations that set the broad guidelines for governing union members and for formulating collective bargaining goals in dealing with management. The only major difference between a national and an international union is that the international union organizes workers and charters local unions in foreign countries. For example, the United Auto Workers is an international union with locals in Canada.

A national union, through its constitution, establishes the rules and conditions under which the local unions may be chartered. Most national unions have regulations governing dues, initiation fees, and the internal administration of the locals.

FIGURE 17–4 STRUCTURE OF THE AFL-CIO

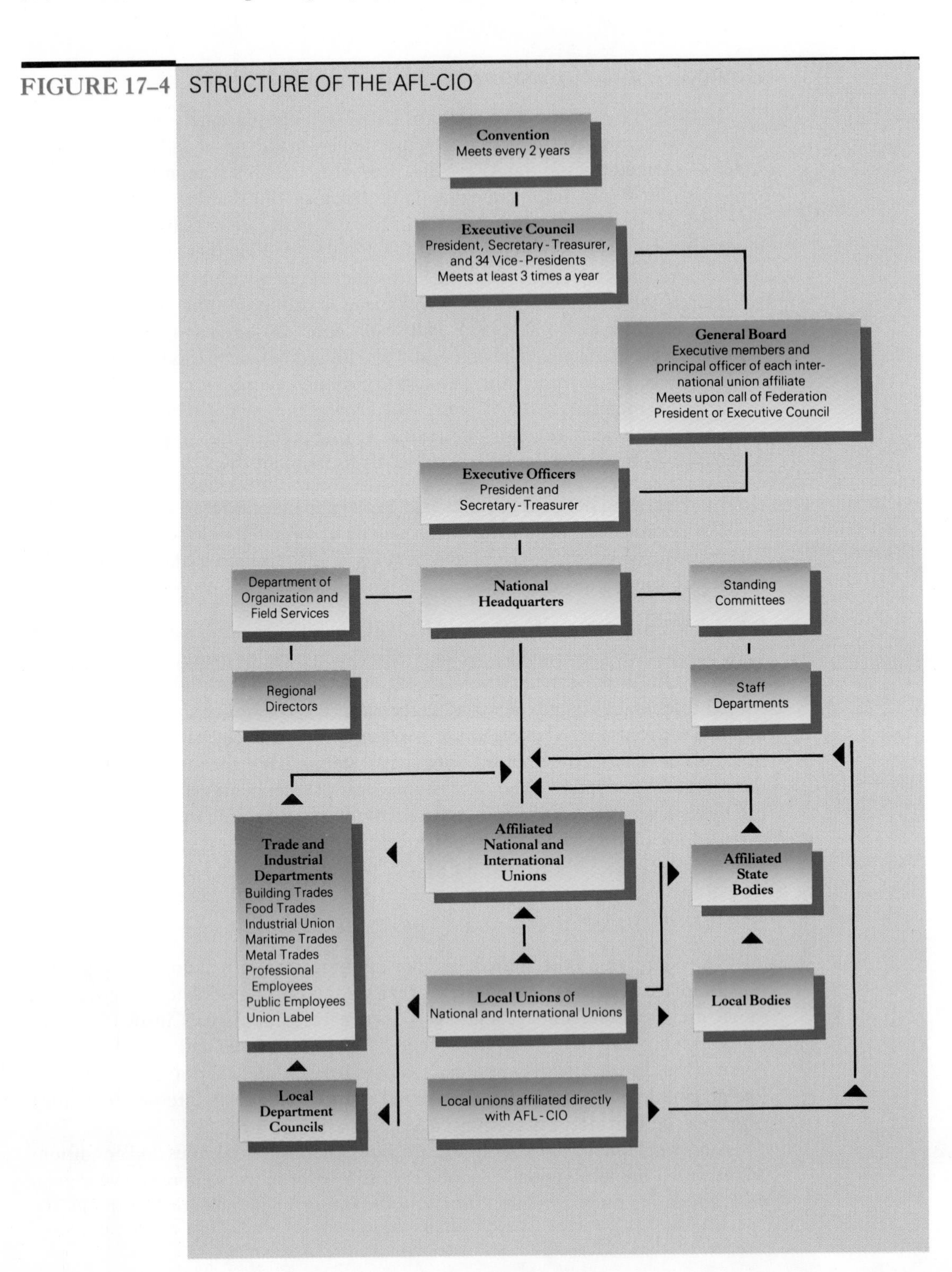

National unions also may require that certain standard provisions be included in labor agreements with employers. In return for these controls, they provide professional and financial assistance during organizing drives and strikes and help in the negotiation and administration of labor agreements. Other services provided by national unions include:

1. Training of union leaders
2. Legal assistance
3. Political activity
4. Educational and public relations programs
5. Discipline of union members

Like the AFL-CIO, national unions hold conventions to pass resolutions, amend their constitutions, and elect officers. This last function is very important to a national union because its president often exerts a large influence—if not control—over the union's policies and direction. Furthermore, many presidents, such as Lynn Williams (United Steelworkers), Richard Trumka (United Mine Workers), and Owen Bieber (United Auto Workers), are highly visible individuals who represent the labor movement to the public. In addition, the president of a national union is responsible for the overall administration of the union and of the different union departments, as shown in Figure 17–5.

Structure and Functions of Local Unions

The officers of a local union are usually responsible for negotiating the local labor agreement and for investigating and processing member grievances. Most important, they assist in preventing the members of the local union from being treated by their employers in way that runs counter to established HR policies and practices.

The officers of a local union typically include a president, vice-president, secretary-treasurer, business representative, and various committee chairpersons. Depending on the size of the union, one or more of these officers, in addition to the business representative, may be paid by the union to serve on a full-time basis. The remaining officers are members who have regular jobs and who serve the union without pay except perhaps for token gratuities and expense allowances. In many locals, the business representative is the dominant power. In some locals, however, the dominant power is the secretary-treasurer or the president.

ROLE OF THE UNION STEWARD The **union steward** represents the interests of union members in their relations with their immediate supervisors and other members of management. Stewards are normally elected by union members within their department and serve without union pay.[18] Since stewards are full-time employees of the organization, they often spend considerable time after working hours investigating and handling member problems. When stewards represent members during grievance meetings on organizational time, their lost earnings are paid by the local union.

FIGURE 17–5 TYPICAL ORGANIZATION OF A NATIONAL UNION

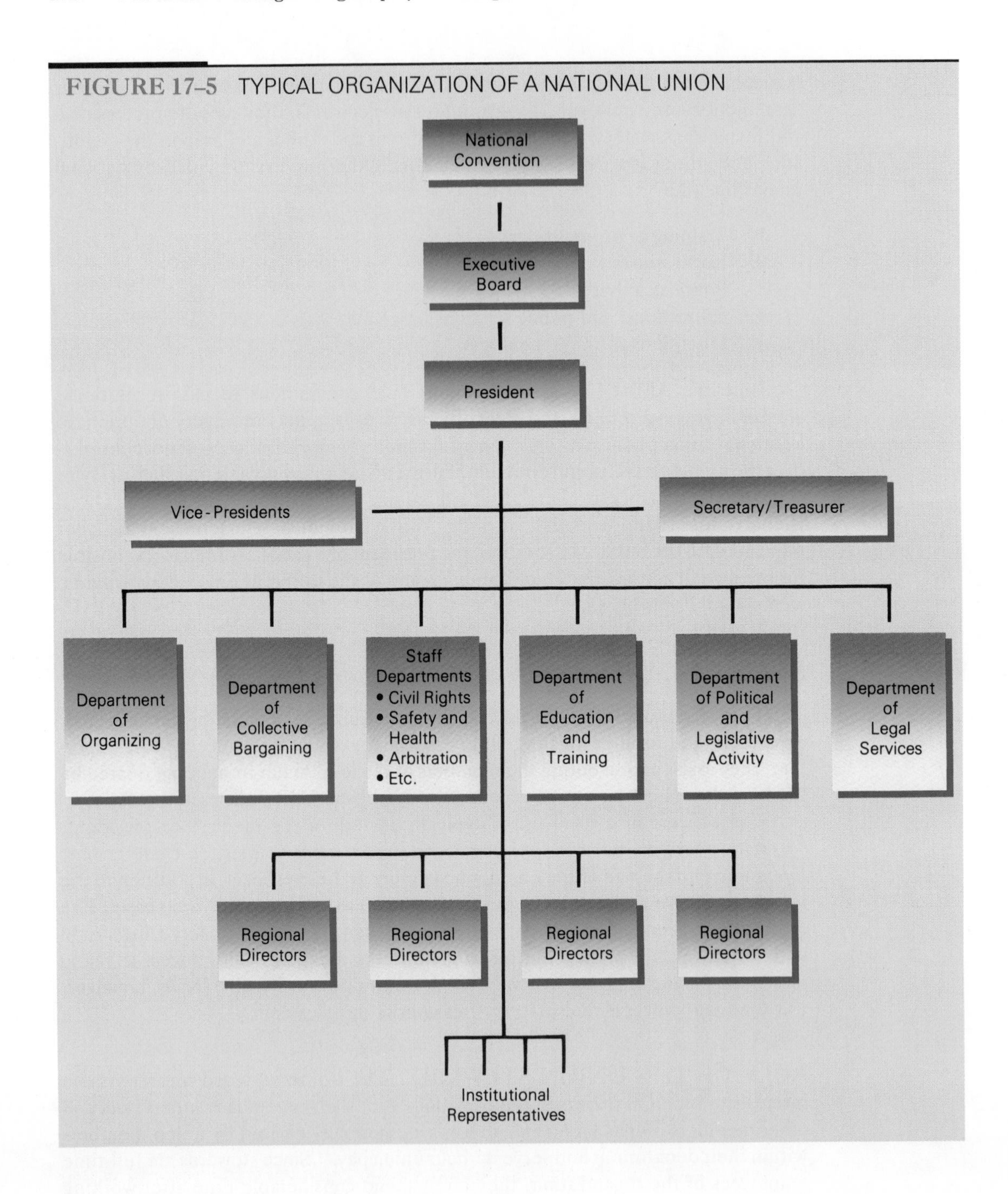

In describing the role of a union steward, Al Nash sees a "man-in-the-middle," caught between conflicting interests and groups. Nash notes:

> The steward's role as grievance handler and maid-of-all-work for the union thrusts him into a number of roles. He represents the workers in the "internal" and "external" government of the union and in negotiating with management. He is an agent of the union leadership within the workplace and, to some extent, a quasi-agent of management in enforcing the collective bargaining agreement and company rules. His role-set, then, consists of members of his own constituency, some of whom may be non-union members, members of immediate management, and higher union officials with whom he must deal.[19]

It is evident from the preceding quotation that if stewards perform their tasks effectively, they serve as important links between union members and their employer. Their attitudes and actions can have an important bearing on union–management cooperation and on the efficiency and morale of the employees they represent.

ROLE OF THE BUSINESS REPRESENTATIVE Negotiating and administering the labor agreement and working to resolve problems arising in connection with it are major responsibilities of the **business representative**. In performing these duties, business representatives must be all things to all persons within their unions. They frequently are required to assume the role of counselor in helping union members with both personal and job-related problems. They are also expected to dispose satisfactorily of the members' grievances that cannot be settled by the union stewards. Administering the daily affairs of the local union is another significant part of the business representative's job.

Union Leadership Approaches and Philosophies

To evaluate the role of union leaders accurately, one must understand the nature of their backgrounds and ambitions and recognize the political nature of the offices they occupy. The leaders of many national unions have been able to develop political machines that enable them to suppress opposition and to perpetuate themselves in office. Tenure for the leaders of a local union, however, is less secure. In the local union, officers, by federal law, must run for reelection at least every third year. If they are to remain in office, they must be able to convince a majority of the members that they are serving them effectively.

Some employers, as well as members of the general public, are prone to equate a union leader's authority with that of an executive in a public or private organization. Consequently, they may exaggerate the power and influence that these leaders exercise over union actions. When employers fail to achieve cooperative employee relations within their organization, they may assume that some union official has led their employees astray. Although it is true that some blame for strikes and other forms of labor strife may be attributed to union leaders, rank-and-file members can and

Polish leader Lech Walesa, here addressing the AFL-CIO regarding social concerns in his country.

often do exercise a very strong influence over these leaders, particularly with respect to the negotiation and administration of the labor agreement. It is important for managers to understand that union officials are elected to office and, like any political officials, must be responsive to the views of their constituency. The union leader who ignores the demands of union members may risk (1) being voted out of office, (2) having members vote the union out as their bargaining agent, (3) having members refuse to ratify the union agreement, or (4) having members engage in wildcat strikes or work stoppages.

To be effective leaders, labor officials must also pay constant attention to the general goals and philosophies of the labor movement. **Business unionism** is the general label given to the goals of American labor organizations, among which are the goals of increased pay and benefits, job security, and improved working conditions. Furthermore, union leaders also know that unions must address the broader social, economic, and legislative issues of concern to members. For example, the United Auto Workers continually lobbies Congress for protective legislation affecting the auto industry. The American Federation of State, County, and Municipal Employees, the International Ladies' Garment Workers' Union, and the Independent Federation of Flight Attendants representing flight attendants at TWA have been active supporters of women's issues at both the state and national levels.

GOVERNMENT REGULATION OF LABOR RELATIONS

Employers who are vulnerable to organizing efforts of labor unions or whose employees are already unionized must be concerned with the growing body of state and federal law on labor relations. These laws have evolved out of common law and civil law, as well as court interpretations. The first federal law pertaining to labor relations was the Railway Labor Act passed in 1926. In 1936, it was expanded to cover employers in the airline industry. Other major laws that affect labor relations in the private sector today are the Wagner Act, the Taft-Hartley Act, and the Landrum-Griffin Act.

Railway Labor Act

The primary purpose of the Railway Labor Act (RLA) is to avoid service interruptions resulting from disputes between railroads and their operating unions. To achieve this end, the RLA contains two extensive procedures to handle these labor–management disputes. First, the National Mediation Board resolves negotiating impasses by using mediation and/or arbitration. The Board is additionally charged with holding secret-ballot elections to determine if employees desire unionization. Second, the National Railway Adjustment Board functions to handle grievance and arbitration disputes arising during the life of an agreement.

Wagner Act

The Wagner Act of 1935 (or National Labor Relations Act) has had by far the most significant impact on union–management relations. It placed the protective power of the federal government firmly behind employee efforts to organize and bargain collectively through representatives of their choice. Although this Act was amended by the Taft-Hartley Act, most of its major provisions that protected employee bargaining rights were retained. Section 7 of the law guarantees these rights as follows:

> Employees shall have the right to self-organization, to form, join, or assist labor organizations, to bargain collectively through representatives of their own choosing, and to engage in concerted activities, for the purpose of collective bargaining or other mutual aid or protection, and shall also have the right to refrain from any or all of such activities except to the extent that such right may be affected by an agreement requiring membership in a labor organization as a condition of employment.[20]

To guarantee employees their Section 7 rights, Congress outlawed specific employer practices that deny employees the benefits of the law. Section 8 of the Act lists five **unfair labor practices (ULPs)** of employers. These practices are defined as follows:

1. Interfering with, restraining, or coercing employees in the exercise of their rights guaranteed in Section 7.
2. Dominating or interfering with the formation or administration of any labor organization, or contributing financial or other support to it.
3. Discriminating in regard to hiring or tenure of employment or any term or condition of employment so as to encourage or discourage membership in any labor organization.
4. Discharging or otherwise discriminating against employees because they file charges or give testimony under this Act.
5. Refusing to bargain collectively with the duly chosen representatives of employees.

Many ULPs are either knowingly or unknowingly committed each year by employers. In fiscal year 1988, for example, 31,453 unfair labor practices were filed with the NLRB. Alleged violations of the Act by employers were filed in 22,266 cases. The majority of all charges against employers concerned illegal discharge or other discrimination against employees.[21] Therefore, it is imperative that managers at all levels receive training in employee rights and unfair labor practices. Where employers violate employee rights, the NLRB can "take such affirmative action including reinstatement of employment with or without back pay, as well as effectuate the policies of the Act, and make discriminated employees whole."[22] For example, in 1987, the NLRB ordered Lundy Packing Company to pay $1.7 million to 46 workers improperly discharged during a union organizing campaign.[23]

Taft-Hartley Act

Because the bargaining power of unions increased significantly after the passage of the Wagner Act, certain restraints on unions were considered necessary. The Taft-Hartley Act of 1947 (also known as the Labor–Management Relations Act) defined the following activities as unfair union practices:

1. Restraint or coercion of employees in the exercise of their rights.
2. Restraint or coercion of employers in the selection of the parties to bargain in their behalf.
3. Persuasion of employers to discriminate against any of their employees.
4. Refusal to bargain collectively with an employer.
5. Participation in secondary boycotts and jurisdictional disputes.
6. Attempt to force recognition from an employer when another union is already the certified representative.
7. Charge of excessive initiation fees.
8. "Featherbedding" practices requiring the payment of wages for services not performed.

In short, by passing the Taft-Hartley Act, Congress balanced the rights and duties of labor and management in the collective bargaining arena. No longer could the law be criticized as favoring unions.

Health care employees represent a large and important part of the work force. In 1974, the Taft-Hartley Act was amended to include coverage of employees working in privately owned hospitals and nursing homes. Because of the critical nature of health care services, the 1974 amendments place special requirements on collective bargaining in this industry. For example, before a union of health care employees can strike, it must give a ten-day notice to the employer. Unions must also notify health care facilities of their intent to renegotiate a labor contract at least 90 days prior to the expiration of the agreement; there is a 60-day requirement for other industries covered by the Act.

ENFORCEMENT OF THE TAFT-HARTLEY ACT The agency responsible for administering and enforcing the Taft-Hartley Act is the National Labor Relations Board. It serves the public interest by reducing interruptions in production or service caused by labor–management strife. To accomplish this goal the NLRB is given two primary charges: (1) to hold secret-ballot elections to determine whether employees wish to be represented by a union and (2) to prevent and remedy unfair labor practices. The NLRB does not act on its own initiative in either function. It processes only those charges of unfair labor practices and petitions for employee elections that may be filed at one of its regional offices or other smaller field offices.

THE FEDERAL MEDIATION AND CONCILIATION SERVICE Because of the high incidence of strikes after World War II, the Taft-Hartley Act created the Federal Mediation and Conciliation Service (FMCS) to help resolve negotiating disputes. The function of this independent agency is to help labor and management reach collective bargaining agreements through the processes of mediation and conciliation. Unlike the NLRB, the FMCS has no enforcement powers, nor can it prosecute anyone. Rather, the parties to a negotiating impasse must voluntarily elect to use the service. Once the FMCS is asked to mediate a dispute, however, its involvement in the process can greatly improve labor–management relations while providing a vehicle for the exchange of collective bargaining proposals.[24] In recent years the FMCS has been highly visible in resolving deadlocks involving the communications, auto, steel, and trucking industries.

Landrum-Griffin Act

As provisions of the Taft-Hartley Act were put into practice and tested in the courts, the need for changes became evident. Congressional investigations into corrupt practices occurring within the field of union–management relations revealed that the existing statutes were inadequate to protect the rights of individual union members. They did not protect the equities of members in union welfare funds, nor did they prevent racketeering or other unscrupulous practices by employers or union officers. To address such abuses of power, Congress passed the Landrum-Griffin Act of 1959 (also known as the Labor–Management Reporting and Disclosure Act).

One of the most important provisions of the Landrum-Griffin Act is the Bill of Rights of Union Members, which requires that every union member must be given the right to (1) nominate candidates for union office, (2) vote in union elections or referendums, (3) attend union meetings, and (4) participate in union meetings and vote on union business. Members who are deprived of these rights are permitted to seek appropriate relief in a federal court. The court's action may include obtaining an appropriate injunction. Union members are also granted the right to examine union accounts and records in order to verify information contained in union reports and to bring suit against union officers as necessary to protect union funds.

The Landrum-Griffin Act also establishes certain ground rules governing the control that national unions may exert over local unions where locals are alleged to have violated member rights. Moreover, under the Act, unions are required to submit a financial report annually to the Secretary of Labor, and employers must report any expenditures that are made in attempting to exercise their bargaining rights.

LABOR RELATIONS IN THE PUBLIC SECTOR

Compared to that in the private sector, heavy unionization among public employees is a relatively recent event, beginning in the early 1960s. Since that time, however, collective bargaining among federal, state, and local government employees has been an area of large growth for the union movement. As unions and employee associations of teachers, police, firefighters, and state employees have

Oklahoma teachers demonstrating at the state capitol building in Oklahoma City, April 1990.

grown in size and political power, they have demanded the same rights to bargain and strike that private-sector employees have.

While public- and private-sector collective bargaining have many features in common, a number of factors differentiate the two sectors. In this section, we will highlight several of the major differences between public-sector and private-sector industrial relations and discuss how these differences affect HRM. Three areas will be explored: (1) legislation governing collective bargaining in the public sector, (2) the political nature of the labor–management relationship, and (3) public-sector strikes.

Public-Sector Legislation

The public-sector legislation affecting HRM includes executive orders, the Civil Service Reform Act of 1978, and state laws.

EXECUTIVE ORDERS Regulations governing labor relations with federal employees have been modeled after those developed for the private sector. However, the rights granted to labor organizations under these regulations are fewer than those accorded by the Taft-Hartley Act.

Issued in 1962 by President Kennedy, Executive Order 10988 contained provisions similar to those in Section 7 of the Taft-Hartley Act. These provisions state that federal employees have the right "freely and without fear of penalty or reprisal to form, join, or assist any labor organization or to refrain from such activity."[25] Included in this Executive Order are provisions for establishing bargaining units within government agencies. Labor organizations also are permitted to bargain collectively with the government in reaching a labor agreement for members.

Issued in 1971 by President Nixon, Executive Order 11491 defined the bargaining rights of federal employees more precisely and provided procedures for safeguarding these rights. This Executive Order created the Federal Labor Relations Council to hear appeals relating to unfair practices and bargaining issues. A body called the Federal Service Impasses Panel also was established to deal with collective bargaining deadlocks.

CIVIL SERVICE REFORM ACT OF 1978 The Civil Service Reform Act of 1978 made the regulation of labor relations in the federal government even more consistent with that contained in the Taft-Hartley Act for the private sector. The Federal Labor Relations Authority (FLRA), an agency similar to the NLRB, was created to decide on unfair practices and representation cases and to enforce the provisions of the Act. An Office of General Counsel, similar to that provided by the Taft-Hartley Act, also was created to investigate and decide which unfair labor practices and complaints are to be prosecuted.[26]

Even with the Civil Service Reform Act, labor organizations representing federal employees do not have rights equal to those provided by the Taft-Hartley Act. Most important, they lack the legal right to strike to enforce their bargaining demands. Furthermore, management rights in the federal government are accorded greater protection than those of employers in the private sector. Rules, procedures, and area restrictions that govern bargaining further reduce the influence that labor organizations can exercise over employment conditions in federal agencies.[27]

STATE LEGISLATION One distinctive characteristic of public-sector collective bargaining at the state level is the great diversity among the various state laws. This occurs because the regulation of public-sector labor–management relations falls within the separate jurisdiction of each state. For example, some states, like Arizona, Utah, and Mississippi, have no collective bargaining laws; other states, like Florida, Hawaii, and New York, have comprehensive laws granting collective bargaining rights to all public employees. Between these extremes are state laws granting collective bargaining rights only to specific employee groups such as teachers and the uniformed services (police and fire). Comprehensive state laws provide for an administrative agency analogous to the NLRB and the Federal Labor Relations Authority.[28] A frequent state restriction concerns the right to negotiate labor agreements. Public employees may only have the right to "meet and confer" with representatives of management for the purpose of developing a "memorandum of understanding."

Political Nature of the Labor–Management Relationship

Government employees are not able to negotiate with their employers on the same basis as their counterparts in private organizations. It is doubtful that they will ever be able to do so because of inherent differences between the public and private sectors.

One of the significant differences is that labor relations in the private sector has an economic foundation, whereas in government its foundation is political. Since private employers must stay in business in order to sell their goods or services, their employees are not likely to make demands that could bankrupt them. A strike in the private sector is a test of the employer's economic staying power, and usually its customers have alternative sources of supply. Governments, on the other hand, must stay in business because alternative services are usually not available. Nevertheless, unions representing government employees are not reluctant to press for financial gains that will be paid for by the public.

Another difference between the labor–management relationship in the public and private sectors is the source of management authority. In a private organization the authority flows downward from the board of directors and ultimately from the shareholders. In the public sector, however, authority flows upward from the public at large to their elected representatives and to the appointed or elected managers. Therefore, public employees can exert influence not only as union members but also as pressure groups and voting citizens.[29]

Strikes in the Public Sector

Strikes by government employees create a problem for lawmakers and for the general public. Because the services that government employees provide are considered essential to the well-being of the public, public policy is opposed to such strikes. Thus, most state legislatures have not granted public employees the right to strike.[30] With few exceptions, court decisions relating to this issue have held that public employees have no rights. This position goes back to the concept of government sovereignty and "the right of kings," which holds that government employees have only those rights given to them by their sovereign. Public-employee unions contend, however, that by denying them the same right to strike as that accorded employees in the private sector, their members are demoted to the role of second-class citizens.

Despite the absence of any legal right to do so, public employees in practice do strike. Teachers, sanitation employees, police, transit employees, firefighters, and postal employees have all engaged in strike action. On August 3, 1981, approximately 11,500 federally employed air-traffic controllers went on strike against the Federal Aviation Authority. President Reagan, declaring the strike to be illegal, fired those members of the Professional Air Traffic Controllers Union (PATCO) who refused to return to work. When a large number of controllers maintained their strike status, the government hired replacements. This action, in effect, broke PATCO and ended one of the most widely publicized strikes by public employees in the United States.

While PATCO members were disciplined for their illegal strike activity, often public employees have struck with impunity. Because this is a potentially critical situation, various arbitration methods are used for resolving collective bargaining deadlocks in the public sector. One is **compulsory binding arbitration** for employees such as police officers, firefighters, and others in jobs where strikes cannot be tolerated. Another method is **final offer arbitration**, under which the arbitrator must select one or the other of the final offers submitted by the disputing parties.[31] With this method, the arbitrator's award is more likely to go to the party whose final bargaining offer has moved the closest toward a reasonable settlement.[32]

CONTEMPORARY CHALLENGES TO LABOR ORGANIZATIONS

Among the changes that pose challenges to labor organizations today are foreign competition and technological change, increased protection of employee rights, a decline in labor's public image, the decline of union membership, and union avoidance by employers.

Foreign Competition and Technological Change

The importation of steel, consumer electronics, automobiles, clothing, textiles, and shoes from foreign countries creates a loss of jobs in the United States for workers who produce these products.[33] Furthermore, foreign subsidiaries of American corporations such as Rockwell, Westinghouse, and Xerox have been accused by labor unions of "exporting the jobs of American workers." As a result, unions are demanding more government protection against imports. Such protection has spurred lively congressional debate between those who argue that protective trade barriers create higher prices for American consumers and those who seek to protect American jobs from low-cost overseas producers.

Coupled with the threat of foreign competition is the challenge to labor brought about by rapid technological advances. Improvements in computer technology and highly automated operating systems have lowered the demand for certain types of employees. Decline in membership in the auto, steel, rubber, and transportation unions illustrates this fact. Technological advances have also diminished the effectiveness of strikes because highly automated organizations are capable of maintaining satisfactory levels of operation with minimum staffing levels during work stoppages.

Increased Protection of Employee Rights

In the 1930s and 1940s, unions succeeded in organizing employees by fighting for increased protection of employee rights. Unions negotiated contract provisions prohibiting managerial favoritism and discrimination toward workers. Other clauses provided increased job protection, discipline and discharge limitations, and health and safety gains. These contract provisions continue to be the hallmark of labor agreements. Today, however, many of the provisions for employee protection found in collective bargaining agreements are provided by federal and state legislation (see Chapter 3). The proliferation of laws that protect employees has robbed labor organizations of a principal bargaining goal and diminished their role as the "champion" of employee rights.[34] Legal scholars conclude that the growth of protective legislation for employees will continue to play an increasingly important role in lessening union influence on today's work force.

Declining Public Image of Labor

In addition to the concerns already mentioned, organized labor has suffered a decline in its public image. For example, critics of labor cite wage increases gained by labor unions as a factor that not only contributes to inflation but also helps to drive American products out of the foreign and domestic markets. The opinion also exists that some unions have become too powerful politically. Moreover, public resentment of strikes by public-employee unions has affected the image of all labor unions. The failure of unions promising higher-paid jobs to recruit women and minorities into their ranks has weakened the support for organized labor from these groups.

Publicized instances of corruption and racketeering by some labor leaders have also generated unfavorable public reaction to labor as a whole.[35] After an extensive study of public opinion toward labor organizations, two researchers concluded that union leaders play a pivotal role in the public view. The personality and characteristics of union leaders were found to be significant factors affecting the image of unions.[36] The general perception is that union leaders are powerful, frequently act in their own self-interest, appear to be contemptuous of the public, are often dishonest and unethical, and are increasingly out of touch with the rank-and-file membership.

Well aware of its negative public image, the labor movement has programs under way designed to communicate to the American public, and especially to a new generation of workers, the benefits and relevance of organized labor. In 1979 the AFL-CIO created the Labor Institute for Public Affairs charged with telling "labor's story" to Congress and the public.[37] The labor movement's "Union Yes" advertisements on prime-time television seek to present a positive, upbeat view of unions. The ultimate goal of the campaign is to create a favorable image of unions that will help organizing efforts. The International Ladies' Garment Workers' Union and the United Auto Workers have also used television commercials to publicize their successes in enhancing product quality and the dignity of workers.

Decline in Union Membership

A major challenge confronting organized labor has been to halt the decline in union membership. The magnitude of the problem is shown in Figure 17–6, which illustrates how union membership has declined in total numbers and as a percentage of the total civilian labor force. The combination of a growing labor force and decreasing rank-and-file union membership dropped organized labor's share of the civilian work force to a new modern-era low of 16.4 percent in 1989. In the industrial sector alone, 2.1 million union jobs were lost between 1980 and 1985. At the same time, nonunion jobs in those industries increased by more than 1.1 million. The loss

The "Union Yes" campaign strives to establish a positive view of unions.

of union jobs reflects, in part, the failure of unions to draw membership from among the white-collar ranks where the labor force is growing more rapidly.

EFFORTS TO UNIONIZE WHITE-COLLAR EMPLOYEES In past years, white-collar employees tended to identify themselves with owners or managers as a group enjoying certain privileges (e.g., not having to punch a time clock) and socioeconomic status that blue-collar workers did not possess. Improvements in working conditions for which union members in the shop had to make sacrifices generally were extended to the white-collar group without any need for collective action on their part. The high turnover rate of employees in clerical jobs also increased the difficulty of organizing them. For these reasons, and because union drives to organize white-collar employees were not attuned psychologically to their needs and thinking, white-collar employees have been slow to unionize. In recent years, however, growth in the size of private organizations has tended to depersonalize the work of white-collar groups and to isolate them from management. The lack of job security during layoffs, together with growing difficulties in attempting to resolve grievances, has helped to push white-collar workers toward unionization.

In response to these changes, unions are stepping up their efforts to organize white-collar workers. Many unions are recruiting employees of small businesses and employees in the so-called pink-collar ghetto, a term describing low-paying clerical

FIGURE 17–6 UNION MEMBERSHIP IN NUMBERS AND AS A PERCENTAGE OF THE CIVILIAN WORK FORCE—SELECTED YEARS

YEAR	MEMBERSHIP (in Thousands)	MEMBERSHIP AS A PERCENTAGE OF CIVILIAN LABOR FORCE
1970	21,248	25.7
1972	21,657	24.9
1974	22,809	24.8
1976	22,662	23.6
1978	22,757	22.3
1980	22,366	20.9
1982	19,763	19.3
1984	17,340	18.8
1985	16,996	18.0
1986	16,975	17.5
1987	16,913	17.0
1988	17,002	16.8
1989	16,900	16.4

SOURCE: *Directory of U.S. Labor Organizations,* 1990–1991 Edition, by Courtney D. Gifford, copyright © 1990 by The Bureau of National Affairs, Inc., Washington, DC 20037, and other issues of the *Directory.*

and sales positions traditionally held by women. Unions are also capitalizing on new health and safety issues in white-collar jobs, such as the effects of working at video display terminals and working with potentially hazardous substances.[38] Unions active in recruiting white-collar employees include the Service Employees International Union; the International Brotherhood of Teamsters; 9 to 5, the National Association of Working Women; the Office and Professional Employees International Union; the Insurance Workers International Union; the United Auto Workers; and the United Steelworkers of America.

DECERTIFICATION ELECTIONS Through a **decertification election,** members of the bargaining unit seek to remove the bargaining representative from the organization. These elections, and their voting procedures, largely parallel those for certification elections. An increase in the number of decertification elections requested by union members is another factor in the decline in union membership. For example, in 1988, labor organizations lost decertification elections by a substantial margin—about three out of four. In 459 elections, nearly a fourfold increase since the mid-1960s, unions lost representation rights for 20,736 employees.[39] The increase in decertification elections is attributed to the following:

- Union members appear more willing to challenge union authority when union officials fail to meet membership expectations.
- Managers are more dedicated to operating union-free.

- Progressive HR policies and practices have been designed to lead employees to question the need for union representation.
- Wage and benefit bargaining concessions reduce the attractiveness of unionization.[40]

Union Avoidance by Employers

A significant trend in U.S. labor relations during the 1980s and into the 1990s has been the growth in union avoidance programs. Managers in all types of organizations are vocal in their desire to maintain a union-free environment. To buttress this goal, HR managers are providing wages, benefits, and services designed to make unionism unattractive to employees. In addition, a participative management style, profit-sharing plans, and in-house grievance procedures are offered to counteract the long-established union goals of improved wages and working conditions.

It is argued that organizations may even go so far as to provoke strikes in order to hire replacement workers and permanently lay off striking union members. The president of the North Carolina AFL-CIO notes, "Strikes are now a weapon of management. In a lot of cases, management wants you to go out on strike so they can bust the strike and bust the union."[41] It seems clear that a hard-line management approach to employee unionization contributes to the defeat of union organizing efforts.

SUMMARY

In our society the right of employees to organize and bargain collectively over conditions of employment is well established. While some employees may join unions because they are required to do so, most belong to unions because they are convinced the unions help them to satisfy various economic and psychological needs.

In order to gain recognition and serve as the bargaining agent for an employer's personnel, unions often must recruit aggressively. This effort may encounter strong resistance from employers, whose position is likely to be stronger if they have been treating their employees in a consistent and equitable manner.

Most local unions with whom members have direct contact operate under a charter granted by the national organization. The majority of these national organizations in turn are affiliated with the AFL-CIO. While the bargaining strength of a particular union is affected considerably by the size of its membership and treasury resources, it is also affected by the caliber of its leaders. Good management and leadership are as important to a union as they are to a business organization. Union leaders must be skillful in administration, leadership, and politics if they are to remain in their elected offices.

Much of the current power of unions has been gained through the Wagner Act (1935), which has helped to protect and encourage union organizing and bargaining activities. The passage of the Taft-Hartley Act (1947) and the Landrum-Griffin Act (1959) has served to establish certain controls over the internal affairs of unions and their relations with employers.

Public-sector bargaining has become an increasingly important aspect of labor relations. Currently, however, most public employees do not enjoy the collective bargaining rights afforded their private-sector counterparts. Part of the difference can be attributed to the lack of uniform labor legislation at the state level. Also, the political nature of public-sector bargaining and the types of jobs held by specific public employees require different bargaining structures.

Union leaders today face numerous problems. Many unions are experiencing a decline in membership. To rectify this situation, union leaders are trying to recruit members in white-collar, professional, and government employment. The changing nature of union membership, furthermore, has created demands by women, minorities, and younger members to have their particular interests served more effectively. Such demands require that these groups be given a greater role in union administration. Also required are leadership practices that are more attuned to the contemporary challenges facing labor and management.

DISCUSSION QUESTIONS

1. How is the management of an organization's human resources likely to be affected by the unionization of its employees?
2. Contrast the arguments concerning union membership that are likely to be presented by a union with those presented by an employer.
3. What are the functions of the national union and of the local union?
4. Under the provisions of the Taft-Hartley Act, which unfair labor practices apply to both unions and employers?
5. What arguments would public-sector managers put forth in opposition to unionization?
6. What are some of the actions being taken by unions to cope with some of the contemporary challenges they face?
7. Why have attitudes toward organized labor on the part of certain segments of our society tended to become less favorable than they were in the past?

MINI-CASE 17–1 The Unfair Labor Practice Charge Against Apollo Corporation

Bob Thomas was discharged after 19 years as a plant maintenance engineer with Apollo Corporation. During that time he had received average, and sometimes below-average, annual performance appraisals. Bob was known as something of a complainer and troublemaker, and he was highly critical of management. Prior to his termination, his attendance record for the previous five years had been very poor. However, Apollo Corporation had never enforced its attendance policy, and Bob had never been disciplined for his attendance problems. In fact, until recently, Apollo management had been rather "laid-back" in its dealings with employees.

Apollo Corporation produces general component parts for the communications industry—an industry beset by intense competitive pressures beginning in 1986. To meet this competitive challenge, Jean Lipski, HR director, held a series of meetings with managers in which she instructed them to tighten up their supervisory relationship with employees. They were told to enforce HR policies strictly and to begin disciplinary action against employees not conforming to company policy. These changes did not sit well with employees, particularly Bob Thomas. Upon hearing of the new management approach, Bob became irate and announced, "They can't get away with this. I wrote the book around here." Secretly, Bob believed his past conduct was catching up with him, and he became concerned about protecting his job.

One night after work, Bob called a union organizer of the Brotherhood of Machine Engineers and asked that a union drive begin at Apollo. Within a week employees began handing out flyers announcing a union meeting. When Jean Lipski heard of the organizing campaign and Bob Thomas's leadership in it, she decided to terminate his employment. Bob's termination paper read: "Discharged for poor work performance and unsatisfactory attendance." Bob was called into her office and told of the discharge. After leaving Ms. Lipski's office, Bob called the union organizer, and they both went to the regional office of the NLRB to file an unfair labor practice charge in Bob's behalf. The ULP alleged that he was fired for his support of the union and the organizing drive.

QUESTIONS

1. What, if any, violation of the law did the Apollo Corporation commit?
2. What arguments will Ms. Lipski and Bob Thomas use to support their cases?

MINI-CASE 17–2 The Union Drive at Apollo Corporation

Jean Lipski, HR director for Apollo Corporation, arrived at work on Monday morning to discover employees handing out flyers announcing a union-organizing meeting. Several employees were carrying picket signs saying that management was "unfair to labor." One sign asked that a former employee, Bob Thomas, be reinstated. As Ms. Lipski drove into the parking lot, she realized that trouble was beginning for her and the Apollo Corporation.

Ms. Lipski was deeply concerned about the employees' activities and immediately called a meeting of managers to determine what caused the organizing drive to begin. The meeting took place at 10:30 A.M. After a 15-minute discussion, everyone present expressed genuine surprise at the unionization effort. Several managers felt betrayed by the employees, while others became belligerent and suggested that disciplinary action was in order for the "disloyal" employees. The meeting ended in general confusion.

Jean Lipski had previously worked for a unionized company but had never been directly involved in a union drive. From working with unions, however, she did know that the organizer would work quickly to unite the employees against the company. She knew she could not simply sit by and let things happen as they might. As she walked to her office, she realized that a plan of action was needed.

QUESTIONS

1. What steps will the union use to organize the employees, and what information will the organizer seek to win employee support?
2. Recommend a plan of action for Jean Lipski to counteract the union drive.

NOTES AND REFERENCES

1. For an expanded model of the labor relations process, see John Dunlop, *Industrial Relations Systems* (New York: Henry Holt, 1958), Chapter 1. This book is a classic in the labor relations field. Also, those interested in labor relations may wish to explore in greater detail the historical developments of the U.S. labor movement. Much can be learned about the current operations of labor organizations and the philosophies of labor officials from labor's historical context. A brief but comprehensive history of labor unions can be found in *A Brief History of the American Labor Movement*, U.S. Department of Labor, Bureau of Labor Statistics, Bulletin 1000.

2. George W. Bohlander, "Satisfaction with Unionism: A Public Sector Response," *Journal of Collective Negotiations in the Public Sector* 13, no. 2 (Summer 1984): 95–107.

3. Jack Fiorito, Daniel G. Gallagher, and Cynthia V. Kukami, "Satisfaction with Union Representation," *Industrial and Labor Relations Review* 41, no. 2 (January 1988): 294–305. See also Carol Keegan, "How Union Members and Nonmembers View the Role of Unions," *Monthly Labor Review* 110, no. 8 (August 1987): 50–51.

4. Stephenie Overman, "Nissan Sees Union's Loss as Management Style's Win," *Resource* 8, no. 10 (September 1989): 1.

5. Kenneth S. Warner, Robert F. Chisholm, and Robert F. Munzenrider, "Motives for Unionization Among State Social Service Employees," *Public Personnel Management* 7, no. 3 (May–June 1978): 181–191.

6. Thomas A. Kochan and Harry C. Katz, *Collective Bargaining and Industrial Relations* (Homewood, IL: Richard D. Irwin, 1988), 91.

7. "Labor, Management Advocates Debate the Future of Unions," *BNA's Employee Relations Weekly* 7, no. 17 (April 24, 1989): 524.

8. Jack Fiorito, Christopher Lowman, and Forrest D. Nelson, "The Impact of Human Resource Policies on Union Organizing," *Industrial Relations* 26, no. 2 (Spring 1987): 113–126. See also Charles A. Wentz, Jr., "Preserving a Union-Free Workplace," *Personnel* 64, no. 10 (October 1987): 68–72.

9. Kenneth Gilberg and Nancy Abrams, "Countering Union's New Organizing Techniques," *Personnel* 64, no. 6 (June 1987): 12–16.

10. Ken Gagala, *Union Organizing and Staying Organized* (Reston, VA: Reston Publishing, 1983), Chapter 4. For a discussion of union organizers, see Thomas F. Reed, "Profiles of Union Organizers from Manufacturing and Service Unions," *Journal of Labor Research* 11, no. 1 (Winter 1990): 73–80.

11. Michael E. Golo, *An Introduction to Labor Law* (Ithaca: New York State School of Industrial and Labor Relations, ILR Bulletin 66, 1989), 29.

12. *Fifty-fourth Annual Report of the National Labor Relations Board – 1989* (Washington, DC: U.S. Government Printing Office, 1991), 6.

13. Cheryl L. Maranto and Jack Fiorito, "The Effect of Union Characteristics on the Outcome of NLRB Certification Elections," *Industrial and Labor Relations Review* 40, no. 2 (January 1987): 225–240.

14. For an expanded discussion of the bargaining unit, see Benjamin J. Taylor and Fred Witney, *Labor Relations Law*, 5th ed. (Englewood Cliffs, NJ: Prentice-Hall, 1987), 325–331.

15. John A. Fossum, *Labor Relations: Development, Structure, Process*, 4th ed. (Homewood, IL: BPI/Irwin, 1989), 112.

16. James B. Dworkin and James R. Fain, "Success in Multiple Union Elections: Exclusive Jurisdiction vs. Competition," *Journal of Labor Research* 10, no. 1 (Winter 1989): 91–101.

17. *AFL-CIO News*, November 13, 1989 (815 16th Street, N.W., Washington, DC).

18. E. Edward Herman, Alfred Kuhn, and Ronald L. Seeber, *Collective Bargaining and Labor Relations*, 2d ed. (Englewood Cliffs, NJ: Prentice-Hall, 1987), 111.

19. Al Nash, *The Union Steward: Duties, Rights, and Status*, Key Issue Series no. 22 (Ithaca, NY: ILR Press, 1983), 11–12.
20. *Labor–Management Relations Act*, Public Law 101, 80th Cong., 1947. For criticisms of union–management labor law, see James T. Grady, "Broken Promises: The Failure of American Labor Law," *Labor Law Journal* 41, no. 3 (March 1990): 151–157.
21. *Fifty-fourth Annual Report of the National Labor Relations Board*, 6.
22. *Labor–Management Relations Act*, Section 10(c), 1947, as amended.
23. "15 Years Later, Meat Cutters Win Back Pay," *Resource* 8, no. 3 (March 1989): 12.
24. Steven Briggs and Daniel J. Koys, "What Makes Labor Mediators Effective?" *Labor Law Journal* 40, no. 8 (August 1989): 517–520.
25. CFR (Code of Federal Regulations), 1959–1963 Compilation, 521.
26. George W. Bohlander, "The Federal Labor Relations Authority: A Review and Analysis," *Journal of Collective Negotiations in the Public Sector* 8, no. 4 (1989): 273–288.
27. Richard C. Kearney, *Labor Relations in the Public Sector* (New York: Dekker, 1983), 74.
28. Robert E. Allen and Timothy J. Keaveny, *Contemporary Labor Relations*, 2d ed. (Reading, MA: Addison-Wesley, 1988): 650–651.
29. Chimezie A. B. Osigweh, "Collective Bargaining and Public Sector Union Power," *Public Personnel Management* 14, no. 1 (Spring 1985): 75–83.
30. Raymond Hogler, "Public Sector Strikes, Labor-Management Relations, and the Common Law," *Public Personnel Management* 17, no. 1 (Spring 1988): 83–90.
31. Michael W. Hirlinger and Ronald D. Sylvia, "Public Sector Impasse Procedures Revisited," *Journal of Collective Negotiations in the Public Sector* 17, no. 4 (1988): 267–277.
32. Fossum, 448.
33. Rod Willis, "Can American Unions Transform Themselves?" *Management Review* 77, no. 2 (February 1988): 14–21.
34. Peter Drucker, "Will Unions Ever Again Be Useful Organs of Society?" *Industry Week* (March 20, 1989): 18.
35. Willis, 19.
36. James A. Craft and Suhail Abboushi, "The Union Image: Concept, Programs and Analysis," *Journal of Labor Research* 5, no. 4 (Fall 1983): 299–314.
37. Kirkland Ropp, "State of the Unions," *Personnel Administrator* 32, no. 7 (July 1987): 36–40.
38. Kenneth Gilberg and Nancy Abrams, "Union Organizing: New Tactics for New Times," *Personnel Administrator* 32, no. 7 (July 1987): 52–56.
39. *Fifty-fourth Annual Report of the National Labor Relations Board*, 12–13.
40. William J. Bigoness and Ellen R. Peirce, "Responding to Union Decertification Elections," *Personnel Administrator* 33, no. 8 (August 1988): 49–53.
41. Willis, 18.

CHAPTER 18

Collective Bargaining and Contract Administration

After reading this chapter you will be able to:

1. *Discuss the bargaining process and the bargaining goals and strategies of a union and an employer.*
2. *Describe the forms of bargaining power that a union and an employer may utilize to enforce their bargaining demands.*
3. *Cite the principal methods by which bargaining deadlocks may be resolved.*
4. *Give examples of the current collective bargaining trends occurring within industry and the reasons for these trends.*
5. *Identify the typical provisions of a labor agreement and the forms of security it may provide for a union.*
6. *Describe a typical union grievance procedure and how grievances are prepared.*
7. *Explain the grievance arbitration process and the basis for arbitration awards.*
8. *Define the key terms in the chapter.*

TERMS TO IDENTIFY

collective bargaining process (598)
pattern bargaining (600)
bargaining zone (602)
boycott (605)
primary boycott (605)
secondary boycott (605)
outsourcing (605)
lockout (606)
mediator (606)
arbitrator, or impartial umpire (606)
reserved rights (611)
defined rights (611)
grievance procedure (614)
grievance mediation (616)
arbitration (618)
fair representation doctrine (619)
submission agreement (620)
due process (620)
expedited arbitration (623)

A major function of labor organizations is to bargain collectively for those in the bargaining unit over conditions of employment. According to labor law, once the union wins negotiating rights for bargaining unit members, it must represent everyone in the unit equally regardless of whether employees subsequently join the union or elect to remain nonmembers. The labor agreement that ultimately is negotiated establishes the wages, hours, employee benefits, job security, and other conditions under which represented employees agree to work.

This chapter is concerned with the process by which an agreement is reached between labor and management. It is concerned also with the changes that are occurring in the bargaining relationship as it has evolved from an adversary relationship to a more cooperative one. Even under cooperative conditions, however, collective bargaining requires negotiators to possess special skills and knowledge if they are to represent their parties successfully. Negotiators for a union must be able to produce a labor agreement that members will find acceptable. An employer's negotiators, on the other hand, must come up with an agreement that will allow the employer to remain competitive. The agreement must be one that can be administered with a minimum of conflict and that can facilitate HRM.

THE BARGAINING PROCESS

Those unfamiliar with contract negotiations often view the process as an emotional interaction between labor and management, complete with marathon sessions, fist pounding, and smoke-filled rooms. In reality, negotiating a labor agreement entails long hours of extensive preparation combined with diplomatic maneuvering and the development of bargaining strategies.[1] Furthermore, negotiation is only one part of the **collective bargaining process.** Collective bargaining also may include the use of economic pressures in the form of strikes and boycotts by a union. Lockouts, plant closures, and the replacement of strikers are similar pressures used by an employer. In addition, either or both parties may seek support from the general public or from the courts as a means of pressuring the opposing side.

Good-Faith Bargaining

Once a union has been recognized as the representative for employees, an employer is obligated to negotiate in good faith with the union's representative over conditions of employment. Good faith requires the employer's negotiators to meet with their union counterparts at a reasonable time and place to discuss these conditions. It requires also that the proposals submitted by each party be realistic. In discussing the other party's proposals, each side must offer reasonable counterproposals for those it is unwilling to accept.

Where an employer argues a financial inability-to-pay position during negotiations, the duty to bargain in good faith requires the employer to furnish relevant financial information to the union if the claim is legitimate and not simply based on unwillingness to meet union wage demands.[2] Finally, both parties must sign the written document containing the agreement reached through negotiations.[3]

The National Labor Relations Board defines the duty to bargain as bargaining on all matters concerning rates of pay, wages, hours of employment, or other conditions of employment.[4] These topics are called *mandatory* subjects of bargaining, and both the employer and the union must bargain in good faith over these issues. The law, however, does not require either party to agree to a proposal or to make concessions while negotiating these subjects. On other topics, called *permissive* issues—matters that are lawful but not related to wages, hours, or other conditions of employment—the parties are free to bargain, but neither side can force the other side to bargain over these topics. A permissive subject might include a union demand to ratify supervisory promotions as well as the right to seek dismissal of these employees. Where labor and management negotiators cannot agree on whether a bargaining proposal is a mandatory or a permissive issue the NLRB will decide the dispute.[5] Figure 18–1 illustrates several prevalent examples of bad-faith employer bargaining.

Preparing for Negotiations

Preparing for negotiations includes planning the strategy and assembling data to support bargaining proposals. This will permit collective bargaining to be conducted on an orderly, factual, and positive basis with a greater likelihood of achieving desired goals. Negotiators often develop a bargaining book that serves as a cross-reference file to determine which contract clauses would be affected by a demand.

FIGURE 18–1 EXAMPLES OF BAD-FAITH EMPLOYER BARGAINING

- Refusing to discuss or consider mandatory subjects of bargaining as defined by the NLRB.
- Using delaying tactics such as frequent postponements of bargaining sessions.
- Withdrawing concessions previously granted.
- Insisting that the union stop striking before resuming negotiations.
- Unilaterally changing proper subjects of bargaining such as wages, organizational rules, or employee benefits.
- Negotiating with individual employees other than bargaining unit representatives.
- Engaging in mere surface bargaining rather than honest negotiations.
- Refusing to meet with duly appointed or elected union representatives.

The bargaining book also contains a general history of contract terms and their relative importance to management.[6] Assuming that the labor agreement is not the first to be negotiated by the parties, preparation for negotiations ideally should start soon after the current agreement has been signed. This practice will allow negotiators to review and diagnose mistakes and weaknesses made during the previous negotiations while the experience is still current in their minds.

SOURCES TO CONSULT Internal data relating to grievances, disciplinary actions, transfers and promotions, layoffs, overtime, individual performance, and wage payments are useful in formulating and supporting the employer's bargaining position. The supervisors and executives who must live with and administer the labor agreement can be very important sources of ideas and suggestions concerning changes that are needed in the *next* agreement. Their contact with union members and representatives provides them with a firsthand knowledge of the changes that union negotiators are likely to propose.

Data obtained from government publications, such as the *Monthly Labor Review*, and agencies such as the Department of Labor's Bureau of Labor Statistics, can help to support the employer's position during negotiations; information from the *Wall Street Journal* and publications of the Bureau of National Affairs and Commerce Clearing House can also be of use. Each of these data sources can provide information on general economic conditions, cost-of-living trends, and geographical wage rates covering a wide range of occupations.

BARGAINING PATTERNS When unions negotiate provisions covering wages and other benefits, they generally seek to achieve increases at least equal to those provided in other agreements existing within the industry or region. For example, the United Auto Workers would negotiate similar contract provisions for workers at Ford, General Motors, and Chrysler. Employers quite naturally try to minimize these increases by citing other employers who are paying lower wages and benefits. Other negotiated labor agreements can establish a pattern that one side or the other may seek to follow in support of its own bargaining position. This practice

Pattern bargaining has become less of an influence on employers in the trucking industry.

is known as **pattern bargaining.** In preparing for negotiations, therefore, it is essential for both the union and the employer to be fully aware of established bargaining patterns within the area or the industry.

Empirical studies of bargaining during the period 1980–1985 did not find the predictable pattern of bargaining relationships that once existed. With the recessions of 1980 and 1982, combined with increased domestic and foreign competition, employers were more willing to resist union demands to "accept the pattern." In the trucking, steel, rubber, and auto industries, for example, pattern bargaining came to assume a lesser role in setting wage and benefit standards among employers. However, pattern bargaining still remains a characteristic of U.S. collective bargaining. Pattern bargaining allows unions to show their members that they are receiving wages and benefits similar to those of other employees doing like work, and employers are assured that their labor costs are comparable to their competitors'.[7]

BARGAINING STRATEGIES Negotiators for an employer should develop a plan covering their bargaining strategy. To ensure adherence to the employer's course of action, this plan should be prepared as a written document. The plan should consider the proposals that the union is likely to submit, based on the most recent agreements with other employers and the demands that remain unsatisfied from previous negotiations. The plan should also consider the goals the union is striving to achieve and the extent to which it may be willing to make concessions or to resort to strike action in order to achieve these goals.

At a minimum, the employer's bargaining strategy must address these points:

- Likely union proposals and management responses to them.
- A listing of management demands, limits of concessions, and anticipated union responses.

- Development of a database to support management bargaining proposals and to counteract union demands.
- A contingency operating plan should employees strike.

Certain elements of strategy are common to both the employer and the union. Generally, the initial demands presented by each side are greater than those it actually may hope to achieve. This is done in order to provide room for concessions. Moreover, each party will usually avoid giving up the maximum it is capable of conceding in order to allow for further concessions that may be needed to break a bargaining deadlock.

Conducting the Negotiations

The conditions under which negotiations take place, the experience and personalities of the negotiators on each side, the goals they are seeking to achieve, and the strength of the relative positions are among the factors that tend to make each bargaining situation unique.[8] Some labor agreements can be negotiated informally in a few hours, particularly if the terms are based on the pattern that has been established by the industry. Other agreements, however, may require months of negotiations before a final settlement can be reached.

BARGAINING TEAMS The composition and size of bargaining teams are often a reflection of industry practice and bargaining history. Normally, each side will have four to six representatives at the negotiating table. The chief negotiator for management will be the vice-president or manager for labor relations; the chief negotiator for the union will be the local union president or union business agent. Others making up management's team may include representatives from accounting or finance, operations, employment, legal, or training. The local union president is likely to be supported by the chief steward, various local union vice-presidents, and a representative from the national union.

Many negotiators, over a period of time, acquire the ability "to read their opponents' minds," to anticipate their actions and reactions. Inexperienced negotiators bargaining together for the first time, on the other hand, may misinterpret their opponents' actions and statements and unintentionally cause a deadlock. Furthermore, those who lack experience may be unaware of the rules, rituals, and steps to be followed to keep negotiations moving toward a mutually acceptable agreement.

OPENING THE NEGOTIATIONS The initial meeting of the bargaining teams is a particularly important one because it may establish the climate that will prevail during the negotiations that follow. A cordial attitude, with perhaps the injection of a little humor, can contribute much to a relaxation of tensions and help the negotiations to begin smoothly. This *attitudinal structuring* is done to change the attitudes of the parties toward each other, often with the objective of persuading one side to accept the other side's demands.[9]

The first meeting is usually devoted to establishing the bargaining authority possessed by the representatives of each side and to determining the rules and procedures to be used during negotiations. If the parties have not submitted their proposals in advance, these may be exchanged and clarified at this time.

ANALYZING THE PROPOSALS The negotiation of a labor agreement can have some of the characteristics of a poker game, with each side attempting to determine its opponent's position while not revealing its own. Each party will normally try to avoid disclosing the relative importance that it attaches to a proposal so that it will not be forced to pay a higher price than is necessary to have the proposal accepted. As with sellers who will try to get a higher price for their products if they think the prospective buyer strongly desires them, negotiators will try to get greater concessions in return for granting those their opponents want most.

The proposals that each side submits generally may be divided into those it feels it must achieve, those it would like to achieve, and those it is submitting primarily for trading purposes. Proposals submitted for trading purposes, however, must be realistic in terms of the opponent's ability and willingness to concede them. Unrealistic proposals may serve only to antagonize the opponent and cause a deadlock.

RESOLVING THE PROPOSALS Regardless of its degree of importance, every proposal submitted must be resolved if an agreement is to be finalized. A proposal may be withdrawn, accepted by the other side in its entirety, or accepted in some compromise form.

For each bargaining issue to be resolved satisfactorily, the point at which agreement is reached must be within limits that the union and the employer are willing to accept. In a frequently cited bargaining model, Stagner and Rosen call the area within these two limits the **bargaining zone.** In some bargaining situations, such as the one illustrated in Figure 18–2, the solution desired by one party may exceed the limits of the other party. Thus, that solution is outside the bargaining zone. If that party refuses to modify its demands sufficiently to bring them within the bargaining zone or if the opposing party refuses to extend its limit to accommodate the demands of the other party, a bargaining deadlock will result.[10]

For example, when bargaining a wage increase for employees, if the union's lowest limit is a 4 percent increase and management's top limit is 6 percent, an acceptable range—the bargaining zone—is available to both parties. If management's top limit is only 3 percent, however, a bargaining zone is not available to either side and a deadlock is likely to occur. Figure 18–2 shows that as bargaining takes place, several important variables influence the negotiators and their ability to reach agreement within the bargaining zone.[11]

The Union's Power in Collective Bargaining

During negotiations, it is necessary for each party to retreat sufficiently from its original position to permit an agreement to be achieved. If this does not occur, the

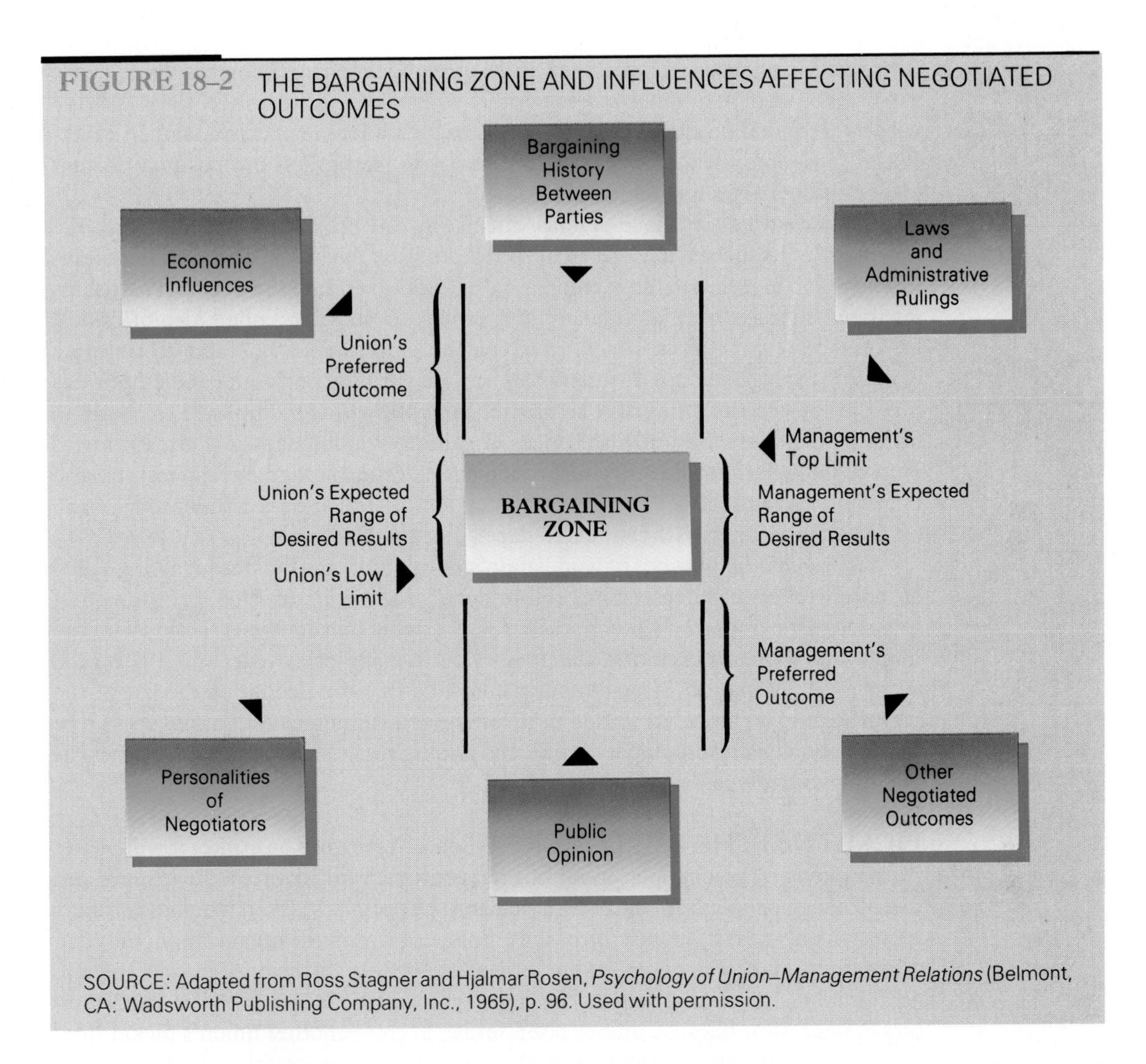

FIGURE 18–2 THE BARGAINING ZONE AND INFLUENCES AFFECTING NEGOTIATED OUTCOMES

SOURCE: Adapted from Ross Stagner and Hjalmar Rosen, *Psychology of Union–Management Relations* (Belmont, CA: Wadsworth Publishing Company, Inc., 1965), p. 96. Used with permission.

negotiations will become deadlocked, and the union may resort to the use of economic power to achieve its demands. Otherwise, its only alternative will be to have members continue working without a labor agreement once the old one has expired. The economic power of the union may be exercised by striking, picketing, or boycotting the employer's products and encouraging others to do likewise. As managers know well, the ability to engage or even threaten to engage in such activities also can serve as a form of pressure.

STRIKING THE EMPLOYER A strike is the refusal of a group of employees to perform their jobs. Although strikes account for only a small portion of total workdays lost in industry each year, they are a costly and emotional event for all concerned. Unions usually will seek strike authorization from their members to use as a bargaining ploy to gain concessions that will make a strike unnecessary. A strike vote by the members does not mean they actually want or expect to go out on strike. Rather, it is intended as a vote of confidence to strengthen the position of their leaders at the bargaining table.

Since a strike can have serious effects on the union and its members, the prospects for its success must be analyzed carefully by the union. It is most important for the union to estimate the members' willingness to endure the personal hardships resulting from a strike, particularly if it proves to be a long one. Also of critical importance is the extent, if any, to which the employer will be able to continue operating through the use of supervisory and nonstriking personnel and employees hired to replace the strikers. The greater the ability of the employer to continue operating, the less the union's chances of gaining the demands it is attempting to enforce through the strike.[12] Failure to achieve a desired settlement can result in the employees' voting either the union officers out of office or the union out of the organization in an NLRB-conducted decertification election.

Since 1985 the number of work stoppages in the United States involving 1,000 or more workers has declined to well under 75 each year. In 1988, the Bureau of Labor Statistics reported 40 such stoppages,[13] a figure that contrasts sharply with the number of strikes reported in the 1960s (282 average each year) and 1970s (288 average each year). HRM practitioners conclude that the decline in the use of the strike by unions can be attributed to the increased willingness of employers to hire replacements when employees strike and the increased availability of workers as unemployment levels have risen.

PICKETING THE EMPLOYER When a union goes on strike, it will picket the employer by placing persons at business entrances to advertise the dispute and to discourage people from entering or leaving the premises. Even when the strikers represent only a small proportion of the employees within the organization, they can cause the shutdown of an entire organization if a sufficient number of the organization's remaining employees (i.e., sympathy strikers) refuse to cross their picket line. Also, because unions often refuse to cross another union's picket line, the pickets may serve to prevent trucks and railcars from entering the business to deliver and pick up goods. For example, a Teamster truck driver may refuse to deliver produce to a food store whose employees are out on strike with the United Food and Commercial Workers' Union.

If a strike fails to stop an employer's operations, the picket line may serve as more than a passive weapon. Employees who attempt to cross the line may be subjected to verbal insults and even physical violence. Mass picketing, in which large groups of pickets try to block the path of people attempting to enter an organization, may also be used. However, the use of picket lines to exert physical pressure and incite violence is illegal and may harm more than help the union cause.

A boycott can be a powerful economic weapon.

BOYCOTTING THE EMPLOYER Another economic weapon of unions is the **boycott,** which is a refusal to patronize the employer. This action can hurt an employer if conducted by a large enough segment of organized labor. In contrast to a strike, a boycott may not end completely with the settlement of the dispute. During the boycott, many former customers may have developed either a bias against the employer's products or a change in buying habits that is not easily reversed.

The refusal of a union to allow its members to patronize a business where there is a labor dispute is a **primary boycott.** Under most circumstances this type of boycott is legal. A union may go a step further, however, and attempt to induce third parties, primarily suppliers and customers, to refrain from business dealings with the employer with whom it has a dispute. A boycott of this type, called a **secondary boycott,** generally is illegal under the Taft-Hartley Act.

The Employer's Power in Collective Bargaining

The employer's power in collective bargaining largely rests in being able to shut down the organization or certain operations within it. The employer can transfer these operations to other locations or can subcontract them to other employers through **outsourcing.** In exercising their economic freedom, however, employers must be careful that their actions are not interpreted by the NLRB to be an attempt to avoid bargaining with the union.

OPERATING DURING STRIKES When negotiations become deadlocked, typically it is the union that initiates action and the employer that reacts. In reacting, employers must balance the cost of taking a strike against the long- and short-term costs of agreeing to union demands. They also must consider the effects that either course of action may have on union demands in negotiating future agreements. The extent to which employers will be forced to suspend operations and the length of time that they and the unions will be able to endure a strike also must be considered. An employer who chooses to accept a strike must then decide whether or not to continue operating if it is possible to do so.

Organizations today seem to be more willing to face a strike than they were in former years. Several reasons have been advanced to explain this change. These include the following:

1. Union members seem less willing to support strike activity. Thus, the union is less able to maintain strike unity among its members.
2. Because organizations are forced to reduce labor costs to meet domestic and foreign competition, unions have no choice but to accept lower wages and benefits.
3. Technological advances enhance the employer's ability to operate during a strike.
4. Organizations are able to obtain favorable, often concessionary, contracts.[14]

USING THE LOCKOUT Although not often used, a **lockout** occurs when an employer takes the initiative to close its operations. The lockout generally is begun when one or more members of an employer association have been struck by a union. It is invoked on the premise that "a strike against one is a strike against all." Lockouts also may be used by employers to combat union slowdowns, damage to their property, or violence within their plants that may occur in connection with a labor dispute.

In an important decision for employers, the NLRB in 1986 granted employers the right to hire temporary replacements during a legitimate lockout. With this ruling, employers acquired a bargaining weapon equal in force to the union's right to strike. As one observer noted, "The availability of a lockout-with-replacement strategy improves management's ability to battle a union head-on in the way that unions have battled employers for decades."[15] Since 1986, businesses such as Deere and Company, USX, Timken Company, Iowa Beef Processors, and the Lockheed Ship Building and Construction Company have used lockouts to support their bargaining position with labor organizations. Employers may still be reluctant to resort to a lockout, however, because of their concern that denying work to regular employees might hurt the company's image.

Resolving Bargaining Deadlocks

When a strike or a lockout occurs, both parties are soon affected by it. The employer will suffer a loss of profits and customers, and possibly of public goodwill. The union members suffer a loss of income that is likely to be only partially offset by strike benefits or outside income. The union's leaders risk the possibility of losing members, of being voted out of office, of losing public support, or of having the members vote to decertify the union as their bargaining agent. As the losses to each side mount, the disputing parties usually feel more pressure to achieve a settlement.

MEDIATION AND ARBITRATION When the disputing parties are unable to resolve a deadlock, a third party serving in the capacity of either a mediator or an arbitrator may be called upon to provide assistance. A **mediator** serves primarily to open up a channel of communication between the parties. Typically, the mediator meets with one party and then the other in order to suggest compromise solutions or to recommend concessions from each side that will lead to an agreement without causing either to lose face. Mediators have no power or authority to force either side toward an agreement. They must use their communication skills and the power of persuasion to help the parties resolve their differences.[16]

An **arbitrator, or impartial umpire,** on the other hand, assumes the role of a judge or umpire and determines what the settlement between the two parties should be. In other words, arbitrators write a final contract that the parties *must* accept. In the public sector, where strikes are largely prohibited, the use of arbitration is one accepted method to resolve bargaining deadlocks.[17] Generally, one or both parties are reluctant to give a third party the power to make the settlement for them.

Consequently, a mediator typically is used to break a deadlock and assist the parties in reaching an agreement. An arbitrator generally is called upon to resolve disputes arising in connection with the administration of the agreement.

GOVERNMENT INTERVENTION In some situations, deadlocks may have to be resolved directly or indirectly as the result of government intervention, particularly if the work stoppage is a threat to the national security or to the public welfare. The Taft-Hartley Act provides that the President of the United States may stop a strike in "an entire industry or a substantial part thereof" if the strike would "imperil the national health or safety." Fortunately, the national emergency strike provisions of the Taft-Hartley Act have not often been used. Rather, the federal government is more likely to become involved in labor disputes through the services of the Federal Mediation and Conciliation Service (see Chapter 17). The FMCS has been highly successful in resolving bargaining deadlocks.

TRENDS IN COLLECTIVE BARGAINING

Observers of the labor environment agree that the 1990s will be a period of great importance to labor–management relations.[18] Advances in technology, management's antiunion posture, and continued competitive pressures will have their impact. These environmental conditions will affect the attitudes and objectives of both employers and unions in collective bargaining. These conditions will also influence the climate in which bargaining must occur and the bargaining power each is able to exercise.

Increased competitiveness in the marketplace will influence labor–management relationships in the 1990s.

Changes in Collective Bargaining Relationships

Traditionally, the collective bargaining relationship between an employer and a union has been an adversary one. The union has held the position that, while the employer has the responsibility for managing the organization, the union has the right to challenge certain actions of management. Unions also have taken the position that the employer has an obligation to operate the organization in a manner that will provide adequate compensation to employees. Moreover, unions maintain that their members should not be expected to subsidize poor management by accepting less than their full entitlement.

Most unions, such as the United Steelworkers bargaining with National Steel Corporation, the Amalgamated Clothing and Textile Workers Union bargaining with Xerox Corporation, and the Office and Professional Employees International Union bargaining with Northwest Natural Gas Company, have been sufficiently enlightened to recognize the danger of making bargaining demands that will create economic adversity for employers.[19] This fact, however, has not stopped these unions from bargaining for what they consider to be a fair and equitable agreement for their members. While the goal of organized labor has always been to bargain for improved economic and working conditions, large layoffs caused by business downturns and domestic and foreign competition have caused both sides to change their bargaining goals and tactics. We are seeing a gradual movement away from direct conflict and toward more labor–management accommodation.

Facilitating Union–Management Cooperation

Improving union–management cooperation generally requires a restructuring of attitudes by both management and unions and, most important, by the union members. The crisis of survival has forced unions, their members, and management to make concessions at the bargaining table and to collaborate in finding the solutions that will ensure survival. If cooperation is to continue after the crisis has passed, however, it must rest on a more solid foundation. For example, it has been noted that cooperation only lasts when both sides undertake the endeavor through a systems approach grounded in developmental activities.[20] Figure 18–3 illustrates a procedure for developing labor–management cooperation.

Furthermore, a review of meaningful labor–management cooperative endeavors indicates that success depends on an open and honest style of communication and that both supervisors and employees must be trained in participative and problem-solving approaches to problem resolution. Finally, a philosophy of trust and respect must underlie the labor–management relationship. It is particularly important that union members believe that management is sincerely interested in their personal well-being. Commenting on the philosophy necessary for successful cooperative programs, one author wrote, "That philosophy emphasizes the building of trust and mutual understanding between key management and union personnel, including

FIGURE 18–3 DEVELOPING LABOR–MANAGEMENT COOPERATION

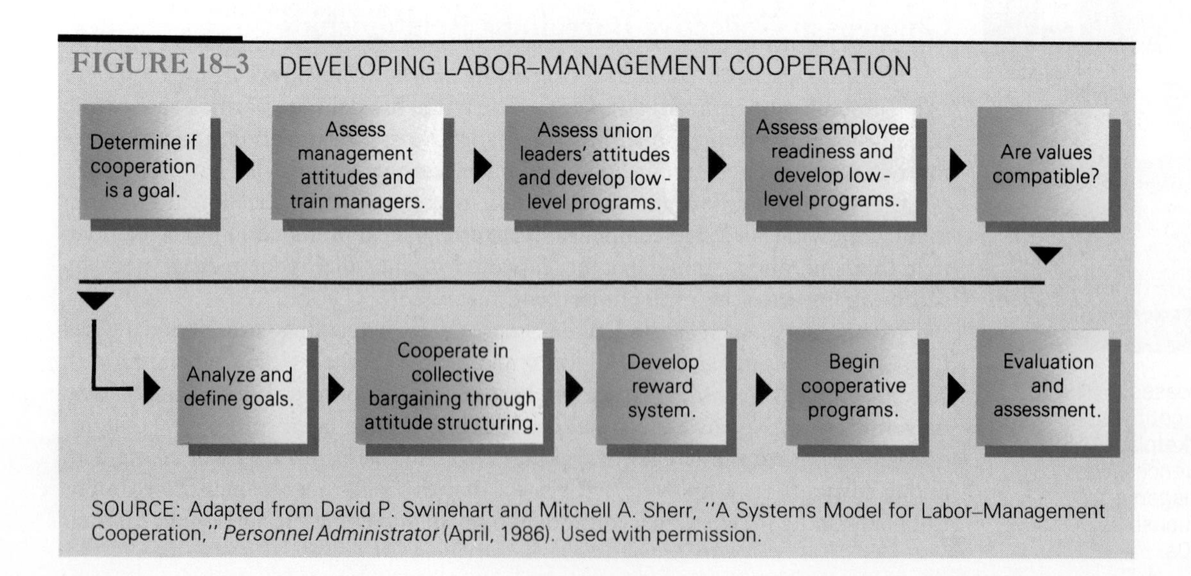

SOURCE: Adapted from David P. Swinehart and Mitchell A. Sherr, "A Systems Model for Labor–Management Cooperation," *Personnel Administrator* (April, 1986). Used with permission.

the common definition of problems, the examination of new approaches to those problems, and the sharing of relevant information."[21]

DEFINITION AND FORMS OF COOPERATION While labor–management cooperation has become a positive trend in collective bargaining, there is no real consensus on how to define this cooperation or what it entails in practice. In one study, managers who were asked to give examples of labor–management cooperation listed union acceptance of wage concessions and union improvement in productivity.[22] On a union leader's list, however, these same elements might appear as evidence of *lack* of cooperation, with union acceptance of wage concessions viewed as capitulation to management's demands and union productivity improvements as the elimination of work rules long cherished by union members. Chamberlain and Kuhn define labor–management cooperation as any mode of bargaining or joint discussion in which the objective is to improve the well-being of both parties.[23] Though this is certainly a good working definition, debate will continue on how the objective can best be achieved.

Management's creation of committees on which employees are represented is the most common approach to collaboration. Shop committees, department committees, and quality circles, to mention a few, are examples of union–management efforts to involve union members in different organizational programs. Moreover, managements are involving union leaders in their attempts to cope with problems such as absenteeism, loafing, and substance abuse. Cooperation between union and management in handling disciplinary problems and in resolving grievances as expeditiously as possible can prove mutually beneficial.

Concessionary Bargaining

To prevent layoffs and plant closures and, it is hoped, put members back to work, enlightened labor leaders recognize the need to help employers reduce operating costs. Getting their members to "give back" any gains received in previous bargaining, however, can prove difficult and politically dangerous for union officers. To reduce this danger, greater emphasis must be placed on educating members regarding the need to cooperate. Members of management often require similar education.

Economic adversity motivates concessionary bargaining and the implementation of cooperative programs. A troubled financial condition, however, may not always bring forth the desired union concessions. In one study, the authors concluded that while union leaders might recognize an organization's financial crisis, their willingness to make concessions depends on (1) a positive labor–management relationship, and (2) their view of management. These authors note:

> Although employers' claims of economic adversity may prompt concession negotiations, getting union officers to agree to make concessions depends on their seeing management as credible. Union officers, who tend to be suspicious of arguments for concessions, often consider such management bargaining positions to be opportu-

nistic. Management generally must persuade unions that a crisis is near. Such persuasion is more likely to succeed in a trustful, not hostile, climate.[24]

CONCESSIONS SOUGHT BY EMPLOYERS Employers in the auto, steel, high-technology, and other highly competitive industries have been seeking labor agreement concessions. This represents a departure from traditional bargaining. The concessions they seek are usually directed toward (1) limiting or lowering compensation payments and (2) increasing employee productivity.

To gain wage concessions, employers may offer gainsharing plans (see Chapter 11) that link compensation to productivity or sales. Profit sharing and stock ownership are other plans being offered to motivate employees and reward improvements in performance. Unfortunately for employers, in the long run job and income guarantees can increase costs, reduce flexibility, and divert funds from equipment that would improve productivity.

Restrictive work rules are particularly troublesome to employers because, in this age of technology, these rules are detrimental to productivity. Changes in these rules represent another area in which unions have been willing to make concessions. In the Plastics Division of Uniroyal, Inc., for example, a labor–management committee established by the company and the United Rubber Workers developed a package of changes in work rules that saved an estimated $5 million.[25]

RECIPROCAL CONCESSIONS SOUGHT BY UNIONS In return for concessions granted to employers, unions are demanding provisions for greater job security. Provisions for such security will be a major union goal in future agreements by such unions as the Teamsters, the Oil, Chemical, and Atomic Workers International Union, the United Rubber Workers, and the United Auto Workers. Unions are also likely to demand provisions restricting the transfer of work, outsourcing (subcontracting), and plant closures by employers. Getting advance notice of shutdowns, as well as severance pay and transfer rights for displaced employees, will be high on the "want lists" of union negotiators. For employees likely to be replaced by technology, unions will bargain for retraining programs as a means to upgrade employee skills.

The Labor Agreement

After an agreement has been reached, it must be put in writing, ratified by the union membership, and signed by the representatives of both parties. The scope of the agreement (and the length of the written document) will vary with the size of the employer and the length of the bargaining relationship. Highlights in HRM 1 shows some of the major articles in the agreement between AT&T Technologies, Inc., and the Communications Workers of America.

Two important items in any labor agreement pertain to the issue of management rights and the forms of security afforded the union.

Employees at General Motors receive a course in robotics.

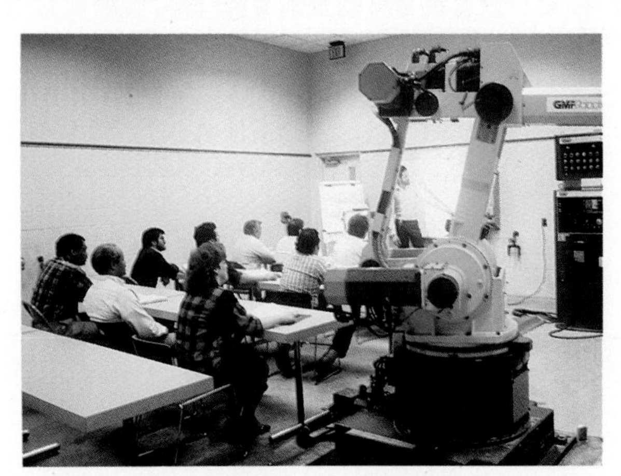

The Issue of Management Rights

Management rights have to do with conditions of employment over which management is able to exercise exclusive jurisdiction. Since virtually every management right can and has been challenged successfully by unions, the ultimate determination of these rights will depend on the relative bargaining power of the two parties. Furthermore, to achieve union cooperation or concessions, employers have had to relinquish some of these time-honored rights.

RESERVED RIGHTS In the labor agreement, management rights may be treated as *reserved rights* or as *defined rights*. The **reserved rights** concept holds that

> management's authority is supreme in all matters except those it has expressly conceded in the collective agreement, or in those areas where its authority is restricted by law. Put another way, management does not look to the collective agreement to ascertain its rights; it looks to the agreement to find out which and how much of its rights and powers it has conceded outright or agreed to share with the union.[26]

Employers who subscribe to the reserved rights concept prefer not to mention management rights in the labor agreement on the grounds that they possess such rights already. To mention them might create an issue with the union.

DEFINED RIGHTS The **defined rights** concept, on the other hand, is intended to reinforce and clarify which rights are exclusively those of management. It serves to reduce confusion and misunderstanding and to remind union officers,

HIGHLIGHTS IN HRM

1 LABOR AGREEMENT BETWEEN AT&T TECHNOLOGIES AND THE COMMUNICATIONS WORKERS OF AMERICA—SELECTED ARTICLES

ARTICLE

1. Recognition
2. Management of Business
4. Collective Bargaining Procedure
5. Access of Union Officials to Company Premises
10. Grievance Procedure
11. Arbitration
12. Work Schedules
13. Overtime
15. Wages
17. Call-in Emergency
20. Vacations
21. Holidays
22. Pay Treatment for Absences

ARTICLE

24. Layoff Allowance
25. Rest Periods
26. Pensions and Benefits
27. Movement of Personnel
28. Suspension and Termination of Employment
30. Payroll Deduction Authorization
36. Lunch Periods
37. Wash-Up or Clothes-Changing Time
38. Responsible Relationship
39. Wage Protection
43. Facility Closing Program
44. Contract Duration

SOURCE: AT&T Technologies, Inc., and Communications Workers of America, June 26, 1986.

union stewards, and employees that management never relinquishes its right to operate the organization. The great majority of labor agreements contain provisions covering management rights. The following is an example of a general statement defining management rights in one labor agreement:

> It is agreed that the company possesses all of the rights, powers, privileges, and authority it had prior to the execution of this agreement; and nothing in this agreement shall be construed to limit the company in any way in the exercise of the regular and customary functions of management and the operation of its business, except as it may be specifically relinquished or modified herein by an express provision of this agreement.[27]

Union Security Agreements

When a labor organization is certified by the NLRB as the exclusive bargaining representative of all employees in a bargaining unit, by law it must represent all employees in the unit, nonunion and union members alike. In exchange for its obligation to represent all employees equally, union officials will seek to negotiate some form of compulsory membership as a condition of employment. Union officials argue that compulsory membership precludes the possibility that some employees will receive the benefits of unionization without paying their share of the costs. A standard union security provision is dues checkoff, which gives the employer the responsibility of withholding union dues from the paychecks of union members who agree to such a deduction.

Other common forms of union security found in labor agreements include the following:

- The *union shop* provides that any employee not a union member at employment must join the union within 30 days or be terminated.
- The *maintenance-of-membership shop* requires that employees who voluntarily join a union must maintain membership during the life of the agreement. Membership withdrawal is possible during a designated escape period.
- The *agency shop* provides for voluntary membership. However, all bargaining unit members must pay union dues and fees.
- The *open shop* allows employees to join the union or not. Nonmembers do not pay union dues.

Few issues in collective bargaining are more controversial than the negotiation of these agreements. The most popular union security clause, the union shop, is illegal in 21 states having right-to-work laws.[28] Right-to-work laws ban any form of compulsory union membership. Section 14(b) of the Taft-Hartley Act permits the individual states to enact legislation prohibiting compulsory union membership as a condition of employment. Generally, right-to-work states are located in the South and West, and are largely agricultural states (see Figure 18–4). The right-to-work argument is a heated one with strong supporters on both sides.[29]

Working side-by-side with the union shop clause are the various seniority provisions of the labor agreement. Unions prefer that many personnel decisions (promotions, job transfers, shift assignments, vacations) be based on seniority, a criterion that limits the discretion of managers to make such decisions based on merit.

ADMINISTRATION OF THE LABOR AGREEMENT

Negotiation of the labor agreement, as mentioned earlier, is usually the most publicized and critical aspect of labor relations. Strike deadlines, press conferences, and employee picketing help create this image. Nevertheless, as managers in unionized organizations know, the bulk of labor relations activity comes from the day-to-day administration of the agreement, since no agreement could possibly anticipate all the forms that disputes may take. In addition, once the agreement is

FIGURE 18–4 RIGHT-TO-WORK STATES

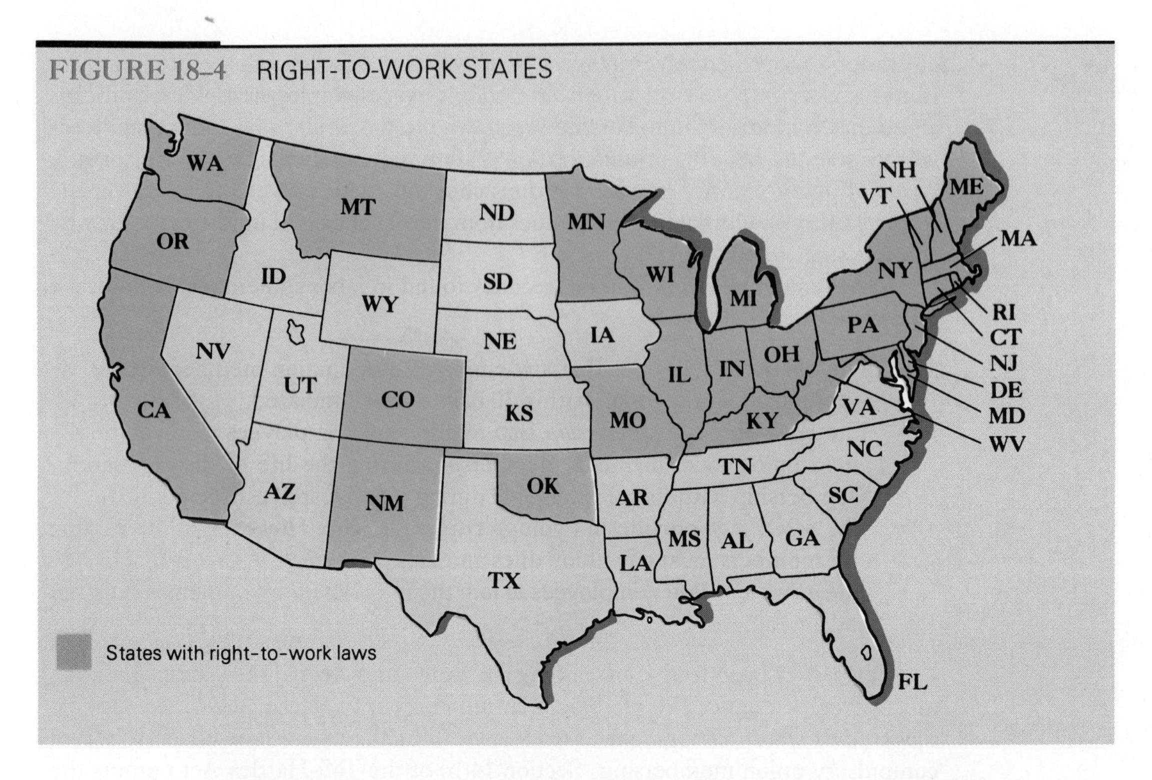

signed, each side will naturally interpret ambiguous clauses to its own advantage. These differences are traditionally resolved through the grievance procedure.

Negotiated Grievance Procedures

The **grievance procedure** typically provides for the union to represent the interests of its members (and nonmembers as well) in processing a grievance. It is considered by some authorities to be the heart of the bargaining agreement, or the safety valve that gives flexibility to the whole system of collective bargaining.[30] When negotiating a grievance procedure, one important concern for both sides is how effectively the system will serve the needs of labor and management. A well-written grievance procedure will allow grievances to be processed expeditiously and with as little red tape as possible. Furthermore, it should serve to foster cooperation, ***not*** conflict, between the employer and the union.

The operation of a grievance procedure is unique to each individual collective bargaining relationship. Grievance procedures are negotiated to address the organization's structure and labor–management philosophy and the specific desires of the parties. Although each procedure is unique, there are common elements between systems. For example, grievance procedures normally specify how the grievance is to be initiated, the number and timing of steps that are to comprise the procedure, and the identity of representatives from each side who are to be involved in the hearings at each step (see Figure 18–5). When a grievance cannot be resolved at one of the specified steps, most agreements provide for the grievance to be submitted to a third party—usually an arbitrator—whose decision is final. It is not the function of an arbitrator to help the two parties reach a compromise solution. Rather, it is the arbitrator's job to mandate how the grievance is to be resolved.

FIGURE 18–5 FIVE-STEP GRIEVANCE ARBITRATION PROCEDURE

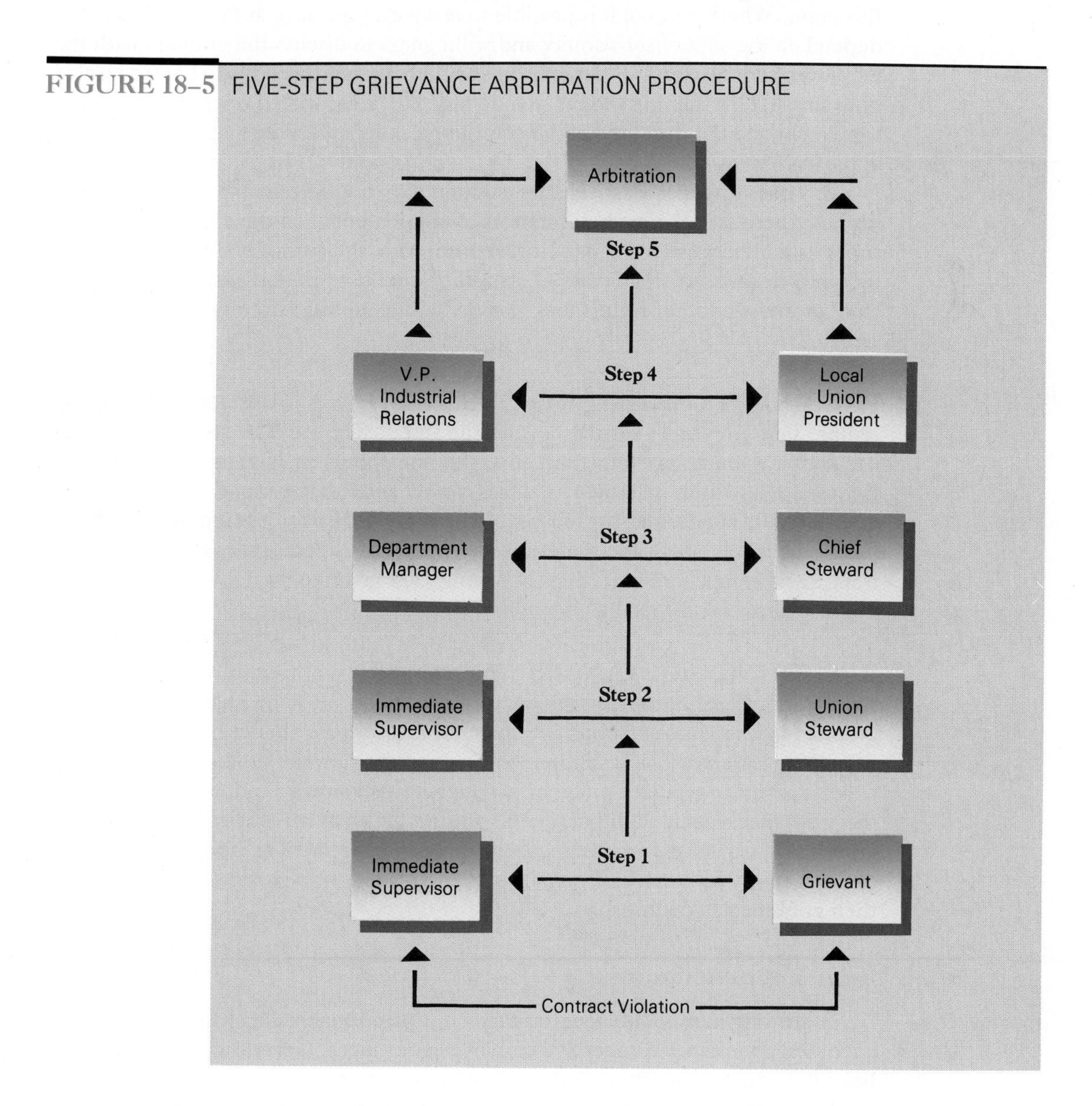

INITIATING THE FORMAL GRIEVANCE In order for an employee's grievance to be considered formally, it must be expressed orally and/or in writing,[31] ideally to the employee's immediate supervisor. If the employee feels unable to communicate effectively with the supervisor, the grievance may be taken to the union steward, who will discuss it with the supervisor. Since grievances are often the result of an oversight or a misunderstanding, many of them can be resolved at this point. Whether or not it is possible to resolve a grievance at the initial step will depend on the supervisor's ability and willingness to discuss the problem with the employee and the steward. Supervisors should be trained formally in how to resolve grievances. This training should include familiarization with the terms of the labor agreement and the development of counseling skills to facilitate a problem-solving approach.

In some instances a satisfactory solution may not be possible at the first step because there are legitimate differences of opinion between the employee and the supervisor or because the supervisor does not have the authority to take the action required to satisfy the grievant. Personality conflicts, prejudices, emotionalism, stubbornness, or other factors may also be barriers to a satisfactory solution at this step.

PREPARING THE GRIEVANCE STATEMENT Most labor agreements require that grievances carried beyond the initial step must be stated in writing, usually on a multicopy form similar to the one shown in Highlights in HRM 2. Requiring a written statement reduces the chance that various versions of the grievance will appear because of lapses in memory. It also forces employees to think more objectively about their grievances. When this is done, grievances that stem from trivial complaints or feelings of hostility are less likely to be pursued beyond the first step.

RESOLVING GRIEVANCES If a grievance is to be resolved successfully, representatives of both management and the union must be able to discuss the problem in a rational and objective manner. A grievance should not be viewed as something to be won or lost. Rather, both sides must view the situation as an attempt to solve a human relations problem. Though neither side should expect to have all the grievances decided in its favor, one study showed, not surprisingly, that grievants' satisfaction with the grievance procedure is related to the outcome of their cases. Those who received favorable settlements reported greater satisfaction with their grievance procedure.[32]

Grievance Mediation

A growing number of labor–management practitioners are championing grievance mediation as a way to resolve employee grievances. **Grievance mediation** has been defined as "an effort on the part of a neutral person to assist two parties in reaching agreement on a grievance that is moving toward or is actually at impasse."[33]

HIGHLIGHTS IN HRM

2 GRIEVANCE FORM: PHOENIX TRANSIT SYSTEM AND TEAMSTERS, LOCAL 104

COMPLAINT RECORD

Transport, Local Delivery and Sales Drivers, Warehousemen and Helpers, Mining and Motion Picture Production, State of Arizona, Local Union No. 104

an Affiliate of the International Brotherhood of Teamsters, Chauffeurs, Warehousemen and Helpers of America

Member's name __________ Date __________

Member's address __________ Home phone __________

City __________ State __________ Zip Code __________

Name of company against whom you are filing complaint __________

Explain complaint in detail __________

If complaint is for discharge (give exact reason given by Co.) __________

This will constitute full authority for Transport and Local Delivery Drivers Local 104 or any employee or agent designated by them as my attorney-in-fact, to fully represent me in the processing of this complaint in any manner they deem is in the best interest of myself as the complainant and the Union, and to receive on my behalf any monies due me.

Should this complaint be processed through the grievance procedure,

(a) I request notification of the time, date and place of hearing ☐

(b) I do not request notification of the time, date and place of hearing ☐

I understand and agree that if I attend any hearing on my behalf, I will do so at my own personal expense, and the Union will in no way be obligated for same.

____
MEMBER'S SIGNATURE

Record of action by Union: __________

Case settled: __________
AGENT

SOURCE: Courtesy of Phoenix Transit System and Teamsters, Local 104, Phoenix, Arizona.

With grievance mediation, a neutral mediator is selected from outside the employment relationship to assist the parties in resolving a dispute voluntarily. The role of the mediator is to help the disputing parties resolve the grievance through compromise as if it were a bargaining deadlock. Grievance mediation may be invoked as one step in the formal labor–management grievance procedure or in an ad hoc situation separate from the labor agreement.

Grievance mediators will attempt to use creative problem solving to resolve disagreements. As one writer noted, "The approach of the mediator may be to bring the parties to a common ground of acceptance or to bring about an understanding between the parties regarding the facts of the case."[34] If an agreement between the parties is reached, it is recorded and signed by the parties as a legally enforceable document. If the issue is not resolved, the mediator may write an advisory opinion regarding a future settlement. The mediator's opinion may be used as a basis for settlement or for proceeding to arbitration.

Arbitrating Grievances

The function of **arbitration** is to provide the solution to a grievance that a union and an employer have been unable to resolve by themselves. As mentioned earlier, arbitration is performed by a neutral third party (an arbitrator or impartial umpire). This third party's decision dictates how the grievance is to be settled. Both parties are obligated to comply with the decision. Even if one of the parties believes the arbitrator's award is unfair, unwise, or inconsistent with the labor agreement, that party may have no alternative but to comply with the decision.[35]

SOURCES OF ARBITRATORS An arbitrator must be an individual who is acceptable to both disputing parties. An arbitrator who is retained on a permanent basis to resolve all grievances arising under an agreement has the advantage of being familiar with the agreement and the labor–management relationship. Most grievances, however, are resolved by arbitrators who are appointed on an ad hoc basis. If both parties are satisfied with an arbitrator's performance, that person may be called upon to resolve subsequent grievances.[36]

Selecting an ad hoc arbitrator frequently involves choosing one whose name appears on a list of acceptable arbitrators submitted by each party. If this method fails to produce an acceptable arbitrator, the two parties may seek recommendations from such organizations as the American Arbitration Association, the Federal Mediation and Conciliation Service, or the appropriate state agency. Typically, arbitrators are professionals such as professors, attorneys, members of the clergy, or retired government labor mediators. Because of their professional backgrounds, they tend to be identified with neither labor nor management and, therefore, are able to occupy a position of neutrality.

THE DECISION TO ARBITRATE If a grievance cannot be resolved through the grievance procedure, each disputing party must decide whether to use arbitration to resolve the case. The alternatives would be for the union to withdraw the grievance or for the employer to agree to union demands.

In deciding whether to use arbitration, each party must weigh the costs involved against the importance of the case and the prospects of gaining a favorable award. It would seem logical that neither party would allow a weak case to go to arbitration if there were little possibility of gaining a favorable award. Logic, however, does not always prevail. For example, it is not unusual for a union to take a weak case to arbitration in order to demonstrate to the members that the union is willing to exhaust every remedy in looking out for their interests. Union officers also are not likely to refuse to take to arbitration the grievances of members who are popular or politically powerful in the union, even though their cases are weak. Moreover, under the **fair representation doctrine,** unions have a legal obligation to provide assistance to members who are pursuing grievances. Because members can bring suit against their unions for failing to process their grievances adequately, many union officers are reluctant to refuse taking even weak grievances to arbitration.

Management, on the other hand, may allow a weak case to go to arbitration to demonstrate to the union officers that management "cannot be pushed around." Also, managers at lower levels may be reluctant to risk the displeasure of top management by stating that a certain HR policy is unworkable or unsound. Stubbornness and mutual antagonism also may force many grievances into arbitration because neither party is willing to make concessions to reach an agreement, even when it may recognize that it is in the wrong. Figure 18–6 lists the prominent types of issues, and their percentages, submitted to arbitration in a recent year.

FIGURE 18–6 ARBITRATION ISSUES REPORTED BY AMERICAN ARBITRATION ASSOCIATION, 1988

ISSUE	PERCENT*
Discipline and discharge	29.45
Arbitrability	11.76
Wages	10.77
Promotions and transfers	8.22
Work assignments and schedules	7.55
Management rights	6.02
Employee benefits	5.43
Layoff and recall	3.03

*Percentages do not add up to 100.

SOURCE: *Study Time,* American Arbitration Association, no. 4 (1988), 3.

THE ARBITRATION PROCESS The issues to be resolved through arbitration may be described formally in a document known as a **submission agreement.** Such a document might read: "Was the three-day suspension of Alex Hayden for just cause? If not, what is the appropriate remedy?" However, grievable issues are also presented orally to the arbitrator by the two parties at the beginning of the hearing. If minutes and memoranda covering the meetings held at earlier stages of the grievance procedure have been prepared, these are sometimes submitted prior to the formal hearing to acquaint the arbitrator with the issues.

In arbitrating a dispute, it is the responsibility of the arbitrator to ensure that each side receives a fair hearing during which it may present all of the facts it considers pertinent to the case. The procedures for conducting arbitration hearings and the restrictions governing the evidence that may be introduced during these hearings are more flexible than those permitted in a court of law. Hearsay evidence, for example, may be introduced provided that it is considered as such when evaluated with the other evidence presented. The primary purpose of the hearing is to assist the arbitrator in obtaining the facts necessary to resolve a human relations problem rather than a legal one. The arbitrator, therefore, has a right to question witnesses or to request additional facts from either party.

Depending on the importance of the case, the hearings may be conducted in either an informal or a very formal manner not unlike that of a court trial. If desired by either or both parties, or by the arbitrator, a court reporter may be present during the hearing to prepare a transcript of the proceedings. After conducting the hearing and receiving post-hearing briefs (should the parties choose to submit them), the arbitrator customarily has 30 days in which to consider the evidence and to prepare a decision. However, times beyond this period are not uncommon.

THE ARBITRATION AWARD The arbitration award should include not only the arbitrator's decision but also the rationale for it. The reasoning behind the decision can help provide guidance concerning the interpretation of the labor agreement and the resolution of future disputes arising from its administration. In pointing out the merits of each party's position, the reasoning that underlies the award can help lessen the disappointment and protect the self-esteem of those representing the unsuccessful party. In short, tact and objective reasoning can help to reduce disappointment and hard feelings.

The foundation for an arbitrator's decision is the labor agreement and the rights it establishes for each party. In many instances the decision may hinge upon whether management's actions were justified under the terms of this agreement. Sometimes it may hinge upon the arbitrator's interpretation of the wording of a particular provision. Established HR policies and past practices also can provide the basis for determining the award.

In many grievances, such as those involving employee performance or behavior on the job, the arbitrator must determine whether the evidence supports the employer's action against the grievant. The evidence must also indicate whether the employee was accorded the right of **due process,** which is the employee's right to

Reprinted by permission of United Feature Syndicate, Inc.

be informed of unsatisfactory performance and to have an opportunity to respond to these charges. Under most labor agreements an employer is required to have *just cause* (i.e., a good reason) for the action it has taken, and such action should be confirmed by the evidence presented.

If the arbitration hearing indicates that an employee was accorded due process and the disciplinary action was for just cause, the severity of the penalty must then be assessed. Where the evidence supports the discipline imposed by the employer, the arbitrator will probably let the discipline stand intact. However, it is within the arbitrator's power, unless denied by the submission agreement, to reduce the penalty. It is not uncommon, for example, for an arbitrator to reduce a discharge to a suspension without pay for the period the grievant has been off the payroll.

Unlike decisions in a court of law, awards—at least in theory—are supposed to be reached on the basis of the facts of the case rather than on the basis of precedents established by previous cases. The reason for this is that no two cases are exactly alike. Therefore, each case should be decided on its own merits. In practice, however, precedents at times do have some influence on the decision of an arbitrator, who may seek guidance from decisions of other arbitrators in somewhat similar cases. These decisions are compiled and published by the American Arbitration Association and by such labor services as the Bureau of National Affairs, Commerce Clearing House, and Prentice-Hall.

How Arbitrators Decide Cases

Because of the importance and magnitude of arbitration in grievance resolution, the process by which arbitrators make decisions and the factors that influence those decisions are of continuing interest to HR managers. Typically, arbitrators use four factors when deciding cases:

1. The wording of the labor agreement.
2. The submission agreement as presented to the arbitrator.

3. Testimony and evidence offered during the hearing.
4. Arbitration criteria or standards (i.e., similar to standards of common law) against which cases are judged.

When deciding the case of an employee discharged for absenteeism, for example, the arbitrator would consider these factors separately and/or jointly. Arbitrators are essentially constrained to decide cases based on the wording of the labor agreement and the facts, testimony, and evidence presented at the hearing.

In practice, however, arbitration decision making is not an exact science. In fact, the decisions of arbitrators can be rather subjective. Arbitrators can, and do, interpret contract language differently (e.g., What does *just cause* discharge actually mean?), they assign varying degrees of importance to testimony and evidence, they judge the truthfulness of witnesses differently, and they give arbitration standards greater or lesser weight as they apply to facts of the case.[37] Each of these influences serves to introduce subjectivity into the decision-making process.

In addition, researchers have also suggested that an arbitrator's gender, age, experience, and training may influence the decision reached.[38] At present, however, the results from these studies are inconclusive. For example, one study investigating the effect of the grievant's gender on the decision of the arbitrator in discharge cases found gender to have a significant effect on the decision reached. In this study, women were twice as likely as men to have their grievance sustained, and 2.7 times more likely than men to receive full rather than partial reinstatement.[39] In a separate but similar study, gender of the grievant was not an influence on the arbitrator's decision. This research concluded that "gender does not systematically bias or influence arbitration decisions in discharge and discipline cases."[40] The researchers took this as a positive comment on the integrity of the arbitration process in a society rife with claims of sex discrimination.

Criticisms of Grievance Arbitration

According to some critics, one of the major problems relating to arbitration is that most grievance arbitration has acquired characteristics that contradict the objectives and needs of the parties. Specifically, arbitration is criticized for taking too much time, becoming too expensive, and often creating frustration for the aggrieved employee and/or the supervisor in the dispute. The busy schedules of the arbitrator and the union and management officers, as well as a backlog of cases, frequently cause long delays in resolving relatively simple disputes. Time spent by the arbitrator reading lengthy transcripts or briefs or attempting to write an impressive opinion also contributes to the expense and delay.

Arbitration has also been criticized for its increasing use of attorneys and legal procedures. In the opinion of its critics, this "creeping legalism" portends a movement away from the original purposes of labor arbitration. Increasing legalism has been fostered, in part, by laws governing equal employment opportunity with their overlapping jurisdictions.

Expedited Arbitration

The steel industry, the U.S. Postal Service, and the maritime industry use **expedited arbitration** as a way of overcoming the high costs, time delays, and legalism of grievance arbitration. While each labor agreement may have its own procedures governing the use of expedited arbitration, the following are typical characteristics of this newer arbitration process:

1. The arbitration hearing will be held within ten days from the demand for arbitration.
2. The hearing will be completed in one day.
3. Awards must be rendered within five days from the close of the hearing, and only short written awards (one or two pages) are required.
4. Hearings are informal, and the use of attorneys, legal briefs, and court reporters is avoided.

Expedited arbitration is an effective way to dispose of disciplinary cases, routine work issues, or cases without a large monetary cost to the parties. Complex contract-interpretation cases may not be amenable to the expedited procedures.

SUMMARY

The rights of employees to unionize, to bargain collectively with an employer over their conditions of employment, and to exert economic pressures to enforce these demands have become firmly accepted by American society. A growing body of law has been developed to protect these rights, to facilitate collective bargaining, to minimize conflicts, and to prevent abuse by either side in the maintenance of a bargaining relationship. While some employers may resent sharing with a union the authority to make various decisions relating to the operation of their organizations, the existence of unions and their participation in these areas have become an established fact. Therefore, it is to the best interests of every employer who must deal with a union to develop the ability to bargain effectively and to maintain a satisfactory relationship with union leaders.

Collective bargaining includes not only the actual negotiations but also the power tactics used to support negotiating demands. When negotiations become deadlocked, bargaining becomes a power struggle to force from either or both parties the concessions needed to break the deadlock. The need of organizations to survive and continue to provide jobs has placed both unions and employers under pressure to make the concessions required to reach an agreement. Concessions made by unions are helping to reduce operating costs, and concessions made by employers are providing union members with greater employment security.

Once the contract has been ratified, both sides must abide by its provisions or grievances will result. When labor and management are unable to resolve their grievances, the problem may then be resolved through the arbitration process. In taking personnel actions, management should be aware of the basis on which its actions may be reversed by an arbitrator. Any action it takes, therefore, must be in accordance with industrial and legal guidelines, as well as sound principles of human relations.

DISCUSSION QUESTIONS

1. Is collective bargaining the same as negotiating? Explain.
2. Of what significance is the "bargaining zone" in the conduct of negotiations, and what are some influences affecting negotiated outcomes?
3. What are some of the possible reasons why an employer may be willing to face a strike that could result in a loss of customers and profits?
4. How does mediation differ from arbitration, and in what situations is each of these processes most likely to be used?
5. What are some of the bargaining concessions being sought by employers and unions in return for the concessions they may grant?
6. What are some of the developments that are posing a threat to union security?
7. At an election conducted among the 20 employees of the Exclusive Jewelry Store, all but two voted in favor of the Jewelry Workers Union, which subsequently was certified as their bargaining agent. In negotiating its first agreement, the union demanded that it be granted a union shop. The two employees who had voted against the union, however, informed the management that they would quit rather than join. Unfortunately for the store, the two employees were skilled gem cutters who were the most valuable of its employees and would be difficult to replace. What position should the store take with regard to the demand for a union shop?
8. What are some of the reasons why a union or an employer may allow a weak grievance to go to arbitration?

MINI-CASE 18–1 Labor–Management Cooperation at NUMMI

New United Motor Manufacturing Co., Inc. (NUMMI), a former Chevrolet plant located in Fremont, California, employs about 2,500 workers and assembles Chevrolet Novas, Toyota Corollas, and GEO Prizms for sale by GM dealers. The company represents a joint venture between GM and Toyota, Japan's largest automaker.

The old GM-Fremont plant closed in March 1982 after ranking at the bottom of GM's U.S. plants in productivity. The plant recorded absentee rates of over 20 percent and accumulated a backlog of over 1,000 grievances. Union–management relations were described by George Nano, UAW Shop Committee Chair, as "ongoing war."

The plant reopened in December 1984 as a partnership between GM and Toyota. Central to the success of the operation was a new cooperative relationship between the United Auto Workers and NUMMI management based on the sharing of information and an increased level of commitment to each other through a process that involves risk taking and trust building.

At the heart of the production system at NUMMI is the "Operating Team System." All workers in the plant, hourly and salaried, are organized into teams of five to eight members. The teams divide up and rotate jobs among their members. Teams meet periodically (every two weeks on average) to discuss how to improve the work, reduce the number of tasks, and improve quality. Teams can also make limited shop-floor decisions, such as how frequently to rotate jobs among the members. Problems on the line are solved, whenever possible, by team members. Workers have the right to stop the line to solve assembly problems. The organization of teams is facilitated by having only one job classification among production workers. Previously at GM-Fremont there had been over 80 separate job classifications. Team leaders chosen by a joint labor–management committee perform many of the duties of first-line supervisors in traditional auto plants.

The cooperation between labor and management has resulted in numerous operating and quality improvements. These improvements have been possible because workers are sincerely interested in making improvements and because management actively solicits and encourages employee suggestions. Cooperation has reduced unproductive conflict between the two sides. Workers report greater job satisfaction, and absenteeism is down. The local union leadership preaches and practices union–management cooperation at NUMMI in a manner that enhances the degree of equality and reciprocity between labor and management in the plant.

SOURCE: From Clair Brown and Michael Reich, "When Does Union–Management Cooperation Work? A Look at NUMMI and GM-Van Nuys." © 1989 by the Regents of the University of California. Reprinted/condensed from the *California Management Review,* Vol. 31, No. 4. By Permission of the Regents.

QUESTIONS

1. What factors led to the development of cooperation at the NUMMI plant?
2. How do you believe labor and management would define "cooperation" at NUMMI?

MINI-CASE 18–2 The Arbitrator's Dilemma

Maria Suarez realized that the first problem she faced following the delivery of the personal computers to the firm was to educate managers and supervisors in their use. Her solution was to close down the entire plant for two days so that all supervisors using the new computers could be sent to the equipment manufacturer for an extensive course of instruction. Managers and supervisors were paid for this shutdown time, but plant employees were not. This led to a grievance filed by the shop steward on behalf of all hourly employees.

The grievance stated that the two-day shutdown constituted a "lockout," which violated the terms of the labor agreement. The steward argued that there was "work to be done, and my employees are willing and able to do it. You can close the plant if you want to, but we are entitled to pay for the hours not worked."

Suarez researched the labor agreement and found no articles providing for a "guaranteed workweek." Rather, the management's rights clause stated in part that "management retains the right to conduct the operations of the plant according to service needs." Suarez answered the grievance by stating: "Management retains the sole right to close the plant for good cause; and training managers and supervisors is a good, logical reason. There is no discrimination against any employee, since all employees in the bargaining unit were laid off equally for the two-day period."

After the grievance was processed through the first four steps of the grievance procedure, the union demanded arbitration.

QUESTIONS

1. What arguments will labor and management use to advance their case before the arbitration?
2. What factors might the arbitrator use to resolve the case?

NOTES AND REFERENCES

1. Thomas R. Colosi and Arthur E. Berkeley, *Collective Bargaining: How It Works and Why* (New York: American Arbitration Association, 1986). See also Francisco Hernandez-Senter, Jr., "Closing the Communication Gap in Collective Bargaining," *Labor Law Journal* 41, no. 7 (July 1990): 438–444.

2. Employers who refuse to pay union demands are not legally required to provide financial data to union representatives. The requirement to provide financial data would normally arise where an employer asserts during negotiations that it cannot survive if it agrees to union wage proposals or has no operating profit. See Katrina L. Abel, "The Duty to Disclose Relevant Financial Information," *Employee Relations Law Journal* 15, no. 2 (Autumn 1989): 281–289.

3. Michael R. Carrell and Christina Heavrin, *Collective Bargaining and Labor Relations: Cases, Practice, and Law* (Columbus, OH: Merrill, 1985), 111–117.

4. *A Guide to Basic Law and Procedures Under the National Labor Relations Act* (Washington, DC: U.S. Government Printing Office, 1978), 16.

5. John Thomas Delaney and Donna Sockell, "The Mandatory-Permissive Distinction and Collective Bargaining Outcomes," *Industrial and Labor Relations Review* 42, no. 4 (July 1989): 566–581.

6. John A. Fossum, *Labor Relations: Development, Structure, Process*, 4th ed. (Homewood, IL: BPI-Irwin, 1989), 239.

7. Daniel Q. Mills, *Labor–Management Relations*, 4th ed. (New York: McGraw-Hill, 1989), 505.

8. Research suggests that the way in which negotiators frame their initial proposals and the confidence they possess can affect bargaining outcomes. See Margaret A. Neale and Max H. Bazeman, "The Effects of Framing and Negotiator Overconfidence on Bargaining Behaviors and Outcomes," *Academy of Management Journal* 28, no. 1 (March 1985): 34–48.

9. For the original description of attitudinal structuring, see Richard E. Walton and Robert B. McKersie, *A Behavioral Theory of Labor Negotiations* (New York: McGraw-Hill, 1965). This book is considered a classic in the labor relations field.

10. Ross Stagner and Hjalmar Rosen, *Psychology of Union–Management Relations* (Belmont, CA: Wadsworth, 1965), 95–97.

11. For a comprehensive discussion of factors influencing the bargaining relationship, see Terry L. Leap and David W. Grigsby, "A Conceptualization of Collective Bargaining Power," *Industrial and Labor Relations Review* 39, no. 2 (January 1986): 202–213.

12. Bruce E. Kaufman, "Labor's Inequality of Bargaining Power: Changes over Time and Implications for Public Policy," *Journal of Labor Research* 10, no. 3 (Summer 1989), 285–297. See also John G. Kilgor, "Can Unions Strike Anymore? The Impact of Recent Supreme Court Decisions," *Labor Law Journal* 41, no. 5 (May 1990): 259–269.

13. *Monthly Labor Review* 112, no. 9 (September 1989): 84.

14. Jack Barbash, "Do We Really Want Labor on the Ropes?" *Harvard Business Review* 63, no. 4 (July–August 1985): 10–17.

15. Thomas P. Murphy, "Lockouts and Replacements: The NLRB Gives Teeth to an Old Weapon," *Employee Relations Law Journal* 14, no. 2 (Autumn 1988): 253.

16. Sam Kagel and Kathy Kelly, *The Anatomy of Mediation: What Makes It Work* (Washington, DC: Bureau of National Affairs, 1989).

17. Homer C. LaRue, "An Historical Overview of Interest Arbitration in the United States," *Arbitration Journal* 42, no. 4 (December 1987): 18–19.

18. Joel Cutcher-Gershenfeld, Robert McKersie, and Richard Walton, "Dispute Resolution and the Transformation of U.S. Industrial Relations: A Negotiations Perspective," *Labor Law Journal* 40, no. 8 (August 1989): 475–483.

19. For example, see Gary Jacobson, "Employee Relations at Xerox: A Model Worth Copying," *Management Review* 77, no. 2 (February 1988): 22–27; "Conference Focuses on Ways to Achieve Labor–Management Cooperation," *BNA's Employee Relations Weekly* 7, no. 16 (April 17, 1989): 493–494; and Anthony J. Rutigliano, "Cooperating to Survive at National Steel," *Management Review* 77, no. 2 (February 1988): 30–38.

20. David P. Swinehart and Mitchell A. Sherr, "A Systems Model for Labor–Management Cooperation," *Personnel Administrator* 31, no. 4 (April 1986): 87–98.

21. Paula B. Voos, "The Influence of Cooperative Programs on Union–Management Relations, Flexibility, and Other Labor Relations Outcomes," *Journal of Labor Research* 10, no. 1 (Winter 1989): 103.

22. Paula B. Voos and Tsan-Yuang Cheng, "What Do Managers Mean by Cooperative Labor Relations?" *Labor Studies Journal* 14, no. 1 (Spring 1989): 3–17.

23. Richard B. Peterson and Lane Tracy, "Lessons from Labor–Management Cooperation," *California Management Review* 31, no. 1 (Fall 1988): 41.

24. Mark S. Plovnick and Gary N. Chaison, "Relationships Between Concession Bargaining and Labor–Management Cooperation," *Academy of Management Journal* 28, no. 3 (September 1985): 697–704.

25. John G. Belcher, Jr., "The Role of Unions in Productivity Management," *Personnel* 65, no. 1 (January 1988): 58.

26. Paul Prasow and Edward Peters, *Arbitration and Collective Bargaining,* 2d ed. (New York: McGraw-Hill, 1983), 33–34.

27. Wabash Fibre Box Company and Paperworkers.

28. Right-to-work states include Alabama, Arizona, Arkansas, Florida, Georgia, Idaho, Iowa, Kansas, Louisiana, Mississippi, Nebraska, Nevada, North Carolina, North Dakota, South Carolina, South Dakota, Tennessee, Texas, Utah, Virginia, and Wyoming.

29. Marc G. Singer, "Comprehension of Right-to-Work Laws Among Residents of the Right-to-Work States," *Journal of Collective Negotiations in the Public Sector* 16, no. 4 (1987): 311–325. See also Edward Brankey and Mel E. Schnake, "Exceptions to Compulsory Union Membership," *Personnel Journal* 67, no. 6 (June 1988): 114–121. For a discussion of right-to-work laws, see Robert E. Allen and Timothy J. Keaveny, *Contemporary Labor Relations*, 2d ed. (Reading, MA: Addison-Wesley, 1988), 468–471.

30. Frank Elkouri and Edna Asher Elkouri, *How Arbitration Works*, 4th ed. (Washington, DC: Bureau of National Affairs, 1985), 153. See also Judith L. Catlett and Edwin L. Brown, "Union Leaders' Perception of the Grievance Procedure," *Labor Studies Journal* 15, no. 1 (Spring 1990): 54–65.

31. For a review of why employees file grievances and the impact of the grievance system on employee behavior, see Brian S. Klass, "Determinants of Grievance Activity and the Grievance System's Impact on Employee Behavior: An Integrative Perspective," *Academy of Management Review* 14, no. 3 (July 1989): 445–457.

32. Michael E. Gordon and Robert L. Bowlby, "Propositions About Grievance Settlements: Finally, Consultation with Grievants," *Personnel Psychology* 41, no. 1 (Spring 1988): 108. See also Ignace Ng and Ali Dastmalchian, "Determinants of Grievance Outcomes: A Case Study," *Industrial and Labor Relations Review* 42, no. 3 (April 1989): 393–402.

33. John C. Sigler, "Mediation of Grievances: An Alternative to Arbitration?" *Employee Relations Law Journal* 13, no. 2 (Autumn 1987): 272.

34. Ibid., 274.

35. Benjamin J. Taylor and Fred Witney, *Labor Relations Law*, 5th ed. (Englewood Cliffs, NJ: Prentice-Hall, 1987), 447–451. Arbitration awards are not final in all cases. Arbitration awards may be overturned through the judicial process if it can be shown that the arbitrator was prejudiced or failed to render an award based on the essence of the agreement.

36. Some labor agreements call for using arbitration boards to resolve employee grievances. Arbitration boards, which may be either temporary or permanent, are composed of one or more members chosen by management and an equal number chosen by labor. A neutral member serves as chairman. See

Peter A. Veglahn, "Grievance Arbitration by Arbitration Boards: A Survey of the Parties," *Arbitration Journal* 42, no. 2 (July 1987): 47–53.

37. Clyde Scott and Trevor Bain, "How Arbitrators Interpret Ambiguous Contract Language," *Personnel* 64, no. 8 (August 1987): 10–14.

38. Clarence R. Deitsch and David A. Dilts, "An Analysis of Arbitrator Characteristics and Their Effects on Decision Making in Discharge Cases," *Labor Law Journal* 40, no. 2 (February 1989): 112–116.

39. Brian Bemmels, "The Effects of Grievants' Gender on Arbitrator's Decisions," *Industrial and Labor Relations Review* 41, no. 2 (January 1988): 251–262.

40. Clyde Scott and Elizabeth Shadoan, "The Effect of Gender on Arbitration Decisions," *Journal of Labor Research* 10, no. 4 (Fall 1989): 427–436.

PART SEVEN

International Human Resources Management and HR Audits

Part Seven focuses on the topics of HR in multinational companies and the auditing of specific HR functions. Chapter 19 deals with the challenges faced by multinational enterprises when they staff managers and executives in overseas assignments. Special considerations are given to understanding cultural, social, and legal differences of job assignments in foreign countries. In Chapter 20 the effectiveness of HR programs is examined. Included here are HR audit procedures available to both department supervisors and HR specialists. Auditing the many HR functions and programs is a prerequisite to the effective utilization of both monetary and human resources.

CHAPTER 19

International Human Resources Management

After reading this chapter you will be able to:

1. *Identify the components of the cultural environment of international business.*
2. *Cite the advantages in using each of the three different types of overseas managers.*
3. *Describe the personal characteristics desired of an international manager.*
4. *Explain the significance of cross-cultural differences in the management of multinational enterprises.*
5. *Describe the training and development needed to become an effective manager in a foreign location.*
6. *Cite some of the differences among countries in the ways that the major HRM functions are performed.*
7. *Define the key terms in the chapter.*

TERMS TO IDENTIFY

multinational corporation (MNC) *(632)*
global manager *(634)*
host country *(635)*
home-country nationals, or expatriates *(639)*
host-country nationals *(639)*
third-country nationals *(639)*
cross-cultural variables *(644)*
culture shock *(649)*
work permit, or work certificate *(650)*
guest workers *(651)*
balance-sheet approach *(654)*
codetermination *(659)*

The emphasis throughout this book has been on HRM as it is practiced in organizations in the United States. Many of these organizations also engage in international trade. A large percentage carry on their international business with only limited facilities and representation in foreign countries. Others, particularly the huge corporations, have extensive facilities and personnel in various countries of the world. Managing these facilities effectively is a challenge to the leadership of these organizations.

In a period in the economic history of the United States in which international business operations are a major concern, it is essential for the reader to be aware of the role of HRM and the contributions it can make to an organization's foreign operations. Recent popular books have suggested that many U.S. companies need to reassess their approach to doing business overseas, particularly in the area of managing human resources. In this chapter we will observe that much of what has been discussed throughout the book can be applied to foreign operations, provided one is sensitive to the requirements of a particular international setting.

The dramatic changes that have occurred in recent years in the Soviet Union and Eastern Europe will have their effects on HRM. Of probably even greater influence will be the scheduled 1992 unification of the markets of 12 European nations into the European Community (EC-92). In concept, EC-92 will turn Europe into a unified buying and selling power that will compete as a major economic player with the United States and Japan. With EC-92, goods, services, capital, and human resources will move across national borders in Europe as freely as they cross state borders in the United States. In the years ahead the reader will have a unique opportunity to observe the effect that EC-92 has on HRM.

The first part of this chapter will present a brief introduction to international HRM and the environmental factors that affect the work of HR managers in the international setting. Since the success of foreign operations depends on the quality of leadership, a major portion of this chapter will deal with the various HR activities involved in the recruitment, selection, and training and development of individuals for managerial positions in foreign locations. An overview of HR functions and the ways in which they are performed in some of the countries where American corporations have facilities will follow. Throughout the discussion the focus will be on U.S. multinational corporations. Finally, some predictions about the role of HRM in the European Community will be presented.

DOMESTIC AND INTERNATIONAL HRM

Internationalization of U.S. corporate activity has grown at a faster pace than the publication of articles about it. While various journals on international business have published articles on HRM over the years, it was not until 1990 that a journal specifically devoted to this area—the *International Journal of Human Resource Management*—was started.

International HRM differs from domestic HRM in several ways. In the first place, it is responsible for a greater number of functions. As shown in Figure 19–1, functions and activities unique to international HRM include relocation, orientation, and translation services to help employees adapt to a new and different environment outside their own country. Assistance with taxation matters, banking, investment management, home rental while on assignment, and coordination of home visits is also usually provided by the HR department.[1]

The HR manager in an overseas unit must be particularly responsive to the external environment. The human and financial consequences of failure in an international business are often more severe than in a domestic business. Other risks to which international HR managers are exposed are financial, e.g., the volatility of foreign exchange rates; political, e.g., the possibility of terrorist attacks on personnel; and the need to change emphasis in HR operations as a foreign subsidiary matures.

MULTINATIONAL CORPORATIONS

While international business operations include various types of financial, marketing, and control arrangements, the emphasis in this chapter will be on multinational corporations. There are several definitions of a multinational corporation. For purposes of this discussion, a **multinational corporation (MNC)** is one that operates in two or more countries, earns part of its profits from its foreign operations, and has part of its assets located in other countries. The most obvious characteristic of MNCs is their size. Some of the largest American MNCs are listed in Figure 19–2.

MNCs are in a strong position to affect the world economy in the following ways: (1) production and distribution extend beyond national boundaries, making the MNCs important channels for the transfer of technology; (2) MNCs have direct investments in many countries, affecting the balance of payments; and (3) MNCs

FIGURE 19–1 DOMESTIC AND INTERNATIONAL HRM FUNCTIONS AND ACTIVITIES

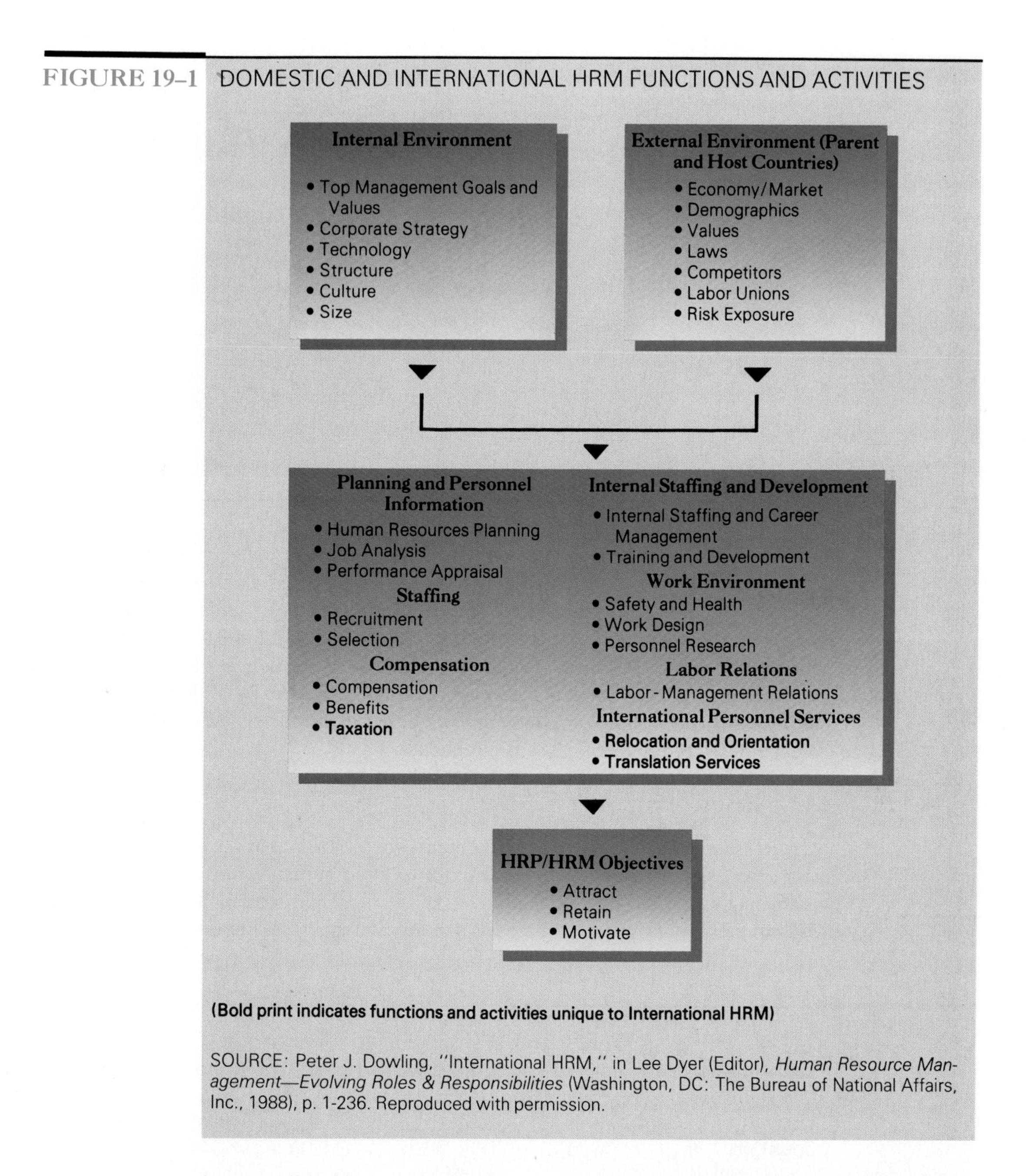

SOURCE: Peter J. Dowling, "International HRM," in Lee Dyer (Editor), *Human Resource Management—Evolving Roles & Responsibilities* (Washington, DC: The Bureau of National Affairs, Inc., 1988), p. 1-236. Reproduced with permission.

have a political impact that leads to cooperation among countries and to the breaking down of barriers of nationalism. The United States has no monopoly on MNCs. They are found in European countries, Japan, and other countries. MNCs of British and Dutch origin are readily found on U.S. soil.[2]

IBM is one of the most widely recognized multinationals in the world.

If these organizations are to be managed effectively, managers will need to be educated and trained in global management skills. Such skills as being able to balance and tune centralized and decentralized activities, generalized expertise across all areas of an enterprise's activities, the ability to see the opportunities and constraints in the big picture, a sense of reality, operational effectiveness, and interpersonal effectiveness are among the skills needed to be a **global manager**. Other skills and personal characteristics essential to the success of a global manager will be described in detail later in this chapter.[3]

The Environment of MNCs

In Chapter 2, the role of environment—both internal and external—in HRM was emphasized. Understanding the external environment is critical to the success of managing an MNC. Certainly the economic environment and the physical environment (population, climate, geography, and so on) are important factors in the

FIGURE 19–2 SOME OF THE LARGEST U.S. MULTINATIONALS

BankAmerica	General Motors	Procter & Gamble
Chrysler	Goodyear	RJR Nabisco
Citicorp	IBM	Safeway Stores
Coca-Cola	ITT	Texaco
E. I. DuPont de Nemours	Mobil	United Technologies
Ford Motor	J. P. Morgan	Xerox
General Electric		

making of managerial decisions. Of special importance in international business, however, is the *cultural environment* (language, religion, values and attitudes, education, social organization, technology, politics, and law). Figure 19–3 is an overview of the complexity of the cultural environment in which international business operates. As indicated by the arrows, any one of the components may be linked with any of the others. Culture should thus be viewed as an integrated phenomenon. By recognizing and accommodating taboos, rituals, attitudes toward time, social stratification, kinship systems, and the many other components listed in Figure 19–3, the HR manager will pave the way toward greater harmony and achievement in the **host country** (the country in which an MNC operates).

Different cultural environments require different organizational behaviors. Strategies, structures, and technologies that are appropriate in one cultural setting may lead to failure in another. Managing relations between an organization and its cultural environment is thus a matter of accurate perception, sound diagnosis, and appropriate adaptation. Several techniques and approaches are available to assist MNC personnel in coping with demands imposed by the cultural environment.[4] MNCs in one location often push aside interorganizational differences to share experiences and to assist each other in resolving conflicts that arise with the host country's culture.

Managing in a Foreign Environment

Managerial attitudes and behaviors are the product of the society in which managers receive their training. Similarly, reactions of subordinates are the result of cultural conditioning. Each culture has its expectations for the roles of manager and subordinate. What one culture encourages as participative management another sees as managerial incompetence.[5] Being successful as a manager depends on one's ability to understand the way things are and to recognize that changes cannot be made abruptly without considerable resistance and possibly antagonism on the part of local nationals. Some of the areas in which there are often significant variations among the different countries will be examined briefly.

EMPLOYEE ATTITUDES AND MOTIVATION While each employee has his or her unique set of attitudes, desires, and goals, certain patterns have been found to prevail in different countries. A wealth of data from cross-cultural studies reveals that countries/nations tend to cluster according to similarities on certain cultural dimensions such as work goals, values, needs, and job attitudes. The underlying factors for clustering are *geography*, *language*, and *religion*. Using data from eight comprehensive studies of cultural differences, Ronen and Shenkar group countries into the clusters shown in Figure 19–4. Countries having a higher GNP per capita in comparison with other countries are placed close to the center.

Ronen and Shenkar point out that while evidence for the grouping of countries into Anglo, Germanic, Nordic, Latin European, and Latin American clusters appears to be quite strong, clusters encompassing the Far Eastern and Arab countries

FIGURE 19–3 COMPOSITION OF THE CULTURAL ENVIRONMENT OF INTERNATIONAL BUSINESS

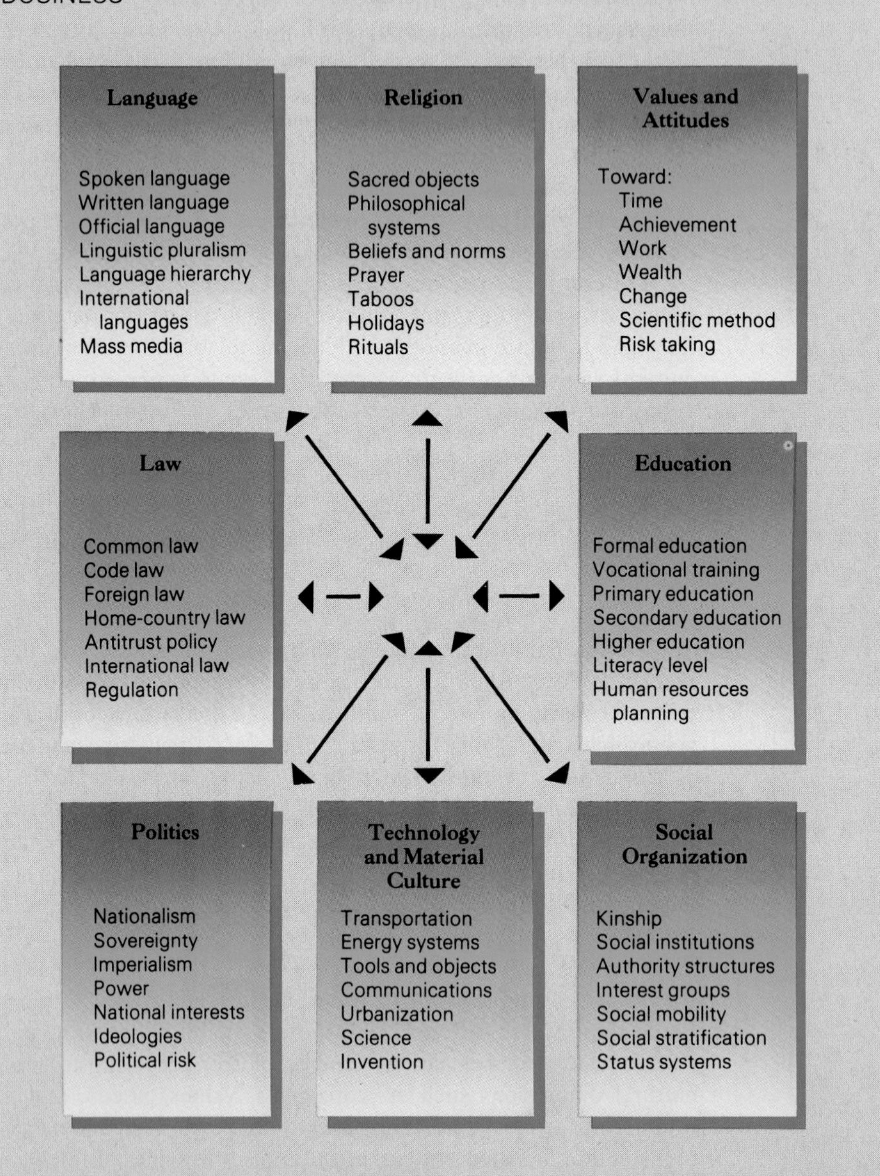

SOURCE: Vern Terpstra, *The Cultural Environment of International Business* (Cincinnati: South-Western, 1978), xiv. Reproduced with permission.

FIGURE 19–4 A SYNTHESIS OF COUNTRY CLUSTERS

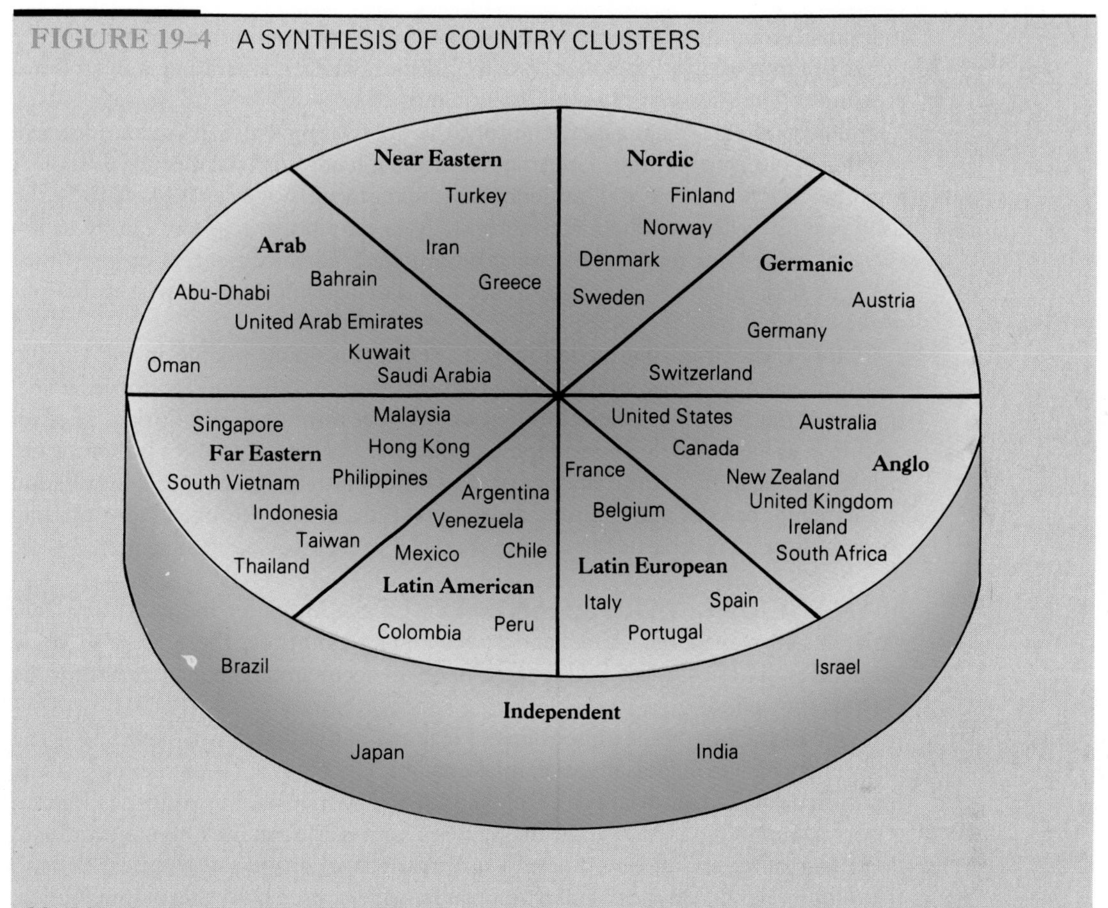

SOURCE: Simcha Ronen and Oded Shenkar, "Clustering Countries on Attitudinal Dimensions: A Review and Synthesis," *Academy of Management Review* 10, no. 3 (July 1985): 435–454. Copyright *Academy of Management Review*. Reprinted with permission of the *Academy of Management Review* and the authors.

are ill defined and require further research, as do clusters of countries classified as independent. Many areas, such as Africa, have not been studied at all. It should also be noted that the clusters presented in Figure 19–4 do not include the Soviet Union and its former satellites.

In spite of these limitations, the cluster approach can be helpful to managers in identifying and understanding differences in work attitudes and motivation in other cultures. In Japan, for example, employees are more likely to feel a strong loyalty to their organization, although recent reports show that this may be changing. Americans, when compared with the Japanese, may feel little loyalty to the organization they work for. On the other hand, the Latin American tends to work not for an organization but for an individual manager. Thus, managers in Latin American countries can get performance only by using personal influence and working through individual members of a group. In the United States, competition is the name of the game; in Japan, Taiwan, and other Asian countries, where cooperation is an art form, creating competition can cause major problems.[6]

Managers should consider carefully the motivational use of incentives and rewards in foreign countries. For Americans, though nonfinancial incentives such as prestige, independence, and influence may be motivators, money is likely to be the driving force. Other cultures are more likely to emphasize respect, family or job security, a satisfying personal life, social acceptance, advancement, or power. Since there are many alternatives to money, the rule is to match the reward with the values of the culture.[7]

Most research on motivation in work settings is about people in industrially advanced nations. Those studies that have been done in third-world countries reveal that work motivation can be attributed to *culture strength* (lack of dilution by other cultures), as well as to the level of industrialization. As Western values influence the culture and as industrialization increases, worker motivation changes.[8] Motivation is a dynamic process and requires continued study in any setting. Understanding work motivation in a particular culture is crucial to the overseas manager.

MANAGERIAL VALUES AND STYLES Although there certainly are variations in managerial values and styles among countries, there are also some similarities. These similarities are most likely to occur among managers within the clusters shown in Figure 19–4.

One of the important dimensions of leadership discussed in Chapter 14 is the degree to which managers invite employee participation in decision making. While it is difficult to find hard data on employee participation in various countries, careful observers report that American managers are about in the middle on a continuum of decision-making styles. Scandinavian and Australian managers also appear to be in the middle. South American and European managers, especially those from France, Germany, and Italy, are toward the autocratic end of the continuum; Japanese managers are at the most participatory end. Because Far Eastern cultures and religions tend to emphasize harmony, group decision making predominates there.[9]

MANAGERS FOR THE MULTINATIONAL CORPORATION

In the preceding section we saw that the operation of an MNC poses many problems in addition to those the manager of a domestic operation is required to handle. Furthermore, because of geographic distance and a lack of close, day-to-day relationships with headquarters in the home country, problems must often be resolved with little or no counsel or assistance from others. It is essential, therefore, that special attention be given to the management staffing of overseas units. Because of the importance of this aspect of international HRM, we will discuss sources of managerial personnel, criteria for selection, training and development, and some special considerations related to managerial staffing that must be handled effectively. Compensation of managers will be discussed later in the chapter.

Sources of Managerial Personnel

There are three sources of managers with which to staff an MNC. First, the MNC can send managers from its home country. These individuals are often referred to as **home-country nationals,** or **expatriates.** Second, it can hire **host-country nationals** (natives of the host country) to do the managing. Third, it can hire **third-country nationals,** natives of a country other than the home country or the host country. For example, a German national may be assigned as manager of an American subsidiary in Japan.

Using each of the three sources of overseas managers presents advantages and disadvantages. Some of the more important advantages are presented in Figure 19–5. Most MNCs use all three sources for staffing their multinational operations, although some companies exhibit a distinct bias for one of the three sources.[10] In making a decision regarding the source to be used, factors to be weighed in addition to those listed in Figure 19–5 are technical competence, functional area of expertise, health status, career plans, personal preferences, and personality attributes. These and other prerequisites for foreign assignments will be examined more thoroughly in the next section.

It should be recognized that while top managers may have preferences for one source of managers over another, the host country may place pressures on them that

FIGURE 19–5 SOME ADVANTAGES OF USING DIFFERENT SOURCES OF OVERSEAS MANAGERS

Host-Country Nationals
Less cost
Preference of host-country governments
Intimate knowledge of environment
Language facility

Home-Country Nationals (Expatriates)
Talent available within company
Greater control
Company experience
Mobility
Experience provided to corporate executives

Third-Country Nationals
Broad experience
International outlook
Multilingualism

restrict their choices. Such pressure takes the form of sophisticated government persuasion through administrative or legislative decrees.[11]

Criteria for Selection

Selecting home-country and third-country nationals requires that more factors be considered than in selecting host-country nationals. While the latter must of course possess managerial abilities and the necessary technical skills, they have the advantage of familiarity with the physical and cultural environment and the language of the host country. The discussion that follows will focus on the selection of managers from the home country.

PERSONAL CHARACTERISTICS The problem facing MNCs is to find managers who can meet the demands of working in a foreign environment. There are no screening devices to identify with certainty who will succeed and who will fail. But there are requirements that one should meet to even be considered for a managerial position in a foreign country. Before examining these requirements, a look at the ideal characteristics of an international manager will illustrate the problem of selecting the right person:

> Ideally, it seems, he (she) should have the stamina of an Olympic swimmer, the mental agility of an Einstein, the conversational skill of a professor of languages, the detachment of a judge, the tact of a diplomat, and the perseverance of an Egyptian pyramid builder. . . . And if he (she) is going to measure up to the demands of living and working in a foreign country, he (she) should also have a feeling of culture; his (her) moral judgments should not be too rigid; he (she) should be able to merge with the local environment with chameleon-like ease; and he (she) should show no signs of prejudice.[12]

An expatriate manager may experience strong cultural differences in a foreign country both professionally and socially.

Obviously it is difficult to find individuals who measure up to this ideal. Nevertheless, careful evaluation of candidates will increase the possibilities of finding the type of person who is most likely to succeed. Several characteristics have been shown to be very important. Tung sent a questionnaire to a sample of American companies in which respondents were asked to identify the criteria they would consider important in selecting personnel for various types of managerial jobs in foreign countries. They were also asked to indicate the most important reasons for an expatriate's failure to function effectively in a foreign environment. The reasons given, in descending order of importance, are shown in Figure 19–6.

It is apparent from the figure that ability to adjust to a different type of environment overshadows technical competence and company experience, motivation, and job responsibilities. This clearly requires the commitment of the whole family, particularly the manager's spouse, to the success of the assignment. Satisfactory adjustment depends on flexibility, emotional maturity and stability, empathy for the culture, language and communication skills, resourcefulness and initiative, and diplomatic skills.

FIGURE 19–6 REASONS FOR AMERICAN EXPATRIATE FAILURES IN FOREIGN ENVIRONMENT (in descending order of importance)

- Inability of the manager's spouse to adjust to a different physical or cultural environment.
- The manager's inability to adapt to a different physical or cultural environment.
- Other family-related problems.
- The manager's personality or emotional immaturity.
- The manager's inability to cope with the responsibilities posed by the overseas work.
- The manager's lack of technical competence.
- The manager's lack of motivation to work overseas.

SOURCE: Rosalie L. Tung, "Selection and Training of Personnel for Overseas Assignments." Reprinted with permission of the *Columbia Journal of World Business* XVI, no. 1 (Spring 1981): 68–78. © 1981.

THE SELECTION PROCESS The first step in the selection process is to identify the job. If the job involves extensive contacts with the community, as with a chief executive officer, this factor should be given appropriate weight. A second set of factors relates to "environmental variables." The magnitude of differences between the political, legal, socioeconomic, and cultural systems of the host country and those of the home country should be assessed and rank-ordered. If a candidate is willing to live and work in a foreign environment, an indication of his or her tolerance of cultural differences should be obtained. If local nationals have the technical competence to carry out the job successfully, Tung advises that they be carefully considered for the job before the organization launches a search (at home) for a candidate to fill the job. She reports that most of the 80 corporations surveyed appeared to realize the advantages to be gained by staffing foreign subsidiaries with local nationals wherever possible.[13]

The selection process that Tung recommends is shown in Figure 19–7. A study of the flowchart reveals the emphasis that should be given to different factors, depending on the extent of contact that one would have with the culture and the degree to which the foreign environment differs from the home environment. Once an individual is selected, the amount of orientation required will vary as shown at the bottom of the chart. The nature of the orientation usually provided will be discussed later.

SELECTION METHODS The most commonly used methods of selection used by MNCs are interviews, assessment centers, and tests.

While some MNCs interview only the candidate, a relatively high percentage of them interview both the candidate and the spouse, lending support to the fact that MNCs are becoming increasingly aware of the significance of the spouse's adjustment to a foreign environment and its contribution to managerial performance abroad. Interviews are best conducted by senior executives who have had managerial

FIGURE 19–7 FLOWCHART OF THE SELECTION-DECISION PROCESS

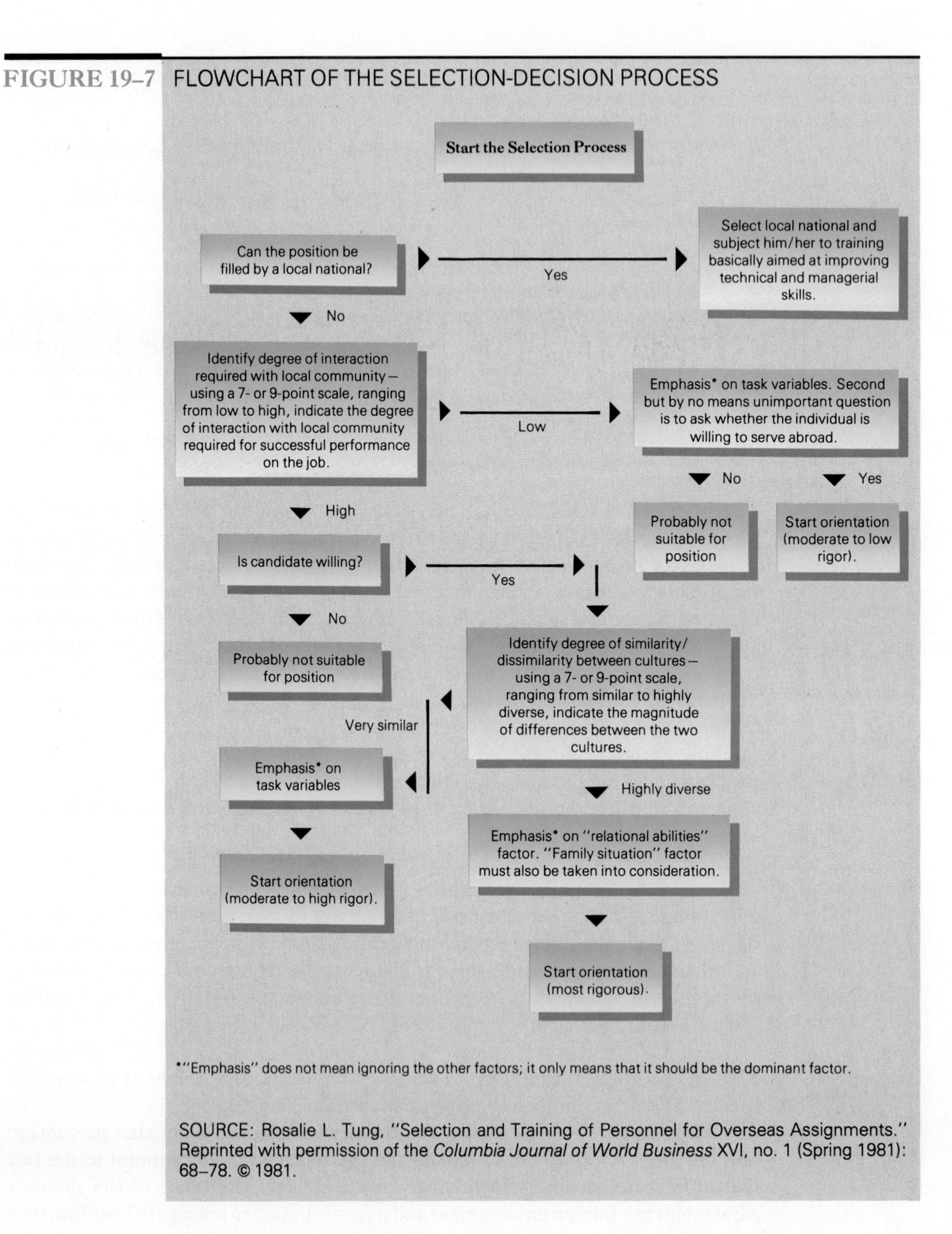

SOURCE: Rosalie L. Tung, "Selection and Training of Personnel for Overseas Assignments." Reprinted with permission of the *Columbia Journal of World Business* XVI, no. 1 (Spring 1981): 68–78. © 1981.

experience in foreign countries. For example, at Mobil Oil the manager of international placement and staffing and two assistants with foreign experience conduct a four-hour interview with the candidate and the spouse to discuss all phases of the job. Emphasis is placed on the culture and the adaptability demands made on the candidate and the spouse.[14]

Assessment centers typically use individual and group exercises, individual interviews with managers and/or psychologists, and some personality and mental ability tests to evaluate candidates. Exercises that reflect situations characteristic of the potential host culture are usually included. The use of assessment centers has been shown to have high face validity and to be an effective tool for selecting from a large pool of international managerial candidates.[15]

Since the early 1970s, the use of tests—especially for higher-level positions—has declined. A study by Tung in 1982 revealed that only 5 percent of U.S.-based MNCs reporting used tests to assess a candidate's abilities to relate to others of a different culture.[16] A variety of psychometric devices, particularly personality inventories that can be used to determine an individual's ability to adapt to a different cultural environment, are available. Such inventories as the *Minnesota Multiphasic Personality Inventory*, the *Guilford-Zimmerman Temperament Survey*, and the *California Test* (the Indirect Scale for Ethnocentrism) are among those recommended. This third test is probably the most promising of these measures, since data suggest that high ethnocentrism correlates with overseas job failure.[17]

In using personality inventories and other types of personality tests, it is advisable to employ the services of a psychologist who is licensed by the state. One New York consulting firm has developed an assessment tool known as the *Overseas Assignment Inventory (OAI)*. Based on 12 years of research involving more than 7,000 cases, the *OAI* helps identify characteristics and attitudes that potential international candidates should have.[18] One test, the *Modern Language Aptitude Test,* predicts with considerable accuracy a person's chances of being able to learn a foreign language. Where it is essential that a person learn a foreign language, employers find that it is important to have some assurance that the prognosis is favorable.[19]

Training and Development

Organizations that are serious about succeeding in global business are tackling the intercultural "chemistry" by providing intensive training. MNCs such as Amoco, Bechtel, 3M, Hyatt, McDonald's, Honeywell, Xerox, and others with large numbers of international personnel prepare employees for overseas assignments. These organizations and others, including Coca-Cola, Motorola, Chevron, and Mattel, are also orienting U.S.-based employees who deal in international markets. The biggest mistake HR managers can make is to assume that people are the same everywhere. An organization that makes a concerted effort to ensure that its employees understand and respect cultural differences will realize the impact of its effort on its sales, costs, and productivity.[20]

Personnel abroad may require training to help them adapt to the new forms of communication they may encounter.

CONTENT OF TRAINING PROGRAMS Because of the many differences even between countries that speak the same language, it is essential for persons preparing for a successful assignment abroad to receive training in many different areas. They need to know as much as possible about (1) the place where they are going, (2) their own culture, and (3) the history, values, and dynamics of their own organization. Highlights in HRM 1, from the book *Going International,* gives an overview of what one needs to study for an international assignment. To illustrate the importance of training personnel, some of the problems that may arise in two areas—cross-cultural differences and communication—will be discussed.

Cross-cultural differences represent the most elusive aspect of international business. Generally unaware of their own culture-conditioned behavior, most people tend to react negatively to tastes and behavior that deviate from those of their own culture. Styles of clothing, housing, and furniture and even the facial expressions and gestures people from other cultures use to communicate are viewed as strange. While there has been much borrowing and integration among people of different national cultures as a result of modern communications technology, especially among the upper classes, all cultures are inherently conservative and foster continuity. Apparent likenesses, such as wearing jeans and drinking Coke, should not be misinterpreted as evidence that others have adopted our American culture.

As exceedingly complex systems, cultures can only be studied in terms of their various dimensions or subsystems. One writer identified 17 **cross-cultural variables** important in international business and shows how their normative content may vary between two countries. Among the variables identified are the following, together with possible differences between two countries (Country A and Country B):[21]

VARIABLE	COUNTRY A	COUNTRY B
Mode of thinking	pragmatic	universalistic
Problem solving	scientific	traditional
Class structure	vague	distinct
Decision-making style	democratic	autocratic
Kinship bondage	weak	strong
Time orientation	intense	casual
Nonverbal communication	passive	active

This selection from a more comprehensive listing of cross-cultural variables serves to illustrate the awareness one needs in order to interact effectively in a foreign environment. Ways of developing this awareness will be discussed later.

In Chapter 15 we saw the types of problems that managers face in communicating with individuals from the same culture who speak the same language. Communication with individuals who have a different language and a different cultural orientation is much more difficult. Most executives agree that it is the biggest problem for the foreign business traveler. Even with an interpreter, much is missed.

HIGHLIGHTS IN HRM

1 PREPARING FOR AN INTERNATIONAL ASSIGNMENT

To prepare for an international assignment, study the following subjects:

1. Social and business etiquette.
2. History and folklore.
3. Current affairs, including relations between the country and the United States.
4. The culture's values and priorities.
5. Geography, especially the cities.
6. Sources of pride: artists, musicians, novelists, sports, great achievements of the culture, including things to see and do.
7. Religion and the role of religion in daily life.
8. Political structure and current players.
9. Practical matters such as currency, transportation, time zones, hours of business.
10. The language.

SOURCE: Lennie Copeland and Lewis Griggs, *Going International* (New York: Random House, 1985), 216. Reproduced with permission.

While foreign-language fluency is important in all aspects of international business, only a small percentage of Americans have facility in a language other than English. Students who plan careers in international business should start instruction in one or more foreign languages as early as possible.[22] Programs designed to train individuals for international business, such as those offered at the American Graduate School of International Management in Glendale, Arizona, and at the University of South Carolina, provide intensive training in foreign languages.

Learning the language is only part of communicating in another culture. One must also learn how the people think and act in their relations with others. Copeland and Griggs's *Going International* includes a myriad of examples. A few of them are cited in the following list to highlight the complexities of the communication process in international business.

1. In England, to "table" a subject means to put it on the table for present discussion. In the United States, it means to postpone discussion of a subject, perhaps indefinitely.
2. In America, information flows to a manager. In cultures where authority is centralized (Europe and South America), the manager must take the initiative to seek out the information.
3. Getting straight to the point is uniquely Western. Europeans, Arabs, and many others resent American directness in communication.

4. In Japan, there are 16 ways to avoid saying "no."
5. When something is "inconvenient" to the Chinese, it is most likely downright impossible.
6. In most foreign countries, expressions of anger are unacceptable; in some places, public display of anger is taboo.
7. The typical American must learn to treat silences as "communication spaces" and not interrupt them.
8. In general, avoid gesturing with the hand.[23]

We observed in Chapter 15 that to understand the communication process, attention must be given to nonverbal communication. Figure 19–8 illustrates that some of our everyday gestures have very different meanings in other cultures. In summary, when one leaves the United States, it is imperative to remember that perfectly appropriate behavior in one country can get one into embarrassing situations in another.

TRAINING METHODS The typical training program for American expatriates employs a variety of training methods. The manager and his or her family can learn much of the host country through books, lectures, and videotapes about the culture, geography, social and political history, climate, food, and so on. The content is factual and the knowledge acquired will at least help the participants to have a better understanding of their assignments. Such minimal exposure, however, does not fully prepare one for a foreign assignment. Training methods such as sensitivity training, which focuses on learning at the affective level, may well be a powerful technique in the reduction of ethnic prejudices. The Peace Corps uses sensitivity training supplemented by field experiences. Field experiences may sometimes be obtained in nearby "microcultures" where similarities exist.[24]

It is important for U.S. managers to learn to work with others in teams. MNCs are increasingly using teams to conduct business, develop strategy, transfer technology, and communicate between headquarters and subsidiaries in different countries. Unlike their counterparts in other parts of the world, U.S. managers are frequently at a disadvantage because they lack experience in working with people with different backgrounds. For cross-functional, cross-cultural, multinational teams to perform well, managers need such qualities as flexibility, a sense of humor, patience, sensitivity, curiosity, a willingness to listen to others, and respect for differences. In short, North American team leaders cannot "shout orders from the dugout."[25]

Special Considerations

Most of the major factors to be considered in the managerial staffing of organizations outside the United States were discussed in the preceding sections. There are, however, other items that deserve attention. These include risks to an employee's career development, reentry problems, managing personal and family life, and terrorism.

FIGURE 19–8 MEANING OF SOME NONVERBAL COMMUNICATIONS IN DIFFERENT CULTURES

Calling a Waiter
In the United States, a common way to call a waiter is to point upward with the forefinger. In Asia, a raised forefinger is used to call a dog or other animal. To get the attention of a Japanese waiter, extend the arm upward, palm down, and flutter the fingers. In Africa, knock on the table. In the Middle East, clap your hands.

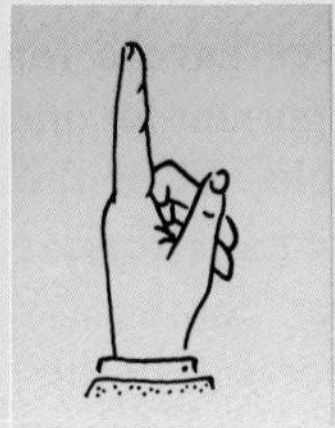

Handshake and Touching
In most countries, the handshake is an acceptable form of greeting. In the Middle East and other Islamic countries, however, the left hand is considered the toilet hand and is thought to be unclean. Only the right hand should be used for touching.

Scratching the Head
In most Western countries, scratching the head is interpreted as lack of understanding or noncomprehension. To the Japanese, it indicates anger.

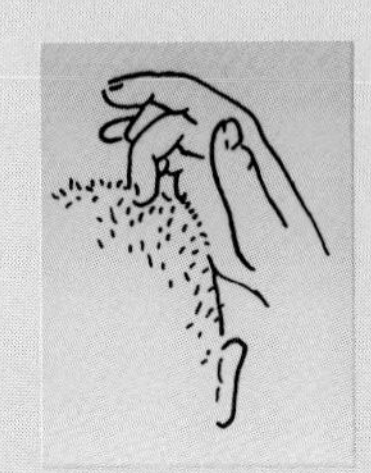

Insults
In Arab countries, showing the soles of your shoes is an insult. Also, an Arab may insult a person by holding a hand in front of the person's face.

A-okay Gesture
In the United States, using the index finger and the thumb to form an "o" while extending the rest of the fingers is a gesture meaning okay or fine. In Japan, however, the same gesture means money. Nodding your head in agreement if a Japanese uses this sign during your discussion could mean you are expected to give him some cash. And in Brazil the same gesture is considered a seductive sign to a woman and an insult to a man.

Indicating "No"
In most parts of the world, shaking the head left and right is the most common way to say no. But among the Arabs, in parts of Greece, Yugoslavia, Bulgaria, and Turkey, a person says no by tossing the head to the side, sometimes clicking the tongue at the same time. In Japan, no can also be said by moving the right hand back and forth.

Eye Contact
In Western and Arab cultures, prolonged eye contact with a person is acceptable. In Japan, on the other hand, holding the gaze of another person is considered rude. The Japanese generally focus on a person's neck or tie knot.

Agreement
In addition to saying yes, Africans will hold an open palm perpendicular to the ground and pound it with the other fist to emphasize "agreed." Arabs will clasp their hands together, forefingers pointed outward, to indicate agreement.

SOURCE: S. Hawkins, *International Management* 38, no. 9 (September 1983): 49. Reprinted with permission from *International Management*.

CAREER DEVELOPMENT RISKS In many cases, an overseas assignment is more risky for the average executive than staying with his or her employer in the United States. Far too often, executives who have been assigned abroad return to corporate headquarters after a few years to find that there is no position for them and they no longer know anyone who can help them. To get the career benefits of a foreign assignment, two key questions about the employer should be asked before accepting an overseas post: (1) Do your organization's senior executives view the firm's international business as a critical part of their business? (2) Within top management, how many executives have a foreign-service assignment in their background, and do they feel it important for one to have overseas experience?

At Dow Chemical, for example, 14 of the firm's 22-member management committee including the CEO have had overseas assignments. Dow appoints what employees refer to as the "godfather" for those who get overseas assignments. The godfather, usually a high-level supervisor in the expatriate's particular function, is the stateside contact for information about organizational changes, job opportunities, and anything related to salary and compensation. At Exxon, employees are given a general idea of what they can expect after an overseas assignment even before they leave to assume it.[26]

REENTRY PROBLEMS The approaches used by Dow and Exxon can serve to relieve the anxiety that many managers experience in returning home. Without providing for transition, a manager may be concerned about what to expect in terms of his or her place in the organization. Certainly, one problem many experience is getting used to working under organizational constraints after having had more freedom and autonomy. Abroad, the manager was probably a very prominent member of the local community. At home, she or he is likely to be just another executive. An expatriate manager may have to incur financial burdens, usually because of inflation in the housing market. These and other reentry problems require close attention by the manager of the international program.

Colgate-Palmolive and Ciba-Geigy make a special effort to keep in touch with expatriates during the period that they are abroad. Colgate's division executives and other corporate staff members make frequent visits to international transferees. Ciba-Geigy provides a full repatriation program for returning employees for the purpose of (1) reversing "culture shock" for the transferee and his or her family and department, (2) smoothing the return to the home organization, and (3) facilitating the readjustment process so that the organization can benefit from the expatriate's knowledge and experience.[27]

Not all companies have well-developed programs for repatriating employees. A study of 175 employers who belong to the SHRM: International reveals that many U.S.-based MNCs are not aware of the need for such programs. Only 31 percent of those included in the survey had formal programs. The reasons most frequently mentioned for not having a program were (1) lack of expertise in establishing a program—47 percent, (2) cost of program—36 percent, and (3) no need perceived by top management for such a program—35 percent. It is interesting to note that the HR managers also did not perceive the need for training and thus did not alert top managers to the problem. Many organizations also fail to debrief returnees, with the result that a considerable amount of valuable information concerning overseas operations is lost. This is a tragic waste of overseas experience.[28]

MANAGING PERSONAL AND FAMILY LIFE The most frequent cause of an employee's failure to complete an international assignment is personal and family stress. **Culture shock**—a disorientation that causes perpetual stress—is experienced by people who settle overseas for extended periods. The stress is caused by hundreds of jarring and disorienting incidents such as being unable to communicate, having trouble getting the telephone to work, being unable to read the street signs, and a myriad of other everyday matters that are no problem at home. Soon minor frustrations become catastrophic events, and one feels helpless and drained, emotionally and physically.

A spouse usually faces a much greater challenge than the employee. She—it usually is she—must grapple with all aspects of the new cultural environment. To do well abroad, one must be highly motivated to succeed. The employee usually is, but the wife often does not see direct payoffs. It is important for her to have her own goals and objectives. The employee must involve the whole family in the decision to go abroad and ensure that their needs are met once there.[29]

In Chapter 8, we observed that more and more employers are assisting two-career couples in finding suitable employment in the same location. Some employers are also providing informal job help to the spouses of international transferees. As women move up in the professional and managerial ranks of MNCs, employers are going to have to pay greater attention to the employment needs of the dual-career couple.[30]

TERRORISM There have been enough incidents of terrorism in recent years to cause MNCs to take steps to protect their overseas employees. Some of the steps they have taken include creating a low employment and public profile, increasing security forces, and advising employees to avoid bars, restaurants, and other facilities known to be American hangouts. Employees are also instructed to watch for anything suspicious at work as well as at home.[31]

HR FUNCTIONS IN MNCs

As with other major managerial functions, HRM in a foreign branch of an MNC is about the same as in the United States. It consists of the same functions and utilizes many of the same techniques to achieve its objectives. But because of cultural differences, economic conditions, and educational, political, and legal constraints, it is necessary for HR managers to modify policies and procedures followed at the home office to fit the local situation.

A comparative analysis of the major HRM functions as they are performed in all of the countries where U.S.-based MNCs are situated would fill a large volume. In this section, some of the differences found among some of the countries will be examined. A look at the differences will serve to acquaint the reader with the importance of modifying what works at home. The HRM functions discussed will

A young Russian woman, newly trained in her position at McDonald's in Moscow.

include recruitment and selection, training and development, compensation, and labor relations.

Recruitment and Selection

Decades ago, American firms abroad imported all of their employees, including janitors and laborers, from the United States. Over the years, and especially as MNCs have evolved, they have steadily shifted to the use of local personnel. There are three reasons for this trend: (1) Hiring local citizens is less costly because the company does not have to worry about the costs of home leaves, transportation, and special schooling allowances. (2) Since local governments usually want good jobs for their citizens, foreign employers may be required to hire them. (3) Using local personnel avoids the problem of employees having to adjust to the culture.

With growth over the years, U.S.-based MNCs have tended to use more third-country expatriates, for example, a Mexican technician working for an American MNC in Peru. Probably U.S.-based MNCs have more third-country expatriates than other MNCs because most of them have been at it longer and American firms emphasize the hiring of qualified persons.[32]

RECRUITMENT In general, personnel recruitment in other countries is subject to more government regulation than it is in the United States. Regulations range from those that cover procedures for recruiting personnel to those that govern the employment of foreign labor or require the employment of the physically disabled, war veterans, or displaced persons.[33] Many Central American countries, as well as other countries, have stringent regulations about the number of foreigners that can be employed as a percentage of the total work force. Virtually all countries have work-permit or visa restrictions that apply to foreigners. A **work permit** or **work**

certificate is a document issued by a government granting authority to a foreign individual to seek employment in that government's country.

As in the United States, various methods are used to recruit personnel from internal sources and external sources. In any country, but particularly in the developing countries, a disadvantage of using current employees as recruiters is that considerations of family, similar social status, culture, or language are usually more important than qualifications for the vacant position. More than one HR manager depending on employees as recruiters have filled a plant with relatives or people from the same hometown. In small towns much of the recruiting is done by word of mouth. Thus, having locals involved is critical. Churches, unions, and community groups also play a role.

MNCs tend to use the same kinds of external recruitment sources as are used in their home countries. While unskilled labor is readily available in the developing countries, the recruitment of skilled workers is more difficult. Many employers have learned that the best way to find workers in these countries is through radio announcements because many of them cannot read or write. The solution is to have a recruiter who uses local methods within the context of the organization's culture and needs or to put an expatriate in charge of recruiting.

The laws of almost all countries require the employment of local people if adequate numbers of skilled people are available. Thus, recruiting is limited to a restricted population. Specific exceptions are granted (officially or unofficially) for contrary cases, as for Mexican farm workers in the United States, and for Italian, Spanish, Greek, and Turkish workers in Germany and the Benelux countries. Foreign workers invited to come to perform needed labor are usually referred to as **guest workers.** The employment of nonnationals may involve lower direct labor costs, but indirect costs—language training, health services, recruitment, transportation, and so on—may be substantial.[34]

SELECTION American organizations have had a very significant impact on foreign HRM practices. The success of the U.S.-based MNCs has caused many local firms and MNCs based in other countries to study the methods of the American firms. Personnel selection practices in U.S. organizations emphasize merit, with the best-qualified person getting the job. Other countries have tended to hire on the basis of family ties, social status, language, and common origin. The candidate who satisfies these criteria gets the job even if otherwise unqualified. There has been a growing realization among foreign organizations, however, that greater attention must be given to hiring those most qualified.

In the industrialized countries, most organizations follow standard procedures of requesting personal information, including work experiences, in interviews and on application forms. Prospective employees may be given a physical examination and employment tests. In many European countries an employer is forbidden to make unfavorable statements about former employees. In Belgium and France, this prohibition was established by legislation; in Germany, by court decision.[35]

Training and Development

In the United States, employers try to recruit individuals who are adequately trained to perform the job for which they are being considered. However, it is often necessary to provide some type of training to achieve the desired level of performance. Employees also may need their skills upgraded or be taught new ones as they continue on the job. Such training may be provided within the organization or outside in some type of educational setting.

DEVELOPING LOCAL RESOURCES MNC subsidiaries have found that good training programs help them attract needed employees. This works both ways, however, as the locally owned firms regularly hire away those workers who have been trained by the foreign-owned organizations. Managers of MNC subsidiaries in Mexico have been heard to complain that "they must be training half the machinists in Mexico."[36]

The general experience of firms operating in different parts of the world is that people who are relatively unsophisticated in a technological sense can learn industrial skills with surprising ease. It is generally necessary, however, to teach new workers from farms and villages to adjust to factory life. They are not accustomed to the scheduled life of the enterprise. Local military training of a technical nature may offer clues about the training methods most effective within the local culture and also clues about trainee motivation.

APPRENTICESHIP TRAINING A major source of trained labor in European nations is through apprenticeship training (described in Chapter 7). On the whole, apprenticeship training in Europe is superior to that in the United States. In Europe, the dual-track system of education directs a large number of youth into vocational training. The German system of apprenticeship training, one of the best in Europe, provides training for office and shop jobs under a three-way responsibility contract between the apprentice, his or her parents, and the organization. At the conclusion of their training, apprentices can work for any employer but generally receive seniority credit with the training firm if they remain in it.[37]

MANAGEMENT DEVELOPMENT One of the greatest contributions that the United States has made to work organizations is in improving the competence of managers. Some years ago, Eugene de Facq, an international management consultant, stated that

> America's greatest contribution has been to provide modern management. An American has a facility for reasoning that is part of his life. He can make decisions on a rational basis and has a better psychological background for decision making. Decisions of European managers, by way of contrast, are sometimes based on engineering-like and short-term thinking.[38]

Foreign nationals have generally welcomed the type of training they have received through management development programs offered by American organizations.

LANGUAGE AND TRAINING Although English is a required subject in many foreign schools, students who use it only in the classroom may not learn to use it effectively. Many MNCs provide instruction in English for those who are required to use English in their jobs. Where trainers are using English to communicate information and instructions about the job, it is essential that they realize the discomfort that foreign trainees may be experiencing. Learning job skills in a second language is usually much more difficult than learning them in one's native tongue. In addition, certain concepts may not exist in the foreign trainees' culture. The word *achievement*, for example, doesn't exist in some Asian and African languages. There is no direct translation for *management* in French.

Several tips for teaching where English is a second language for the trainees are presented in Highlights in HRM 2. Many of the tips may also be applied in interpersonal communication on and off the job with people who have a limited understanding of American English. By placing oneself in the foreigner's position, one can soon learn how far to go in applying the tips.

Compensation

One of the most complex areas of HRM in multinational corporations is compensation, particularly with regard to expatriate managers. After a brief discussion of compensation practices for host-country employees and managers, we will focus on the problems of compensating expatriate and third-country nationals.

COMPENSATION OF HOST-COUNTRY EMPLOYEES Host-country employees are paid on the basis of productivity, time spent on the job, or a combination of these factors. In the industrialized countries, pay is generally by the hour; in the developing countries, by the day. The piece-rate method is quite common. In some countries, including Japan, seniority is an important element in determining employees' pay rates. When MNCs commence operations in a foreign country, they usually set their wage rates at or slightly higher than the prevailing wage for local companies. Eventually, though, they are urged to conform to local practices to avoid "spoiling" the local workers.

Employee benefits in other countries are frequently higher than those in the United States. In France, for example, they are about 70 percent of wages and in Italy 92 percent, compared with 37 percent in the United States. Whereas in the United States most benefits are awarded to employees by employers, in other industrialized countries most of them are legislated or ordered by governments.[39]

In Italy, Japan, and some other countries, it is customary to add semiannual or annual lump-sum payments equal to one or two months' pay. These payments are not considered profit sharing but an integral part of the basic pay package. Profit sharing is legally required for certain categories of industry in Mexico, Peru, Pakistan, India, and Egypt among the developing countries, and in France among the industrialized countries.[40] Compensation patterns in Eastern Europe are in flux as these countries experiment with more capitalistic systems.

HIGHLIGHTS IN HRM

2 TIPS FOR TEACHING WHERE ENGLISH IS A SECOND LANGUAGE

- Speak slowly and enunciate clearly.
- Do not use idioms, jargon, or slang.
- Repeat important ideas expressed in different ways.
- Use short, simple sentences; stop between sentences.
- Use active, not passive, verbs.
- Use visual reinforcement: charts, gestures, demonstrations.
- Have materials duplicated in the local language.
- Pause frequently and give breaks.
- Summarize periodically.
- Check comprehension by having students reiterate material.
- Encourage and reward, as appropriate to the culture.
- Never criticize or tease.

SOURCE: Lennie Copeland and Lewis Griggs, *Going International* (New York: Random House, 1985), 149. Reproduced with permission.

COMPENSATION OF HOST-COUNTRY MANAGERS In the past, remuneration of host-country managers has been ruled by local salary levels. However, increased competition among different MNCs with subsidiaries in the same country has led to a gradual upgrading of host-country managers' salaries. Overall, international firms are moving toward a narrowing of the salary gap between the host-country manager and the expatriate.

COMPENSATION OF EXPATRIATE MANAGERS Compensation plans for expatriate managers must be competitive, cost-effective, motivating, fair and easy to understand, consistent with international financial management, easy to administer, and simple to communicate. To be effective, an international compensation program must:

1. Provide an incentive to leave the United States.
2. Maintain an American standard of living.
3. Facilitate reentry into the United States.
4. Provide for the education of children.
5. Maintain relationships with family, friends, and business associates.[41]

Expatriate compensation programs used by most U.S.-based MNCs rest on the **balance-sheet approach,** a system designed to equalize the purchasing power of employees at comparable position levels living overseas and in the home country, and to provide incentives to offset qualitative differences between assignment locations. The balance-sheet approach comprises four elements:

1. *Base pay*—essentially equal to pay of domestic counterparts in comparably evaluated jobs.
2. *Differentials*—to offset the higher costs of overseas goods, services, and housing.
3. *Incentives*—to compensate the person for separation from family, friends, and domestic support systems, usually 15 percent of base salary.
4. *Assistance programs*—to cover added costs such as moving and storage costs, automobile, and education expenses.[42]

The *differentials* element is intended to correct for the higher costs of overseas goods and services so that in relation to their domestic peers expatriates neither gain purchasing power nor lose it. It involves a myriad of calculations to arrive at a total differential figure. Fortunately, employers do not have to do extensive work to have comparative data. They typically rely on data published quarterly by the U.S. Department of State for use in establishing allowances to compensate American civilian employees for costs and hardships related to assignments abroad.[43]

The costs of utilizing expatriate managers are higher today than ever before. For example, the employer's typical first-year expenses of sending one U.S. executive to Great Britain, as shown in Highlights in HRM 3, are $200,000 above the base salary. Many American MNCs are sending fewer managers overseas, often by substituting host-country managers. Others are reducing allowances, benefits, and overseas pay incentives.[44] An increasing number of MNCs employ foreign graduates from U.S. M.B.A. programs. The many foreign graduate students enrolled in business programs at U.S. universities are a pool of potential managers who combine the training and enculturation of an American M.B.A. with their own native background.

COMPENSATION OF THIRD-COUNTRY MANAGERS As the number of third-country nationals in MNCs increases, their compensation level is also approaching that of expatriates. One of the problems peculiar to third-country nationals, however, is defining them. In the past, they have been defined in terms of their home country, but there is an increasing trend to define them in terms of cultural identity. Some companies establish cultural zones; for example, Western Europe is considered to be one zone, Africa another, and so on. Other companies use a combination of geographic and language zones. Thus, a manager remains a national (not a third-country national) unless he or she moves to a different geographic zone and a different language zone as well.[45]

Labor Relations

Labor relations in countries outside the United States differ significantly from those in the United States. Differences exist not only in the collective bargaining

HIGHLIGHTS IN HRM

3 THE PRICE OF AN EXPATRIATE

An employer's typical first-year expenses of sending a U.S. executive to Britain, assuming a $100,000 salary and a family of four

Direct compensation costs	
Base salary	$100,000
Foreign-service premium	15,000
Goods and services differential	21,000
Housing costs in London	39,000*
Transfer costs	
Relocation allowance	$5,000
Air fare to London	2,000
Moving household goods	25,000
Other costs	
Company car	$15,000
Schooling (two children)	20,000
Annual home leave (four people)	4,000
U.K. personal income tax	56,000*
TOTAL	**$302,000**

Note: Additional costs often incurred aren't listed above, including language and cross-cultural training for employee and family, and costs of selling home and cars in the U.S. before moving.

*Figures take into account payments by employee to company based on hypothetical U.S. income tax and housing costs.

SOURCE: Reprinted by permission of *The Wall Street Journal* © 1989 Dow Jones & Company, Inc.

process but also in the political and legal conditions. An American who works as an executive or as an HR manager in an MNC soon learns the differences and learns how to operate effectively under conditions that are quite different from those at home. These executives also learn that there may be no assistance of value from headquarters and that they must rely heavily on local personnel with expertise in labor–management relations.

To acquaint the reader with the nature of labor–management relations in MNCs, we will look at the role of unions in different countries, multinational bargaining, international labor organizations, and the role of labor participation in management.

THE ROLE OF UNIONS The role of unions varies from country to country and depends on many factors, such as the level of per capita labor income, mobility between management and labor, homogeneity of labor (racial, religious, social class), and level of employment. These and other factors determine whether the union will have the strength it needs to represent labor effectively. In countries with relatively high unemployment, low pay levels, and no union funds for welfare, the union is driven into alliance with other organizations: political party, church, or government. This is in marked contrast to the United States, where the union selected by the majority of employees bargains only with the employer, not with other institutions.

Even in the major industrial countries one finds national differences are great with respect to (1) the level at which bargaining takes place (national, industry, or workplace), (2) centralization of union–management relations, (3) the scope of bargaining, (4) the degree to which government intervenes, and (5) the degree of unionization.[46]

Labor relations in Europe differ from those in the United States in certain significant characteristics:

1. In Europe, organizations typically negotiate the agreement with the union at the national level through the employer association representing their particular industry, even when there may be local within-company negotiations as well. This agreement establishes certain minimum conditions of employment which frequently are augmented through negotiations with the union at the company level.
2. Unions in many European countries have more political power than those in the United States, with the result that when employers deal with the union they are, in effect, dealing indirectly with the government. Unions are often allied with a particular political party, although in some countries these alliances are more complex, with unions having predominant but not sole representation with one party.
3. There is a greater tendency in Europe for salaried employees, including those at the management level, to be unionized, quite often in a union of their own.
4. Unions in most European countries have been in existence longer than those in the United States. Consequently, they occupy a more accepted position in society and need be less concerned about gaining approval.[47]

Like the United States, European countries are facing the reality of a developing global economy. It has been increasingly evident in Europe that workers are less inclined to make constant demands for higher wages. The trend has been to demand compensation in other ways: through a proliferation of benefits or through greater participation in company decision making.[48] Various approaches to participation will be discussed later.

MULTINATIONAL BARGAINING We saw in Chapter 18 how the collective bargaining process is typically carried out in organizations operating in the United States. When we look at other countries, we find that the whole process can vary widely, especially with regard to the role that government plays. In the United Kingdom and France, for example, government intervenes in all aspects of collective bargaining. Government involvement is only natural where parts of industry are nationalized. Also, in countries where there is heavy nationalization there is more likely to be acceptance of government involvement even in the non-nationalized companies. At Renault, the French government–owned automobile manufacturer, unions make use of political pressures in their bargaining with managers, who are essentially government employees. The resulting terms of agreement then set the standards for other firms. In the developing countries it is common for the government to have representatives present during bargaining sessions to make sure that unions with relatively uneducated leaders are not disadvantaged in bargaining with skilled management representatives.

While local workers often see MNC plants and offices as highly desirable places to work because of the good wages, labor-saving equipment, and amenities such as air conditioning and clean cafeterias, such benefits do not preclude strikes, union demands, and labor unrest. Since the managers at headquarters usually are not knowledgeable about labor relations in a specific country or area, it is almost mandatory that those responsible for labor relations in an MNC subsidiary be local personnel who speak the language, know the laws and customs, and be able to communicate effectively with local union officials and attorneys.[49]

INTERNATIONAL LABOR ORGANIZATIONS The fact that MNCs can choose the countries in which they wish to establish subsidiaries generally results in the selection of those countries that have the most to offer. Certainly cheap labor is a benefit that most MNC strategists consider. By coordinating their resources, including human resources, and their production facilities, MNCs operate from a position of strength. International unions, such as the United Auto Workers, have found it difficult to achieve a level of influence anywhere near that found within a particular industrial nation. Those that have been successful operate in countries that are similar, such as the United States and Canada.

The most active of the international union organizations has been the International Confederation of Free Trade Unions (ICFTU), which has its headquarters in Brussels. Cooperating with the ICFTU are some 20 International Trade Secretariats (ITSs), which are really international federations of national trade unions operating in the same or related industries. The significance of the ITSs from the point of view of management lies in the fact that behind local unions may be the expertise and resources of an ITS. Another active and influential organization is the International Labor Organization (ILO), a specialized agency of the United Nations. It does considerable research on an international basis and endorses standards for various working conditions, referred to as the International Labor Code. At various times

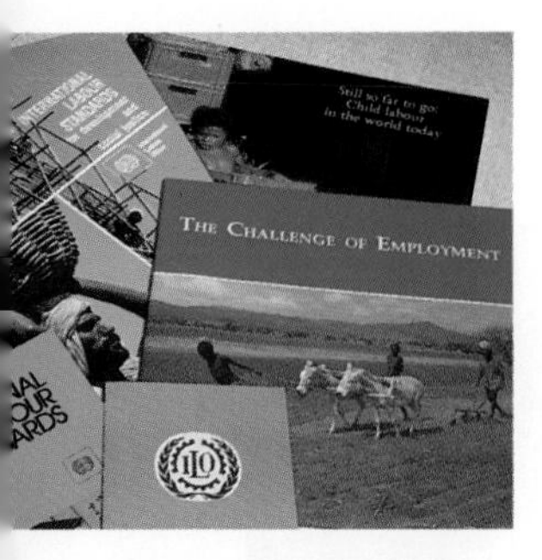

Books and pamphlets published by the ILO set standards for the international labor community.

and places this code may be quoted *to* management as international labor standards to which employers are expected to conform.

LABOR PARTICIPATION IN MANAGEMENT In many European countries, provisions for employee representation are established by law. An employer may be legally required to provide for employee representation on safety and hygiene committees, worker councils, or even on boards of directors. While their responsibilities vary from country to country, worker councils basically provide a communication channel between employers and workers. The legal codes that set forth the functions of worker councils in France are very detailed. Councils are generally concerned with grievances, problems of individual employees, internal regulations, and matters affecting employee welfare.

A higher form of worker participation in management is found in Germany, where representation of labor on the board of directors of a company is required by law. This arrangement is known as **codetermination** and often by its German word *Mitbestimmung*. Power is generally left with the shareholders, and shareholders are generally assured the chairmanship. Other European countries and Japan either have or are considering minority board participation.[50]

HRM IN THE EUROPEAN COMMUNITY (EC-92)

At the beginning of the chapter we mentioned the unification of the markets of 12 European nations into the European Community (EC-92). Numerous articles have appeared in recent years about the unification process and what it will mean in terms of the movement of goods, services, capital, and human resources. The effect that unification will have on the European nations involved as well as on the rest of the world has also been examined in detail in many publications.[51]

Progress toward a single European market has been steady since 1985. With December 1992 as the deadline, EC-92 has compiled almost 300 directives aimed at reducing regulations, simplifying standards, and eliminating hidden barriers that now stand in the way of free access to markets. At the headquarters of EC-92 in Brussels, the 12 member nations listed here have been actively engaged in negotiations over the directives that will ultimately become the law for the Community.

- Belgium
- Denmark
- France
- Germany
- Greece
- Ireland
- Italy
- Luxembourg
- Netherlands
- Portugal
- Spain
- United Kingdom

Each star represents one of the member countries of the European Economic Community.

Some experts have predicted that the EC will probably include 14 countries by the mid-1990s and possibly 18 by the year 2000. The newest candidates are countries of Eastern Europe that are struggling to become democracies. Labeling EC-92 "an extraordinary phenomenon," Naisbitt and Aburdene report that "the excitement in Western European government and business circles is almost euphoric."[52]

In the past few years a number of articles concerning the HRM aspects of EC-92 have appeared in the journals. Many writers have attempted to predict how the HR functions and the role of HR managers will be affected by the unification process. Excerpts from several articles presented in Highlights in HRM 4 will give the reader a feel for the issues involved.

From the brief statements quoted from the seven articles as a representation of the issues involved in the unification of the EC, it is apparent that HR managers are facing many challenges. If they are to meet these challenges, it is essential that they assume a proactive stance in their organizations and utilize their professional skills to the fullest.

HIGHLIGHTS IN HRM

4 HRM ISSUES OF EC-92

General Statements

Personnel specialists [in European companies] are often not informed about the business planning and strategy in their own companies and rarely have direct contact with corporate planners. . . . After 1992, companies who wish to survive the intense competition will need to adopt strategic HRM.[a]

It does no good to ignore that 1992 will demand sacrifices and pain for certain industries and labor forces.[b]

Small businesses have provided virtually all the new employment in the United States during the Reagan boom of the 1980s. In the single European market, they are likely to play an equally significant role.[b]

Selection and Development Issues

1992 means that students will be able to study at universities of their choice knowing that their degrees and diplomas will be recognized in all 12 countries.[c]

Bringing education up-to-date to prepare Europe's youth and to eliminate the bottlenecks that already exist in many advanced industries will not be simple.[b]

There will be a big need for "Euro-executives"—[those who speak] English plus one or two European languages. Mobility, initiative, creativity, team building, and independence are all musts. The ability to initiate change and get results is critical.[d]

1992 means creating an EC-wide job market for professionals, technical personnel, and skilled workers.[c]

Compensation and Security Issues

Governments, unions, and enterprises will face a major and unavoidable change in pay distribution. . . . The high-pay economies of Europe such as West Germany will adjust downward, and the low-pay economies, such as Spain and Greece, will move upward.[e]

Some firms are modifying their benefit packages and perquisites to match the needs of the increasing proportion of the work force that is female.[f]

The creation of a single economic market will most likely affect compensation and benefits practices throughout that region and may have ripple effect in the United States as well. U.S. firms and subsidiaries in Western Europe will, of course, be directly affected.[f]

Several directives on occupational safety and health already exist and a significant harmonisation of European minimal standards is expected.[g]

Labor Relations Issues

A growing number of European trade union leaders warn that if labor is forced to bear the brunt of the pain, industrial conflict is inevitable.[b]

Western European firms have less scope for concession bargaining than U.S. firms, but they may obtain important concessions from their governments on costly social benefits.[f]

Concerns about "social dumping" [the migration of work to the low-wage, limited benefit nations of southern Europe] will motivate some actions. These concerns will be coupled with historically vigorous union involvement.[e]

The issues that labor unions brought before the EC in the 1970s—such as worker participation on corporate boards and increased worker rights to information and consultation—are almost entirely overlooked in the documents. It disregards the labor unions' proposal for a 35-hour week and contains no mention of plant closures or layoffs, two practices against which labor unions would like more protection.[f]

SOURCE: (**a**) Jan S. Krulis-Randa, "Strategic Human Resource Management in Europe After 1992," *International Journal of Human Resource Management* 1, no. 2 (Spring 1990): 131–138. (**b**) Leigh Bruce, "1992—The Bad News," *International Management* 43, no. 9 (September 1988): 22–26. (**c**) John Naisbitt and Patricia Aburdene, *Megatrends 2000* (New York: Morrow, 1990), 48–61. (**d**) Rae Sedel, "Europe 1992: HR Implications of the European Unification," *Personnel* 66, no. 10 (October 1989): 19–24. (**e**) Frank P. Doyle, "People-Power: The Global Human Resource Challenge for the '90s," *Columbia Journal of World Business* 25, nos. 1 and 2 (Spring–Summer 1990): 36–45. (**f**) Beverly J. Springer, "1992: The Impact on Compensation and Benefits in the European Community," *Compensation and Benefits Review* 21, no. 4 (July–August 1989): 20–27. (**g**) Hugh G. Mosley, "The Social Dimension of European Integration," *International Labour Review* 129, no. 2 (1990): 147–164.

SUMMARY

In the management of foreign subsidiaries of an MNC, special attention should be given to understanding the external environment of the host country, especially the cultural environment. Different cultural environments require different managerial styles, strategies, structures, and technologies.

Because of the special demands made on managerial personnel in an MNC, many factors must be considered in their selection and development. Though hiring host-country nationals or third-country nationals automatically avoids many potential problems, expatriate managers are preferable in some circumstances. The selection of the latter requires careful evaluation of the personal characteristics of the candidate and his or her spouse. Once an individual is selected, an intensive training and development program is essential to qualify that person for the assignment. Wherever possible, development should include sensitivity training and field experiences that will enable the manager to understand cultural differences better. Those in charge of the international program should provide the help needed to protect managers from career development risks, reentry problems, culture shock, and terrorism.

A review of HRM functions in MNCs reveals many differences among countries that require HR managers to modify home-office policies and procedures to fit the local situation. In this review we observed some of the differences in the functions of recruitment and selection, training and development, compensation, and labor relations. The unification of the 12 European nations into the European Community will mark a new era for world business that will have many challenges for HR managers.

DISCUSSION QUESTIONS

1. Describe the effects that different components of the cultural environment can have on HRM in MNCs.

2. In what ways are American managers likely to experience difficulties in their relationships with employees in foreign operations? How can these difficulties be minimized?
3. This chapter places considerable emphasis on the role of the spouse in the success of an overseas manager. What steps should management take to increase the likelihood of a successful experience for all parties involved?
4. What are the major differences between labor–management relations in Europe and those in the United States?
5. In recent years we have observed an increase in foreign investment in the United States. What effect are joint ventures, such as General Motors–Toyota, likely to have on HRM in the United States?
6. What is codetermination? Do you believe that it will ever become popular in the United States? Explain your position.
7. If you were starting now to plan for a career in international HRM, what steps would you take to prepare yourself for overseas assignments?
8. Talk with a foreign student on your campus, and ask about his or her experience with culture shock on first arriving in the United States. What did you learn from your discussion?

MINI-CASE 19–1 The 1992 HR Decision

Chuck Waldo is the HR vice-president for Teleco Electronics. His company is heavily involved in sales of its computer and electronic equipment in Europe. At this time, Teleco's international sales account for 31 percent of its total sales, and almost half of those sales are in the European Economic Community (EEC) countries. Because of the large volume of sales in Europe, his company has decided to build a manufacturing operation in one of the EEC countries. There are a number of advantages that Teleco can derive from this decision. Currently, because the company must work through numerous middlemen, sales within Europe are very complicated and expenses are high. By building a manufacturing operation, Teleco can reduce some of these sales expenses. Furthermore, Teleco can take advantage of the Single European Act of 1992 by avoiding the taxes associated with imported products if its products were manufactured within one of the EEC countries.

An important part of the decision to expand is the choice of which EEC country would provide the best location for the facility. Labor laws still vary widely among EEC member countries, and despite the Single European Act, there is disagreement among member countries on which of the labor laws are to become common across countries. Even with considerable commonality, cultures and languages will still affect labor practices to a great extent. In deciding which country to choose for the manufacturing plant, Chuck charged his staff with considering several important issues associated with the management of human resources in the EEC. Among the issues to be considered are the social policies of the countries.

Germany represents one extreme in the area of social policy. It has very strong labor unions and one of the best-protected labor forces among EEC member states. Its workers receive a minimum of 18 days of vacation per year; the maximum hours of work per day are 8, and 48 per week. Spain represents the other extreme in social policy associated with labor protection. Its work force has much less protection than Germany's in the areas of wages, health, and safety. Unemployment in Spain is about 20 percent, and labor costs are much lower than elsewhere. By contrast with Germany, however, its minimum vacation is longer—2.5 days per month—and while its maximum workday is 9 hours, the maximum per week is 40 hours. Ireland represents still another labor environment. Its per capita income is low and unemployment is high, somewhat like Spain's. However, the educational level of its citizens is very high. Minimum vacation is 3 weeks per year, and there is no maximum on the number of hours that one may work per day or week.

Despite differences among the countries, there is pressure from the labor unions for a common social charter among EEC member states. The implementation of common social policy in the form of an EEC-mandated social charter has important implications for HR decisions. The charter has the potential for drastically changing the way a firm operates in the EEC. A common charter would remove the competitive advantages of a given country. For example, Spain would no longer be able to offer the advantage of cheap labor with the implementation of a common wage and salary structure. The likelihood of these social issues being settled soon is still low despite the Single European Act of 1992, and many observers believe that adoption of a common charter prior to the year 2000 is very unlikely.

QUESTIONS

1. What considerations led Teleco to decide to expand its manufacturing to Europe?
2. What considerations should Chuck Waldo take into account in choosing among EEC member states for the location of the manufacturing plant?

MINI-CASE 19–2 The Female Touch

Starting around 1970, a few major companies began to hire female managers. Actually, the Civil Rights Act of 1964 banned sex discrimination in employment, but it took a while for the word to get around and for companies to realize that the government and the women were very serious. At first, relatively few female managers were hired, given the limited supply of women with the requisite managerial training, but Doris McCall was one of them. She went to work for the Mammoth Corporation in New York and quickly proved to be a superior manager. At first, many men resented having to take orders from a woman, but Doris had the right supervisory touch. And she has been steadily promoted so that now she is general manager of the consumer goods division for North America.

Mammoth needs a vice-president for its total Latin American operation, and after careful consideration of the available personnel, the company's personnel management specialist has concluded that Doris is the best candidate. She even speaks fluent Spanish, having majored in that subject before she obtained her M.B.A. at Harvard. Indeed, there isn't a close second for the job.

But Mammoth's CEO is still hesitating. "After all," he said recently to a close friend, "we have very different attitudes toward women in North America than the Latins do. There just aren't any female managers in any Latin American country, and this job involves very close liaison with all sorts of government people, our Latin managers, suppliers, and others. How will Mammoth look when a charming lady shows up as manager? She can handle almost anything. . . . I've seen her do it, and she's very sharp, but those male chauvinists down there will die before they'll work for or cooperate with a woman! I just don't see how we can do it. They don't have any Civil Rights Act in Latin America, and we just can't force social change down their throats!"

SOURCE: Reprinted with permission from Richard N. Farmer, *Incidents in International Business,* 4th ed. (Bloomington, IN: Cedarwood Press, 1984), 60–61.

QUESTIONS

1. Should Mammoth appoint Doris as its Latin American manager? Why or why not?
2. Can an American company force social change in another culture? Is this the time to do it?

NOTES AND REFERENCES

1. Peter J. Dowling, "International HRM," in *Human Resource Management—Evolving Roles & Responsibilities,* ed. Lee Dyer (Washington, DC: Bureau of National Affairs, 1988), 1:228–1:242. See also A. G. Kefalas, *Global Business Strategy—A Systems Approach* (Cincinnati: South-Western, 1990), Chapter 12.
2. Martin C. Schnitzer, Marilyn L. Liebrenz, and Konrad W. Kubin, *International Business* (Cincinnati: South-Western, 1985), 13. See also Taylor Cox, Jr., "The Multicultural Organization," *Academy of Management Executive* 5, no. 2 (May 1991): 34–47.
3. Robert Albanese, *Management* (Cincinnati: South-Western, 1988), 151. See also Peter Blunt, "Recent Developments in Human Resource Management: The Good, the Bad and the Ugly," *International Journal of Human Resource Management* 1, no. 1 (June 1990): 45–59.
4. Vern Terpstra and Kenneth David, *The Cultural Environment of International Business,* 3d ed. (Cincinnati: South-Western, 1990).
5. Lennie Copeland and Lewis Griggs, *Going International* (New York: Random House, 1985), 119–120.
6. Fred Luthans, Harriette S. McCaul, and Nancy Dodd, "Organizational Commitment: A Comparison of American, Japanese, and Korean Employees," *Academy of Management Journal* 28, no. 1 (March 1985): 213–218.
7. Ibid., 130–131.
8. Simcha Ronen, *Comparative and Multinational Management* (New York: Wiley, 1986), 184–186.
9. Copeland and Griggs, 123–126.
10. Arvind V. Phatak, *International Dimensions of Management,* 2d ed. (Boston: PWS-Kent, 1989), 106.
11. Ibid., 93–94.
12. Jean E. Heller, "Criteria for Selecting an International Manager," *Personnel* 57, no. 3 (May–June 1980): 48.
13. Rosalie L. Tung, "Selection and Training of Personnel for Overseas Assignments," *Columbia Journal of World Business* 16, no. 1 (Spring 1981): 68–78. See also Rosalie L. Tung, *The New Expatriates: Managing Human Resources Abroad* (Cambridge, MA: Ballinger, 1988).
14. Ronen, 184–186.
15. Ibid., 539.
16. R. L. Tung, "Selection and Training Procedures of U.S., European, and Japanese Multinationals," *California Management Review* 25, no. 1 (Fall 1982): 57–71.
17. Tung, "Selection and Training of Personnel," and Ronen, 536.
18. Madelyn R. Callahan, "Preparing the New Global Manager," *Training & Development Journal* 43, no. 3 (March 1989): 29–32.
19. Terpstra and David, 41.

20. Lennie Copeland, "Cross-Cultural Training: The Competitive Edge," *Training* 22, no. 7 (July 1985): 49–53. See also Mark Mendenhall and Gary Oddou, "The Dimensions of Expatriate Acculturation: A Review," *Academy of Management Review* 19, no. 1 (January 1985): 39–47; "Learning to Accept Cultural Diversity," *Wall Street Journal* (September 12, 1990); and Barry Rubin, "Europeans Value Diversity," *HR Magazine* 36, no. 1 (January 1991): 38–41, 78.

21. Endel-Jakob Kolde, *Environment of International Business* (Boston: Kent, 1985), 420, 428–429.

22. Lee H. Radebaugh and Janice C. Shields, "A Note on Foreign Language Training and International Business Education in U.S. Colleges and Universities," *Journal of International Business Studies* 15, no. 3 (Winter 1984): 195–199.

23. Copeland and Griggs, 99–118.

24. Tung, "Selection and Training of Personnel." See also S. Ronen, "Training the International Assignee," in *Training and Career Development,* ed. I. Goldstein (San Francisco: Jossey-Bass, 1989), 430; and Gary W. Hogan and Jane R. Goodson, "The Key to Expatriate Success," *Training & Development Journal* 44, no. 1 (January 1990): 50–52.

25. Victoria J. Marsick, Ernie Turner, and Lars Cederholm, "International Managers as Team Leaders," *Management Review* 78, no. 3 (March 1989): 46–49. See also Terpstra and David, 5; and Spencer Hayden, "Our Foreign Legions Are Faltering," *Personnel* 67, no. 8 (August 1990): 40–44.

26. Carey W. English, "Weight the Risks First on That Job Abroad," *U.S. News & World Report* (December 2, 1985): 82. See also Philip R. Harris, "Employees Abroad: Maintain the Corporate Connection," *Personnel Journal* 65, no. 8 (August 1986): 106–110; Paul L. Blocklyn, "Developing the International Executive," *Personnel* 66, no. 3 (March 1989): 44–47; and Mark E. Mendenhall and Gary Oddou, "The Overseas Assignment: A Practical Look," *Business Horizons* 31, no. 5 (September–October 1988): 78–84.

27. Blocklyn, 47.

28. Michael G. Harvey, "Repatriation of Corporate Executives: An Empirical Study," *Journal of International Business Studies* 20, no. 1 (Spring 1989): 131–144; and Robert T. Moran, "Corporations Tragically Waste Overseas Experience," *International Management* 43, no. 1 (January 1988): 74.

29. Copeland and Griggs, 196–199.

30. Joann S. Lublin, "More Spouses Receive Help in Job Searches When Executives Take Positions Overseas," *Wall Street Journal* (January 26, 1984): 29.

31. "Multinational Firms Act to Protect Overseas Workers from Terrorism," *Wall Street Journal* (April 19, 1986): 31. See also Michael Harvey, "A New Corporate Weapon Against Terrorism," *Business Horizons* 28, no. 1 (January–February 1985): 42–47.

32. Richard N. Farmer and Barry M. Richman, *International Business,* 4th ed. (Bloomington, IN: Cedarwood Press, 1984), 250–251.

33. Herbert J. Chruden and Arthur W. Sherman, Jr., *Personnel Practices of American Companies in Europe* (New York: American Management Association, 1972), 25.

34. Richard D. Robinson, *Internationalization of Business: An Introduction* (New York: Dryden Press, 1984), 104–106.

35. Chruden and Sherman, 32–33.

36. Donald A. Ball and Wendell H. McCulloch, Jr., *International Business—Introduction and Essentials,* 4th ed. (Plano, TX: Business Publications, 1990), 628.

37. Chruden and Sherman, 40–41.

38. Ibid., 7–8.

39. Ball and McCulloch, 640.

40. Robinson, 108–113.

41. Raymond J. Stone, "Pay and Perks for Overseas Executives," *Personnel Journal* 65, no. 1 (January 1986): 64–69.

42. Calvin Reynolds, "Compensation of Overseas Personnel," in *Handbook of Human Resources Administration,* 2d ed., ed. Joseph J. Famularo (New York: McGraw-Hill, 1986), 56–2, 56–3. See also Lin P. Crandall and Mark I. Phelps, "Pay for a Global Work Force," *Personnel Journal* 70, no. 2 (February 1991): 28–33.

43. *U.S. Department of State Indexes of Living Costs Abroad, Quarters, Allowances, and Hardship Differentials* (Washington, DC: Bureau of Labor Statistics, published quarterly).

44. Joann S. Lublin, "Companies Try to Cut Subsidies for Employees," *Wall Street Journal* (December 11, 1989): B1. See also Neil B. Krupp, "Overseas Staffing for the New Europe," *Personnel* 67, no. 7 (July 1990): 20–24; and Kate Gillespie, "U.S. Multinationals and the Foreign MBA," *Columbia Journal of World Business* 24, no. 2 (Summer 1989): 45–51.

45. Phatak, 133.
46. Robinson, 94–97.
47. Chruden and Sherman, 116.
48. Reginald Dale, "International Forces Will Prevail, but Will Unions Be Able to Change with New Global Workplace?" *Personnel Administrator* 28, no. 12 (December 1983): 100–104.
49. Ball and McCulloch, 643.
50. Robinson, 86.
51. For a comprehensive overview of EC-92 designed to assist managers in planning a strategy for the European market, see Heinz Weihrich, "Europe 1991: What the Future May Hold," *Academy of Management Executive* 4, no. 2 (May 1990): 7–18. See also Robert O'Connor, "Britain Trains to Compete in a Unified Europe," *Personnel Journal* 70, no. 5 (May 1991): 67–70.
52. John Naisbitt and Patricia Aburdene, *Megatrends 2000* (New York: Morrow, 1990), 60–61. See also André Laurent, "Managing Across Cultures and National Borders," in Spyros G. Makridakis and Associates, *Single Market Europe—Opportunities and Challenges for Business* (San Francisco: Jossey-Bass, 1991), Chapter 8.

An excellent glossary of terms used in international human resources management may be found in Peter J. Dowling and Randall S. Schuler, *International Dimensions of Human Resource Management* (Boston: PWS-Kent, 1990), 169–184.

CHAPTER 20

Auditing the Human Resources Management Program

After reading this chapter you will be able to:

1. *Discuss the contributions of audits to an organization.*
2. *Describe the approaches used in auditing the major HR functions.*
3. *Identify the types of information used in audits.*
4. *Explain the formulas for computing the rates of employee turnover, absenteeism, injuries, and illnesses.*
5. *Describe the methods used to assess employee attitudes.*
6. *Describe the methods used in analyzing audit findings.*
7. *Define the key terms in the chapter.*

TERMS TO IDENTIFY

cultural audit *(678)*
employee turnover *(678)*
turnover rate *(678)*
exit interview *(679)*
post-exit interview *(680)*
absenteeism rates *(681)*
attitude surveys *(684)*
personnel staff ratio *(690)*
cost-benefit analysis *(691)*
cost-effectiveness analysis *(691)*

Now that we have completed the discussion of the functions that make up the HR program, it is appropriate to analyze the ways in which the value of this program to an organization may be assessed. Auditing the HR program will be the focus of this chapter.

Like financial audits, audits of the HR program should be conducted periodically to ensure that its objectives are being accomplished. An HR audit typically involves analyzing data relative to the HR program, including employee turnover, grievances, absences, accidents, employee attitudes, and job satisfaction. The most effective audit is one that provides the maximum amount of valid information concerning the overall effectiveness of the HR program in contributing to the strategic objectives of the organization.

While it typically focuses on the HR department, an HR audit is not restricted to the activities of that department. It includes a study of the functions of HRM as they are performed in the total organization, including those performed by managerial and supervisory personnel. More emphasis, however, should be placed on evaluating the effectiveness of the HR department at the operating level because of its impact on employee attitudes and behaviors and its services to managers and employees. As shown in Figure 20–1, the decisions and activities of HR managers influence the effectiveness of the HR function as well as overall HR—and ultimately organizational—effectiveness.

CONTRIBUTIONS OF THE HUMAN RESOURCES AUDIT

Traditionally, management has been concerned primarily with the efficient and economical use of financial and material resources in the achievement of organizational goals. In the last two decades, however, increasing attention has been given to human resources and the contribution they make to the achievement of organiza-

FIGURE 20–1 INTEGRATIVE MODEL OF HR EFFECTIVENESS

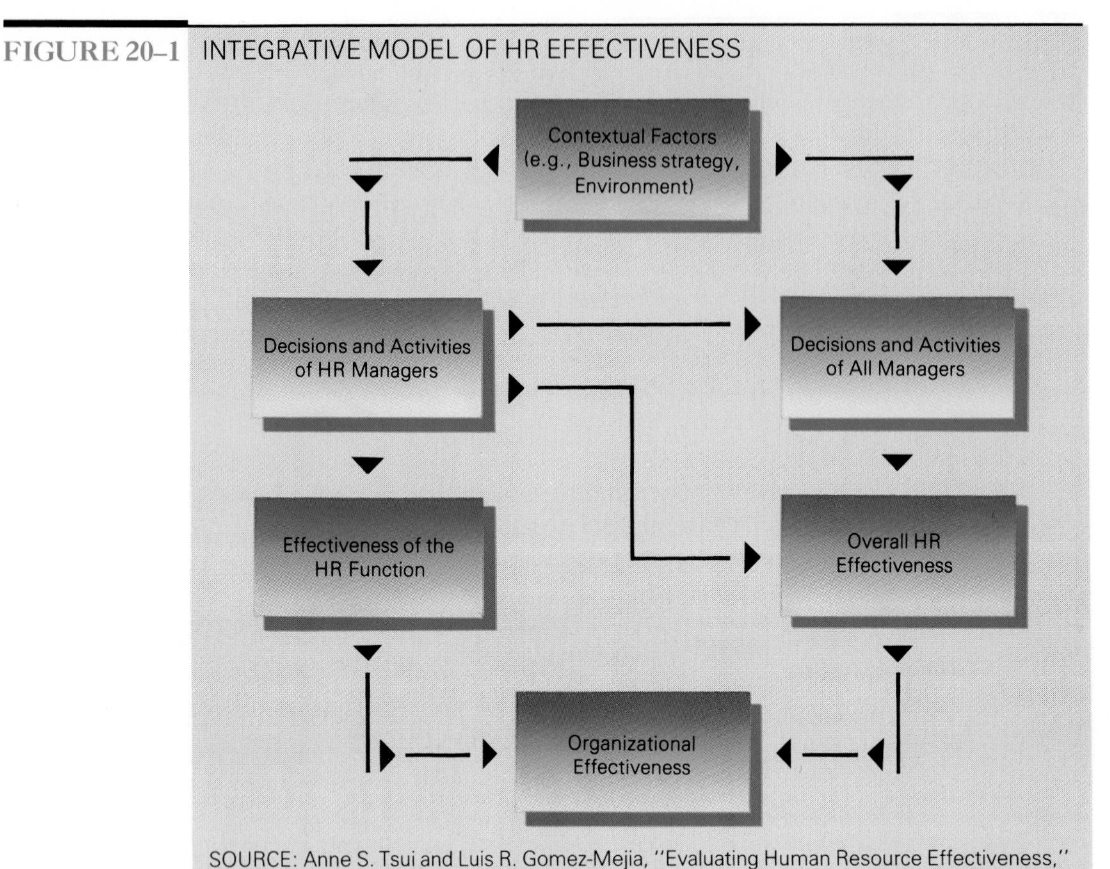

SOURCE: Anne S. Tsui and Luis R. Gomez-Mejia, "Evaluating Human Resource Effectiveness," in Lee Dyer, editor, and Gerald W. Holder, consulting editor, *Human Resource Management—Evolving Roles & Responsibilities* (Washington, DC: The Bureau of National Affairs, 1988), 1–211. Reproduced with permission.

tional success. The HR audit is a method of ensuring that the human resources potential of the organization is being fulfilled, while providing an opportunity to:

1. Evaluate the effectiveness of the HR functions.
2. Ensure compliance with laws, policies, regulations, and procedures.
3. Set guidelines for establishing standards.
4. Improve the quality of the HR staff.
5. Enhance the image of the HR function.
6. Promote change and creativity.
7. Assess the financial advantages and disadvantages of various HR functions.
8. Focus the HR staff on important issues.
9. Bring HR closer to the line functions of the organization.[1]

When asked how things are going, the traditional HR manager is likely to report, "Things seem okay, people are smiling." One expert advises that when the HR department stops reporting feelings and begins to report efficiency and productivity data, it will be perceived as a mainline function and not as a nice-to-do activity.[2] The HR audit can contribute to the professionalization of the HR function in many ways.

If an organization is to remain competitive, it must undergo continual change. An audit of its HR program can help managers identify variances between actual and expected or desired conditions. The audit thus becomes a data-based stimulus for change. Not only can the audit facilitate change, but also it can be used as an instrument of change. For example, if it is desirable that the HR manager make changes in the department, an audit can be used as a neutral medium for the views of superiors, peers, subordinates, and non-HR personnel in the organization. Thus, multiple pressures for change are brought upon the manager.

CONDUCTING THE AUDIT

Audits may be conducted by internal or external personnel. There are advantages and disadvantages to each approach. Insiders know more about the organization and are in a better position to determine which aspects require evaluation. They are also less likely to be viewed as a threat by those being audited. How objective the insiders will be, however, is always a question. External auditors are likely to be more objective and have less ego involvement.

The fact that legal and HR considerations have become inextricably intertwined makes it desirable for employers to consider using the services of an external auditor who has substantial experience in both HR and employment law.[3] At the present time, however, only about 3 percent of companies surveyed use outside consultants. Corporate or executive management, corporate HR administration, or the HR research department typically performs the audit.[4]

Steps in the Audit Process

Before discussing the various aspects of the HR program that provide the content for an audit, we will first take a look at the steps that are typically followed in an organizational audit.

One auditing specialist proposes that the audit process should consist of the following six steps:

1. Introduce the idea of the audit and emphasize the benefits to be derived from it.
2. Select personnel with a broad range of skills for the audit team and provide training as needed.
3. Gather data from different levels in the organization.
4. Prepare audit reports for line managers and HR department evaluation.

5. Discuss reports with operating managers who then prepare their own evaluation.
6. Incorporate corrective actions into the regular company objective-setting process.[5]

Since auditing is a form of research, it is important that the findings be based on objective, reliable, and valid data. HR records of all types are available for use in audits. In addition to analyzing these records, interviews are usually conducted with managers at different levels, the HR manager, the HR staff, and a selected number of supervisors and nonmanagement personnel.

Approaches in the Human Resources Audit

The most important function of the HR audit is to determine the effectiveness with which the objectives of the HR program are being met. Before starting the audit, the objectives and standards of the program should be stated clearly. This is especially important if external auditors are used. An audit should include at least three major approaches: determining compliance with laws and regulations (external requirements), measuring the program's compatibility with organizational goals, and evaluating the performance of the program.[6] In addition, policies and procedures should be examined carefully to determine whether they are adequate in meeting objectives.

DETERMINING COMPLIANCE WITH LAWS AND REGULATIONS

As we have noted throughout this book, the number of laws and regulations affecting HRM has increased dramatically in recent years. Organizations typically establish programs and procedures for achieving compliance with them. Top management needs to be aware of the manner in which managers at all levels are complying with the laws and regulations. Equal employment opportunity, safety and health, and pension plans are among the compliance areas often investigated in comprehensive audits.

Employers are required to maintain records for these programs in specified formats for examination by compliance investigators from federal and state agencies. In addition, many employers have learned to keep current as much information as possible about their performance in order to avoid last-minute crises in data-gathering projects.

To illustrate the types of demands on employers that government agencies can make, here are a few items among a total of 26 that one employer facing an EEO compliance review had to provide:

1. A listing by ethnic group of minority promotions in a 12-month period, giving "from" and "to" position titles, along with effective dates.
2. Copies of seniority lists by plant, division, and department with minority members identified.

Employers must keep careful records of ethnic hiring practices to prove compliance with EEOC laws and regulations.

3. An explanation of how tests were validated, by whom the tests were validated, and the scores used to make employment decisions.
4. A listing of craft jobs from the EEO-1 Report, broken down to show totals and minorities by ethnic group.
5. Names of those who referred minority candidates, and how many were refused.
6. Information on how many employees by ethnic grouping were in the summer employment program.[7]

The 20 other requests appeared to require just as much work on the part of the HR department as the six listed. It is essential, therefore, that managers of HR departments anticipate the types of information that will be required by government agencies and establish systems for maintaining such information in a computer file.

Employers should take a proactive approach to compliance with laws and regulations. It is important not only to establish effective policies and procedures but also to make sure that subordinates understand them thoroughly. Sexual harassment, discussed in Chapter 3, is a good example of a problem area. Problems often arise from lack of knowledge of the specific on-the-job behaviors that constitute sexual harassment under the law. Through a questionnaire it is possible to test employee understanding of what is and is not sexual harassment. Highlights in HRM 1 is a sampling of items from such a questionnaire. Such an instrument, part of which is essentially a test, is a valuable tool for determining what employees know and do not know about important areas.

Too often it is assumed that workers know all about the policies and procedures that relate to their job or work environment. Just as employees are tested on their

HIGHLIGHTS IN HRM

1 QUESTIONNAIRE USED IN AUDITING SEXUAL HARASSMENT

	Would it be sexual harassment?			Are you currently aware of or have you observed this behavior within the organization?	
1. Mr. (Ms.) X (Supervisor) posts cartoons on the bulletin board containing sexually related material.	Yes	No	Uncertain	Yes	No
14. Mr. (Ms.) X (Supervisor) habitually calls all female employees "sweetie" or "honey."	Yes	No	Uncertain	Yes	No
18. Mr. (Ms.) X (Supervisor) fails to promote a female (male) subordinate for not granting sexual favors.	Yes	No	Uncertain	Yes	No
21. Mr. X (Supervisor) leans and peers over the back of a female employee when she wears a low-cut dress.	Yes	No	Uncertain	Yes	No
25. Mr. (Ms.) X (Supervisor) gives a female (male) subordinate a nice present on her (his) birthday.	Yes	No	Uncertain	Yes	No

SOURCE: Paul J. Champagne and R. Bruce McAfee, "Auditing Sexual Harassment," *Personnel Journal* 68, no. 6 (June 1989): 124–139. Reproduced with permission.

understanding of matters related to safety and security, their understanding of other relevant matters should be audited.

MEASURING COMPATIBILITY WITH ORGANIZATIONAL GOALS

For many years managers of HR departments were viewed by top management as being out of touch with the goals of the organization. Consequently, as noted in Chapter 1, their role often was not considered nearly as important as that of other staff personnel. In the past several years, however, labor costs, government intervention, and a recognition of the need for greater productivity have caused executives to revise their view of the importance of the HR function. Concurrently, managers of HR departments have developed the expertise and have revised their orientation to be more in tune with the major goals of their organizations.

The process of setting goals requires close coordination with top management. This ensures that the policies and procedures of the HR department are consistent with top management's goals and objectives. The audit provides an opportunity to assess the extent to which objectives are being met and to revise policies and procedures accordingly.

EVALUATING PROGRAM PERFORMANCE Each of the functional areas of HRM that have been described in detail throughout this book should help to meet the overall objectives of an HR program. It is important, therefore, to audit each of these functions to determine how effectively and economically they are being performed. Since it is not possible to discuss in this text all the details involved in the audit of each functional area, we suggest in Figure 20–2 the general types of questions that should be answered in an audit. The sources of in-house information—usually records and reports—that are available for use in the audit are also included in the figure.

Most of the sources of information listed in Figure 20–2 yield statistical data that are readily available in many organizations. Where electronic data processing (EDP) facilities are being utilized, such information can be kept current for analysis and reporting, and should be used. We have made numerous references throughout the book to the increased use of EDP in HRM. One can expect even greater use of EDP in carrying out the various HR audit functions. One need only turn to the *Personnel Journal* or *HR Magazine* to find articles with specific recommendations for the use of EDP as well as advertisements of companies specializing in software for HR activities.

As valuable as the information sources listed in Figure 20–2 are in measuring the effectiveness of the major HRM functions, overreliance on quantitative measures may yield conclusions that seem objectively valid but fail to assess whether HR clients are really satisfied with the services they receive. This suggests using periodic studies of clients' perception of services rendered. Clients may include line executives and managers, employees, applicants, or even union officers.[8] User reactions may be obtained through attitude surveys, discussions with employees, group meetings, manager and supervisor comments, and similar approaches.

Employee benefit packages are one of the human resources programs that must be accounted for when budgets are being drawn up.

MEASURING HUMAN RESOURCES COSTS Management is typically interested in the costs of the activities that are required to meet the HR objectives. Standard cost-accounting procedures can be applied to all of the HRM functions. Cost savings are easily demonstrated in (1) compensation policies and procedures, (2) benefit programs and insurance premiums, (3) personnel taxes (e.g., unemployment taxes), (4) recruiting, training, and management development, (5) affirmative action, and (6) turnover and outplacement.[9]

In establishing a program for measuring HR costs, it is important to enlist the participation of the HR staff. Many staff members will not be measurement-ori-

FIGURE 20–2 AUDITING THE MAJOR FUNCTIONS IN HRM

HUMAN RESOURCES FUNCTION	SOURCES OF INFORMATION
Planning and Recruitment • Do job specifications contain bona fide occupational qualifications? • Are job descriptions accurate, periodically reviewed, and updated? • Are there any human resources that are not being fully utilized? • Is the affirmative action program achieving its goals? • How effective is the recruiting process? • How productive are the recruiters?	• HR budgets • Recruitment cost data • Job descriptions and specifications • Hiring rate
Selection • How valid are selection techniques? • Is there evidence of discrimination in hiring? • Are interviewers familiar with the job requirements? • Do interviewers understand what questions are acceptable and unacceptable to ask of job applicants? • Are tests job-related and free from bias? • How do hiring costs compare with those of other organizations?	• Employment interview records • Applicant rejection records • Transfer requests • EEOC complaints
Training and Development • How effective are training programs in increasing productivity and improving the quality of employee performance? • Are there sufficient opportunities for women and minorities to advance into management positions? • What is the cost of training per person-hour of instruction? • What is the relationship between training costs and accidents?	• Training costs data • Production records • Accident records • Quality-control records
Performance Appraisal • Are the performance standards objective and job-related? • Do the appraisal methods emphasize performance rather than traits? • Are the appraisers adequately trained and thoroughly familiar with the employees' work? • Are the appraisals documented and reviewed with employees? • Are the performance appraisal data assembled in such form that they can be used to validate tests and other selection procedures?	• Performance appraisal records • Production records • Scrap loss records • Appraisal interview records • Attendance records • Disciplinary action records

ented. At first they may fail to understand that all HRM functions are measurable and that their costs can be determined and related to the benefits that accrue to the organization. Through participative approaches the staff can identify a large number of measurable activities that can be included in formulas for measuring costs. Costs of orientation, for example, can be computed per employee per department (or HR

FIGURE 20–2 continued

HUMAN RESOURCES FUNCTION	SOURCES OF INFORMATION
Compensation	
• Does the pay system, including incentive plans, attract employees and motivate them to achieve organizational goals? • Do the compensation structure and policies comply with EEO, ERISA, and IRS requirements? • Is the choice of weights and factors in job evaluation sound and properly documented? • Do benefits costs compare favorably with those of similar organizations?	• Wages and benefits data • Wage-survey records • Unemployment compensation insurance • Turnover records • Cost-of-living surveys
Labor Relations	
• Are supervisors trained to handle grievances effectively? • Is there ongoing preparation for collective bargaining? • What is the record of the number and types of grievances, and what percentage of grievances have gone to arbitration? • What percentage of disciplinary discharges have been challenged?	• Grievance records • Arbitration award records • Work stoppage records • Unfair labor-practice complaint records

department orientation expense). The cost of various recruiting and hiring procedures can likewise be computed. For example, the source cost of recruits per hire (SC/H) can be computed by the following formula:

$$SC/H = \frac{AC + AF + RB + NC}{H}$$

where AC = advertising costs, total monthly expenditure (e.g., \$28,000)
AF = agency fees, total for the month (e.g., \$19,000)
RB = referral bonuses, total paid (e.g., \$2,300)
NC = no-cost hires, walk-in, nonprofit agencies, etc. (e.g., \$0)
H = total hires (e.g., 119)

Substituting the example numbers in the formula:

$$\begin{aligned} SC/H &= \frac{\$28{,}000 + \$19{,}000 + \$2{,}300 + \$0}{119} \\ &= \frac{\$49{,}300}{119} \\ &= \$414 \text{ (source cost of recruits per hire)} \end{aligned}$$

The basic formula can be varied by changing total hires to include only exempt hires (EH) or nonexempt hires (NEH). The example of source costs per hire is only one of many formulas available.[10]

CULTURAL AUDIT With the increased interest in the areas of organizational culture, it is only natural that these have also become subjects of audits. The **cultural audit** essentially involves discussions among top-level managers of how the organization's culture reveals itself and how the culture may be influenced. It requires a serious examination of such questions as, What reports are filled out? What do employees spend their time doing? How do they talk with each other? And, Who is given what responsibility? In studying organizational culture, according to Wilkins, we should focus on the underlying assumptions and orientations of a group of people. Conducting in-depth interviews and making observations over a period of time are the ways to learn about the culture. Wilkins emphasizes that in studying the culture of an organization it is important to recognize the existence of subcultures. Subcultures within an organization may well have quite different views about the nature of the work and how work is to be done. He cites an example of an electronics firm with a Subculture A, made up of the majority, that focuses on the importance of innovation and displays an abhorrence of rigid objectives or structure that would deter the creative urge. Subculture B, which comprises a minority of the people, focuses on the importance of accountability along with the need for objective and quantified information.[11] Larger organizations may have even more subcultures that should be studied to determine the extent to which different orientations are shared.

In addition to the study of the culture that involves philosophical discussions, there are objective data that are indicators of the quality of work life. These are discussed in the next section.

INDICATORS FOR EVALUATING THE WORK ENVIRONMENT

Throughout this book we have emphasized that the work environment can have a significant effect on the motivation, performance, job satisfaction, and morale of employees. It is possible to assess the quality of the environment within an organization by studying certain indicators. These indicators, which may also be used to assess the HR functions, are widely used in all types and sizes of organizations. They include employee turnover rates, absenteeism rates, injury and illness records, and responses from employee attitude surveys.

Employee Turnover Rates

Employee turnover refers to the movement of employees in and out of an organization. It is often cited as one of the factors behind the failure of U.S. employee productivity rates to keep pace with those of foreign competitors.

COMPUTING THE TURNOVER RATE The **turnover rate** for a department or an entire organization is an indicator of how employees respond to their work environment. The U.S. Department of Labor suggests the following formula for computing turnover rates:

$$\frac{\text{Number of separations during the month}}{\text{Total number of employees at midmonth}} \times 100$$

Thus, if there were 25 separations during a month and the total number of employees at midmonth was 500, the turnover rate would be:

$$\frac{25}{500} \times 100 = 5\%$$

Turnover rates are computed on a regular basis for more than four out of five organizations responding to a BNA survey. More than three-fourths of them use the data to compare rates among specific groups within the organizations such as departments, divisions, and work groups. In half of these organizations, comparisons are made with data provided by other organizations. The BNA's *Quarterly Report on Job Absence and Turnover* is used by the majority as a source of comparative turnover data.[12]

Another method of computing the turnover rate is one in which the rate reflects the avoidable separations. Unavoidable separations (US) are those occurring for reasons over which the organization has no control (e.g., pregnancy, return to school, and separations due to illness, death, or marriage). The formula for this method is as follows:

$$\frac{(S - US)}{M} \times 100 = T \text{ (turnover rate)}$$

For example, if there were 25 separations during a month, 5 of which were US, and the total number of employees at midmonth was 500, the turnover rate would be:

$$\frac{(25 - 5)}{500} \times 100 = 4\%$$

This method yields what is probably the most significant measure of the effectiveness of the HR program, since it can serve to direct attention to the portion of employee turnover that management has the most opportunity to control by means of better selection, training, supervisory leadership, improved working conditions, better wages, and opportunities for advancement.

The quantitative rate of turnover is not the only factor to be considered. The quality of personnel who leave an organization is also important.

The exit interview provides a forum for discussing an employee's motives for leaving the job.

DETERMINING CAUSES OF TURNOVER To determine why employees leave, many organizations conduct an **exit interview** during the employee's final week of employment. One study of a limited number of organizations found that 83 percent of these interviews are conducted by the HR department. In most cases the interviewers are employment recruiters. This is advantageous for two reasons: (1) Employees are likely to be more open when speaking with someone with whom they have had previous contact, and (2) recruiters are usually experienced interviewers.[13] Topics covered in exit interviews are shown in Figure 20–3.

The validity of the reasons for leaving that employees give during the exit interview has to be questioned. Many employees follow the rule of leaving on good terms and may consider frank discussion detrimental to their interests. Standardizing the interview by asking the same questions, advising exiting employees that information will be used in a constructive, not retaliatory, manner, and checking reasons with supervisory personnel and co-workers can help to improve the reliability and validity of data.

One writer suggests that a follow-up or **post-exit interview** should be conducted several months after the employee leaves. The meeting may be face-to-face or by telephone. The purpose of the interview is to review the information presented during the exit interview.[14]

Because of the importance of managers to an organization, special attention should be given to turnover among managerial personnel. In one electronics firm, responses to a questionnaire about managerial experiences were given to 143 current managers and 140 former managers. The former managers, with a few exceptions, were still in the organization but holding nonmanagerial positions. Compared with current managers, former managers describe their managerial experiences in terms of (1) less satisfying job characteristics, (2) greater degrees of difficulty in adjustment and socialization, (3) more unmet job expectations, and (4) greater degrees of job stress. While these findings do not account for all of the differences between the two groups, they provide the basis for practical recommendations to reduce turnover among managerial personnel.[15]

COSTS OF TURNOVER Replacing an employee can be time-consuming and expensive. Costs can generally be broken down into three categories: separation costs for the departing employee, replacement costs, and training costs for the new employee. These costs are conservatively estimated at two to three times the

FIGURE 20–3 TOPICS COVERED DURING EXIT INTERVIEWS

- Reasons for departure
- Relationships with supervisors
- Fairness of performance appraisal reviews
- Evaluation of pay and advancement opportunities
- Rating of working conditions
- Things liked best about job/organization
- Things liked least about job/organization
- Communication from management
- Evaluation of training received
- Organizational climate
- Suggestions

monthly salary of the departing employee, and they do not include indirect costs such as low productivity prior to quitting, and lower morale and overtime for other employees because of the job vacated. Consequently, reducing turnover could result in significant savings to an organization.[16] Highlights in HRM 2 details one organization's costs associated with the turnover of one computer programmer. Note that the major expense is the costs involved in training a replacement.

Absenteeism Rates

How frequently employees are absent from their work may also indicate the state of the work environment and the effectiveness of the HR program. A certain amount of absenteeism is, of course, unavoidable. There will always be some who must be absent from work because of sickness, accidents, serious family problems, and for other legitimate reasons. However, considerable evidence indicates that there are many other absences which can be avoided.

COMPUTING ABSENTEEISM RATES It is advisable for management to determine the seriousness of its absenteeism problem by maintaining individual and departmental attendance records and by computing **absenteeism rates.** Neither a universally accepted definition of absence nor a standard formula for computing absenteeism rates exists. However, the method of computing absenteeism rates most frequently used is that recommended by the U.S. Department of Labor:

$$\frac{\text{Number of worker days lost through job absence during period}}{\text{Average number of employees} \times \text{number of workdays}} \times 100$$

If 300 worker days are lost through job absence during one month having 25 scheduled working days at an organization that employs 500 workers, the absenteeism rate for that month would be:

$$\frac{300}{500 \times 25} \times 100 = 2.4\%$$

The Department of Labor defines *job absence* as the failure of employees to report to work when their schedules require it, whether or not such failure to report is excused. Scheduled vacations, holidays, and prearranged leaves of absence are not counted as job absence.

COMPARING ABSENTEEISM DATA The Bureau of Labor Statistics of the U.S. Department of Labor receives data on job absences from the Current Population Survey of Households conducted by the Bureau of the Census, and analyses of these data are published periodically. These analyses permit the identification of problem areas—those industries, occupations, or groups of workers with the highest incidence of absence or with rapidly increasing rates of absence. Comparison with other organizations may be made by referring to Bureau of Labor Statistics data reported in the *Monthly Labor Review* or by consulting such reporting

HIGHLIGHTS IN HRM

2 COSTS ASSOCIATED WITH THE TURNOVER OF ONE COMPUTER PROGRAMMER

Turnover costs = Separation costs + Replacement costs + Training costs

Separation Costs

1. Exit interview = cost for salary and benefits of both interviewer and departing employee during the exit interview = \$30 + \$30 = \$60
2. Administrative and recordkeeping action = \$30

Separation costs = \$60 + \$30 = \$90

Replacement Costs

1. Advertising for job opening = \$2,500
2. Preemployment administrative functions and recordkeeping action = \$100
3. Selection interview = \$250
4. Employment tests = \$40
5. Meetings to discuss candidates (salary and benefits of managers while participating in meetings) = \$250

Replacement costs = \$2,500 + \$100 + \$250 + \$40 + \$250 = \$3,140

Training Costs

1. Booklets, manuals, and reports = \$50
2. Education = \$240/day for new employee's salary and benefits × 10 days of workshops, seminars, or courses = \$2,400
3. One-to-one coaching = (\$240/day/new employee + \$240/day/staff coach or job expert) × 20 days of one-to-one coaching = \$9,600
4. Salary and benefits of new employee until he or she gets "up to par" = \$240/day for salary and benefits × 20 days = \$4,800

Training costs = \$50 + \$2,400 + \$9,600 + \$4,800 = \$16,850

Total turnover costs = \$90 + \$3,140 + \$16,850 = \$20,080/turnover

SOURCE: Michael W. Mercer, "Turnover: Reducing the Costs," *Personnel* 65, no. 12 (December 1988): 36–42. Reproduced with permission from Michael W. Mercer, Ph.D., Industrial Psychologist, The Mercer Group, Inc., Chicago, IL.

services as the Bureau of National Affairs, Prentice-Hall, and Commerce Clearing House.[17]

Nearly six out of ten organizations responding to a BNA survey reported that they compute absence rates on a regular basis for at least one employee group. These organizations encouraged their supervisors to compare their department rates with those of other departments and with the company average so that problems could be promptly identified and corrected.

COSTS OF ABSENTEEISM Traditional accounting and personnel information systems often do not generate data that reflect the costs of absenteeism. To call management's attention to the severity of the problem, absenteeism should be translated into dollar costs. A system for computing absenteeism costs for an individual organization is available. Organizations with computerized absence-reporting systems should find this additional information easy and inexpensive to generate. The cost of each person-hour lost to absenteeism is based on the hourly weighted average salary, costs of employee benefits, supervisory costs, and incidental costs. For a hypothetical company of 1,200 employees with 78,000 person-hours lost to absenteeism, the total cost was found to be $560,886. When this figure is divided by 1,200, the cost is $467.41 per employee for the period covered.[18] (In this example the absent workers were paid. If absent workers are not paid, their salary figures are omitted from the computation.)

REDUCING ABSENTEEISM While an employer may find that absenteeism rates and costs are within an acceptable range, it is advisable to study the statistics and determine exactly where the numbers are rooted. Rarely does absenteeism spread itself evenly across an organization. A fairly high percentage of workers may have perfect attendance records, while some may be absent frequently. Effective HRM requires that individual attendance records be monitored by supervisors, that incentives be provided for perfect attendance, and that progressive discipline procedures (see Chapter 16) be used with employees having a record of chronic absenteeism. The direct and continuing involvement of all managers and supervisors is essential.[19]

A record of every recordable workplace injury or illness provides a starting point for analyzing problems that may not be so obvious.

Occupational Injuries and Illnesses

We noted in Chapter 13 that employers are required by OSHA to maintain a Log and Summary of Occupational Injuries and Illnesses and to prepare a Supplementary Record for every recordable injury or illness. Detailed information about accidents and illnesses provides a starting point for analyzing problem areas, making changes in the working environment, and motivating personnel to promote safety and health.

From the records that are maintained, the Bureau of Labor Statistics and other organizations, such as the National Safety Council, compile data that an employer can use as a basis for comparison. In order to make such comparisons, it is necessary to compute for an individual organization the *incidence rate,* which is the number of injuries and illnesses per 100 full-time employees during a given year. The standard formula for computing the incidence rate is shown by the following equation where 200,000 equals the base for 100 full-time workers who work 40 hours a week, 50 weeks a year:

$$\text{Incidence rate} = \frac{\text{Number of injuries and illnesses} \times 200{,}000}{\text{Total hours worked by all employees during period covered}}$$

Incidence rates thus provide a basis for making comparisons with other organizations doing similar work. These rates are also useful for making comparisons between work groups, between departments, and between similar units within an organization. Application of this formula to the experience of one organization and the use of a table for comparative purposes are illustrated in the following example.

Shannon's Concrete Company, with an average annual employment of 80 individuals during 1987, experienced 15 recordable injuries and illnesses in that year. The total hours worked by all employees during this period were 127,000 (from payroll or other time records):

$$\frac{15 \times 200{,}000}{127{,}000} = 23.6 \text{ incidence rate}$$

Therefore, Shannon's Concrete experienced an incidence rate for total recordable cases of 23.6 injuries and illnesses per 100 full-time employees during 1987.

By examining the line marked off in Figure 20–4, which gives data from organizations with 50 to 99 employees, we find that Shannon's incidence rate of 23.6 is higher than the median (15.4) but lower than that in at least one-quarter of the establishments. It should be noted that the same formula can be used to compute incidence rates for (1) the number of workdays lost because of injuries and illnesses, (2) the number of nonfatal injuries and illnesses without lost workdays, and (3) cases involving only injuries or only illnesses.

Employee Attitude Surveys

The influence of attitudes and values on employee behavior is well recognized. In assessing attitudes, employers are typically interested in those attitudes that relate to the job, supervision, communication, and special organizational concerns. With such information it is possible to make organizational changes that will, it is hoped, increase employee satisfaction. One of the most objective and economical approaches to obtaining data for use in making organizational changes is through **attitude surveys.** These surveys are usually conducted on an organization-wide or plant-wide basis and usually involve the administration of a questionnaire (or inventory) or the use of interviews.

Traditionally, large organizations have been the primary users of employee surveys, but this is no longer the case. In a survey of 429 HR managers, 70 percent report that they have been involved in employee attitude surveys at least once during the past ten years. Six out of seven respondents believe that employee attitude surveys are particularly useful in addressing issues related to communication, motivation, effectiveness of supervisors, or compensation. A surprising finding is that the large majority also value research on corporate culture.[20]

USE OF QUESTIONNAIRES Questionnaires are intended to gather employee opinions that reflect attitudes about various aspects of their work situation. The steps in conducting a questionnaire survey are described in Figure 20–5.

One commercially available questionnaire used by several large organizations is the *SRA Attitude Survey*. It consists of a questionnaire known as the Core Survey,

FIGURE 20–4 EXAMPLE OF COMPARISON DATA FOR INJURIES AND ILLNESSES

Occupational injury and illness incidence rates of total recordable cases for construction industries by employment size and quartile distribution, 1987

Industry, SIC code(1), and employment size	Incidence rates per 100 full-time workers			
	Column A	Column B	Column C	Column D
	Average incidence rates for all establishments: (mean)	One-quarter of the establishments had a rate lower than or equal to: (1st quartile)	One-half of the establishments had a rate lower than or equal to: (median)	Three-fourths of the establishments had a rate lower than or equal to: (3rd quartile)
Special trade contractors Concrete work (SIC 177)				
All sizes	13.2	0.0	0.0	0.0
1 to 19	6.2	.0	.0	.0
20 to 49	15.1	.0	7.5	24.2
50 to 99	19.6	5.6	15.4	30.9
100 to 249	25.9	11.3	21.2	31.4
250 to 499	22.7	(2)	(2)	(2)
500 to 999	19.3	(2)	(2)	(2)
1,000 to 2,499	19.0	(2)	(2)	(2)

Note: (1) *Standard Industrial Classification Manual,* 1972 Edition, 1977 Supplement (Washington, DC: Office of Management and Budget).

(2) Quartile rates were not derived because fewer than 25 establishment reports were included in the industry employment-size group.

SOURCE: *Evaluating Your Firm's Injury and Illness Record—Construction Industries* (Washington, DC: Bureau of Labor Statistics, Report 776, March 1990), 4.

which contains 78 items sampling the 15 categories listed in Highlights in HRM 3. There are also provisions for supplementary items of concern to individual organizations, as well as for use with supervisors and salespersons. Respondents are asked to indicate their degree of agreement (from strongly agree to strongly disagree) with statements such as the following:

FIGURE 20–5 STEPS IN CONDUCTING AN ATTITUDE SURVEY

1. *Planning the Survey.* A careful planning of the survey is essential to its success. The objectives of the survey should be clearly determined and discussed by representatives of the various groups concerned, namely, managers, supervisors, employees, and the union.
2. *Designing the Questionnaire.* The questionnaire or inventory used in a survey should cover all phases of the employment situation that are believed to be related to employee satisfaction and dissatisfaction. Attitude surveys are better accepted by employees when employees at all levels participate in the development of the questionnaire items.
3. *Administering the Questionnaire.* The conditions under which the attitude questionnaire is administered are of vital importance to the success of the survey and to the morale of the participants. Employees should be fully oriented so that they understand the purpose of the survey. Prepublicity should be given through newsletters, special bulletins, and mailers. The usual procedure is to administer the questionnaire anonymously to large groups during working hours.
4. *Analyzing the Data.* A tabulation of results broken down by departments, male versus female employees, hourly versus managerial personnel, and other meaningful categories is the starting point in analyzing the data. If data are available from previous surveys, comparisons can be made. Comparisons are usually made between departments within the organization.
5. *Taking Appropriate Action.* Once problems are identified, appropriate action should be taken. Feedback on survey results and follow-up action that management has planned should be given to employees.

"If I have a complaint to make, I feel free to talk to someone up the line."
"My supervisor sees that employees are properly trained for their jobs."
"Changes are made here with little regard for the welfare of employees."[21]

Another commercially available questionnaire is the *Campbell Organizational Survey* (COS), published by National Computer Systems, Inc. Like the *SRA Attitude Survey*, the COS asks for responses to statements about working life such as the following:

"I have a lot of freedom to decide how to do my work."
"Many of my co-workers are under a lot of pressure."
"My supervisor keeps me up-to-date about what is happening."[22]

The 44 items in the COS cover the 13 scales listed in Highlights in HRM 4. According to the developer's research, these scales are related to job satisfaction and productivity.

The COS provides not only summary statistics for an entire working group but also a personal profile of each respondent. Thus the COS can serve as both an attitude survey and a job satisfaction questionnaire. The manual for the COS

HIGHLIGHTS IN HRM

3 CORE CATEGORIES IN THE SRA ATTITUDE SURVEY

Job demands
Working conditions
Pay
Employee benefits
Friendliness and cooperation of fellow employees
Supervisor–employee interpersonal relations
Confidence in management
Technical competence of supervision
Effectiveness of administration
Adequacy of communication
Security of job and work relations
Status and recognition
Identification with the company
Opportunity for growth and advancement
Reaction to the inventory

SOURCE: *SRA Attitude System Handbook*, Copyright © Science Research Associates, Inc., 1984. Reprinted by permission of the publisher.

contains considerable information on the reliability and validity of the COS, the use of the instrument for one-on-one counseling and in small group discussions, and the implementation of the results.

Getting the most from the answers obtained in a survey requires careful analysis of the data (see Step 4 in Figure 20–5 on page 686). While data on the total population will probably reveal areas of HRM that need improvement, problems of small critical groups of employees can be lost when ratings of all employees are combined and averaged. Ratings of those who are very dissatisfied will be offset by the ratings of those who are extremely satisfied. To obtain a clear picture of the strengths and weaknesses of the organization and provide a guide to solutions, analysis by groups is essential. One organization, for example, tabulated the results of a special attitude study of terminated employees on the basis of the following distinct groupings:

1. *The Job Hoppers.* They were most likely to be white, single, and male. They usually left because they were looking for a new job.
2. *The Dissatisfied Minority.* This group comprised the "best work performers." They left because they were generally dissatisfied with promotional opportunities as well as job-related and supervisor-related dimensions.

HIGHLIGHTS IN HRM

4 CAMPBELL ORGANIZATIONAL SURVEY SCALES

The work itself
Working conditions
Freedom from stress
Co-workers
Supervision
Top leadership
Pay
Benefits
Job security
Promotional opportunities
Feedback/Communications
Organizational planning
Support for innovation

SOURCE: David Campbell, *Manual for the Campbell Organizational Survey* (Minneapolis, MN: National Computer Systems, 1990), 6. Reproduced with permission.

3. *The Young, Career-oriented Women.* These individuals left because opportunities for promotion and advancement were limited.
4. *The Contented Veterans.* Most of these employees were terminated because of retirement, relocation, family needs, or reduction in staff.

The attitude ratings for these four groups are shown in Highlights in HRM 5. Findings from this study clearly indicate that a better understanding of organizational problems can be obtained by a careful analysis of the patterns of ratings for different groups within an organization, however the groups are defined.[23]

USE OF INTERVIEWS Another way to learn about employee attitudes is through an interviewing program. Interviewers should make it clear that the object of the interviews is to ascertain how to make the organization a more productive and satisfying place to work. The emphasis is on listening and encouraging participants to speak freely. A list of items requiring action is maintained, and concrete and prompt feedback to employees on the action taken is essential. Organizations such as Xerox, Copperweld, Kraft Foods, and General Electric have found that the upward communication system utilizing interviews has paid off in terms of reduced absenteeism and turnover, less waste and spoilage, improved safety records, increased productivity, and higher profits.[24]

HIGHLIGHTS IN HRM

5 ATTITUDE RATINGS OF FOUR DIFFERENT GROUPS IN ONE ORGANIZATION

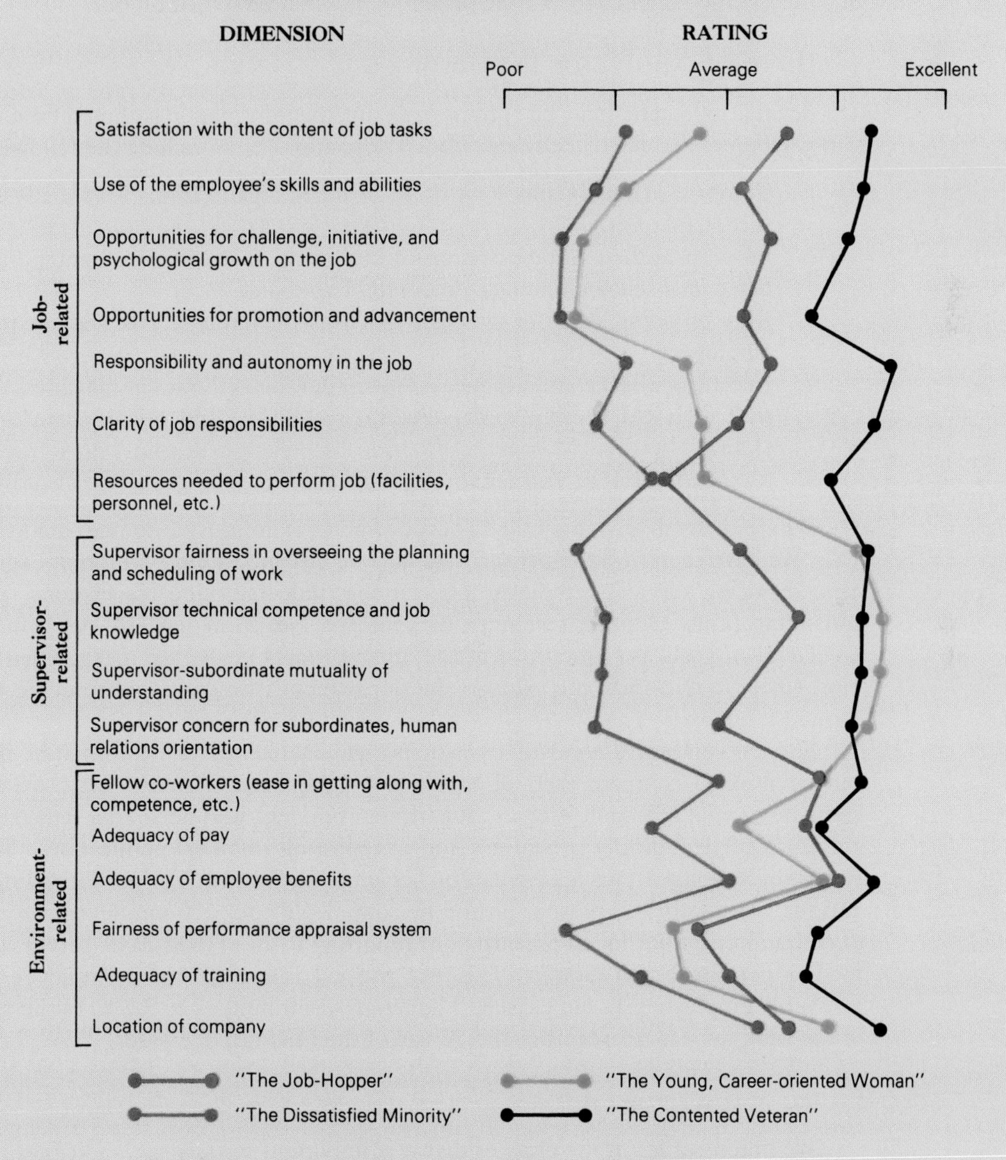

SOURCE: Reprinted from the May, 1985 issue of *Personnel Administrator*, copyright 1985, The American Society for Personnel Administration, 606 North Washington Street, Alexandria, VA 22314.

UTILIZING AUDIT FINDINGS

In the preceding discussion we observed that there are many sources and indicators from which information may be obtained about the overall effectiveness of the HRM program. This information must then be analyzed to identify the types of corrective action needed and the personnel best suited to carry it out.

Methods of Analyzing the Findings

Several approaches may be used in analyzing the information gathered from the various sources that have been described. These approaches include the following:

1. Compare HR programs with those of other organizations, especially the successful ones.
2. Base an audit on some source of authority, such as consultant norms, behavioral science findings, or an HRM textbook.
3. Rely on some ratios or averages, such as the ratio of HR staff to total employees.
4. Use a compliance audit to measure whether the activities of managers and staff in HRM comply with policies, procedures, and rules—an internal audit.
5. Manage the HR department by objectives and use a systems type of audit.[25]

Where the comparison method is used, figures from outside sources are available. We have seen that comparison data may be obtained from government agencies, reporting services, employer associations, industry trade associations, and consulting firms. Odiorne recommends approach No. 5. When HR department objectives or goals are supportive of the organizational goals, top management is more likely to recognize the value of the department's functions and provide the support it needs.

Surveys conducted regularly by various organizations provide information that can be used to compare costs of the total program and its parts. Data on the compensation of HR professionals, department budgets, and personnel staff ratios are reported periodically in journals and in reporting services' publications. The Bureau of National Affairs reports data on personnel staff ratios. The **personnel staff ratio** is the number of persons on the personnel staff per 100 employees on the organization payroll. For all organizations reporting in an SHRM-BNA survey, the median personnel staff ratio in 1987–1988 was 1.1 HR department employee for every 100 employees on the payroll. The range was from 0.02 to 7.7.[26] As the size of the work force increases, the relative size of the HR staff decreases.

Costs of the Program

We noted earlier in the chapter that it is important to translate audit findings into dollar costs wherever possible. Saying that turnover is "expensive" is not enough. When cost data are available, it is possible to make informed decisions about how much should be spent to improve existing programs or institute new ones, such as a program to reduce turnover. HR specialists should take the lead in preparing cost figures for as many of the HR activities as possible. With such figures the relationship between costs and benefits, and between costs and effectiveness, of the proposed activities can be clearly demonstrated. A **cost-benefit analysis** is the analysis of the costs of a particular function—e.g., training—in monetary units as compared to nonmonetary benefits such as attitudes, health, and safety. A **cost-effectiveness analysis** is the analysis of the costs of a particular function in monetary units as compared to monetary benefits resulting from increases in production, reductions in waste and downtime, etc.

If HR managers are to be effective and valued as part of the management team, they must have a measurement orientation.[27] According to Fitz-enz, since value in organizations is most often expressed in financial terms, "HR professionals are gradually giving up vague, subjective terms for the more specific, objective language of numbers."[28] Innovative HR departments are increasing their influence within their organizations by moving beyond the traditional administrative role and practicing "human value management"—helping their organizations to achieve important human, production, and financial objectives by using people's skills and talents to the best advantage.

Preparation of Reports and Recommendations

One of the most important activities of the audit team is the preparation of reports of their findings, evaluation, and recommendations. The reports should include everything that is pertinent and will be useful to the recipients. One report

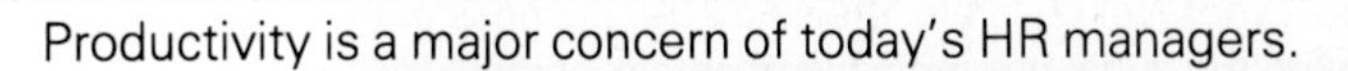

Productivity is a major concern of today's HR managers.

is usually prepared for line managers. A special report is prepared for the HR department manager, who also receives a copy of the report given to line managers.

The value to be derived from information obtained from audits lies in the use made of it to correct deficiencies in the HR program. An analysis of the information may reveal that procedures for carrying out some of the HR functions need to be revised. It is even possible that certain parts of the total program should undergo a thorough revision if they are to meet the objectives that have been established for them. Finally, the policies for each of the various functions should be examined to determine their adequacy as part of the overall HR policy.

SUMMARY

The HR audit offers a method for evaluating the effectiveness of the HR program and for improving its quality. It is used to determine the degree to which an organization is complying with laws and regulations and the degree to which the HR program is contributing to organizational goals by performing its functions effectively with a favorable cost-benefit ratio. The many aspects of HR planning and recruiting, selection, training and development, performance appraisal, compensation, and labor relations require careful study and evaluation.

By making special studies of turnover, absenteeism, occupational injuries and illnesses, and employee attitudes, it is possible to evaluate the quality of the work environment. Surveys of employee attitudes, which may be conducted through interviews and/or questionnaires, and a study of the organizational culture provide the basis for making changes in specific areas of the work environment such as the nature of supervision, adequacy of communication, and working conditions.

There are several approaches in analyzing audit findings. These include making comparisons with HR programs of similar organizations and relying on personnel staff ratios. Wherever possible, the cost effectiveness of the HR program should be assessed. Through the audit, it is possible to obtain insights that will be useful in planning for future operations.

DISCUSSION QUESTIONS

1. Why is it important to audit the HRM program periodically?
2. Some organizations employ specially trained consultants to conduct HR resources audits.
   a. What are the advantages and disadvantages of using consultants for this purpose?
   b. Consultants often compare the audit findings from an organization with those of other organizations with which they are familiar. Of what value are such comparisons?

3. Many organizations have found it necessary to be prepared for compliance audits by government agencies.
   a. How can the HR department best prepare itself for such an audit?
   b. How much effort should be devoted to preparing for compliance audits?
4. What types of information should be included in audit reports to management?
5. Describe the type of information available in records and reports that can be used in auditing the major HR functions. Give some examples of data that are easily computerized.
6. Explain the difference between an exit interview and a post-exit interview. What are the advantages and disadvantages of each method?
7. Why is it important to compute absenteeism rates? What steps can management take to reduce absenteeism?
8. What are the advantages of conducting periodic employee attitude surveys? Are any problems likely to arise over a survey? Explain.

MINI-CASE 20–1 Kelly's Attendance Bonus Plan

Kelly Marine Services, a builder of offshore support vessels, instituted an Attendance Bonus Plan to reduce absenteeism by recognizing and rewarding employees who come to work on a regular basis. The plan, as outlined in a letter to employees, is based on perfect attendance Monday through Friday of each week. If the shipyard does not work for reasons beyond the employees' control, the attendance bonus is not affected, provided the employees have punched in for that particular day. Any personal absence, excused or otherwise, will cause an employee to lose the attendance bonus for that week.

The attendance bonus is 10 to 15 cents per hour, depending on an employee's hourly rate. In the letter announcing the plan, employees were advised: "When you are absent, we are going to send a letter to your home showing exactly how much money you have lost. . . . Absenteeism of any kind will cause you to lose the attendance bonus. Unexcused absences may cause you to lose a raise or possibly even your job. Come to work every day and let the Attendance Bonus Plan pay you cash."

QUESTIONS

1. What effect is such a plan likely to have on production? On morale?
2. Why does the company send a letter home? Is this an advisable procedure?
3. Should such a plan include office employees as well as production employees?

MINI-CASE 20–2 Complaints from Crew X-31

The management of Midwest Cannery, employing 1,500 individuals to prepare and can baby foods, decided it was time to survey its employees to determine their attitudes toward their jobs and general working conditions. For about two weeks the assistant HR manager, who had had experience with surveys, met with representatives of management, of the employees, and of the union to discuss all aspects of the proposed survey. A definite date was set for conducting the survey, and all employees were given details about the purposes of the survey and how it would be conducted.

On the scheduled day, employees assembled in the company auditorium in groups of 200. After a brief orientation by the assistant HR manager, a questionnaire containing about 100 items was administered. The employees answered the items by checking "agree," "disagree," or "undecided." Provision was also made for employees to write their comments on the form. The only identification required on the questionnaire was the individual's crew number.

After all employees had participated and data were tabulated and summarized, reports were prepared for submission to the department heads and the plant manager. The reports were broken down by each major department and by crews. The comments that employees had written on the form were summarized to facilitate their use by those concerned.

The following is an extract from the company report that was sent to the manager of the Preparation Department. It concerned a crew of 30 employees (Crew X-31) who prepared meats and vegetables for canning. The crew was under the supervision of a general supervisor, who had three lead persons also responsible to him. Crew X-31 employees were paid on the basis of straight time plus incentive bonuses.

Extract of Report

The statistical analysis of the questionnaires for this crew reveals that attitudes toward the company as a whole, top management, and other areas measured are quite favorable. Employee attitudes toward the following areas, however, are quite unfavorable:

- Friendliness and cooperation of fellow employees
- Supervisor and employee interpersonal relations
- Technical competence of supervision

The comments that employees wrote on their answer sheets concerning the three areas viewed unfavorably were summarized as follows.

Friendliness and Cooperation of Fellow Employees. There are apparently older employees who adopt a bossy and domineering manner regarding those with less seniority. These employees boss others around.

A second complaint among the employees is that some employees are given better-grade ingredients to process.

Those ordinarily engaged in the preparation of vegetables resent being transferred, when necessary, to the preparation of chicken on the basis that they cannot make a sufficient bonus. They suspect favoritism at such times.

Supervisor and Employee Interpersonal Relations. The general supervisor often bypasses the lead persons in contacts with employees.

There are frequent changes in work that come up without warning or explanation, allowing only enough time to give orders to change what is being done and to transfer employees to other types of work where perhaps less bonus is to be made. The lead person, therefore, becomes more often than not the harbinger of bad news rather than the motivator.

Scheduling of rest periods is a problem.

Technical Competence of Supervision. Although there is possibly enough equipment available for the employees to do their jobs, equipment does not seem to be in the right place at the right time. Food carts are one of the main shortages, and any change in work amplifies this.

Employees do their job the same way day after day, but the inspectors can change their minds in interpreting procedure. They then write a note about an employee, giving name and badge number to the plant manager. The employee sometimes gets a written reprimand, and this causes friction. Employees feel that it should be brought to the employee's attention in some other way. There have been times when the employees tried to retaliate by damaging the product.

QUESTIONS

1. If you were the manager of the Preparation Department, what immediate action would you take on the basis of this report? What long-range action would you take?
2. What role should the HR department play in the follow-up of the critical aspects of the attitude survey?
3. Was this survey necessary? Couldn't management obtain the same type of information by just keeping its eyes and ears open? Discuss.

NOTES AND REFERENCES

1. Anne S. Tsui and Luis R. Gomez-Mejia, "Evaluating Human Resource Effectiveness," in *Human Resource Management—Evolving Roles & Responsibilities*, ed. Lee Dyer (Washington, DC: Bureau of National Affairs, 1988), 1:187–1:189; Jac Fitz-enz, *How to Measure Human Resources Management* (New York: McGraw-Hill, 1984), 28–29; and Vytenis P. Kuraitis, "The Personnel Audit," *Personnel Administrator* 26, no. 11 (November 1981): 29–34.

2. Fitz-enz, 28–29.

3. Johnathan A. Segal and Mary A. Quinn, "How to Audit Your HR Programs," *Personnel Administrator* 34, no. 5 (May 1989): 67–70.

4. Tsui and Gomez-Mejia, 1:198. See also Margaret E. Cashman and James C. McElroy, "Evaluating the HR Function," *HR Magazine* 36, no. 1 (January 1991): 70–73.

5. Walter R. Mahler, "Auditing PAIR," in *Planning and Auditing PAIR*, ASPA Handbook of Personnel and Industrial Relations, ed. Dale Yoder and Herbert G. Heneman, Jr. (Washington, DC: Bureau of National Affairs, 1976), 2-91–2-107.

6. Kuraitis, 32–33.

7. George R. Wendt, "Questions Compliance Officers Ask," *Personnel Journal* 54, no. 7 (July 1975): 385–387. See also Wayne K. West, "A Self-Audit for Affirmative Action Programs," *Personnel Journal* 57, no. 12 (December 1978): 688–690, 699.

8. Tsui and Gomez-Mejia, 1:194, 1:195.

9. Wayne F. Cascio, *Costing Human Resources: The Financial Impact of Behavior in Organizations*, 3d ed. (Boston: PWS-Kent, 1991), 8–9. See also Eric G. Flamholtz, *Human Resource Accounting—Advances in Concepts, Methods, and Applications*, 2d ed. (San Francisco: Jossey-Bass, 1985).

10. Fitz-enz, 61–62.

11. Alan L. Wilkins, "The Culture Audit: A Tool for Understanding," *Organizational Dynamics* 12, no. 2 (Autumn 1983), 24–38.

12. This Quarterly Report is part of *BNA Bulletin to Management*.

13. Pamela Garretson and Kenneth S. Teel, "The Exit Interview: Effective Tool or Meaningless Gesture?" *Personnel* 59, no. 4 (July–August 1982): 70–77.

14. Robert A. Giacalone and Stephen B. Knouse, "Farewell to Fruitless Exit Interviews," *Personnel* 66, no. 9 (September 1989): 60–62. See also Steve Jenkins, "Turnover: Correcting the Causes," *Personnel* 65, no. 12 (December 1988): 43–48.

15. Michael A. Campion and Michelle M. Mitchell, "Management Turnover: Experiential Differences Between Former and Current Managers," *Personnel Psychology* 39, no. 1 (Spring 1986): 57–69.

16. Garretson and Teel, 74–76.

17. The reader has probably observed that the loose-leaf services of these organizations are sources of invaluable information for the HR professional. As noted in Chapter 1, these services may be found in most libraries containing reference books in business.

18. Frank E. Kuzmits, "How Much Is Absenteeism Costing *Your* Organization?" *Personnel Administrator* 24, no. 6 (June 1979): 29–33.

19. John Putzier and Frank T. Nowak, "Attendance Management and Control," *Personnel Administrator* 34, no. 8 (August 1989): 58–61; and Paul Sandwich, "Absenteeism: You Get What You Accept," *Personnel Journal* 66, no. 11 (November 1987): 88–93. For a BLS study of absences over a five-year period, see Bruce W. Klein, "Missed Work and Lost Hours, May, 1985," *Monthly Labor Review* 109, no. 11 (November 1986): 26–30. For an interesting longitudinal study of reasons for absences, see Rick D. Hackett, Peter Bycio, and Robert M. Guion, "Absenteeism Among Hospital Nurses: An Idiographic-Longitudinal Analysis," *Academy of Management Journal* 32, no. 2 (June 1989): 424–453.

20. George Gallup, "Employee Research: From Nice to Know to Need to Know," *Personnel Journal* 67, no. 8 (August 1988): 42–43. See also Thomas Rotondi, "The Anonymity Factor in Questionnaire Surveys," *Personnel Journal* 68, no. 2 (February 1989): 92–101; Leland G. Verheyen, "How to Develop an Employee Attitude Survey," *Training and Development Journal* 42, no. 8 (August 1988): 72–76; and Robert J. Sahl, "Company-Specific Attitude Surveys," *Personnel Journal* 69, no. 5 (May 1990): 46–51.

21. From the *SRA Employee Inventory*. Copyright, 1951 by the Industrial Relations Center of the University of Chicago, as reprinted in the *SRA Attitude Survey*, © 1972, 1962 by Science Research Associates, Inc. Reprinted by permission of the publisher.

22. From the *Campbell Organizational Survey* © 1988 David Campbell, Ph.D. Published by National Computer Systems, Inc., P.O. Box 1416, Minneapolis, MN 55440. Reproduced with permission.

23. Robert C. Ernest and Leonard B. Baenen, "Analysis of Attitude Survey Results: Getting the Most from the Data," *Personnel Administrator* 30, no. 5 (May 1985): 71–80.

24. Woodruff Imberman, "Letting the Employee Speak His Mind," *Personnel* 53, no. 6 (November–December 1976): 12–22.

25. George S. Odiorne, "Evaluating the Human Resources Program," in *Handbook of Human Resources Administration*, 2d ed., ed. Joseph J. Famularo (New York: McGraw-Hill, 1986): 9-1.

26. *BNA Policy and Practice Series—Personnel Management* (Washington, DC: Bureau of National Affairs, 1989): 251: 159.

27. Cascio, 119–121.

28. Jac Fitz-enz, *Human Value Management* (San Francisco: Jossey-Bass, 1990), 311–312.

Cases

CASE 1 EAST MEETS WEST IN A JAPANESE SUBSIDIARY

Helen Stein was a graduate of the University of Texas with a major in HRM. Unable to obtain a position in her major field, she took a job in the operations department of a large oil company. Eventually, however, she was successful in obtaining a position as an employment interviewer with an aerospace company. In this company she advanced to the position of assistant manager of the HR department. She remained in this position until employed by the Tormaru Electronics Company. When Tormaru Electronics established a manufacturing plant on the West Coast, she was hired by the plant manager, Ichio Konaga, as the HR manager for the plant.

Although Mr. Konaga was a citizen of Japan, he had worked for several years in the United States and had become familiar with American management practices. His engineering and operations managers, however, had been brought directly from Japan nine months earlier to help open the West Coast plant. In the opinion of Ms. Stein, they were still "very Japanese" and somewhat suspicious of American management practices. The plant supervisors, all of whom were Americans, had been hired from other electronics firms or recently promoted from within Tormaru Electronics. Generally, Ms. Stein was able to work well with Mr. Konaga in establishing an HR program which reflected the management philosophies of the parent company. However, she did encounter a number of frustrations in attempting to implement the quality circle program that Mr. Konaga and his Japanese managers strongly supported. Several of her problems and frustrations can best be described in Ms. Stein's own words:

> A few months after I assumed my position, several of the first-level supervisors from the manufacturing department stopped by my office to complain about the quality circle program. Overall, they believed the concept had merit, but they thought that perhaps it functioned better in Japan, where workers and managers worked under a more consensus and interactive management system. They believed it just "didn't fit" within the American enterprise system. Almost all of the supervisors felt uneasy about discussing the situation with middle- and upper-level management for fear of being criticized by their Japanese superiors. Company policy required that "all departments and management personnel will implement and support the quality circle program." Furthermore, the Japanese managers were proud of the accomplishments of the quality circle program in their Japanese firm, and they firmly believed it to be a logical employee-management system for American organizations.
>
> Unfortunately these early complaints persisted, and, in fact, more supervisors from other departments began expressing additional concerns about the quality circle

efforts in their areas. After several supervisors threatened to quit if something wasn't done, I realized that I had to approach Mr. Konaga about the objections expressed to me. Before this meeting could take place, however, specific reasons for the dissatisfaction with the quality circle program had to be documented. Over the next week I outlined what seemed to be the problems. These included the following:

1. Supervisors feel they are losing control over the direction of their work units. Employees now recommend production changes directly to upper management rather than having supervisors make these recommendations. Supervisors believe top management might see employees as doing the supervisors' jobs, namely, proposing production changes.
2. Supervisors object to the supportive role they have to assume during quality circle meetings. During these sessions employees seem to be "the boss," and some employees are highly critical of various supervisory practices. Supervisors see this as a reversal of how American organizations should be run.
3. Sometimes quality circle meetings do not focus on production and quality issues; rather, they turn into employee gripe sessions. Employees discuss HR-related topics including employee appraisals, salary increases, or disciplinary matters. Petty gripes concerning parking facilities, lunchroom menus, and break privileges are regular topics of discussion.
4. Finally, supervisors believe that they have little or no voice regarding the implementation or development of the quality circle program. As one supervisor complained, "The program was shoved down our throats whether we liked it or not." Supervisors show little enthusiasm for making the system work.

An executive committee composed of top- and middle-level managers is responsible for the success of the quality circle program. According to the policy manual governing circle operations, all problems relating to the program are to be brought to the attention of the committee. Because of Mr. Konaga's experience with American managers, however, Ms. Stein decided to see him first before going to the executive committee.

CASE QUESTIONS

1. How would you account for the beliefs of the supervisors? Do their concerns sound rational?
2. If you were Mr. Konaga, what action, if any, would you take to resolve this dilemma?

CASE 2 THE EEO CHARGE

On June 24, 1989, Ms. Patricia Welch, vice-president of human resources for the Phoenix Publishing Company, was notified by the regional office of the Equal Employment Opportunity Commission (EEOC) in Chicago that a sex discrimination charge had been filed against the company. The charge form (see Exhibit 2–1) alleged that Phoenix discriminated against female employees by refusing to grant

EXHIBIT 2–1 CHARGE OF DISCRIMINATION

CHARGE OF DISCRIMINATION SAMPLE

This form is affected by the Privacy Act of 1974; see Privacy Act Statement on reverse before completing this form.

ENTER CHARGE NUMBER

☐ FEPA

☐ EEOC

_______________________________________ and EEOC

(State or local Agency, if any)

NAME *(Indicate Mr., Ms., or Mrs.)*		HOME TELEPHONE NO. *(Include Area Code)*
Mrs. Sandra Long		(312) 555-6675
STREET ADDRESS	CITY, STATE AND ZIP CODE	COUNTY
1972 West Walnut	Chicago, IL	Cook

NAMED IS THE EMPLOYER, LABOR ORGANIZATION, EMPLOYMENT AGENCY, APPRENTICESHIP COMMITTEE, STATE OR LOCAL GOVERNMENT AGENCY WHO DISCRIMINATED AGAINST ME *(If more than one list below.)*

NAME	NO. OF EMPLOYEES/MEMBERS	TELEPHONE NUMBER *(Include Area Code)*
Phoenix Publishing Company	2,300	(312) 555-0000
STREET ADDRESS		CITY, STATE AND ZIP CODE
174 South Baseline		Chicago, IL
NAME		TELEPHONE NUMBER *(Include Area Code)*
STREET ADDRESS		CITY, STATE AND ZIP CODE

CAUSE OF DISCRIMINATION BASED ON *(Check appropriate box(es))*

☐ RACE ☐ COLOR ☒ SEX ☐ RELIGION ☐ NATIONAL ORIGIN ☐ AGE ☐ RETALIATION ☐ OTHER *(Specify)*

DATE MOST RECENT OR CONTINUING DISCRIMINATION TOOK PLACE *(Month, day, year)* June 4, 1989

THE PARTICULARS ARE *(If additional space is needed, attached extra sheet(s)):*

The Phoenix Publishing Company discriminated against me by refusing to promote me to the position of Senior Press Operator. I am a woman, and the company does not promote many women in the printing department. Almost all of the promotions to Senior Press Operator go to men.

I bid on this job, and I feel I am fully qualified to perform the duties and responsibilities of the job. I feel that the company does not provide equal promotional opportunities to women.

☐ I also want this charge filed with the EEOC.

I will advise the agencies if I change my address or telephone number and I will cooperate fully with them in the processing of my charge in accordance with their procedures.

NOTARY - (When necessary to meet State and Local Requirements)

I swear or affirm that I have read the above charge and that it is true to the best of my knowledge, information and belief.

I declare under penalty of perjury that the foregoing is true and correct.

June 15, 1989 Sandra Long

Date Charging Party *(Signature)*

SIGNATURE OF COMPLAINANT

SUBSCRIBED AND SWORN TO BEFORE ME THIS DATE (Day, month, and year)

EEOC FORM 5 MAR 84 PREVIOUS EDITIONS OF THIS FORM ARE OBSOLETE AND MUST NOT BE USED them equal promotional opportunities within the printing department. The letter from Edward Valenzuela, regional director for the EEOC, informed Ms. Welch that a specialist from the Chicago office would be investigating the sex discrimination charge on behalf of the complainant.

The Phoenix Publishing Company, with headquarters in Chicago, employed almost 2,300 employees throughout the United States. Most of these employees were located in regional and district offices performing administrative and sales tasks. Approximately 950 employees worked in the Chicago office, a large number in the printing department. HR policies and procedures for the company were written by the HR staff in Chicago. However, large departments, like the printing department, were given some autonomy to implement company policies according to their departmental needs.

Over the past 15 years Phoenix had supported a policy of promotion from within. Company executives strongly believed that employees should be given every opportunity to advance their careers according to their individual abilities and talents. The policy was outlined in the following statement:

> The Phoenix Publishing Company adheres to a policy of promotion from within. Employee morale and loyalty are strengthened when individuals have the opportunity to advance within the organization. The company and its customers also benefit by having employees use their abilities to the fullest extent possible. As with all its employment policies, the Phoenix Publishing Company maintains and supports a policy of equal employment opportunity. The company promotes individuals solely on their talents, knowledge, and/or skills. Promotion based upon favoritism or any form of discrimination is unfair according to company policy and illegal as stated in federal and state laws.

This policy had always been well received by employees, and it had provided the organization with many outstanding employees.

While the promotion policy served as a guide for departments to follow, department managers were free to set their own promotion standards and to establish the procedures by which employees were upgraded. In the printing department, employees bidding on higher-rated jobs were evaluated and selected by a five-member departmental promotion board consisting of two hourly employees elected by their peers by secret ballot and three supervisors appointed by the department manager. According to the promotion procedures of the printing department, the department manager had the authority to overturn the decision of the promotion board, but in practice this rarely happened. All open positions were posted for ten working days, after which the promotion board reviewed each bidding employee's total work record and educational history. The successful employee was the one whose job experience, education, and work record were superior to those of other bidding employees. Where employees were judged to have equivalent employment and educational records, the senior employee, as determined by length of service within the printing department, was awarded the job.

The sex discrimination charge was filed by Sandra Long, an assistant press operator in the printing department. Sandra was hired by Phoenix three years ago after graduating from Advanced Technical Institute, a trade school specializing in training for the printing trades. Over this three-year period, Sandra's performance ratings were all above average. Her supervisor, Wade Hageman, noted on her evaluation forms that the quality of her printing work was excellent. She seldom made printing errors, and her production runs were always set up according to company procedures. Compared with that of other assistant press operators, her scrap rate was marginal. However, on each of her performance appraisal forms, Hageman noted that her production setup time was always slow, which sometimes created production bottlenecks and scheduling problems. On two occasions during the past year, Sandra missed customer delivery dates by several hours.

It was no secret to her fellow employees or management that Ms. Long enjoyed her job. She often shortened her breaks and lunch periods to watch the senior press operators perform difficult printing operations. Sandra continued to expand her knowledge of press operations by taking night classes at North Central Community College. Furthermore, she had recently received a certificate for completing a correspondence course on press setup and maintenance offered by the Association of Press Operators, a national trade association.

The sex discrimination charge was filed with the EEOC after Ms. Long had bid on an opening for senior press operator and was turned down by the departmental promotion board. The all-male promotion board made its decision after thoroughly reviewing the employment and education records of two candidates, Ms. Long and Mr. Keith Ormrod, another assistant press operator. The report of the promotion board noted the following:

1. Both candidates possessed similar work records for the past three years. However, the promotion board unanimously found that, although their work was generally comparable in quality, Mr. Ormrod always completed his production runs on time.
2. Ms. Long and Mr. Ormrod were approximately equal in educational attainment. While Ms. Long held a certificate in press setup and maintenance, Mr. Ormrod had obtained a certificate from the Association of Press Operators in ink composition. Ms. Long was taking a correspondence course in ink.
3. Both individuals had good attendance records, although Mr. Ormrod had one extended medical leave of nine weeks for a kidney infection.

The promotion board also noted that, while Sandra was well liked by her fellow employees, she did not associate on a personal basis with her peers. Sandra once told John Feinstein, a close friend and fellow employee, that family responsibilities and educational commitments made it very difficult for her to get together with the gang after work. Several employees remarked that Sandra was a "die-hard feminist," and her support for various women's causes was often discussed and joked about among the other press operators.

After deliberating for nearly two hours, the departmental promotion board selected Mr. Ormrod for the senior press operator position. In addition to the title upgrade, Mr. Ormrod's hourly rate of pay increased from $11.36 to $15.55 per hour. The promotion was to be effective beginning with the next payroll period. Ms. Long was told of the promotion board's decision by her supervisor shortly after the board completed its deliberations. The HR department also sent her an official notice of the bid outcome, along with a statement that promotion requests would again be considered when other senior press operator vacancies occurred and employees elected to bid on the positions. Neither the discussion with her supervisor nor the letter from HR helped to lessen Ms. Long's disappointment at being denied the promotion. Later she told John Feinstein, "I wouldn't have bid on the position if I didn't think I was the best qualified for the opening."

After several discussions with other female employees in the printing department, and at the urging of her husband, Sandra Long decided to file the sex discrimination charge with the EEOC in Chicago. The charge was based on two points:

1. The Phoenix Publishing Company committed sex discrimination against her when it denied her the promotion to senior press operator because she was a woman.
2. The Phoenix Publishing Company discriminated against females as a class because of its past promotion record in the printing department. (See Exhibit 2–2).

Ms. Long charged the company with past and present sex discrimination against female employees in violation of Title VII of the Equal Employment Opportunity Act of 1972.

CASE QUESTIONS

1. Does Sandra Long have a logical basis for pursuing a sex discrimination case successfully?
2. How does the *Uniform Guidelines on Employee Selection Procedures* pertain to Sandra's case?
3. If you were the EEOC investigative officer, how would you evaluate Sandra Long's charge?

CASE 3 RAPID EXPANSION AT GALVEZ RETAIL GROUP

The Galvez Retail Group, a large specialty clothing store chain with headquarters in Portland, Oregon, operates 28 stores throughout the western United States. Dorothy Galvez, president and CEO, started the organization in Orange County, California, in 1980 when she opened a small specialty store selling fashion sportswear. Merchandise for the store was selected for those with a "discriminating taste"

EXHIBIT 2–2 EMPLOYMENT NUMBERS AND PROMOTION RECORD OF THE PRINTING DEPARTMENT

Number of employees in the printing department classified by sex as of December 31, 1988 (all printing job classifications)

	NUMBER
Male	93
Female	17

Promotion of employees within the printing department classified by sex since January 1, 1981 (all print job classifications)

YEAR	MALE	FEMALE	TOTAL
1981	2	2	4
1982	9	3	12
1983	3	1	4
1984	2	1	3
1985	6	2	8
1986	3	2	5
1987	4	0	4
1988	6	1	7
	35	12	47

in sports clothing. Prices were well above those charged for sportswear in discount outlets or department stores. Dorothy Galvez's first store was highly successful, and within a two-year period she had expanded her line to include evening wear and related accessories and had a staff of 9 full-time and 4 part-time employees.

Ms. Galvez was an exceptional entrepreneur. After graduation from high school in 1977, she had enrolled at South Coast Community College and received an Associate of Arts (A.A.) degree with an emphasis in business administration. She excelled in her finance, marketing, small-business management, entrepreneurship, and HR classes. Her professors described her as hard-working and goal-directed. Ms. Galvez was selected to present the graduation address at the school's spring commencement ceremony, an honor bestowed only upon the most outstanding students. It was shortly after receiving her A.A. degree that she opened the Orange County store.

Ms. Galvez's business and educational experiences afforded her many opportunities to become involved in civic and community work. She considered her directorship of the Orange County United Way Campaign in 1987 and her leadership on the executive board for the expansion of the county's recreational facilities to be two of her highest civic achievements. She also believed that her many contacts with prominent community leaders had helped her business to grow.

The Orange County store was such a large success that Ms. Galvez decided to expand her business by opening two more stores. In 1984, a store was opened in Los Angeles, and in 1986 another store held its grand opening in Del Mar, California. Dorothy promoted two supervisors from the Orange County store to manage these new facilities. Both new store managers possessed strong merchandising backgrounds; however, as Ms. Galvez confided to a business friend, "They need to develop their human resources skills."

Ms. Galvez received some exciting news in 1989 when she was approached by the West Merchandising Corporation with an offer to buy into her growing business. West Merchandising was a multimillion-dollar retail organization managing large department stores nationwide. West had recently announced an ambitious expansion program. Part of the expansion program involved investing in specialty clothing stores. The offer made by West to Ms. Galvez was relatively simple. West would extend a $40-million line of credit in exchange for a 49 percent share of the new joint venture. Ms. Galvez would retain complete control of the organization and be given the titles of president and CEO. The new venture would be called the Galvez Retail Group in recognition of Dorothy's contribution to the organization. A seven-person board of directors would be formed, with three board positions filled by West Merchandising executives.

The West purchase offer was attractive to Ms. Galvez for several reasons. First, the money extended through the line of credit was very generous. Second, it allowed her to expand the organization in a very short period of time. Indeed, West management granted the large money offer because of the tremendous expansion potential of these specialty clothing stores. If Ms. Galvez accepted the proposal, she had to agree to expand the number of her stores to 28 by 1994—an average of five new stores each year for the next five years. West agreed to have its marketing department help identify new store locations. The initial plan called for new stores to be opened in Seattle, the Los Angeles area, San Diego, Portland, Palm Springs, Las Vegas, Denver, Phoenix, and the San Francisco area. Beyond West's assistance with store locations, Ms. Galvez would be totally responsible for developing store layouts, local advertising campaigns, operating procedures, and HR policies.

After several exploratory meetings between Ms. Galvez and West executives, Ms. Galvez was given three months to consider the offer and develop short-range (one year) and long-range (five years) plans for execution of the proposed venture. West's acceptance of Ms. Galvez's plans depended upon the thoughtfulness and detail of these plans. While the final report submitted by Ms. Galvez was to cover many areas, it specifically had to discuss the following topics:

1. *A complete human resources plan for meeting staffing requirements for the next five years.* Recruiting sources for both hourly and management personnel were to be identified.
2. *Development of a training program for store management personnel.* Since store managers were to be completely responsible for store operations, their training would include all aspects of HRM.

3. *A career planning program for store managers, staff managers, and executive personnel.*

Because of the short time available to prepare the strategic plans, Ms. Galvez employed three HR consultants, each with experience in HR planning and training activities. Their responsibility, along with input from Dorothy, was to formulate the plans to present at the meeting with West executives in three months.

CASE QUESTIONS

1. Working in teams of three or four, formulate an HR plan for meeting staffing requirements in 1994. Identify possible environmental constraints to the plan, and list recruitment sources.
2. Propose a management training program for new store managers identifying various HR topics to cover.
3. Develop a career planning program for store managers.

CASE 4

COLLEGE RECRUITING AT LANDSTAR

Three months after graduating from Greenview State University's College of Business, John Schroder and David Ludwig met for dinner to discuss their job-hunting experiences and to talk about their newly found jobs. John and David had met at Greenview while taking a required business statistics class and became close friends during the remainder of their college days. John's area of specialization was marketing, while David's interests were in communication and general business management. After college, both graduates were fortunate to have found employment with large national companies in the St. Louis area, and, therefore, were able to continue their friendship.

During the last semester of their senior year, John and David registered with University Career Services in order to be interviewed by organizations wishing to recruit graduating seniors. Both John and David scheduled ten interviews with organizations they were interested in. After these initial campus meetings, John received invitations to visit four companies and David received three.

On April 19, 1988, both graduating seniors received plant interviews with Landstar Communications, Inc., a growing telecommunications organization employing approximately 3,200 employees with headquarters in Atlanta. The letter from Ms. Elizabeth Shepard, director of human resources, advised them that the interviews would take place in Atlanta on May 21, 22, and 23, and that Ms. Shepard would coordinate their interview schedule and act as host during their stay. The letter to John said he was being considered for an opening in the marketing department; the letter to David said he was being interviewed for a first-line supervisory position in the manufacturing department. Both candidates were to make their own transportation and accommodation arrangements and report to the HR office at 9:30 A.M. on May 21 to begin the interview process.

Business students at Greenview State generally considered Landstar an excellent employer. The company had a reputation as a growth organization with good advancement opportunities and was noted for the high starting salaries it paid to college graduates. It also offered its employees an excellent cafeteria-type benefits package.

Shortly after their interviews in May, John and David received offers of employment with starting dates of July 1, 1988. They met for lunch on June 17, and after a lengthy and involved conversation they both decided to reject the Landstar offers. Both starting salary offers were well above average, and the jobs appeared to be exciting and personally rewarding. However, it was the three-day interview process and the impression they received from the company visit that led to their decision to turn down the employment offers. John described his interviewing experience like this:

> I was really "pumped up" for the Landstar visit. When I arrived at the human resources office at 9:30, I was surprised to find 11 other college graduates waiting to see Ms. Shepard. Somehow I thought our first meeting would be a little more personal. Her secretary gave each of us an employment application and medical history form to complete, after which she informed us that Ms. Shepard would begin briefing us individually in 15-minute time slots starting at 11:00 A.M. The employment forms were very complex, and most of us hadn't brought all of the information needed to complete them. I felt uneasy about the sections I left blank because I didn't want to make a negative impression right off. Since the employment forms could be completed in about one hour, we spent the remaining 30 minutes engaging in nervous conversation to kill time.
>
> My briefing with Ms. Shepard was very structured, and she seemed somewhat aloof. The only purpose of this meeting was to give me my personal preemployment schedule for the three-day visit. My schedule consisted of seven interviews, a physical examination, testing by the HR department, a group interview conducted by top managers from the marketing department, and several management exercises which I assumed were given to evaluate my managerial and leadership skills.
>
> My first interview that afternoon was with Mr. Steven Rayford, director of marketing. The interview was a marathon event lasting almost three hours. He quizzed me about my career goals, marriage and family plans, college classes, extracurricular activities, and how I felt about coming to work for Landstar. He seemed interested in my answers although our meeting was often halted by phone calls and interruptions by other marketing department personnel. He was always polite to those people and answered their questions with added comments on matters concerning their families or personal lives. Mr. Rayford seemed friendly to me, but my impression was that he had more important things on his mind than our interview. In fact, I had this impression about many of the marketing people I met with. Furthermore, one manager was late to our interview because of a "personal" meeting with one of his employees. I don't know, perhaps these incidents were simply a characteristic of a busy, growing company.
>
> I was looking forward to my interview on Thursday morning with Ms. Simpson, sales manager for the East Coast. In fact, I really prepared for our meeting since her

department had the opening I was interviewing for. Unfortunately this interview was very superficial. Ms. Simpson and I mostly discussed her personal likes and dislikes and her travel experiences to Europe and Africa, where Landstar has several clients. She also was very impressed with my Christian youth work and my affiliation with the Young Republican Club at Greenview. Toward the end of our meeting, she asked me some general questions about three of my marketing classes, and that's about all.

We spent the afternoon of May 22 with Ms. Shepard in human resources. She asked four of us to take personality tests and to fill out some forms which were explained to us as a new method of honesty testing. I felt uneasy that only four of us were required to undergo these employment procedures, but I felt I had no other option but to complete the testing if I wanted the job. If I refused, they might think I was uncooperative or had something to hide. Ms. Shepard then asked all of us to take some general aptitude tests, which she explained were given to all future Landstar employees regardless of the position applied for. The day ended in the HR medical office where we were required to take a drug screening test.

My schedule on May 23 consisted of several more short interviews which I thought went well except for the one with Ms. Gloria Winkler. The interview with Ms. Winkler, director of advertising, was strange, to say the least. After my introduction to her, she simply sat there and let me talk about anything that seemed important to me. Her total involvement in the interview was to gesture approval of my statements and to ask three or four follow-up questions. After 30 minutes I had nothing more to say, and the interview was terminated.

We finished the employment process in Ms. Shepard's office at 3:00 P.M. She was very polite and thanked each of us for coming to Landstar. My impression of this final meeting was that it seemed very canned and perfunctory. After the meeting I asked some of the other applicants if they had any final questions to ask of Ms. Shepard, and they all said yes but that the atmosphere just didn't seem right to ask them. At 3:30 I was on the way to the airport for the return trip to Greenview State.

CASE QUESTIONS

1. Comment specifically on the interviewing, testing, and overall scheduling procedure used at Landstar.
2. Discuss the interview procedure used by Gloria Winkler. Is this an effective interview method?
3. Design a successful employment selection system for Landstar Communications.

CASE 5

THE CASE OF THE SECOND APPRAISAL

Marcus Singh, a naturalized U.S. citizen from India, is a research economist in the City of Rock Falls Office of Research and Evaluation. He is 40 years old and has worked for the City of Rock Falls for the past ten years. During that time, Marcus

This case was prepared by James G. Pesek and Joseph P. Grunenwald of Clarion University of Pennsylvania. Reprinted with permission.

has been perceived by his supervisors as an above-average performer, although no formal personnel evaluations have ever been done in his department. About ten months ago he was transferred from the department's Industrial Development unit to the newly formed Office of Research and Evaluation. Other employees also were transferred as part of an overall reorganization. The organizational chart for the department is depicted in Exhibit 5–1.

Out of concern for equal employment opportunity, the department director, Victor Popelmill, recently issued a directive to all of the unit heads to formally evaluate the performance of their subordinates. Attached to his memorandum was a copy of a new performance appraisal form to be used in conducting the evaluations. Garth Fryer, head of the Office of Research and Evaluation, decided to allow his subordinates to have some input in the appraisal process. (In addition to Garth Fryer, the Office of Research and Evaluation comprised Marcus Singh and another research economist, Jason Taft, and one secretary, Connie Millar.) Garth told each of the researchers to complete a self-appraisal and a peer appraisal for the other. After reviewing these appraisals, Garth completed the final and official appraisal of each researcher. Before sending the forms to Mr. Popelmill's office, Garth met with each researcher individually to review and explain his ratings. Each researcher signed his appraisal and indicated agreement with the ratings.

About one week after submitting the appraisals to the department director, Garth Fryer received a memorandum from Mr. Popelmill stating that his evaluations were unacceptable. Garth was not the only unit head to receive this memorandum; in fact, they all received the same note. On examination of the completed appraisal forms from the various departments, the director had noticed that not one employee was appraised in either the "fair" or "satisfactory" category. In fact, the vast majority of the employees were rated as "outstanding" in every category. Mr. Popelmill felt that his unit heads were too lenient and asked them to redo the evaluations in a more objective and critical manner.

Garth Fryer explained the director's request to his subordinates and asked them to redo their appraisals with the idea of being more objective this time. Once again, after reviewing his subordinates' appraisals, Garth formulated his ratings and discussed them individually with each employee.

Marcus Singh was not pleased at all when he found out that his supervisor had rated him one level lower on each category. (Compare Exhibits 5–2 and 5–3.) Although he signed the second appraisal form, he clearly indicated on the form that he did not agree with the evaluation. Jason Taft, the other researcher in the Office of Research and Evaluation, received all "outstanding" ratings on his second evaluation. Like Marcus, Jason has a master's degree in economics, but he has been working for the City of Rock Falls for less than two years and is only 24 years old. Jason also worked closely with Garth Fryer before being transferred to his new assignment ten months ago. Recently, the mayor of the city received a letter from the regional director of a major government agency praising Jason Taft's and Garth Fryer's outstanding research.

EXHIBIT 5–1 ORGANIZATIONAL CHART OF THE CITY OF ROCK FALLS, OFFICE OF RESEARCH AND EVALUATION

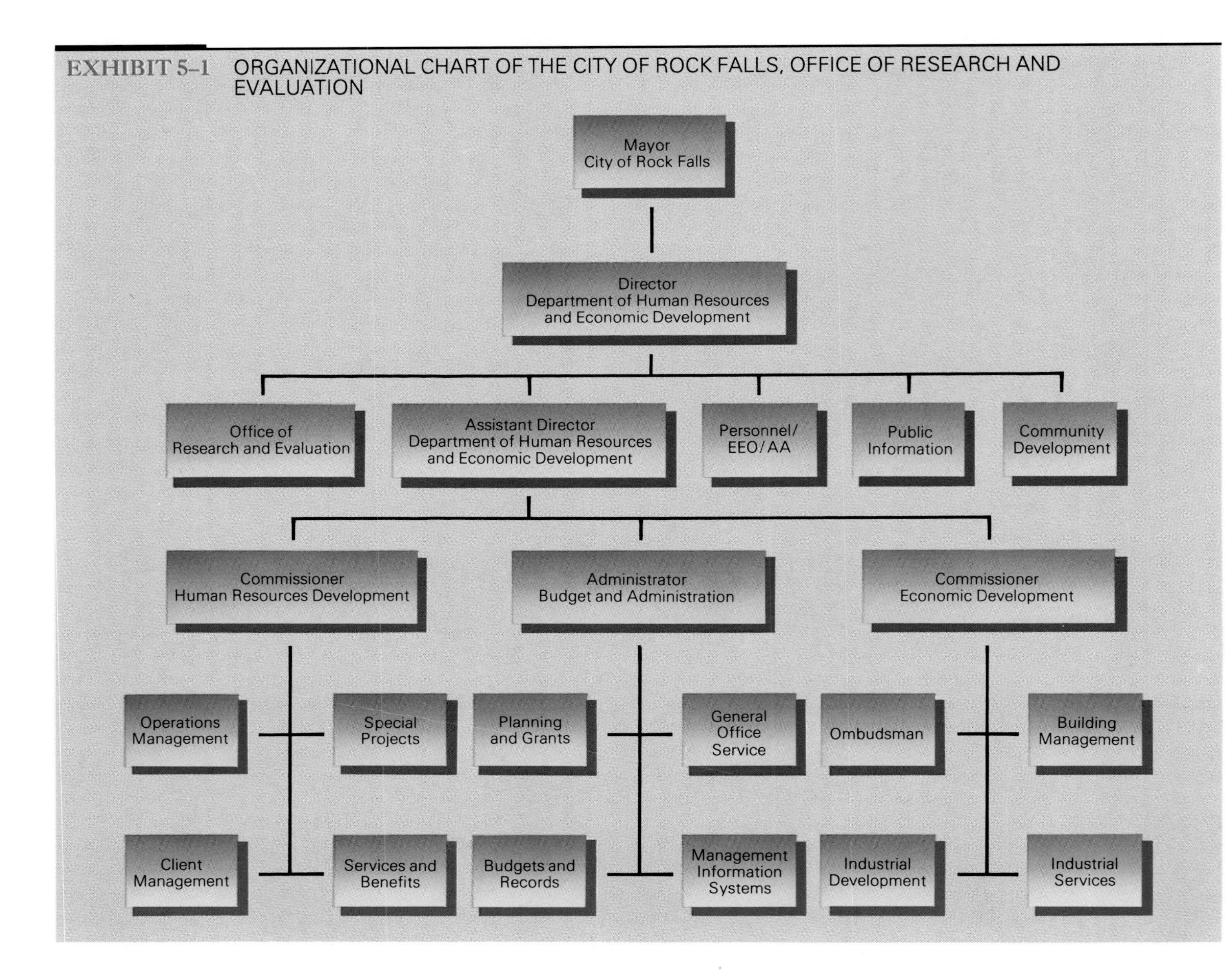

EXHIBIT 5–2 EMPLOYEE APPRAISAL FORM

Employee Name: Marcus Singh Date: October 4, 1989

Job Title: Economist/Researcher

Please indicate your evaluation of the employee in each category by placing a check mark (✓) in the appropriate block.

	Outstanding	Good	Satisfactory	Fair	Unsatisfactory
KNOWLEDGE OF JOB Assess overall knowledge of duties and responsibilities of current job.	☑	☐	☐	☐	☐
QUANTITY OF WORK Assess the volume of work under normal conditions.	☐	☑	☐	☐	☐
QUALITY OF WORK Assess the neatness, accuracy, & effectiveness of work.	☐	☑	☐	☐	☐
COOPERATION Assess ability & willingness to work with peers, superiors, & subordinates.	☐	☑	☐	☐	☐
INITIATIVE Assess willingness to seek greater responsibilities & knowledge. Self-starting.	☐	☑	☐	☐	☐
ATTENDANCE Assess reliability with respect to attendance habits.	☑	☐	☐	☐	☐
ATTITUDE Assess disposition & level of enthusiasm. Desire to excel.	☑	☐	☐	☐	☐
JUDGMENT Assess ability to make logical decisions.	☐	☑	☐	☐	☐

Comments on ratings: Valuable employee!

Supervisor's Signature: Garth Fryer Date: Oct. 4, 1989

Department: Office of Research and Evaluation

Employee's Signature: Marcus Singh

Does the employee agree with this evaluation? X Yes ______ No

EXHIBIT 5–3 EMPLOYEE APPRAISAL FORM

Employee Name: Marcus Singh Date: October 18, 1989

Job Title: Economist/Researcher

Please indicate your evaluation of the employee in each category by placing a check mark (✓) in the appropriate block.

	Outstanding	Good	Satisfactory	Fair	Unsatisfactory
KNOWLEDGE OF JOB Assess overall knowledge of duties and responsibilities of current job.	☐	☑	☐	☐	☐
QUANTITY OF WORK Assess the volume of work under normal conditions.	☐	☐	☑	☐	☐
QUALITY OF WORK Assess the neatness, accuracy, & effectiveness of work.	☐	☐	☑	☐	☐
COOPERATION Assess ability & willingness to work with peers, superiors, & subordinates.	☐	☐	☑	☐	☐
INITIATIVE Assess willingness to seek greater responsibilities & knowledge. Self-starting.	☐	☐	☑	☐	☐
ATTENDANCE Assess reliability with respect to attendance habits.	☐	☑	☐	☐	☐
ATTITUDE Assess disposition & level of enthusiasm. Desire to excel.	☐	☑	☐	☐	☐
JUDGMENT Assess ability to make logical decisions.	☐	☐	☑	☐	☐

Comments on ratings: Marcus needs to increase the quantity of his work to receive higher ratings. Also, he should take a greater initiative in his job.

Supervisor's Signature: *Garth Fryer* Date: *Oct. 18, 1989*

Department: Office of Research and Evaluation

Employee's Signature: *Marcus Singh*

Does the employee agree with this evaluation? ____ Yes X No

Marcus Singh's working relationship with Garth Fryer and Jason Taft and with others in the department has been good. On some occasions, though, he found himself in awkward disagreements with his co-workers in areas where he held strong opinions.

After Marcus and Jason had signed the appraisals, Garth Fryer forwarded them to Mr. Popelmill's office, where they were eventually added to the employees' permanent files. When pay raises were awarded in the department three weeks later, Marcus Singh did not receive a merit raise for the next year. He was told that it was due to his less-than-outstanding appraisal. He did, however, receive the general increase of $500 given to all employees regardless of their performance appraisal.

Marcus has refused to speak one word to Garth Fryer since they discussed the appraisal, communicating only through Ms. Millar or in writing. Marcus has become unmotivated and has complained bitterly to his colleagues about his unfair ratings. While he reports to work at 8:00 A.M. sharp and does not leave until 5:00 P.M. each day, he has been observed to spend a lot of time reading newspapers and books while at work.

CASE QUESTIONS

1. What is the problem in this case? Who is to blame?
2. How would you have reacted if you were Marcus Singh?
3. Could this problem have been avoided? How?
4. Critically evaluate the rating form used in this case. Suggest specific improvements.
5. What can be done to motivate Marcus Singh?

CASE 6 AN ESOP AT WORLD INTERNATIONAL AIRLINES

The fortunes of World International Airlines (WIA) changed drastically with the deregulation of the airline industry in the early 1980s. Prior to this period, the airline had been regarded by passengers as a high-quality carrier with an excellent service and on-time record. Safety and service complaints filed with the Civil Aeronautics Board were low, and employee morale was high. Employees enjoyed wages, benefits, and work rules on a par with those of employees of other major U.S. domestic and international carriers. Unfortunately, the airline was slow to take advantage of a deregulated environment, and new "start-up" carriers began to cut into WIA's domestic market. In addition, other major U.S. airlines entered WIA's international markets, further increasing competition.

World International Airlines began losing large sums of money in the early and mid-1980s. In 1985, the airline became the target of a takeover attempt by a

This case is adapted from an actual experience. The background information is factual. All names are fictitious.

corporate raider. After a prolonged and highly publicized battle, the takeover was completed. This occurred shortly before the start of collective bargaining negotiations with the pilots, machinists, and flight attendants. Under the direction of new management, WIA negotiators adopted a hard-line position during bargaining sessions. Union leaders were asked to grant large concessions to the company, mainly through productive work rule changes and large monetary "give-backs." The pilots were asked to reduce their wages by 25 percent, the machinists by 15 percent, and the flight attendants by 22 percent. After difficult bargaining discussions, both the pilots and machinists reached agreement on wages, accepting wage cuts of 25 percent and 15 percent respectively. Negotiations with the flight attendants, however, were unsuccessful, and in 1986, six thousand flight attendants struck the airline. Management immediately began hiring permanent replacements under a newly implemented two-tier wage schedule. Under this compensation plan, B-scalers (new hires) were paid $1,000 per month; under the previous labor agreement the lowest pay for a flight attendant was $1,136. After nine weeks the strike was halted when the union agreed to return to work. Flight attendants returned to their jobs by accepting a 22 percent cut in wages and benefits. The company implemented work rule changes and also increased the flying hours of all flight attendants by ten more hours per month.

Shortly after the strike, employee morale dropped dramatically. Senior flight attendants complained of having to fly more hours with less pay. New hires felt inequitably treated since they received B-scale pay while performing job duties identical to those of senior flight attendants. Pilots and machinists were largely unhappy with their lower pay rates and work rule changes.

Since 1986, WIA has reported profits in a few selected quarters. The overall financial position of the airline has, however, continued to decline. To meet operating expenses and service a heavy debt, management sold profitable routes and other valued assets, including planes and a state-of-the-art reservation system. Unfortunately, these measures did not stem the flow of red ink, and in early 1990 an airline analyst predicted that WIA was close to financial disaster.

Senior management continued to seek employee wage concessions, arguing that employees should be willing to "help with" the company's financial burden. Specifically, in 1990, management asked for additional wage and benefit cuts totaling $50 million. This time, however, pilots were reluctant to reduce their earnings. At union meetings, various pilots, machinists, and flight attendants expressed adamant opposition to further wage reductions. The feeling of employees could generally be summed up as "Enough is enough." Management countered by claiming that without these concessions the airline could not survive in its present financial position.

In 1990, senior airline management indicated a willingness to sell WIA if the right buyer could be found. It was generally acknowledged by airline financial analysts, however, that finding a buyer would be difficult because of the carrier's poor financial position. One possible strategy to financially strengthen WIA is an employee buyout of company stock through an employee stock ownership plan

(ESOP). The machinists have been leaders in suggesting an ESOP leveraged buyout. Other employee groups regard an ESOP as preferable to selling the airline to outsiders, who might institute unwelcome changes. Both labor and management are now exploring the feasibility of implementing a leveraged ESOP.

CASE QUESTIONS

1. In light of WIA's poor financial position, why are employees reluctant to grant additional concessions to management?
2. What are the apparent advantages to employees of establishing a leveraged ESOP?
3. What risks might employees assume if the ESOP is implemented? How might these risks be minimized?

THE FRUSTRATED MANAGEMENT TRAINEE

Jack Mitchell sat at his desk puzzled and disheartened. When he joined Liberty Airlines two years ago, it was the fulfillment of a lifelong vocational dream. To join a growing regional airline with its travel benefits and high-status image was something he had planned since his high school graduation. Furthermore, Liberty Airlines' college recruiter had painted a bright picture of the rewarding jobs in the airline industry and, in particular, the exciting work assignments and advancement opportunities with Liberty Air. Now Jack felt deceived and frustrated as he finished writing his resignation letter.

Jack Mitchell's background and vocational aspirations were ideally suited to a career in the airline industry. Until his retirement in 1988, Jack's father, Donald Mitchell, had been a pilot for 23 years with Southeastern Airlines. During the last four years of his employment, Mr. Mitchell had been the director of airline scheduling and fleet operations. With his experience in this executive position, Mr. Mitchell was able to tell Jack about many of the ins and outs of the airline business. This experience, plus Jack's summer employment in ramp operations with Southeastern, gave him what he believed was "a leg up" on the other management trainees hired by Liberty Air.

In 1989, Jack Mitchell graduated from Longmore State University with a degree in business administration. His field of specialization was HRM, with classes in recruitment and selection, labor relations, compensation administration, training and development, and employee motivation. The motivation classes were particularly engrossing, because Jack was deeply interested in the study of various motivational theories and their practical application to different organizational settings. In addition to his HR classes, Jack also took four courses in psychology.

This case is based on the actual experience of a former management student at Arizona State University.

Jack Mitchell's long-range goal was to become an HR vice-president for a major international airline. He believed that his educational background, combined with his interest in working with people, qualified him for a high-level HR position. Although Jack realized that all new employees had to "pay their dues," he believed his rise up the corporate hierarchy would be relatively fast.

Liberty Airlines was an "upstart" regional airline serving the North Central and Northeastern states. Its founders, George Ryan and Chris Holden, capitalized on the deregulation of the airline industry by serving various cities largely untouched by the major carriers. Starting with two planes, the company had grown to a fleet of 24 planes and 1,123 employees in five years. In 1986, Liberty Air began a management training program in order to staff current management openings and to develop future executive talent.

Jack Mitchell described his two years in Liberty Air's management training program as "boring and a waste of time and energy." As a management trainee he had expected to be placed in meaningful jobs where his talents and abilities could be utilized and developed. Unfortunately his initial jobs were routine and clerical, offering no opportunity to use his educational background or develop his managerial talents.

Jack's first trainee position was on the ramp as assistant to Juan Sanchez, manager of ramp operations. Jack recalled that all Mr. Sanchez wanted him to do was tag and load bags and to get the planes off on schedule. After six months Jack was transferred to in-flight scheduling, a department of flight operations. Here his assignment was to work with four hourly employees reconciling flight attendants' monthly bids with their company seniority in order to establish flight staffing schedules. At lunch one day, Jack told another management trainee that any high school graduate could learn the job in three days. When he asked Marsha Fetzer, manager of in-flight scheduling, for additional duties and responsibilities, he was told that the management training program in her department consisted of crew scheduling only. After ten months in scheduling, Jack was assigned to his final training position in commissary. Again, in Jack's words, "All I seemed to do was record meal numbers and make arrangements for service necessities." At no time during any of the three training positions did Jack have the opportunity to supervise employees or perform basic managerial tasks. Furthermore, personnel in the HR department never discussed his career aspirations with him, nor did they ask him what different job experiences he might wish to explore. Jack signed his resignation letter and left for the day.

CASE QUESTIONS

1. After reviewing the different motivational theories discussed in Chapter 14, explain how each might apply to Jack Mitchell.
2. What could the three managers have done to create motivating conditions within their job areas for the management trainees?

3. What can managers do to reduce frustration and conflict that inhibit productivity?
4. Do you believe Jack Mitchell's experience is unique with management training programs? Explain.

TOXIC SUBSTANCES AT LUKENS CHEMICAL INDUSTRIES

With 53 plants operating in 15 countries throughout the world, Lukens Chemical is a multinational corporation and a world leader in the production of standard and specialty chemicals. Highly committed to chemical research and development, Lukens also has 19 research laboratories worldwide. A partial listing of the company's chemicals includes the following:

Agricultural	insecticides, herbicides, fungicides, phosphate and nitrogen fertilizer products
Specialty chemicals	dyes, plastic additives, aerospace and manufacturing chemicals, organic and inorganic paint pigments, and chemicals for residential and commercial water treatment
Consumer	personal care chemicals, home cleaning and maintenance aids
Medical products	steroids, antibiotics, vaccines, various pharmaceuticals

Because of the nature of its products and general public criticism of the chemical industry, senior management has adopted a proactive stance toward the handling and distribution of toxic substances. The company has taken extensive efforts to protect the health and safety of its employees while complying with OSHA standards applicable to toxic substances in the chemical industry. Environmentalists have spoken approvingly of company actions to protect both its employees and the environment.

Under the direction of a dynamic president and CEO, Lukens Chemical has experienced a 12 percent annual growth in plants and facilities. Managerial, engineering, technical, and other professional employees needed to staff the company have come largely from competitors and college recruiting. In order to develop its HR personnel, in 1984 the company started a specialized management training program for HR specialists. Individuals selected for this program are rotated every six months through the functional areas of recruitment and selection, compensation administration, training and development, labor relations, and equal employment opportunity. Upon completion of these assignments HR specialists are assigned as

This case is adapted from an actual experience. The background information is factual. All names are fictitious.

plant HR assistants. One or more of these field assignments normally lead to the HR directorship at a major chemical plant.

In early 1989, Paul Chavis was promoted to the position of HR director of the New Orleans plant of Lukens Chemical. During Paul's interview with Chad Welker, plant manager of the New Orleans facility, he was told that the major HR concerns were a high level of union grievance activity, high turnover, and the need to recruit new engineering and technical personnel. It was not long after assuming his new assignment, however, that a more pressing problem developed. The problem began shortly after a lengthy meeting with Dr. Howard Loy, the plant's health and safety physician. The following is part of the conversation between the two.

Howard: Paul, as you know, our corporate management is always concerned about the problems of employees coming into contact with toxic chemicals. Part of my job is to monitor the facilities here and to report any work-related health problems. Since the lead pigments department is a highly suspect area, I keep a very close watch on this particular facility.

Paul: I know that it is an important area to us. Besides supplying important products, the lead pigments department employs over 150 employees.

Howard: My personal study, and those of other researchers, shows a relationship between lead exposure and serious health conditions, especially various female reproductive dangers.

Paul: Howard, this could be a real problem for us. We have 17 women between the ages of 23 and 45 working in lead pigments. What medical problems might women encounter from exposure to lead?

Howard: Pregnant women who have been exposed to lead may miscarry or give birth to children with serious defects. The possibility of sterility is another danger. I believe we are running a real risk by continuing to employ women in these jobs.

Additionally troublesome was that the department used a lead chromate pigment process which can be especially dangerous to women. Furthermore, the problems described by Dr. Loy have been confirmed by the National Institute of Occupational Safety and Health (NIOSH).

Shortly after the meeting with Dr. Loy, Paul wrote to Dr. Kathryn Long in Houston recommending that some policy be developed regarding the exposure of women to lead. In July 1989, the company established a policy that only women beyond childbearing years or those surgically sterilized could hold jobs involving exposure to lead. All women in the lead pigments department were told of this policy. Those women not accepting the company's offer of surgical sterilization could transfer to jobs involving no contact with lead. Unfortunately, those jobs were largely in clerical and maintenance positions, jobs paying considerably less than the technical positions in the lead pigments department. Management established this policy with the belief that it was being institutionally responsive to women's health needs.

Shortly after the policy was announced, nine women filed an EEOC sex discrimination charge against the company alleging that it was forcing them to be surgically sterilized as a condition to retaining their jobs. The complaining employees noted in the charge, "No female should be forced to give up her reproductive rights in order to keep her job." The EEOC suit came as a complete surprise to management, since no women in the lead pigments department had indicated displeasure with the policy, and the company had acted with what it felt was a responsible and humane concern for its female employees.

CASE QUESTIONS

1. Given the recommendations of Dr. Loy, what possible courses of action could the company take regarding women's exposure to lead?
2. Evaluate the rights and responsibilities of both the company and the employees in this case.

ILL-FATED LOVE

Nancy Miller-Canton never imagined she would lose her job at Centrex Electronics Corporation (CEC), and certainly not under such unpleasant circumstances. Unfortunately, after 11 years of employment, the last two as a senior product engineer in the firm's military/space division in Atlanta, she made a mistake: she fell in love.

Nancy joined Centrex Electronics shortly after graduating from Georgia State University in 1980. At that time she was married to Tom Canton, her college sweetheart. In 1986, Tom died suddenly. As a single parent, she became dependent upon her job for the majority of her family's support.

Nancy had enjoyed rapid promotions through various engineering positions until reaching her present job as senior product engineer. In 1990, the year before her dismissal, she was awarded the firm's Engineering Distinction Award for her research and development work in metallography. In January 1991, one week after receiving a 14.2 percent raise, she was called on the carpet. The question from the military/space division manager was clear and direct: "Are you dating Mike Domzalski?" Mike was a former CEC senior engineer who had changed employment in 1990 to work for International Technologies, a direct competitor of CEC. There was no denying the romance. The two had dated while Domzalski was with CEC, and he still played on CEC's softball team. It was widely known among

This case is adapted from an actual situation known to the authors. All names are fictitious.

Nancy's friends that she was "extremely fond" of Mike. At the conclusion of the meeting Nancy was ordered to forget about Mike or be demoted. After the meeting she told a friend, "I was so socialized in CEC culture and my devotion to my job that I thought seriously about breaking up with Mike." As she later testified in court, however, she never got the chance because she was dismissed the next day.

Human resources professionals agree that CEC is highly regarded as a quality employer in the electronics industry. It is a multinational corporation with engineering services and production facilities in Spain, Canada, Hong Kong, Mexico, and West Germany. With more than 12,000 employees in the United States, several studies have named the firm as one of the country's top 100 organizations to work for. Centrex Electronics is known as a top-paying corporation with proactive employee relations policies. Kathryn Garner, V-P Human Resources, is credited with establishing many positive employee rights policies, including those covering drug testing, search and surveillance, employee files, and employee smoking. The corporation permits marriage between employees except in cases where "one employee is in a direct reporting relationship with the other."

At the root of Nancy's dismissal is a corporate policy regarding the leakage of confidential product information. The policy seeks to avoid situations where an employee of CEC might be compromised into providing sensitive or confidential information to an employee of a competing organization. Nancy's work in research and development makes her subject to the following CEC policy:

> Employees performing jobs where they have access to sensitive or confidential information which could benefit competitors are prohibited from being married to or from having a romantic relationship with individuals employed by competing organizations.

Since Mike Domzalski's work at International Technologies is similar to Nancy's at CEC, the corporation felt their "romantic relationship" made Nancy's discharge appropriate.

Feeling aggrieved, Nancy engaged the services of an attorney specializing in employee rights claims. In preparing her wrongful-discharge suit, the attorney told her that, given the nature of her case and the continuous erosion of the employment-at-will doctrine, he believed she would win the lawsuit. Furthermore, while gathering background information for the trial, the attorney discovered something that her former division manager didn't know. Shortly before her discharge, no less an authority than former CEC chairman Joseph M. Torell had declared that "CEC employees are responsible for their own off-the-job behavior. We are concerned with an employee's off-the-job conduct only when it reduces the employee's ability to perform normal job assignments."

A jury trial in state court upheld the wrongful-discharge suit and awarded Nancy $425,000 in back pay and punitive damages. Like other trials, however, this one took its toll on Nancy. "I couldn't function for four or five months after the trial I was so emotionally upset and drained," she said. Nancy is now employed as an engineer for a computer company; she and Mike are no longer dating. "It was a bad experience all around," she says. "There was a real sense of belonging and a feeling of personal job worth at CEC. If I had my way, I'd take my old job back today."

CASE QUESTIONS

1. What exceptions to the employment-at-will doctrine would the attorney have used to file the lawsuit?
2. Comment on the confidential information policy adopted by Centrex Electronics. Do you agree with the way it is used?
3. Is dating a "romantic relationship"? How might this term become a problem for the corporation?

CASE 10 THE LAST STRAW

The meeting lasted only ten minutes, since all those present quickly agreed that Tom Kinder should be fired. According to management, Tom had caused the company numerous problems over the last 18 months, and the incident on Saturday was "the straw that broke the camel's back." Plant management believed it had rid itself of a poor employee—one the company knew it had offered numerous opportunities for improvement. It seemed like an airtight case and one the union couldn't win if taken to arbitration.

Tom Kinder had worked for the Aero Engine Company for 14 years prior to his discharge. He was initially employed as an engine mechanic servicing heavy-duty diesel engines. For his first nine years with Aero Engine, he was considered a model employee by his supervisors and plant management. Tom also was well liked by his fellow employees. His performance appraisals were always marked "exceptional," and his personnel folder contained many commendation letters from customers and supervisors alike. Supervisor Mark Lee described Tom as "devoted to his job of building and repairing engines." Through company-sponsored training classes and courses taken at a local trade school, Tom acquired the knowledge and experience to build and repair specialty engines used in arctic oil exploration.

The Aero Engine Company, with headquarters in the Midwest, was engaged primarily in the production and maintenance of specialty engines used in drilling, heavy manufacturing, and diesel transportation. The company had experienced very rapid growth in sales volume, number of products produced, and the size of its work force since 1970. (At the time of Tom Kinder's termination, the company employed about 1,700 employees.) Aero Engine avoided hiring new personnel and then laying them off if they should no longer be needed. Company policy stated that layoffs

This case is based on an actual arbitration heard by George W. Bohlander. All names are fictitious.

were to be avoided except in extreme circumstances. When heavy workloads arose, the natural solution to the problem was to schedule large amounts of overtime and to hire temporary employees who could be obtained through one of the local temporary help services.

Tom Kinder's work problems began approximately five years ago when he went through a very emotional and difficult divorce. A devoted family man, the divorce was a shock to his values and his way of life. The loss of his children was particularly devastating to his mental well-being. He became sullen, withdrawn, and argumentative with his supervisors. An absenteeism problem developed which continued until his discharge. Over the 18 months prior to this termination, Tom was absent 27 complete days and 9 partial days and was tardy 19 times. Twelve months ago he was given a written warning that his attendance must improve or he would face further disciplinary action, including possible discharge. Unfortunately his attendance did not improve; however, he received no further disciplinary action until his discharge on Monday, June 15, 1988.

Management also experienced other problems with Tom Kinder. His quantity and quality of work decreased to only an acceptable level of performance. His supervisor discussed this with him on two occasions, but no disciplinary action was ever instituted. Furthermore, during heavy production periods Tom either would refuse to work overtime assignments or, once assigned, would often fail to report for work. It was an incident which occurred during a Saturday overtime shift that caused his discharge.

On Saturday, June 13, Tom was assigned to a high-priority project that required him to build a specialty engine for a large and loyal customer. The new, large engine was needed to replace a smaller engine that had exploded on an Alaskan drilling rig. The engine was being built in a newly constructed plant building located one-half mile from the company's main production facilities. At approximately 9:15 A.M. on Saturday, Gordon Thompson, Tom's supervisor, walked over to the new building to check on the progress of the engine. As Mr. Thompson passed by a window, he noticed Tom Kinder sitting at a desk with his feet up reading a magazine. The supervisor decided to observe Tom from outside the building. After about 25 minutes Tom had not moved, and Mr. Thompson returned to the plant to report the incident to Glenn Navarro, the plant production manager. Neither the supervisor nor the production manager confronted Tom about the incident.

At 8:15 A.M. on Monday morning, supervisor Thompson and production manager Navarro met with the director of human resources to review the total work performance of Tom Kinder. After the short meeting mentioned at the beginning of this case, all those present decided that Tom Kinder should be fired. Tom's discharge notice read, "Terminated for poor work performance, excessive absenteeism, and loafing." At 10:15 A.M. on Monday, Tom was called into Mr. Navarro's office and told of his discharge. Then Mr. Navarro handed him his final paycheck, which included eight hours of work for Monday.

CASE QUESTIONS

1. Comment on the handling of this case by the supervisor, production manager, and director of human resources.
2. To what extent were the concepts of good discipline and "just cause" discharge applied?
3. If Tom Kinder's discharge went to arbitration, how would you decide the case? Why? What arguments would labor and management present to support their respective positions?

HIRING STRIKE REPLACEMENTS AT PALO VERDE MINING

The right of employees to strike their employers is an established guarantee under the National Labor Relations Act. Consequently, strikes have long been an accepted part of the labor–management collective bargaining setting. Traditionally, when employees elected to strike, the organization would shut down its operations entirely or continue to operate with a limited complement of supervisory personnel. While this practice continues today, increasingly employers are hiring strike replacements to keep facilities running when strike action occurs. The Greyhound Corporation, Trans World Airlines (TWA), Phelps Dodge, Hormel, and the National Football League are recent examples of organizations that were willing to hire replacement workers in order to maintain operations. One labor relations scholar has noted, "No longer can unions expect the strike to provide the force needed to make employers capitulate to union demands. The growing anti-union attitudes of managers, technological advances, and foreign and domestic competition have made the strike weapon largely ineffective in many situations." Unfortunately, with this change has come a new period of labor–management unrest accompanied by violence, threats of strikebreaking, and other hostile labor–management interactions. The following case illustrates these points.

For 40 years labor negotiations between the Palo Verde Mining Company and the International Mine Workers Union had concluded without a major incident. While both sides had had their differences, and several short strikes had taken place, negotiations had ended with both labor and management believing that a fair bargain had been reached. This changed dramatically in 1986, when copper prices fell and company management bargained hard to hold down wage increases and obtain productive work rule changes.

This case is adapted from an actual experience. The background information is factual. All dates and names are fictitious.

In February 1986, shortly before the contract was to expire, tentative agreements had been reached on all important bargaining items except one, contractual arrangements granting employees a cost-of-living allowance (COLA). Management demanded elimination of the COLA wage provision since it caused uncontrollable wage increases and other copper companies had successfully removed this costly wage guarantee from their contracts. Union officials argued that the COLA was needed to keep pace with inflation and maintain employees' purchasing power. During the last week of negotiations no progress was made on the COLA issue and on February 23, 1986, 2,300 union members began striking the company's mining facilities at Queen Creek, Desert City, and the Salt River Basin. The company immediately announced that it would hire strike replacements, an action not taken during previous strikes. With unemployment high and the good wages and benefits available to new hires, the Palo Verde Mining Company was able to return to 80 percent operations within seven weeks.

During the strike, tensions between management, strikers, and strike replacements were extremely high. Violent outbreaks between union strikers and strike replacements were common, as was the destruction of company property by striking employees. The strike received national attention in March when a small child was accidentally shot by an unknown individual. Further violence caused the governor of the state to send in the National Guard and state police to restore order in the mining communities.

Capitalizing on its success in hiring strike replacements, Palo Verde management changed its bargaining agenda in subsequent negotiations to include items not previously discussed. In addition, management negotiators insisted on reopening many of the tentative agreements reached in bargaining during late January and early February. Labor relations experts regarded this action as a way of backing the union into an unacceptable position to resolve the strike. When the bargaining talks broke down, the union immediately filed unfair labor practice charges with the National Labor Relations Board (NLRB). These charges alleged that the company was refusing to bargain in good faith.

Tensions remained hostile between union members, management, and strike replacements during April, May, and June of that year. In July, the Palo Verde Mining Company issued eviction notices to strikers to leave their company-owned homes. Providing subsidized company housing has been a common practice in predominantly southwestern mining communities. As the strike continued, many former employees began to cross the union picket lines, heightening tensions between family members and fellow striking employees.

In March 1987, one year after the strike began, employees of the Palo Verde Mining Company petitioned the NLRB to hold a decertification election. The NLRB held this election on May 14, 1987. An overwhelming number of miners voted to decertify the union. Since decertification of the union the company has operated as a nonunion employer, and recent organizing attempts at Palo Verde have been unsuccessful. While the bitterness of the strike still plagues families in the mining communities, operations at the mines have returned to normal.

CASE QUESTIONS

1. Comment specifically on the company's decision to hire strike replacements. What are the advantages and disadvantages of this action to the company?
2. Discuss the effectiveness of the strike in light of today's labor–management environment.
3. How do you think the NLRB will resolve the unfair labor practice charge filed by the union? What criteria might the NLRB use to settle the charge?

CASE 12 EXPATRIATE MANAGERS AT INTERNATIONAL MINING, INC.

International Mining (IM), Inc., is a multinational company with large mining operations in North America, Africa, and South America. In all countries where IM has mining interests, company operations are jointly managed by American managers and engineers and host-country management personnel recruited from within the country. HR policies and procedures at IM emphasize a close working relationship between American managers and their foreign counterparts. The company works hard at training and promoting its foreign personnel while providing them with a substantial voice in the management of the host-country mine. IM has avoided much of the anti-American feeling voiced against other U.S. enterprises owning foreign operations—a fact it attributes to its proactive HR policies.

IM has most of its foreign mining operations in Peru. Peru has great mineral wealth, with most of the mineral deposits located in the rugged central highlands that were once the heart of the Inca empire. Peru is rich in copper ore, but it also has large deposits of iron, coal, vanadium, and zinc. The largest mine operated by IM lies near the city of Cerro de Pasco. The city is located in the central mountain region of Peru, 14,000 feet above sea level and about 200 miles northeast of Lima, the capital.

The Republic of Peru extends 1,500 miles along the western coast of South America. The country is bounded on the north by Ecuador and Colombia, on the east by Brazil and Bolivia, on the south by Chile, and on the west by the Pacific Ocean. The Andes Mountains extend across the country from northwest to southeast and divide Peru into three distinct regions: a coastal lowland, the Andean highlands, and the upper Amazon basin. The Andean highlands, where most of Peru's mineral wealth is found, has a varied topography with an average annual temperature of 60° F and an average annual rainfall of about 32 inches in the Sierra, which lies in the southeastern part of the highlands.

Peru's 17 million inhabitants are predominantly Indian or mestizo (a mixture of Spanish and Indian heritage). The country is largely Roman Catholic. Approximately one-half of the population speaks Quechua (the original Inca language), and the remaining population speaks mostly Spanish. In 1980, the population of Peru was 76 percent literate. The life expectancy in 1980 for women was 59 years; for men, 56 years. Considerable progress has been made in reducing epidemics and improving sanitation and health care facilities. In the small towns and cities, however, medical facilities are far below Western standards.

Citizens in the larger cities of Peru enjoy swimming, golf, tennis, polo, and horse racing. Bullfighting is also a popular sport. For people in Peru's outlying regions, however, the only forms of recreation are church services, carnivals, and fiestas.

Peru has a republican form of government, although the political stability of the country has been somewhat shaky since the mid-1980s. The government has nationalized some industries, causing a strained relationship between the governments of the United States and Peru. How complete the nationalization movement will be and what industries will be affected in the future is unknown.

International Mining annually transfers about 45 managers and engineers to its mining facilities throughout South America. Of these, approximately 25 are transferred to mines or smelter plants in Peru. These expatriate employees are critical for the effective operations of the mines and for maintaining the cooperative relationship between American and host-country personnel. Owing to the large costs associated with moving and housing expatriate managers and their families overseas, the average assignment of IM personnel to Peru is 2½ years. To advance within the corporate ranks of the company, managers are expected to accept foreign assignments when they occur. In fact, refusing an overseas position is viewed as greatly limiting one's advancement opportunities within IM. Therefore most managers or engineers accept these assignments, although many do so begrudgingly.

IM conducts a general orientation program for all managers and their families prior to their departure from the United States for their foreign assignment. This eight-hour presentation consists largely of lectures, slides and movies, and discussions with employees who have recently returned to the United States. The purpose of the employee discussion periods is to give departing personnel an idea of what life is really like in a foreign country. The entire orientation program is designed to give a broad overview of overseas living; however, the HR department does give all expatriate employees pamphlets and books about their country of assignment.

Like other multinational organizations, IM has not had overwhelming success with either the experiences of its expatriates or the completion rate of their tour assignments. The premature return rate for IM managers or engineers is about 30 percent, a figure approximating the premature return rate experienced by other United States multinational corporations.[1] Senior management at IM also believes that those expatriates who do complete their assignments, but are unsuited for or simply unhappy with the experience, finish their tours with reduced job efficiency. Although exact figures are unavailable, these individuals cost IM in lost money and diminished reputation. Interviews with returning overseas personnel reveal that

---

1. Afzalur Rahim, "A Model for Developing Key Expatriate Executives," *Personnel Journal* 62, no. 4 (April 1983): 312–317.

radical differences in the culture, economics, politics, and social factors of the host country contribute to the high early return rate. These interviews also find that family members often exhibit high stress, caused in large part by the difficulties of adapting to a foreign culture.

CASE QUESTIONS

1. Discuss some of the difficulties you think American managers and their families might experience living in Peru or any South American country.
2. Comment on the overseas orientation program used by IM. What specifically should be done to improve the "socialization" of American managers in foreign countries?
3. List and discuss some HR policies that should be used when selecting and preparing expatriate managers.

Name Index

A

B

C

D

E

F

G

H

I

J

K

N

O

P

T

U

V

W

Y

Z

Organization Index

A, B, C

D, E, F

P, Q, R, S

T, U, V

W, X, Y, Z

Subject Index

A

B

D

E

Q

R

Acknowledgments

PART ONE Courtesy, University of Akron Archives, 8; Courtesy, AT&T Archives, 10; David Hathcox, 18; SWP, 22; SWP, 27; ABB Robotics Inc., 40; Genentech, Inc., 49; Courtesy, Salt River Project, 55; Nissan Motor Manufacturing Corporation, U.S.A., 57; © Michael Melford, 1989, 62; Courtesy of NAACP National Public Relations Department, 75; Stephen Pumphrey, 79; Inland Boatmen's Union of The Pacific, 88; SWP, 96; Ed Streeky/Camera 5, 100.

PART TWO Courtesy, Hewlett-Packard Company, 111; SWP, 118; NASA, 126; Saturn Corporation, 131; Good Samaritan Hospital, 134; Kevin Horan/Picture Group, 143; Video courtesy Internal Revenue Service, 154; Courtesy, University of Cincinnati, 157; Courtesy of AT&T Archives, 161; United States Air Force, 162; Courtesy of The Lincoln Electric Company, Cleveland, Ohio, 172; Courtesy of the Lafayette Instrument Company, Inc., 179; Brad Bower/Picture Group, 182; SWP, 193.

PART THREE SWP, 208; Shane Gamble/Bethesda Oak Hospital, 216; Courtesy, IIT Research Institute, 222; SWP, 226; SWP, 231; SWP, 241; Courtesy, California Highway Patrol, 246; David Hathcox, 252; R.I.T. Communications Department, 258; SWP, 262; U.S. Postal Service, 278; SWP, 293.

PART FOUR SWP, 304; Courtesy, Eastern Michigan University, 306; Pamela Price/Picture Group, 314; Courtesy of Chevron Corp., 324; State Historical Society of Iowa, 335; Photograph courtesy of Steelcase Inc., 350; SWP, 357; Rob Nelson/Picture Group, 361; Courtesy of The Lincoln Electric Company, Cleveland, Ohio, 366; Courtesy of Chevron Corp., 372; SWP, 383; Aetna Casualty and Surety Company, 388; Courtesy, Amtrak, 396; Courtesy, Good Samaritan Hospital, 403; SWP, 408; The Prudential Insurance Company of America, 411; U.S. Department of Labor/OSHA, 422; Courtesy, Westmorland Coal Company, 430; SWP, 436; Poster courtesy g.Neil Companies, 443; SWP, 450.

PART FIVE Courtesy Carnival Cruise Lines, 461; SWP, 464; Courtesy, America West Airlines, 475; Courtesy of International Business Machines Corporation, 478; Courtesy, Chrysler Motor Corp., 486; SWP, 498; SWP, 501; Courtesy, AT&T Archives, 505; Courtesy, g.Neil Companies, 508; Courtesy, Toastmasters International, 513; SWP, 529; Jim Knowles/Picture Group, 534; SWP, 535; SWP, 544.

PART SIX SWP, 568; Zephyr Pictures/Melanie Carr, 571; P. F. Gero/Sygma, 580; Jim Argo/Picture Group, 584; Courtesy AFL-CIO, 589; The Martin-Brower Company, 600; P. Forden/Sygma, 605; Peter Freed/Picture Group, 607; General Motors Corporation, 611.

PART SEVEN Courtesy of International Business Machines Corporation, 634; From film GOING INTERNATIONAL, Copeland Griggs Productions, 640; From film GOING INTERNATIONAL, Copeland Griggs Productions, 644; F. Hibon/Sygma, 650; SWP, 659; European Community Delegation, Washington DC, 660; Courtesy, Hewlett-Packard Company, 673; Courtesy of Chevron Corp., 675; SWP, 679; SWP, 683; John Zoiner, 691.